W9-BUX-818

THE MARK TWAIN PAPERS

THE MARK TWAIN PAPERS

Of the projected fifteen volumes of this edition of Mark Twain's previously unpublished works the following have been issued to date:

Mark Twain's Letters to His Publishers, 1867–1894
edited by Hamlin Hill

Mark Twain's Satires & Burlesques
edited by Franklin R. Rogers

Mark Twain's Which Was the Dream?
edited by John S. Tuckey

Mark Twain's Hannibal, Huck & Tom
edited by Walter Blair

Mark Twain's Mysterious Stranger Manuscripts
edited by William M. Gibson

Mark Twain's Correspondence with Henry Huttleston Rogers
edited by Lewis Leary

Mark Twain's Fables of Man
edited by John S. Tuckey
text established by Kenneth M. Sanderson
and Bernard L. Stein

Mark Twain's Notebooks & Journals, Volume I
edited by Frederick Anderson
Michael B. Frank
and Kenneth M. Sanderson

Mark Twain's Notebooks & Journals, Volume II
edited by Frederick Anderson
Lin Salamo
and Bernard L. Stein

Editorial Associates

ROBERT PACK BROWNING

VICTOR FISCHER

MICHAEL B. FRANK

ALAN GRIBBEN

BRUCE TAYLOR HAMILTON

KENNETH M. SANDERSON

MARK TWAIN'S NOTEBOOKS & JOURNALS

VOLUME II (1877–1883)

Edited by Frederick Anderson
Lin Salamo and
Bernard L. Stein

Mark Twain

UNIVERSITY OF CALIFORNIA PRESS
Berkeley, Los Angeles, London 1975

Editorial expenses for this volume have been in large part supported by grants from the National Endowment for the Humanities of the National Foundation on the Arts and Humanities administered through the Center for Editions of American Authors of the Modern Language Association.

University of California Press
Berkeley and Los Angeles, California

University of California Press, Ltd.
London, England

Library of Congress Catalog Card Number: 72–87199
ISBN: 0–520–02542–3

Designed by Adrian Wilson
in collaboration with James Mennick

Manufactured in the United States of America

Acknowledgments

AMONG the research and editorial assistants employed in the Mark Twain Papers, Evan Alderson, Robert Hirst, Linda Mullen, Susan Severin, and Robert Schildgen made important contributions to this volume through their preliminary research, translations, or checking of obscure readings. Dahlia Armon and Wendy Won patiently typed the various stages of text, tables, footnotes, headnotes, and index.

The project has been supported by the financial aid of the University of California and of the Samuel Charles Webster Memorial Fund, made available through the generous bequest of Mrs. Webster. The Center for Editions of American Authors, under the directorship of Matthew J. Bruccoli, has supplied necessary grants in support of the preparation of texts for this volume.

Notebooks 15 and 16 are reproduced with the kind permission of Donald Gallup, Curator of the American Literature Collections in the Beinecke Library, Yale University.

A complete list of all those whose information contributed to this edition would be impossible to prepare, but recognition of specific indebtedness appears throughout the editorial material.

Contents

Abbreviations

THE FOLLOWING abbreviations have been used for citations in this volume. Unless otherwise indicated, all materials quoted in the documentation are transcribed from originals in the Mark Twain Papers, The Bancroft Library, University of California, Berkeley.

AD	Samuel L. Clemens' Autobiographical Dictation(s) (typed manuscript in MTP).
DV	Prefix designating literary manuscripts in the Mark Twain Papers.
MS	Manuscript
MT	Mark Twain
MTP	Mark Twain Papers, The Bancroft Library, University of California, Berkeley.
MTM	Mark Twain Memorial, Hartford, Conn.
OLC	Olivia Langdon Clemens
PH	Photocopy
SLC	Samuel L. Clemens
TS	Typescript
Yale	American Literature Collections, Beinecke Library, Yale University, New Haven, Conn.

Published Works Cited

A1911	"The Library and Manuscripts of Samuel L. Clemens," Anderson Auction Company catalogue no. 892—1911, 7–8 February 1911.
HH&T	*Hannibal, Huck & Tom,* ed. Walter Blair (Berkeley and Los Angeles: University of California Press, 1969).
LE	*Letters from the Earth,* ed. Bernard DeVoto (New York: Harper & Row, 1962).
LLMT	*The Love Letters of Mark Twain,* ed. Dixon Wecter (New York: Harper & Brothers, 1949).
MTA	*Mark Twain's Autobiography,* ed. Albert Bigelow Paine, 2 vols. (New York: Harper & Brothers, 1924).
MTB	Albert Bigelow Paine, *Mark Twain: A Biography* (New York: Harper & Brothers, 1912).
MTBus	*Mark Twain, Business Man,* ed. Samuel C. Webster (Boston: Little, Brown and Co., 1946).
MTE	*Mark Twain in Eruption,* ed. Bernard DeVoto (New York: Harper & Brothers, 1940).
MTHL	*Mark Twain-Howells Letters,* ed. Henry Nash Smith and William M. Gibson (Cambridge: Harvard University Press, Belknap Press, 1960).
MTL	*Mark Twain's Letters,* ed. Albert Bigelow Paine (New York: Harper & Brothers, 1917).
MTLP	*Mark Twain's Letters to His Publishers,* ed. Hamlin Hill (Berkeley and Los Angeles: University of California Press, 1967).
MTMF	*Mark Twain to Mrs. Fairbanks,* ed. Dixon Wecter (San Marino, Calif.: Huntington Library, 1949).
S&MT	Edith Colgate Salsbury, *Susy and Mark Twain* (New York: Harper & Row, 1965).

Calendar

In an effort to clarify the numbering of the notebooks, a new sequence has been substituted for that originally used for the typescripts in the files of the Mark Twain Papers. Since the typescript numbers have been frequently cited in print, this calendar lists both the previous and the present numbering systems.

The calendar also contains the inclusive dates for each of the notebooks published in this volume and provisional dates, in brackets, for notebooks to be published in forthcoming volumes. The dating comes from references made by Clemens and from internal evidence when there was no specific notation of a beginning or a terminal date. While many of the notebooks begin or end on specified days, the dating for many is so vague that only the month that Clemens started or finished an individual notebook is known. Therefore, only the month and year that a notebook covers have been listed here. The headnote for each notebook discusses the period of its use.

Notebooks in Volume I

No.	Former No.	Date	Location
1	1A	June–July 1855	Missouri, Iowa
2	1	April–July 1857	Mississippi River
3	2	November 1860–March 1861	Mississippi River

4	3	January–February 1865	California
5	4	March, June–September 1866	San Francisco, Sandwich Islands
6	5	March–April 1866	San Francisco, Sandwich Islands
7	6	December 1866–January 1867	San Francisco to New York City
8	7	May–June 1867	New York City, *Quaker City*
9	8	August–October 1867	*Quaker City*
10	9	August–December 1867	*Quaker City*, Washington, D.C.
11	10	July 1868	San Francisco to New York City
12	10A	June–July 1873	England, Belgium

Notebooks in Volume II

No.	Former No.	Date	Location
13	11	May–July 1877	New York City, Bermuda
14	12	November 1877–July 1878	Germany
15	12A	July–August 1878	Switzerland
16	12B	August–October 1878	Switzerland, Italy
17	13	October 1878–February 1879	Italy, Munich
18	14	February–September 1879	Paris, Belgium, Holland, England
19	15	July 1880–January 1882	Hartford, Canada
20	16	January 1882–February 1883	Hartford, Mississippi River, Elmira
21	16A	April–May 1882	Mississippi River

Forthcoming Notebooks

No.	Former No.	Date
22	17	[May 1883–September 1884]
23	18	[October 1884–April 1885]
24	19	[April–August 1885]
25	20	[August 1885–January 1886]
26	21	[May 1886–May 1887]
27	22	[September 1887–July 1888]
28	23	[July 1888–September 1889]
29	24	[May 1889–December 1890]
30	25	[October 1890–June 1891]
31	26	[August 1891–July 1892]
32	26A	[May 1892–January 1893]
33	27	[March 1893–July 1894]
34	28	[March–December 1895]
35	28A	[May–October 1895]
36	28B	[December 1895–March 1896]
37	29	[January–April 1896]
38	30	[May–July 1896]
39	31	[September 1896–January 1897]
40	32	[January 1897–July 1899]
41	32A	[January–July 1897]
42	32B	[June 1897–March 1900]
43	33	[1900]
44	34	[1901]
45	35	[1902]
46	36	[1903–1904]
47	37	[1904]
48	38	[1905–1908]
49	39	[1910]

Introduction

THE TWELVE notebooks in volume 1 provided information about the eighteen years in which the most profound, even dramatic, changes took place in Clemens' life. He early achieved the limits of his boyhood ambition by becoming a steamboat pilot on the Mississippi River, a position there is no reason to believe he would have abandoned if the Civil War had not forced him to do so. In fleeing from a war which principle and temperament prevented him from supporting, Clemens entered into the first stages of his literary career by serving as a reporter for newspapers in Virginia City and San Francisco. When the restricted experiences available to a local reporter had been thoroughly explored, he moved on as a traveling correspondent to the Sandwich Islands and then still farther to Europe and the Near East. The latter travels provided him with material for *The Innocents Abroad*, the book that established Mark Twain as a popular author with an international reputation in 1869. In 1872 he further exploited his personal history by publishing *Roughing It* and in the same year visited England to gather material on English people and institutions. He returned to England the following year, this time accompanied by his family and by a secretary who would record the observations printed as the last notebook in volume 1.

The book on England was never written and in an interview published in the New York *World* on 11 May 1879, Mark Twain explained why:

> I have spent a good deal of time in England . . . and I made a world of notes, but it was of no use. I couldn't get any fun out of England. . . . One is bound to respect England—she is one of the three great republics of the world—in some respects she is the most real republic of the three, too, and in other respects she isn't, but she is not a good text for hilarious literature. No, there wasn't anything to satirize—what I mean is, you couldn't satirize any given thing in England in any but a half-hearted way, because your conscience told you to look nearer home and you would find that very thing at your own door. A man with a hump-backed uncle mustn't make fun of another man's cross-eyed aunt.

Although there aren't any notebooks to document Clemens' activities between 1873 and 1877, the intervening years were spent in consolidating the effects of the preceding years of growth and change while the author extended his literary and financial position. He wrote *The Gilded Age* in collaboration with his Nook Farm neighbor Charles Dudley Warner in 1873 and followed it with two collections of sketches in 1874 and 1875 and with *The Adventures of Tom Sawyer* in 1876.

Mark Twain drew material from *The Gilded Age* for a play, usually called *Colonel Sellers,* which was a financial success from its first performance in 1874. Continuing profits from that play and persistent problems with pirated editions of his books led Mark Twain to report to his English agent, Moncure Conway, on 13 December 1876, "We find our copywright law here to be nearly worthless, and if I can make a living out of plays, I shall never write another book. . . . Have just written a new play with Bret Harte, which we expect great things from, tho' of course we may be disappointed" (Columbia University Library, New York, N.Y.). The play, *Ah Sin,* written in 1876/1877, was neither a popular nor a financial success, and, in addition, precipitated the final rupture in the two authors' friendship.

Volume 2 of *Mark Twain's Notebooks & Journals*, documenting

Clemens' activities in the years from 1877 to 1883, consists largely of the record of three trips which would serve as the source for three travel narratives: the excursion to Bermuda, a prolonged tour of Europe, and an evocative return to the Mississippi River. Despite the common impulse to preserve observations and impressions for literary use, the contents of the notebooks are remarkably different in their vitality—and the works which developed from the notes are correspondingly varied.

Notebook 13 records the Bermuda trip in rather full narrative form, reflecting a leisurely and interested contemplation of landscape and people and local customs. The material moved smoothly into a series of four pieces published in the *Atlantic* with the appropriate title, "Some Rambling Notes of an Idle Excursion." Both the original notes and their literary development are pleasant and consistently entertaining, making little demand upon either the author or the reader.

The Bermuda notebook concludes at the time that Clemens was supervising final rehearsals for the New York opening of *Ah Sin* on 31 July 1877. The failure of that play and the total lack of professional interest in the script for *Cap'n Simon Wheeler, The Amateur Detective* at least temporarily convinced Clemens that he could not "make a living out of plays." Further discouraged by criticism of his speech at the Whittier birthday dinner in December 1877, Clemens decided to take the family to Europe for an extended tour, which would also allow him to gather material for another travel book. Five journals are composed of notes made while traveling through Germany, Switzerland, Italy, France, Belgium, Holland, and England, an itinerary entirely too ambitious for Clemens' limited patience. His flagging interest and energy and the demands of a tour prolonged to an unwelcome length are apparent in the European notes and "the troublesome book" which grew out of them. *A Tramp Abroad*, despite occasional stretches of really fine material usually entirely extraneous to the travel narrative, engages the reader's attention less often than most of Mark Twain's travel books.

Upon the family's return from Europe in 1879 Mark Twain commented with indirect accuracy upon the desultory nature of the book he was still trying to put together:

> It is a gossipy volume of travel, and will be similar to the "Innocents Abroad" in size, and similarly illustrated. . . . It talks about anything and everything, and always drops a subject the moment my interest in it begins to slacken. It is as discursive as a conversation; it has no more restraints or limitations than a fireside talk has. I have been drifting around on an idle, easy-going tramp—so to speak—for a year, stopping when I pleased, moving on when I got ready. In a word, it is a book written by one loafer for a brother loafer to read. (New York *World*, 11 May 1879)

During the tour of Europe, Clemens' notebook entries had recurrently expressed his desire to return to the familiar comforts and activities of the United States. The positive effect of Clemens' weariness with Europe was the appetite aroused in him for a return to those books derived from his early experiences—*Life on the Mississippi* and *Adventures of Huckleberry Finn*. But upon arrival in Hartford, Clemens found himself confronted with the business affairs that had helped drive him to Europe. His investments in the Kaolatype engraving process and his scrapbook enterprise consumed more and more of his time and money. He also found himself embroiled in the extensive redecoration of the Hartford house. Against the background of these distractions, Clemens finally completed *A Tramp Abroad* in 1880. This was followed by *The Prince and the Pauper* in 1881 and by *The Stolen White Elephant*, a collection of sketches published by James R. Osgood in 1882.

In April 1882 Clemens finally returned to the Mississippi, this time with the congenial company of Osgood, and with a secretary, Roswell Phelps. This volume ends, as does volume 1, with a secretarial notebook, a transcription of Clemens' remarks made while traveling. The secretarial notebook and the author's own journal of the pilgrimage record Clemens' joy as he rediscovered life along the river. The familiar vernacular situation aboard the steamboats and the gruffly masculine companionship of his old river friends, combined with the freedom of dictating narrative passages, provides a direct sense of the author's presence so disappointingly absent in the 1878/1879 record of European travel. With an affectionate, amused, but accurate eye, Clemens verified the truth of memory while he appraised present reality. With little tolerance for the folly of nostalgia which clung to the remembered beauty of "the moon before the war," Clemens assembled his resources for completing *Life on the Mississippi* and *Huckleberry Finn.* The immediate stimulation he needed was found when, while standing an occasional watch at the wheel in the pilot house of the *Gold Dust,* Clemens was able "to dream that the years had not slipped away" (*MTB*, p. 738).

The Text of the Notebooks

In order to avoid editorial misrepresentation and to preserve the texture of autograph documents, the entries are presented in their original, often unfinished, form with most of Clemens' irregularities, inconsistencies, errors, and cancellations unchanged. Clemens' cancellations are included in the text enclosed in angle brackets, thus <word>; editorially-supplied conjectural readings are in square brackets, thus [word]; hyphens within square brackets stand for unreadable letters, thus [--]; and editorial remarks are italicized and enclosed in square brackets, thus [*blank page*]. A slash separates alternative readings which Clemens left unresolved, thus word/word. The separation of entries is indicated on the printed page by extra space between lines; when the end of a manuscript entry coincides with the end of a page of the printed text, the symbol [#] follows the entry. A full discussion of textual procedures accompanies the tables of emendation and details of inscription in the Textual Apparatus at the end of each volume; specific textual problems are explained in headnotes or footnotes when unusual situations warrant.

Annotation of the Notebooks

A series of documents encompassing Mark Twain's adult life, a life which ranged from Missouri villages to European capitals, must contain many references so obscure they cannot be annotated, or so well known their explanation would offend the reader's intelligence. Every effort has been made to recover the obscure and to strike a balance in anticipating the reader's need for information not available in standard books of reference.

The erratic nature of the notebooks, with their diverse and often almost compulsive record of minute matters, allows us access far closer than more formal documents to the movements of a man's mind at a distant time. In order to guide the reader through this cryptic record of activities and observations, the documentation often is necessarily longer than the original entry. Since so much of the information in the notes has been assembled from a variety of sources, themselves often unpublished or otherwise very nearly inaccessible, citation to these is customarily confined to material directly quoted, with a bibliography of the most useful related material in the headnote where that seems appropriate.

Apart from the general discussion in headnotes concerning published material which derives from each notebook, no attempt has been made to collate notebook entries with their development in literary form except when such reference is necessary for an understanding of an entry. Occasional references to specific literary themes or topics which are not readily identifiable are made when it seems likely they might otherwise escape the reader's notice. Even these are selective and do not pretend to identify each instance in which ideas for characters or episodes are reworked in the various phases of the author's writing. What appear to be tag lines for jokes persist throughout the notebooks. Variant repetitions when assembled sometimes provide the substance of the anecdote, but since the form and language of these stories were doubtless adjusted for the raconteur's audience, their full versions have been left to each reader's imagination.

When no useful information can be assembled to document a troublesome entry, there is no statement of editorial failure. Mark Twain's comments on persons, events, or other subjects out of any recoverable context may result from spontaneous recall or anticipation, proposed literary projects, pure association, or his diverse reading. On one occasion Clemens himself remarked: "One often finds notes in his book which no longer convey a meaning—they were texts, but you forget what you were going to say under them" (Notebook 17, p. 259). Later editors can seldom be more successful than the original inscriber in recovering the intention behind such entries.

XIII

"To Get the World & the Devil Out of My Head"

(May–July 1877)

NOTEBOOK 13 is primarily the record of Clemens' ten-day vacation trip to Bermuda with the Reverend Joseph Hopkins Twichell. The flyleaf and endpaper entries and a few final pages in the notebook were made immediately before and after the trip. A full account of the Bermuda journey, developed from this notebook, appeared in the *Atlantic Monthly* from October 1877 through January 1878 as "Some Rambling Notes of an Idle Excursion."

In the weeks preceding his departure for Bermuda Clemens was working on the production of *Ah Sin,* which, due to a disagreement with Bret Harte, had fallen almost entirely into his hands. At the end of April he was in Baltimore rehearsing the piece—and again rewriting it—for its Washington opening on 7 May. Theatrical manager J. T. Ford of Baltimore wrote to Clemens the morning after the opening: "With help the play can be made an assured success You ought to be here to be its wetnurse until it can do for it's self. . . . Some improvements can easily be made

Some features more distinctly brought out, and your presence and watchfulness will ensure both" (Ford to SLC, 8 May 1877). Clemens, however, had no inclination to "wetnurse" the play any further. The week-long trial run in Washington showed receipts of over two thousand dollars and Clemens gladly postponed revision for several weeks. His weary and harassed state was evident in the short note he wrote to his sister-in-law, Sue Crane, at about this time: "I am going off on a sea voyage. . . . It is to get the world & the devil out of my head so that I can start fresh at the farm early in June." On 16 May 1877, on the eve of his departure for Bermuda, Clemens began Notebook 13. He continued to use it throughout his stay on the island and until shortly after the New York opening of *Ah Sin* on 31 July 1877.

This was Clemens' first extended excursion with Twichell. The two left New Haven for New York by overnight boat on 16 May. Several pages of entries describe their adventures in New York on the morning of 17 May before the sailing of the S.S. *Bermuda*. Throughout these notes Twichell figures as an ingenuous and inquisitive tourist and Clemens manifests an uneasy consciousness of his companion's provincial manners and dress. Similar examples of comic ineptitude are attributed to a character Clemens called the Fool later in this notebook. He figures in the shipboard sequence of "Some Rambling Notes" as the Ass, a callow young man who halts conversation with his exasperatingly inappropriate remarks.

Clemens and Twichell arrived in Bermuda on 20 May and secured rooms, under false names, in Mrs. Kirkham's boardinghouse in Hamilton. The next four days were spent in companionable walks and drives around Bermuda. Clemens would write to Twichell shortly after their return: "It was much the joyousest trip I ever had, Joe—not a heartache in it, not a twinge of conscience" (27 June 1877). His notes—written in a conversational style reminiscent of the letters which he wrote to Livy when traveling—reflect his enjoyment of the island. Unlike his other notebooks, there are no references here to current work or business affairs. Clemens claimed in "Some Rambling Notes" that this was the first trip he had ever undertaken "for pure recreation, the bread-and-butter element left out." Despite this disclaimer, he began expanding the detailed notes which he made during this period of ostensible idleness immediately upon his return from Bermuda. He wrote to Howells on 29 May, two days after his return: "If you had gone with me & let me pay the $50 which the trip, & the board & the various nick-nacks & mementoes would cost, I would have picked up enough droppings from your conversation to pay me 500 per cent profit in the way of the *several* magazine articles which I could have written, whereas I can now write only one or two" (*MTHL*, p. 179).

The Clemens family left for Quarry Farm on 6 June. By 27 June Clemens had completed most of his work on the four installments of "Some Rambling Notes" and had plunged into a new play, *Cap'n Simon Wheeler, The Amateur Detective*, which he completed in six and a half working days. Clemens boasted to Howells that it was a "prodigious dash of work" and added: "If the play's a success it is worth $50,000 or more—if it fails it is worth nothing—& yet even the worst of failures can't rob me of the 6½ days of booming pleasure I have had in writing it" (6 July 1877, *MTHL*, p. 188). Clemens revised and edited the play, informing Howells: "You see I learned something from the fatal blunder of putting Ah Sin aside before it was finished" (11 July 1877, *MTHL*, p. 189).

On 15 July Clemens arrived in New York for a two-week stay, during which he tried unsuccessfully to interest his theatrical acquaintances in *Cap'n Simon Wheeler*, which never was produced. Meanwhile he was "licking that dreadful play of Ah Sin into shape & rehearsing it 4 hours a day with the actors" (*MTMF*, p. 205). The play opened at the Fifth Avenue Theatre on 31 July for a brief and unprofitable run and Clemens was almost relieved to announce to Howells several weeks later that it was a "most abject & incurable failure!" (15 October 1877, *MTHL*, p. 206). Clemens' hopes for a theatrical success to equal that of his *Gilded Age* play were never realized, but he continued to sketch out plans for dramatic works. His note for *The Prince and the Pauper* in Notebook 13 indicates that he originally planned that as a play also.

Notebook 13 now contains 108 pages, 22 of them blank. They measure 5¾ by 3 7/16 inches (14.6 by 8.7 centimeters). Because the notebook is hinged at the top, tablet-style, facing pages are upper and lower rather than left-hand and right-hand. The pages are ruled with blue horizontal lines, twenty on the upper page below a wide top margin and twenty-two on the lower page. The page edges are gilded. The cover is stiff, glazed, red-brown calf with blind stamped borders on the front and back. Two slits in the front cover probably once held a strap that is now missing. The pages are bound together as a unit but are not permanently attached to the cover. They are held inside the cover by a cardboard tab, bound to them at the back, which slips into the hollow back cover through a slot at the hinge. A bellows pocket with sides of a red-violet textured fabric is attached to the back endpaper. This pocket, the back endpaper itself, and the outer sides of the flyleaves are lined with a shiny white paper with a brocade grain. The front endpaper is lined with a smooth, shiny white paper. The inner sides of both flyleaves are lined with cream-colored paper. A second flyleaf of matching cream-colored paper originally followed the front flyleaf. It has been torn out and is missing, as are two ruled leaves.

During the Bermuda trip Clemens used the notebook from back to front. After his return to New York he turned the notebook and used it briefly from front to back. The text is presented here in that chronological sequence, beginning with entries from the back endpaper. After the trip, the second sequence begins with entries in order from the front endpaper and flyleaf (pp. 37.2–40.3), followed by the entries on the remaining pages running from front to back.

The entries are neatly written in pencil, with some brief additions in purple ink. Clemens drew lines, spirals, Ws, and Xs, in pencil and purple ink, through most of the first Bermuda entries; there are black ink marks on some of the final Bermuda notes and a paragraph marked "Close" in black ink. These use marks were almost certainly added by Clemens in Hartford, as he was incorporating the notebook material into his manuscript of "Some Rambling Notes."

Albert Bigelow Paine wrote "Idle Excursion" on the back flyleaf.

J. R. Locke[1]
243 Broadway—2 [#]

---

[1] David Ross Locke (Petroleum V. Nasby) was an editor of the New York *Evening Mail* from 1871 to 1879 and maintained a business office at 243 Broadway. Locke and Clemens had known each other since 1869. It is probable that the two met to discuss an idea which Clemens mentioned in a letter of 7 August 1877 to F. D. Millet: "Petroleum V. Nasby wanted me to write a play with him, but I didn't believe we'd amount to anything together, & I see by the papers he has got another collaborateur" (Houghton Library, Harvard University, Cambridge, Mass.). This and the following entries through "Frank Fuller" were written on the notebook's bellows pocket.

Dan Slote[2]

St James[3]

Frank Fuller[4]

First actual pleasure trip I ever took. 16th May.

Bar-keep on boat who showed all comers a foul misprint in a play bill.

<Backed out>

Gobbled the youth's place in the line & was proud of my <ass> manly assertion of my rights. When he yielded & looked so meek & abashed, felt infinitely ashamed of myself. Did not get through blushing for an hour.

People sitting about saloon waiting for beds & looking forlorn.

---

[2] Slote, whose friendship with Clemens dated from the *Quaker City* excursion, was a partner in Slote, Woodman & Company, "Blank Book Manufacturers," of New York City. During this period, Clemens and Slote were involved in the manufacture of "Mark Twain's Patent Self-Pasting Scrap Book," an invention which Clemens had enthusiastically announced to his brother Orion on 11 August 1872: "My idea is this: Make a scrap-book *with leaves veneered or coated with gum-stickum* of some kind; wet the page with sponge, brush, rag or tongue, and dab on your scraps like postage stamps. . . . [A] great humanizing and civilizing invention" (*MTL*, pp. 196–197). The sales of the scrapbook were steady, if not extraordinary. Slote, Woodman & Company's statement for the period ending 31 December 1877 shows that twenty-five thousand copies of the scrapbook were sold (Slote, Woodman & Co. to SLC, 12 January 1878). The scrapbook was Clemens' only commercially successful invention.

[3] Clemens may have planned to stay at the St. James Hotel at Broadway and Twenty-sixth Street in New York before sailing for Bermuda. He had stayed briefly at the hotel in April 1877 and would stay there again in July while he was putting the final touches on the production of *Ah Sin*.

[4] Fuller, former acting governor of Utah, had been acquainted with Clemens in the West and had served occasionally as Clemens' lecture agent. For some time he had been looking about for "some little patented thing which you & I can make some money out of" (Fuller to SLC, 21 August 1874). In 1877, Fuller, currently president of the Health Food Company in New York City, was the business manager for a steam-generating invention whose development Clemens was financing. Fuller wrote to Clemens on 15 May 1877 asking for a meeting before Clemens sailed for Bermuda, but Clemens did not find time to see him. The two finally met during Clemens' stay in New York in late July.

<Moved most quietly>

Undressed. A warm night. Opened window & partly closed shutter.—Two elderly men, brothers, sat on guard in hearing, & discussed & finally jawed over Charlie's cemetery business.[5]

Slow railroad[6]

Moved silently away frn N Haven near midnight, with far lightning flashing & paling the scattered red lights, then distant thunder.

In morning T[7] on main deck asked mulatto <stew> stewardess a question not in her line—the scorn she threw into the fact that it was out of her line.

T asked 5 people where the baggage room on the dock was—one was enough. Then he wanted to go there & *see* if our trunks were there, as if our <checks> cks weren't sufficient.

Started up town. T to policeman 123, (suspicious overcoat & green manners

Can you tell me where pier 12 is? (We didn't need to know where it was, yet.)

P.—Pier 12 East river?

T—No, Pier 12 north river.

P—Suspiciously & eyeing T from head to foot—*This*—is *East* river! (watching for the effect.)

T.—O! <(with the air of one> (as much as to suggest, he hadn't thought of that—& yet with a manner that would lead one to suspect that he was ignorant that there was an East river & therefore *couldn't* have thought of it.

P—Pier 12 north river is on <[o]the>the other side of town. You *can* go there by car, but—

---

[5] In "Some Rambling Notes" Clemens recounts a conversation between two brothers about the location of long-dead and still-living family members in a new burial plot. Each brother's concern is to get a prime position for himself and closest kin.

[6] Clemens squeezed these words in at the top of the manuscript page (above "Two elderly men" in the preceding paragraph). His meaning and his intended placement of the note are unclear.

[7] The Reverend Joseph Hopkins Twichell.

T (interrupting)—We only only wanted to know, you know. We don't want to go there<—>. <we>We—

P—(very suspiciously.) You don't want to go there?

T—No. That is, not now—not just now. But if we knew the way—

P—Do you know <Old> Trinity Church?

T—(with uncertainty) O yes.

P—Well, you strike down the first street before you come to Trinity & that will take you there.

T (Going.) Thanks. Many thanks.

I.—Now we didn't need to ask those questions. We have caused that man to suspect us. Where we are really bound for, is William street near Fulton.—Come along, now & let's not ask any more questions until we want to find out something. (<So>By this time we had gone a block & then we turned in the <opposite> wrong direction & walked a blazing hot three hundred yards before observing it.

T. Didn't you say William near Fulton?

I—Yes; & if you hadn't stopped to fool with that policeman we would be there by this time instead of plowing along in this fiery weather.

T. Well I only wanted to ask—

I—Yes, you're always wanting to ask. That's the trouble.

T. Well I don't mean any harm by it. I want to ask this man here if—

I—If what?

T. If we are going in the right direction?

I—You don't need to ask him—I know all about it.

T (to fellow sweeping sidewalk.) My friend <if> are we going right to strike Fulton street?

Man—No you are going right away from it.

The man was right. I saw it in a moment. So we turned, & T asked the direction <of ever> every now & then & I was I was tongue-tied & had to let him go on.

Presently we observed that P. 123 was following us. He talked to a man in plain clothes, then disappeared & so did the plain clothes man (to <disguis> slip on a false moustache) & after that we had the pleasant conviction that we were being "shadowed."

The overcoat & the early hour brought us under suspicion at the restaurant. The large & solitary waiter on second floor kept his ancient-mariner eye steadily & accusingly on us while our breakfast cooked. It was uncomfortable. <With> I began to talk of men & things likely to give him an idea of our respectability & was humiliated to notice that he was not believing in my men & things. I went on, in a sort of desperate way, telling matters that occurred between myself & distinguished people—the waiter's unbelief coldly growing; I desperately *increased* & enlarged my men—spoke of intercourse with exceedingly great men—& in such a way as to show that that intercouse was the familiar intercourse of <ad> old friends.—It was a failure. <I seemed> The waiter was implacable. I saw that his original doubts & suspicions of me were becoming petrified certainties. And now I had a happy thought. Luckily my comrade was a clergyman. *That* would be respectable enough company to satisfy even such a purist as this waiter. So I said to my friend, keeping a furtive eye on the waiter to observe the effect—

"When you were preaching the morning sermon last Sunday—

That waiter turned away with the <indignant> look of one who had received the last feather & could carry no more in the way of shameless humbug. Then I noticed that T didn't look clerical.

How grateful I was <wa>when an old customer of the place came in, recognized me with effusion & gave me an opportunity to introduce my friend "the Rev. Mr—" What a sense of victory I had; what a triumph it was to look into that waiter's face & see him mutely taking back all the injurious things he had been saying to himself about us.

Russian Fleet[8] [#]

---

[8] The Russian fleet sailed from New York Harbor on the morning of 17 May for an undisclosed destination. The New York *Tribune* speculated that the fleet was planning to intercept vessels suspected of carrying arms for Turkey for use in the Russo-Turkish War (16 May 1877).

"Part of a pack but not a whole one.[9]

Policeman still on our track.

Bought cards.

Left at 3.$^{30.}$ Blazing hot till we got outside—then cold rain; put on seal skin coat & tied up the collar with silk handkercf.[10]

Steamer came out with us, went ahead.

Hearty supper at 6.

Chat in smoking cabin till 8.$^{30.}$ Then whisky & to bed.

Had a lantern hung at my head & read self to sleep with Motley's Netherlands.[11]

Kept waking up with nightmares all night—coffee for supper—finally fell to reading at 2 or 3 & read till sunrise.

2^{d} day.

Bright, sunny, mild—put on light overcoat for the deck.

Mother Cary's chicks very beautiful; bronze, shiny, metallic, broad white stripe across tail; <fr>—built & carry themselves much like swallows. After luncheon I commenced feeding crumbs to a few over the stern, & in 15 minutes had a thousand collected from nobody knows where. We are very far from land, of course. They *never* rested a moment. This stormy Petrel is supposed to sleep on the water at night.

Played a little Euchre, then undressed & slept all the afternoon. <On deck before supper> Tried hard to keep awake & read. Said to myself presently, "Come it's a recreation trip—*why* should I

---

[9] This line anticipates an anecdote about playing cards in "Some Rambling Notes."

[10] The S.S. *Bermuda*, commanded by Captain Angrove, left New York on the afternoon of 17 May and arrived in Bermuda on 20 May.

[11] In a letter of 6 August to Mrs. Fairbanks' daughter Mollie, Clemens commented: "I read as much of Motley's Dutch Republic as I could stand, on my way to Bermuda, & would have thrown the book into the sea if I had owned it, it did make me so cordially despise those pitiful Dutchmen & their execrable Republic" (*MTMF*, p. 208). It is unclear whether Clemens was reading Motley's *History of the United Netherlands* or his *Rise of the Dutch Republic*.

torture myself to store up knowledge about people dead 300 yrs ago? Go to, I will sleep."

On deck, before supper. Very fine & sunny, but a breeze has sprung up—we have up a fore & main spencer, a staysail & fore-topsail. Shall have a sea to-morrow which will retard us. Have been making great speed up to this time.

Man asks when I think we shall get in. Discover that I wasn't thinking or caring—so, gave an offensive reply indicative of that indifference.

Engine stopped—everybody interested, I indifferent, caring not a dam.

Capt Ro[unce]ville—8 days—7 men—one coat—wife & child lost—Portyghee comforts him with pats.—wear coat turn about—the barrel of magnesia—the *onion* (5th day)—put it into Capt's hands for division—8th day—1st ship—far away—2^{d} ship very close but went on—3^{d} vessel just at sunset—Capt reading prayer book—raft & signal passed into red disk resting on water—went about—could hear boat's oars in dark & officer close by saying Hollo!—tongues swollen, couldn't answer—"we must pray"—Portyghee pats him again—then a united whisper makes noise enough—boat comes—dimly remembers that & being carried up vessel's side.

A little French brandy was the thing.

The real health-giving property of a sea voyage is, that a man eats like an animal & sleeps a dead dreamless stupor <d>half the day & all the night.

There, that engineer has sat down to rest again—lazy. (Machinery stopped.)

Two men talking. It is the nature of women to ask trivial irrelavant & pursuing questions.

Yes, & to think they have logical, analytical minds & argumentative ability. You see 'em whet up when they smell argument in the air. [#]

6 A.M. Sunday.—Making land.

Unreasonable fury to think a ship could ship a sea in next to a dead calm. Presently another. (The men were washing decks & my port was open.)

<La>Whaling yarns last night.

Boston student's Governor Gardiner[12] fine clothes & spectacles—man that wanted lantern & umbrella to go aloft. Man wouldn't go above foretop—no ladder—wanted him go to fore-to-galan Xtrees.

"You might heave her down & keep her hove down 6 months & she wouldn't shed a tear."

That a New Bedford built vessel—but "down East" (Bath, &c) they don't build 'em so well. <[¶]S> Send 'em to sea & they wet their oakum first trip.

"Think it was to-day week ago"—everybody waiting—the date entirely trivial.

Pilot—What's price onions.

Citizens—What's price onions.

Narrow channel, between 2 points of rock.

Sea-sick resurrection.

Man with ancient plug hat came aboard—effusive meeting with friends long absent.

"Don't you know me?"

"Well there *is* something about you that looks familiar, but then I haven't been here for 15 years—O, it's your hat!"

Mighty well dressed people of both sexes & colors & all ages.—Men all put one foot up on a barrel.

Many use little dandy canes.

---

[12] Clemens identifies the "Boston student," here and in "Some Rambling Notes," as "Governor Gardiner," probably meaning Henry J. Gardner, governor of Massachusetts from 1855 to 1858. This anecdote about his youthful experiences is considerably expanded in the published piece.

Fine colored complexions & handsome faces & easy carriage.

Corrugated iron roof over a great freight of onions in boxes.
3^{d} to take us four yards in boat—charged us 1^{s} a piece.
Beautiful English girl at Agent's, very tastefully dressed.

Hotel closed.

No vehicle to take us or baggage to Mrs. Kirkham's. Hired little darkey boy to show us. He had seat of pants like a township map <done in co> chromolithographed.

He wound in & out & here & there—once through very narrow lane. Charged <1^{s}> double.

Houses painfully white—town & houses & verandahs all Spanish style.

They cut this porous stone out in blocks of any shape <& it h>with a saw & it hardens afterward. Then they put on a blinding coat of whitewash.

English naval officers & fine ladies returning from a fine large church on the hill.

Roses, morning glories, papaias, <& a> lemons, figs, bananas, & a sort of spreading palm & India rubber tree.

Got a darkey to <c>hand-cart our baggage up. Charged us double ($1) but he sweated the worth of it, for it is very hot.

Got two large cool, well lighted rooms, & now the calm Sabbath is being profaned by the crowing & clucking of chickens, the wauling of cats & the clanging of a metallic neighboring piano & people singing "Only an Armor Bearer" &c with power.

"What's the war news?
"And the price of onions?

Pop. 12000, half of them colored.

Couldn't sleep—got to feeling low & far from home—went into next room to find a cheerful book—got one in the dark—"Meditations on Death & Eternity."[13] Looked again & found books better suited to my mood.

Fine calla lilies in the gardens.

Beautiful rose & splendid red foliage plant climbing rock wall near Gov's.

Every man has a quarry behind his house—can take long chisel & cut out the beautiful white blocks of coral (full of <a periwi> a larger shell.) The roofs are terraced or tiled with apparently the same stuff & are snow white. They catch the rain in <cis> cisterns. Few or no good wells. No springs, no streams.

Everywhere these snow-white houses peeping from the dull green vegetation—everywhere the hard gleaming white road—cut through <[--]>the 6-inch soil, smooth off & you have a hard paved road. <so> This glare of whiteness pained our eyes. Presently a soothing blessed twilight <lai> spread its balm around; looked up & saw it proceeded from an intensely black negro. We answered his <bow> military salute gratefully in the cool shade of his near presence & passed on into the pitiless white glare again.

Flags in the swamp ten feet high. Everywhere the pleasant pink of the oleander ten to 15 ft high & with stem like a tree.

Beautiful red bird with a crest—didn't know him. Graceful cat bird—songs of unknown bird. All the birds tame—not afraid of us.

Bewitching view of the sea—pale blue in shoal—brown over rocks.

Handsome red blossom of the pomegranate

Orange in back yard

Bridal, Annunciation Day lily

Magnolia (but saw none)

A ragged palm is one of the picturesquest of trees.

To church—fine. ½ darks, ½ whites—house full ("turn^{d} people way from the door)." [#]

---

[13] The English edition of these essays by Heinrich Zschokke, translated from German by Frederica Rowan, was published in London in 1862 and reprinted in Boston in 1863.

The bride & bridegroom.

The organ-blowing boys.

The universal good dressin—the exceedingly tasteful dresses of the young women—must be plenty tailors & milliners here.

Fool[14] Walked to <g>ship, got a bot. of beer, drew cork, but couldn't succeed in carrying it home. It kept foaming up & had to keep stopping to drink off surplus. Finished & threw bottle away.

Read self to sleep with The Lady's Book of 44 yrs ago—such pieces as The Broken Vow (Mrs. Norton) The Lone Indian &c.[15] They were a sad & sentimental lot in those days. Then I woke Joe up snoring & he came in & after a world of row & trouble got me awake. I apologized.

Monday

Was awaked at <6:30> 6 AM Monday by our ambitious young rooster—looked out saw him swelling around a yellow cat asleep on ground. Birds, a bugle, & various noises. Then a piano over the way which

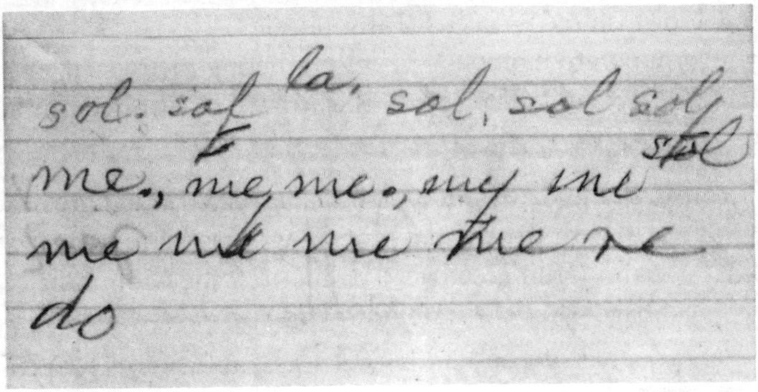

sol. sol la, sol, sol sol sol
me, me me, me me
me me me me re
do

[14] Clemens wrote "Fool" in purple ink to identify the subject of this entry. He added the word sometime after writing the entry, probably as he worked on "Some Rambling Notes" in Hartford.

[15] Caroline Norton's "The Broken Vow" as well as the anonymous "The Last Indian" appeared in the February 1834 issue of *Godey's Lady's Book*.

Glare reflected from white <ground> road makes you want to sneeze.

Bought white shoes & pipe-clay. Walked till hurt heel. After noonday dinner

Drove along shore—one horse & intelligent young colored man. The sea-view always enchanting—light green water striped here & there with brown where rocks lie near surface. Sail boats flying over the rippled water. Distant glimpses[16] of brilliant green water through narrow gaps between the many little islands.

Close to shore on shallow water where light colored bottom, that marvellous transparency that crystal brilliancy & diamond like play which the wavelets cast—& the brilliant distinctness of the rocks on bottom.

That fool with us sees "Onions Wanted" & innocently gets out to tell man plenty along the road.

Geranium (scarlet) is simply almost a weed here. So is the lantana (yellow & brownish red)—in S. I.[17] it is purple.

Indian corn, potatoes onions—people gathering the two latter (May 21) in every field. The corn & the arrow root just beginning to grow.

Bermuda bamboo—lemon, fig, papaia, mangrove (with the twisted roots in water)—date palm, cocoa palm (fruit green yet) palmetto & the Mountain cabbage palm the stateliest of all.

---

[16] The placement of two pages of pencil drawings which, in the notebook, interrupt this entry suggests that they predate Clemens' Bermuda notes. The scrawled signature on the drawings is possibly that of John O'Brien Inman, a still-life and genre painter and son of fashionable portrait painter Henry Inman. There is, however, no evidence of Clemens' association with Inman. The drawings, which are unrelated to the surrounding text, have not been reproduced here.

[17] Sandwich Islands.

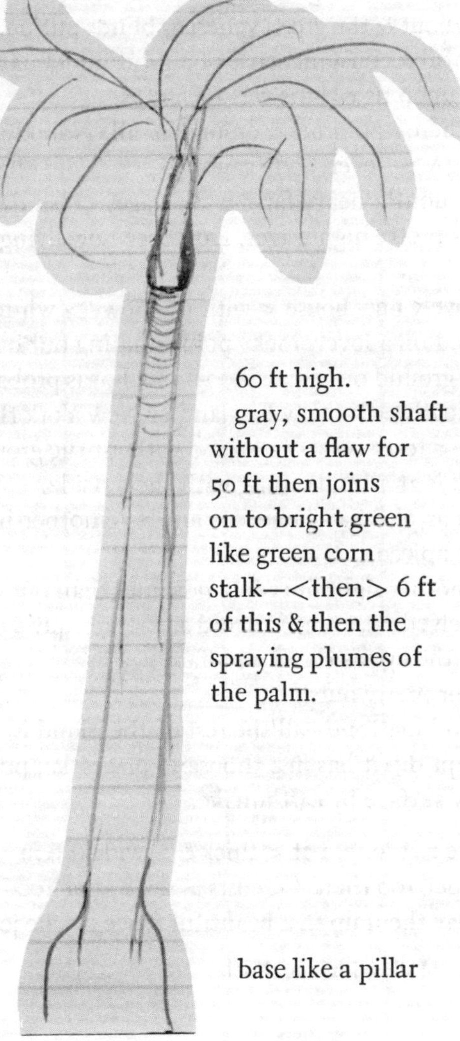

60 ft high.
gray, smooth shaft
without a flaw for
50 ft then joins
on to bright green
like green corn
stalk—<then> 6 ft
of this & then the
spraying plumes of
the palm.
base like a pillar

Century plant—dead.
Splendid tamarind tree.

The whitest, loveliest chimneys, with soft shade on shady side. They <are n>don't look like marble <or snow>, but something whiter, daintier, richer, <s>—white sugar is the nearest to it. No sign of <join> mortar-joints or any joints of any kind in house or chimney—just solid seamless white sugar carved out of a single cake. —then the windows sawed out & the green venetian blinds put on.

There is <not> a painful & constant sense of a great undefinable lack here—at last it burst upon us what is was—*Tramps!*

Living is very cheap & there's potatoes & onions for all. Nobody can starve. Plenty of schools <&>—everybody can read.

Rent a cottage for $5 a month; heavy farm work wages 5^{s} per day —lighter work 4^{s} per day—pretty high wages. Don't see how living can be so cheap.

Yet we were shown a lovely new house <with its snowy> white as the driven snow, situated on a lovely rocky point running out into the sea—said the house & ground only cost $900—which was probably a lie.—<In Hartford or nearly> In New England or New York that house would cost $10,000 <to 15,000> to 15,000 without the ground —that is if the inside work is at all in keeping with the outside.

Two new cottages, neat as pins $480 apiece <ano>—another lie. They must have cost 2500 apiece.

That $900 house was another sight finer & handsomer than our stable.—There are not twelve houses in Hartford as picturesque & as beautiful & captivating to the eye as this $900 affair.

Hamilton is the place for pretty outsides.

Saw one outcrop of hard limestone—all the rest of the island is coral. By the queer & abrupt dip it has in a thousand places, suppose it was hove up from below surface by earthquake.

The blocks at quarry are 2 ft long, 1 ft <thick &> wide & 6 in thick—worth 28 shillings per 100 there—<costs> say $7 per 100—costs 24^{s} or $6 per 100 to lay them up in a beautiful fence by the job.

Digs out blocks with long chisel.

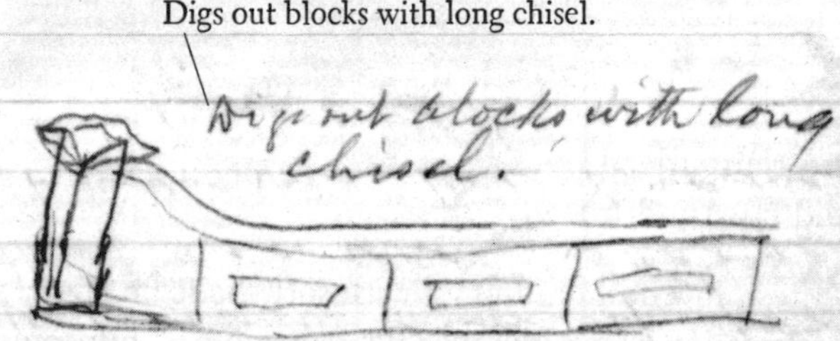

Early rose is the early crop. Garnet<s> potatoes the second crop.

Our darkey said that here everybody knows everybody. Presently (away on a country road) T said "There's a little dog seems lost & is worn out."

"He belongs to an old man named Yokes"—so the driver is acquainted with all the dogs, too.

Well, he doesn't need to know many, for <they> dogs are very scarce. However, they make it up in cats.

Plenty red coats & English faces.

Cedar is a pretty enough tree except when it<s> is the prevailing tree, then it is not so pleasant. In fact the cedar is so <thick> *every*where that you almost get the impression that it is the *only* tree here.

Pretty little bird on wall—had to stir him up with whip handle to make him stir—so he stirred, a foot & grumbled about it—so we left him there.

With all this luxuriance of vegetation, <s>no vines seem to ever climb these white houses—perhaps they can't get hold of the smooth hard coat of whitewash.

A country cottage here with its cosy comfort bedded in among a wealth of brilliant scarlet geraniums & other flowers & the pink oleander is <or> a mighty pretty thing. In other countries you'd know the cottage was worm-eaten & rotten—here you know it is as sound as if bran new.

Pigs, chickens, cows, horses, goats, donkeys, all anchored out on hillsides grazing—mighty poor grazing too.

The tidiness the marvellous cleanliness & neatness of this town & people.

No hog wallows, no puddles, no stinks.

The whitest & tidiest town in N. E. is shabby compared to this.

Capt. Angrove (<[-]>35) has had 7 children & never saw but 3<.> of them. Wife lonely & a shadow, got agent's permission & took her to Bermuda. The Co reprimanded him & fined him $50. [#]

The old couple who made fortune with a dairy farm in Australia & talked all the way home to England (95 days) how they were going to live & die in peace in comfort in their native village. Ship sailed 6 weeks later & here they were, going back. England changed!

The Captain of the condemned ship (53 years) went to sea at 15—been 18 times to Mediterranean, several times to India, &c & was at raising of Bear Flag at Monterey under Fremont in 1846 (or 7?) For last 12 years has quieted down & "staid at home"—quit roving—that is, has traded from Boston to Surinam all that time!

Old Capt West hunting for his ship.[18]

Most colored folks of all ages & sexes bow—the men often give the military salute—from seeing so much of it here among the soldiers.

Pleasantly assailed by young darkeys with missionary cards—especialy one night in a dark avenue—Come on Annie

Never occurred to us to ask anybody if it was dangerous to go these dark alleys at night—the aspect of the people & their homes was a sufficient guaranty.

Private roads & walks about houses too clean to expectorate in—have to step aside.

Tuesday.

That same old tune & that same rooster this morn.

The bugle was a pedlar's.

Mosquito bars—T sits slapping mosquitoes which I think are imaginary.

Rat & delirium tremens experiment. [#]

---

[18] The three captains mentioned in these entries appear in somewhat altered form in "Some Rambling Notes." A letter from Clemens to Howells identifies two of his Bermuda acquaintances as "Capt. West the whaler, & Capt. Hope . . . wanderer in all the oceans for 43 years" (*MTHL*, pp. 178–179). These two men became the captains Tom Bowling and Ned Brace in "Some Rambling Notes." The history of Captain Brace incorporates that of the S.S. *Bermuda's* Captain Angrove.

Tuesday

Day-dreaming for Patti[19]—Generals & finally Princes saving life of sweetheart.

No bugs here to speak of, & comparatively few buggers.

Started with basket of lunch to go yachting—turned back to get soft hats—took a back street to avoid passing a second time the negro man who is building the fence & to whom we talked yesterday. What might he think—though he said nothing. We were not brave enough to brave his secret & depreciatory thoughts about us. Got the hats & took another back street.

Couldn't get a yacht, so returned home with that basket, & this time boldly passed the negro—arguing inwardly, "There has been time enough now for him to imagine we have done the thing we set out to do."

That is it. You are a coward when you even *seem* to have backed down from a thing you <av>openly set out to do.

Seemingly none but blue or purple morning glories—very large—a fine effect where one had climbed *through* a very thick green tree & merely *dotted* it with an occasional blossom.

Morning glory blossoms remain open all day.

The scarlet geranium that grows everywhere is the *double* variety.

Calla's & day or bridal lilies grow everywhere too.

Saw a fine sweet pea.

And a tree wholly naked of leaves but with brilliant red flowers <shap> <like> <somewhat like a rimless> of a shape that

---

19 Adelina Patti had appeared in a number of operas in Covent Garden when Clemens and Livy were visiting London in 1873. At the time of Clemens' Bermuda trip, Mme Patti had just opened a new season at Covent Garden (New York *Times*, 17 May 1877). Clemens' entry is cryptic. It is possible that the reference is to Patti's relations with her husband, the Marquis de Caux, who had been ordered out of Russia by the emperor in February 1877 for subjecting the popular opera star to "all the grosser offences against propriety that husbands commonly commit" (New York *Herald*, 24 and 28 February 1877).

rather more suggested a star than anything else—<so> the flowers were wide apart—so the tree was a sort of constellation.

Very large locust trees.
India rubber tree.

Sent for horse to be brought *immediately* to go to St George's—<r>that was <around the corner> an hour ago—horse not here yet. Happy land, where that word means little or nothing.

Abstemious in dogs.

Devil's Hole—angel fish, blue & yellow.—

Bays with water like rolling blue smoke.

Palatial front fence of Vice Consul.

Bamboos 40 ft high.
1 Mahogany tree.
Wild grape tree.
Beautiful road, substantially walled.
The custom of wearing canes comes from the prevalence of the British soldier with his little cane.
The same with the half military salute of the negro men.

2 or 3 patches of forest clothed, draped, festooned with blue morning glories—fine effect.

Turn to left as in England when meet carriage.

Cat-poisoning case, where chickens got some of the poison—(after warning) & woman whose cat got some, egged on the negro woman to bring suit. Slander of magistrate who gets <$150> £150 & half the <fees> fine—so decides against the client who is ablest to pay the fine. That's the dimensions of the country!

Wretched wooden houses in edge of St George's—villanous constrast to the tidy coral ones.
One can't imagine where the poor live—in these bewitching cottages? [#]

Sensible Venetian shutter—not double & hung at sides of window, like ours, but single & hung at top—push it out from bottom & prop with stick.

Everywhere the solid substantial suggestion of England & English prosperity & good order.

Globe Hotel, St. George's—explained that they had but one boarder & were unprepared for an inundation of two strangers. No fish for sale to-day. Wanted to decline our custom, but we insisted & they yielded, taking an hour's grace to get dinner. Iron clad chicken.

Globe Hotel piano same aged pattern. Must have been a musical epidemic here some 30 years ago, which died early. The pianos & the songs are all of that date.

3 prize onions shown us—man patted the onion with pathetic affection and praised it.

The onion standard for all things—"Strive to become an Early Rose, my boy"—in youth & you may become a Garnet in maturity.

Cat had been delivered of her Early rose (first crop) & was big with her Garnet crop.

Enlarge on the onion.

Most captured the only flea in the islands, but failed. Saw him but didn't get him.

"Drive ahead of him."

<"He only goes>

"He'll turn out in a minute."

I wondered how the driver knew.—But he did know. Because he knew the man & where he lived. He knows everybody. The man did turn out.

The houses & roofs are like the white frosting or icing on a cake.

The different parishes (8) are jealous of & blackguard each other—playfully & otherwise. [#]

Man was lame from having got a jigger in his foot. Dreadful

Went to St George's in Irish linen suit & returned at 4 in 2 overcoats.

Quail wouldn't fly.

The ship can't carry all the onions & potatoes that offer.

These potatoes (Early crop) sell at $2.50 a bushel <($3.> ($7.50 a bbl) in New York, now.

The sword tree.
The tamarisk.
Lemon, lime & orange trees—handsome fresh green foliage a contrast to the prevailing dull foliage & parched grass.

Hedge of oleanders *20 ft high* & in lavish bloom.

Bewitching place on a lovely inlet where the consul lives.

Dose of No. 15—the old whaler was out of No 15 so gave the man half a dose of No. 8 & 7 & was surprised that it killed him.

We chased a huge spider all over the room to-night & killed him—Joe said "My! here's a spider as big as a rat!—gone under your bed!" (*Mem*—There *are* vermin here.)

The soup at George's (says the fool) had hellfire in it or something that tasted like it.

Put Mr. West in Bermuda—& everything on shipboard—say nothing about the voyage—well, I don't know—better think this over—it is a *relaxation* trip—& what more relaxing than—bosh! leave the *voyage* out!

Something in the soup which the fool recognized—ah, it's hellfire.

The fool tells of a young fellow who wasted away from unrequited love & then found it was a tapeworm.

The pet prides of men—money, horse, tapeworm &c. Article. [#]

Apparently few or no Irish in the islands.

Wednesday

That piano & that tune & that rooster were silent this morning. Somebody's been telling.

Flags at ½ mast for a citizen.

Rained like everything. Couldn't go sailing. Dined aboard the ship.

Belleck dessert set for £2.^{10}—carried off to England.[20]

The fool—"Do they make arrows of the arrowroot?

The fool—"Does this arrowroot make better arrows than any other material?"

Flag at ½ mast—"I reckon one of their boarders is dead."

Simple Negro—"Go up this street, turn to right, up a block & into next street then go along till you come to a house where you hear a piano & a young woman playing this tune" (He whistles.) Recognized the tune, but asked him to do it again, which he gravely did.

Locate it in St. George's.

<Thursday.>

Rained all day— —came home middle of afternoon—

Bright moonlight night. We started at 8 & walked to North Shore & then around west & across to town, Joe stepping in an occasional puddle, to my intense enjoyment. Got caught in rain. Walked 5 or 6 miles in new shoes. They were 7^{s} when I started & 5^{s} when I got back.[21]

---

20 Presumably Clemens was struck by the irony of the English carrying home Irish porcelain (Belleek) from Bermuda.

21 A year later Twichell would write accepting Clemens' invitation to join him on the walking tour in Europe which became the basis for *A Tramp Abroad*: "*Shoes*, Mark. . . . Don't fail to have adequate preparation made in that department. Recall the tears we have shed over the discomfort you suffered the day we wandered by the Bermuda shore" (8 June 1878).

Dogs don't run out & bark at you as you go along nights.

Mrs. Kirkham had a grandchild born to her in the middle of the night—that is, 1 <this mor> Thursday morning, the Queen's birthday, May 24.

Thursday.

Cool nights here, but hot days—that is, they *would* be hot but for the breeze.

White *and* pink oleanders.

AT SEA.[22]

Went to sea 4 PM.

Mr. Allen, the American consul, came aboard to inquire after Charly Langdon & mother.[23]

A doctor aboard has an infallible remedy—is going from lady to lady on upper deck, administering it & saying it never fails. This as we go out over the reef.

7 P.M. All the ladies are sea-sick & gone to bed except a Scotchman's wife.

7.30. The Scotchman's wife has "caved."

8 P.M. The doctor is emptying himself over the side. (So much for infallible preventives of sea sickness.

Friday—

Jonas Smith, 10 days out from Bermuda, 250 M—distress signal, union down in the main rigging—went out of our course to see her—

---

[22] Clemens and Twichell sailed on the S.S. *Bermuda* on 24 May and arrived in New York on Sunday the twenty-seventh.

[23] Charles M. Allen was the United States consul to Bermuda from 1861 to 1888. His son William H. Allen was Clemens' host on the dying author's last trip to Bermuda in 1910. There is no information regarding Allen's acquaintance with the Langdons.

they launched their boat stern first & then swung themselves down the tall empty sides into her—a high & heaving & somewhat [*blank*] sea—& bailed her out. Crew & owners all negros. Bought her (condemned) for <$> £42. Somebody said she left port with only 5 days provis—One of our sea captains says she had only one bbl potatoes when she sailed. He was aboard & knows. She was about out, now—a little bread, &c & 1½ cask water,—we gave them 4 bbl potatoes & 2 or 300 lb salt junk & saw the sun set on her, & then saw the last glimpse of her in the broad track of the moon, presently.

Fool asked if had any passengers.

How handy sailors are—getting those bbls down our side.

Spanish sailor.

Evidence of the foolhardiness of man. Shall we ever hear of these negroes again?[24]

---

[24] As an example of the use which Clemens recurrently made of his notebook entries, the following presentation of these fragmentary notes appeared in a letter which he wrote to the Hartford *Courant* on 19 September 1877:

> I hunted up my old note-book of our Bermuda voyage and turned to the date May 25. There I found a rude pencil sketch of a disabled vessel, and this note concerning it:—"*Friday,* 25.—Jonas Smith, ten days out from Bermuda, 250 miles. Signal of distress flying (flag in the main rigging with the Union down.) Went out of our course to see her. Heavy ground swell on the sea, but no wind. They launched their boat, stern first, from the deck amidships (of course it filled with water at once), and then a man took hold of a rope that was rove through a block at the starboard end of the foreyard arm, and swung himself off over the sea like a spider at the end of his thread. The vessel's deck stood up as high as a house, she was so empty. Naturally, she rolled fearfully in the ground swell. That man would swing far out over the waves and then go rushing back again like a pendulum and slam against the ship's side. The boat never was there when he arrived. However, he made his trip at last, and began to bail out. Two others followed him in the same precarious spider fashion. They pulled off to our ship, and proved to be two colored men and a Portuguese, who was blacker than both of them put together. They said they had sailed from Bermuda for New York ten days before, with five days' provisions! They were about out of everything now—had a little bread left and a cask and a half of water. The vessel had an absurdly large crew—we could see as many as a dozen colored men lying around taking it easy on her deck. We loaded four barrels of potatoes into their boat, together with some 300 pounds of salt junk and a great quantity of sea-biscuit, but no water, for it was stowed where we could not well get at it. We saw the sun go down on the rolling and tumbling hulk, and later caught a final glimpse of her,

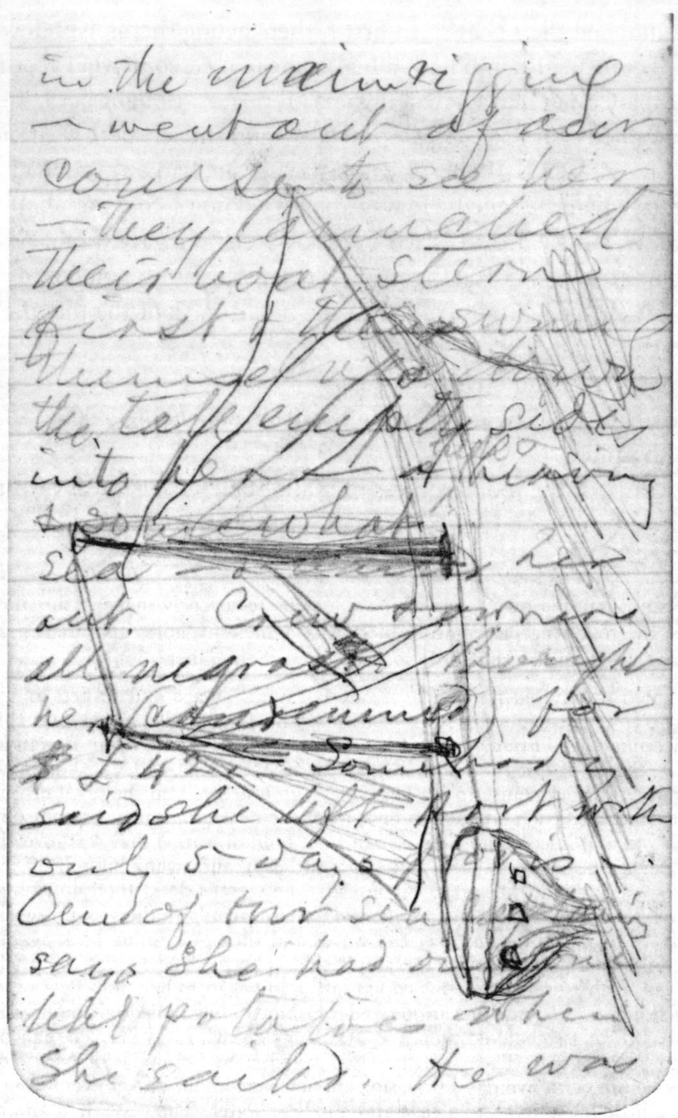

black and ragged, in the broad track of the moon. Shall we ever hear of those negroes again?"

The occasion for the letter was a report which had appeared the previous day that the *Jonas Smith* had been sighted in apparent distress. On the basis of his informa-

Friday.

Woke sad to see how smooth sea had become—but was grateful to see there was nobody notwithstanding. Enlarge on it?

Miss K smuggles gloves & laces in newspapers.

<J>The country roads were so clean & white Joe wouldn't spit in them. Conversation disjointed in consequence.

Albert's answers were so short & <to the po> exact that they did not leave a doubt to hang conversation on—[25]

Worst market in the world except <Hartford.> the town I live in.

Give Capt Duncan a shot.[26]

The Admiral's secretary & the angel fish.

Pitch into quarantine. [#]

---

tion Clemens attempted to clear up the mystery surrounding the ship as well as to elicit sympathy for its crew from the readers of the *Courant*. On 19 September he also wrote to Howells, promising: "When I hear that the 'Jonas Smith' has been found again, I mean to send for one of those darkies to come to Hartford & give me his adventures for an Atlantic article" (*MTHL*, p. 203).

[25] In two letters, one to Howells on 29 May (*MTHL*, p. 179) and the other to Twichell (27 June), the eleven-year-old "little white table-waiter" of "Some Rambling Notes" is called Alfred. He is not named in the *Atlantic* articles. Oddly enough, this entry is in Livy's hand. It is therefore clear that this and the following entries through "God's laughter" (p. 37.1) were written after Clemens' return to Hartford.

[26] Captain C. C. Duncan of the *Quaker City* had made a speech about the Holy Land excursion earlier in 1877 containing a reference which Clemens considered uncomplimentary to himself. Clemens wrote two letters to the New York *World* in February 1877 attacking Duncan and exposing his corrupt practices as shipping commissioner for the port of New York (see *MTHL*, pp. 865–867). Perhaps Clemens planned to connect Duncan with the irksome delay of the ship in quarantine which he wrote about in "Some Rambling Notes." In his letter of 31 October 1877 to Mrs. Fairbanks concerning her proposed book on the *Quaker City* voyage, Clemens wrote: "You must always refer offensively to Capt. Duncan; & when it comes my turn in the introduction I will give him a lift that will enable him to find out what Mars's new moons are made of" (*MTMF*, p. 213).

Capital situation. Young wife or sweetheart <asking> writing a very particular & ceremonious letter & asking him (whose back is to her, reading a newspaper) How do you spell "My new ruff"—"rough."—Now rough—"ruff" &c. Are you *sure* it is "tough?"

Perfectly sure. After a moment—Please tell me how to spell snuffers: "Snoughphers." Close with that or worse. Thank you dear, you're ever so good.

He—What a villain I am.

(Situation—The reception of that letter by the august person.) Comments & perplexity.

Old Wakeman's stories[27] about Isaac & Dan'l

They economise by selling us their own potatoes at $7.50 per bbl & eating our own at much less. Ours are "stronger."

Two dying soldiers winking at each other—each thinks the coffin is for *him.* & he has got the best of the other.

K'lyle; Carlyle

Flag at half-mast "for a boarder." <Proved to be> This shows the simplicity of the place.

I beg the Rev. to <make> keep down any possible doubts by swearing a little occasionally.

Close[28]

Bermuda is free (at present) from the triple curse of railways, telegraphs & newspapers—but this will not outlast next year. I propose to spend next year there & no more.[29] [#]

---

27 In "Some Rambling Notes" the burlesque story of Isaac and the prophets of Baal is attributed to Captain "Hurricane" Jones, easily recognizable as Clemens' old friend Ned Wakeman. Wakeman's memoirs contain his version of this story and the story of Daniel and the lions (Edgar Wakeman, *The Log of an Ancient Mariner* [San Francisco: A. L. Bancroft & Co., 1878], pp. 253–254).

28 Clemens modified and expanded the following paragraph for the closing of "Some Rambling Notes."

29 Clemens' next trip to Bermuda, once again accompanied by Twichell, was not until January 1907. He made several subsequent short visits to the island from 1907 to 1910.

The Deity filled with humor. Kingsley. God's laughter.[30]

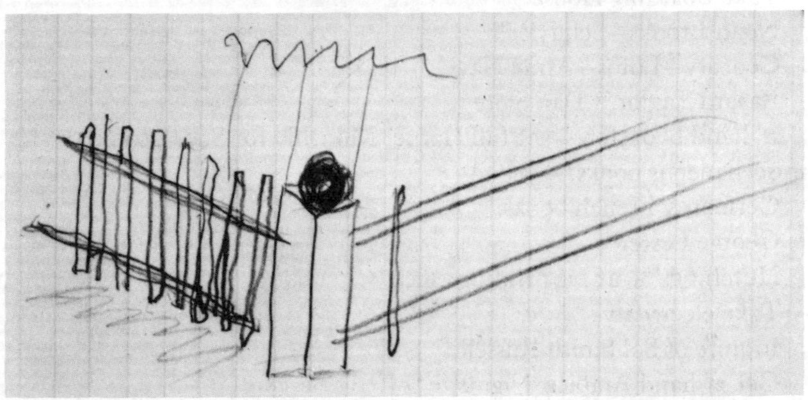

Pen-knife for Livy;[31] 2—Toys.[32]
Boucicault—felony & England[33]
Bergen,[34] 20 Cross st. Newark.

---

[30] Clemens' note was probably suggested by the discussion of divine humor in Mrs. Kingsley's biography of her husband, *Charles Kingsley, His Letters and Memories of His Life* (London: Henry S. King & Co., 1877). In a letter to Mollie Clemens on 29 July 1877 Livy mentioned that she and Sue Crane were currently reading "The Life and Letters of Charles Kingsley."

[31] The remaining entries are memoranda concerning Clemens' stay in New York from 15 July until after the opening of *Ah Sin* on 31 July. They are written from the front toward the back of the notebook, reversing the notebook's prevailing order. The entries begin on the front endpaper and continue on both sides of the front flyleaf and on the recto of each of the next two remaining leaves.

[32] Susy and Clara were each sent a doll with a toy bathtub by their father along with letters (19 July 1877) giving the names and medical histories of both dolls whose ailments required a good deal of bathing.

[33] Clemens visited with Dion Boucicault while in New York. He described the meeting in a letter to Howells on 29 August: "I read passages from my play [*Cap'n Simon Wheeler*], & a full synopsis, to Boucicault, who was re-writing a play which he wrote & laid aside 3 or 4 years ago. . . . Then he read a passage from his play, where a *real* detective does some things that are as idiotic as some of my old Wheeler's performances" (*MTHL*, p. 200).

[34] H. W. Bergen acted as Clemens' agent for the production of *Colonel Sellers* for a share in the profits. The play, which was frequently revived, had been performed in the New York area from 30 April to 16 June 1877 (Bryant M. French, *Mark Twain and "The Gilded Age"* [Dallas: Southern Methodist University Press, 1965], p. 334, n. 5).

Mrs. M. J. Shoot & Mollie.[35]

Take Boarding House.

Noah Brooks—Schuyler[36]

Century—Lotos—Army Navy

Bayard Taylor.[37] Dan Slote

2ᵈ hand bookstore—get full Harper Monthly for Sue, & some miscellaneous books.

German & French books.

George Lester[38]

Hutchings[39]—at big printing office

Take electricity.

Inquire of Sol Smith Russell.[40]

Get 2ᵈ hand Arabian Nights.[41] [#]

---

[35] Possibly a member of the Shoot family from Hannibal. Clemens was acquainted with the family in his youth (*HH&T*, pp. 34 and 366).

[36] Montgomery Schuyler of the New York *World* and Brooks of the *Times* were old newspaper acquaintances of Clemens.

[37] At this time Taylor was professor of German at Cornell University and also a contributing editor to the New York *Tribune*.

[38] George B. Lester and Clemens were both directors of the Hartford Accident Insurance Company. Clemens had put money into the company on the assurance that his investment would be secured against loss in return for the prestige his name would give the board of directors. The company failed, and Lester maintained that he was attempting to recover Clemens' twenty-three thousand dollars from its former president, Senator John P. Jones, Lester's brother-in-law (AD, 24 May 1906). Senator Jones finally returned Clemens' investment in March 1878.

[39] On 22 August 1877 William C. Hutchings, agent for the Aetna Life Insurance Company of Hartford, wrote to Clemens requesting approval of his plan to dispose of "the entire lot of 'Sketches' pamphlets to the Aetna Life Ins. Co." which had offered to pay $300 for the right to use them as a medium for company advertisements. The second state of the first edition of *Mark Twain's Sketches, No. 1*, a pamphlet collection of short pieces published in 1874 by the American News Company, had the advertisement for the insurance company on its back cover (Merle Johnson, *A Bibliography of the Works of Mark Twain*, rev. ed. [New York: Harper & Brothers, 1935], p. 23).

[40] Clemens wanted Russell, a well-known comic actor, to play the part of the old detective in the play he had just written, *Cap'n Simon Wheeler, The Amateur Detective*, and was trying, unsuccessfully, to arrange a meeting with him.

[41] Clemens purchased a copy of the three-volume first edition of Edward Lane's *The Thousand and One Nights* (London: Charles Knight & Co., 1839) in 1877 ("Books from the Library of Mark Twain . . . ," Zeitlin & Ver Brugge catalogue no. 132, May 1951, item 29).

Capt Angrove
A. E. Outerbridge
29 Broadway.[42]

Write Prince & Pauper in 4 acts & 8 changes.[43]

Get Froude & notes.[44]

Get Methuselah.[45]

Go to N. Y. Eve Post.

Bring Hume's Henry VIII

& Henry VII[46]

Butter-tongue/mouth sugar-teat
Slate-face.
Tumble-bug

---

[42] The name of the S.S. *Bermuda's* captain and the name and address of A. E. Outerbridge and Company, the agents for the ship, are written at the top of the endpaper. They are upside-down in relation to the other entries on the endpaper and flyleaf and were almost certainly written earlier.

[43] It was not until 1889 that Abby Sage Richardson adapted *The Prince and the Pauper* successfully for the stage.

[44] In a letter to Mrs. Fairbanks written on 5 February 1878, Clemens mentioned his current work on the manuscript of *The Prince and the Pauper* and added: "I have been studying for it, off & on, for a year & a half" (*MTMF*, p. 218). James Anthony Froude's *History of England from the Fall of Wolsey to the Defeat of the Spanish Armada,* 10 vols. (New York: Scribner & Co., 1865–1871) was evidently part of his background reading for the novel ("Mark Twain Library Auction," Hollywood, Calif., 10 April 1951, item D76). Clemens' reminder to "get Froude & notes," and the similar notes about "Methuselah" and Hume's *History of England* which follow, suggest that Clemens wrote these entries about material in his home library just before he made a short visit to the Hartford house on 16 and 17 July. Reports of a burglar in the house brought Clemens hurrying from New York just a day after he had arrived in the city from Quarry Farm.

[45] During this period Clemens was working on a burlesque diary of Methuselah which was first published as part of the "Papers of the Adam Family" in *Letters from the Earth*.

[46] Clemens owned a six-volume set of David Hume's *History of England* (A1911, item 255) which contained several chapters on Henry VII and Henry VIII. Many of Clemens' notes for *The Prince and the Pauper* (DV 115) are keyed to page numbers in Hume's *History*.

Gum-drop
Ash-cat
Leather head

The fairy gives young Johnny Smith the patent duster, it being the turning point of his life—he gets the girl.

The cleanest man gets her. Tother fellow took palace car with wire sieve. This fellow used a shingle in smoking car.

That letter from Plunkett[47] must be reduced to a single sentence—
Shant be a single long speech.
Hunt them out. Cut them down.

Chas must get deaf & dumb signs[48]

---

47 "Uncle Billy" Plunkett was one of the main characters in *Ah Sin* which Clemens was readying for its New York debut on 31 July at Augustin Daly's Fifth Avenue Theatre. The reading of Plunkett's letter occurs in the first act of the play, and is limited to a one-line quotation ("*Ah Sin*," ed. Frederick Anderson [San Francisco: Book Club of California, 1961], p. 11). Clemens' emphatic note to "hunt" out the long passages in the play probably refers to those written by Bret Harte. Clemens wrote to Howells on 3 August: "I have been putting in a deal of hard work on that play in New York, & have left hardly a foot-print of Harte in it anywhere" (*MTHL*, p. 192).

48 The comic sequence in which Charles Dexter, one of the characters in *Cap'n Simon Wheeler, The Amateur Detective,* attempts to interpret some bogus deaf and dumb sign language occurs in the third act of the play (*Mark Twain's Satires & Burlesques,* ed. Franklin R. Rogers [Berkeley and Los Angeles: University of California Press, 1967], pp. 269–270).

XIV

"Fly to Some Little Corner of Europe"

(November 1877–July 1878)

IN APRIL 1878 the Clemens family closed up the Hartford house and set off for an extended trip that would take them through Germany, Switzerland, Italy, France, Belgium, Holland, and England. Notebook 14 provides a record of the period immediately preceding the Clemenses' departure for Europe, comments on their journey to Hamburg, and ends in late July 1878 just as they are about to leave Heidelberg. The notebook also includes a few pages of notes dating from November 1877.

An event at the end of 1877 may have contributed to Clemens' decision to make the trip abroad. On 17 December, he made a speech at John Greenleaf Whittier's birthday dinner which contained irreverent references to Emerson, Holmes, and Longfellow. The speech was received coldly and Clemens was convinced he had gravely offended his audience. He wrote to Howells gloomily: "I feel that my misfortune has injured me all over the country; therefore it will be best that I retire from before the public at present." He admitted that he hadn't "done a stroke of work" and had only "moped around" since the dinner (*MTHL*, pp. 212, 215). The idea of a lengthy stay abroad was understandably attractive to Clemens at this time. The European trip would provide him with the time and privacy to complete some of his literary projects and would allow him a respite from the business and social obligations which interrupted his work. By the middle of February 1878 Clemens wrote to his mother: "Life has come to be a very serious matter with me. I have a badgered, harassed feeling, a good part of my time. It comes mainly of business responsibilities and annoyances. . . . There are other things also that help to consume my time and defeat my projects. Well, the consequence is, I cannot write a book at home. This cuts my income down. Therefore, I have about made up my mind to take my tribe and fly to some little corner of Europe and budge no more until I shall have completed one of the half dozen books that lie begun, up stairs" (17 February 1878, *MTL*, pp. 319–320). The unfinished manuscripts probably included drafts of "Captain Stormfield's Visit to Heaven," *The Prince and the Pauper*, the novel "Simon Wheeler, Detective," "The Autobiography of a Damned Fool," a burlesque diary of Methuselah, and *Huckleberry Finn*.

Within a few weeks, however, Clemens' plans had changed considerably. The unfinished manuscripts were forgotten again and a new project—a book about his European travels—became his chief concern. On 8 March 1878, a month before his departure for Europe, Clemens secretly signed a contract for the new book with Frank Bliss, son of the American Publishing Company's president, Elisha Bliss. The secret contract—prompted by dissatisfaction with the American Publishing Company—was Clemens' attempt to bring the publication of his books more firmly under his own control. But Frank Bliss's short-lived publishing company was not equipped to market Clemens' new book. In November 1879 Clemens and Frank Bliss would agree to transfer the contract for *A Tramp Abroad* to the American Publishing Company. Bliss returned to his position as secretary of the company.

Most of March 1878 was spent in packing and making hurried farewell visits to the Langdons and the Cranes in Elmira and to Clemens' mother and sister in Fredonia, New York. At about this time, Livy began compiling lists of gifts and purchases commissioned by family and friends in her own memorandum book. The book includes measurements of the Hartford house, with suggestions for furniture and bric-a-brac to be bought in Europe. Once the trip was under way, Livy kept accounts of purchases made in each city, ruling her memorandum book in ledger-fashion and usually entering total expenditures at the bottom of each page. The lists are extensive, ranging from an elaborate music box "for Mr C's birthday" bought in Geneva for $400 to a $2.50 gift of "Amber beads for Aunty Cord," the Crane's cook at Quarry Farm. The memorandum book is narrow, with gilded edges and a patterned black and gold cover labeled "Henry Penny's Patent Improved Metallic Books." It is encased in a leather wallet. The first fifteen pages of the book contain an itinerary of Clemens' 1871/1872 lecture tour in an unidentified hand. Livy's memorandum book is not included in this series of Clemens' notebooks, but occasional references are made to it when it provides useful information about the Clemenses' expenditures abroad.

The Clemens party, including Livy, Susy, Clara ("Bay"), Clara Spaulding, and Rosina Hay, the nursemaid, sailed for Hamburg on the S.S. *Holsatia* on 11 April 1878. Clemens wrote glowingly of the joys of going abroad—of his "deep, grateful, unutterable sense of being 'out of it all' " (*MTHL*, p. 227). From Hamburg the party went by easy stages to Frankfort on the Main and then on to Heidelberg where they stayed during May, June, and July.

The party took rooms at the imposing Schloss-Hotel in Heidelberg and Clemens soon found himself a small "work-den" across the Neckar River from the hotel. The hotel, he wrote Howells on 26 May, was "divinely located"; he was fascinated by the "marvelous prospect" from the glass-enclosed balconies. "It must have been a noble genius who devised this hotel. Lord, how blessed is the repose, the tranquillity of this place! Only two sounds: the happy clamor of the birds in the groves, & the muffled music of the Neckar. . . . It is so healing to the spirit." Clemens' few weeks of contented idleness revived his energy for writing. "I have waited for a 'call' to go to work," he continued in his letter to Howells, "I knew it would come. Well, it began to come a week ago; my note-book comes out more & more frequently every day since; 3 days ago I concluded to move my manuscripts over to my den. *Now* the call is loud & decided, at last. So, tomorrow I shall begin regular, steady work" (*MTHL*, pp. 229, 230, 231). Clemens' notebook entry for 27 May states simply: "Wandered through Castle grounds, then to my den & began work."

At first Clemens thought of writing a travel diary, as his notebook indicates, and he evidently wrote a number of chapters—including descriptions, garnered from his notebook, of the *Holsatia* voyage, Hamburg, Cassel, Frankfort on the Main, and Heidelberg—following the diary format. Much of this material was later eliminated from *A Tramp Abroad* or extensively revised. The fragments of this early manuscript which survive are barely fictionalized and rather commonplace.

Clemens' enthusiasm for the manuscript waned as the weeks passed in Heidelberg. The book was progressing unevenly, primarily because he had not yet found a focus for it. The entries in Notebook 14 evidence Clemens' lack of engagement and are for the most part disjointed and perfunctory. In his notebook Clemens experimented intermittently with a character called the Grumbler, later named John, who was to have functioned as the comic counterpoint to Clemens in the book and also as the vehicle for his attacks on the opera, the theater, European art, German food, and the German language. In Notebooks 15, 16, and 17 Clemens would continue his efforts to develop such a character—evolving finally the figure of Mr. Harris, a rather dull compromise between the outspoken Grumbler and Twichell.

Clemens' letter of 13 July to Frank Bliss was noncommittal: "I am making fair progress, but of course it isn't *great* progress, because it costs me more days to *get* material than to write it up. I have written 400 pages of MS—that is to say about 45 or 50,000 words, or one-fourth of a book, but it is in disconnected form and cannot be used until joined together by the writing of at least a dozen intermediate chapters. These intermediate chapters cannot be rightly written until we are settled down for the fall and winter in Munich" (*MTLP*, p. 108).

The *Tramp Abroad* notebooks—Notebooks 14 through 18—are chronologically continuous and overlap in subject matter. Notebooks 15 and 16 and the first half of Notebook 17 contain the notes Clemens made during his tramp through Germany and Switzerland with Twichell and his travels with the family party in Italy. The second half of Notebook 17 and the notes in Notebook 18, while continuing the chronological account of Clemens' travels, also include evidence of his progress in revising and expanding the manuscript of *A Tramp Abroad* in Munich and Paris. Because entries are frequently repeated the notebooks should be consulted in sequence; references are usually documented only the first time they appear. Since Clemens' revisions of the manuscript were circuitous and much of the discarded material survives, quotations from the rejected sections—most of them now in the Mark Twain Papers—often appear in the footnotes. No attempt has been made, however, to align the notebooks with the published work except when necessary for the understanding of a notebook entry. Clemens' sometimes eccentric spellings of European place names have not been altered. The footnotes provide approximate translations of Clemens' more extended passages in German in accord with his expressed view: "I have a prejudice against people who print things in a foreign language and add no translation. When I am the reader, and the author considers me able to do the translating myself, he pays me quite a nice compliment,—but if he would do the translating for me I would try to get along without the compliment" (*A Tramp Abroad*, chapter 16).

Notebook 14 now contains 192 pages, 19 of them blank. Seven pages have drawings that are not reproduced here. Most of these drawings are clearly the work of a child; some may possibly be by Clemens; but none is related to the text. The pages measure 6¹¹⁄₁₆ by 4¹⁄₁₆ inches (17 by 10.3 centimeters) and are ruled with twenty-four blue horizontal lines and divided by red vertical lines into four unequal columns in account book fashion. The endpapers and flyleaves are white. The page edges are tinted red. The notebook is bound in stiff, light brown natural calf. The penciled dates "1877–78" and "1877" appear on the front and back covers respectively, and there are two or three very faint illegible penciled words on the front cover. Notebook 14 is heavily worn with use, the spine has completely deteriorated, and the covers, the page gatherings, and many single leaves are loose. Portions of five leaves have been torn out and are missing, and it is possible that further leaves are missing. There are numerous pencil inscriptions on the endpapers and flyleaves. With the exception of three pages in purple ink (the first writing in the notebook) and a few brief notes in black, blue, and purple ink, all the entries are in pencil. Clemens evidently jotted down some of the brief notes in ink while developing his manuscript for *A Tramp Abroad* from the notebook material.

There are a great number of Clemens' use marks, both in pencil and in ink, throughout the notebook. These marks, which often take the form of large Xs or lines drawn through entire entries, are not reproduced.

The first entries in this notebook, a list of literary projects (pp. 49.1–51.9), were written with the notebook held right side up, the wide margin at the top of the page, and are in the purple ink that Clemens used most frequently during this period when he was working at home in Hartford. After these entries, Clemens inverted the notebook and started writing from the back, with the wide margin at the bottom of the page. He may have inverted the notebook to keep space at the end of his list of projects for the addition of new ideas. Two penciled entries at the end of the purple ink list may be such later additions (p. 51.4–9). The word "Written" penciled over the entry at page 49.2–5 suggests that the author originally intended the list to be a working record where ideas for stories could be entered as they occurred to him and later checked off as they were used.

With the exception of a few short entries, the earliest writing in the notebook (through p. 65.6) is on right-hand pages only. In the remainder of the notebook Clemens wrote consistently on both sides of the leaves.

It is possible that Clemens laid the notebook aside for a time after compiling the list of literary projects. After the initial date ("Nov. 23, 1877."), no entries in the notebook can with assurance be dated earlier than mid-February 1878, when Clemens began preparing in earnest for the European trip. It is unlikely that he would have used the notebook even sporadically during that interval without referring to appointments and engagements, in particular the Whittier birthday dinner of 17 December 1877.

The notebook is accompanied by three loose slips of paper: the magazine clipping quoted in note 86, the list of German words quoted in note 128, and a child's drawing not reproduced here.

The itinerary of the 1878/1879 European trip follows. The excursions which Clemens and Twichell made without the other members of the party have been marked with asterisks.

European Itinerary, 1878–1879

11 April 1878	*Holsatia* sails from New York
25–[30] April	Hamburg
[1–3] May	To Cassel, via Hanover and Göttingen; excursion to Wilhelmshöhe
4 May	Frankfort on the Main
6 May–23 July	Heidelberg
24 May	Excursion to Mannheim
30 May	Excursion to Mannheim
10 July	Excursion to Worms
23 July	To Baden-Baden

24–[27] July	Black Forest carriage trip, via Forbach, Schönmünzach, and Allerheiligen; return to Baden-Baden
1 August	Twichell arrives in Baden-Baden
2 August	*Excursion to Favorite Schloss; return to Baden-Baden
4 August	*Excursion to Gernsbach, via Ebersteinburg and Neuhaus; return to Baden-Baden
5 August	*To Allerheiligen, via Aachen and Ottenhöfen
6 August	*To Heidelberg, via Oppenau
8 August	*To Heilbronn
9 August	*Neckar boat trip from Heilbronn to Hirschhorn
10 August	*Return to Baden-Baden
12 August	*To Lucerne; rejoin the family party
15–16 August	Excursion to the Rigi-Kulm; return to Lucerne
21 August	To Interlaken
23 August	*To Kandersteg
24 August	*Over Gemmi Pass to Leukerbad
26 August	*To Saint Niklaus, via Visp
27 August	*To Zermatt (Matterhorn)
28 August	*Excursion to Riffelberg and Gorner Grat
29 August	*Excursion to Gorner Glacier
30 August	*Return to Visp, via Saint Niklaus
31 August	*To Ouchy, via Bouveret; rejoin the family party
2 September	Excursion to Castle of Chillon
4 September	*To Martigny
5 September	*To Chamonix (Mont Blanc), via Tête-Noir and Argentière
6 September	*Excursion to the Montanvert

7 September	*To Geneva; rejoin the family party
8 September	Twichell departs for home
10 September	To Chamonix
12 September	Return to Geneva
14 September	To Chambéry
16 September	To Turin
18–[24] September	Milan
24 September	Bellagio on Lake Como
25 September–17 October	Venice
17–28 October	Florence
28 October–11 November	Rome
11 November	Return to Florence
13 November	To Bologna
14 November	To Trento, via Modena, Mantua, and Verona
15 November 1878–27 February 1879	Munich
27–28 February 1879	To Paris, via Strasbourg
28 February–10 July	Paris
10 July	To Brussels
12 July	To Antwerp
14 July	To Rotterdam
15 July	To Amsterdam
17 July	To The Hague, via Haarlem
19 July	To Flushing to catch the night boat to England
20–28 July	London
28 July–2 August	Stay at Condover Hall near Shrewsbury
2–3 August	Excursion to Oxford
4–18 August	London
18–20 August	Excursion to the English Lake District—Windermere and Grasmere
21 August	Arrive in Liverpool
23 August	S.S. *Gallia* sails from Liverpool

3 September Arrival in New York; leave immediately for Elmira

Nov. 23, 1877.[1]

Sketch, story, farce or drama, in which the telephone plays a principal part. Fellow listening around telephones to find his lost girl by hearing her play "In the Sweet By & By" with a peculiar discord in it, she a thousand miles away.[2]

Written

Edward VI & a little pauper exchange places by accident a day or so before Henry VIIIs death. The prince wanders in rags & hardships & the pauper suffers the (to him) horrible miseries of princedom, up to the moment of crowning, in Westminster Abbey, when proof is brought & the <e>mistakc rectified.[3]

Biography of Whitelaw Reid.[4] [#]

---

[1] The entries through "The two Dromios" (p. 51.9), a list of literary projects planned or in progress, apparently predate the rest of the notebook. Through "Leathers, Earl of Durham" (p. 51.3) the entries are in purple ink and presumably were all written on or soon after 23 November 1877. Although the entries at page 51.4–9 are clearly part of the list, they are in pencil and may have been added later.

[2] The germ of Mark Twain's story "The Loves of Alonzo Fitz Clarence and Rosannah Ethelton" which was published in the *Atlantic* for March 1878. The newly developed telephone fascinated Clemens who had one installed to connect his home with the Hartford *Courant* office shortly after this entry was written.

[3] Mark Twain had been working on *The Prince and the Pauper* since the summer of 1877. According to Albert Bigelow Paine, he completed four hundred pages of the manuscript that summer before laying it aside (*MTB*, p. 598). This note of November 1877 and a letter to Mrs. Fairbanks on 5 February 1878—"What am I writing? A historical tale, of 300 years ago. . . . I swear the Young Girls' Club to secresy & read the MS to them, half a dozen chapters at a time, at their meetings" (*MTMF*, p. 218)—suggest that he was working on the manuscript until shortly before his departure for Germany in April 1878. The novel was not completed until 1881.

[4] This note anticipates the venomous biography of Whitelaw Reid which Clemens would begin in 1881 (see Notebook 19, pp. 417–425), but the specific incident that goaded Clemens to contemplate writing the biography at this date is lost. Clemens and Reid had earlier clashed over Edward House's review of *The Gilded*

Ditto of Oakey Hall, in very brief chapters, each signalizing one of his failures. To be entitled "The Genial Thief."[5]

My Autobiography.[6]

The Diary of Methuselah.[7]

About Undertakers.[8]

A man sent to superintend a private mad-house takes charge of a sane household by mistake. It is in England, & when they call him the "keeper" <it suggests [ne]> they do so because they think he is the new gamekeeper (who, by mistake, <[--]> is <in> now in charge of the maniacs in the other house & <[--]> vastly perplexed, too.)

<Dion Bouccicault>

Dion Boucicault the dramatist gave me this idea & told me to use it.[9] [#]

Age in 1873 (see Notebook 19, note 196), after which Clemens referred to Reid as a "contemptible cur" (*MTLP*, p. 76) who was "capable of stealing pea-nuts from a blind pedlar" (*MTHL*, p. 92).

[5] Abraham Oakey Hall was mayor of New York City from 1869 to 1872. In 1872 he was indicted and tried for collusion with "Boss" Tweed but won acquittal by conducting his own defense. "Elegant Oakey" Hall was many times caricatured by Thomas Nast in his Tweed Ring cartoons. In his biography of Nast, Albert Bigelow Paine characterizes Hall as "a frequenter of clubs, a beau of fashion, a wit, a writer of clever tales, a punster, a versatile mountebank, a lover of social distinction and applause. . . . the dashing bandit" of the Tweed Ring (*Th. Nast: His Period and His Pictures* [New York: Harper & Brothers, 1904], p. 143). Hall was president of the Lotos Club from 1870 to 1873; undoubtedly Clemens became acquainted with him there. Among Hall's "failures" was his 1875 debut as actor and playwright in *The Crucible*, which despite favorable reception closed after three months.

[6] In 1877, Clemens wrote a chapter of his autobiography (*MTA*, 1:7–10), a project which he worked on intermittently until his death.

[7] DeVoto dated the two existing extracts from Methuselah's diary between 1876 and 1878 (*LE*, pp. 59–75).

[8] Probably a reference to Mark Twain's unpublished story "The Undertaker's Tale" which he was revising about this time. He had written to Howells in October asking his advice about the story (*MTHL*, p. 206).

[9] Clemens consulted with Boucicault in the summer of 1877 about his play *Cap'n Simon Wheeler, The Amateur Detective* and probably got this idea for a play from the dramatist at that time.

Publish scraps from my Autobiography occasionally.

Skeleton Novellettes.[10]

Leathers, Earl of Durham[11]

bell
No longer ushers souls to Heaven
Or other sls to N. J.
dam
[cent]

The two Dromios.[12]

Tie up in Siena,[13] Italy, in summer.

---

[10] Mark Twain came back to this idea many times without ever bringing it to fruition. His plan for a series of "Blindfold Novelettes" by major authors to be based on a plot outline which he would supply is described in his letter to Howells of 12 October 1876 (*MTHL*, p. 160). In April 1876 Mark Twain wrote one version following the skeleton-plan entitled *A Murder, A Mystery, and A Marriage* (privately printed, 1945 [copy in MTP]). He hoped to enlist Charles Dudley Warner, Howells, Harte, Henry James, Oliver Wendell Holmes, and James Russell Lowell to write other versions. Notes in the Mark Twain Papers dated 1893 (DV 128) indicate that Clemens was still considering the idea at that date.

[11] In 1875 Jesse M. Leathers, a distant cousin of Clemens, wrote to him in hopes of enlisting his sympathy and aid for a claim on the Lambton estate in England. Leathers believed himself to be the rightful heir to the Lambton fortune and earldom. Clemens had no interest in furthering Leathers' claim, but he considered the eccentric Kentuckian prime literary material and later used Leathers' story as a basis for *The American Claimant*.

[12] The twin servants in Shakespeare's *Comedy of Errors*, Dromio of Ephesus and Dromio of Syracuse, who served twin masters, are examples of the double identity theme which persistently intrigued Clemens. A number of the preceding notes contain variants of the theme: the exchange of clothes and identities in *The Prince and the Pauper*, the mix-up of gamekeeper and mad-house superintendent in Boucicault's story, Leathers' claim of being the rightful heir, and the crucial mistake in telephone voices in "The Loves of Alonzo Fitz Clarence and Rosannah Ethelton."

[13] The itinerary for the Clemens family's trip abroad was never firmly established in advance. In a letter to Mrs. Howells in February 1878 Clemens maintained that even the vague itinerary which existed at that point was drafted by Livy (*MTHL*, p. 220), for he never had "anything quite so definite as a plan." Despite his disclaimer, it seems clear from his notes here and on pages 59 through 61 that Clemens was taking a very active interest in the planning of the trip.

Also Nuremberg 60 or 70 m from Munich.

<J[--]>Sol Smith Russell[14]
care Lee & Shepard
Boston or Dorchester, Mass.

Saalfeld—in Thuringia. Very old & delicious village

Frau Emma Roehn[15]
16 Christian strasse
1st & 2d story, Dresden.

Fraulein German
15 Johannes Platz
Dresden.

Frau Dr. Salzenburg
4 Puttskammer strasse
Berlin.

Carl Weise<r> (GUIDE)[16]
80 Bolivar st
London [#]

---

[14] Clemens had been sounding Russell's interest in the leading role in *Cap'n Simon Wheeler, The Amateur Detective* since the summer of 1877, but had been unable to arrange a meeting with the actor. Russell wrote on 30 September 1877 to inform Clemens that he would be in New England in February 1878 and "I shall run up and see you so soon as possible." Although he had supplied Clemens with a mailing address in Jacksonville, Illinois, Russell's mail now evidently reached him through the Boston book publishers Clemens noted here.

[15] This and the next two entries are probably the names of *pensions* that had been recommended to Clemens. He had questioned Howells about accommodations in Germany; Howells replied on 24 February 1878: "I never was in Berlin and don't know any family hotel there. I shd be glad I didn't, if it would keep you from going" (*MTHL*, p. 218).

[16] Livy's letter to Charles Langdon of 21 July 1878 probably refers to Weise: "Mr Clemens is going to write your Courier in London to see if he is disengaged and can come to us for from three to four months—I don't entirely approve of having a courier but since your letter I feel as if we *might* be able to afford it" (MTM). The Clemenses eventually did engage a courier, deciding against Weise in favor of George Burk, who was the *portier* at the Schloss-Hotel in Heidelberg. Clemens discharged Burk, whom he called a "worthless idiot" (SLC to Twichell, 20 November 1878, Yale), at Venice with much bad feeling on both sides.

£11 per month & railway fares—he grubs & lodges himself.

From Zurich by rail to Coire (Hotel Steinbach—excellent—the best.); then by Vettura through the Splugen Pass—tell your vetturina you want to stop ½ way at a good hotel; from Splugen Pass to Thusis; from there in a carriage to the Via Mala & back to Thusis in one day. From Thusis by Shywn Pass to Samaden, (Hotel Bernina,). From there by Maloya Pass to Khievenna—from there to Colico, then take steamer down Lake Como to Bellagia, to Hotel Grand Bretagne & tell them you want rooms in Villa Serbelloni—from thence to Venice.

Mch 15/78

Maj. Goodwin falls dead in street-car.[17]—My first thought (& upon talking with others they had had at times similar thoughts) "If it was me I should think with my last gasp, 'So I have had all this dreadful teeth-scraping for nothing.'

Mem—I had lately had most all the enamel cleaned off my teeth, by Dr. Riggs, an old fool who helped Dr. Wells, of Hartford, make in 1835, the first application of anesthesia to surgical purposes that was ever made in the world.[18]

The Bayard Taylor banquet is to be Apl. 4.[19] [#]

---

17 Major James Goodwin, one of the wealthiest men in Hartford, was president of the Connecticut Mutual Life Insurance Company. The story of his sudden collapse in a Hartford streetcar and his subsequent death appeared in the Hartford *Courant* and the New York *Times* on 16 March 1878.

18 A page from Twichell's diary dated February 25–26, 1878, tells of Twichell's visit to Dr. John Mankey Riggs and gives a short account of the experiments with anesthesia made by Riggs and Horace Wells. Twichell correctly dates the first successful experiment as 1844. It seems likely that Clemens borrowed the anecdote and information from Twichell and in making this note misremembered the date. A few years later, in "Happy Memories of the Dental Chair," Clemens retold the story of the anesthesia experiments (again mistaking the date) and included an amusing description of "tooth-scraping" at the hands of Dr. Riggs as a treatment for pyorrhea alveolaris—also called Riggs's disease. In the fragmentary "Discovery of Anesthetics" he wrote at length of Riggs and Wells, properly dating their achievement.

19 The dinner honoring the newly appointed minister to Germany, Bayard Taylor, was on 4 April 1878 at Delmonico's in New York City. Clemens and Taylor would be fellow passengers on the *Holsatia*.

40 thieves—charged $1—greeny paid it but declined to enter—said he didn't care to see the other 39.

Catch a Canadian Belford[20] in a disgraceful matter on ship or in Europe.

Write book in diary form.[21]

The First German Principia[22]
—A First " Course.
Harper

People of such a mild form of good breeding as to notify you on the back of a postal card that you are elected "honorary member" &c

The wretched autograph business. <Nobody (in America)> Say very little on this delicate subject—& put *that* into somebody else's mouth—say the beginning of the voyage was saddened by the killing of an autograph hunter.

Mch. 19.—Susie's birthday.

" " Lester was to have written me last Friday what he said to the lying thief US Senator Jno P Jones, & what said thief said in reply. It is now Tuesday, & (as usual) not a word from Lester yet. These two men are habitual liars. Have telegraphed Lester to meet me at Rossmore Hotel N.Y. to-morrow between 12 & 1, & to answer "with positiveness." (Sometimes I have crowded him into actually keeping an appointment.)

Mch. 13 (I think it was, that Lester & I talked at Rossmore & he made promises.[23] [#]

---

[20] Clemens had ample cause to dislike the Canadian publishers for, despite his efforts to foil pirates, Belford Brothers had managed to publish pirated editions of *Old Times on the Mississippi* and *Tom Sawyer*.

[21] The book was of course *A Tramp Abroad*.

[22] *A First German Course* (New York: Harper & Brothers, 1856) was part of Harper & Brothers' series based "on the plan of Dr. William Smith's 'Principia Latina' " and was probably one of the books Clemens used in his study of German.

[23] Clemens' meeting with George Lester at the Rossmore Hotel in New York concerned the recovery of Clemens' twenty-three thousand dollar investment in

Mch 19. Lester writes (from Washington) one of the regular Jones-Lester non-committal letters half-promising for the 26th.

Mch 20

Twichell, at the farewell Pentecost[24] meeting yesterday, urged people to keep on going to church—<they> *we* can't give you such preaching, "but you come nevertheless & take what God can give you through us (the local preachers), remembering that ½ a loaf is better than no bread.<"> You know that the ravens brought food to Elijah, & when he got it it was as nutritious as if it had been brought by a finer bird."

An awkward new arrival brushes Wakeman in the eye with his wing.

Have all sorts of heavens—have a gate for each sort.

One gate where they receive a barkeeper with artillery salutes, swarms of angels in the sky & a noble torch-light procession. *He* thinks he is *the* lion of Heaven. Procession over, he drops at once into awful obscurity<,>. <& thinks this> But the roughest part of it is, that he has to do 30 weeks penance—day & night he must carry a torch, & shout himself hoarse, to do honor to some poor scrub whom he wishes had gone to hell.[25] [#]

---

the failed Hartford Accident Insurance Company, of which both Clemens and Lester had been directors. Lester was supposedly acting as intermediary between Clemens and Senator John P. Jones, president of the company, and continually assured Clemens that repayment was imminent. J. D. Slee of the Langdon coal company agreed to act as Clemens' agent in the matter and through his intervention a meeting was arranged with Senator Jones in New York on 26 March 1878. It was apparently at that time that Jones made complete restitution to Clemens. It is not clear whether Clemens was present at the New York meeting with Jones or whether Slee attended for him.

24 The Reverends George L. Pentecost and George C. Stebbins held gospel meetings at the Hartford Skating Rink from 10 February through 19 March 1878 with immense success (*Geer's Hartford City Directory and Hartford Illustrated* [Hartford: Elihu Geer, 1882], p. 425).

25 Clemens was once again revising "Captain Stormfield's Visit to Heaven," the story based on one of Edgar Wakeman's anecdotes which he had worked on intermittently since 1868 (see the headnote to Notebook 7 in volume 1 for a discussion of the evolution of this piece). The manuscript, published in *Report from Para-*

Wakeman visits these various heavens.

W. is years & years in darkness *between* solar systems.

Give American dry-goods clerks *rats*.—Quote some of their insolences to ladies.

One feels so cowed, at home, so unindependent, so deferential to all sorts of clerks & little officials, that it is good to go & breathe the free air of Europe & lay in a stock of self-respect & independence.

Note the system of the customs officers.

Also as to management of baggage on German railways

Note the cars, & the people in them.

How Jones[26] was grandly going to make all his kin rich—broke up all their business to flock at his heels, & killed them broken hearts. He meant well, but he was a fool.

Noble system, truly, where a man like R H Dana[27] can't be confirmed, & where a person like Jones, whose proper place is shyster in a Tombs court, is sent to the US Senate. <Where>
Where it is impossible to reward the most illustrious & fittest citizens with the Presidency. [#]

---

dise, ed. Dixon Wecter (New York: Harper & Brothers, 1952), ends abruptly with a description of the barkeeper's grand entry into heaven.

[26] Clemens' feelings about the "lying thief," Senator John P. Jones, were to undergo a complete reversal within a few days when Jones, upon being approached by Clemens' agent J. D. Slee, immediately wrote a check for the amount owed Clemens. Clemens' recollections of Jones in an Autobiographical Dictation of 24 May 1906 cast a more kindly light on the senator's character and on his treatment of his relatives. There Jones figures as a "big-hearted man with ninety-nine parts of him pure generosity" who had filled his hotel, the St. James in New York, with poor relations who were "waiting for Jones to find lucrative occupations for them."

[27] Richard Henry Dana, Jr., author of *Two Years Before the Mast*, was appointed minister to England by President Grant in March 1876. Dana was to replace General Robert Schenck, who was implicated in a mining stock fraud. Dana's nomination was rejected by the Senate in April 1876 despite public approval of the choice both at home and abroad. The only real charge the Senate made against Dana was the groundless one of literary piracy.

Look at the list:
Polk, Tyler, Pierce, &c &c, & *almost* Tilden, with a suit pending for swindling the revenue. Half the nation voted for him.

Put these things in the mouth of critical foreigner, else they will have no force & teach no lesson.

"The Senator"[28] "the Senator"—always "the Senator"—& he a thief.

Our adoration of titles. "Hon"—procured in legislature 30 yrs ago.
No congressman is entitled to a title.

This beggarly Congress of Ignorance & fraud.
The back-pay gang of thieves

Congregational singing reminds one of nothing but the dental chair

$11/1 \times 1/4 \quad 11/4$

$4\overline{)11}$

$2\,3/4$

No such pictures in Europe as you get in Scribner.[29]

Put in the undertaker yarns.[30]
Yank woman in Florida to Rev. Knight:[31]
"Do her good? Why she's down in the cabin on ice.

---

[28] Clemens seems to have briefly considered drawing on his experience of the Washington scene to write a critique of congressional practices using Jones as the central figure. His attack on the office of senator was never written, possibly because he had changed his opinion of Senator Jones.

[29] *Scribner's Monthly* was internationally known for its illustrations and for the excellence of its innovative wood-engraving techniques.

[30] Clemens evidently intended to develop a humorous chapter on undertakers for *A Tramp Abroad* from this list of anecdotes. The only story which he wrote out in full for inclusion in the book was his "Limberger cheese story about box of guns" (p. 59), which he eventually decided, on Howells' advice, to leave out. Howells had apparently been instrumental in an earlier suppression of this story, for Mark Twain later claimed that it had been omitted from the *Atlantic Monthly* version of "Some Rambling Notes of an Idle Excursion." He restored the story before including his Bermuda sketch in *The Stolen White Elephant* (1882).

[31] Probably Cyrus Frederick Knight (1831–1891), a member of the Hartford Monday Evening Club and later bishop of Milwaukee. At the time he and Clemens

Sent husband home in box with turnips as vegetable freight—corpses being costly.

Geo. Robinson's child coffin passed round to view—absent minded stranger dropped a nickel in, thinking it a contribution box.

His farmer who came & priced a coffin for his wife who was only *sick*.

"What <wi> wi' the cost o' <bringin> fetchin <[en]> 'em in & the cost o' takkin 'em oot agin, there's nae sae muckle prawfut in it after a'."

"He had a rat!"[32]

"A breadth or maybe two."

<Buried> Coffined in another man's short coat.

"The Casket."

List of undertaker <visitor's>visitors to Casket sanctum. The "urbane" the "popular" &c—& references in every paragraph to "the profession."

Falling off in Rochester death-rate—makes the profession sad.

Knight's Jerseyman & his coffin plates.

SF man who politely measures dying man for coffin, straightens him out Xes his hands & asks him to die so.

Pupil Könnt—Fahrt—draw the line at <a hole>[33] [#]

---

were acquainted, Knight was the rector of the Church of the Incarnation in Hartford and was known for his oratorical ability and warmth of personality. Clemens recalled Knight as a "most delightful man" and "almost a rival of Twichell in the matter of having adventures" in an Autobiographical Dictation of 15 March 1906.

[32] Clemens used this phrase in the anecdote about a howling dog who disrupts the funeral service in chapter 27 of *Huckleberry Finn*.

[33] Clemens' sly wordplay was not included in the passages of *A Tramp Abroad* dealing with the "awful German language." The last reference in the note is to the assonance of "hölle" and "hohle"—hell and hole. Clemens merely permitted himself a passing reference to "hölle" in Appendix D of *A Tramp Abroad*, denouncing the word as "frivolous and unimpressive."

Breaking news of Maj Goodwins death—Finally—
"Is that all?"

Limberger cheese story about box of guns.

Queer names—
Sir Harbottle Grimstone[34]

"The Moncoon."[35]

Stick to you <&>as pitilessly as a man you have done a benevolence to.

As sure to do you ultimate insult & injury as a <suf>supplicating sufferer whom you have helped out of his distress.

Hamburg) HOTEL (Hamburg)[36]

Hotel <di Le> de l'Europe on the Alster Basin—or Hotel de Russe

Altona. (5 m from Hamb.

Alt Markt (old houses.)

The Bourse (biggest in Europe.)

Zoological Garden. Dine there in Pavilion

Lubec.—1½ hour from Hamburg.

Write Robt. Watt.[37] 2 Nordgate

Copenhagen is 12 hours from Lubec by steamer.

Then <cros> back by rail, Xing Great Belt by water-ferry. [#]

---

34 An English baronet and member of Parliament (1603–1685). Clemens probably came across the name in the course of his reading for *The Prince and the Pauper*—it is mentioned by Samuel Pepys in his diary entry of 26 April 1660. The name appears, without comment, in Clemens' working notes for *The Prince and the Pauper*.

35 This is the first of many mentions of this name throughout Clemens' notebooks. The name usually appears without comment and has not been identified.

36 The entries through page 61 record a possible itinerary from the Clemenses' trip abroad.

37 Robert Watt, Danish translator of Clemens' works, had carried on a very friendly correspondence with Clemens in 1875.

The 2 streets of prostitutes on plate-glass exhibition in Hamburg.

Ancient costumes & carriages remain in Hamburg—not to be seen elsewhere.

Hamburg old fashioned, & thoroughly German.

Begin chapter with Ollendorff & First German Reader.

Mighty nice steamer with excellent living, from Copenhagen to Christiania, Norway. Steamer calls at Gottenberg on the way. (Twenty-four hour voyage.) Nowhere in the world where living is so good as on that steamer.
<Upsala in Sweden>
<Stockholm.>

Go down from Christiania to <Frederichs-Thal>Frederichshal & take <little steamer> wagon 20 miles to the beginning of the Dalsland Canal & take little steamer around into Lake Werner—delicious living on steamer—perfectly lovely trip. Very few people go. <Gott> You pass through Lake Werner & this steamer lands you at Gottenburg where you take your original steamer back to Copenhagen.

Prettiest trip in all the world.

Then to Hamburg by rail from Copenhagen if you choose.

Or, go from Lake Werner by canal to Stockholm, a lovely trip—then by rail to <Co> Malma & thence across to Copenhagen by boat.

Hotel Rydberg in Stockholm.

This town is a Venice with penny steamers instead of gondolas—Very gay city.

Dine at the Deer park.

Live in Frankfort-on-the-Main, *not* Dresden. Frankforkt is central, old, picturesque, wholly German, filled with interest—is near the

<Rin> Rhine, Heidelberg, Switzerland, &c.—Dresden is away off yonder, near to nothing.

Go from Hamburg to Cologne by rail—then to Frankfort by water (Rhine)

In the freshness of May go up the Rhine—don't wait later, for then the boats are crowded.

Cologne, <Mayence> Mainz (fresh) & Coblentz should be seen. & Heidelberg.

A very short trip.

A great thing to do, is to stop at Bingen on the Rhine in May—then, at day-dawn, go down the bank of the river (*walk*) 3 miles, then you will see the castle of <Königsberg> Rheinstein on the hill overhead—walk up to it through woods by a zig-zag path. It belongs to crown prince of Germany who has restored to its *middle-age* state & one can see *perfectly* what a medieval fortress <wh> was in middle ages when <garrisoned &> ready for service. & occupation.

Then come down to river & get man to row you across, where is an old ruin & fine river & vista-views—young girl will drive your donkey & act as guide.

Then go south on the <dong[--]>donkey to Rudesheim & get drunk on real Rudesheim.

Then re-cross in boat to Bingen.

Grumbler.[38] [#]

---

38 One of Clemens' early newspaper pseudonyms dating back to his apprenticeship on the Hannibal *Journal* in 1853 (Edgar M. Branch, *The Literary Apprenticeship of Mark Twain* [Urbana: University of Illinois Press, 1950], pp. 17–18). Clemens seems to have briefly considered reviving the Grumbler in *A Tramp Abroad* as a vehicle for critical observations on the American and European scene. Here Clemens added the name lengthwise beside the previous entry, indicating that he intended to attribute the Rudesheim and Bingen activities to this character. In several later entries the Grumbler is simply referred to as "Gr" and a few Grumbler-style remarks are ascribed to the character John. The Grumbler and John are stages in the evolution of Mr. Harris.

Phila, Mch 24—Mrs. <Spelliesy,> the lady from whom the felt hat was purchased, was taken to Camden & identified Hunter. The lady attendant in the store also identifies Graham as being with Hunter at the time."[39]

Nowhere but in a republic could these titles be so ridiculously applied. It comes of cowardice. These people might be offended if they warn't called ladies.

"Help," meaning servants (which latter is a perfectly honorable term & applies to *every*body, where menial is not used because it carries a slur) is contemptible.

"The Senator"

The Congressional graveyard at Washington—stones for even *ex*-MC's buried elsewhere. Chuckleheaded vanity of brief grandeur can no further go. Congressman is the trivialest distinction for a full grown man.

When silver bills & the talk of declining to pay the $5,000,000 fisheries award to England get to be unbearable, go away awhile & get out of it.[40]

Going abroad we let up on the weight & wear & responsibility of housekeeping—we go & board with somebody who is suffering it, but it touches us not.

Here, we are helping the *nation* keep house—we go abroad & become another nation's guests—we don't have to feel any responsibility about his housekeeping, nor about our nation's that we've left behind. So, to go *abroad* is the true rest—you cease *wholly* to keep house, then, both national & domestic. [#]

---

[39] Clemens copied the report almost verbatim from the New York *Times* of 25 March 1878. The case involved the murder of John M. Armstrong in Camden, New Jersey, for his insurance money. The crime was committed by Thomas Graham and Benjamin Hunter, Armstrong's former business partner, who hired Graham and also participated in the fatal assault. The "lady" is identified as both Mrs. Spellissy and Mrs. Spellesy in the newspaper accounts.

[40] The controversies over the remonetization of silver and the $5.5 million Halifax fishery award were raging in Congress before Clemens' departure for Europe and for some months thereafter.

1.75
 5
8.75
 30
262.50

How insignificant a creature a Senator or MC is, in New York—& how great a personage he is in Washington!—

We should have a much better sort of legislation if we had these swollen country jakes in New York as their capital. Congress *ought* to sit in a big city.

I remember how those pigmy Congressmen used to come into the Arlington breakfast room with a bundle of papers & letters—you could see by their affection for it & their <[--]>delight in this sort of display that out in the woods where they came from they warn't used to much mail matter.

They always occupied their seats at table a level hour after breakfast, to be looked at, though they wore a weak pretence of settling the affairs of Empires over their mail—contracting brows, &c. "The Senator"

How New York would squeeze the conceit out of those poor little Congressmen.

There a chirk & natty something about New York dress & carriage male & female which can't be <mistaken in the native o> <imitated su> <attain> imitated by the outsider. On a railway, steamboat, or elsewhere there can always be a question as to where a lady or gentleman hails from *unless* he hails from N.Y—then there's no question. Getting your millinery made by the N.Y. milliner doesn't help—you can't fool anybody—you're a provincial in disguise & any blind man can see it.[41]

[G]rumbler. [#]

---

[41] The Clemens party stayed at the Gilsey House hotel in New York for at least one day before the *Holsatia* sailed on 11 April. The New York *Times* of 12 April 1878 mentions the conspicuous arrival of the Clemens party at the dock in the Gilsey House's gilt coach on the morning of the *Holsatia's* sailing.

Write an Englishman's Tour in America[42]

To go abroad has something of the same sense that death brings—I am no longer of ye—what ye say of me is now of no consequence—but of how much consequence when I am with ye & of ye! I know you will refrain from saying harsh things *because* they can't hurt me, since I am out of reach & cannot hear them. This is why we say no harsh things of the dead.

Deadly light on your face the match called <s>Safety Parlor Fusees of Erie Pa maker.

Some Characters.[43]

Mr. Nye,—Mary Nye.
Mrs. Gridley.
Peruvian dollars
Mr. <G[--]> Gillette, Roe, Beach.
Orion. Raymond. Lester

Baggage-smasher on Erie road.[44]

Transfer the little teapot storms of Fredonia to a German village.

Sea-sick man—to Capt, every day, "I am Daniel Pratt, I'm from Elmira, Chemung Co, N.Y"—repeat this every day—"please take care of my effects—I shall not live to see land." Let him say it to me.

In modern times every house has a clock, yet they continue the exasperating church bell [#]

---

[42] Three leaves (p. 64.1–22), two loose and the third glued to the following leaf, have been placed here. They belong to the period of Clemens' visit to his mother in Fredonia at the end of March 1878. A number of leaves, perhaps as many as five, are missing from this gathering of the notebook.

[43] Clemens' list of characters spans the periods of his experiences in the West, on the *Quaker City*, and in Hartford. However, the relationship among these persons cannot now be established.

[44] Clemens probably made this note on the rail trip to Fredonia in western New York State. The Clemens family arrived in Elmira on 29 March 1878. From there Clemens set out alone for Fredonia to visit his mother and sister before the European trip.

Taken for McClellan at Hornellsville.[45]

Put in the undertaker yarns.

Capt. Brand's[46] experiences with Capt. Horn of the Marmion of Newcascle upon Tyne born at Sh'ids[47]

Stewardess is wife of purser & has had 12 children.

Capt Horn murdered by his wife wh made him take nitric acid while asleep & burnt his insides out.

The evidence of 145 persons as to what sea-sickness is, who & why it affects, how to prevent & how to cure it. (What cures one gives it to another.)

<S>Farewell speech in German.[48]

The excellent stewardess.

An exceedingly steady ship in an ordinary sea is the Holsatia—rolls very little.

Jim Gillis's yarn[49] about the <jay-birds>blue jays that tried to fill Carrington's house with acorns—

---

[45] Clemens retold the anecdote about "Mistaken Identity" in a speech at the Papyrus Club in Boston a few years later (*Mark Twain's Speeches*, ed. Albert Bigelow Paine [New York: Harper & Brothers, 1910], pp. 258–261). The incident in which Clemens was mistaken for "Jenuel McClellan" and given preferential treatment by the black train porter probably occurred in January 1870 when Clemens was en route to Hornellsville, New York, on a lecture tour.

[46] Captain C. L. Brandt commanded the S.S. *Holsatia* on which the Clemenses sailed for Hamburg on 11 April 1878, paying "$450 Gold" for "4 Adults including 2 Children" (Dan Slote to SLC, 25 February 1878). This and the following notes (through p. 71.2) were undoubtedly written on board ship.

[47] South Shields, the seaport near the mouth of the Tyne river in northern England.

[48] Clemens wrote to Howells from Heidelberg on 26 May 1878: "It occurs to me that I made a great mistake in not thinking to deliver a very bad German speech (every other sentence pieced out with English,) at the Bayard Taylor banquet in New York; I think I could have made it one of the features of the occasion" (*MTHL*, p. 231). Clemens had been invited to speak at the Taylor banquet but was too "jaded and worn" to deliver his speech (*MTL*, p. 327). He later employed this idea in his speech to the Anglo-American Club in Heidelberg on 4 July 1878.

[49] Clemens included the yarn in chapter 3 of *A Tramp Abroad*, changing the

"By George this lays over anything *I* ever struck" says the jay. I've put <5>460 in there.

Unberufen! & knock *under* the table or other wood 3 times—the superstition being that the evil spirits hear you say "What fine weather it is!" They will immediately change it unless you ward it off the invocation "Unberufen!"

Wakeman comes across Ollendorff & proceeds to learn the language of a near-lying district of Heaven—people of Jupiter?

17th April a most remarkable day—frequent hail, sleet, snow & wind-squalls, with dark lowering <sk> Himmel, und mit hölle <Sonnenschien>Sonnenschein zwichen. Sehr hohe See-wellen, mit blenden grün in dem zerbrochenen Spitze.[50]

Der Mench welche versuchte zum bild sein lebens-conduct bei die New York Nation. Die fatal Folgung.[51]

Grumbler.

"Gesegnete Mahlzeit!"

Die Baronin hat gefallen athemlos <dieses>dieser Morgen, vom Müde & Wacht. Sie fliegt <fr> vom <sie>seiner Mann, der Baron ihrer Eltern zu. Sie is ein Countess in seiner Eigenen right in Silesia. Sie war sehr reich, aber ihrer Mann, der Baron, wer <also

---

name of his friend to Jim Baker. Robert and Thomas Carrington were early settlers of Jackass Hill where Clemens had stayed in December 1864 and January 1865.

[50] The German ("Himmel . . . Spitze.") reads: *sky, and with bright sunshine between. Very high sea-waves, with brilliant green in the shattered peaks.*

[51] The *Nation*, a liberal political weekly, was founded by E. L. Godkin in 1865. Clemens had sketched out the unfortunate results of modeling one's life according to the principles of the *Nation* in his working notes for his play, *Cap'n Simon Wheeler, The Amateur Detective* (*Mark Twain's Satires & Burlesques*, ed. Franklin R. Rogers [Berkeley and Los Angeles: University of California Press, 1967], p. 296). He evidently intended the Grumbler to demonstrate the same folly, for he added the next entry lengthwise in the margin beside this German note, which reads: *The person who tried to fashion his life according to the New York Nation. The fatal result.*

rei> <ac> auch reich war, hat ihrer gelt squandered in gambling & dissipation, so ist die arme Weibe nun geltlos & hat <ze>zwei<n> Kinderlein mit bringen ihrer alte heimat zu. Ihrer Mann hat sie grausam treated.[52]

John McDowell:[53] "Ich habe einander Niger gelickt!"

Im Rauchzimmer verstehe ich nur genug von dem Unterhaltung zu mich puzzle.[54]

Der alte französiche beast.

Meist-rückwärts Kammer—shriek-Stimme Kinder,[55] the ceaseless metallic clatter of that old cracked kettle of a piano, & the thunder <of> <& thump> & pounding of the screw, with an occasional avalanche of crashing crockery as the ship lurches—this is the afternoon hell in this ship, daily.

But the piano is the *special* hell—how it racks one's head!

Until it stops—then you think the scream-voiced boy is it.

There goes the b's crying baby!
Now a guffaw of beastly laughter—
Now the little Spanish boy is hurled headlong down into our gangway by a lurch of the ship, & fetches up against the bulkhead with a heavy bang & a pile of books & rubbish tumbles down. [#]

---

[52] *This morning the baroness fell breathless from fatigue and vigilance. She is fleeing from her husband, the baron, to her parents. She is a countess in her own right in Silesia. She was very rich, but her husband the baron, who was also rich, squandered their money in gambling and dissipation, so the poor woman is now penniless and has to bring her two small children with her to her old home. Her husband has treated her cruelly.*

[53] Clemens recalled young Dr. John McDowell in his "Villagers of 1840–3" (*HH&T*, p. 33). Clemens' sentence, written in pidgin German, reads: "*I have licked another nigger!*"

[54] *In the smoking-room I understand only enough of the conversation to be puzzled.*

[55] *Room farthest back—shriek-voiced children.*

(20th Apl.)

3 days of heavy sea, now, & the above is my first attempt to get an afternoon nap, after being hawked out of the smoking room by the French hog.

German good-society conversation, in which both sexes say Lord God, how good it is! Jesus C! By God! Est ist verdammt gut! (the soup) D—d good.—Said by a lady.

3d day out, Bayard Taylor's colored man, being constipated, applied <fo> to the ship's doctor for relief, who sent him 6 large rhubarb pills, to be taken one every 4 hours; the pills came by a German steward, who delivered the directions in German, the darkey not understanding a word of it. Result: the darkey took all the pills at once & appeared no more on deck for 6 days.

22d Apl—It breaks our hearts, this sunny magnificent <E>morning, to sail along the lovely shores of England & can't go ashore.

inviting

Have some people <an> dissatisfied because Heaven is an absolute monarchy, with many viceroys, when they expected a leatherheaded Republic with the damnation of unrestricted suffrage.[56]

It is a marvel that never loses its surprise by repetition, this aiming a ship at a mark 3000 miles away & hitting the bull's-eye in a fog—as we did. When the fog fell on us the Capt. said we ought to be at

---

56 Clemens elaborated on his vision of heaven as an absolute monarchy in "Captain Stormfield's Visit to Heaven" (*Report from Paradise*, pp. 64–65): "Down there they talk of the heavenly King—and that is right—but then they go right on speaking as if this was a republic and everybody was on a dead level with everybody else. . . . How tangled up and absurd that is! How are you going to have a republic under a king? How are you going to have a republic at all, where the head of the government is absolute, holds his place forever, and has no parliament, no council to meddle or make in his affairs, nobody voted for, nobody elected, nobody in the whole universe with a voice in the government, nobody to take a hand in its matters, and nobody *allowed* to do it? Fine republic, ain't it?' "

such & such a spot (it had been 18 hours since an observation was had) with the Scilly islands bearing so-&-so & about so many miles away. Hove the lead & got 48 fathoms—looked on the chart & sure enough this depth of water showed that we were right where Capt said we were.

Another idea. For ages man probably did not know why God carpeted the ocean-bottom with sand in one place, shells in another, & so on.—But we see, now; the kind of bottom the lead brings up shows where a ship is when the soundings don't—& also it *confirms* the soundings.

Lying story-books which make boys fall in love with the sea. Capt. Brandt's experience & that of Young Cooper in the English paper, & a million other instances show 2 things (Dana's & that of the young Canadian of the Astor expedion)—: that a common sailor's life is often a hell; & that there are probably more brutes in command of little ships than in any other occupation in life.[57]

Those vulgar, ignorant, wealthy Irish Californians, old man & several daughters. The old man has income of $100,000 a year. He bought a bottle of Champagne to make farewell to his friends—poured it himself ½ glass at a time, but it didn't hold out—so he put some in his & his especial comrade's glasses from the glasses of his daughters.

The daughters' first act was to show the stewards[58] that they carried a great load of diamonds inside their bosoms (to astonish Paris with) & told her if she was diligent & care-taking they would make her a nice present. When they got off at Cherbourg the entire Irish party bunched together & gave her $2! They had <n>doubtless recently seen the time when a gift of ½ the sum would be a memorable thing.

---

[57] Clemens often criticized romantic sea and adventure fiction. Here he refers to more realistic sea stories: R. H. Dana's *Two Years Before the Mast* and Gabriel Franchère's *Narrative of a Voyage to the Northwest Coast of America*, trans. and ed. J. V. Huntington (New York: Redfield, 1854). "Young Cooper" has not been identified.

[58] Evidently this is Clemens' abbreviation for "stewardess."

The girls wore huge <d>solitaire finger-rings, & were always furtively glancing at them & turning them in the sunlight—also half or whole-consciously posing their hands—the sure sign that they were new to <Califo> diamonds.

The old man unwillingly drew for beer & lost. He evidently was so grieved I was sorry for him.

A jewess from Cal (in the same party) was sea-sick all the way, & was constantly waited on by stewardess—carrying her up & down stairs, & *always* buttoning her shoes in the morning—sent for her to button them the last morning when sh was for the first & only time not seasick to button them. *She* gave stewardess *nothing*.

Hamburg-Americanische Packet*fahrt* Actien Gesellschaft.

Lady teaches gentleman how to pronounce the words, one after the other.

Draw the line at - - - -

Weer gaen yuber die Brooky. (Wir gehen über die Brücke.)[59]

3 agents of the same Hamburgh house, scattered over Mexico, all came in the Holsatia, neither knowing the others were coming, & never saw each other before. They were excellent fellows, one from Chihuahua, one from Colima, & the other from another place.

With pretended ignorance I asked Degetan if he had any brothers & sisters. He zuct die Achseln[60] & said—

"Altogether we are 14!" said he had brothers ranging from 30 to 65—by 2 mothers.

History of the Spanish German.

Ditto of the China consul's wife.

The meeting at Hamburg between the Spanish German & his sister—

"It hurts <my heart!"> me here!" putting her hand on her heart.

The dandy of the second class—with specs, & hat tipped on head. [#]

---

59 *We are going over the bridge.*

60 *He shrugged his shoulders.*

Two histories which cannot be told in print—the Baroness's & the Stewardess's.

Hamburg.[61]

<St Michaeel>

Church St. Nicholai, very beautiful open-work stone spire (said to be <the> next to the highest in the world) set upon a huge brick edifice. One account says this spire is the *highest* in the world. Well, no matter, the Church can claim one pre-eminence, I think, which cannot safely (successfully) be disputed—that inside it is the dismalest, barrenest, ugliest barn that exists in the boundless universe of God.

Grumbler[62]

200 people present (forenoon) <of the> commoners of the commoners, not a gentleman or lady—what they <ne> seem to need at St N is more congregation & not quite so much steeple.

Haven't seen or been accosted by a beggar.

Haven't seen a tramp—what luxury this is! It is what *used* to attract attention at home.

No peddlers accost you—they stand where you can accost *them* if you see fit. This is perfection.

The "Landerin" stand at the hotel door with their flowers but never <show th> accost you or shove their wares in your way.

Perhaps in the trains we are going to miss the familiar train-boy.?

Got lost yesterday, wandered many miles & returned by water through the Alster.

Watched a man on spire of St. Petri 400 ft above ground to see him fall, as he was handling a heavy rope & wind blowing—but was disappointed. [#]

[61] The Clemens party arrived in Hamburg on 25 April 1878 after almost two weeks at sea and stayed in the city for about a week at the Crown Prince Hotel.

[62] Added lengthwise in the margin beside the previous entry, an observation for potential attribution to this character.

The "portier"[63] is not an institution I have met before. Seems to be chief officer. Speaks several languages, wears nice uniform, is always at hand at the door, orders carriages, instructs driver, sends for everything, pays for everything—will have a hotel of his own in time.

Gr:=The Kronprinz of Germany knows how to keep hotel, anyway.

The Crown Prince the best hotel I know.

(Daily <a>bill.)

Chickens the size of sparrows—perfect.[64]

Parlor stove & mantel combined—peat. Can't get it very warm.

Best of beds—the famous upper feather-bed is loosely filled with down—6 inches thick—as light as a cobweb, & very comfortable & excellent thing.

View of Alsterbassin from front window.

Races begin to-day, Sunday. Sunday the great day—no work, all play—sensible. Some of the theatres charge 25% extra on Sunday.

Wanted slippers—called for Kartoffeln instead of pantoffeln.

Man called for some "Hanschuhlager" that being the sign over door. "Lager" over every door that hasn't "Handlung" there.

Bergedorf to.

Neuengamme.

The hackman lifted his hat when we left.—A perfectly astounding & gratifying piece of politeness.

Pissoir. [#]

---

63 Appendix A of *A Tramp Abroad* describes the *portier* in detail.

64 Most of Clemens' notes on Hamburg were incorporated into two chapters of manuscript which he did not include in *A Tramp Abroad*. In the unpublished manuscript chapters he made note of the "Hamburg spring chickens" which he found "a shade superior to anything strictly earthly" adding that he could not "think of anything that *could* taste so good, unless it might be a cherubim."

Hotel <- - - ->du Nord Cassel[65]

Who is buried here?

Nobody.

Then why the monument?

It is not a monument. It is a stove.

We had reverently removed our hats. We now put them on again.

Stove 8 ft high—female bust in a circle in the side midway,—3½ ft by 2¼. Very ornamental - - - - around the top.

Huge parlor & bedroom. Silk quilts & top-beds. Two beds in curtained alcoves.

Parlor, vast—looks out on great paved space before the stately RR station. 2 red silk sofas; 4 tables; writing desk; 12 chairs. Polished floor with rugs; 3 large windows; 2 ditto mirrors; 2 candelabra with 3 candles each against the walls; 2 with 4 each <against> before the mirrors; chandelier with <2[-]>12 candles.

Susie—"I wish Rosa was made in English."[66]

Every town in the world has its peculiar hack.—The hacks of Hamburg, Hanover & Cassel are different—so are those of London & Edinburgh. Why *is* this?

Hamburg has the best *&* the worst. Its oldest are its only antiquities.

These great German hotels remind me of the Imperial Hotel at Belfast, because <there>they resemble it so little.[67]

Fine autograph book at Hanover.

In Europe they use safety matches & then entrust candles to drunken men, children, idiots, &c., & yet suffer little from fires,

---

65 After leaving Hamburg, the Clemens party traveled by rail to Heidelberg, stopping briefly in Hanover, Wilhelmshöhe, Cassel, and Frankfort on the Main.

66 The punchline of a story about Susy and the German nursemaid included in Clemens' letter of 4 May 1878 to Howells (*MTHL*, p. 228) illustrating the children's difficulties with the German language, "which they hate with all their souls."

67 Clemens' unfavorable recollection of Belfast's Imperial Hotel dates from 1873 when he visited Belfast to see his journalist friend Frank Finlay.

apparently. The idea of an open light in one of *our* houses <gives> makes us shudder.

Heinrich's[68] history of siege of Weinberg, near Heidelberg—<su>stubborn resistance & final surrender. Terms, women & children could march out of the gates & go free, but every man must die. Upon entreaty the Emperor <further> granted as a grace that each woman might convey forth whatever thing among her possessions she considered most precious—& behold, every woman fetched out her husband on her back! The Emperor's generals ran to him to have him nip this thin evasion, but he very finely said in the latin of the day, "The King's word is immutable."

Woman at Napoleon's prison-palace at Wilhelmshöhe—Heinrich <(stu[r]> (zucht die Achseln) said "If she look at you, if she say something, if she do anything, she all time look like a cat which is <unw> unwell."

"He not sing, he cry."

Heard cuckoo in woods at W, May 2—Heinrich said, "How long shall I live?" The cuckoo went on cuckooing for the next 20 minutes—wherefore H is a Methuselah, each yell meaning a year.—first cuckoo I ever heard outside of a clock. Was surprised to see how closely it imitated the clock—& yet of course it could never have <se> heard a clock. The hatefulest thing in the world is a cuckoo clock.

The prettiest effect is a cloud-ceiling in fresco in our parlor at Frankfort.[69]

The so-called German "cream"

German cleanliness reaches an altitude to which we may not aspire. These peasants are as cleanly in their houses as the <pro-> Yankee of romance, & more cleanly than the reality.

---

[68] Evidently a guide. Clemens may have intended to use him as the basis of a character in *A Tramp Abroad*. In a later note he appears as Henry (p. 80).

[69] The Clemens party arrived in Frankfort on the Main on 4 May 1878 and rested a day or so before moving on to Heidelberg.

Even in the narrow crooked lanes of the old parts of the cities, where the poor dwell, the children are neat & clean—much white stockings on the little girls.

7 gray cats in one small house in Frankfort-on-the-Main.

Each city has its peculiarity—F's is its ancient town pumps.

Goethe's house—the<y> courier had the effrontery to propose we visit birthplace of Rothschild. My dear sir, 2 or 300 years ago, they'd have skinned this Jew <instea> in old Frankfort, instead of <vis> paying homage to his birthplace—but it is an advance—we have quit loathing Jews & gone to worshiping their money.—Come, let<s> us exhibit the birthplaces of Vanderbilt & Stewart to admiring foreigners.

The <Geutenburg>Geutenberg &c trinity stand opposite our windows.[70]

Er lebt we Gott in Frankreich.[71]

Nun ist Holland in Noth

Er hat das Pulver nicht erfunden.

Der Jude, by Carl Spindler

Ghetto up to 1830.

Frankfort does not own Goete's house—this is very American

Legend that Charlemagne arrived at the Main with his army chasing the Saxons, or chased by them—early in the morning—fog, & could not see well, <how>—saw a deer taking her young along, judged she would seek a ford—so she did—C crossed there & resolved to build a city—which he named the ford of the Franks—Frankfort—there's an old bridge there with <his> C's statue on it. [#]

---

[70] The Gutenberg Trinity, a grouping of statues representing Gutenberg, Fust, and Schöffer, associates in the invention of printing, stood in Frankfort's Rossmarkt.

[71] This and the two following entries are idiomatic expressions: *He lives a life free from care; Now we are in a fine mess; He will never set the Thames on fire.*

Roland's statue, one of the Paladins, at chapel, Wilhelmshöhe.

Buchstaben, the alphabet—so called because the first movable types of <Gutenburg>Gutenberg were made <on> on birch sticks, Buchstabe.

Gutenberg was born in Frankfort (they don't know just where) <& d[e]> <M> & did his work in Mainz. (Mayence).
The Trinity.

Bay say, "I brang you some flowers—no, I bring'd 'em.

Susie has composed a poem.

In the meadow below us,[72]

Students at Göttingen with dreadfully scarred faces. Here you can't tell whether a man is a Franco-Prussian war hero, or merely has a university education.

In Frankfort, hotel chandelier with 9 burners, but you had to light 8 of them in order to see the other one. Bad gas has no nationality.

Boxes established in beer saloons for nubs of cigars for orphans—the result in money is enormous.

Fresco our drawing-room simply with light clouds, nothing more, except a distant balloon.

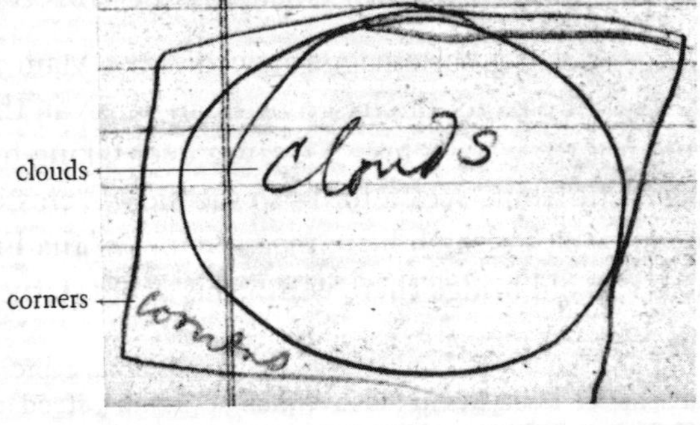

[72] This entry, possibly the first line of Susy's poem, is followed by several blank lines in the manuscript, presumably reserved for the balance of the poem.

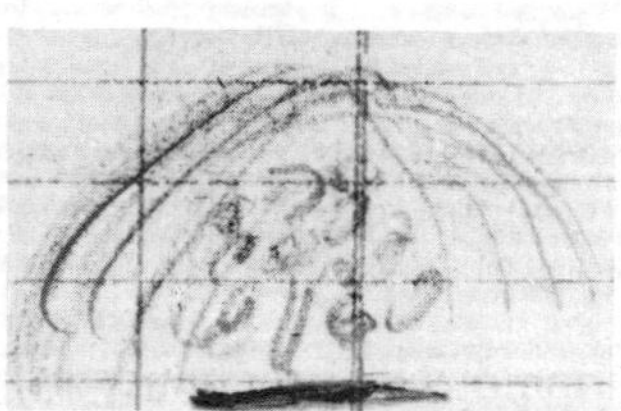

Bouquet under umbrella fountain jet.

The people have such good faces.

The uniforms are all bran new.

Street-car conductor wears bright new uniform, & is as polite as —as—but there is nobody at home to compare this politeness with.

—& politeness costs so little. Our national impoliteness is not natural, but acquired. It would be a curious study, *how* <& whence> & from whom & why we acquired it.

The bank in Hamburg was up a stable-yard, apparently. If ours were as modest they wouldn't fail so often, maybe.

A melancholy place, the old Ghetto, with its ancient wall.—8 pm no exit, even for a doctor, 1830.

Men in garb of gentlemen stare at ladies here in Frankfort just as they do in London.

Everywhere the evidences of great freedom & superb government.

The "Anlage" full of song-birds.

Bought good cigar for 2 cents, though my friends say I don't know a good cigar when I see one.

The very schoolboys wear uniform cap.

The lower-class women, however nicely dressed, wear nothing on the head in this hot sunshine.

The schoolboys carry books in knapsack, apparently.

<[Ha]>Frankfort is flourishing, & fast being rebuilt & extended.

The first Rothchild's house in the Ghetto. [#]

Picturesque old buildings

They charged me $7.50 for paper-covered German books worth $2, which fell to pieces in my hands, so badly bound, & $12.50 for a water-color worth $75—so I came out ahead.

Funny times with the good-faced chambermaid, who pronounced anziehen (to put on clothes) like Ansehen—called the Fraulein (Clara) & finally Rosa.

When a body sneezes they say "Gezundheit!" (meaning "Zur -----")

They look surprised when I order a second armful of wood for the monument. Proper enough; for I find that one small armfull, if it be good brisk-burning wood,) heats the entire monument & it *stays* <[--]> <so> hot, for 6 to 9 hours, <th>—a more economical stove than exists elsewhere in the world, perhaps. No wonder it has held its own for several hundred years.

A fire was made in our monument at 11.30 this morning; it is now 7 P.M., & I cannot bear my hand on the lower part of the monument. <This>The room has been uncomfortably warm all that time, & is yet. <It is not> <(& there's a window open> It is not cold weather, but with *no* fire the room is quite uncomfortable—chilly.

The Portier is a most useful & wonderful being. He starts as waiter, then head waiter, then Portier, then gets a hotel of his own.—Speaks 5 or 6 languages. Let somebody else say this.

The Grand Duke of Baden.

"Slow freight" in Germany.[73]

People lift their hats slightly, to ladies driving in a cab, almost without looking at them—perfect strangers. It is pleasant here, but

---

[73] Clemens bitterly recalled his experiences with the German freight system in *A Tramp Abroad* (chapter 20): "If you tell a German to send your trunk to you by 'slow freight,' he takes you at your word; he sends it by 'slow freight,' and you cannot imagine how long you will go on enlarging your admiration of the expressiveness of that phrase in the German tongue, before you get that trunk."

would be an offense at home. This morning a gentleman in reading room bowed to me, & later to the ladies when they entered. Every servant bows & chambermaid says good-night. I find it difficult to learn to expect these pleasant bows & be ready to return them without too sudden awkwardness.

Ordered red pepper in German—waiter acted happy & intelligent, but returned no more. Rang up head waiter & ordered red pepper in English—he sent the portier up with 1 sheet paper. *He* understood & sent up the pepper.

"The <father-> mother-dog is the <mother-> father-dog's brother."

The Heidelberg view by night—& day.[74]

Indignant. Saw a man of 30 pass a Wirt of 50 (who had his pipe in mouth) & take of his hat & bow. The Wirt took not the slightest notice.

Lot of students in little pale red caps playing cards in porch of very old house at end of bridge—little boys in street below singing the same old song & looking up—hoping for pennies.

The washerwoman has given Livy a title: "die Frau Baronin."

6 trunks, <10>12 days coming 300 miles by slow freight—charges, $1 apiece. Cheap for the time—12 days.

To bring one trunk 50 miles, along with us, (*no* baggage allowed free,) 4 M <40>20 pf.

My attempt to open the trunks—no key would fit, & I had no keys for Clara's 2 trunks.

Swimley's Boarders.[75] [#]

---

[74] The Clemenses stayed at the imposing Schloss-Hotel overlooking Heidelberg Castle and the Rhine valley from early May till 23 July 1878.

[75] The name Swimley appears in an early sketch, "A Complaint About Correspondents," as part of a burlesque letter purportedly from Mark Twain's eight-

Henry's account of how the great ladies of Heidelberg fared in the public market when the French took the town & zerstört the castle.

John Hay attempting German with a stranger all day, on a diligence—finally stranger (after trying for 20 minutes to frame a sentence,) "Oh, God damn the language!" Hay—embracing him—"Bless my soul, you speak English!

Church bells are usually hateful things—these of Heidelberg are also, no doubt, but are softened by distance.

Eavesdropping at table d'hote, in eagerness to learn the language.

A great business is growing up in bringing sugar-cured hams to Germany—they are much better & greatly cheaper than they can make in Germany. Also the croquet equipment which can only be made in G. of G. wood at 27 M, are made of better wood in America & sold here at 17.

Hellishly beautiful—remark of an English-learner upon seeing Heidelberg through the red glass—it was so very expressive without his knowing it.

Took 1st class tickets, first day but had to ride 2^{d} class—the other days bought 2^{d} class.

He said that when it came to declining a German - - - - -/verb? he could as easily (or would as soon) decline a drink.—Or, he would rather decline 2 drinks than one German verb.

Hang a carpet with a figure in it, for a study<,>!—you walk the floor & you can't think connectedly for unconsciously stretching & spreading your legs trying to step the figures. I have sometimes been made lame in this way. [#]

---

year-old niece: "Sissy McElroy's mother has got another little baby. She has them all the time. It has got little blue eyes, like Mr. Swimley that boards there, and looks just like him" (*Mark Twain's San Francisco*, ed. Bernard Taper [New York: McGraw-Hill Book Co., 1963], pp. 242–243). Swimley is not otherwise identifiable.

Student says, "It's a good (phrase) book to get the Ich habe gehabt's out of."

A residence here must make one softer, kinder, where <peo> strangers bow respectfully to you when you sit down at the table or they get up to go. Not frozen, like England & America.

Germans can't seem to pronounce *pr*<*o.*> if an o comes after it. —they call it *po,* as in ponnounce—looked in dic—7 columns of pro's —all most all, I think *all,* were foreign words.

We spoke first to the sweet German lady at the head of the table yesterday—& to-day when she took her departure from here she shook hands. It is a kindly people.

The Dauern & Halten families.[76]

Clara's episode of the ½ dozen students at table in beer garden (with white caps) who rose up when *the* middle-aged man in plain clothes came.

Significance of student's cap-colors.

Faces full of new & old <c>scars. A duel every day (or every week.)

The wise fashion here of giving wine to children at dinner.

Some of the words are so long that they have a perspective. When one casts his glance along down onc of these, it gradually tapers to a point like the receding lines of a railway track.

So much elegant swearing over dinner tables &c is explained: it crept in, originally to stay & support the pupil while learning the language. [#]

---

[76] Clemens was exasperated—and amused—by the multiple and contradictory meanings of certain German words, like the verbs *dauern* and *halten*. In Appendix D, "The Awful German Language," of *A Tramp Abroad* Clemens shows the usefulness of such words, giving *Schlag* and *Zug* as examples. He concludes that "when you load your conversational gun it is always best to throw in a *Schlag* or two and a *Zug* or two; because it doesn't make any difference how much the rest of the charge may scatter, you are bound to bag something with *them.*"

One knows a college bred man by his scars.

Clara reading in the sun in Castle grounds—fine old gentleman hesitated, passed on, came back & said he *must* tell her she was injuring her eyes.

Students send 2 to Berlin, & 2 come here from Berlin to fight. This morning 8 couples (May 17) fought—2 spectators fainted. One student had a piece of his scalp taken. The others faces so gashed up & floor all covered with blood.

They only wear protecting spectacles.

Mr Pfaff had a 6-inch piece of sword, broken in fight. It was 2-edged, & wonderfully whetted up & sharp.[77]

They fight twice <a f> a week—in a wirtschaft up a little road opposite hotel on other side of river.

No baths in hotel.

Lovely in castle grounds at 4 every afternoon—music.

Students at tables—white caps to themselves & blue caps. Very polite to each other—<s>take off caps.

Chinese umbrellas, & led dogs.

Little girl received me & my wild flowers so enthusiasticaly I gave her some—mother said "Danke schön"

Alway put verb at far end & fill in between with ( ) within (—).

Told 2 German gentlemen the way to the Wolfsbrunnen, in elaborate German—1 put up his hands & solemnly said, "Gott im Himmel!"

Said he—"Mein Fämilienigenthümlichkeiten—"

Said I—"Life is short. I'll have to get you to abbreviate some of your words." [#]

---

77 Clemens included his own sketch of the broken sword in chapter 7 of *A Tramp Abroad*.

From Das Geheimniss Der Alten Mamsell[78]—by Marlitt: (the hyphens are mine):

.... "wenn er aber auf der Strasse der in-Sammet-&-Seide-gehüllten,-<y>jetz-sehr-ungenirt-nach-der-neuesten-Mode-gekleideten-Regierungsrathin begegnet, &c"[79]

*Um*gehen, to associate. Gehen <s>Sie <mit> mit jenem Manne um.

Um*gehen,* (to evade!) die Gesellschaft jenes Mannes.[80]

<— —>godam godam language with 16 THE's in it.

& where a <girl> turnip has a sex & a <girl> young lady hasn't. (Die Rübe—Das Mädchen).

Very neat bug called Maikäfer—superior in some respects to the June bug of North America.

Where is the turnip?
She has gone to the kitchen.
Where is Arabella Victoria Templeton?
It has gone to church.

One must learn the *sex* of every noun in the language.

Concave windows of Heidelberg. [#]

---

[78] A novel by the German writer Eugenie John whose pseudonym was "E. Marlitt."

[79] Clemens translates this sentence in Appendix D, "The Awful German Language," of *A Tramp Abroad*: "I will make a perfectly literal translation, and throw in the parenthesis-marks and some hyphens for the assistance of the reader,—though in the original there are no parenthesis-marks or hyphens, and the reader is left to flounder through to the remote verb the best way he can: 'But when he, upon the street, the (in-satin-and-silk-covered-now-very-unconstrainedly-after-the-newest-fashion-dressed) government counsellor's wife *met.*'"

[80] The German reads: *Associate with that man. Avoid the company of that man.* In Appendix D, "The Awful German Language," of *A Tramp Abroad* Clemens remarks: "There is a word . . . which signifies to *associate* with a man, or to *avoid* him, according to where you put the emphasis,—and you can generally depend on putting it in the wrong place and getting into trouble."

Dreamed <he went to> all bad <p>foreigners went to German Heaven—couldn't talk & wished they had gone to the other place.

Great pump factory in Frankfort used to employ 500 men—employ only 15 now. Reason—America sends better & cheaper pumps & floods the market—has taken their trade all away.

May 21—Pink sunset through haze—black cloud with fringe circling over end of ridge at <Nun> that town.

May 21—At breakfast we saw the fields & villages or landslides (whichever they were) on the great sides of the Haard Mts, 35 or 40 miles away—the first time these mountains have shown anything but dark blue distance & nothing definable.

· Put it in the Accusative (*any*thing) & <be d—d to it!>—says Grumbler

<D—d> Dative son of a gun.

The windows in restaurant Erie depot Jersey City are blue—the meats look horrible.

To make a German sentence complete & beautiful, you have only to add <Vo> Wollen haben sollen Werden to it<.>, after you have got through with what you wanted to say.

(May 22)

Mannheim, 13 Mai. Der "Bad. Beob." berichtet Folgendes: In vorletzer Nacht ist dahier die Wirtschaft "Zur Landkutsche" niedergebrannt. Als die Flamme an dem auf dem brennenden Hause befindlichen Storchen-Nest emporschlug, flogen die *Storchen* auf. Als aber das Nest selbst in Brand gerieth, stürzte das Weibchen sich in die Flammen und starb, die Flügel über die Jungen ausbreitend.[81] [#]

[81] Clemens illustrated the "ponderous and dismal German system of piling jumbled compounds together" in Appendix D of A *Tramp Abroad*, presenting an exaggerated translation of this paragraph from his notebook: "'In the daybefore-yesterdayshortlyaftereleveno'clock Night, the inthistownstandingtavern called "The Wagoner" was downburnt. When the fire to the onthedownburninghouseresting

I find this pretty incident among the "Kleine Mittheilungen" of the Frankfurter Journal of this morning (May 22, '78). It is very neatly stated for a mere country sheet like the "Bad. Beob." (Badische Beobachter?)

How the mother-heart was wrung!

Gr delighted—"I pricked up my ears & glowed with delight—I <could har> doubted my ears—no, it was perfectly true, I <unde> was understanding every word he said ------ <G-d d— him,> he was talking English!

(Used to hearing nothing but German, naturally thought they were talking German.)

Gr—<Go[e]s>Hires at stevedore teach him to swear in German

Blanch recognized a hair of the poor Mr. Degetan in the butter & burst into tears.

(Suggestion for a sentence to be inserted in a German novel with pathetic effect.)

May 24—Theatre, Mannheim[82]—Lear—performance began at 6 sharp. Never understood a word—Gr grumbling—by & by terrific & perfectly natural peal of thunder & vivid lightning. Gr—"Thank<s> heaven <they> it thunders in English, anyway."

At home—Sat 3 hours & never understood a word but the thunder & lightning." [#]

Stork's Nest reached, flew the parent Storks away. But when the bytheraging, fire-surrounded Nest *itself* caught Fire, straightway plunged the quickreturning Mother-Stork into the Flames and died, her Wings over her young ones outspread.' " The German of Clemens' notebook entry is actually much simpler: *Mannheim, 13 May. The Baden Observer reports the following: The night before last the establishment "At the Stage-Coach" here burned down. As the blaze beat up around the storks' nest on the burning house, the storks flew up. But when the nest itself caught fire, the little mother threw herself into the flames and died, her wings stretched out over her young.*

82 Mannheim and its famous theater were only a half hour by rail from Heidelberg. Clemens made at least two excursions to the city—once for a performance of *King Lear* and once for *Lohengrin*. The entries about *King Lear* are scrawled and nearly illegible. Clemens may have been taking these notes in the dimly lit theater during the performance.

Only 4 or 5 ladies with hats on—some held them in lap.

No music at all after beginning of play.

Curtain always dropped with every change of scene.

It was down only 1 minute. Down 1½ to 3 minutes between acts.

Scenes were changed utterly without noise.

Applause only once in the midst of an act, though at the end of acts there was <twi> thrice applause & <tw>once the king was recalled & once twic recaled.

No lights except on the stage

No ushers.

Very quiet well behaved audienc

They rustled papers occasionally.

Lear's great speeches sounded mighty flat. (Quote one.)

Quote some ads from newspaper.

We were the last in—5 or 10 m after play began.

5 balconies & a parquet.
Excellent house though no celebrated actor.
Gentleman in train said a Shaks play was a feast in G.

May 25.

How we miss our big wood fires, these raw cold days in the end of May. In all this region I suppose they've nothing but their close stoves, which warm gradually up & then stink & swelter for hours. It is the same vile atmosphere which a furnace has which has no cold-air box & so heats & re-heats the same air.

Gr. delighted—found *one* sensible German word, anyway—damit. Disappointed to find the accent is <on> not on the first syllable.

"O höll!" is good & sound, any way.
O höllish maid!

Write in diary form. [#]

This tea isn't good
" coffee " "
" bread seems old
Isn't there a curious smell abt
In't that something in the butter?
<J[-]>Jim—<Wait what you want is a micro>
Quietly lay a microscope by Gr.

<Gr. creates a swear sentence>

Wedge under head of bed & 2 pillows

By far The *very* funniest things that ever happened or were ever said, are unprintable (in our day). A great pity. It was no so in the freer age of Boccacio & Rabelais.
"Right!—if you can't catch him, shoot him!"
Man on ladder says—
<"Er ist in ihr aftern.">
The funniest scene I ever saw was when my poor parson struck up a talk with the hostler at Ashland.
You raise pretty fine horses around here?
"*Fine!* Well, — — — — — — — — —"
Try the whole story, with dashes to represent swearing & obscenity.[83]

P.S. Next morning hostler comes in with ice in his hand.

Write it out in full, <& *th*en> for private reference.

Have you any objection to riding an Englishman?
Gr—found he meant a bob-tailed horse. [#]

---

[83] Clemens often deplored the "sad, sad false delicacy" which robbed literature of the "two best things among its belongings: Family-circle narratives & obscene stories" (*MTHL*, p. 203), yet he consistently censored even his notebook entries. The anecdote of the profane Ashland hostler and the parson (the parson was Twichell, the year 1874, and the town Westford, Connecticut) is retold in *Mark Twain in Eruption* (pp. 366–372).

The marks * [signature marks], &c are correspondent's signatures. Required by law?

The thunder generally preceded the lightning last night at theatre, which was wrong.

Mr Pfaff—The Americans make things first good, & *then* cheap—but the Germans reverse this.

May 25—Not a star to-night—consequently the display of lights in town is particularly <zahlreis>zahlreich & vivid—strong reflections in water, from the lights on both bridges.

And the bahnhof! What to liken it to!

But nothing in the world is so overpoweringly beautiful is a tree in ice storm in sun & gentle wind It is worth crossing 3 oceans to see.

The clerk of a first class hotel in America accomplishes everything you can possibly desire—& that is what the German portier does—but there is this difference—if the clerk chooses, he can clog & slight you, but the portier can't afford that, or his fees would suffer.

Was told that the portier of one great Berlin Hotel paid $5000 a year (not *marks*, but $) for his place.

The Grand Duchess of Baden passed through to-day—streets & <bahnhoof>bahnhoff decked with bunting & cannon fired. She is the Emperor's daughter & was in the carriage with him last week when that communist fired on him.[84]

May 26

A coin, sleeve-button, collar<s> button lost in bedchamber mighty hard to find. Will hide in a conspicuous place & *stay* hid. Handkerchief in bed can't be found. A square of chalk will roll clear across billiard room, <missing> steering safe among heels & cuspidors, <& hide in some cons> (especially if you are nervous, angry & in a hurry [#]

---

[84] The Grand Duchess Louise of Baden was returning from a drive with Emperor William I on 11 May 1878 when an alleged socialist, Max Hödel, made an attempt on the emperor's life. The emperor was unharmed.

All this loveliness is too good for sinners.

Bought 2 cigars & 4 boxes fancy matches—gave 48 cent piece and got 42½ cents change. Shant import any more cheap cigars into Germany for economy's sake.

A dog is *der* <h>Hund *the* dog;; a <cat> woman is *die* Frau <a>the wom[an]; a horse is *das* Pferd, *the* horse; now you put that dog in the Genitive case, & is he the same dog he was before? *No* sir; he is *des* Hundes; <*the*> put him in the Dative case & what is he? Why, he is *dem* Hund. Now you snatch him into the Accusative case & how is it with him? Why he is *den* Hunden (?) <Sup> But suppose he happens to be twins & you have to pluralize him—what then? Why sir they'll swap that twin dog around thro' the four cases till he'll think he's an entire International Dog-Show all in his own person. I don't like dogs, but I wouldn't treat a dog like that. I wouldn't even treat a borrowed dog that way. Well, don't you know, it's just the same with a cat. They start her in at the Nominative singular in good health & fair to look upon & they sweat her thro all the 4 cases & the 16 the's, & when she limps out through the Accusative Plural, you wouldn't recognize her for the same being. Yes, sir, once the German grammar gets hold of a cat, it's good-bye cat—that's about the amount of it.

May 26.—Prof. Ihne, Mrs. Ihne & daughter called—a very pleasant call, indeed.[85]

May 27. Wandered through Castle grounds, then to my den & began work.

The moss covered walls overflowed by cascades of ivy. [#]

---

[85] Wilhelm Ihne was the author of several works on Roman history. Livy described this visit in a letter to her mother written on 26 May 1878: "This afternoon Mr Clemens and I were just starting for the castle grounds when we met Prof. Ihne (he is the prof. of English in the University here, Mr Clemens went to see him about a teacher for us when we first came) & his wife & daughter coming to call on us—Prof Ihne is a German but his wife is English, they were *perfectly charming* . . . she reminded me a good deal of our Mrs Beecher" (MTM).

Woman & little girls at work in Schloss Garden at table—music—bird lit there for crumbs

Sunday 26, the steam tug began on Neckar
Came down Tuesday on return trip.

"Diplomé donné et signè de l'Empereur Arnolphe petit-fils de Charlemagne, dans l'année <996>896."
Clean, nice seal. Beautiful writing.
(Domesday Book.)

<A>May 28—Another curious sunset. Blazing hot sun approaching the top of the Heiligenberg—all the mountains beyond the plains shut utterly out by an interposed dead leaden sky—(all the plain between vague & indistinct) a hole in the horizon-edge of that leaden sky just over the slop of the Heiligenberg & in that hole 2 tall black factory chimneys 20 miles away, in the plain, pouring out black smoke. Have often seen what looked like spectral chimneys there, shadowy & indistinct, but now they are black as ink & strongly defined & are sending off long streamers of black smoke & grey. The little patch of Rhine to their right under the horizon, shines strong & clear.—No air stirring in Heidelberg—as I look down on its old dark brown roofs, I see them through <the curling s> a curling & twisting pale blue veil of smoke-wreaths which there is no wind to blow away. The effect is exceedingly odd, & very pretty.

Our term "star." I have often wondered what could suggest it. I perceive, now. Here, in the programme you find, in the list of names & characters—
Lohengrin X
<[---] & nothing more>
Then at bottom .... X Loh
Heinrich .... Herr Mödlinger.
Lohengrin X
<L>Elsa .... Fräulien Ottiker
Herzog Gottfried, ... " Ullmicher

Friederich .... Herr Plank
Ortrud .... Frau Seubert.

X LOHENGRIN .... Herr ALBERT NIEMANN

Doors open at half past 4 p.m. Performance begins at half past 5. Perf^{ce} closes at 10 P.M.

Significant that on<[-]> Monday, no seats left except the 6 M (highest price) for Opera next Thurday—all cheaper ones gone. <They> <It>Opera is not a fashion, but a passion & it isn't <j>dependent upon the swells, but upon every body.

At Lear, the whole 6 tiers were pretty full—the 6th as full as any.

Zug, Schlag, & <aufge>aufheben—let John curse these words—always asking what Zug means & always getting a fresh meaning—finally goes to dictionary & finds a <c[--]> column & a half of Zug, ¾ col. of Schlag,—Very little of aufheben, but its direct *contradictions* <are what get John.>

John says let a man post himself thoroughly in Zug & Schlag, & then throw in aufheben for style & ornament & you are qualified to carry on a German conversation on any sub- without fear. Yes, sir, then you've got a command of language which places you forever out of trouble.

Slender breakfasts & suppers.
Table d'Hote.

We get the Frankfort daily the day it is published—get Heidelburg daily the day after.[86] [#]

---

86 The following clipping from the July 1878 issue of *Harper's New Monthly Magazine* was pinned to the notebook page at this point. The extract is from "An Adventure in a Forest; or, Dickens's Maypole Inn" by James Payn (pp. 298–302), an account of the unsuccessful attempts of a party of American tourists to visit the Maypole Inn which figures in *Barnaby Rudge*.

Upon our second application, the clerk gave us tickets to Epping, though, as it were, under protest, and giving us notice that we should have to change at Bethnal Green—the dismalest, ugliest, and most abject portion of London, and

May 28—Bought a couple of gorgeously dressed ancient horrors in Castle museum, to start a portrait gallery of my ancestors with. Paid a dollar & a quarter for the male portrait & $2.50 for the lady. <It> The gentleman a most self-satisfied smirk—but if he had known he would be sold to a base untitled republican 100 yrs later for a dollar & a half, would it have taken some of the tuck out of that smirk.

And this fair young creature, with her lavish finery, & her hair stood straight up on end <& piled into> <in a wheat-sheaf> in a druggist's-mortar shape, with a bed of red roses on top—what has become of her & her graces in these hundred years? <No doubt the wrinkles came, & the teeth went,> Very likely <her> the gallants praised this picture & said it was destined to grow in value & fame with the centuries, like the works of the old masters, & by & by be within the purse-reach of none but kings & successful brewers. And now she goes for $2.50!

Rücken—V.N. To move, to proceed, to advance; <to move by a short impulse,> to push.

Rücken—back.

May 30—Mannheim—<Lohengrin, a shivaree, whose> Went to a shivaree—(this is John) polite name, Opera.

In midst of it John who had not moved or spoken from the beginning, but looked the picture of patient suffering, was asked how he was getting along. He said in a tremulous voice <tremulous with tears> that he had not had just such <ano> a good time since the time he had his teeth fixed.

I will say this much for Lohengrin on my own account: it accomplished for me what no circumstance or combination of circumstances has ever been able to do before, since I <s>first saw the light of this world: it gave me the headache.

The bugle blasts were martial & stirring—& the 4 buglers stood on the stage & blew sure-enough bugles. I had never seen anything of

---

wholly unconnected with literature, except by an ancient ballad, "The Beggar of Bethnal Green," a specimen of early English poetry, singular to say, comparatively unknown in the United States.

the kind before. In my experience buglers have always pretended to blow but the sound came from the orchestra.

Orchestra of 60 pieces.

The great theatre jammed—standing room all sold.

The bridal song very sweet & beautiful—not another strain in the whole Opera that was pretty except <so> choruses & some of the instrumental parts. It's an "historical" Opera, so to speak. First one & then another "relates" either in a linked scream, long drawn out, or (male) in a succession of war-whoops, with appropriate action. There seems to be little of that where the tenor & the soprano, sweetly & appealingly warbling, alternately hold<s> out <her>their arms toward <the tenor> each other as if <she was> preparing to catch a flour-sack, & then <clasp<s> them together & hitches up her left breast> impressively spread them, first over one breast & then over the other, & pour their souls out in a blended strain. No, it was every <fellow> rioter for himself, & no blending to speak of.—I recognized nothing I had ever heard before, except the bridal song.

I have attended Operas whenever I could not help it, for fourteen years, now, & I am sure I know of no agony comparable to the listening to an unfamiliar Opera. <The uncul> I am enchanted with the airs in Trovatore & other old operas which the hand organ & the music box have made entirely familiar to my ear—I am carried away with delighted enthusiasm when they are sung at the Opera—but O, how far between they are! & what long, arid heart-breaking & head-aching between-times <expanses>expanses of that sort of <extreme> intense but incoherent noise <who>which <always> so reminds me of the time the orphan asylum burned down.

It was well put on the stage, & very beautiful.

Delivered my order for tickets—a gentleman made me understand I must pay 18½ M. Was a great rush—expected to get lost, as there are no ushers—but we found there *are* ushers—the men & women <what>who attend in the dressing rooms & take care of the hats & bonnets.

<Op> We arrived in the house at 5.30,—they were playing an overture—2 minutes later, curtain went up.

3-acts. Just ½ hour between acts—people seemed to know this perfectly well—theatre half empty, clear up to 2 minutes of time—all full & quiet every time curtain went up. I could see that the changes of scenery required no ½ hour, nor even the half of it, they way *they* handle scenery in this country.

Out promptly at 9.30.

No lights except a chandelier in ceiling—& *it* was always shut down very low & dim except between acts. This is very pleasant. You are in twilight & stage is brilliant—Theatre is not so hot, by this method.

Angewöhnung—assuefaction—this fm Dictionary

June 2/78. <A week> 10 days ago a socialist fired 4 shots at the Emperor in Berlin without effect. He was captured. The Emp. was driving out with his daughter the Grand Dutchess of Baden.

To-day he was fired upon again—this time by an under-officer of the government it is said. Wounded in cheek & arm & lost good deal of blood. He is so old the shock may kill him. A crowd rushed at the house & were received with a shot from the assin which hit a landlord; then assassin wounded himself, but not fatally.[87]

60,000 communists drilling in Cin. Chic. & St. Louis.

June 4—Rented & paid for a room for a month at the pretty little <Wirth> Wirtschaft under the Königstuhl.[88] [#]

---

[87] The second attempt on the life of Emperor William I occurred on 2 June 1878. The would-be assassin, Karl Nobiling, a young "Doctor of Philosophy and Scientific Agriculturist" with socialist sympathies, reportedly had been refused employment at the Ministry of Agriculture (London *Times*, 3 and 4 June 1878). He wounded the emperor in the arms, back, and head with buckshot. The assassination attempt caused a furor throughout Germany; hundreds of arrests were made, not only of Nobiling's suspected accomplices but of people who ventured any disrespectful remark about the emperor or his government.

[88] Clemens described his work arrangements in a letter to Bayard Taylor (10 June 1878): "We still live at the Schloss-Hotel . . . but I only eat & sleep there; my work-den is in the second story of a little Wirthschaft which stands at the base of the Tower on the summit of the Königsstuhl. I walk up there every morning, at 10, write until 3, talk the most hopeless and unimprovable German with the family till 5, then tramp down to the Hotel for the night."

Ch. 8 begins with 93.[89]

6 pr slippers—6 colors—2 No 4^{s} & 4 No. 19^{s}·—had to go elsewhere.

How <miene>meine Lehrerinnen haben gelacht when I said I supposed der Thurm war <60> <unge> <*gefëhr*> *gefähr* 60 Fuss hoch, statt <*ungefëhr*>*ungefähr* 60 Fuss hoch![90]

Die höhe des Thurmes übermeer ist 1836 Fuss.—Der Wirtschaft 1756 Fuss[91]

Livy—200 years ago Hei^{g} had a something which we have lost this beautiful Castle, but they lacked something <—they>which we have, a noble & pathetic ruin to contemplate & muse over. (A natural thought)

I—no, they visited ruins which had been peopled 500 yrs before—& these had ruins to visit. Find one stone of a ruin 1000 yrs old—even *they* had ruins to muse over.

No beggars, but plenty flower-peddlers, which is infinitely better if it *is* a trifle troublesome.

Mohlkenkuhr.[92]

Bay—*Why* musn't I?
Because I said *not*.
Bay—But that's no *why*.

Susie—Nein! nein! Es ist nicht *meine* Geburtstag, aber <die des> meine Schwesters[93] [#]

---

[89] The discarded manuscript chapter 3 on Hamburg which began on page 19 was first numbered chapter 8 and began on page 93.

[90] *How my teachers laughed when I said I supposed the tower was* danger 60 *feet high, instead of* about 60 *feet high!*

[91] *The height of the tower above sea level is 1836 feet.—The house 1756 feet.*

[92] The Molkencur was a popular restaurant and resort above the castle on the Königsstuhl.

[93] The German reads: *No! no! It is not* my *birthday, but my sister's.* Clara Clemens' fourth birthday was celebrated with toys, strawberries, and a donkey-ride on 8 June 1878.

Mr. Albert[94]—Why your papa would let you have wein.
Susie—Yes—but we do as mamma says.

Ein Englanderin—should be *eine*—which is simply saying this person is a she-Englishwoman. It may be good grammar, but it ain't good sense.

Englander*in* describes the sex—therefore why describe it *twice*.

Met boy with roses—said he had earned nothing to-day—& added that his mother was sick. Ungraciously bought a bud, paid 3 prices, mentally said his yarn was too thin, hated him for interrupting me—& darted on. Had misgiving presently, climbed hill again, found the boy crying.

Wirthschaft is 1756 ft high—
top of Tower 1836 " " uber See.

Luther, Diet of Worms—thought, as a boy he ate the worms.

Edel—Esel—Thought man said I was Ameri— noble—no, ass.

Slave Ship—Cat having a fit in a platter of tomatoes.

Bought some ancestors for 15 M

Sunday, 9th <Ma> June—Pfinxten[95]—big crowd at dinner

Freundschaftsbezeigungen—24.[96]

Fish is *he*—his scales are *she* & a fish wife has no sex—neither has wife, Weib.[97] [#]

---

[94] In a letter to her mother (7 May 1878) Livy identified Mr. Albert as the Clemenses' landlord at the Schloss-Hotel. He was an attentive host, accompanying the Clemens group on sightseeing and riding excursions when Clemens was unavailable. However, Clemens' note on a return visit to Heidelberg in 1891 (Notebook 31, entry dated 2 September) indicates that Albert was not entirely amiable: "Albert is gone—he was a brute & hammered the servants."

[95] Pfingsten, or Whitsunday, the seventh Sunday after Easter.

[96] Elsewhere in the notebook Clemens noted several equally imposing German words as evidence to be used in his comic attack on the German language in *A Tramp Abroad* (Appendix D).

[97] In "The Sad Tale of the Fishwife" in *A Tramp Abroad* (Appendix D), Clem-

To have a great crow heave up his shoulders & drop his head between them to look down & scold at me in the solemn mystery of the pines in the Odenwald & say to another crow, O here, d—n this fellow what can he be up to"—it was embarrassing & forced me to move on.[98]

June 10—Emperor ready to leave his bed again—this is wonderful. 8 days after receiving such lacerating wounds in arm, shoulder & side—with buckshot—& at *his* age.[99]

June 10.—Author's Congress meets in Paris to-morrow, Victor Hugo presiding. My invitation has been to America—started May 8, <&> recrossed & got to me June <8.>in Heidelberg. I can't attend. Invitation is signed by Edmond About.[100]

Mind acting upon mind—De Quille, Millet—dream of Henry, &c.[101] [#]

---

ens mocked what he considered the unreasonable and unpredictable use of genders in German.

98 Clemens told of the disdainful ravens who forced him to flee the Heidelberg woods in chapter 2 of A *Tramp Abroad*.

99 The same day, Clemens wrote to Bayard Taylor and spoke of the eighty-one-year-old emperor's quick recovery: "The Emperor is a splendid old hero! That he could survive such wounds never once entered my head. . . . I have not seen anything like this outburst of affectionate indignation since Mr. Lincoln's assassination gave the common globe a sense of personal injury" (Cornell University Library, Ithaca, N.Y.).

100 The president of Le Comité de la Société des Gens de Lettres de France invited Clemens to join in the International Literary Congress that had been arranged as part of the Paris Exposition of 1878 (Edmond About to SLC, 8 May 1878). One of the major topics of discussion at the congress was copyright legislation. Victor Hugo's remarks on the copyright question at the closing session of the congress, to the effect that an author's published work was that author's exclusive property until his death, at which time it fell rightfully into the public domain, were widely publicized. The speakers included About, Turgenev, Blanchard Jerrold, and Jules Simon. Clemens wrote Charles Dudley Warner on 16 June 1878: "I dreadfully wanted to go to the Paris Literary Congress & see Victor Hugo, but I declined because it would break into my work—which would be bad, now that I am just getting into the swing of my book on Germany."

101 Clemens was fascinated by cases of telepathic coincidence for which he employed the term "telegraphy." He explored the phenomenon in his essays "Mental Telegraphy" and "Mental Telegraphy Again," published in *Harper's New*

Unintelligibility

<Stadtver> Stadtverordnetenversammlung.—27 tape-worm

XXX cat cradle. Do it yourself. Perfectly simple.

He had a memory like a memorandum book.

June 11—30 or 40 little school girls at the Wirthschaft to-day when I left, all drinking beer at the tables in the open air. What at an atrocious sight to the total abstinent eye!

I am going *in der* Sweitz.
No, in die Sweitz (movement
It is very pretty in die Sweitz
No, *in der* Sweitz. (quiet)

Man who wouldn't go out in the rain for fear he would wet his new umbrella.

German cream—the cows don't seem to give it.

I think that only God can read a German newspaper.

Now there is that <confounded> blistered word Vermählt. I never know whether it means despised, <married,> painted, or suspected.—(Yes, it is married.)

Be talking in forei-gn tongue & be suddenly let down by running out of words—hideous!

On 10th Shah visited <emp> President both in citizen's dress—Shah in blue specs! O how different frm when I saw him 4 yrs ago.[102] [#]

Monthly Magazine for December 1891 and September 1895. When he wrote this note, Clemens was working on the first of these essays, which he intended to include in *A Tramp Abroad*. Clemens decided against its inclusion since he "feared that the public would treat the thing as a joke and throw it aside" (*Harper's,* December 1891, p. 95). The telegraphic incidents involving Frank Millet and Dan De Quille are discussed in "Mental Telegraphy." The incident of Clemens' prophetic dream of his brother Henry's death is in Paine's biography (*MTB*, pp. 134–144).

102 The shah of Persia arrived in Paris on 10 June 1878, visited the Paris Expo-

Schoolmaster banging army of children with umbrella racing down Castle-road.

June 11—Fraulein's brother asked me what State from, then drew map of Am & S A—marked & named states & rivers—boy of 10—must ask his exact age.

Barring spelling & pronouncing, one ought to learn English in <[24]>30 hours—French in 30 days, G in 30 yrs.

Clemens Müller on the sewing-machine.[103] Stamped in raised iron.

Es <sind> waren heute <hier> viele Amerikanisher Landsleute <<heir>hier gewesen—landslide.> hier ge*wesen*.[104]

<Win>Wunderschön—windowshade![105]

We say Guten Morgen to a servant who replies Good morning—then we blush.

Say Ja, also.

Called me *edel* American—no, may *Esel*. [#]

---

sition, and met with Marshal MacMahon, the French president, as part of his six-month tour of Europe. According to the London *Times* of 24 May 1878, there seemed to be much less public enthusiasm for the shah than there had been on his previous tour in 1873. Clemens had reported the shah's gaudy arrival in London for the New York *Herald* in 1873, remarking at the time that the bejeweled monarch "shone like a window with the westering sun on it" ("O'Shah," *Europe and Elsewhere* [New York: Harper & Brothers, 1923], p. 67).

103 Clemens wrote to Warner on 16 June 1878: "My landlord's name is Müller. My room opens into what may be called the parlor,—with a sewing machine in it. Day before yesterday I wrote a long chapter on curious accidents, correspondences & coincidences—then stepped in there & happened to notice the manufacturer's name, stamped in gilt letters on that machine: '*Clemens Müller.*' I must add that to my chapter—never thought of it before."

104 *There were many American compatriots here today.*

105 Clemens' 16 June 1878 letter to Warner describes Livy's struggle with the German language: "The thing that distresses Livy is that the more she learns of the language the less she understands of it when spoken; but the other morning as we sat at table, waiting for our breakfast & admiring the fine display of fruits & flowers on another table, an old German gentleman & lady stepped in & the former hauled down the window curtain at the same moment that his wife threw up her hands in presence of the fruits & flowers & ejaculated '*Wunderschön!*' Livy said, gratefully, 'There—Gott sei dank, I understood THAT, anyway—*window-shade!*' "

The chief German characteristic <of>seems to be kindness, good will to men.

(Sweet petting-sounding <[n]>talk of birds & flowers & leaves & trees & fields—& it is not mere *talk* from a poet's attic, they *do* live in the open air.

The best English characteristic is its plucky & persistent & individual standing-up for its rights. No other people approaches England in this <grand,> this admirable, this manliest of all traits. It is makes every man in the whole nation a policeman—the administration of law can never grow lax where every individual sees to it that it grows not lax in his own case or in cases which fall under his eyes.

Ponderous & marble jaws.[106]

noble *un* sound[107]

Great big *guns*<!>.
L*on*don
Th*un*der D*on*ner

Blitz is good as Lightning.
The spitting of the lightning
—Blitz.

Grosse Gewehre
Battle Schlacht
Boom
Burst
Crash
Hell—Hölle
Cannon
Artillery
Bellow—<bark—bellt:> bellt
is stronger than bark.

The roar & boom & crash! The booming of the <be>alarm bells The long roll of the dr*ums*. The shout. The yell. The groan. The c*ur*se. The howl. Cry—schreit (short) Donner (short) The r*u*sh & roar. The h*u*sh. und r*u*hig peacefully fliesst. der Rhine[108] [#]

---

[106] Although written over the preceding paragraph, this phrase from *Hamlet* was probably associated in Clemens' mind with the notes that follow concerning the sounds of words.

[107] The items in these lists appear here in positions that approximate their placement on the notebook page. But Clemens apparently added to the lists haphazardly as new ideas occurred to him, and the order of inscription is unclear.

[108] The German words are from the first verse of Heine's "Lorelei" which Clemens translated in chapter 16 of *A Tramp Abroad*.

Damn (long)—<W>Verdammtes (sh)
The wolf's long howl on Oo[s] shore
Song (long) Lied (short)
<Hieligen>Heiligen, holy (equal) selig, better ″ blessed[109]
wind Blows (long) bläst (sh)
Stormy (<long>strong) stürmish <(sh)>(weak)
Storm—Gewitter—
Explosion—
The tolling of the knell
Modert—molders
Er starb—grisly!
Heilig
Selig
Starb
ruhig

(Per literature)

France seems to interest herself mainly in high art & seduction.

English swore (Misses Berry?)[110] <within a generat> <la> up to end of last century—the rest of Europe still swears—a custom inherited from pagan times—"Per Bacco."

The Trinkhalle.

German politeness.

The Rhine valley, view.
We can look at 100 acres of soldiers 10 miles away in the Rhine plain & feel that they move. We look at 1000 acres trees & do not—

[109] The ditto marks refer to a previous word in this line but the precise parallel that Clemens intended is uncertain. They appear here in approximately the same spatial relationship to the preceding line as they do in the manuscript.

[110] Clemens may be recalling the description of Mary and Agnes Berry in Harriet Martineau's *Autobiography*: "While up to all modern interests, the old-fashioned rouge and pearl-powder, and false hair, and the use of feminine oaths of a hundred years ago were odd and striking" (ed. Maria Weston Chapman [Boston: James R. Osgood & Co., 1877], p. 278).

their force for a second, put under a church would lift it into the air <Stole that, perhaps.>

Fool, to <hunt> go a-hunting Emperors with bird-shot.
Emp well—June 18.

June 17 & 18—Grass full of hopping weak young birds—& woods full of their feeble chirping, like insect.

I will jetzt mein Satz vor Ihnen ausbreiten.[111] (spread.) out.

The tyranny of protecting people from explosions.

June 19—Dreamed Rosa & Esel-woman complained in German of Fraulein Bühler—good, fluent German—I could not understand it all, but got the sense of it,—could hardly scare up words enough to reply in, & *they* were in very bad grammar. Very curious.[112]

June 14—Suit of clothes for $18—cheaper than stealing.

The unspeakably nasty woman-fashion of towing dog by a string.

In early times some sufferer had to sit up with a toothache, & he <ha> put in the time inventing the German language.

Is half Germany near-sighted, or do they wear glasses for style?[113] [#]

---

[111] *I will now spread my proposition out before you.*

[112] The characters of Clemens' dream were familiar figures during the Heidelberg stay. Rosa was the children's German nurse who came with the family from Hartford; the "Esel-woman," whose donkeys were a source of great delight to the Clemens children, is mentioned in Susy's letter of 12 May 1878 to her grandmother: "One day this week we went out on some little donkeys, it was a woman leaded us and Rosa stood on the other side–they had some little red saddles on their backs. . . . The donkeys belonged to the woman that led them" (*S&MT*, p. 79); Fräulein Bühler was probably the young lady whom Livy hired in Heidelberg to be with the children for three hours each day (OLC to Mrs. Langdon, 26 May 1878, MTM).

[113] Clemens wrote the farcical "Legend of the 'Spectacular Ruin'" (*A Tramp Abroad*, chapter 17) to explain the prevalence of spectacles in Germany. He included several German legends in *A Tramp Abroad*, some invented, some reprinted from F. J. Kiefer, *The Legends of the Rhine from Basle to Rotterdam*, trans. L. W. Garnham (Mainz: David Kapp, 1870).

I will take my um—in case nobody wants it—*brella.*

Big Tun holds 200,000,000—what?
Barrells.

Millet's story of two men hunting the same grave.

June 22—Man hanging to boat in Neckar—people rescued him.

From a German paper:
"What constitutes official disgrace in America?"
Ans—God knows.

There is only one thing on earth which is worse than H coffee: that is H cream.

Efforts to make coffee with a patent pot—no success.

Walldürn
take cars to Seckach[114]

Picture of Savior on Leibtuch

Dilletantenaufdringlichkeit.

Antique oak chair & table bought very cheap in Heidelberg. (Made last year of pine & stained this year in water color black which rubs off.) <Ro>Rubbed off all the antiquity in 6 weeks.)

Superstitions lasting from old mythology.
Must not climb a tree on St John's Day (22^d June?)—nor go on the water 8 days before up to 8 days after.[115] Rock & swirl above here at the bend. [#]

---

114 The towns of Seckach and Walldürn are respectively to the east and northeast of Heidelberg. The entry is in an unidentified hand.

115 The feast day of Saint John the Baptist on 24 June has long been associated in Europe with Midsummer's Day rites. Numerous myths surround Saint John's Eve and Saint John's Day but no trace has been found of the legends which Clemens notes here.

found out the mystery.

The Great Tun is filled with water, then a 50-cent can of condensed milk is added. This accounts for the cream in the hotels.

To be accurate—which is a great thing—they slant a little more than a ladder & not quite as much as a mansard roof.—

They work the cows in wagons—maybe they *can't* give good milk. Would like to put one in a hydraulic press & squeze her

Unverfälscht, unadulterated, not genuine—
Exact opposites?

Superior light[g] bug.

Breakfasted down town. Things pretty neat, though I noticed the butter had not been combed.

German laundry <[let]> could not have acquired this *perfect* ignorance of how to do up a shirt without able instruction—one easily sees England in it. <W> Your collar is like a horse-collar; <when> your shirt can stand alone; & when you get into it you feel ready for crime. It is a wonder they do not have more crime here. But it is increasing, as <the knowledge> adoption of clean shirts spreads among the Social Democrats. Acids eat up linen & turn colored socks white.

Who has the butcher's darning needle? <The> <Neither> the sexless young lady <nor the> has it not but the she-Englishwoman has it.

June 29—6 students entered the Schloss grounds this afternoon in single file, each solemnly towing a big dog.

We usually spend from 5 to 7 pm in the grounds, knitting, embroidering, <&> smoking, & hearing the music. Pretty warm, now.

Das Socialdemokratische Central Wahl-Comité für Berlin *hielt* <pre-> with-/de- gestern Abend in der Privatwohnung eines im

Potsdamer Viertel wohnenden Parteigenossen seine erste Konstituirende Versammlung *ab.*[116] (vented)./held/layed

Frankfurter Zeit. 30 Juni

I will take my um . . . . . brella.

Parroquet & 4 pups. People who get up at 6 & sing, whistle & talk loudly.

But even when it is quiet we can't sleep soundly more than 4 & sometimes 5 hours—then drowsily cat-nap it 4 or 5 more & get up jaded—but it soon wears off.

July 2 It did not rain to-day. <(Furnish a date for this.)>
July <3>7—Forgot to mention that the remark under date of 2ᵈ proved incorrect. It was entered in the diary at 5 PM

July 2—Heard Prof. Fisher[117] at University, on Leibnitz—plenty names & dates, from birth 1646 to death, 1717.

German hotels & houses are as brilliantly light as English are dark.

Carcer[118]

III Tage ohne Grund angeblich aus Neugierde.

F. Graf Bismarck (sign of his corps) <—IIII '74—>— 27—29—IIII '74.

IV <w>Wochen, wegen, misverstandener galanterie. [#]

---

116 *Yesterday evening the social democratic central election committee for Berlin held its first constitutional meeting in the private dwelling of a party member living in the Potsdam quarter.*

117 Probably Professor Kuno Fischer, noted German historian of philosophy and lecturer at Heidelberg University. Professor Fischer's extensive *Geschichte der Neuern Philosophie* includes a section on Leibnitz' life and work.

118 Clemens copied these inscriptions from the walls of the college prison in Heidelberg and provided translations for most of them in Appendix C of *A Tramp Abroad*. He wrote to Frank Bliss on 13 July: "I have been gathering a lot of excellent matter here during the past ten days (stuff which has never been in a book) and shall finish gathering it in a week more" (*MTLP*, p. 108). The "excellent matter" was evidently the college prison information.

Im 10ten Semester,
Mein Bester,
Musste ich hierher wandern
Wegen Verklagens von *andern.*

Nachfolgern zur Warnung.

F. Humelsheim (with blue (cap) portrait in colors—face well scarred) 3 Tage weil er den Dctr Köpke[119] nicht kannte.

F. Kopfer, VI Tage <(now false> (original inscription erased & WEGEN MORD! <s>written over it in black.

K. Gallo.

Lerne schweigen, o Freund!
dem Polypenthum gegenüber—
Sind deine Worte auch *wahr,*
es geht ihr Diensteid doch drüber.
(3 days, 1873.

Lib trans—You may as well save your breath, because no matter if you do testify the truth the policeman's testimony outweighs yours.

E. Frey, VI Tage, weil es am III. I. 75 im Theater gezogen hat.

J. Guimaraes e Silva, 3 quälvolle Tage unschuldig Eingespert!!! (This on back of rule placard.)

R. Diergandt, Aus Liebe IV Tage.

Martin Gerber, wegen Diebstahl IV Tage.

11 cartes de visite inserted in the door & covered with glass.

So lange Rosabella treu mir bleibt,
Bin ich bedeint, beritten und beweibt.[120]
Fridolin. [#]

---

[119] Clemens identifies the caricatured Dr. Köpke in Appendix C of *A Tramp Abroad* as a "certain unpopular college dignitary."

[120] *As long as Rosabella remains true to me/ I am in her service, broken in and wedded.*

Rache! (What for?)

Originally corps were <the> nobles (aristocrats) <of [-]>from the several States named & 2 Burschenschafts spring up in democratic opposition—but now that corps receive everybody these dying out.

Laws.

For every day spent in the Carcer, prisoner must pay 50 pf. For the priv. of entering, <5>90 pf. For privi. of going out, 90 pf.

Fire & light <5> 50 pf per day.

You send out for your dinner & supper. The jailer furnishes coffee in morning some small price.

Dreadful old straw tick, no sheets or anything. But you are privileged to bring your own bedding.

Pine table with oaken top elaborately whittled with names, &c.

An oak table, ditto.

Two *hard* wood chairs.

One fellow II Tage for disturbing peace.

VIII for being at the dueling place. XIV for something which is erased. Summa: XXIV Tage unschuldig im Kerker geschmachtet!!!

E. Glinicke, IV T. wegen zu eifrigen Zusehens bei einer Prügelei.

A picture of rear elevation of a green cap with <2 bottle> bottle champagne in each hand, & under & bween outspread legs, "Was kan das schlechte Leben nutzen!"

American arms & E pluribus unum.

K. Müller W.S. 76/77 II Tage weg. Beleidig. eines gross. Mannes. Dieser Reformer hatte nicht 2, sondern III Tage.

E. Flügge.

Ceilings frescoed with the candle.

In 2^{d} Room. [#]

The entire door inset with cartes de visite.

One a green-cap Philadelphian, with ribbon in for 3 days.

Another bit of humor—Picture of 2 corps students & a dog rushing off with a cart to put it in the Neckar—policeman captures them. Underneath is the judgment of the court—

Reichenheim III Tage.
Salzmann—III "
Nero—freigesprochen.

Liepmann had to be imprisoned because his dog Cesar "Who knows everything" would not "bark gently."

Dr Köpke hanging on a gallows. (See other room.)

One "hat hier 2 Tage *slept* & 3 nights lain awake wegen Dr Köpke.

Avery, May 31. 78 Tyler July 78

Keep a parlor in Schloss hotel—you *can't* teach them to send up cards.

Perils of women riding in these compartment cars.

July 10—Worms.[121]

Sharpen your razor on your hand[122]

All Rhine wines are bad, but some worse than others—that is, less vinegary.

July 13—51 Americans arrived & made less noise than 10 Germans.

10 minutes in Rome, 15 in Greece.

Prof. (?) Loomis—a very superior party, a credit to their country. [#]

---

[121] Clemens evidently made an excursion to the historic city from nearby Heidelberg on the date noted.

[122] Clemens discussed the art of putting an edge on his razor by whetting it successively on an oil-stone, on a razor strop, and on his hand, in a letter to Twichell written several months after this note (*MTL*, pp. 357–358).

Geisberg Tower, July <21>22.—Rhine valley rag carpet & township map.

Heidelberg hack fares very high—<same price as illuminating the castle—a mark a> ½ mark a minute. From town to castle, 10 minutes, 3.50—back, 5 minutes, $3.^{50.}$ To Königsstuhl & back, 15 M. I can walk it in less than 1½ h.

But we have *gas.* in hotel.

German stone houses full of rheumatism—go regularly once a year to the baths & sweat it out.

Wohnung zu verheirathen.

<*ëchzen*>*ächzen*—achtzehn

Meine Herren—<*herr*[rs]>*herr*.

Matriculation fee 13 M only. Attend lectures or not, just as you please. Pay for only the single lectures you *do* attend. Pay 420 M for examination—get about 100 back if you fail. Ceremonies.

Day before leaving Heidl.[123] Where is that, this, & the other thing? It is *packed*—& so we live without a convenience.

Doctor's bills in H.[124]

One part of breakfast always hot—handle of coffee pot.

Tabaksuntersuchung.

Landeshauptmannschaft. (District of a Governor General)

Witterungsbeobachtungen.

Unabhängigkeitserklärunge[n]

---

[123] The Clemens party left Heidelberg on 23 July 1878 and proceeded to Baden-Baden where on 1 August Twichell joined it.

[124] During the last weeks of the Clemens family's stay in Heidelberg, Clemens was bedridden with a severe attack of rheumatism. Livy described the treatment in her letter to Charles Langdon of 21 July 1878: "He had perfectly terrible pain in his foot and leg—the ankle was very much swollen & the cords & veins all distended—We sent for the Dr. & he put on a plaster of paris bandage that made in a few minutes a boot as hard as a stone, in a few hours the pain was better" (MTM). Throughout their stay in Europe the Clemens party was plagued by minor illnesses and mishaps.

Actienbierbrauereigesellschaft
Lebensversicherungsgesellschaft[125]

Get up a Pottery "Collection" of 50-cent rubbish made in Bridgeport—tear-jugs,[126] rare—only one more—in the collection of Smith the Grocer.

Hotel Grand Bretagne (or preferably,) the Villa *Serbelloni*, Lake Como.

Madame Marie Rieu
Beaulieu près
  Lausanne.
Miss Olivier address[127]

    8 gr.
    4
<16>32[-]

Familieneigenthümlichkeiten.
Freundschaftsbezeigungen
Dilletantenaufdringlichkeiten
Stadtverordnetenversammlungen[128] [#]

---

[125] Clemens continued to collect examples of long German words. The five words for which he provided no translation read: *Tobacco research, Weather observations, Declarations of independence, Joint-stock brewing company, Life insurance company.*

[126] Clemens included his own drawing of an Etruscan tear jug in chapter 20 of *A Tramp Abroad*. In fact, Clemens did own such a relic (now in the Mark Twain Papers) which he had brought back from his 1867 *Quaker City* trip. A list describing Clemens' *Quaker City* souvenirs mentions it: "Tear jug from an Etruscan city near Civita Vecchia, buried before Herculaneum was built—buried 2000 years ago —This jug is 4000 years old" (TS in MTP).

[127] Miss Sophia J. Olivier's name appears on the passenger list of the *Holsatia* (New York *Times*, 11 April 1878). She was probably the "young lady passenger" placed under Livy's charge during the voyage to Hamburg (SLC to Jane Clemens, 7 April 1878, *MTL*, p. 327). The name appears to be in Livy's hand; the Lausanne address above Miss Olivier's name is in an unidentified hand.

[128] The German reads: *Family characteristics, Displays of friendship, Dillet-*

eternal punishment

2 P.M, foot of 3^d st. Hoboken.

Marine to Mrs. Perkins.[129]

Rose ″ ⎫
Pretorium ⎬ Twichell
Winter pic ⎭

Flower Girl ⎫
Oak tree ⎬ Geo. Warner
Millet Inte ⎭

Hotel Schrieder
Heidelberg.

Howells.
Chas. L. Mead[130]
35 Chambers st [#]

---

tante's obtrusiveness, Town council. Another list of long German words, written on a piece of scrap paper in brown ink and in an unknown hand, is pinned to the notebook page at this point:

Fernglaskraftmesser
Hauptgebirgsketten
Wellenbewegungen
<Eq>Aequatorialstromungen
Generalstaatenversammlungen
Waffenstillstandsunterhandlungen
Alterthumswissenschaften
Kinderbewahrungsanstalten
Unabhängigkeitserklärungen
Wiederherstellungsbestrebungen

The German reads: *Binocular dynamometer, Principal mountain ranges, Undulations, Equatorial currents, Meetings of the parliament, Armistice negotiations, Sciences of antiquity, Children's nursery, Declarations of independence, Efforts to restore.*

129 Livy's notebook (in MTP) contains extensive lists of pictures and other European purchases for family, friends, and neighbors.

130 Clemens' note about Charles Mead, Howells' brother-in-law, was presumably made in anticipation of a visit.

Frank Harris, (Engl.) Marcus Stine, bei Franz Mai, Wrede Platz.[131]

---

[131] Clemens met young Frank Harris, then a student in Heidelberg, when Harris came to the hotel to invite him to address the Anglo-American Club on the Fourth of July. Harris recalls having been accompanied by a brother of Sir Charles Waldstein (probably Martin Waldstein) on his first encounter with Clemens. The "Marcus Stine" of Clemens' note is presumably a misrendering of that name. Harris comments on his unfavorable impression of that encounter and on Clemens' work in general in his *Contemporary Portraits (Fourth Series)* (New York: Brentano's, 1923), pp. 162–173.

XV

"A New and Better Plan for the Book"

(July–August 1878)

Notebook 15 extends from 24 July through 27 August 1878—a short period, but one which marks a decisive change in the development of *A Tramp Abroad*.

On 23 July the Clemens party left Heidelberg and arrived at Baden-Baden, the Black Forest resort. Nine days later Twichell, who had come to Europe at Clemens' invitation and expense, joined the group. Twichell's visit had been projected even before the Clemenses left Hartford and the offer was renewed by Clemens from Heidelberg on 23 May. Twichell's reply of 8 June was ebullient: "*Do* you realize, Mark, what a symposium it is to be? . . . Nothing replenishes me as travel does. Most of all I am to have my fill, or a big feed anyway, of *your company*—and under such circumstances! To walk with you, and talk with you, and sleep with you, and say my prayers with you, and see things with you, for weeks together, —why, it's my dream of luxury."

After two short walks in the neighborhood of Baden-Baden, Twichell and Clemens set off on two longer excursions: one through the Black

Forest and then on to Heidelberg by rail (5–6 August); and another along the Neckar River from Heidelberg to Heilbronn and back, accomplishing part of the trip by boat (8–9 August). They returned to Baden-Baden on 10 August. After an interlude in Lucerne with the rest of the party, Clemens and Twichell set off on their longest walking tour together: from Kandersteg over the Gemmi Pass to Zermatt–a trip that took them five days (23–27 August). Notebook 15 ends as the two friends approach Zermatt.

The weeks in Heidelberg had enabled Clemens to write steadily and in detail. Once on the road with Twichell, however, he had neither the time nor the energy to "write up in full every night" as he had hoped (SLC to Frank Bliss, 13 July 1878, *MTLP*, p. 108). He produced little or no manuscript. The only extended entries in Notebook 15 were those written during a quiet Sunday in Baden-Baden on 11 August (pp. 135–140).

The arrival of Twichell is reflected in the notebook by the influx of personal and anecdotal material, the result of conversations and reminiscences shared by the two men during their hours of tramping. It is clear that Twichell played a decisive role in the development of *A Tramp Abroad*, acting as a catalyst for Clemens' invention. Clemens later wrote to his companion: "One of my discouragements had been the belief that my interest in this tour had been so slender that I couldn't gouge matter enough out of it to make a book. What a mistake. . . . the mood is everything, not the material" (26 January 1879, *MTL*, p. 349). Moreover, Twichell's arrival provided Clemens with a unifying theme for his book of travels. He wrote to Frank Bliss from Lucerne on 20 August 1878: "Since Twichell has been with me I have invented a new and better plan for the book. . . . I have instructed Twichell to keep the title and plan of the book a secret. . . . They are in themselves a joke" (*MTLP*, p. 109). Clemens later revealed his plan in a letter to Howells: "In my book I allow it to appear,–casually & without stress,–that I am over here to make the tour of Europe *on foot*. I am in pedestrian costume, as a general thing, & *start* on pedestrian tours, but mount the first conveyance that offers, making but slight explanation or excuse, & endeavoring to seem unconscious that this is not legitimate pedestrianizing" (30 January 1879, *MTHL*, p. 249).

The weeks spent with Twichell, described in Notebooks 15 and 16, provided Clemens with matter for chapters 11 through 46 of *A Tramp*

Abroad. Indeed, Clemens relied so heavily on these notebooks that when he lost one of them briefly he felt he couldn't write the book (SLC to Twichell, 26 January 1879, *MTL*, p. 349). Notebooks 15 and 16 were later given to Twichell and are now in the American Literature Collections in the Beinecke Library at Yale University.

Notebook 15 now contains 162 pages, 1 of them blank. The pages measure 5½ by 3¼ inches (14 by 8.4 centimeters) and are of unruled pulp paper. The endpapers and the sides of the flyleaves that face them are yellow. The inner sides of the flyleaves match the notebook's pages. There is a black leather pencil holder attached to the outside margin of the back endpaper. The stiff covers are faced with black pebbled cloth with blind stamped borders. The word "NOTES" is stamped in gold on the front cover. Also on the front cover is a paper label, apparently pasted there by Twichell, who wrote on it in ink:

Notebook of M. T.
"Tramp Abroad"

The words "Mr Twichell—" have been added to the label in faint pencil by an unknown hand. There are two short lengths of narrow black cloth ribbon attached near the top and bottom of the back cover, apparently the remnants of ties designed to hold the notebook closed. Notebook 15 is heavily worn with use. All of the leaves are loose, and it is possible that leaves no longer traceable are missing. All the entries are in pencil. There are a number of Clemens' use marks, including large Xs and wavy lines drawn through entire entries. Someone other than Clemens has numbered the pages in pencil in the upper outside corners.

Miss Elizabeth N. Stevens
Monroe & Co
7 rue Scribe
Paris.[1] [#]

[1] This name and address and the following entry ("Miss Roosevelt.") were written on the front endpaper, upside-down in relation to the other entries in the notebook. Neither woman has been identified.

Miss Roosevelt.

Heiliger Gott im Himmel! schrie H plötzlich aus.

Es ist eine gottverdammte <n>Nacht![2]

July 24—Start to Blk Forest. from Baden.[3]

Niederländisch-Americaniche Dampschifffahrtsgesellschaft.

Stopped at Forbach at noon—trout under a grape arbor, & 3 Germans eating in general room.

The village assembled to see a tinker mend a tin boiler.

School where they sang—something like our singing geography—one monotonous tune of ½ doz. notes.

Through fine gorge scenery by a brook to Post-inn at Schonmünd[4] or some such name. Nice pictures on walls, nice paper, hand-crocheted counterpanes.

How can they have such nice inns in the woods.

Openau to Appenweier & change—then to Ofenberg & change.[5]

This cursed way of stating all distances by minutes & hours—it means nothing. You don't know whether it is 15 M by telegraph, <hor> or lounging, or with sheriff after you.[6] [#]

---

[2] These German phrases, written on the front flyleaf, read: *Holy God in heaven! H suddenly cried out* and *It is a goddamned night!*

[3] The Clemens party had traveled from Heidelberg to Baden-Baden on 23 July 1878. The next morning they started out on a three-day carriage trip through the Black Forest, staying at inns along the way; they returned to Baden-Baden by rail on 26 or 27 July. Clemens and Twichell would tramp over part of the same route in early August.

[4] The Clemens party followed the scenic carriage route, from Baden-Baden to Allerheiligen via Forbach, Schönmünzach and Ottenhöfen, described by Baedeker (*The Rhine from Rotterdam to Constance* [Coblenz: Karl Baedeker, 1873], pp. 250–253).

[5] Clemens is outlining the return route which the party would follow after leaving Allerheiligen. There was a direct rail route from Appenweier to Baden-Baden, but he evidently intended to include Offenburg in the tour and take the train for Baden-Baden from there.

[6] In Baedeker's guidebooks distances for pedestrian excursions are given in terms of "the time they occupy" (Baedeker's *Rhine*, p. VI).

25th
Allerheiligen

Hotel with nobody visible—one (very nice) room-girl for 3 floors—& an awful bell to call folks to supper

I wish I could hear myself talk German.

Pretty girl here. An infernal cuckoo clock in hotel where we took dinner Offenbosen 1½ hour before Allerheiligen.

2 young ladies who walked 9½ to 12 hours a day.

Plenty crucifixes.

Maps in railway carriage—very useful.

Green theatrical fine forest before Allerheiligen.

Steep slope clothed in green velvet—before theatrical forest.

Saw a small deer here.

Superb view from Teufelstein, <Luisa R>Luisaruhe & Engelkanzel.

C went down & visited the waterfalls.

A ruin where a Kloster was built 700 yr ago. Leave the monks alone, every time, to pick out the loveliest spots.

People gardening high above our heads before Allerheiligen.

Beautiful bright green grass everywhere.

Lovely valley & quaint thatched houses in Thal befor Seeberg[7] or some such name.

Drenching rain all down the Schlectes Weg which approaches All^{n}. Bright holly bushes.

---

[7] Seebach was on the route to Allerheiligen. Occasionally throughout the notebook, Clemens records a random word or two of his entry in German ("Thal" in this entry and "Kloster," "Schlectes Weg," and "Gipfel des Berges" in nearby entries).

Fine aspect of Gipfel des Berges[8] faintly through drifting mists.

Gushing little torrents of clear water everywhere, & everywhere they were turned this way & that to irrigate.

Sometimes the cows occupy the first floor, sometimes the family Saw a cow's rump projecting from what should have been the drawing room.

Journal of a youth of 20 & a man of 60 who visited the Teufelstein[9] in a pouring rain.

Troops of students & young gentlemen walking.

To call a butcher a gentleman is as absurd as it would be to call an English Earl a prince. These titles signify station, not worthiness or manly excellence.

Not a grain of dust on us after 3 days driving in open carriage in dead summer. Think of it!

If they had Schwarzwald bread, the feeding the 5,000 was hardly a miracle.

Only 18. M. for large parlor & 2 large chambers on 1st floor, Hotel de France.[10]

Music at 7 AM & from 4 PM till late toward about 10 or 11. Very fine.

Guidebook says no tourist should fail to climb the mountain & enjoy the view. Hired boy to climb the Mt & examine (or enjoy?) the view.[11] <For 6 marks> He felt well repaid for all his trouble. [#]

---

[8] This phrase, "peak of the mountain," occurs in the first verse of the "Lorelei" which Clemens had recently learned from Bayard Taylor on board the *Holsatia*.

[9] Clemens is probably referring to the Teufelskanzel, "a huge isolated block of rock rising from a grassy ravine," near Baden-Baden (Baedeker's *Rhine*, p. 199). The Teufelsstein, in the Haardt Mountains just north of Durkheim, was not on Clemens' German itinerary.

[10] These notes were written in Baden-Baden after the Clemens party returned from their Black Forest excursion. Clemens remembered the hotel as a "plain, simple, unpretending, good hotel" in chapter 21 of *A Tramp Abroad*.

[11] "One of the most agreeable [excursions], and usually the first taken, is that

In Odessa I gave blind woman in a church a Napoleon—& sneaked back afraid I had been seen & got my change.[12]

<People look so surprised> Am addressed in German & say I can't speak it—immediately the person tackles me in French & plainly shows astonishment when I stop him. They naturally despise such an ignoramus. Our doctor, here, speaks as pure English as I.

Jno Arnot[13] gave $450 wʰ he won at Monaco to poor young girl in Paris who was struggling with a musical education.

28ᵗʰ *July*—Sat in the next seat behind the Empress of Germany & one of her maids of honor, in the English Church. She contributed 20 marks & snapped her smelling bottle a good deal & curtsied at the name of the Savior instead of merely inclining the head, as others did. <T>She is apparently about 60. The maid of honor had a very sweet face.

Our coachman was gotten up rather gorgeously—hence, no doubt, we were taken for a ducal family & placed in the seat of honor.

Church not crowded—the Empress does not "draw" well for an Em[press.][14] O[ur] pew for six had but 3 in it. E's pew wa[s] the uppermost one on left of chancel. [#]

---

to the . . . *Altes Schloss* . . . the conspicuous ruin which rises out of the woods on the summit of the hill above the town. . . . The view . . . is the most pleasing and extensive in the neighborhood of Baden" (*Handbook for North Germany and the Rhine* [London: John Murray, 1877], p. 422). Clemens repeated his idea of sending an agent or "scout" as his proxy several times in this notebook and in *A Tramp Abroad*.

12 Clemens included the story of his embarrassing recovery of a coin from a blind beggarwoman in chapter 47 of *A Tramp Abroad*. He claimed that the incident occurred in 1867 during his trip abroad with the *Quaker City* excursion, but there is no mention of it in *The Innocents Abroad*.

13 Clemens is probably referring to the elder John Arnot, a very successful Elmira banker and businessman who in 1870 was instrumental in saving the Langdon family business from financial ruin (*MTA*, 2:135–138). Arnot traveled in Europe before his death in 1873.

14 The outside edge of one notebook leaf has been torn, obliterating a number of letters in the text (pp. 119.18–120.8). The missing or partially obliterated letters have been supplied in square brackets.

Germans are exceeding polite by day, but at night, in these thin-partitioned hotels, they <move>make a world of noise, with loud talk, &c, regardless of their neighbors' comfort.

July 28—Hotel de France, [B]aden—We went to [ta]ble d'hote, to-day—[(S]unday) all Amer[i]cans except one [o]ld lady, 2 superb young ones & a young gentlemen [b]eyond & opposite us. Waited for them to leave as it was my place (they say,) to bow to these strangers if I go first. Fin[ally] I started—& pulled through safely—they responding handsomely to my bow.

Flower-sellers "Nach Beliebe" & Baden Trinkhalle "What you please"—dirty vile customs.

The German 1st class gentleman's bow to another gentleman is very elaborate, even gaudy. Describe it.

New & infallible way to sharpen rasors.[15]

July 29—Lot of loud Americans at breakfast this morning—loud talk & coarse laughter. Talking *at* everybody else. "Well, *good*-bye, old fellow—if I don't run across you in Italy you hunt me up in London before you sail."[16]

Nice portier, but woman with disagreeable look & manners at the great Friederich's Bad.

It is pleasant to be in a country where you can break the Sabbath without sin.

Ridicule the pretentious Friederich's Bath—& mark swindles

The servants read & write nicely.

---

[15] Clemens' new method, which entailed whetting the blade in succession on an oil-stone, razor strop, and hand, is also mentioned in Notebook 14, p. 108.

[16] In order to give immediacy to his travel narrative, Clemens occasionally quoted entries from his notebooks. This entry, slightly expanded, appears in chapter 21 of *A Tramp Abroad* with Clemens' preface: "I open my note book to see if I can find some more information of a valuable nature about Baden-Baden, and the first thing I fall upon is this." He continues with a revised version of the entry about Indians on page 121 of this notebook.

Washerwoman list.

"From the French" explained the chambermaid.

July 29—Took a nasty glass of hot mineral water at 7 AM, with teaspoonful of Carlsbad salt dissolvd in it.

July 29—Sat from 8 till 10 last night hearing the music & watching the crowds drift by. Pretty girls & beautiful women hardly exist in Germany, but many have beautiful forms.

From a little distance the throng & the lights make a pretty sight.

Never knew before what Eternity was made for. It is to give some of us a chance to learn German.

The 51 Americans came, slept, & departed & all put together did not make as much noise as 2 G ladies or 7 G gentlemen.

With all their daylight politeness (w^h is faultless,) their go-to-bed & get-up manners are execrable. So they have a noisy good time they don't care a cent who suffers. Doubtless I should find the case the same at home if our hotel walls were so *hörbar*—but then we are not a good-mannered race & much cannot be expected of us.

The fact that we have but 1200 soldiers to meet 6,000 Indians is well utilized here to discourage immigration to America. The common people think the Indians are in New Jersey.

Nothing can stop the Irish from coming, alas!

It is very pleasant the way the landlord, the portier & the head-waiter come out & receive the tired traveler when he arrives. It pays the hotel to be polite. Lord, the difference between this & the way an American clerk or a she-hotel clerk in London or Liverpool recives the stranger!

Wrote the portier[17] 29th that he needn't come till 6th—of course

---

[17] Clemens hired George Burk as a courier to accompany the family on its travels, particularly for the periods when he and Twichell would be away. Livy wrote to her mother on 5 August: "We go with a *good* Courier (he was the Portier at the Schloss Hotel [in Heidelberg]) all the time that we were there)" (MTM). Clemens is once again noting instances of coincidence or "mental telegraphy" (see Notebook 14, note 101).

the letters crossed—he writing to ask permission to delay his coming till 4th or 6th.

Some time ago Lilly Warner wrote, saying her mother would presently send on a commission. A few days later she aded a postscript saying "The picture you sent is what mother was going to ask you to supply."

I was going to write Carter to-night (July 30) about that student table;[18] as I was fetching the paper & Ink, Livy suggested that I write Carter about that table!

You can smoke anywhere but in the car marked Ladies' Car—but here in B B smoking is prohibited in the baths & the <Promenade &> Conversation building.

Herzog von Hartford.

The Fraulein, the Weib & the Turnip, et al. Ring in all the she's & he's—make an extended talk on the model of "Where is the turnip gone?"

The shopmen are as impertinent in Baden as in New York. Germans tell me they despise Ams so much that an Am lady unattended is pretty sure to have offense offered her.

July 31.

Got swindled at the 'Fr B'[19] again (not only by a 6^{d} book for 2 M,

---

[18] In Appendix C of *A Tramp Abroad* Clemens tells of his visit to the college prison in Heidelberg: "I very much wanted one of the sorry old tables which the prisoners had spent so many years in ornamenting with their pocket knives, but red tape was in the way." He mentioned such a table in a 30 July letter to a Mr. Tyler: "The rheumatism staid with me . . . so I failed in the matter of the table; but I have not given that relic up; I expect to be at Lang's Hotel on the 6th [Clemens and Twichell would arrive in Heidelberg on 6 August to begin their boat trip on the Neckar]. . . . At that time I hope to have a chance to see you & collar that piece of furniture" (Middlebury College, Middlebury, Vt.). It is likely that Tyler and Carter were American or English students at Heidelberg University, possibly members of the Anglo-American Club that Clemens addressed on 4 July. Clemens noted Tyler's name among those scratched on the walls of the college prison in Notebook 14, p. 108.

[19] Mark Twain's abbreviation for "the great Friederich's Bad" (p. 120).

but in changing a 100 M note they put off some Fr money on me w[h] won't go. Also swindled me out of a M. or so.

Orion's queer bath in Hartford.[20]

He was thoroughly noble, being descended from a king through a prostitute.

Dismally cold & rainy in B, <&>with alternations (at very wide intervals,) of hellish heat.

The Schwartzwald is too close to B to be endurable. Still, by going to it one gets out of B.

The Ams & English are particularly detested.

See Naples & then die.—but endeavor to die *before* you see B. B.

Would like to have 2 monopolies[—]umbrellas in England & specs here. I would rather be a spectacle-maker in Germany than anything else.—These people <can> <could> might possibly get along without clothes, or Bibles, or even beer, but they've got to have spectacles.

When 12 or 13 Germans are gathered together, <behold> if there be one without glasses, suspect him for a foreigner.

They comb themselves as they walk to their places at dinner—but these may be a commoner sort. [#]

---

[20] Throughout his *Tramp Abroad* notebooks, Clemens noted anecdotes, usually unconnected with his European travels, to be expanded for possible incorporation in the book. Some, like "Baker's Blue-Jay Yarn," were included in *A Tramp Abroad*, providing a humorous digression from the travel narrative. The episode which Clemens notes here was not described in *A Tramp Abroad*, but it appears in the Autobiographical Dictation of 6 April 1906 where Clemens tells of Orion taking a bath in a Hartford boardinghouse without locking the door: "It was his custom, in summer weather, to fill the long bath-tub nearly full of cold water and then get in it on his knees with his nose on the bottom and maintain this pleasant attitude a couple of minutes at a time. A chambermaid came in there, and then she rushed out and went shrieking through the house, 'Mr. Clemens is drowned!' Everybody came flying out of the doors, and Mrs. Clemens rushed by, crying out in agony, 'How do you know it is Mr. Clemens?' And the chambermaid said, 'I don't.' "

Have seen 1 pretty girl & one beautiful one in 3 months—the former German, the latter Russian. <Sent> Seen a dozen pretty Am girls <in> in the meantime.

B B.—Thousands of yelping & barking dogs, & here & there a black cat. ("Here & there" is ironical.)

Occasionally a swell <deli> in the street deliberately takes on a wee little opera glass, plants himself & stares up at a lady in a balcony.

Aug 1. The noisy G. savages in the next room chattered till well after midnight, & were at it again at 6 this morning. They took a carriage at 10—to go to hell, I hoped,—but found they were only going to the Favorita.[21]

(Some of these notes may be attributed to a foreigner's diary which I found—some to the young fellow of 20, others to the old fellow of 60.

(These diaries save me the making of some notes, as they reflect my own opinions.

Pretty rows of brilliant little shops,—booths, with the whole front wide open & crammed with pretty (& generally worthless) gimcrackery—& chairs in the street outside the sidewalk. This <[noi]> street is shops on both sides & is in the "Conversation" grounds.

What pretty forms <some> many of the young German ladies have.

Through the town winds a very swift stream of <cl> limpid water. It is not allowed to sprawl around, but flows in a trough of dressed stone 4 or 5 ft wide & 18 in. deep. It fills this trough to the brim. Its surface is not smooth but tumbled with waves—because of the swiftness, of course, as the bottom of the stone trough is smooth

---

[21] The Favorite, a castle built by the Margravine Sibylla of Baden, was about six miles from Baden-Baden and was a popular destination for excursions.

& without obstructions. It flows exactly as fast as a man can walk at his best gait.

Restaurant keeper at Strasburg so polite to Joe—it reminded him of similar experience at home—where man simply said "Go to H!"

"That person" who always meets with runaway accidents—New York, Elmira, Heidelberg, & finally Worms.[22]

Furnish the music to "Ich weiss nicht was soll es <beteud> bedeutend,"[23]—& ask everybody to learn, it. Very popular in Germany. 30 years old, but the bands all play it.

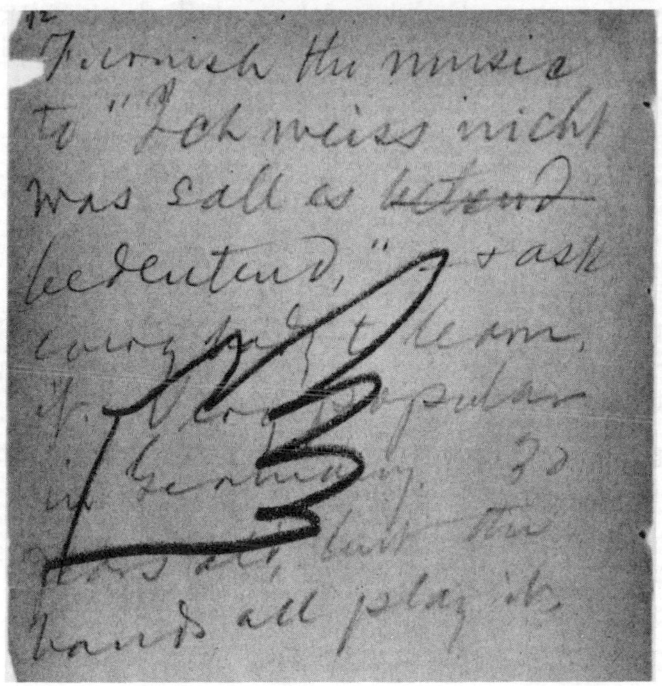
12
Furnish the music
to "Ich weiss nicht
was soll es ~~beteud~~
bedeutend," & ask
everybody to learn,
it. Very popular
in Germany. 30
years old, but the
bands all play it.

---

[22] "That person" was Clara Spaulding. In his autobiography (*MTA*, 2:140–142) Clemens recalled her bad luck with horses and carriages, describing at length the runaway incident of July 1878 in Worms.

[23] This is the first line of Heinrich Heine's "Lorelei." Clemens included the words and music to the song in chapter 16 of *A Tramp Abroad*.

Undershirt which is merely a fish net—set to cure & keep of rheumatism.

"Poor Tom"—judge—dead bone—Home Guard—Gettysburg, Harrisburg—wound, hero,—3 days—girl—went to tell uncle—uncle told *him*, going to marry *his* girl—did so—*he* went & engaged to a make-shift—& a week later the uncle's wife died.

A real honor—Jim Gillis gave all the squaws in Tuolumne Co ½ dollar to name their cubs after me.

Engaged man fell in love with another girl—original insisted on the marriage—storm—English service—"anybody objects, declare it now or hold your piece"—no answer—repeated—lightning killed the bride.

Institutions to be proud of—West Point & Annapolis—plenty of ceremony—fortitude taught there as in Heidelberg dueling—my enthusiasms & desires are dying out, but I do want to see the boys at West Point. I remember yet how they impressed me at the Centennial.[24]

The girl at the Favorita Schloss (May 2)[25] was so pretty & alas spoke in French—I could only understand it, couldn't speak in reply. This is the girl who so pleased Livy & Clara.

Aug 2—Went to Favorita Schloss (6 m.) with Joe & walked back thro' the woods.

G P R James's "Heidelberg"[26] is rot.

Girl at Favorita (built in 1725 by Margravine Sibilla,) spoke French but I could not reply. [#]

---

[24] The West Point Cadets had participated in the Centennial Exhibition held in Philadelphia in 1876. Clemens had attended as a member of the Congress of Authors.

[25] Clemens must have meant August.

[26] George Payne Rainsford James's *Heidelberg*, first published in 1846, is a mannered and melodramatic novel about seventeenth-century Heidelberg.

1725 is just the time of the Margravine of Baireut,[27] who was born [1]707.

"He that sitteth on the circle of the heavens shall laugh."

Bushnell said "Sedan was God laughing at France." France had put forth such bombastic proclamations.[28]

The monkey

Big mouth fish.

Bee that impregnates that tubular plant.

I guess God will laugh when he sees this horse.

God made man *in his own image.*

Christ, a man, was the *son of God*—& possessed humor of course.

Bushnell said God makes a little flower in the midst of an untrodden wilderness for himself to look at.

Ici
repose en Dieu
Caroline de Clery,
ancienne religieuse à St. Denis,
agèe de 83 ans & aveugle.
Elle fut rendue à la
lumière
à Baden le 5 Janvier
1839.[29]

(This is beautiful.)

It is on a stone set against the wall. [#]

---

27 Frederica Sophia Wilhelmina, sister of Frederick the Great. Clemens had received a copy of her autobiography from William Dean Howells who wrote the introduction for an edition published by James R. Osgood and Company in 1877.

28 Evidently the line from Psalms 2:4 ("He that sitteth in the heavens shall laugh: the Lord shall have them in derision") called to mind a statement made by Horace Bushnell about the battle of Sedan in 1870 when the French people, expecting victory, were stunned by France's disastrous loss to Germany. Bushnell, who died in 1876, had been a prominent and controversial minister in Hartford, well known to both Clemens and Twichell.

29 Clemens copied this "quaint and pretty" tombstone inscription in the cemetery at Baden-Baden and included it, in English, in chapter 21 of *A Tramp Abroad.*

Ordered one of my force to go & drink the goats milk for the information of the public. State what he thought of it.

Ordered another to experiment with different kinds of salts in hot water—till a very complicated dose killed him. He had been wasting away before.

God does great blessings in such severe methods (rude?)—Instance, Strong's experience in collecting money for his college.)[30] Names no names—everybody alive yet.

The lady with an imaginary invalid daughter—filled us from day to day with deep sympathy. Told us the different kind of baths she took.

Sent for soap & the waiter brought *soup*.

Sent one of my scouts to observe the Trinkhalle ball.

Tried to get Stanley[31] for a scout, but too expensive.

"The foot of the Country"—the redheaded girl had it—at Gernsbach [#]

---

[30] Twichell probably told this story to Clemens as the two walked to the Favorite Schloss on 2 August. A former classmate of his, James W. Strong, had come East looking for money for the small Christian college in Minnesota of which he was president. While visiting Hartford, Strong was severely injured in a railroad accident, and his subsequent near-miraculous recovery induced a wealthy Massachusetts acquaintance, Mr. William Carleton, to donate fifty thousand dollars to the college, which was then named in his honor (Delavan L. Leonard, *The History of Carleton College* [Chicago: Fleming H. Revell Co., 1904], pp. 182–189). In *The History of Carleton College,* Twichell recalled telling the story to Clemens:

> It was our wont in our long days' walks to entertain one another with various discourse . . . often with tales of personal reminiscence. I chanced one day to call up out of the past this foregoing story of President Strong. . . . I was just finishing it . . . when a sharp turn in the road brought us abruptly face to face with President Strong himself! so that I was able, after a momentary pause of speechless astonishment, to say: "And here is the very man! President Strong, let me introduce you." He was also there on a pedestrian tour, yet neither of us knew that the other was in the country. My friend was something of a believer in telepathy; and as presently we resumed our journey, he said: "You felt him coming. That's the reason why that story rose to the surface just now." (p. 186)

[31] Clemens first met Henry M. Stanley in 1867 and the two men saw each other again in London in 1872 after Stanley had returned from finding Livingstone.

Sunday walk[32]—Aug 4—From B B to Edelsteinburg—to Zum Neuhaus—to Gernsbach—took beer &c & sent telegram to Livy at Hotel de France

Joe's speech at the 3ᵈ corps re-union.[33]

Fellow said been here several months & got no German but zwei lager—but got that *solid.*"

Aug 6 Walked fm Allerheiligen to Oppenau. By measurement, 10 m—by Joe's pedometer 164.[34]

Aug 6—From Oppenau to Heidelberg through clouds of dust (by rail.)

Only one bath-room in an entire hotel—& generally not that. It takes 1 hour to get a hot bath ready in a G. hotel.

Napoleon's Invasion medal.[35] [#]

---

[32] A one-day walk by Clemens and Twichell in the neighborhood of Baden-Baden. The next day they left for a week-long tramp, spending two days in the Black Forest, then traveling by rail to Heidelberg and from there following the Neckar River, again by train, to Heilbronn. They made the return trip by boat down the Neckar as far as Hirschhorn, then proceeded by railroad and carriage to Heidelberg. Clemens used the one-day Neckar boat trip as the source for the raft excursion in chapters 14 through 17 of *A Tramp Abroad.* Clemens and Twichell returned briefly to Baden-Baden after their excursion before rejoining the rest of the party in Lucerne.

[33] In May 1873, Twichell had been present at the fifth annual reunion of the Society of the Army of the Potomac in New Haven, Connecticut. He delivered the blessing at the commencement of the general ceremonies and, evidently, also addressed the third corps at their individual reunion. Twichell had been one of the chaplains of General Daniel Sickles' third corps brigade during the Civil War.

[34] In *A Tramp Abroad* Clemens recurrently pointed out the difference between the mileage given in the guidebook and the pedometer readings.

[35] In anticipation of his invasion and conquest of England, in preparation since 1803, Napoleon I had a medal struck in 1804: one side showed the laurel-crowned head of the emperor and the other side, inscribed "Descente en Angleterre," depicted Hercules vanquishing a marine monster (catalogue of the *Collection du Prince d'Essling: Monnaies—Médailles* [Paris, 1926], p. 91, plate 28; William H. Jervis, *A History of France* [New York: American Book Co., 1862], p. 611).

Church in Hei[d] with partition—one side Cath—other side Protestant.[36]

Church on Neckar—must hold service once a year. in it.

Aug 8 Very sweet girl in train—Joe told me so in German, to keep her from understanding. This is very neat. Most G's *do* understand English, but very few of them can understand our German.

Heilbron, Aug. 8.—At hotel ordered one red wine & they brought another. We called attention to it. Head Waiter—"Here, bring another label!" (Fact is the <w>label had just been put on & was still wet.

2000 labels sent to one American firm so they can furnish any wine desired.

The Clock.[37]

The church—old carvings—mural tablets of 1598 &c in brass & iron with coats of arms.

Handwriting of Tilly, <Alfa>Alva, Chas XII, Ney, Götz von - - - &c.—& Ms of 1402, 1440, &c, kept lying on an old table in portfolios.[38]

Wild boars killed 200 yrs ago.

Pictures of modern French soldiers.

Fine portico to Rathhaus & 2 old figures in armor. Roof 3 stories high. The whole place looked so old (built 1550). It must make a clerk feel as fleeting as a butterfly to sit & work where so many have wrought & died before. [#]

---

[36] The Church of the Holy Ghost employed the nave for Protestant worship, the choir for Roman Catholic.

[37] Clemens described the ornate and unusual clock on Heilbronn's Rathhaus in chapter 12 of *A Tramp Abroad*.

[38] The count of Tilly, the duke of Alva, and Michel Ney were generals involved in various battles fought in Germany during the preceding centuries. Götz von Berlichingen was a sixteenth-century knight who became a folk hero and was immortalized by Goethe in his drama *Götz von Berlichingen*. The documents which Clemens mentions were displayed in the archives of the Heilbronn Rathhaus.

At Wimpfen am Berge the Red Tower (legend.)[39] By church the crucifixion (300 yr old) one thief dressed in height of fashion with sleeves of his doublet slashed & a prominent codpiece.

In this church was a lively picture of the final judgment.

Saw Weinberg in the distance; & above it Weibertreu, an old wall enclosing trees on top of a sort of Dilsberg

Vast carpetless room at Hotel zum Falkan, opening into a kind of theatre on one side.

1000 noises.

No street lamps & no use for them.

I heard the ¼ hours struck & the sweet trumpet blow, from <4> 10.15 to 4.30.

Got up in night to get my feather bed & barked my brow on <the> an ornament of the tall stove. I could not do it justice, so said absolutely nothing.

No carpet, but a rabbit skin before each bed & a rug under the table.

Green colored plums the size of a hen's egg, better than oranges—that is why the plum, which is with us a worthless fruit, holds such a place in G literature.

The cherries are black & delicious. Their other fruits are about like ours, neither better nor worse.

In old times here people waited some time for a boat—but we can have one at 9 AM.

The hotel about 300 years old is a comparatively modern building —but some of the stenches were <antiques> quite old—they were antiques, I should say. [#]

---

39 Murray mentions "an ancient tower . . . the foundations of which are said to be of Roman construction" in Wimpfen am Berg (*A Handbook for Travellers in Southern Germany* [London: John Murray, 1871], p. 11). No legend is known about the tower, but Clemens was planning to include legends in *A Tramp Abroad* about ruined castles and other landmarks, relying on his own invention where local history was lacking.

Inlaid & carved great sideboard in pantry <250 (1570> 1570 (300 yrs old.) One on 2^d^ floor of <1747> 1747.

Stone pavement worn gutter 3 inch deep by feet of swinging children

Smith[40] to boatman Kan man boat get here?

"Machen Sie a flat board."

Stopped for beer at <Neckar> Jagtfeldt & took a nooning of beer &c & a new & smaller boat.

A little below found a dozen naked little girls bathing, with an old mother in charge.

Tower (tall & square & old) of Ehrenberg on left bank an hour below Wimpfen—100 ft above river in middle of the steep bank. The town (not visible, is called Heinsheim Write legend.) An ancient roofless vine-clad ruin adjoins the tower.

Slopes of Neckar very steep here & covered thick with grape vines.

All Rhine wines are disguised vinegar.

Schloss Gutenberg on left bank below town on right where 20 little girls were bathing. Little left of it but ivy clad small tower.

The boatman talks constantly to me in G which I can't understand & I reply sociably in English which *he* can't understand.

Have a character who uses <irre> meaningless big words w^h^ exasperate me. "That is a mighty duplex tower."

Hassmersheim (?) town where we tarried & took beer & H[41] went swimming above where 25 girls were & was warned away. Below this town on right bank, 200 ft up on top of the steep bank, castle of

40 Edward M. Smith, United States consul at Mannheim, with whom Clemens and Twichell undertook the boat trip down the Neckar. In chapter 18 of *A Tramp Abroad* Clemens elaborates this entry.

41 Probably Clemens' fictional agent Haggerty, later Harris.

Hornberg, high old <w> vine clad walls enclosing trees, & one peaked tall tower 75 ft high. (Legend.)[42]

The whole hill side terraced in grape vines under Hornberg castle.

New RR will pass under it.

2 mile below Hornberg on left bank is a cave in low cliff—girl <wh> of Hornberg whose lover was gone to Xsades, was persecuted by lovers till she fled there & lived alone (on fish?) till lover returned & they were married.

The cave is by the Denkmal<l> to 3 preachers whom schiffer <meant to> say were drowned <but did>.

No Name.

2 hours above Eberbach, on right bank, a low small square tower, ruined, standing above a low rock or cliff—tower 150 ft above Neckar. Name it.—(Legend.) Call it the Nameless Tower?

Nice old ruin  right on <st>peak of very steep hill ½ hour above Eberbach—(legend) left bank.—From above toward twilight looks like 2 persons (heads against sky) <tou> leaning forward & touching forheads to talk confidentially. Put that in as a point in legend.

2 or 3 miles below the above, a castle composed of a stately pile of massed buildings, the older parts pink stone. Right bank. 200 ft above river.—200 yds of front wall, ivy clad. Thick round tower at lower end & tall square pointed tower at upper. A round white tower in midway. <A> In good condition & still inhabited. [#]

---

[42] Götz von Berlichingen died at Hornberg Castle in 1562. In chapter 15 of *A Tramp Abroad* Clemens describes the Hornberg region and recounts a local legend, "The Cave of the Spectre," outlined below.

<½ m below>

At this castle passed a raft.

½ m below man yelled at us to hurry—several blasts smoking in hill side. We seemed to move rather slowly, though schiffer laid in vigorously. The blasts did us no damage.

10th Aug—Back to Heidelberg after spending night at Hotel zum Naturlistes, in Hirschhorn—<[pa]> carriage to Neckargemünd—rail to H.

To Baden Baden to "wash & pray"[43]

Slender naked girl snatched a leafy bow of a bush across her front & then stood satisfied gazing out upon us as we floated by—a very pretty picture.

Baden

American who watched till nobody was in sight in the Lichtenthal allè, then got under that furiously spraying fountain, seated himself on the black rocks, with umbrella raised, & proceeded to plunge himself deeply in his book. This fountain is where allè joins town. Audience collected, then the police interfered.

10th Aug—Baden. Blazing hot in train—2 Amer youths—met another on stret, a student in Stuttgart for Veterinary surgeon—he ranged alongside, & said "Americans?" We said Yes. How long in G? 4 mos. Tired? No—are you? O, *hell*, yes. &c.

Awfully hot all day. Took a bath at Friedrich. In Evening to bed early, with the new home magazines, which I had saved all day & wouldn't cut a leaf.[44] Twichell the ass, writes & goes to the music. I lie & smoke & am wise. [#]

---

[43] Clemens and Twichell arrived back in Baden-Baden on Saturday, 10 August. The rest of the Clemens party had meanwhile gone on to Switzerland.

[44] The magazines included the July 1878 issues of *Harper's New Monthly Magazine* and the *Atlantic Monthly* (see Notebook 14, note 86, and note 48 of this notebook).

File meerschaum with crape.
My ivory cards. 120 M. made by <St> Stüber.

Invented a note-book in May.[45]

Sharpen without strop in June.

Sunday, AM, Aug. 11.[46] Been reading Romola yesterday afternoon, last night, & this morning; at last I came upon the only passage which has thus far *hit me with force*—Tito compromising with his conscience & resolving to do, not a bad thing, but not the *best* thing. Joe entered the room 5 minutes, no, 3 minutes later, & without prelude said, "I read that book you've got there, 6 years ago, & got a mighty good text for a sermon out of it—the passage where the young fellow compromises with his conscience & resolves to do, not a bad thing, but not the *best* thing." This is Joe's first reference to this book since he saw me buy it 24 hours ago in Heidelberg. So my mind operated on his, in this instance. He said he was sitting yonder in the reading room, 3 minutes ago (I have not got up, yet,) thinking of nothing in particular & didn't know what brought Romola into his head—but into his head it came, & that particular passage. Now I, 40 feet away, in another room, was reading that particular passage at that particular moment. I couldn't suggest Romola to him earlier, because nothing in the book had taken hold of me till I came to that one passage on page 112 Tauchnitz edition.

Only he knows the real & permanent joy of life who has a specialty —the miser, the Latinist, the oculist, <the> a particular branch of Keramics or other Alterthum—Seth Green's fish,[47] &c. But to have

---

[45] Clemens designed a notebook with a tab projecting from the top corner of each leaf; the tab could be torn off so the writer could easily find his place. Notebooks 16 through 20 were made in Germany to Clemens' specifications. He had additional notebooks with this tab device made to order in Hartford.

[46] Clemens spent his Sunday in Baden-Baden making the notes on the succeeding pages (pp. 135–140). In his working notes for A *Tramp Abroad*, he referred to this entry: "Under date of Sunday, Aug 11, is a pretext for lugging in Mind-Reading—(old note book)—other references in newer books."

[47] Green, who fished for sport as a young boy in his native New York, dedicated his life to the development of practical and profitable fish hatcheries.

many interests weakens them all. See what an intense life was the Scotch naturalist's![48]

Always Went in a procession by himself, like Smith's hog.

The Angel's Camp constable who always saw everything largely. Two men walking tandem was a procession; <2> 3 men fighting was a riot; 5 <a riot; 15> an insurrection, & <25> 15 a revolution.[49]

Drawing a tooth in the army—with a brigade of yellers for audience. The patient doesn't wince, then.

The chap who always went bawling like a baby into battle—& if there was a wavering or sign of retreat, the Col would order him to cry.

Feeling religious, this morning, I sent a scout to church. He saw the Empress & heard a poor sermon.

The stuffed great gray cat with staring, intelligent glass eyes, in the moonlight, that wouldn't let young Smith go to sleep (he was on the floor & it above on a bracket) till he got up & turned its head away. This at the Naturalists inn[50]—every room & hall full of stuffed creatures, & the back yards full of odd living ones. [#]

---

[48] Clemens may be referring to the Scottish-American ornithologist Alexander Wilson. An edition of Wilson's writing, *The Poems and Literary Prose of Alexander Wilson, the American Ornithologist* edited by the Reverend Alexander B. Grosart, was reviewed at length in the July 1878 issue of the *Atlantic Monthly*. Clemens probably saw the review while reading the "new home magazines" on 10 August (p. 134). The review dwelt on Wilson's fascination with birds during his youth in Scotland and his later years in America: "It is this enthusiasm, bearing him up above the vicissitudes of a somewhat depressing life, which makes the atmosphere in which we now see Wilson's fine spirit. . . . The birds which he loved with so natural and genuine an ardor seem fit emblems of a life which alighted on the earth only for necessary food and rest" (*Atlantic*, p. 124).

[49] These exaggerations are typical of Constable Bilgewater who is the subject of "Angel's Camp Constable," an unpublished early sketch. Bilgewater "always liked to have people pay him a good deal of respect, & he liked to have them call things belonging to his line by big names. . . . There warn't anything small about him—names nor anything" (DV 408, TS in MTP).

[50] Clemens, Twichell, E. M. Smith, and "young Smith" spent the night of 9 August at the Hotel zum Naturalisten in Hirschhorn.

The rooms & bedding wonderfully nice, but the old man rich & indifferent. Trying to get his nephew from America to take the place & be his heir, but he won't. He is the boy in green-faced hunting coat who said "I'm an American!" & shook hands & sat down with us without further introduction. Nice boy.

In the garden fruit trees, which the boy knocked down for us; & odds & ends of ancient stone carvings damp & mildewed lying around, & then a swift stream literally alive with trout—but you can't fish there, because it belongs to Heidelberg & an individual rents it at $200 a year—& every fish in it is worth a dollar or thereabouts.

That poor raven <all> all louse-eaten, & so humble & ashamed of his bare-sterned condition. he was Pathetic.

What *is* the law of accidents? Got up in the dark, (to save trouble of striking a match) to get my "plumeau"—knocked my head against stove—put up hand to feel wound, & knocked <vase off mantelpiece> pitcher off commode—grabbed at pitcher & <fetched down> touched lamp, <with globe &c>—grabbed at that, of course, <—>thinking it was falling, & knocked it down—grabbed at it again as it went & fell over a chair & knocked down a 6-foot hat rack which destroyed the remaining furniture in its fall. I then struck a match & got my plumeau. My comrade springing to a sitting posture out of a sound sleep & exclaiming, Heavens, what has happened, I answer irritatedly, "Nothing! I never *saw* a man so eaten up with <idle> foolish curiosity as you." Then I blow out light, lie down, & for an hour, those incidents make procession & re-procession through my mind till I am burnt up with helpless fury.

Still Aug. 11—Gave my[51] about an hour's nooning & sent him to the Prot. Evangelical church, I being still filled with churchly longings.

Man's an ass who does not carry an agent.

Put T by the window so he could listen to the wagons.

Law of accidents again: crushed a grape-seed up between my

[51] Mark Twain inadvertently omitted a word, evidently "scout" or "agent."

teeth & had to eat on other side of mouth—every bite shoved my whole upper jaw—nothing so uncomfortable as such a wedge between one's teeth. Not used to *beginning* a bite with other side of mouth—presently bit right down in the thick part of left <side> half of my tongue—never had such a crushing & cruel bite before. Presently forgot & poured some wine into the bite—raised my foot to stamp, in the sudden infuriation caused by the pain, & overthrew the small table & all its dishes. I <sho> siezed the table to throw it through the window—but that would never do, I might kill somebody—so I glanced feverishly around for something to wreak my fury on—a chair stood convenient—<with a sudden> I launched a kick, & the next moment the chair was lying bottom up on the other side of the room & I was on the sofa nursing my instep, rocking to & fro, with <the> tears of anguish standing in my eyes & a torrent of spontaneous eloquence pouring from my lips. What *is* the law of accidents?

How Nicodemus Dodge sold the skeleton to traveling quack for $5.

"I should have liked to (have known) know more about him."[52]

Notes which you start to set down & they vanish. Others which you start to set down & say "Hold on, you lie there a moment till I set down these others, which are elusive—& by George the note so laid down is gone when you want it.—Notes or names which are at your fingers' ends & you can't quite get them.

Sunday Night, 11th. Huge crowd out to-night to hear the band play the Fremersberg. I suppose it is very low grade music—I know it *must* be low grade music—because it so delighted me, it so warmed me, moved me, stirred me, uplifted me, enraptured me that at times I

---

[52] In chapter 23 of *A Tramp Abroad*, "Harris" discusses the use of multiple "haves" as a grammatical construction in writing. Chapter 23 ranges over several topics unconnected with the European trip, including the tale of Nicodemus Dodge's adventures. Clemens introduces this digressive chapter by simply remarking "what a motley variety of subjects a couple of people will casually rake over in the course of a day's tramp!"

could have cried & at others split my throat with shouting.[53] The great crowd was another evidence that it wa low grade music; for only the few are educated up to a point where high class music gives pleasure. I have never heard enough classic music to be able to enjoy it; & the simple truth is, I detest it. Not mildly, but with all my heart. To me an opera is the very climax & cap-stone of the absurd, the fantastic the unjustifiable. I hate the very name of opera—<mere> partly because of the nights of suffering I have endured in its presence, & partly because I want to love it and can't. I suppose one naturally hates the things he wants to love & can't. In America the opera is an affectation. The seeming love for [it] is a lie. Nine out of every ten of the males are bored by it, & 5 out of 10 women. Yet how they applaud, the ignorant liars!—

What a poor lot we human beings are, anyway. If base music gives me wings, why should I want any other? But I do. I want to like the higher music because the higher & better like it. But you see, I want to like it without taking the necessary trouble & <laying out the> giving the thing the necessary amount of time & attention. The natural suggestion is, to get into that upper tier, that dress circle, by a lie: <—> we will *pretend* we like it. This lie, this pretense, gives to opera what support it has in America.

And then there is painting. What a red rag is to a bull, Turner's "Slave Ship" is to me. Mr. Ruskin is educated in art up to a point where that picture throws him into as mad <a rap> an ecstasy of pleasure as it throws me into one of rage. <To> His cultivation enables him to see water in that yellow mud; his cultivation reconciles the floating of unfloatable things to him—chains &c—it reconciles him to fishes swimming on top of the water. The most of the picture is a manifest impossibility—that is to say, a lie; & only rigid cultivation can enable a man to find truth in a lie. A Boston critic said the Slave Ship reminded him of a cat having a fit in a platter of tomatoes. That went home to my non-cultivation & I thought here

---

[53] Clemens included a discussion of "high" and "low-grade" music and art in chapter 24 of *A Tramp Abroad*. Further evidence of Clemens' musical taste at this time occurs in the lists of selections for a music box (Notebook 16, pp. 211–213).

is a man with an unobstructed eye. Mr R would have said This person is an ass.

How much we do lose by cultivation! It narrows us down till a single false note can spoil an evening's entertainment. And what will the cultivated people do in heaven?—for in the nature of things they will have to have "popular" music there because of the crowd. And I wonder where they will have the "classic" music.

When they play Martha, the liars applaud all along—but when The Last Rose of Summer drops in, they forget & the applause is something tremendous.

The first thing to remind us we were out of Germany was the sign in depot beyond the Rhine in Switzerland:

Vor Taschendieben wird gewarnt.
Méfiez vous des Voleurs
Beware of Pickpockets.

The hated Cuckoo-clock.

Aug. 12th, came from Baden to Luzerne.

About 14th, Rigi.[54]

17th, Joe to St. Gottard Pass.[55]

19th Aug—The Yale cub who asked so many idiotic questions on the lake steamer.[56] DON'T FAIL. [#]

---

[54] The Clemens party spent the night of 15 August in a hotel on the Rigi in order to watch the sunset and sunrise. Livy and Clara Spaulding went up in "an open car in which we were pushed by a steam engine up the mountain, we were all obliged to ride backward and that was rather trying to Clara and me" (OLC to Mrs. Langdon, 18 August 1878, MTM). Clemens wrote to his mother and sister: "Twichell & I took a stroll . . . to the summit of the Rigi, where the rheumatism captured me once more & we had to come down with the others by rail. It was a good deal like coming down a ladder by rail. I did not like it" (20 August 1878).

[55] While Clemens rested and wrote letters in the hotel at Lucerne, Twichell went off on a three-day trip in the Alps by himself.

[56] Clemens described this traveler at greater length in Notebook 16, p. 168.

Rhone glacier—
glazier
glaceer
glasher
gletcher
" G. (telegram).

Disgusted to find that an invalid lady walked up Rigi & back. American? No—English.

Aug. 21. Left in 4-horse ambulance. Proprietor gave children box.

Aug 22—At Jungfrau Hotel, Interlaken—Superb view of the Jungfrau.

Confounded crow woke us all up at daylight.

Set your umbrella up on these polished wood floors, down it goes. Step suddenly on them, down *you* go.

The lowest snow on the Jf seems but little above the valley level—

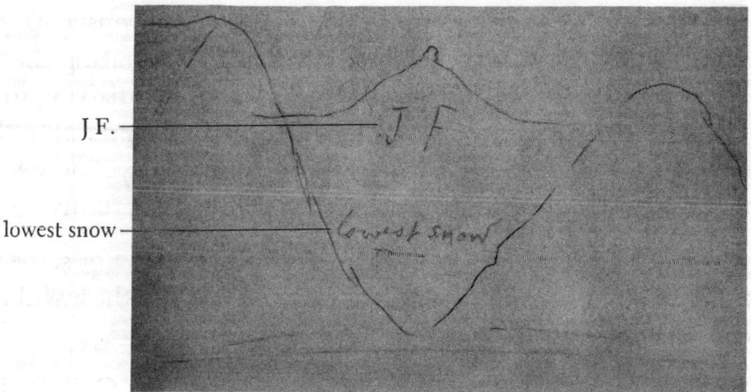

& on the left towers a huge rampart 2 or 3000 ft high (close to us)—& it seems absurd to say that that lowest snow is higher than that (apparently) vastly higher rampart—but so it is—for the one is on the eternal snow altitude & the other isn't—as the absence of snow shows.

Ice does not make water (except soda) cold in this country. [#]

Halls of hotel paved with great rough flags of granite—upon which you slip.

Runaway twice in an omnibus—once Worms, once N.O., where saver said, "You G— d— fool, you might ruined that lamp post."[57]

Women are the meanest creatures—they wrinkle up their noses in so faint a way (scorn) that you can only detect it as they come into profile—at each other's dresses—men hardly glance at each other—(apparently). They *do* glance & see all, though.

Waiter woman with side whiskers reaching (finger-breadth) half way to chin.

Sent scout to see Giesbach falls illuminated. You leave here by little steamboat at 8 & get back about 11

Young woman after table d'hote tackled an old rattle trap piano with such vigor & absence of expression with Battle of Prague & favorites of the same age that she soon cleaned out the great reading room—but I staid, at first to watch the grimaces & unconscious squirms of people when she fetched a particularly lacerating chord—& afterwards I staid because the exquisitely bad is as satisfying to the soul as the exquisitely good—only the mediocre is unendurable. The pun is like mediocre music, neither wit nor humor—& yet now & then one sees a pun which comes so near being wit that it is funny.

She was a new bride & her man sat manfully by her. For some time I was sorry for him—but presently discovered he *liked* the awful noise & considered it music.

Scout killed by flea in principal hotel. <Removed> Collected remains by microscope.

Chamois is only a flea—hence our word sham.[58] [#]

---

[57] A reference to Clara Spaulding's omnibus mishaps (see note 22).

[58] Clemens elaborated his identification of the chamois with a flea in chapter 25 of *A Tramp Abroad*.

Out-door bench is 2 boards slanting with crack in middle for rain to run thro'.

23^d Aug—Drove in rain around Lake Thun to Kandersteg.[59]

Here there is always a foot of clothes-line next the thills.[60]

Make frequent reference to the Chamois.

24th—up, shaved breakfasted, before 8—everybody gone but us.

Don't forget that jolly tight driver looking over hack top to explain scenery & give his card to the family, his horses flying down hill. He walked & talked with our driver. Tongue ran incessantly. Sang a song.[61]

Girls laughed at Joe asleep.

Ink in G & S is black mud—the inkstand still has a sandbox.

Men wear Edelweiss in their hats—not a pretty flower.

Visited Gasternthal—gushing waterspout from rock. Sun shining on green ice & blazing snow

Chased a chunk down stream[62] [#]

---

[59] Clemens and Twichell left the others in Interlaken and started a five-day tour which took them, partly on foot, from Kandersteg over the Gemmi Pass to Leukerbad, along the Rhone Valley to Visp, then up through Saint Niklaus to Zermatt where they stayed several days. They rejoined the rest of the party, which had gone to Ouchy on Lake Geneva, on 31 August.

[60] Clemens also comments on the use of clothesline to piece out harness in Notebook 16, p. 175.

[61] Mark Twain gave an exaggerated account of the "tight driver" in chapter 33 of *A Tramp Abroad*. To Livy, however, he wrote a tamer version of the incident: "Livy darling, we had a lovely day—jogged right along, with a good horse and sensible driver—the last two hours right behind an open carriage filled with a pleasant German family—old gentleman and 3 pretty daughters" ([23] August 1878).

[62] Twichell described the boyish enthusiasm with which Clemens pursued some floating driftwood: "Mark was running down-stream after it as hard as he could go, throwing up his hands and shouting in the wildest ecstasy, and when a piece went over a fall and emerged to view in the foam below he would jump up and down and yell. He said afterward that he hadn't been so excited in three months" (*MTB*, p. 629).

Cows wear church bells, torrents roar so.

Rainbow on water fall—like illuminated thin smoke.

24th Aug—8.30 A.M. Started—had a grand time thro' the Gemmi Pass—reached summit at 1 & looked down on steep precipice & town of <Leuch> Bad-Leuk.

Denkmal—guide saw the tragedy. Bridal tour.[63]

Reached B.-L 3.30—7 hours.

Our girls are here.

Saw people in the bath playing a game.[64]

Raw & rainy here to-night—miss our library fire.

Sunday morning 25th Aug. visited the King of the World's palace[65] & drew its outline, seated on a grassy bench (a precipice) 2 or 300 ft high,) with 2 or 3 trees projecting above its edge.

In the gorge a wooden (small) platform stuck against a straight precipice 500 ft high, 50 ft from ground—reached by a pole with pegs in it resting 25 ft from ground[66]—how did they get up to the

---

63 Chapter 35 of *A Tramp Abroad* quotes the following description of this incident from Baedeker: "The descent on horseback should be avoided. In 1861 a Comtesse d'Herlincourt fell from her saddle over the precipice and was killed on the spot" (*Switzerland and the Adjacent Portions of Italy, Savoy, and the Tyrol* [Leipzig: Karl Baedeker, 1877], p. 153).

64 Baedeker describes the bathing customs at Leukerbad: "In order to avoid the tedium of a long and solitary immersion, the patients, clothed in long flannel dresses, sit up to their necks in water in a common bath, where they remain for several hours together. Each bather has a small floating table before him, from which his book, newspaper, or coffee is enjoyed. The utmost order and decorum are preserved. Travellers are admitted to view this singular and somewhat uninviting spectacle" (Baedeker's *Switzerland*, p. 154).

65 Clemens' reference is to a natural cliff formation whose romantic description in chapter 35 of *A Tramp Abroad* concludes: "If there were a king whose realms included the whole world, here would be the palace meet and proper for such a monarch. He would only need to hollow it out and put in the electric light. He could give audience to a nation at a time under its roof."

66 "On the face of a rock . . . the remains of a hut are pointed out, in which, it is said, a hermit once lived. He had to climb to it up a pole" (*A Handbook for*

pole? Boy told me they were going to throw a bridge across the chasm—paid him 15 cent. for this doubtful information—he thanked me & asked for 10 more (pointing to his holes) to get a new blouse. Gave him 20 & he kept on bowing, taking off cap & saying Merci Monsieur, Merci beaucoup—adie" for 50 yards.

Another man, a guide, said it was for a sentinel to watch for the French in 1795. <*That* won't> Went up by rope ladder. *That* won't explain it. The guard had better & more accessible places. Paid this one 10 cent, & 10 more to get *him* a blouse. This thing is put here just to pique curiosity & cause the tourist needless expense in blouses.—

Give further explanations—for blouses.

Single bar left of an old fence—young fellow leaned on it & it gave way a foot.

The baths—people eating breakfast on boards.

At Visp, girl who had removed the guideboard & substituted hersef (in rain & mud)—one man *thanked* her.

Describe man a little tight—tries to pour wine from a corked bottle—tries 3 times to say a word, then changes to one which he *can* pronounce.

Stone walls do not a prison make—grave man interrupts (matter of fact) "but they assist"

Give other instances of his interruptions.

Joe lost hat & found opera glass.

Got down to 4000 ft above sea, came into October & found fringed gentian.

Runaway stage-coach on plains—driver on the thills.

Gigantic French Countess—did wish I might venture to ask her for her dimensions.

Travellers in Switzerland, and the Alps of Savoy and Piedmont [London: John Murray, 1871], p. 135).

She said one woman with hands 6 inches thick reduced them greatly by 5 baths.

The fatlings bathe 3 hours in AM & 2 in PM

Monday, Aug. 26.

From Leukerbad to <Visp> Locchi-Suste in a buggy—<driver pretended> shoved the horse down with the carriage.

French count with one eye-glass, hair parted in middle—had 5 dogs & a flying squirrel (in his bosom.

Curse the eternal hotel fashion of noisy pets. The caged cooking doves or pigeons woke me both mornings at Leukerbad.

Barking little dog, & a <ba> crying baby—didn't mind the baby, because these are necessary.

Alas! while we were up the mountain yesterday (Sunday) gathering gentians for our German girls, they vamosed to Visp.

Describe Joe's bowing to them at table d'hote in Kandesteg.

Village ½ hour out of Leukerbad, w^h they climb to up ladders—up a cliff 3 or 400 ft.

The streams in Switzerland are such a lovely gray color! And they tumble along so lively.

Met English family[67] at Leukerbad, going same day with us to St Nicholas.

Also American & 2 ladies going tother way.

If a bird *should* stick one of these Swiss village spires in his eye.

Muddy walk to-day & bad roads—the first we have had in Europe.

Waitress at hotel with considerable *side* whiskers.

Joe to pretty waitress (with pantomime of drinking) (L'eau froid—frisches Wasser—cold water, please—to drink, you know!" [#]

---

67 This was John Dawson, a wholesale boot and shoe dealer, his son and three daughters. The Dawson family called on the Clemenses later in Ouchy and Twichell visited them in London on his way home.

There was a *hotel* de Chamois—we avoided it.—The accommodations are sufficient where it is not made a specialty.

Can't we ring in Jim Wolf & the cats, simply, unobtrusively, & *not* in dialect—& then tell how Maj. Wadsworth bummed on me as long as he could in London & then sold that sketch to Tom Hoods Annual (for 1874) in Tom's absence for £1 & signed his 3 stately names to it?[68]

That yarn *always* fetches an audience.

Everybody, very old wrinkled women too, work a field in Schweiz, & carry vast loads in baskets 3 ft high on their backs

The cabins picturesquely dot the mountains in the midst of the greenest grass clear up the precipices to the snow & clouds. How do they cling there.

Drat this stupid "yodling."

Avalanch of small boys & girls with little casks strapped to their backs poured down into Leucherbad in procession at dusk—been far up on the mountains to milk goats.

Avalanche destroyed the whole town 50 yrs ago & killed 120 people. A semi-centennial avalanche would clean the town & do good.

Sheep like slugs on the dizzy green precipice under Gemmi summit.

A pleasant swing the palanquin has to it—also one's feet.

None but Americans declined to bow.

The vulgar women who don't return our bow don't know the difference between reverence & familiarity—a sure sign of vulgarity. They plainly feel insulted by our respectful homage. But we have

[68] Mark Twain's story about Jim Wolf had already appeared in several American newspapers in the 1860s before it was published in *Tom Hood's Comic Annual for 1874* as "A Yankee Story" under the name of G. R. Wadleigh. Clemens describes the plagiarism in his autobiography, but makes himself the agent who convinced his friend Hood to publish Wadleigh's manuscript as a favor, ignorant of its contents (*MTA*, 1:141–143).

learned this in Germany & don't intend to lose it—it is a valuable possession.

Crazy wooden Bridge over <a> the foaming Visp—if I had an elephant that was a keepsake I wouldn't want to ride him over it.

<Every>

Arrived at St. Nicholas at 4 PM 6 hours through mud & rain from Visp.

All the gentlemen stripped & went to bed & sent down their clothes & boots to be dried. These got mixed & went to various rooms. I came near going down with one striped & one white sock, like a convict.[69] I lost the chance to bespeak rooms for our English friends—the young brother beat us in. Glad they all go to Zermat to-morrow.

English gentleman remarked that a man can command no respect without his pantaloons. So he waited for his & it made him last at dinner.

The moment you step out of Berne (on the Gemmi) & into this wretched canton[70] (the Arkansas) of Sw, you notice the difference. No guideboards whatever—except one—in that nasty little town[71] where the aged castle was; a fine for trotting a horse down its steep streets—& (in German) a fine for "beschädigt" the "Bonne." If that is street, how *could* anybody injure it. This is the lazy canton, the worthless canton. In that village where Hotel du Raisin was,[72] the carpenter must be asked 20 times a day the road to *this* inhabited privy—& yet he doesn't put up a guide-board.

The dangerous descent of the Gemmi & the dangerous road here for the last 5 miles. The village<s> alleys run liquid dung—these

---

69 In chapter 35 of *A Tramp Abroad,* Clemens elaborately developed the confusion of garments so that he presents himself as having appeared in the dining room unwittingly dressed in women's underclothing.

70 The Valais.

71 The village of Leuk, south of Leukerbad and a short distance from the Rhone.

72 The town of Stalden, on the route to Saint Niklaus, had a Traube ("Grape") Inn.

villages are the shackliest & vilest we have seen anywhere. This canton may be called the fundament of Switzerland.

How strange! to plow through dung & decay & squalor & come plump upon an excellent hotel & be received by a maitre d'hotel in swallowtail & elegant manners.—These people think it a palace, no doubt.

These roads and bridges must have made themselves. These fools have got a great show here, & if they knew anything they would make good roads & then keep door as if it was a circus. It <may> would pay better than dung.

St. Nicklaus Aug. 27—Awakend at 4.30 by the clang & jangle of a church bell wh rang 15 min. Went to sleep no more. At 7 it rang again 15.

It is an ugly little whitewashed church with a queer tin dome <on its> <which> like a turnip growing with its root in the air.

Damn all ch bells! At 7.25 they rang again!

(All town clocks in S have but one long, stiff hand, so the very devil can't tell the time by them.)

Still that ringing goes on. I wish to God that church w^{d} burn down. It is not fifty yards from the hotel. I hope an earthquake will topple a mountain on it. *Why* was it absent from Go[nau]?

<Ger> Girl came up to find lost clothes—talked both languages. So also our driver—<who> everybody in this region does.

At 8 the bell rang again. Let us hope there is a hell.

Man who lost no moment to pour out obscenity, so as to keep himself pure *within*—could not abide those impure people who keep it inside.

This canton is Catholic, Berne Protestant.

<V>*Go by* Mont Blanc—so used to bigger Mountains, did not notice it.

Left St Nicholas at <8.45> 9.15, 27th.

The girls right ahead [#]

Corporal McGwyre, with the tears of an injured spirit in his eyes—"Chaplain, do you take me for a G— d— Catholic?"[73]

Treasurer Spinner & the widow committee—swearing.[74]

About half way to Zermat we saw on top of a near mountain a perpendicular wall of ice (pale green) & were forced to reflect that if Strasburg Cathedral, stood at its base, a man on top of the wall could reach out & hang his hat on top of the spire—& he could look *down* on St Pauls or St Peters or Capitol of W.

Here in this canton they take care of nothing—let their glashers get so dirty—never whitewash them—in the Prot canton[75] [#]

---

[73] Clemens told a similar Civil War anecdote about Twichell in his autobiography. There the role of "McGwyre" is assigned to the father of Tammany leader Richard Croker. Twichell, as chaplain of the brigade, expressed delight that Croker occasionally could "put aside his religious prejudices and manifest the breadth and tolerance" to come to listen to his services. Whereupon Croker "flushed, and said with eloquent emphasis, 'Mr. Twichell, do you take me for a God damned papist?' " (*MTA*, 2:205–206).

[74] Francis Elias Spinner, treasurer of the United States from 1861 to 1875, was notorious for his profanity. The anecdote referred to here is fully reported in a clipping probably dating from 1867 or 1868 (Walter Frear Scrapbook, Yale) in which Mark Twain says: "It began to be whispered around that under very trying circumstances, General Spinner was guilty of swearing a little, sometimes. The church . . . appointed a discreet sister (the grieving mourner of a husband and three gallant brothers slain in the war) to inquire into the matter." The widow "posted herself among a crowd of waiting ones in the General's office." One of the treasurer's petitioners was a soldier who had deserted the Union army to fight on the Confederate side and was now applying to the government for back pay. Spinner looked over the man's documents wrathfully, and then denounced the "sneaking hound of a deserter" in fluent and colorful language. "And the mourner of the Union dead went back and reported. She said no, the General didn't swear exactly—and yet didn't exactly pray; but the words he said were the next most soothing words to a beautiful prayer that ever she heard in all her life."

[75] Mark Twain elaborated humorously on the superiority of Protestant cantons over Catholic cantons in chapter 36 of *A Tramp Abroad* with Harris as his spokesman. Harris' conclusions repeat many of the complaints in the notebook entries on Valais: " 'In the Protestant cantons you never see such poverty and dirt and squalor as you do in this Catholic one; you never see the lanes and alleys flowing with foulness; you never see such wretched little sties of houses; you never see an inverted tin turnip on top of a church for a dome; and as for a church bell, why you never hear a church bell at all.' "

At N. Y. Metropolitan Museum, they charge 25^{c} but have one free day for the poor. <Atten> Attendance slim on pay day but street blocked with carriages <for> of the rich on free day.[76]

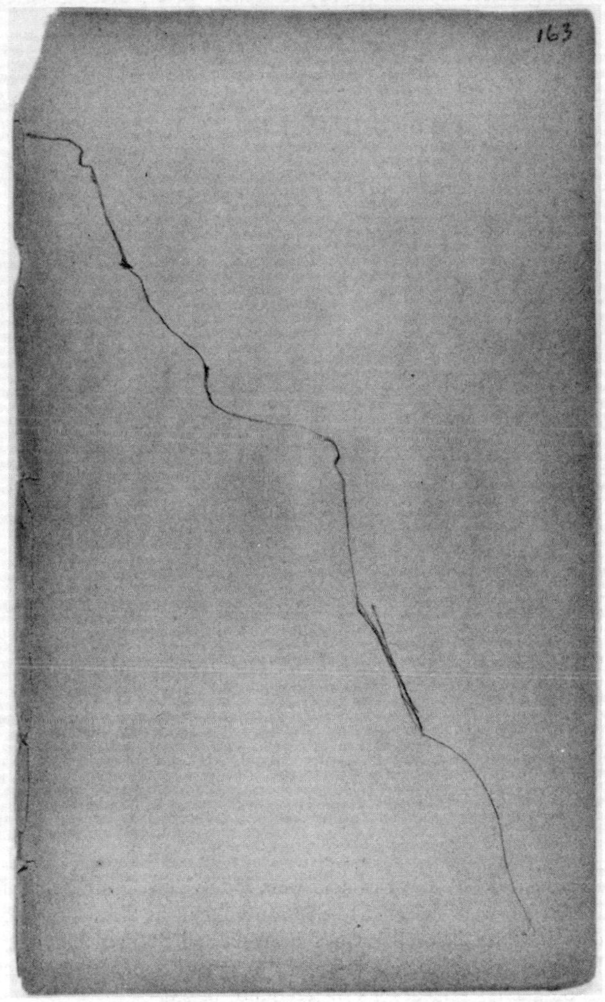

[76] In the manuscript this outline of mountainous terrain follows the notebook's last entry ("The Rhone glasher . . . the tidiest glasher in S.") and is followed by the drawing on page 152.

At monasteries in Holy Land our pilgrims contributed pennies.

See Baedecker as to stinginess of tourists at Hospice St. Bernard.[77]

The Rhone glasher is neat & tidy & clean—the tidiest glasher in S.

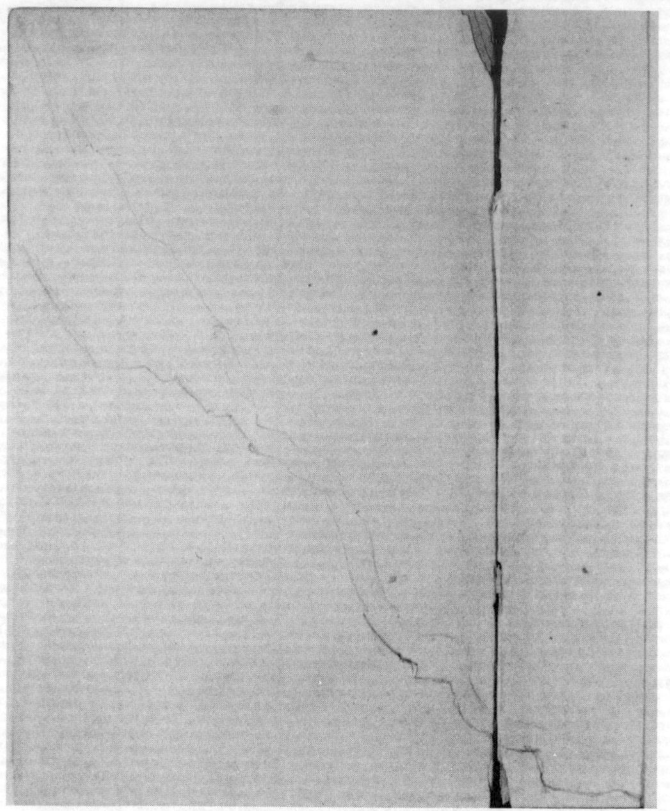

[77] Baedeker pointed out that travelers were lodged and boarded gratuitously by the brotherhood, but were expected to deposit alms in the almsbox. He continued: "Of late years 16–20,000 travellers have been annually accommodated, while the sum they have contributed barely amounts to what would be a moderate hotel charge for 1000 guests" (Baedeker's *Switzerland*, p. 244).

XVI

"Poking About with Red Guidebooks"

(August–October 1878)

NOTEBOOK 16 continues the account of Clemens' and Twichell's trip to Zermatt begun in Notebook 15 and provides details of the Clemens family's travels in Switzerland and Italy between 27 August and 13 October 1878. Like Notebooks 14 and 15 it is a combination of professional notes to go into A *Tramp Abroad* and personal ones that reflect the pleasures and aggravations of so lengthy a trip. The correspondence between notebook entries and A *Tramp Abroad* is pervasive, and in addition to individual incidents some of the continuing jokes in the book are alluded to or developed here, such as the alleged disparity between guidebook and "actual" distances and the confusion of the chamois and the flea.

On 30 August 1878, after three days of observing the Matterhorn, the Riffelberg, the Gorner Grat, and the adjacent mountains, Clemens and Twichell left Zermatt "in a wagon & a shower." They stopped in Saint Niklaus for lunch, walked to Visp where they spent the night, and on the next day traveled by train and boat to Ouchy on Lake Geneva to rejoin the family. The reunion was brief, for on 4 September the two men set out on their last Alpine tramp, taking the train to Martigny on the way to Chamonix. The following day an eight-and-a-half-hour walk brought them to Argentière where they hired a wagon for the last six miles to Chamonix, arriving at dark but finding Mont Blanc and the other high peaks in "a fine luminous daylight sort of light." On 6 September Clemens and Twichell took the one-day excursion recommended by Baedeker, climbing the Montanvert, from which they "crossed the Mer de Glace & ascended the confounded moraine." The climb, tiring but not difficult, proceeded without mishap in spite of Clemens' discomfort because of his smooth-soled shoes, and the descent was easily made except for one spot at the Mauvais Pas, a formerly hazardous point rendered secure by a system of iron rails.

On 7 September Clemens and Twichell returned to Geneva. The summer tramp had come to an end, and Twichell departed for home by way of Paris and London. The two friends were effusive in their recollections of the pleasure of each other's company. On 9 September Clemens wrote to Twichell:

> It is actually all over! I was so low-spirited at the station yesterday, and this morning, when I woke, I couldn't seem to accept the dismal truth that you were really gone, and the pleasant tramping and talking at an end. Ah, my boy! it has been such a rich holiday to me, and I feel under such deep and honest obligations to you for coming. I am putting out of my mind all memory of the times when I misbehaved toward you and hurt you: I am resolved to consider it forgiven, and to store up and remember only the charming hours of the journeys and the times when I was not unworthy to be with you and share a companionship which to me stands first after Livy's. (*MTL*, p. 338)

On 13 September Twichell wrote from Liverpool: "My heart was mighty heavy, I can tell you, when the train moved out of Geneva after I bade you goodbye. That I was starting for home I could not make seem the fact. I had not got far enough. I felt only what I was leaving behind." And in a letter from Hartford on 22 October he professed ignorance of any offense by Clemens and commented: "There's nobody that I want to travel with henceforth but you, even at my own charges." On 12 September, having brought Livy to Chamonix to appreciate the scenes he had already enjoyed with Twichell, Clemens was moved to inscribe in this notebook a glowing, but somewhat ambivalent tribute to his now distant friend: "M[ont] B[lanc] is like the great qualities of a friend—they sink low when close by & the du Midi defects & Doms tower above—but down the vally of time

& distance, *they* sink & old M B. soars into heaven with the glory of the sun on his crown."

The effect of Twichell's presence on *A Tramp Abroad* also seems ambivalent, though Clemens was unsparing in acknowledging his companionable assistance. "If I can make a book out of the matter gathered in your company over here," Clemens wrote from Rome on 3 November, "the book is safe; but I don't think I have gathered any matter before or since your visit worth writing up" (*MTL*, p. 339). He inscribed a presentation copy of that book: "My Dear 'Harris'—No, I mean My Dear Joe . . . I was collecting material in Europe during fourteen months for a book, and now that the thing is printed I find that you, who were with me only a month and a half of the fourteen, are in *actual* presence (not imaginary) in 440 of the 531 pages the book contains!" (*MTB*, p. 666). But this pervasiveness of Twichell-Harris may account for much of the flatness of *A Tramp Abroad*. Desirous of presenting his clergyman friend in a kindly and favorable fashion, Clemens created the genteel Harris, who bears no resemblance to Mr. Brown, the earlier travel companion whose follies and bizarre personality provided an outlet for unrestrained and sometimes bawdy observation. In *A Tramp Abroad* these elements of Clemens' humor, when they do appear, are distributed among a number of ephemeral characters, leaving Mr. Harris passive and undeveloped and consequently limiting the delineation of the character of Mark Twain through the author's usual method of sustained contrast.

Clemens and Livy returned to Geneva from Chamonix on 12 September. There Clemens reflected apprehensively on the next stage of the tour, a journey into "Italy the home of art & swindling; home of religion & moral rottenness." While the family and Clara Spaulding went on a last round of shopping, Clemens computed the cost of living in Europe and confessed that "we get discouraged every time we add up expenses." Indeed, Notebook 16 is almost as much the record of Clemens' futile struggle against expense as it is of his efforts to write *A Tramp Abroad*. A succession of purchases of personal items and objects for the Hartford house, in addition to a steady accumulation of small gifts for family and friends led Clemens to remind himself on several occasions that at least "we economise on pew-rent while abroad." Many of the unsympathetic entries about places visited in the period covered by this notebook may be the product of Clemens' recurrent sense of economic frustration.

The Clemenses and Clara Spaulding left Geneva on 14 September and traveled by rail to Chambéry where they stopped for a day. Clemens found it "the quaintest old town out of Heilbron" and marveled at the architecture that seemed "to have wandered out of old engravings of towns in the middle ages," but Livy complained to her mother of the poor accommodations, "the worst beds that we have had on our journey & very poor food" (15 September 1878, MTM), and she and Clara Spaulding spent a good part of the day foraging for food to satisfy their longings for American cooking. Clemens would take up their lament at length in his discourses on food in chapter 49 of *A Tramp Abroad.*

In contrast to Clemens' expectations, this segment of the Italian tour was generally agreeable and the ill humor that characterized part of the stay in Switzerland was dissipated. The streets and architecture of Turin, where the family arrived on 16 September, were so impressive and exhilarating that Clemens judged it "the finest city I have ever seen," taking special satisfaction in noting that there were "more books for sale here than I have seen anywhere in Europe." He was surprised at Italian honesty and could even decide that the high prices of railway tickets "were justifiable" because of the ingenious and costly construction of the many tunnels, although later he would complain bitterly of the price and quality of Italian cigars. After Turin, the next stop was Milan, where the Clemens party stayed from 18 to 24 September. Clemens' good humor persisted. He commented disparagingly on the Old Masters he encountered, but was pleased by Milan's galleries and arcades, found its public transportation excellent, again commented appreciatively on Italian honesty, and viewed the flamboyant aspects of Italian character with an amused, if critical, eye. Following a day's stop at Bellagio on Lake Como, the Clemens party arrived in Venice on 25 September.

In Venice Clemens unavoidably set reality against recollection. Eleven years before he had described Venice as "a great city, with its towers and domes and steeples drowsing in a golden mist of sunset" (*The Innocents Abroad,* chapter 21), but now he observed that "Venice is changing fast —can see it myself." His notes register his displeasure with architectural alterations along the Grand Canal and elsewhere in the city. Nevertheless, after the strenuous traveling of the past two months, Clemens welcomed a respite. On 27 September he wrote to Howells: "I wish you were Consul here, for we want to stay a year, & would do so in that case—but as it is, I suppose we shall stay only 3 or 4 weeks" (*MTHL,* p. 239). The family was taken with Venice; the children made friends with the family's gondolier, spending many hours out on the water, and Livy reported enthusiastically to her mother: "It is so fascinating, so thoroughly charming—I sit now before a window that opens on to a little piazza; where I can look right on to the Grand Canal . . . We have the morning sun in our rooms and the weather for three days has been perfect" (29 September 1878, MTM). She did complain that in Venice "we are worst pushed than Hartford," but the family thrived on the very things they protested at home and the attention they received was undoubtedly part of the delight of Venice, particularly after Mark Twain's sometimes disappointing anonymity in Switzerland. The increase in social obligations was matched by an increase in expenditure which also made life in Venice like life in Hartford. The pace of acquisition increased considerably here with purchases of furniture, dishes, glass, and brassware for the Clemens home. In addition to visits with Livy to well-known commercial establishments like Besarel and Salviati, Clemens frequented old shops, rummaging through "many small rooms crowded with images, armor, pots, lanterns, &c," motley storehouses which seemed the hallmark of Venice. His note about the miscellaneous architectural and decorative elements of Saint Mark's provides an implicit parallel to his own acquisitions for the Hartford house: "The church seems to have gone on the highway to build this gaudy scarecrow of St Mark—instructing all shipmen sailing to pagan lands to bring back pillars & stones—so it is a combination of robberies—it seems to have been the fashion in that day to build churches by robbing pagan temples."

Further confrontation with the Old Masters was unavoidable. On 4 October and again five days later Clemens visited the Palace of the Doges where he made exasperated notes on a number of paintings. Nevertheless, his comments on art in Notebook 16 are not entirely scathing or satirical. He reversed his earlier preference, expressed in *The Innocents Abroad,* for copies over the originals, and he responded with admiration for some of the paintings he viewed. Always, however, his taste was independent. He found a special favorite in Tiepolo but remained unstintingly critical of the cult of the Old Masters, using this notebook to draft the first version of the burlesque of "The Hair Trunk" which was later included in *A Tramp Abroad.*

The final entries in this notebook were recorded on 13 October, four days before the Clemens party left for Florence.

"Invented a note-book in May," Clemens wrote in Notebook 15 (p. 135). Three months later, in August 1878, he began using Notebook

16, the first of at least twenty notebooks that he eventually had made according to his new design. These notebooks hardly differ from many Clemens had used before: his "invention" is simply a small tab projecting from the upper corner of each leaf. The tab is to be torn off when the leaf is filled so that the writer can easily open the notebook to his current place. The tabs on Notebook 16 measure 1⅟16 by ¼ inch (2.7 by .7 centimeters).

Notebook 16 now contains 194 pages, all of them inscribed. The pages measure 6⅝ by 3¾ inches (16.9 by 9.5 centimeters). Three leaves and portions of four others have been torn out and are missing. The pages are ruled with twenty blue horizontal lines, and their edges are tinted red. The cover is of pliable, black, grained leather with blind stamped borders on the front and back. The endpapers and flyleaves are light green. With the exception of a few brief notes in brown ink, all the entries are in pencil. There are a number of Clemens' use marks in the notebook, almost all of them on entries written before Clemens left Switzerland for Italy. They take various forms, mostly large Xs or lines drawn through entire entries.

Fred'k Martin's Statesman's Year Book.—15 years.[1]

John Bellows (Gloucester) Bona-fide Pocket Glossary, Eng. & Fr.[2]

Hotel de l'ecu
Geneva.[3]

Lauchletts 18 John st.
Agent for Hess, Geneva watches. Send watch there for repairs.[4] [#]

---

[1] *The Statesman's Year-Book: Statistical and Historical Annual of the States of the World*, edited by Frederick Martin, had begun publication in 1864. Notebook entries through "Les deux Tours Verona" (p. 159.6–7) were made on different occasions on the front endpaper.

[2] John Bellows' *Dictionary for the Pocket: French and English, English and French* (London: Trübner & Co., 1877), printed in Gloucester, originally appeared in 1873 as *The Bona-fide Pocket Dictionary of the French and English Languages.*

[3] The Clemens family's residence while visiting Geneva in September.

[4] Clemens would pay $180 for a watch for himself in Geneva. The full name of the manufacturer is noted on page 213 of this notebook.

Hotel Minerva, Rome.

Take carriage for the whole day.

Hotel Washington, Florence.

Salmiac water for musquitoes

Sticks or candles to burn to kill mosquitoes.

Les deux Tours
Verona.

Geo. C. Wilde,[5]
4 Gt. St. Thomas Apostle,
London EC.

2 trunks in Hamburg.
1 box china in Frankfort.
1 " at Zimmerman's Heidelberg.
3 pkgs sent fm Baden to Munich.
2 " " " Interlaken to "
1 carving left with Geo. Baker,
6 rue Bonivard, Geneva.
1 trunk sent to Munich from Geneva.

"*C. H. S. 776*"—"Zerbrechlich"—box with Interlaken carving in it.

Hotel Italie—Bauer und Grunwald.—Venice.

Mr. Meyer, of Vienna[6] [#]

---

[5] Beginning with this entry, the notes through "Mr. Meyer, of Vienna" (p. 159.21) appear on the recto of the front flyleaf. George C. Wilde of Slote, Woodman & Company had left for England in March 1878 to take charge of the company's new London office and to oversee the firm's exhibit at the Paris Exposition (*Publishers' Weekly*, 30 March 1878, p. 355). Plans for extending their market to England and the Continent were ended when Slote, Woodman & Company failed in July 1878. Clemens probably intended to write or visit Wilde to discuss the failure.

[6] The Clemenses met G. K. Mayer and his wife in Bellagio and traveled with them to Venice by boat, train, and omnibus. Mayer's name also appears, evidently in his own hand, near the end of this notebook.

Marks—S. C. H., No. 17—this seems to be the first box which Sarfatti sent from Venice.[7]

Aug 27. <Beyond> At a bridge say 9 miles fr[om] St Nicholas, we crossed over to the left bank of the stream. A little distance further, came to a long piece of fence. Three children were approaching; a little girl started to run toward us & fell. She slipped actually under the bottom rail & her sprawling feet for a moment overhung a precipice 40 ft high. She scrambled out while my heart stopped beating. She laughed & ran by. We examined the place & there were her tracks where her foot had torn the dirt right to the verge. Below were great rocks. We came so near witnessing her death. She would have fallen straight down a built wall 15 ft, then rolled 30 down a steep bank into the howling torrent & been pounded to a jelly in 2 minutes.

I am perfectly satisfied that those church bells are rung from 4.30 to 7.30 in the interest of the hackmen—a piece of deliberate scoundrelism. From loss of sleep a man feels jaded & unequal to walking—so he hires a hack, at considerable expense. There is nothing these <priestly rascals won't do.>

An English gentleman kindly took our bags in his carriage to Zermat.

Joe has no spirit of self-denial. He continually expresses gratitude that that child was not killed—never caring a cent for *my* feelings & my loss of such a literary plum hanging ready to fall into my mouth. His selfishness puts his own gratification in being spared suffering clear before all concern for *me*. Apparently he does not reflect upon the valuable details which would have fallen like a windfall to me: fishing the child out—witnessing the surprise of the parents & the stir the thing would have made among the peasants; then a Swiss funeral

[7] Gustavo Sarfatti was the Venetian shipping agent responsible for dispatching many of the Clemenses' purchases. This note is written on the verso of the front flyleaf; the following entry is the first in the regular sequence of the notebook text.

—then the denkmal to be paid for by us & with our names mentioned in it. And we would have gone into Baedecker & been immortal.

The iron integrity of Baedeker, who tells the petrified truth about hotels & everything. A wonderful guide book—a marvelous faithful & pains-taking work—you can go anywhere without a human guide, almost. And this book is absolutely correct & reliable.

The poet & the enthusiast have probably over-aggrandized the goitre. I have not seen one on any woman's neck yet which you could not get into <an ordinary> a hat.[8]

Gray & bent man of 80 with vast basket of faggots on back put up his trembling finger in salute. Blind of an eye.

Very old woman ahead, similarly laden.

But it is very hard to guess ages here, where almost everybody looks old & hungry & tired out. Saw one child with a face of the *size* & age of 40.

The English family[9] & Mr. Eden & his ladies remain here at Zermat over night.

We reached Zermat at 3 PM after a lazy walk & did not feel like trying the 3 hours to Riffle to-night.

We strolled out & took a long look at that wonderful upright wedge, the Matterhorn. Its precipitous sides were <cover> powdered over with snow & the upper half hidden in thick clouds which often *threatened* to dissolve, & *did* give flitting glimpses of the mighty tower, but proceeded no further toward dissolution. [#]

---

[8] Clemens drew a wavy vertical line, like some of his use marks on earlier pages of this notebook, through this paragraph. Across the paragraph he also wrote the instruction "STET," possibly indicating a change of mind about whether or where to use the passage and signaling to himself that it was again available for use. He ultimately included a version of the passage in chapter 36 of *A Tramp Abroad*.

[9] Clemens and Twichell met the Dawson family in Leukerbad on August 26 (see Notebook 15, p. 146). They also met Mr. Eden, rector of the English church in Lausanne, at about the same time.

Chapel by Church with charnelhouse under it—& a ⅛ acre graveyard *blasted out*.

Mr. Eden says a family can't bury one body on top of another, but must take up the old one & stow it in the cellar.—

Saw a black box with <scull>skull & crossbones painted on it in white—no doubt the thing they move the old bones in.

In cellar stack of bones & skulls corded up—18 ft long, 7 ft high, 8 ft wide—hundreds of people. Mr. E. says in some of these receptacles these skulls are marked, & if a man wants his grandfather he can go & get him.

He says that this is the cradle of compulsory education—but that the English idea that it will reduce bastardy & intemperance is a mistake—it does not do it. The drinking here is not troublesome as it does not make them quarrel & kill. But few high crimes.

More seduction in Prot that in Cath cantons—the confessional protects the girls.

Here because of poverty, they will cast lots as to which of the boys shall marry & increase the burdens—then the others camp down <& don't> & help support that family.

Often a poor couple who are engaged draw freely on matrimonial joys but do not really marry till babies are imminent. I a man should desert a girl after she is enciente, the place would be too hot to hold him.

"Unto us a child is born."

Mr. Eden has lived in Sw 3 years.[10]

---

[10] On 13 September 1878, while in Liverpool on his way home, Twichell wrote Clemens:

> The Dawsons had learned all about *Mr Eden*. Livy was right. Her instinct, or insight, was true, perfectly so. He *did* have an unhappy domestic experience. He ran away with his wife, in the first place. After they went to Lausanne, he took private pupils, and with one of these private pupils—the son of some aristocratic house, she eloped. He made every effort to get her to come back to him, went after her, offered her forgiveness, but in vain. She is now dead. Poor, poor, Mr. Eden. No wonder he had that look about him. But Livy is a seer.

Sw with 4,000,000, can call 200,000 men into the field at 48 hours notice, well armed & equipped, & admirable soldiers.

Saw the graves of a young English Lord (19) a young clergyman, who, with 3 guides, were killed on the <m>Matterhorn July 14 '65. See Baedeker.[11]

The little goats looking out of hole in cabin.

The instances of mind-telegraphing are simply innumerable. This evening Joe & I sat long at the edge of the village looking at the Matterhorn. Then Joe said "We ought to go to the Cervin hotel & inquire for Livy's telegram." If he had been but one instant later *I* should have said those words instead of <he.>him.—

To-night I began to write the top-lines on preceding page when Joe said "Let me read you the catastrophe on Matterhorn in '65"—& *did* it, from Baedeker.

What nonsense fame is! In New York or London I am courteously invited into the banker's private office when I have business.—Here I am utterly unknown & must stand around & wait with Tom Dick & Harry—& lucky if not received at last with rude impertinence.

But it is pleasant to see that whenever English or Americans learn my name by any accident, their good offices begin at once, & with such heart-warming cordiality. Text for a paragraph The fact is, I am spoiled by <ten> <ten> 10 years' petting.— I needed to come to a country where I was unknown to get the tuck taken out of my self-complacency. [#]

---

11 "The Matterhorn was ascended for the first time on 14th July 1865, by the Rev. Mr. *Hudson*, Lord *Francis Douglas*, Messrs. *Whymper*, and *Hadow*, with the guides *Michael Croz* and the two *Taugwalders*. In descending Mr. Hadow lost his footing not far from the summit, and was precipitated along with Mr. Hudson, Lord Francis Douglas, and Croz, to a depth of 4000′ towards the Matterhorn Glacier. Mr. Whymper and the two other guides escaped by the breaking of the rope" (*Switzerland and the Adjacent Portions of Italy, Savoy, and the Tyrol* [Leipzig: Karl Baedeker, 1877], p. 288).

I am well known in Sweden & Norway but not in Germany, Sw. &c.

Here, the English go first to see the grave of the unfortunate young lord. I, too am descended from the Earls of Durham through my mother. Mr. Leathers is the rightful lord Durham, not I.

About hotels & the servants & ways—& differences from our so-called hotels "on the European plan."

Aug. 28

"The Alps without a Guide"[12]—the author a long, wiry, whiskered man, was going to England this morning, but he had to have one more dose, <she> so he was just starting up some new break-neck place with a friend. They had ropes, steel picks, & what they called flasks of milk.

Get his book.—& Whymper's.[13]

It is whispered that the survivors *cut* the rope—which I believe. I lay an hour last night trying to imagine how it could break—or how the survivors could by any possibility haul the others up.[14]

The Oxford man[15] so frightened with his crime. [#]

---

[12] *The High Alps Without Guides: Being a Narrative of Adventures in Switzerland* (London: Longmans, Green, and Co., 1870) written by the Reverend Arthur Gilbert Girdlestone.

[13] *Scrambles Amongst the Alps in the Years 1860–69* (London: John Murray, 1871) by Edward Whymper, who was one of the survivors of the first ascent of the Matterhorn. On 25 April 1879, when Clemens reached the point of incorporating his Switzerland notes into his manuscript, he would write to his London publishers, Chatto & Windus, for copies of both the Girdlestone and Whymper books (TS in MTP).

[14] In fact the rope did break, but only because one of the surviving guides, ignorant of the strength of the available rope, had tied on with a weak line. Suspicions such as Clemens' persisted for years even though informed opinion acquitted the guide of willful neglect and of intent to sacrifice his companions to save himself. Whymper was not himself suspected of foul play, but his published remarks about the surviving guides, who had angered him with their quick recognition of the increased patronage their fame would bring, helped perpetuate controversy about the Matterhorn tragedy.

[15] A reference to the Reverend Arthur G. Girdlestone, whom Clemens notes

They show the ropes yet.

If somebody would set up a good strong telescope here, he make money.

The Alpenstock is not necessary & yet must be carried in deference to custom. This rendered it expensive to me as I had to hire a boy to carry it for me.

They ought to tax the travel 5 years & make good roads.

Neither pictures, paintings nor the imagination can give one any idea of the glittering splendor of the snow with the sun on it—the dazzling, intense whiteness of it.

Matterhorn's tall sharp peak very well represents a volcano, with <the> his vast wreaths of white cloud circling about his summit & floating away from it in <roc>rolling & tumbling volumes twenty-mile wreaths floating slanting toward the sun. When one of his sides is clean another is sure to be densely clothed from base to summit in thick smoke-like cloud which feathers off & blows around his sharp edge like <sm>the smoke around the corners of a burning building.

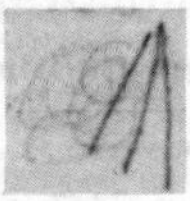

Electric light (sun)—colored one should be on his summit & blow horn to get people up.

The guide-book said it was 12 M <to>from St. Nicholas to Zermat, but we found by the Pedometer it was 72.

The guide-book calls it 7 miles from Zermat to Riffel, but we found by the Pedometer it was only 800 yards. So in everything but distances the G. B. is to be depended on. It took us 6 hours to go the 800 yds, though. [#]

---

seeing above. Girdlestone, a former fellow of Magdalen College at Oxford University, was well acquainted with Edward Whymper. Although illness had prevented his participation in the disastrous climb of the Matterhorn, he was one of the first to hear Whymper's account of the tragedy. A comment by Girdlestone about the guide may have reinforced Clemens' suspicion that the rope had been cut.

I keep a clergyman to remonstrate against my drinking—it gives zest & increase of appetite.

From <the> the base of a glacier flowed away a great many gray long graves many hundred feet down mountain side. Sharp backs —all look like fine sand,—but it is a moraine made of great broken rocks.

The young Lord Francis Douglas has the stateliest monument in the world, & his name will be forever connected with it.[16] If he is found 3000 years from now he will still be as sound & perfect as the flesh of the Siberian elephants.

We have been mightily favored. On the Grornergrat (1870 ft) above our Riffel Hotel, we <fre> <[--]> saw the whole world of circling mountains free from cloud. <O[n]> Often the Matterhorn was free for nearly a minute at a time. Just at sunset on our way down he was utterly free & against a pure blue sky.

But there are people here who have remained 2 weeks waiting for a clear day.

Matterhorn so steep the snow can't stay on it.

Other mountains suggest being made of rocks packed together—this suggests being *one solid rock.*

Coming down, a lamb came fearlessly up & without waiting for introduction examined my pants (to see if they were lambs wool, w[h] they ain't) examined the inside of my hat, then licked both my hands & wrists all over (sweat) & would have been obliged to me to strip. He went off to his flock & came back presently & repeated his operation and wanted to lick my face—grew familiar & insisted but I wouldn't have it. I said we must draw the line somewhere. All these sheep & lambs were white with black faces, <black> white head, black ears, tongues, & legs. Prettiest sheep I ever saw. [#]

---

16 "Think of a monument a mile high, standing on a pedestal two miles high! This is what the Matterhorn is,—a monument. Its office, henceforth, for all time, will be to keep watch and ward over the secret resting-place of the young Lord Douglas" (*A Tramp Abroad*, chapter 36).

Man fell off cliff 4,000 ft high—we threw arnica after him.

Burlesque trip with ropes, guides, &c 1800 ft up from Zermat to Riffel Hotel.[17]

Didn't venture up to Gorner Grat, Eh?

At that village out of Leukerbad on Sunday Joe wanted to go to the woods near the ladders & sing. We began—some people were coming down the ladders laden but when they heard the music they climbed back.

To-day Aug 29 we climbed up on end of Gorner glacier which is joined in its course by 10 glaciers. The Visp issues from it.

No flowers about the houses in this canton of Valais—only saw one box, red flowers on top of a peasant's house. Houses pretty & full of flowers from Luzerne to Interlaken

We left Zermatt about 10 A.M. in a wagon & a shower, for St. Nicholas—Aug. 30.

In this canton all is sordid, mean, & hard, hard work—every person with a basket of dung or faggots on shoulder.

The very filthiest villages & people on earth are these in Valais. The narrow ill paved alleys or streets run with liquid manure. The only clean members of the family are the cattle.

This queer region on both sides of the gorge above & abreast St Nicholas—houses & villages perched on awful cliffs 1000 to 12 & apparently 1500 ft above the valley.

Think of a courtship from cliff to cliff.—Shoot love-letters with

---

[17] In chapters 37 through 39 of *A Tramp Abroad*, Mark Twain presents an account of a lengthy expedition from Zermatt to the Riffel Hotel and the Gorner Grat undertaken by Harris and himself composed of "198 persons, including the mules; or 205, including the cows." In fact this was a four-hour walk which brought the pedestrian to "an elevation of over 10,000 feet without the slightest semblance of a difficulty" (*Cook's Tourist's Handbook for Switzerland* [London: Thomas Cook & Son, 1876], p. 162).

a rifle. <How> We could see no place which even a goat could climb to those houses.

Our friends the Dawsons will come on this afternoon & stay all night at St. N. where we (1 PM) are lunching. Johnson[18] has gone through to Visp—left Z at 6 AM.

Speak of a sweet patient pious Swiss family consisting of parents 3 children & a hog.

Vin d'enfer (wine of hell?—hellish wine?)—drank it at St Nicholas to-day—the very tamest sort of claret.

Found a mud avalanche to-day—a stream away up on mountain had changed its course last night with the heavy rains & broken through & brought down several acres of big stones & mud—buried & skinned bushes, used up a meadow &c & destroyed the road.

In another place stream swept over a bridge & carried off a railing.

Another place print of horses' hoofs & stone of outside wall displaced, showing struggle to regain footing. I looked hopefully 1000 feet below, but disappointed—no remains. Again Joe thanked Heaven. I was too provoked to reply.

Wretched & dangerous path. We kept saying, "In Baden this would be a beautiful road, firmly walled, &c"

The banks of rivers are *paved* from source to end,—a curious thing.

Livy & Clara's young man at Lucerne—student of Yale—would make the same statement 3 or 4 times—& forget it. Ask about him before writing him up.[19]

Also drunken Jew at Interlaken at hotel—table d'hote.[20] [#]

---

[18] A friend met in the mountains with whom Twichell later spent some time in London.

[19] While in Ouchy, Livy mentioned this young man, who appears in chapter 27 of *A Tramp Abroad*, in a letter to her mother: "We met again the American boy that asked so many questions that I wrote Sue about. We hoped he would not discover us but there was no such good luck for us" (2 September 1878, MTM).

[20] Clemens is reminding himself of an incident he recorded in Notebook 15, page 145, which he developed as an anecdote in chapter 35 of *A Tramp Abroad*.

"Coinciders"—people who always eagerly coincide with every proposition you make—& sometimes too soon, coinciding with a yes when a no would have been the proper thing if he had waited.

Put in Ed's Sunday street car.

Ed & the girl's playing the Expulsion from Eden.[21]

30th Aug., we walked from St. Nicholas to Visp & staid all night at hotel du Soliel.

Aug. 31. Took train at 10.51 & came to Beveret with the Dawsons—then by boat to Ouchy-pres de Lausanne, arriving at 5 P.M.[22]

Sunday, Sept. 1, went to the English church, AM. At 5 P.M. Rev. Mr. Eden called, & in the evening our friends the Dawsons took coffee with us in our room in the Hotel Beau Rivage. A pleasant evening.

In early days the Scotch used to try to jew down the railroads—then wait for next train & jew again.

DRUNK Saw 2 punts & stepped into the wrong one & caught cold.

Sept 2—To Chillon—humbug—no chamois—hired Bonneval[23] for his role. Enterprise of the canton in <B>building a castle around the living rock to fit Byron's poem. This dungeon is much cleaner & pleasanter than Visp or any of those places.

The old steward, crying "Yes, lord bless you I wish I had as many thousand pounds as your father loved horses!"

Charity sermon—plate about to be passed—minister said, "Hold! see that you apportion your contribution according to your estate—lest the Lord apportion your estate according to your contribution."

Man shot a "chamois." [#]

---

21 Clemens gives an account of Twichell's ten-year-old son and his Sabbath activity in chapter 42 of *A Tramp Abroad*.

22 Twichell and Clemens rejoined the Clemens family and Clara Spaulding at this point.

23 François de Bonnivard was the subject of Byron's "The Prisoner of Chillon."

Band played in front of hotel evenings at Ouchy, as at Lucerne. When they play marches I hone my razor (on my hand)—as a king might who kept a band for that purpose. A march is best to strop by.

My new note-book is a mighty success.[24]

Picture of it. Patent applied for, simply to keep somebody else from patenting it.[25]

Have invented various things, but think the most of my note-book, scrap-book & method of stropping razor.

Mrs. Slawson's negro—"Samson had a knack."
Mary <McDowling>McDillon[26]
Love letter "From a Young Gentle

Furious at breakfast (Beau Rivage, Ouchy, Sept 4) have read French 25 years & now could not say "breakfast"—could think of nothing but aujourdhui—then demain!—then—& so on, tearing my hair (figuratively) and raging inwardly while outwardly calm—one idiot french word after another while waiter stood bewildered.

In "ostensible" German.

There were indications wh showed that this egg was an antique.

Fleas won't bite me—or Wallace.

Sept. 4—9 PM arrived by rail at Martigny[27]—hotel Clerc. Badgered the chambermaid with English to no effect—presently grateful to find she knew German.

Speak now & then of the alleged Chamois [#]

---

[24] Clemens has used thirty-eight pages of this first notebook made with corner tabs according to his own design. (See Notebook 15, note 45.)

[25] Of Clemens' inventions, the only ones for which he made patent applications were a self-pasting scrapbook, an adjustable garment strap, and a history game; only the scrapbook proved financially profitable.

[26] Clemens' pun on the name of Mary Magdalen is recorded more explicitly in Notebook 17, p. 269.

[27] Clemens and Twichell took a trip of several days to Chamonix and Mont Blanc and then on 7 September rejoined the family which had moved on to Geneva.

Going through the towns we could always have made better time but for the signs, "Defense de trotter<—>, amende de 3 a 6 fr."

Here was the grave of a poor fellow who was plowing in his field, not in the <steep> perpendicular part of it, but in a place where it leaned a little—& so being over-confident on this account he either let go his handles or stumbled against a cornstalk & plunged 5000 ft to the valley below.

People have said the English not polite race, but the Rev. says he notices he has not stepped on one of them's dress this morning but she apologised.

The misery of people, who have a wagon this awfully hot morning —having hired it they feel obliged to use it—& they do, till driven out of it by the sun. Nothing could induce me to ascend to the tete noir[28] by *any* conveyance but my legs.

Snow<y>-touched mountains are majestic & magnificent with the sun on them & in some other aspects, but in others they are not. In some lights the spots & stripes look as if somebody had started to whitewash them & got tired—or run out of stuff.

They feed bread to the horses in Ger & Switz.

To-day, Sep. 4,[29] when nearing Argentiere, we saw exquisite prismatic colors playing upon white clouds which were so delicate as to resemble shredded gossamer webs. The dainty faint pinks & greens were particularly beautiful—none of the colors were deep, they were the lightest shades. They were bewitchingly commingled. *Now* I know what they were like—they were exactly like the dainty coloring of a soap-bubble—& to my thinking, the play & nature of the colors of the soap bubble are the very climax, the ultima thule of the daintily beautiful. [#]

---

[28] The route Clemens and Twichell took to Chamonix from Martigny passed along the flank of the Tête-Noire mountain.

[29] Actually 5 September, since, as Clemens noted above, they arrived in Martigny the evening of the fourth.

The little children seem to have no dolls—they haven't even little make-believe baskets on their backs.

Mont Blanc framed in a strong V shaped gorge ½ hour before Argentiere was very grand—one wast dome of snow with the sun blazing on it.

Neighboring peaks were peculiarly pinnacled—some like fingers whittled to a point.

One mighty sugar-loaf resembled a bishop's mitre—too steep to hold snow, but had some in a hollow in its side.

Very picturesque glaciers all about.

Dined at Argentiere—paid our porter 6 f for a hard 8 hours' tramp—hired a returning wagon, 6 m to Chamounix for 4 f. Driver very drunk but a good driver—went like the wind—said in French he was the King of drivers. The other chap, very drunk too (both good-natured) called himself the Captain of Mont Blanc—had made more ascents than any man—48 & his brother 37. He spoke German. Driver invited a nurse & baby in as we approached Chamounix.

Secured a room at hotel <dan> d'Angleterre & diligence for 6th (on 2d floor is a room marked in French, *Albert Smith's Room*[30]—after the Creator he made Mont Blanc) went to post office & telegraphed Eden to know if I left my letter of credit at Bank.

When I came out it was dark in the valley & all the lamps lit, but there was a fine luminous daylight sort of light on the high peaks & Mont Blanc but all the flanks of the mountains in deep shadow.

There was a bright moonlight on the <other> back side of these peaks & one *thumb* standing up in the midst of a strong luminous spot—so I thought the moon was about to rise there. I waited, a full hour, but she never came. She was going down, perhaps.

The great snowy dome of M B was like a volcano casting up a rich greenish light upon its own smoke—ie, <clouds> white shreds &

---

[30] Albert Richard Smith, English lecturer and humorist, made an ascent of Mont Blanc in 1851. From this experience he created an immensely popular platform entertainment. He also wrote "A Handbook of Mr. Albert Smith's Ascent of Mont Blanc" in 1852 and *The Story of Mont Blanc* in 1853.

ribbons of ethereal clouds which sprang aloft  vast spreading fan-shaped shadows. in an explosive form. Presently they looked like a pale green <fa> flames waving above a chafing dish. A very beautiful spectacle.

There was a red light up on the Grands Mulets where the hut is. 6,500 ab Cham

Oceans of people in these hotels.

We came through the Tete Noir to-day—a wild & picturesque piece of gorge & mountain country.

We walked from Martigny to Argentiere <in> from 8 a.m. to 4.30 pm—8½ h.

Our French Countess—so big & majestic I hung around to see the moon rise over her.

The roar of the little river here at M. B. is deafeningly oppressive, & yet pleasant.

That Hartford flying machine[31] will soon knock the romance out of this Alp-climbing & kill the guide's business. There will be no towns of hotels, then—parties will <go &> come from the European capitals & return the same day, or to neighboring capitals.

The telescope—the tired party of 3 sinking down for ½ hour while still far from summit—glass was moved along up the profile to show us how far they had still to go—distance not perceptible to naked eye. How distinct the figures are!

Joe afraid he will over-exert himself walking with me. This is flattering but not true. I sat down half an hour & tried to show him by argument that he was wrong. We then resumed our journey—he presently remarking that he had meant to be satirical. [#]

---

[31] On 13 June 1878, Professor C. F. Ritchel's "Flying Car," the "Only reliable 'Air Line' to all parts of the world. . . . pronounced the GRAND TRIUMPH OF GENIUS AND MECHANISM of the 19th Century" (Hartford *Courant*, 8 June 1878), made a flight of fifty minutes duration from the Hartford baseball grounds to Newington, Connecticut, a distance of approximately nine miles. The "aeronaut" who operated Ritchel's machine, which was a gas bag controlled only vertically by a pedal-driven propeller, estimated the highest point of his wind-driven flight at two thousand feet. Clemens must have received news of this event from Twichell.

Sept. 6—Half way up mountain, on way to Montanvert, <[co]>took soda at a chalet where they had a French sign up "One may here see a living Chamois for 50 ct. But *we* wanted the satisfaction of seeing a dead one.

Sent agent up Mt. B & watched him thro' telescope, feeling *with* him all the time. Many expressed their sympathy for me.

Crossed the Mer de Glace & ascended the confounded moraine. Was not comfortable on the ice with my smoothe shoes & was still less comfortable on the moraine, 70 ft above the glacier—my feelings made it 700. Of course in the worst place the guide had to observe a glove down a piece & sprang to capture it—springing back his foot slipped & I thought he was going over the precipice.

In one place *on the glacier* we passed along a place only 2 feet wide with precipitous walls on both sides—a plunge of 6 feet.

The Mauvais pas—a villainous place protected by iron rails—otherwise a body might tumble 50 ft—& mind you 50<o> ft is <a[m]>as effective as 5000 tho' it does not look so fine in a book.

The chamois would not haunt these frightful places to make a living—& he certainly, being an animal, wouldn't do it to observe the scenery—now these are arguments against the possibility of such a creature as the chamois which the poet cannot get over. There is not & never was, a chamois.

The fraud who chopped steps in the Mer de Glace & collected for it.

Sept. 6.—The moon showed its brilliant rim twice above depressions about Mont Blanc but descended again. Evidently she is trying to get beyond (south) of M B to the open country & *then* rise.

Guide-Chef Bureau in the public building. German gentleman, No. 685 who said he ascended M B Sept. 4 was there to get his diploma, duly signed & sealed.

I bought a diploma for an invalid friend at home who has never traveled & whose desire all his life has been to ascend M B. [#]

This evening du Midi (the vast peak to left of M B threw a shadow on the heavens—a long, slanting, cleanly-cut dark ray—with a suggestion of *force* such as the squirt from a fire engine or the ray from a Drummond light affords. <[¶]Later when> I never knew before that a shadow of an earthly object could be cast upon so intangible an object as the atmosphere. idyllic odic[32]

Later the peaks to right & left of the M B depression *both* shot prodigious shadows, while between them flared up a mellow glare where the invisible moon was.

Looked at Jupiter & his moons thro' telescope.

Monument to Jacques Balmat before Church Statues to Balmat & de Saussure in hall of Hotel de Londres & <d'>de l'Angleterre. They ascended (guide-book says otherwise,) 3d Aug. 1787.[33]

In record at Chef's Bureau is the accidents from 1820 to 1877.

Velley—o ful[34] (English pro)

Glad came to Switz so early—for the mountains are wasting away —in time they will be gone

Saw the pretty little creature—then a herd—waved sock & <scared> they escaped.

Even the diligence <horses> harness is pieced out with clothes line—cheaper & as good or better than leather. [#]

---

32 Clemens was apparently so moved by the spectacle that in brown ink he interlined "idyllic" above "ray" and "odic" after "affords"; the description in chapter 43 of *A Tramp Abroad* uses much the same phrasing.

33 "[Mont Blanc] was ascended for the first time in 1786 by an enterprising guide named Jacques Balmat. . . . In 1787 the ascent was made by the celebrated naturalist De Saussure, accompanied by seventeen guides" (Baedeker's *Switzerland*, p. 227). Clemens evidently assumed that 3 August 1787 was the date of the first successful ascent of Mont Blanc, and was disputing Baedeker. Actually, the first ascent to the summit was made by Michel-Gabriel Paccard, a local physician, accompanied by Balmat on 8 August 1786; Balmat was a member of the second ascent party on 5 July 1787, and returned with De Saussure a month later.

34 Mark Twain would illustrate some of the peculiarities of English pronunciation, including this rendering of "awful," in chapter 31 of *A Tramp Abroad* and more elaborately in a discarded section of that work later published as "Concerning the American Language" in *The Stolen White Elephant* (1882).

Grateful to the shoes I wore in Switz. Make a list of ways in which shoes can torture a man when they are not right.

It is questionable if it pays to have a courier. Perhaps better have an intelligent servant & *pay his way* specially—with a courier they put him indirectly (& *largely*) in your<s> bills.

The *one* evidence of high civilization must surely be to *not lie*.—

At the Riffel the nice landlady talked French so carefully that I could understand it—& I talked English, which she easily understood.

Sept. 9—Bought a wonderful music box for 2000 fr.[35]
Describe trading with Mr. Geo. Baker for a music box when we both had the belly ache. Pleasant gentleman—an Englishman.
(Samuel Troll Fils.
6 Rue Bonivard
Geneva.

Describe the stubborn manliness of the old English gentleman at Chamonix who refused to be cheated,—put on his glasses & examined his bill in detail, comparing it with the carte of prices. He spoke of a case where he was over charged. "And did you pay?" "Indeed I didn't." I wish we had some of that pluck.

They examine passports on the Italian frontier for fear an honest man may slip in. [#]

---

[35] Livy's list of purchases indicates that this music box, acquired in Geneva, cost $400. Clemens described the transaction in a chapter omitted from *A Tramp Abroad* in which he wrote of Mr. George Baker:

> He had probably been bothered a good deal with tourists who came merely to sample his goods for curiosity's sake, without any intention of buying; for he exhibited a most composed indifference concerning the matter in hand. He was not rude—very far from it; indeed he was endowed with an enviable stock of polite graces & affable superiorities—he was indifferent to matters of commerce, that was all; he was not indifferent to other things, such as the weather, the war-news, the opera, & so on; in fact he showed a cheery & vivacious interest in these. Consequently, while we progressed well enough, socially, we did not get along very fast, commercially.

See pages 211 to 213 for further references to Clemens' music box.

Bay said "It was very delicate in papa to give me that ring."[36]

Wash houses in the Rhone—woman behind smooth board—cold water—saw one pounding or slapping garment on this board—& one scrubbing garment with shoe brush & soap. Do they ever get clothes clean?—Perhaps, though evidently no nation but ours really understands the art & has polishing irons.

Human face on mountain under Mont Blanc—perfect—no disproportions.

Bay—Papa gives me a good deal of trouble—wants me to get in his bed—I can't do that with gelmuls—I don't like g's—Uncle Theo isn't a g'l—he is a *friend*[37]

Sept 10—Started to Chamonix with 2 horse-wagon, 9.30.[38]

As soon as you strike French territory out of Geneva you find the road strewn with crosses & beggars. [#]

---

[36] In a letter to Mrs. Langdon on 13 September 1878, Clemens wrote of four-year-old Clara Clemens:

> The other day I gave Bay a small gold ring. Afterward she said to Clara [Spaulding]: "It was very delicate in papa to give me that ring."
>
> We can't quite make out what she meant by that stately word, unless she meant that it was a "delicate attention" on my part. (MTM)

[37] This is a further reference to Clara's conversation which Clemens elaborated in the 13 September letter to Mrs. Langdon:

> The other day she had a private conference with Clara [Spaulding], & said, impressively: "Aunt Clara, I am going to tell you something. Papa gives me a good deal of trouble lately."
>
> "Why, *Bay!*"
>
> "Yes, he does, Aunt Clara; papa is a good deal of trouble to me. He interrupts me when I am busy; & he wants me to get in bed with him—and I can't do that with jelmuls" (gentlemen;) I don't like jelmuls."
>
> "Why Bay, you like Uncle Theodore, don't you?"
>
> "O yes, but *he* ain't a jelmul, he's a *friend*."

[38] After rejoining the family in Geneva and seeing Twichell off for home, Clemens went back to Chamonix with Livy: "A day or two ago Livy & I drove there in a two-horse carriage & remained a day—9 hours' drive thither & 9 hours back. . . . At Chamouny she ascended part of a mountain in a chair borne by men, & then walked to an ice-cavern in the great glacier below the Grandes Mulets, & back again" (SLC to Mrs. Langdon, 13 September 1878, MTM).

Dr. Hamel, a Russian ascended in 1820—3 guides fell 400 ft—41 yrs afterward, their remains were shoved into view by the glacier.[39]

1860—2 Englishmen & their guide perished in crossing the Col du Géant.[40]

However, there is *no* question about it. To travel with even the stupidest & most expensive courier is inexpressibly pleasanter than to go without.

Moon last night, 10th Sept.

The dim spiritual, unreal look of some of the gigantic peaks above us while the others were painfully white with snow & moonlight was an enchanting spectacle.

Ordered George[41] to get me a 2-horse carriage to ascend M B. "My God!—It has never been done!" "Very well, it is time it *was* done—attend to it."—"Mother of God! it *can't* be done!" &c. String it out.

Climbing to the Glacier des Bossons—blazing sun.—"George, you look chilly—put on this shawl." Wiping off perspiration—"My God, sir, I am dying with heat." "No—it is cold—put on the shawl." He put it on, looking unutterable things.

Grotto tunnel was blue & beautiful, like Blue Grotto of Capri.

Picture from tunnel beautiful. Fine echoes. [#]

---

39 "In 1820, Dr. Hamel, a Russian, accompanied by two Englishmen, met with a sad accident. . . . An avalanche swept four of the guides into a crevasse. One only, Marie Couttet, was rescued. The remains of the others were turned up by the ice in 1861 and 1863, in the latter year on the Glacier des Bossons 5½ m. from the scene of the disaster" (*A Handbook for Travellers in Switzerland, and the Alps of Savoy and Piedmont*, 14th ed. [London: John Murray, 1871], p. 433).

40 "To the rt. is the snow-slope on which occurred the fatal slip of 1860, when three travellers and Frédéric Tairraz were lost because the rope was not tied to the guides but merely held by them" (Murray's *Switzerland*, p. 435).

41 George Burk, their courier, accompanied Clemens and Livy to Chamonix.

Little girl was climbing about a steep path she had made for herself on steep <s> side of moraine—imitating the perils the guides encounter—this is the first time I have seen a child imitate grown people as a sport—(her father patted her head & called her little chamois)—except boys who crack whips & say "Hii!"—ambitious to be those great men the cab & diligence drivers.

27th April 77 a guide 27 yrs old fell fatally down a precipice leaving young wife, & 2 chn under 18 months, & a feeble & lame mother.—

Upon this follows a sequel:

On 13th June the young widow died of grief & exhaustion.

Jacques Balmat made first ascent 5th Aug 1787[42] & his last *climb* nearly 50 yrs later in 1834—fell from du Midi while hunting for minerals & was killed—72 yrs old. The "hardy mountaineer" indeed!

Sept. 12—Saw 3 people far up on the forehead of M B through the glass waved hdkf

You see the first house with naked ey—then from that to the house on Grands Mulets is 3300 additional altitude

M B is like the <defects> <wh> great qualities of a friend—<think> they sink low<er> when close by & the du Midi defects & Doms tower above—but down the vally of time & distance, *they* sink & old M B. soars into heaven with the glory of the sun on his crown.

Joe's chief defect,—secret profanity.[43] Name some others.

---

[42] See note 33 for the correct dates of Balmat's ascents.

[43] Twichell playfully defended himself on this score in a letter of 22 October 1878. In describing his voyage home, he told Clemens of J. F. Beilstein, a Pennsylvania butcher, one of his cabin mates, whose opinions of the rough trip were expressed "somewhat as follows":

> "Blank blank the blank blanked sea to H.!!!" . . . Well, the elements that were exhibiting themselves so handsomely outside couldn't hold my attention at all, there was so much finer a show of its kind going on within. . . . Oh, forgive me, Mark. Its too bad. Of course I *didn't* take pleasure in Mr Beilstein's profanity. I speak of it in this light way, under the influence of other impressions and memories of the man, later formed, that *are* pleasurable. He didn't suspect at

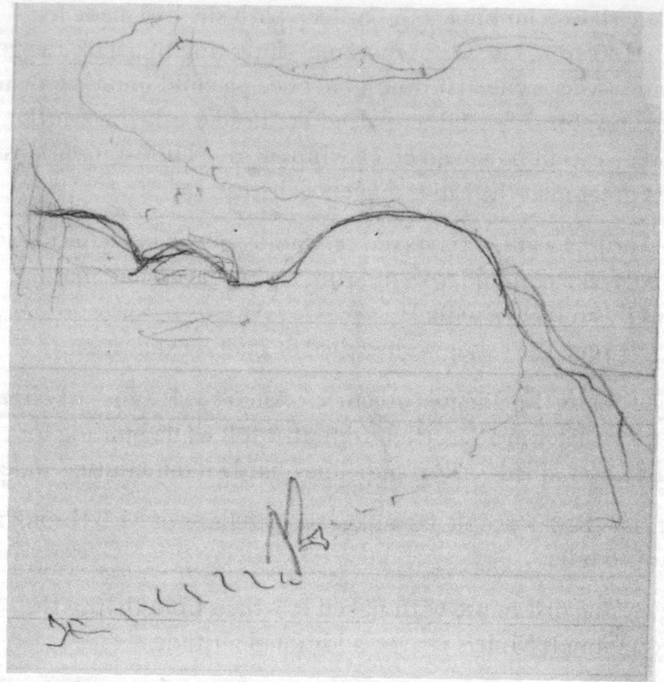

The frivolity of these French sticks out in their keeping up their unceasing "Hii!" & whip snapping all the way down hill 51 miles

Forgot to look at the great human face under du Midi.

Started back to Geneva at 9.

Study the *profiles* of mountains.

A most noble one between St. Gervais & Sallanche, on opposite side of valley.

If we never allowd a foreigner to vote or hold office our integrity

---

this time that he had a minister in his audience. He never so much as said "Oh, my," after he found that out.

In an early autobiographical fragment, apparently written in the 1880s, Clemens would delightedly recall a similar incident involving Twichell and a profane hostler (*MTE*, pp. 366–372).

would be irreproachable. <The>Our foreigners have taught us rascality & now it is our *habit.*

Hire no private conveyance in Geneva without making a long written contract. They changed horses only once to-day—the last horses came 30 miles—very hot.

"140 or 50 frs—& something for the driver."

Drivers are always a little tight after nooning.—If they bring a shilling's worth of custom to the inn the landlord's gives him a shillings worth of beer.

Boat darted after drowned man to-day—caught him before he got to the chain-buoys. Crowd of 500. <Co> 10 men sailing last Sunday —8 drowned—this is one of them.

<Would prefer to be>

In Switzerland the express trains make upwards of 3 miles an hour. <Dreadfully dangerous> But they are not dangerous

3 little narrow streets in Geneva named Hell, Purgatory & Paradise. <The> "Paradise" is sarcastic, no doubt, but the others fit.

Pay nothing through a courier. The first week's wash bill at Interlaken was $14 (70 f). The washerwoman said "Don't the courier pay the bill?" This excited suspicion. The second week she wanted the former bill to make out the bill by.

Sept. 13—In Genève, on the Grand Quay, a puppy[44] walked deliberately across the pavement & compelled Clara to separate from me.

We buy first-class tickets in Italy, the 1er cl compartments here being no better than 2^{d} cl in Germany.

Beautiful string of white crystal beads; 40 fr.—you may have them for 35—take them to hotel with you—you may have them for 30!—

[44] Described in chapter 47 of *A Tramp Abroad* as "a trim dandy" who deliberately "lounged lazily across my path."

(to Bay)—if you come back with the lady to buy the beads, I will give you a pretty little house.

Times are hard—whether we like expatriation or not we *must* stay abroad till pew-rent cheapens.

From Geneva to Venice, 200 miles, RR tickets for the 5 grown members of my family, over $100—N.Y. to Boston, 212 m, would be $30.

"Well, we've got the wood-carving."

And always remember that we economise on pew-rent while abroad.

We get discouraged every time we add up expenses.

We have seen the principal features of S. scenery—Mont Blanc & the goitre.

Sept 14—Wakened at 3 AM by the fearful braying of a jackass in the market square in front of the hotel de l'Ecu de Genéve—it was like sawing a very wide & ill-supported plank in two with a wood saw. Jacks thence till 8.

Watched 2 swans swim the swift river this morning, ¼ m wide—powerful swimmers,—occasionally they got nearly down on the chain & had to face about & swim straight up stream.

In this headquarters of clockdom the town clocks are 2 or 3 minutes apart.

Sept. 14—P.M.—One dreads going into Italy because of its reputation.

What small & frivolous & trivial countries these are over here.

Italy the home of art & swindling; home of religion & moral rottenness; home of the

Hotel bill, Geneva, 9 days, 812 fr—of this, a little over 100 was "paid out—therefore the expense for living was less than 100 f per day. [#]

This is the correct average—in Germany 60 marks (or $15) per day; in Switzerland 75 francs (or $15) per day.

Having Cook's tickets, we were charged for the children for the first time.

Cook's agent *did not know* whether they would be charged for or not.

We were four hours going from Geneva to Chambery,[45] & had infinite difficulty to get seats with 1er class tickets.—

Changed cars once, were herded like cattle through a douain & had a long wait & as much trouble as ever to secure seats.

On arrival I felt like the man whose oxen ran away over a stumpy road—if ever I have to go to h— I want to go by the Chambery railway, I'll be so glad to get there."

They wouldn't furnish Geoge a 2^{d} class seat on a Cook's ticket—so he had to pay extra & go 1st cl.

If I am forgiven for traveling in this region I won't offend again.

Chambery, interesting, crooked narrow lanes—more different uniforms in one hour here than I saw in 4 months before—& all of them ugly, slouching, ill-fitting & the very reverse of neat & clean. But in G a soldier always looks as if he had just stepped out of a band box.

A dirty, shabby Hotel de France, but the best in town—& good enough, too, for so small a town.[46]

White cats, with light eyes. [#]

---

45 The Clemens party stayed one day in Chambéry, France in order to break the long rail journey into Italy. They continued on, staying in Turin, Milan, Bellagio on Lake Como, and Venice.

46 Livy was not so willing to forgive the hotel's deficiencies for she wrote her mother from Chambéry on 15 September 1878:

> I felt sure that today I had material for a long letter to you but all day I have been too dead to write. I think probably partly the accumulation of weariness after our Chamouny trip—& partly the poor beds & poor food. We found here the worst beds that we have had on our journey & very poor food. (MTM)

The man in Geneva who was offended because I found fault with his prices had pirated copies of my books for sale—hence he was a "fence" for stolen goods. One book had my name but none of my stuff in it.

Chambery, the quaintest old town out of Heilbron.

The soldiers' uniforms are *not* soiled, but are awkward, clumsy & ugly.

Saw the 97th regt go by—a marching regiment, the men deeply bronzed & their uniforms showing hard wear. Their dark faces contrasted strongly with the white complexions of the 14th here in garrison.

An old cathedral with houses built against it. Another public building showed hoary age.

The Elephant monument (bronze & marble) to a soldier distinguished in India.[47]

The idiotic fashion in America of teaching pupils only to read & write a foreign language—this *was* actually the case at Vassar, one of the first if not *the* first Female college in America. There may be a justifiable reason for this—God knows what it is. Any fool can teach<in> *himself* to read a language—the only valuable thing a school can do is to teach how to *speak* it.

In the German gymnasiums <—think of their> they even compel the pupil to speak Latin & Greek.

Some of these quaint streets, buildings, doors, windows & stairways seem to have wandered out of old engravings of towns in the middle ages.

In one crooked one to-day (Sunday) a very picturesque one 8 ft

---

47 "On the promenade between the railway and the town rises a large monumental *Fountain*, adorned with life-size elephants, in memory of General *de Boigne* (d. 1830), who bequeathed to Chambéry, his native town, a fortune of 3½ million fr. which he had amassed in the East Indies" (Baedeker's *Switzerland*, p. 215).

wide, I saw a boy watching over 3 fat, sleeping hogs, the only living beings visible —from queer windows along the curve projected boxes of flowers. It was a *very* picturesque street.

There seem to be rather more soldiers than citizens, here.
There is a deal of hallooing & racket at night.

Our youngest always gets mixed & says "take"—corrects & says "keep"—then "keep"—"take." I think the Lord smiles every time he hears that prayer,—which is 365 times a year.

Horribly creaking doors everywhere on the continent.—Drives a body crazy.

The most delicious drink of water I have had in Europe was from a limpid crystal depression on the Mer de Glace.

From Chambery to Turin—(100 m?)—<7> 75 f ($15) 28 f each for 2 little children.

They take 8 hours to go this 100 m. Being in a hurry, Thompson walked

It is all down hill I think—it *must* be, else it would take them longer.

"Observers" (ie geographers) say it is up hill—but plainly this is an error, for the reason set forth in the above paragraph.

Left Chambery Monday Sept 16 at 10.14 for Turin by the fast express which makes 4 miles an hour—the other trains make only 3¼. By 11 we were out of sight of Chambery.
Here the courier, who had been left, overtook us. He had been obliged to run during the last 15 minutes—being fat, he was blown.
3 hours from Turin we had a race with an ox team—they had the best of it at first, but we eventually tired them out.

6 hours—at 4 m—distance from Cham to Turin probably 24 m.

The "sick" woman whom we got rid of where we changed <cars>

cars. She was huge & had hair the color of faded hay—done up in a net.[48]

The nice head porter who got us a nice compartment & held it for us against all comers clear till the train left—a kindness which gave me the first sense of pleasure I had had during the day—even tho' it *was* interested & was paid for. I wanted to give him all the money I had & some of my clothes.

One needs a lantern to observe Italy by rail—on account of the tunnels.

Arrived at Turin near 7. Beautiful city—*vast* squares Enclosed with yellowstone huge blocks of palaces.

Hotel d'Europe—wonderful rooms—great parlor with walls & windows upholstered in red silk damask 4 sofas upholstered in the same stuff—lot of chairs *do.*—4 big mirrors—chandelier for a raft of candles.

Followed the wonderful arcade ½ m this eve, without seeming to approach the end of it.

Therere was an open air concert (Caffe<e> Romano)—a fanciful little house & stage & a yard full of chairs & tables where people drank & smoked. Good orchestra & excellent male & female operatic singing—(can hear them from hotel—2 or 300 yds)—No admission—could not think of the name of the delicious native wine (Barõlo) we had at supper, so did not go in. It is better music than one usually hears in opera at home for $2.50 a ticket.

Crowds of people in the arcades, & soldiers in handsome uniforms. Arcades 15 ft wide & 20 high on great piers 5 × 4 shops on both sides—flagged side walk outside.

Struck through & entered a great oval with <g>lofty glass roof & stone pavement laid in ornamental patterns—brilliantly lighted

[48] Described in Mark Twain's virulent account in chapter 47 of *A Tramp Abroad* as "a ponderous tow-headed Swiss woman who put on many fine-lady airs, but was evidently more used to washing linen than wearing it."

with gas—pretty shops all around—went through & struck into another fine arcade—a vast square with equestrian statue—noble building over the arcade, with the facade of a palace.

Punchinello show—watched it—2 ten-^{c} pieces, copper, French, & one Swiss nickel, 20 centimes—gave one 10 & the 20—the incident —& I had just been thinking of Italian dishonesty![49]

Saw two picturesque old castles on peak of two hills on our way this afternoon.

This Turin is the very livest town we have seen since Hamburg. In its pavements, squares, arcades & commercial palaces, it is the finest city I have ever seen. And yet I suppose it is but a copy (inferior) of Milan.

They *did* charge big railway fares to-day, but when I saw that the way was nearly all through tunnels (some outside ones with windows) & magnificent work, too, & inexpressibly costly, I was obliged to confess that the high prices were justifiable.

More books for sale here than I have seen anywhere in Europe.

The majority of the Italian officers are very handsome—black hair & eyes & well cut features & good complexions.

Ranzoni 250 f[50]

Barbera[51] [#]

---

[49] In chapter 47 of A *Tramp Abroad*, after telling how the puppeteers attempted to return his money to him because they thought he had mistakenly given more than he meant to, Clemens concludes: "Then I retired to make a note to the effect that in Italy, persons connected with the drama do not cheat."

[50] Daniele Ranzoni, a contemporary Italian painter who specialized in portraits, often of young girls, characterized by effects of diffused light and rich coloring. Among the list of purchases made in Milan Livy noted "Mr C. bought a young girls head in watter color for my birth day." This portrait, purchased in the Galleria Vittorio Emanuele (see p. 188), was the work of Ranzoni. The Clemenses later referred to it humorously as "Emmeline."

[51] As with the earlier note on Barolo, and intermittently later, Clemens records the name of an Italian wine unfamiliar to him.

<Arriv> Left Turin 18th Sept at 9.15, arrived at Milan 1.30.

The guard stood by us firmly & drove away all applicants for the vacant seats.

The vast & beautiful Arcade or Gallerie of Victor Emmanuel. Statues around.

Crowds there at night.

I think the arcade system is borrowed from Turin.

Saw a starchy suit of clothes marked $9—doorway full of dummies dressed—stepped in to order one like the $9—nothing inside! The old man hauled in the dummy, stripped him & I ordered the clothes sent to the hotel.[52]

In the arcade stumbled on a water color in a window which was without form—just random dull-colored splotches—like a palette which hadn't been cleaned. Stepped back 15 feet was so carried away with rapture over the beauty of the picture & the sweetness of the face that I said to myself, "I know by my perfect joy in this thing that it is the very worst <painting tha> piece of art that has ever defiled the world. But to my vulgar & ignorant eye it is divine. I wish it were within the possibilities of my purse. But of course it isn't. I will go out of the reach of its fascinations. Ah, if I could only get it for a thousand francs I would snatch it & fly—& economise in clothes. Then the pew-rent occurred to me—I could stand 2000. I went in & asked the price: 250 francs! My soul stood still for gladness. I said "I will give you 200." After some talk he said, "Take it for 200." So I took it.

Smoth parallel stones for carriage wheels to run on—a most excellent idea.

Omnibuses have a sign "Completo" when they are full.—I wish we had such laws.

Saw 6 Italians go into a furious quarrel, with terrific gesticulations.

---

52 Mark Twain attributes this episode to Harris in chapter 48 of *A Tramp Abroad* although Twichell did not accompany the Clemens family to Italy.

Turned <up> back my sleeves & prepared to cord up the dead. By & by they embraced & all was over.

In the Italian & Swiss hotels they furnish plenty of ice—but in Germany they charge a mark for it.

One of the conveniences, in almost all the German hotels we have seen, was not as cleanly as it might have been.

That same old door-frame of the Cathedral still fascinates me above any other part—with its wonderful life-like carvings of snakes, insects, fruits &c. Could look at it weeks without tiring. It must be very bad art.

The chambermaid at Turin (Hotel D'Europe) spoke French, German, English & Italian.

The children find probity here, too. They gave a toy man 50^{c} in copper & a silver ½ fr, <—> (& took 2 fans)—"but he didn't need so much, so he gave me back my silver piece & gave Clara back one of her copper moneys."

The strong ray falling on red priest, gilded cross & <t> yellow candle flames, very effective.

Priests in red & blue vestments sitting further back in a dimness, helped the picture. Stepped aside & behind these the great pictured window flamed out, a conflagration of intense color.

Shafts of blue light <tra> bridging the heights of the nave from *white* panes.

Omnibus conductor took 10^{c} & afterwards showed me by the tarif that it was right.

Watched a chattering gesticulating man—over a covered box which he frequently *almost* uncovered—for 15 minutes, expecting to see a wonderful legerdemain performance. Alas he finally uncovered the box, chattered over a liquid in a spoon some time—which I supposed he was going to set fire to & swallow, & so got a centime ready in one hand & a florin in the other, in great excitement, intending to give him the former if he survived & the latter if he killed himself (which I greatly desired)—& lo, he ended by adding some white powder & *polishing the spoon.*—I kept my money.

Saw a vast pyramid of furniture on two almost invisible wheels—went around to hunt for the moving impulse & found a donkey the size of a rabbit—the driver was riding.

Old barefooted man & two young street Arabs "laying for" cigar-stubs in the grand Gallerie Vittorio Immanuel to-day. One boy got out his stubs (the whole inside of their coats were pockets, apparently) & counted them—15.

Skin mostly off my friends—effect of the Chamois.

My undershirt of fish net trips up the Chamois.

The Eye-stone—cinder in 48 hours.

Friday, Sept. 20—Went again to see the Last Supper—it was well worth the trouble, because we heard the military bugle.[53]
If there is anything worse than the original, it is the 15 or 20 copies in oil & water. Bran new table cloth—each copyist provides his own bill of fare. Red & yellow wine.

The Crucifixion,[54] at the other end is much finer & livelier—it has been contemptibly neglected by writers.

Bartholomew James the Less, Andrew, Judas, Peter, John, <Thomas> Savior, Thomas, James the Greater, Philip Matthew, Thaddeus, & Simon.

"VIETATA L'AFFISSIONE"[55] [#]

---

[53] Clemens saw Da Vinci's "Last Supper" in the refectory of the monastery of Santa Maria delle Grazie in Milan which had been converted into a cavalry barracks.

[54] A large fresco painted in 1495 by Giovanni Donato Montorfano was also in the monastery of Santa Maria delle Grazie. Clemens' opinion of the relative merits of the Da Vinci and Montorfano works was undoubtedly influenced by the superior state of preservation of the latter.

[55] Essentially, "Post No Bills." Clemens may have been amused by the placement of this sign on walls displaying works by the Old Masters.

To the great picture gallery[56] where I jumped into the midst of the same old St Sebastians, spitted in all sorts of fashions with arrows; & in one place a bowman shooting more into him at a 3-foot range. There is small merit in martyrdom which don't hurt. These Sebastians all either smile or else look as if they don't care a damn.

About the first thing you strike upon entering, is a small room upholstered mainly with atrocities by a person by the name of Luini —not one of the old masters but one of the old apprentices—he was a pupil of Leonardo.

<One or two>Two or three of his faces have quite a human look —but his legs & arms & attitudes are those of bad wax figures.

Person with the deadly complexion which a safety match <affords> communicates when you light it in a person's face.

The head of Christ is beautiful—the face expresses the man of sorrows—there is nothing uncertain about it. <Wh> This was a sketch for the Last Supper—then why was it not used instead of the characterless head which *was* used?

The above is the head of the common autotype—which latter <would be> lacks the color w[h] is very soft & fine

There are artists in Arkansas to-day who would not have had to paint signs for a living if they had <been> had the luck to live in the time of the old masters.

Luini chose for a subject, Noah's sons uncovering his nakedness![57] The grapes are there, one idiot is laughing, & the ark reposes peacefully on an ash-pile in the middle distance. Noah has a quart bowl by him, & a tub. What sense was there in such a subject?

The vast picture by the Bellini family[58]—<these artists> (*loud color*)—dreadful drawing & perspective—that camel & that

---

[56] The Pinacoteca, the picture gallery of the Brera, or Palazzo delle Scienze ed Arti, in Milan.

[57] Bernardino Luini's "Noah Drunk and His Sons."

[58] "St. Mark Preaching at Alexandria," begun by Gentile Bellini and completed by his brother, Giovanni.

camelepard—these artists could have made a good living in our day painting the big pictures for the side-shows which accompany circuses.

There are pictures here as bad as the Slave Ship. They give you the belly-ache.

This Hotel de Ville is excessively dirty—if you drop anything, it is befouled. Fleas, *mice* & mosquitoes abound.

<Reubens'>Rubens' <Last Supper> <(Institution of the Eucharist> Last Supper[59] is (to the ignorant eye) far superior to that of Leonardo.

Gentleman split peach (stone & all) then put half on a long wooden toothpick, (without peeling) soaked it in his claret & ate it. Perceiving that my attention was riveted upon him, he proceeded to furnish me with several startling items of custom—<wh> but I presently saw his drift & went him one better in the way of strange foreign customs—I took his audience away from him & <f>at the same time joined him to it.

Sept. 21.

Made a rare & valuable addition to my bric-a-brac collection at breakfast. It was an egg. There was a something about it which satisfied me that it was an antique.

Added to my collection of BB or Keramics an iron pot with one leg gone—supposed to be by Higgins, but some judges contend that it is in the manner of Snodgrass. Got it "restored" by Smithers

Also a jug—contents not old enough to have a fancy value—therefore, transferred them.

The Italians all seem to go to work before daylight—& all in couples, singing tenor & bass or alto duet—all got strong voices &

---

59 Baedeker describes this picture as "a late work of admirable colouring, but somewhat coarse" (*Italy: Handbook for Travellers; First Part: Northern Italy*, 5th rev. ed. [Leipzig: Karl Baedeker, 1879], p. 126).

many good ones—don't sing simple airs but starchy opera-stuff—they wake you up & *keep* you awake.

The Milan clocks not useful. This morning one struck 2, another 3, another 1, another 2, two others 3—all this occupied 10 minutes—so I got up & looked at my watch—correct time 4.15. <Twenty> 15 minutes later, the procession of striking began again.

The ladies wear black veils <(embroidered or> (figured) from the forehead back & spread over the shoulders.

Hotel libraries are only novels & hymn books.

24th Sept, Bellagio, lake of Como, Grand Bretagne Hotel—Rainy, sour, cold, dreary. Removed a screen in our room & discovered a regular fire-place—for *wood*. Right away we had the first wood fire we had seen since we left our own house. This made the day cheery.

Russian lady comes to table with 3 <[shin]ing> pretty children, an old German nurse & an English governess.—The mother & children talk together in German, French, English & Rus'n.

The two young girls are very prettily & picturesquely dressed; their gowns do not reach down to their knees; the eldest (10) wears very long stockings; the other (8) none.

Make a chapter showing what curious & useful details Baedeker goes into for the protection of the tourist. He has run Murray out of Europe.

Magnificent picture of group of steep pyramids shutting out end of lake, yesterday evening, they in a deep, dark blue of rain & cloud, & the water a very dark blue—a single intense white little sail, & the pale yellow of a <gr> terraced group of houses on the point of a pyramidal island jutting into lake, the whole island thick with verdure.

A glacier moves 6000 feet in say 40 years—one can travel on it for nothing, but it is too slow & cold.

Saw a boulder as big as a house on a glacier—it had been half a century coming there, perhaps. [#]

Prof. Forbes, (who *discovered* the movement of glaciers, (?)[60] states that a knapsack lost in 1836, was carried down in ten years, to another locality, 4300 ft, and having descended through 1145 ft of elevation. *Quick.*

Mauvais Pas—see 256, Hinchliff's book.[61]
Moonlight—257

The Prodigal son & Co in the costume of 1750 or 1770—ruffles, kneebreeches, buckled shoes, bell crowned hats, claw-hammer coats, & laced sleves & bosoms. Playing cards with prostitutes, with piles of coin on the tables.

The very thing for a London lawyer[62] to rest his fatigued mind, is to climb the Alps—but for <idiots> idle idiots—*no.*

Movement of Glaciers, see 306[63] of Hinchliff's book.

Valpolicella wine.

Left Bellagio Sept 25 (stormy & rainy) at 10 AM, arrived at Venice at 7.30 PM

Would have been left at Lecco & one or two other places but for Mr. Mayer.

Sept 26—These Italian thieves have charged me $8 duty on $4 worth (100) of cigars & $1 worth of tobacco.—

I must stop smoking, for no right Christian can smoke an Italian cigar. Only the wrappers are grown—the insides are of stubs collected

---

[60] James David Forbes was the first person to specialize in the study of glacial phenomena, and much of his work was done in the Alpine region Clemens had visited.

[61] The book is *Summer Months Among the Alps: With the Ascent of Monte Rosa* (London: Longman, Brown, Green, Longmans, & Roberts, 1857) by Thomas Woodbine Hinchliff. A description of the author's encounter with a frightened American on the Mauvais Pas appears on pages 255 and 256, while page 257 has a description of the moon throwing a shadow of a mountain on the sky similar to the scene Clemens describes on page 175 of this notebook.

[62] Hinchliff was a barrister in Lincoln's Inn, London.

[63] This is a discussion of James D. Forbes's study of glaciers.

on the pavements by the younger sons of the nobility—stubs from Switzerland—bad enough.

Ridiculous Venice! (under anger at the swindle.)

Faschirtes Beefsteak with yellow of egg.

Ementhaler cheese

too much—troppo caro[64] (too dear.)

The blind musicians at Bellagio—little Russian girl passed the plate.

The charming singing of the men at night in Venice.

Give specimen of conversation made up of utterly inane stuff—such as the tourist has to endure from the chance acquaintance.

Vice-Consul, Venice, $400 worth of fees—no more.
<Re>Say government is extravagant—people live here for 3 cents a week.

The naval officer who came home after 3 years & fell over the mud pile in the front yard when rushing to embrace his wife.

The church seems to have gone on the highway to build this gaudy scarecrow of St Mark—instructing all shipmen sailing to pagan lands to <b> bring back pillars & stones—so it is a combination of robberies<—as>—it seems to have been the fashion in that day <for> to build churches by robbing pagan temples.
Woman showing off her piety, holding her dirty child up to lift its hands toward a black crucifix & watching the effect on us.
It is a queer place, devout people kneeling & crossing themselves & muttering prayers, the priests mumbling & bowing before the altar, boys swinging censers & ringing <dinner> bells, priests chanting litanies, & amidst it all, the gawking gangs of tourists poking about

[64] The Italian words appear to be in the hand of G. K. Mayer whom the Clemenses had met in Bellagio on the way to Venice (see note 6).

with red guidebooks up to near-sighted eyes, & pointing with umbrellas over the heads of the devout at the barbarous mosaics in the sides of the building.

Middle all broken up & corrugated.

Christ riding on an ass.

I think they renew the mosaics every little while on the old patterns.

One girl saw St Peter's & said she'd got her eyes opened—the Pope could not need any more of her hard earnings & would get none.

A Hartford servant did not go to church at all—for it was always "Money, Money" for the pope—& she could afford none—& remarked that if *she* were in trouble the Pope wouldn't send *her* a cent—very true, for Hartford & other priests take no care of the poor.

The bronze man on the clock tower[65] once killed a workman with his hammer. It is said he was tried—& acquitted because he did it without premeditation. Not so—he had been getting ready an hour.

Fenzo Spiridione[66]
Gondoliere,
al Traghetto della Salute<, Num>
Num. 137.

His partner was No. 146.

48 cats born in one house this year—& not a good year for cats, either.

Lachryma Christi—Jack—if anything would make him shed 'em, this is it."[67]

Speak<s> of Smith of Arks foreshortening, hindshortening, &c.

Criticise old masterpieces gravely, hurling in "tone" & other

[65] "On the platform [of the clock tower] are two Vulcans in bronze, who strike the hours on a bell" (Baedeker's *Northern Italy*, p. 225).

[66] The first gondolier employed by the Clemens family.

[67] Clemens may be recalling an opinion of this wine expressed years before by Jack Van Nostrand, one of his *Quaker City* companions.

technicalities & soberly contrast the Sampson & the Lion &c with Smith's Van Amburg in the Den, painted for Barnum's Menagerie.[68]

The big picture in Great Council Chamber seemed to be a riot in Heaven, but not so.[69]

<Riley> Myer told conductor I was a French Duke

Ran across the Prince of Montenegro again to-day. At tomb of Napoleon in 67.[70]

Great Square of St Mark & interior of St Peters about the same size.

They've built a vile iron bridge over the Grand Canal.

Have not seen a wheeled vehicle—not a wheelbarrow or a man or child's velocipede.

Tearing down bridges everywhere.

<Conyellyana>Conyellyano WINE

New plain yellow front house opposite the Mosaic place <([il]> with the illuminated front on Grand Canal—an insult to Venice.

Oct. 1.—Poor George discharged. Gave him 100 franks extra.[71] [#]

---

68 Isaac A. Van Amburgh was the first prominent American animal trainer, the originator of a number of routines, among them one in which he placed his head in a lion's mouth. In 1867, two years after Van Amburgh's death, his company joined with Phineas T. Barnum to form the "Barnum and Van Amburgh Museum and Menagerie Company." Although Le Grand Smith was at one time one of Barnum's agents, the Smith in this entry, as in the preceding one, is Mark Twain's fictional Arkansas artist (also see p. 191).

69 "On the E. wall [of the Hall of the Great Council in the Doges' Palace is] *Jac. Tintoretto's* Paradise, said to be the largest oil-painting in the world, containing a perplexing multitude of figures, several of the heads of which are admirably done" (Baedeker's *Northern Italy*, p. 227).

70 The prince of Montenegro was in Paris during the summer of 1867 for the International Exposition. Although not specifically mentioned in *The Innocents Abroad*, the prince had been a member of the cortege accompanying the sultan of Turkey and Napoleon III (*Figaro*, 10 July 1867) who are described in chapter 13 of that book.

71 On 20 November 1878 Clemens wrote Twichell from Munich: "I discharged

Bought to-day.

1. Carved Bedstead[72]		1,000
1. " Table		800
1 " "		200
1 " Shebang		100
1 " "		00[73]
2 " Chairs		90
1 " Table		90
1 " Bellows		50
1 small picture		375
Francs		2,705

These things are amazingly cheap.

How they make cisterns in Venice.

Old curio-shops. describe

Saw men drag great laden baskets—ought to have had little wheels on them.

Lenzo Spiridione charged me 10 f when 5 was right—hasn't appeared since.

Use a stage-plank when tide is up.

Haven't seen the great snowy mountains in the east but once.

Venice is changing fast—can see it myself.

We like our new gondoliers—one has superb eyes. No. 123. [#]

George [Burk] at Venice—the worthless idiot—& have developed into a pretty fair sort of courier myself since then" (Yale). On page 208 of this notebook Clemens registered Burk's request for additional payment; he elaborated upon Burk's incompetence on pages 210–211.

72 In his autobiography Clemens describes this as an "old elaborately carved black Venetian bedstead—the most comfortable bedstead that ever was, with space enough in it for a family, and carved angels enough surmounting its twisted columns and its headboard and footboard to bring peace to the sleepers, and pleasant dreams" (*MTA*, 2:86). Livy's list of purchases indicates that this bed cost $200.

73 This item is noted on Livy's list of purchases as "1 stand thrown in."

The Great Face on the mountain peak at Mont Blanc. It was perfect.

A Few easy signs by which the ignorant may tell a fine picture from a bad one.

Two pegs on top of house shows, no taxes. In old pictures these abound to the extent of 3 or 4 houses.

Another queer old Curio shop, up 6 flights stairs—many small rooms crowded with images, armor, pots, lanterns &c.

Lottery on a priest who jumped out of a window last week & killed himself. The newspapers publish his age, &c, & the people buy tickets according to age, jump, &c.

I was in Venice too brief a time to learn for myself the character of the people—but I got friends to tell me & this way I have got at the absolute truth.—

Smith—They are divine.
Jones—They are devilish—&c.

They all say "Never offer a Veneetian more than half—<he'll> but I notice they all weaken & *don't*.

Livy's Oriental purchase[74]—<60.> asked 160—got it for 60.

Dittura Agostino
Gondoliere
Traghetto della Salute. No. 123.
Venezia
(The last word unnecessary.)

Oct 4—Great Council Chamber, Ducal Palace. Immediately at right of the door as you enter, <is a> in the big picture over the

---

[74] Among the purchases made in Venice was a "Japanesse bowl for Mrs Harris" for which Livy paid ten dollars. Mrs. John Harris, the wife of the United States consular agent in Venice, was an old friend of Mrs. Charles Dudley Warner, and the Clemenses visited her while staying there. In this and the subsequent notebooks kept on this trip Clemens calls her "Mrs. H."

book shelves, is a fisherman in the foreground in a green dress holding one basket of fish against his body & resting another basket of fish on a woman's head. This Fisherman has but one leg—but that is not the singularity, but the fact that it is the *port* leg, attached to the *starboard* side of his body.[75]

Tintorets 3-acre picture of Saturday Night in Heaven.[76] Now this is *my* idea of heaven—everybody at work. There is not a reposeful figure in the entire 10,000. Everybody is hard at it & full of energy as if this was the *last* Sat Night. Some are diving, with clasped hands, others swimming through the cloud-shoals, some frog-fashion, some on back, some <[b-]> throwing hand-springs,—nobody is idle, nobody is exercising in a moderate way—every soul in the picture must be in a profuse perspiration<.>—a most tremendous state of activity.

Contrast—look at the gorgeous Doge & the gorgeously robed City Government in the G. Council pictures & then see the present <Gover>Gov't, all in shining plug hats (the only ones in Venice,) arrive in 3 black gondolas flying little blue silk flag of St Mark's & ascend the steps of the Prefecture—(formerly a grand palace.

Agent's report: The Riot—The 15 or 20 people scattered around who are trying to read, show plainly that there is so much noise they can't keep their attention on their books.

One person in the centre of the picture is holding out his book offering it to somebody else—a grand general offer to the whole insurrection—but you dont see anybody going for it.

Next to this person is the Lion of St Mark, with *his* book (he always has a book—you never see him in stone or paint without it. His book is open. Next is St. Mark with his usual pen, elevated—he & the lion are looking each other earnestly in the face, evidently disputing about the way to spell a word. The lion looks up in <w>

---

[75] This figure appears as Clemens describes him in a painting by pupils of Paolo Veronese of Pope Alexander III and the Doge Sebastiano Ziani meeting at the Monastero della Carità.

[76] Tintoretto's "Paradise" mentioned earlier (see p. 197).

rapt admiration while St M spells. Saturday Night in Heaven—have a good time now, because to-morrow they got to be quiet.

Conquest of Smyrna—P. Veronese—2 utterly impossible dogs—all the horses in the Ducal palace (& all in this picture) are blown up like bladders & are in impossible attitudes. No models.

They say there is a horse here in Zoological Gardens.

Emperor <kning> prostrate before Pope[77]—3 men in foreground 30 or 35 feet high, judging by the size of a kneeling little boy in foreground centre) Pope 7 ft high, Doge a little dried-up insignificant dwarf of 4 ft.

Graham[78] gave his stick to a man, who thanked him.

Pretty much all the portraits of the Doges appear to have been painted from the same model.[79]

About Oct 1st I told the North's that if they didn't cable it would be months before they heard—but if they would cable San Francisco at once they would get a letter from there inside of 48 hours—& my prophecy was correct.[80]

George Burk the guide swindled Rosa out of ten marks. [#]

---

[77] A painting by Federigo Zuccaro of the reconciliation in Venice in 1177 of Frederick Barbarossa with Pope Alexander III is in the Hall of the Great Council in the Doges' Palace.

[78] Evidently William Graham, an American painter of Venetian scenes long resident in Venice and Rome, whom Clemens met in Venice and planned to use as a basis for a character in A *Tramp Abroad* (see p. 209 of this notebook and Notebook 17, p. 240). It is Graham who figures as "G" in the following conversation about the Old Masters (pp. 202–203) which was revised for chapter 48 of A *Tramp Abroad*.

[79] The portraits of seventy-six doges appear in the frieze of the Hall of the Great Council.

[80] Mark Twain adapted this note in "Mental Telegraphy," an article written in 1878 but "pigeonholed" for fear of ridicule until December 1891 when it appeared in *Harper's New Monthly Magazine*. There he recalled an occasion when he advised distraught parents that a cable directed anywhere would be certain to bring word from their uncommunicative distant son by the "telegraphic" phenomenon of "letter-crossing."

Put in the American woman who kicked up her dress in Milan Cathedral amid the gravities of that solemn place.[81]

The vile Italian long-nine, black & strong, with a straw through it, which the gov't forces you to smoke by its high duties. They are sold at $2 a hundred—cheap enough, in all conscience—& bad enough, God knows.

St Mark resembles nothing Christian, with its squat bulk. The campanile is a mere brick factory chimney, yet it is spoken of as "architecture." "Built by" so & so in such a century.

I said, "What *is* it people see in the old masters?—I can't see *any*thing in them. Been in the Doge's Palace & saw the worst drawing, the worst proportions, worst Paul Veronese dogs & other artists horses.—(left-legged man

G.—Yes, they often drew badly, they didn't care much for truth & exactness in minor details. <But> But that hair trunk—

<Yes,> Now THERE! That hair trunk is the finest thing in Italy. *I* think it far better than <Raphael's> Titian's Assumption that is so bragged about.

(*Note*—Compare all art with that hair trunk.) Speak of Raphael's Transfiguration, Tintoretto's (?) Hair Trunk,[82] & Titian's Assumption as if they were the 3 great <art trea> pictures of the world. Complain that Ruskin could rave over the Slave Ship but had not a word for the Hair Trunk.)

G. But considering their *time*, the old Masters—

---

81 "The scene was one to sweep all frivolous thoughts away and steep the soul in a holy calm. A trim young American lady paused a yard or two from me, fixed her eyes on the mellow sparks flecking the far-off altar, bent her head reverently a moment, then straightened up, kicked her train into the air with her heel, caught it deftly in her hand, and marched briskly out" (*A Tramp Abroad*, chapter 48).

82 In chapter 48 of *A Tramp Abroad* Mark Twain burlesques the inflated style of contemporary art critics in his extravagant appreciation of "Bassano's immortal Hair Trunk." The hair trunk is actually an insignificant detail in Leandro Bassano's huge painting of "Pope Alexander III and the Doge Ziani, the Conqueror of Emperor Frederick Barbarossa" in the Hall of the Council of Ten in the Doges' Palace.

I—*Ah*—considering their *time*—then why call them the Old Apprentices—they produced the masters of our day.

G—But after all, in spite of bad drawing, & subjects which no longer appeal to people as strongly as 300 yrs ago, there is a *something* about their pictures which is divine—a something which is above & beyond the art of any epoch since—a something which would be the despair of artists but that they never hope or expect to attain it & therefore do not worry about it.

I—I can believe that & I *do* believe it. I believe that true artists, & people with a true & deep cultivation in art, can & do see that—& I reverence it; but *I* can't see it & I will not believe that the average tourist<s> can see it—so when they pretend, it makes me wroth.

<S><Church> Scuolo of Rocco—The Magdalen in the corner —(see Ruskin) Stones of Venice) If that tree[83] had been made for a theatre T would never been paid

The tree where the Virgin is is not a palm tree, but an exploding rocket. The running water[84] is about as such things are done in oil cloth window shades.

Good jackass in the Flight & Mary is beautiful.[85] [#]

---

83 Ruskin noted that in "The Magdalen," in the Scuola di San Rocco in Venice, "the laurel-tree, with its leaves driven hither and thither among flakes of fiery cloud, has been probably one of the greatest achievements that [Tintoretto's] hand performed in landscape: its roots are entangled in underwood, of which every leaf seems to be articulated, yet all is as wild as if it had grown there instead of having been painted" (*The Stones of Venice*, 3 vols. [London: Smith, Elder and Co., 1873–1874], 3:330).

84 About "St. Mary of Egypt," also in the Scuola di San Rocco, Ruskin wrote: "The water painting is exceedingly fine. Of all painters that I know, in old times, Tintoret is the fondest of running water; there was a sort of sympathy between it and his own impetuous spirit" (Ruskin, *Stones of Venice*, 3:331).

85 Clemens does agree with Ruskin's evaluation of Tintoretto's "Flight into Egypt":

> I have never seen any of the nobler animals—lion, or leopard, or horse, or dragon —made so sublime as this quiet head of the domestic ass, chiefly owing to the grand motion in the nostril and writhing in the ears. . . . I had not any conception, until I got near, how much pains had been taken with the Virgin's head; its expression is as sweet and as intense as that of any of Raffaelle's, its

Dear Mrs. H—If I have a talent it is for contributing valuable matter to works upon cookery.[86]

Oct 9.—A swell *big* gondola, trimmed from stem to stern with black & white drapery, stripes, rosettes &c.—Catafalque on it trimmed likewise—everything looked attractive, sumptuous, new & swell. 4 gondoliers, in white <jackets,> sailor jackets & trowsers & white hats with black band—deep turnover sailor collar of black—broad black band around sleeve—black scarf around waist, ends hanging to knees—all mighty handsome & swell.

We had seen the funeral procession before, filing through the square & into the Cathedral—red robes & black do. & caps, & white lace jackets—red pall-bearers, <every>—all bearing candles on poles 7 ft high, &c.

This was a 2^d^ class or 150 f funeral, so the guide said. A first-class is still more swell & costs 300; a third-class is 60; a fourth is 30; a 5th 10; the lowest class & price is 3 f.

Gentleman said,—so & so is building that—mentioning an ancient Dogical name which was perpetuated hundreds years ago by allowing a monk, the last male, to marry. He said this is the same family & is still rich.

Our guide says the Moncenigo's furnished 11 of the 120 Doges of Venice (between 697 & 1797)—& still flourishes in wealth here & owns 4 palaces on the Grand Canal.

Somebody told me there were still Gradenigos in Venice.

I was more reconciled to the Ducal palace pictures to-day—I mean the unhistorical. They are beautiful—perhaps because they have all been "restored" with a whitewash brush & haven't much Old Master left in them. [#]

---

reality far greater. The painter seems to have intended that everything should be subordinate to the beauty of this single head. (Ruskin, *Stones of Venice*, 3:328)

86 This note, perhaps for a postscript to a letter from Livy to Mrs. Harris (see note 74), suggests that Clemens was already thinking of the mock recipes he would include in chapter 49 of *A Tramp Abroad*.

But Tiepelo is *my* artist.[87] In that palace near the Bella Arti<e>—in that chapel of San Giovanni e Paolo—& in the Jesuit church where the marbles are, these are all beautiful.

The little boys & the pedlars of folding pictures won't take "No," but persist & pester the life out of you.

Besarel, in the Grand Canal—2 brothers, sculptors the one in wood the other in marble—their father & grandfather great in <the same speci> wood sculpture.[88]

Began with Dittura[89] Oct 8 by the day at 5 f a day & 50[c] pour-boir—we to have him day & evening both.

The Count Pisani is old & the last of his race. The palace is vast—immense.—One wonders what they did with these mighty mansions, until he remembers that they kept 150 retainers or servants.

The persons who take hold of your gondola when you land, hold out their hat—& if you are a native you drop in <5> 2 centimes—if a foreigner, more—but you have not the slightest use for him.

The Mocenigo Doges were 7, *not* 11, of the 120.

Romance of the Grimani palace (praised by Ruskin.)[90] Courted

---

87 Clemens here shows evidence of the aesthetic sensitivity he elsewhere denies having, for this brilliant eighteenth-century artist was generally ignored by Ruskin and other nineteenth-century commentators.

88 The Clemenses bought a number of pieces of carved wooden furniture from Besarel for their Hartford house while in Venice. Before leaving home, Livy had recorded the dimensions of various rooms with the intention of buying furniture for them while abroad. Her list of purchases includes the note "Venice Furniture value $753."

89 Dittura Agostino was the second gondolier retained by the Clemens family.

90 "Of all the buildings in Venice, later in date than the final additions to the Ducal Palace, the noblest is . . . the Casa Grimani. It is composed of three stories . . . on so colossal a scale, that the three-storied palaces on its right and left only reach to the cornice which marks the level of its first floor. . . . It is to the majesty of the Casa Grimani that the Rialto itself, and the whole group of neighbouring buildings, owe the greater part of their impressiveness" (Ruskin, *Stones of Venice*, 3:32).

a girl over the way under assumed name. Parents said their daughter must live in a palace as fine as theirs. Grimani took his leave saying he would build a palace whose windows should be bigger than their front door—hence the huge Grimani-palace. This was told us by Ditturo—who said that the piles under the palace cost more than the palace itself.

There was a little cat,
And she caught a little rat,
Which she dutifully rendered to her mother—
Who said Bake him in a pie
For his flavor's very high,
Or confer him on the poor, if you'd druther.[91]

The Hair Trunk is in <what I think was> the Chamber of the Council of Ten. The picture is one of three 40-foot fellows that stretch around 3 sides of the room. The far end of the picture is <filled up with a woman> a couple of women, (one with a child looking over her shoulder at a wounded man sitting with bandaged head on the ground. By these women marches a gorgeous procession of grandees, biships, halberdiers & banner-bearers, <flocking> toward the pope, <w> in the centre, who is talking with the bonnetless Doge.—To the right of this tranquil party, & within 12 ft of it, man is beating a drum & in the neighborhood of the drummer two scabs are blowing horns; <w> horsemen are plunging about; in fact 22 ft of this great work is all a deep & happy holiday tranqullity & Sunday School procession; then we come suddenly upon 11½ ft of turmoil & racket & powwow; now at the <s>very end of this section of riot, within 4 ft of the end of the picture & as much as 36 ft from the beginning of it (note the incredible modesty) we come upon the immortal Hair Trunk. The Bassano has done everything he could think of to *apparently* distract attention from

---

[91] Mark Twain incorporated this as a "morning-song" in "A Cat Tale" which he wrote in 1880 (*Concerning Cats*, ed. Frederick Anderson [San Francisco: Book Club of California, 1959], p. 8).

it & ostentatiously pretend that it is not the great feature of the picture. For instance, to the right of it he has placed a stooping man with a cap so red it snatches your eye to that locality the moment you enter the room—then to the left, some <8>6 ft he has placed a dropsical white horse <which prances w> with a man on him in a glaring red hot coat<—>which snatches your eye the moment it leaves the red cap, & so jumps clean over the trunk. Now you *may* wander back between these objects—so B hurls in between the trunk & the red horseman a man naked to his waist, carrying a fancy flour sack on <his> the middle of his back instead of on his shoulder. This feat of course interests you—keeps you at bay a little longer like a sock or a jacket to the pursuing wolf—but at last & in spite of all distractions & detentions your eye falls of the world's masterpiece & you totter to a chair or lean upon your guide for support.

The top of the trunk is arched—the arch is a perfect half circle, in the <[---]>Roman style of architecture. It is bound or bordered with leather all around where the lid joins the main body.—<It is said> Many critics consider this leather too cold in tone; but I consider this its highest praise since it was evidently made so to emphasize by contrast the impassioned heat/fervency of the hasp. The <hair> brass nail heads are in the purest & noblest style of the early renaissance. The handle/High lights on the end of the trunk has evidently been retouched—I think with a piece of chalk—but you can still see the <true> inspiration of the <true> old Master in the tranquil, almost too tranquil, hang of it.—The hair of this trunk is *real* hair—white in patches, brown in patches. So divinely real & genuine is this exquisite trunk, that when the baggagemaster of the Erie road was brought into its presence 2 yrs ago he could hardly keep from checking it. <No inspector> To prove still further its power, an inspector of customs brought before it; he gazed upon it rapt, for some moments, <like the> then slowly & unconsciously placed <his left> one hand behind him <in the form> with palm <significantly> uppermost & got out his chalk with the other.

The villains have placed this right where the sun shines on it, nearly if not almost every now & then. This should be remedied.

The picture opposite is marked (just over the door) Pax Italiæ Bononiæ, inita mdxxix.[92]

This room in little pieces of varicolord marble laid in <s>cement & then ground off smooth, re-laid in 1804.

<[Hi]>

From 10 to 12 M I must have seen 20 or 25 different guides taking parties through the Ducal Palace in various languages.

And O, the style of them!—& the dress of them!—& the various styles & actions & diffidences of the various tourist's—especially new and painfully self-conscious brides & grooms.—Describe in detail.

Oct 10—To-day received an impudent letter from George Burk asking for <7>175 francs more—but it furnishes me his address, which I want.[93]

Afternoon—3 of the very worst & most dismal solo singers in the world have been on the masonry platform ½ hour apart—never heard anything <worst>worse in the <most celebrated> opera. One man with a wheezy accordeon—man with a guitar—woman with a screechy voice who strummed a guitar with her right hand but touched neither fret nor string with her left—only held the machine in position. Another guitar & a discordant man & woman have come. [#]

---

[92] Marco Vecellio's "The Peace of Bologna, concluded in 1529 between Pope Clement VII. and Emp. Charles V." (Baedeker's *Northern Italy*, p. 229).

[93] Burk's 8 October letter reads in part:

> Excuse me for writing does few Lines to you, on the first of October at the time you told me that you dit not requirer me annymore, I was so suprisd that I was not abel to speak to you, as I never Exspected to be treated by a Gentleman in your Postiion. You will Remember Sir that you heave a famalie of you own, so you may Put your own Self in my Position to be turnd away withouth anny particular reason I heave Wife and Childern to Keep and I must Work for, and Know it is a very bad time for me to get Work and the Winter is very near.
>
> I beg you to be so Kind and Send me the rest of the Months Wages of October as I Supose you Know the rights of Law in Germany, you owe me by right and by your worth of honeur 175 franc.

He concluded with a request to be reimbursed also for outlays he had made on behalf of Clemens.

Hotel della Allemania[94]

Piazza di Spania

<The> Bible for the Young. Philip Wickstead, translator. Published by the Manchester Sunday School Union.—Dr. Oort of Amsterdam is one of the writers—7 vols.[95]

Marks—S. C. H. No. 17

Small stage-plank used at high tide.

Sunday Oct 13—Took Dittura & Graham's gondolier & started for the mainland at a point (Fusina) 2 hours away. A steady, heavy rain. Had the casa on & the windows closed. <Put> Lit my best cigar, put on my slippers, propped my feet on the little starboard bench which brought them within a foot of the ½ glass door—wonderfully snug & cosy. Looked out on the ruffled & rainy seas a while after I was beyond the shipping & fairly away from Venice—then recognizing that I could never be so cosy again, got out Marryatt's Pacha of Many Tales & read.

But the seas grew very rough.

Made the trip in 35 minutes, having a strong wind on our beam & the tide with us—went mainly sidewise. <Arr.> <Start> Arrived at 10.45

Tide changed & I started back at 12.30 in a driving storm of rain

---

94 The hotel in Rome at which the Clemens family would stay from 28 October to 11 November.

95 Henricus Oort, Isaac Hooykaas, and Abraham Kuenen, *The Bible for Young People,* trans. Philip Henry Wicksteed, 6 vols. (London and Edinburgh: Williams and Nordgate, 1873–1879). After returning home, Clemens evidently sent the American edition of this work (*The Bible for Learners,* 3 vols. [Boston: Roberts Brothers, 1878–1879]) to his brother Orion who was writing a refutation of the Old and New Testaments. An excerpt from the manuscript, presented as a lecture entitled "Man, the Architect of Our Religion," had recently led to Orion's excommunication from the First Westminster Presbyterian Church of Keokuk, Iowa. In a letter to Clemens on 23 November 1879 Orion gratefully acknowledged receipt of *The Bible for Learners*: "It is going to be of inestimable value to me, if there is any value in my work." Orion eventually submitted his manuscript to Roberts Brothers, but on 23 March 1880 reported its rejection.

& a strong head wind & heavy sea. The customs officers stood in the door & declined to visit & inspect the boat. My fear was that the casa would catch the wind & blow the boat over—then how could I get out of captivity?

We passed inside the 2 big hulks & it was nip & tuck—made hardly any headway & came near drifting across & against their bows.

Arrived home at 2.30—went in 35 minutes—returned in 2 hours.

Every person who brings a package from his employer or does anything for you requires a pour-boire.

1.50

Pension Suisse <Op>

10 f per day apiece

Always the last man out of the train;[96]

Seldom comes at way stations to see how you are getting along, or keep your door against intruders.

Has the impudence to alter your telegram, sign his own name to it & then say *they wouldn't send yours*—a very thin lie.

Was the last out of the steamboat at Bellagio & the train at Como.

Said there was no place to break the 14-hour journey between Interlaken & Ouchy, & afterwards said he mentioned Berne.

Said the hotel in Berne was 10 min from station—it wasn't 10 seconds (*they took a cab*)—he always lets on to know but doesn't always know.

The only time I got no premium on gold was when he took me to the bank—Luzerne.

At Berne, he said there was 10 m to spare when there were only 5—but for Mrs. C they would have been left.

---

[96] This begins a list of Clemens' grievances about Burk's performance as a courier. The incidents relative to Berne and Strasbourg occurred when Clemens was off with Twichell, and Burk was alone responsible for getting the women and children of the Clemens party safely from place to place. In the manuscript the complaint is interrupted by a number of entries which are printed after it in the present text (see Details of Inscription for a full account).

At Strasburg he told them the train left at 7.30 AM, when fortunately Mrs C remembered it left at 6.30.

At Como (last man out of the train) didn't know whether we took omnibuses to go to boat or not—had to inquire.

At Bellagio he was nowhere to be seen when I left the boat in the storm—all the party (Miss C with baggage) reached the omnibus *ahead* of him, *with his umbrella* & nothing else. I carried Clara, Rosa carried Susie.

After 2 days, didn't know the price of a boat 2 hours, & so took portier's word & paid 7 f for what was only 5.

Paid that hackman 4 f for bringing our coats from Kanderstegg in place 2 f as agreed.

Hotel Grand Bretagna
Bellag.

$$\begin{array}{r} 83 \\ 285 \\ 125 \\ \hline 493 \end{array}$$

San Stefano—Palazzo Barbero—Consul.

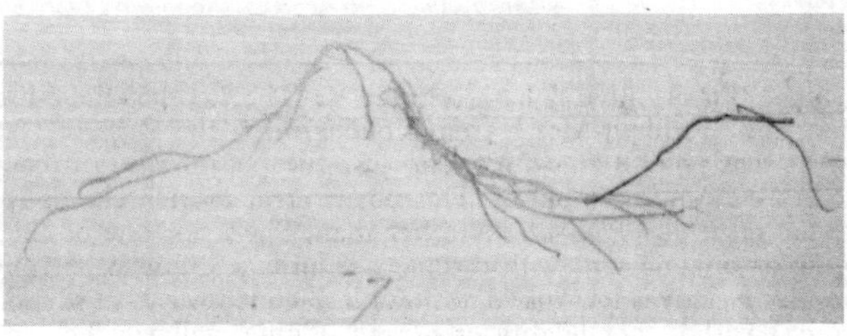

<Father in Heaven, the day is declining.>[97]

[97] In a 20 November 1878 letter to Twichell, Clemens enclosed a note to Susan Warner, an accomplished musician:

> I ordered a perfect love of a music box in Geneva, & for 2 months have been trying to select the 10 tunes for it.—Won't you help me? Its best hold is not loud, or staccato or rapid music, but just the reverse—a soft, *flowing* strain—its

Tannhaüser. (where the heroine is taken into the lower regions.
Wedding March—Lohengrin
<Ich weiss nicht>
The Lorelei.
Miserére—Trovatore.
Irish Immigrant's Lament
Russian National Hymn
Way down in Tennessee
Day after Day.
The Fremersberg
Bonny Doon
Last Rose of Summer.
Overture—Wm Tell
Auld Lang Syne
Long, Long Ago.
Schubert's "Wanderer"
Ouverture—Caliph of Bagdad.
<Mendellson's>Mendelsson's Hymn.

G. K. Mayer.
Vienna

1. America.[98]

---

strong suit is the plaintive. I have selected 4: The Lorelei, the Miserère from Trovatore, the Wedding March from Lohengrin, & the Russian National Anthem—& at that point I *stuck*. You are just the person who can suggest some tunes to get the wanting 6 out of. This box is great on rich chords—pours them out like the great god Pan—or any other man. She's not one of the thumping or banging or tinkling sort, with castanets & birds & drums & such-like foolishness—no, her melody is low-voiced, & flows in blended waves of sound. Her forte is to express pathos, not hilarity or hurrah. Come, will you help me? I shall wait to hear from you. (Yale)

This is a list of melodies Clemens was considering for the four-hundred-dollar music box acquired in Geneva.

[98] This list, on the verso of the back flyleaf and not in Clemens' hand, offers selections for the music box. In an unpublished chapter from *A Tramp Abroad*, Clemens commented:

I thought I had ten favorite tunes, but easily found I had only four. It took me eight months to furnish the other six. Meantime I suppose that that young man

2. The Wedding March.
3. I would that my Love.
4. Luther's Chorale.
5. Maritana. Alas those chimes so sweetly singing
6. The Russian Nat. Hymn.
7. Flower Girl. Waltz
8. Rigoletto. Introduction
9. William Tell. Andante from Overture.
10. La Fille de Wm Angot. Waltz.

75
9
———
705

From Visp 10.51 AM <to> arrives at Bouveret, at 2.35. Boat from at 3. for Ouchy, arriving at 4.40 or 4.50[99]

Go from Chamouni to Glazier des Bossons.

Hess & Metford,
Watchmakers
Geneva.

C. Flury,
vis-a-vis dem Bahnhof
(cigars) Berne

<Golden> Colombo d'Oro, Verona.[100]

---

had forgotten what kind of a box I had ordered. At any rate when I at last opened the blessed thing in America, the first turn of the crank brought forth an agonizing jingle & squawk & clatter of bells, gongs, drums, & castanets, with never a solitary strain of flute or fiddle! It was like ordering a serenade of angels, & getting a shivaree in place of it.

[99] These notes concerning the route Clemens and Twichell took to rejoin Livy and the others on Lake Geneva after their trip to Zermatt in late August were written on the recto of the back endpaper as were all of the remaining notes.

[100] In Notebook 17 Clemens warns himself to avoid this hotel (p. 245).

XVII

"To Get Through with This Painful Trial"

(October 1878–February 1879)

NOTEBOOK 17, which covers the period from 14 October 1878 to February 1879, documents the progress of the Clemenses' European tour from Venice through Florence and Rome and on to Munich, where they settled for the winter of 1878/1879. Ranging from brief travel impressions to extended passages later incorporated in *A Tramp Abroad*, the entries in this notebook follow the pattern of those in the preceding European notebooks and show Clemens in the role of roving observer, dutifully visiting public monuments, churches, and art galleries in pursuit of material for the travel book he was not sure he wanted to write. His preoccupation with certain subjects—for example, his plan to burlesque the Old Masters by comparing them to an Arkansas sign painter—carries over from Notebook 16. Notebook 17 is significant not only as a repository of material for *A Tramp Abroad*, however, but also as an aid in understanding Clemens' composition of that work since he actually began writing the major portion of the book while keeping this notebook.

In addition, Notebook 17 provides a view of the personal side of the Clemens family's tour. Having discharged his courier in Venice, Clemens was faced with the task of leading his party of five through foreign lands, and he can be seen attending to the related responsibilities in a variety of mundane situations—shopping for curiosities, comparing hotel rates, checking train schedules and arranging for private accommodations, grumbling about tipping, struggling with unfamiliar languages, occasionally giving in to an attack of exasperated weariness. Clemens' nostalgia for America becomes apparent here in his repeated laments about the absence of home comforts, particularly in regard to lodgings and food. At one point he notes: "The greatest charm we have found in Europe, by all odds, are the open fire places in Florence & Rome." Despite earlier complaints of excessive social demands, Clemens welcomed the company of congenial American travelers and foreign service officials and, perhaps to fill the void left by the departure of Twichell, visited with several expatriate American artists, on one occasion spending a beer-drinking, tale-spinning evening in Rome with Elihu Vedder, the raconteur and painter.

Clemens' tolerance for travel, already strained by six months in Europe, was further tested during this segment of the tour of Italy. The family left Venice on 17 October and traveled by train to Florence for a stay of eleven days. Clemens was temporarily buoyant, responding with enthusiasm to "this little town" of "Davinci, Buonarotti, Benvenuto, Machiavelli, Giotto, Amerigo Vespucci, Dante, Petrarch, &c." In Florence he appreciated those works by the Old Masters which met his strictly realistic standards, commenting approvingly on Cellini's "beautiful Perseus" and awarding lengthy praise to portraits by Titian and Bronzino.

The pleasant experiences of Florence were clouded, however, by uneasiness about the prospect of Rome. Clemens read William Wetmore Story's *Roba di Roma* and noted that "Rome seems to be a great fair of shams, humbugs, & frauds. Religion is its commerce & its wealth, like dung in the Black Forest." His mood plummeted upon his arrival in Rome on 28 October. By the following day he was already commenting disdainfully: "It is the most ridiculous spectacle to see a Virgin or a copper Apostle stuck on top of every stately monument of the grand old 'pagan' days of Rome." Clemens was irreverent during visits to the Pantheon, the Coliseum, Saint Peter's and the Vatican, the Barberini Palace, and the catacombs on the Appian Way. He confided to Twichell in a letter of 3 November:

> I do wish you were in Rome to do my sight-seeing for me. Rome interests me as much as East Hartford could, and no more. That is, the Rome which the average tourist feels an interest in; but there are other things here which stir me enough to make life worth living. Livy and Clara Spaulding are having a royal time worshiping the old Masters, and I as good a time gritting my ineffectual teeth over them. (*MTL*, p. 339)

This letter and the notebook entries show that Clemens did not share Livy's view: "We have enjoyed Rome immensely & wish so very much that we were going to spend three months here" (OLC to Mrs. Langdon, 10 November 1878, MTM).

On 11 November the Clemens family left Rome and returned to Florence for a short rest before setting out for Munich on 13 November. With overnight stops at Bologna and Trento and "a solid 12-hour pull through the loveliest snow-ranges & snow-draped forests," they finally arrived at their winter quarters "in drizzle & fog" on the evening of November 15. Clemens wrote to Howells on 17 November: "Munich did seem the horriblest place, the most desolate place, the most unendurable place!—& the rooms were *so* small, the conveniences so meagre, & the porcelain stoves so grim, ghastly, dismal, intolerable! So Livy & Clara sat down forlorn, & cried, & I retired to a private place to pray." But, he continued, "that was simply fatigue. Next morning the tribe fell in love with the rooms, with the weather, with Munich" (*MTHL*, p. 240).

In Munich all the members of the Clemens party were productively occupied. Livy and Clara Spaulding engaged teachers for lessons in German and drawing, the children also studied German, and Clemens rented a workroom at 45 Nymphenstrasse, where he planned to write his travel book. But he received an unexpected reprieve explained in a 20 November letter to Twichell:

> Well, I have lost my Switzerland note-book! I have written to Rome and Florence, but I don't expect to find it. If it remains lost, I can't write any volume of travels, & shan't attempt it, but shall tackle some other subject. I've got a workroom, a mile from here, & am all ready to go to work, but shall lie on my oars till I hear from Rome & Florence. (Yale)

The first notebook entry made in Munich is dated 30 November, two weeks after arrival. Soon after that, having found the lost notebook, Clemens went steadily to work on his travel book, ideas for which fill the rest of this notebook. Among these notes is one that registers his final selection of Harris as the name for the fictional travel partner based on Twichell. To some degree Notebook 17 becomes a composite of the previous European notebooks at this point as Clemens read through them, selecting items and often re-recording them here before extracting them yet again into his working notes for the book. Most of an extant eighteen-page sequence of *Tramp Abroad* working notes were in fact copied from Notebook 17. Although Mark Twain sometimes copied and sometimes expanded notebook entries in these working notes, he most often simply condensed them, occasionally adding a reminder to "See notebook" or to "See book," in effect producing an index to useful notebook material. Notebook 17 thus affords an unusual insight into the continuing importance of Clemens' notebooks at the various stages of literary composition.

By the third week of January, Clemens had written 900 pages of satisfactory manuscript, and thought the book was half-finished. On 26 January he reported to Twichell:

> I found the Swiss note-book, some time ago. When it was first lost I was glad of it, for I was getting an idea that I had lost my faculty of writing sketches of travel; therefore the loss of that note-book would render the writing of this one simply impossible, and let me gracefully out; I was about to write to Bliss and propose some other book, when the confounded thing turned up, and down went my heart into my boots. But there was now no excuse, so I went solidly to work —tore up a great part of the MS written in Heidelberg,—wrote and tore up,— continued to write & tear up,—and at last, reward of patient and noble persistence, my pen got the old swing again!
>
> Since then I'm glad Providence knew better what to do with the Swiss note-book than I did, for I like my work, now, exceedingly, and often turn out over 30 MS pages a day and then quit sorry that Heaven makes the days so short. (*MTL*, p. 349)

This renewed confidence is substantiated by Livy's remark, in a 15 December letter to Mollie Clemens, that "Mr Clemens hopes to have certainly one and perhaps two books ready when we go home." This second book may have been the story about Ned Wakeman's adventures in heaven which Mark Twain had been writing intermittently for a decade and for which he made two notes in this notebook.

But of course the writing did not always go so smoothly and Clemens found the hardship of being "yoked down to the grinding out of a 600-page 8-vo. book" compounded by problems of perspective and emotion. He described those difficulties to Howells on 30 January 1879, the day of his last dated entry in Notebook 17, thereby also venting his feelings about the entire European period:

> I wish I *could* give those sharp satires on European life which you mention, but of course a man can't write successful satire except he be in a calm judicial good-humor—whereas I *hate* travel, & I *hate* hotels, & I *hate* the opera, & I *hate* the Old Masters—in truth I don't ever seem to be in a good enough humor with ANYthing to *satirize* it; no, I want to stand up before it & *curse* it, & foam at the mouth,—or take a club & pound it to rags & pulp. (*MTHL*, pp. 248–249)

The family remained in Munich for another four weeks before going on to Paris on 27 February 1879.

Notebook 17 is the second of Clemens' notebooks to be made with page tabs according to his design. Except for a slight difference in the size of the tabs, it is identical in design and format to Notebook 16. It now contains 194 pages, all of them used. Three and one-half leaves have been torn out and are missing. All the entries are in pencil. There are occasional use marks in pencil throughout the notebook, some entered by Clemens but most of them probably by Paine.

Telegraph hotel.[1]
½ dozen gloves
Book for Dittura.
Go to Ponti about Megaloscope.[2]
Railway tickets.
Go to Sarfatti.[3]

---

[1] Clemens' list of final Venetian errands and the notes through "In certain public . . . perceptible." are written on the front endpaper and flyleaf.

[2] Carlo Ponti, formerly optician to King Victor Emmanuel II, had a photograph studio in the Piazza of Saint Mark in Venice. Clemens apparently intended to inquire there about purchase of a megascope, also called an aphengescope, a type of magic lantern which projected images of objects placed within it.

[3] Gustavo Sarfatti was a shipping agent who dispatched many of the Clemenses' Venetian purchases, including glassware and dishes made by Salviati and furniture made by Besarel.

Go to Salviatti
" Besarel
Pay Bunce.[4]
Speak of man to see us off.

Picture 400 M.

Douvernak[5]—go to best studio on right hand side in the court.

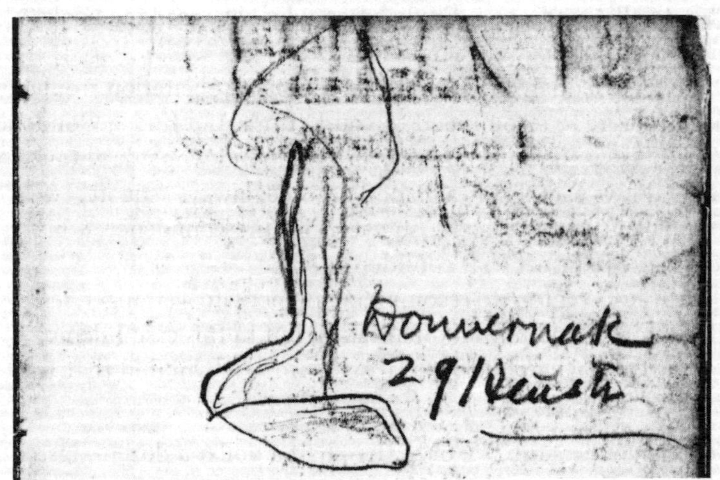

Douvernak
29 Heustr

Hume's Essay on Miracles, and Paley's Evidences of Christianity[6]

Josephus.[7] [#]

---

[4] William Gedney Bunce, a cousin of the Hartford banker Edward M. Bunce, was an American painter living abroad and specializing in views of Venice. Clemens may have bought or commissioned a painting from Bunce who called on the family in both Venice and Paris.

[5] Frank Duveneck, the influential American painter whose studio was a focal point for American art students in Munich.

[6] "Of Miracles," section 10 of David Hume's *An Enquiry Concerning Human Understanding*; William Paley's *View of the Evidences of Christianity.*

[7] Clemens' library included a copy of the two-volume 1829 edition of *The Works of Flavius Josephus* translated by William Whiston (*A1911*, item 271).

Herzogspital st. 11. for blotting paper & ink.

Oct 14/78.

Ich wallt meine Lieb ergösse sich (Mendellsohn)[8]

In certain public indecencies the difference between a dog & a Frenchman is not perceptible.

Oct 14.

This, to all Americans & Englishmen who have read my books & been made wiser & better thereby:

Of my own motion, & without suggestion or solicitation from any quarter, I desire to recommend to you Dittura Agostino, a Gondolier of Venice. He is the only gondolier I have found who was always prompt, always willing, always good natured, always "square," & never indolent. His is a face & an eye to inspire confidence, & his is a character to justify that confidence.

I hardly ever venture to recommend anybody to a stranger, lest I do that stranger an unintentional harm; but in this case I do not feel afraid. If you employ Dittura Agostino, you will find that you have done wisely & well.[9]

Venetian oysters the size of beans—half a dollar a dozen—tasted 4 dozen.

Emerson using up his wife's comb, taking the teeth for matches.[10] [#]

---

8 The Mendelssohn setting for "Ich wollt' meine Lieb' ergösse sich" ("I would that my love") by Heinrich Heine was another possible selection for Clemens' music box (see Notebook 16, pp. 211–213). It wasn't until 23 February 1879 that Clemens could inform Mrs. Langdon: "I've got the airs for my music box selected at last, thanks to goodness" (MTM).

9 Clemens' draft of a testimonial, perhaps to be inscribed in the book he planned to give to his gondolier, Dittura Agostino, is the first entry in the body of the notebook.

10 An anecdote probably told by Augustus P. Chamberlaine or his wife—"wonderfully delightful people great friends of Mr Emersons"—whom the Clemenses had recently met (OLC to Mrs. Langdon, 13 October 1878, MTM). The Chamberlaines knew Emerson at least well enough to have written to him from Venice on 4 October seeking advice on acquisitions for the Concord and Harvard College libraries (*The Letters of Ralph Waldo Emerson*, ed. Ralph L. Rusk, 6 vols. [New

Venetian Goods.

Shipped from Rietti's.

Articles contained in carved box: (Rietti.)

	cost.
Dishes	$20.
1 brass plate	16
1 Claud-Lorraine	6
1 <Conve>Concave Mirror	10
Tapestry	8
Venetian glass	6
	$66

Shipped from Besarel's.

Jardiniere	36
Copper openwork plate	6
<2> 1 brass bowl<s>	10
1 brass waiter	5
1 brass dish	5
Silver & copper bowl	5
Incense burner	12
Wood bambino	10
	$<85>89

Shipped from Salviatti's.

Venetian glass .... $100. [#]

York: Columbia University Press, 1939], 6:248). Their acquaintance with the aging writer enabled the Chamberlaines to assure Clemens that his Whittier dinner speech of 17 December 1877, in which he had burlesqued Emerson, was not the social affront he considered it. In an Autobiographical Dictation of 11 January 1906, Clemens recalled: "I perceived with joy that the C.'s were indignant about the way that my performance had been received in Boston. They poured out their opinions most freely and frankly about the frosty attitude of the people who were present at that performance, and about the Boston newspapers for the position they had taken in regard to the matter" (quoted in *Mark Twain's Speeches*, ed. Albert Bigelow Paine [New York: Harper & Brothers, 1923], p. 69). The Chamberlaines were making a tour of Italy and are mentioned recurrently in this notebook, often with the abbreviation "Ch."

Shipped from Florence.

One box containing large oil painting & frame<.>,—<80.00> & 2 small pictures—136. (Holy Family, Rembrandt & 3 Fates.)[11]

Besarel, shipped about April 1, 1879, 4 cases, No. 79, 80, 81, 82. Cost, <$>a little under $400<.>, gold, for this is the sum in depreciated Italian paper.

Saml. Troll Fils ship 2 packages, "Mark Twain"
about Apl. 17 .... one cost $140.
Music box .... " 400.
(No 1611 is music box—the other, 1612, is the wooden picture).

Oct 15—Dittura—Boom! (finger to temple.)—Morté—<B> Signor Bismarck—to-day—(laying head in palm of hand.)

Over right hand door in St Mark's, a mosaic "Multiply & replenish the Earth"—man & woman on a bed, he with his left hand pawing her right breast, which is naked. She leans her head upon her hand, manifesting no discontent. The sequel picture, alongside, might with propriety be labeled "9 Months later."

Close to the end of the red stone bench (where a strip of embedded iron <holds> clamps a new corner, the shape & size of a brick, to the rest of the bench, I discovered in the mottled surface, polished by the seats of loiterers of several centuries, another antique! one which made the hoary mosaics of St Mark but novelties born of yesterday <[(]>—<one> an antique which was already an antique when these fables pictured over my head were invented!—an antique which was already an antique a hundred thousand years or so before, &ccc—it was a fossil shell nearly as large as the crown of my hat.—It

---

[11] In Florence the Clemenses purchased copies of three paintings: a Rembrandt self-portrait, Andrea del Sarto's "Holy Family," and Rosso Fiorentino's "The Three Fates," long attributed to Michelangelo. This entry, like the following two made some time after the family's departure from Venice, occupies a page of the notebook set aside for information concerning Clemens' various shipments of purchases home.

had been polished down until it was of the appearance of <a peri> the section of a periwinkle—(for its form was a spiral.

Dittura Agosturo "Very good man"—"pol*ee*cyman!—no good for <me> you—good for me" (lighting his lamp.)

Oct 15—Very magnificent sunset & lamp effects (Piazza) coming from San Lazzaro.[12]

Oct. 16—For two days we have been doubting Dittura's reliability as a news gatherer—but to-night I heard a news-man crying a paper —understood "Count Bismarck" & bought a copy—spelled out the fact that 2 days ago, Carlo<,> Conte di Bismarck, a citizen of Venice, committed suicide by shooting himself through the head with a revolver. So D. was 2 days ahead of the newspaper.

Crude petroleum is an infallible cure of rheumatism—applied externally.

A man dreadfully poised by poison oak—(poison ivy) was urged to eat the leaves of it & was thoroughly cured—since then he rubs his hands & face or eats the leaves with impunity—never gets poisoned.

Oct 17—Belli Arti—It is not possible that anybody could take more solid comfort in martyrdom that St. Sebastian did.

The loveliest picture is Paul Veronese showing his sketches to Titian.[13]

---

[12] The island of San Lazzaro, two miles southeast of Venice, was the site of the Armenian monastery where the Clemenses visited Padre Giacomo Issaverdenz, a friend of Howells. In a letter to Howells on 17 November 1878, Clemens reported: "The first time we called at the convent, père Jacopo was absent; the next . . . time, he was there, & gave us preserved rose-leaves to eat, & talked about you, & Mrs. Howells, & Winnie, & brought out his photographs. . . . He expects to spend this winter in Munich & will see us often, he said" (*MTHL*, p. 241). On 30 January Clemens wrote from Munich: "Père Jacomo is here & has called twice, but I was out both times. Mrs. C was out once & lying down in undress uniform the other time & had to excuse herself. He has never come near us since" (*MTHL*, p. 250).

[13] "The Meeting of Titian and Paolo Veronese" by Antonio Zona, a nineteenth-century work on display at the Accademia di Belle Arti in Venice. The next paintings mentioned are Jacopo De Andrea's "The Prophet Daniel Interpreting King

The next is the King bowing down before Daniel. The next is (apparently) the destruction of Jerusalem. All these are modern & recent.

You know a saint (among the Old Masters by his having his head <in a ho> sometimes in a hoop & sometimes in a brass platter—its technical name is nimbus.

The Old Master's horses always rear <like the> after the fashion of the kangaroo.

500 Last Suppers—they all have new table cloths with the fold wrinkles sharply defined

The fig leaf & private members of statues are handled so much that they are black & polished while the rest of the figure is <[r]> white & unpolished. Which sex does this handling?

When you are in R do as the Romans do. Describe what they do. When you are in Venice & Florence one says don't go in the sun in Rome; another, don't go in the shade; don't go out after dark; *go* out after dark as much as you please; get up early; *don't* get up early &c &c

A 1000 f note is as big as a note-paper page.

Angelo Bratti Guide
Cafe Florian

The Baroness D'oyley—formerly Doyle—her husband a brother of Evans the Paris dentist. Her little son created a count by the Pope. She put on her card the tribe (clan) her ancestors trained with in their shirt tails in Scotland.[14] [#]

Nebuchadnezzar's Dream" and Francesco Hayez' "Destruction of Jerusalem," nineteenth-century works also in the Venice Accademia.

[14] Annie Alexis Macdonald of Baltimore, descendant of dispossessed Scottish gentry, was married to John H. Evans of Philadelphia, whom Pope Leo XIII had confirmed as Marquis D'Oyley of the Holy Roman Empire in October 1879. The Marquis D'Oyley was the nephew of Thomas Wiltberger Evans, a distinguished American dentist whose Parisian practice included most of Europe's royal families.

Mrs. H's gondolier—was absent one day because "his wife was sick"—next day because she was confined—got an advance of wages & leave of absence till child was born—more money & leave of absence, 8 days later, to have the child christened—more advance & another leave, a few days later, for funeral of the child—then he disappeared—it transpired later that he had neither wife nor child —he was 22 yrs old.

Oct 17—Left for Florence. Good by, Dittura Agostino!

In 1406 Francesca da Carrara was treacherously executed in prison by the X. Among his papers was found a receipt for 400 ducats lent by the great Carlo Zeno—the X condemned the later to lose all his offices & be imprisoned 2 yrs—a hideous government.[15]

S. Clemens (with <port> mosaic portrait of a pope over a door of St Mark.[16]

Preserved rose leaves at the Arminian convent.[17] [#]

---

[15] Although as commander he had been responsible for the series of military successes in Venice's war against Padua, Carlo Zeno ("the Unconquerable") was imprisoned for two years by Doge Michele Steno for suspected collusion with Francesco Carrara, the captured prince of Padua. Carrara was strangled in his prison cell along with his two sons. Their deaths were officially attributed to "attacks of catarrh" (Aubrey Richardson, *The Doges of Venice* [London: Methuen & Co., 1914], pp. 196–200).

[16] "*DOORWAY OF ST. CLEMENT*: The two, beautiful *bronze doors* with saints and Greek inscriptions inlaid in silver, are fine pieces of Byzantine art of the XIV century, sent, it is believed, as a gift by the Emperor Alessio Comneno of Constantinople. In the lunette: *St. Clement*, mosaic by VALERIO ZUCCATO (1532)" (Giulio Lorenzetti, *Venice and Its Lagoon*, trans. John Guthrie [Rome: Istituto Poligrafico dello Stato, 1961], p. 176).

[17] In *A Foregone Conclusion* (1875), William Dean Howells describes a typical visit to San Lazzaro. There Padre Girolamo—the fictional counterpart to Giacomo Issaverdenz, whom the Clemenses visited on 15 October (see note 12)—leads his guests "through the garden environing the convent, to a little pavilion perched on the wall that defends the island from the tides of the lagoon. A lay-brother presently followed them, bearing a tray with coffee, toasted rusk, and a jar of that conserve of rose-leaves which is the convent's delicate hospitality to favored guests" (16th ed. [Boston: Houghton, Mifflin and Co., 1889], p. 28).

About 1440–45, a Candian named Stammato, in the suite of a Prince of the House of Este, was permitted to view the treasure collection of <the> St Mark, & concealed himself behind an altar in the body of the Cathedral, but was discovered by a priest. Then he entered by false keys. After numerous difficulties & the labor of many nights, he removed a block of the marble paneling which walled the lower part of the treasury. This <stone> panel he fixed so as to be removable at will.—Then night after night he visited this magnificent mine, inspected it at his own sweet pleasure & carried away <su> jewels & gold worth 2,000,000 golden ducats or $8,000,000—say, at present valuations, $50,000,000. He even carried off a unicorn's horn (a mere curiosity,) & had to saw it in two, with great patience & difficulty. It shows how perfectly secure & undisturbed he was. He could have gone home the richest private citizen of his country & it might have been years before the plunder was missed. But he could not enjoy his delight alone. So he exacted a solemn oath from a Candian noble named Crioni, then took him to an obscure lodging & astounded his eyes. Great carbuncle—(afterward in Ducal cap.) He detected a look on C's face which excited his suspicion & was about to slip a stiletto into him when <he>C. saved himself by saying the display so astonished him. He excused himself for a moment, went & showed the carbuncle at the palace & denounced the criminal, who was hanged with a gilded rope (he having such a fancy for gold,) between the Columns.—*All* the booty was recovered. Make a Legend?[18]

Mr. Chamberlain's[19] excellent description of the candle man in St Mark's, the priest with the big handkerchief, the Hercules sailor who sang so well & was "not well paid" & the "cue" of <st>people from the church to the Campanile to draw in the lottery. [#]

---

[18] Clemens revised this tale for chapter 49 of *A Tramp Abroad.*

[19] On 21 October Livy wrote to her mother: "This evening Mr & Mrs Chamberlain were in for an hour & we sat about a wood fire & chatted—then Mr Clemens read to us—then to bed—where I am now—Florence is much more restful than Venice, because we have no social demands—and one ought to know no one when they are visiting picture galleries—The Chamberlains are a perfect delight, they never tax us in the least they are helpful to us and are bright beyond expression" (MTM).

The sergeant who nearly starved himself for nine months, selling & pawning everything to buy lottery tickets, & (lately) was not surprised to learn one morning that he had drawn 240,000 francs.

The lottery is a government institution & the poor its best patrons. This is an evil—but the Monte de <Piete>Pieti also a gov. ins^{t}. is a good thing, no doubt.[20]

Fine old necklace I saw in Venice w^{h} an old family had pawned—then the law was changed to allow only 6 months for redemption (owner supposed he had a year, as of old) but when he came with his money it was sold.

Florence is the city of Benvenuto Cellini (what an interesting autobiography is his!), Michelangelo, Dante, &c—& Raphael & Leonardo have been here.

Leech's picture[21] of 2 French examining a washbowl. "What is it for?" Picture of Italian chambermaid examining a broom. "What is it for?"

These people are not polite—at least in one way. Neither sex is disposed to yield an inch when meeting. So you get the habit of insolently caroming on people. Folks stand talking in middle of sidewalk & yield not an inch to passers.

At first, standing <in>at front door of the graceful tower, you are sure that the Perseus's arms are outrageously disproportioned to his legs & body—but ½ an hour's inspection convinces you that they are not. It is the gracefullest & shapeliest of men.[22]

It is wonderful how many celebrated men this little town of Florence has produced. In niches in the arcades of the Uffizzi they have life-size statues of 24 of them—20 of them being names familiar to every school-boy in the Christian world—Davinci,

---

20 The *mónte di pietà* was the name given to Italian pawnbrokers' establishments.

21 John Leech (1817–1864), English illustrator and cartoonist for *Punch*.

22 Clemens was viewing Cellini's statue of Perseus in the Loggia dei Lanzi from the tower of the Palazzo Vecchio.

Buonarotti, Benvenuto, Machiavelli, Giotto, Amerigo Vespucci, Dante, Petrarch, &c.

Two gallus old statues in front of the front door—<it is> one male & the other female. It is the smut on their faces that gives them such a gallus leer.[23]

Swell turn-out with 12 beautiful bay horses—never saw <the equal> anything like this outside the circus.

Saw the Misericordia or whatever their name is, marching with a coffin & torches—white dresses, masks & eye-holes. Kind of freemasonry for charity's sake.[24]

The Hercules & Cacus so mercilessly blackguarded by Benvenuto.[25] It is by Bandanello, who got Clement VII to <give> transfer to

---

[23] In the following working note for A *Tramp Abroad*, Mark Twain contrasted the effect of these figures with that of Titian's "grossly obscene . . . wholly sensual" Venus (see Notebook 18, p. 319): "2 gallus old smut-faced male & female fig-leafed statues before door—could excite nobody—& T's V inside."

[24] Baedeker describes the Misericordia as "the long established order of brothers of charity, who are frequently seen in the streets garbed in their black robes, with cowls covering the head and leaving apertures for the eyes only, while engaged in their missions of mercy" (*Italy: Handbook for Travellers; First Part: Northern Italy*, 5th rev. ed. [Leipzig: Karl Baedeker, 1879], p. 374).

[25] This statue by Michelangelo's rival and imitator Baccio Bandinelli is located at the right of the entrance to the Palazzo Vecchio. Cellini's remarks to Bandinelli about the "Hercules and Cacus" resemble Mark Twain's scornful appraisals of the Old Masters:

> "If the hair of your Hercules were shaved off, there would not remain skull enough to hold his brains. With regard to his face, it is hard to distinguish whether it be the face of a man, or that of a creature something between a lion and an ox. . . . His great brawny shoulders resemble the two pommels of an ass's pack-saddle; his breasts and their muscles bear no similitude to those of a man, but seem to have been drawn from a sack of melons. As he leans directly against the wall, the small of the back has the appearance of a bag filled with long cucumbers; it is impossible to conceive in what manner the two legs are fastened to this distorted figure, for it is hard to distinguish upon which leg he stands." (*Memoirs of Benvenuto Cellini*, trans. Thomas Roscoe [London: Henry G. Bohn, 1850], p. 408)

Mark Twain's comment on the history of this sculpture borrows language as well as information from a note in Roscoe's translation of Cellini's memoirs (p. 407).

him the job after it had been given to Michelangelo, who had even begun to study a design for it.

That most entertaining of books, Benvenuto's. It will last as long as his beautiful Perseus.

Pretty litte statue of Michel Angelo as a boy doing some sculping —the artist has made him right-handed which is an error.

The Secretary says that the proprietor of this Hotel de New York pays to the owner a Baron 32,000 f rent per annum, & he pays out of this, 13,000 *municipal* tax—say 40 p.c.!

Oct 23—In Santa Croce to-day a well dressed young woman followed us, begging for centimes.

An old frowsy woman watched where I laid my cigar, then approached us with it as Chamberlaine & I came out & said she rescued it from some boys (who had found it in the dark!) & wantd 5 cents for her trouble. She followed us into the street & finally cursed us & called down sudden death upon us.

The Secretary of the N.Y. Hotel made a swan, a pig, an ostrich & a mouse (mounted on an apple) out of bread, perfect.

Man passed counterfeit 50^{c} stamps on Rosa[26] & Mrs Chamberlain.

An artist reminded Mrs Ch. that she had paid 50 francs too much.

One of the richest men in America got Ch to take home a hat in a hat box for him—& Ch told the Collector it *was* a hat & nothing else—he afterwards found he had been imposed upon & that it was a costly French bonnet.

Another wealthy merchant brought a dozen silk umbrellas & gave his word that they were presents for friends (his other baggage was being passed. The umbrellas were afterward found for sale in the merchant's store.

The scoundrel who was to build ten feet of snow fence on our

---

26 Rosina Hay, the Clemens children's nurse.

roof & re-slate a small place—heard hammering for three days, went up there & he had slated an acre of roof & fenced the whole place in & was proposing to fence the stable.

The same man who got under the fountain at Baden Baden goes to the great galleries with a pallette & proceeds to copy the old masters & listens to the disgusted comments of the people.

The wretched continental lamp, which you must wind up, like a clock & which is full of mysteries & <all>always goes out when you meddle with it.

I did not dare to do it, lest I make my cold better.

St Luke was one of the old Masters—the earliest & not the best.

Roba di Roma. Rome seems to be a great fair of shams, humbugs, & frauds. Religion is its commerce & its wealth, like <cowdung>dung in the Black Forest. The Bambino.
Read the chapter "Christmas"—& think of this Bambino rot existing in 19th century.[27]

The eternal repetition of Virgin & Child affect me at last much as an eternity of Washingtons Crossing the Delaware by an infinitude of Artists would. View from down the river; from up the river; cross-ways; at sunrise, sunset, after dark, in the rain, front view, hind view, &c &c, but the main feature always the same—W. standing

---

[27] In the chapter titled "Christmas Holidays" in *Roba di Roma,* 7th ed. (London: Chapman and Hall, 1876), William Wetmore Story describes the Bambino which Clemens would later see in the church of Santa Maria di Ara Coeli in Rome:

> The Santissimo Bambino is a wooden image, carved, as the legend goes, from a tree on the Mount of Olives, by a Franciscan pilgrim, and painted by St. Luke while the pilgrim slept. The carving of this figure gives us by no means a high notion of the skill of the Pilgrim as a sculptor, and the painting is on a par with the carving. But whatever be its merit as a work of art, the Bambino is, according to the popular belief, invested with wonderful powers in curing the sick; and his practice is as lucrative as any physician's in Rome. . . . certain it is that a cure not unfrequently follows upon his visit; but as the regular physicians always cease their attendance upon his entrance, and blood-letting and calomel are consequently intermitted, perhaps the cure is not so miraculous as it might at first seem. (p. 81)

the bow of the boat with his eagle eye on the distant shore, & another person poling ice.

The soft, mellow colors seem to please so many—I simply think the people in these pictures are too much tanned.

Roba di Roma—A rich discourse upon Beans[28]—under the head of "Games."

Italian cigars with straws in them. "Virginias."

"All the languages I know, I can write. I do not consider that I know a language when I can only speak & read it."—Père Jacopo.[29]

Hall of Mars, Pitti Palace—No. 92, Titian, "Portrait of a man"—½ length, dressed in black<,> robe, a trifle of lace at neck & wrists, short brown hair, thin, handsome, manly features, full of character & firmness; blue eyes, oval face, thin <unpretentious m> hair making a<n> fence around <the>upper lip & chin.—& along his jaw—full of a most noble dignity.—chain large links, falling on breast—This person is so *human*—you recognize in him at once the very highest type of man—he is a person who commands instantly your respect & your homage—& lord, how sappy & gushy & chuckleheaded & theatrical the <saints> surrounding saints & angels & Holy Families of the other old Masters do look in his august company!

---

28 "I cannot conscientiously omit to state to all my Roman friends who draw auguries and numbers for the lottery from dreams, that a possible reason why they are so often deceived in their divinations may be found in the fact that they are too much given to the eating of beans. Apollonius Dyscolus, whose testimony on this subject can scarcely be impeached, declares solemnly that beans hinder the mind from the reception of true dreams, and rather open the way to those which are lying and false. And Diogenes Laertius, in his 'Life of Pythagoras,' says that this philosopher strictly prohibited his disciples from the use of beans for various very singular reasons. Cicero also declares that they prevent 'that tranquillity of mind which is necessary in investigating truth.' And Aristotle, Pliny, and Dioscorides, agree that 'whoever wishes to divine the future should strictly abstain from beans.' Plutarch goes further, and says that the 'head of polypi,' as well as leeks, are also to be avoided" (Story, *Roba di Roma*, p. 144).

29 Actually Padre Giacomo Issaverdenz of the Armenian monastery on San Lazzaro (see notes 12 and 17).

What a stomach-ache St Peter has got, just above him, & how poorly he bears it; how sappy Mary Magdalen over in the corner, looks, with her novel in one hand & a skull in the other—& how you wish she would trade off those non-essentials for a blanket <shirt>.[30]

The way those saints used to go around was scandalous.

Hall of Apollo—Murillo, 40, V & child. Most beautiful—the colors & the draperies are surpassingly soft & rich & beautiful—so were those in del Sarto's (58) Des from the Cross until <w>I saw this.[31] Two men were making fair copies of this Murillo, but their glare & gaudiness <were> only made the soft richness of the original the more apparent & the more eloquent & fascinating.

Comes of judicious retouching

I knew that other was a del Sarto because I recognized in one of visiting women the same party who is the Madonna in the Holy Family which we bought.

The lovely & marvelous mosaic tables scattered so freely through these halls interrupt my investigations.

1st Hall (Venus) has not got anything among its great names but a marine view by Rosa & a Landscape by Rubens. The Marriage of St Catherine, by Titian[32] will not bear comparison with the most careless works of the sign<s>-painters of Arkansas.—either in the matters of color, imagination, fearful perspective, or absence of the ridiculous.

Went to <Belli>Belle Arti to see David—found him in a board closet 50 ft high,[33] after a long hunt through uninteresting acres of

---

[30] Clemens' references are to Titian's "Portrait of Ippolito Riminaldi" (also known as "The Man with Blue Eyes," "The Englishman," and "The Duke of Norfolk"), to Carlo Dolci's "Saint Peter Weeping," and to "Saint Mary Magdalen" by Lodovico Cardi da Cigoli, in the Pitti Palace. In notes about paintings, Clemens sometimes included their gallery numbers.

[31] "Madonna with Child" by Bartolomé Murillo; "Descent from the Cross" by Andrea del Sarto.

[32] "Betrothal of St. Catherine" by the School of Titian. Clemens here takes up the comparison of artistry and Arkansas sign painting begun in Notebook 16.

[33] By 1879 Michelangelo's "David" had been "placed under a glass building

picturesque. An official showed the way, & as I did not give him ¾ of a cent he didn't seem to like it.

When the Italians paint the sale of the Savior for 30 pieces of silver, <they ought to> one would think instinct would force them to insert an intermediary chap striking Judas for a pour-boire for having "assisted" at the trade. Or when Elias starts up in the chariot of fire, a "hooker" standing abject, with hat in hand, expecting a <5-centime> 2-centime piece for having closed the chariot door, for him.

(Say I *saw* such pictures & recognized their truth. Describe them seriously & with feeling like hair trunk[34]—say they are in the studio of a rising young Italian painter named so & so—the only Italian who is now anything more than a copyist.

Picture dealer passed a counterfeit 50^{c} piece on Mrs. Ch—& tried to make her believe she bought 2 pictures instead of one—dramatic scene.—

Another scoundrel swindled Rosa.

It is like old times to look in the local Italian guide-books & find the Savior naively referred to as "J. C."[35]

Young good looking left-handed girl painting a very small & very pretty copy of Raphael's Chair Madonna & Child—the other artists —the he-ones fooled away a good of their time (& hers) talking with her.

Strangers, guide book in hand, go up CLOSE & look over artist's shoulders—infernal impertinence. They also plant themselves directly in front of other strangers who are looking at pictures. I have learned

---

covered with a dome" in the Second Court of the Accademia di Belle Arti in Florence (Baedeker's *Northern Italy*, p. 391).

[34] An early draft of Clemens' *Tramp Abroad* discourse on the "immortal Hair Trunk" appears in Notebook 16, pp. 206–207.

[35] Here and in his autobiography (*MTA*, 2:276–282), Clemens recalls the irreverence of Wales McCormick, a fellow apprentice in the Hannibal *Courier* printshop, who, when reproached for abbreviating the Saviour's name to "J. C.," retaliated by expanding it to "Jesus H. Christ."

a good dodge from Ch which I played to-day—stepped directly in front of my annoyer, & he left.

Those galleries are mighty in extent—& the bridge gallery over the Arno, connecting the 2 palaces is a wonderful thing, so long, so crooked & so finely adorned with paintings, sketches & beautiful & wonderful Gobelins. See little Guide to Florence.

Send to Chatto for Roba di & Benvenuto.
Make extract about God the Father & the diamond, &c.[36]

<Su>*Bay*—When the waiter brought my breakfast this morning, I spoke to him in Italian.
Mama.—What did you say?
B—I said "<Parlez> Polly-<vou>voo <francay>fransay."
M—What does it mean?
B—I don't know. What does it mean, S?
Susie—It means "Polly wants a cracker."

Oct 27 Uffizzi Gallery, Sunday (free day,)
What a shamed look people have who go along with a guide—they nod annoyedly at every statement he makes, & they scarcely look at the object he points at; often not at all; neither look they to one side or the other, or at anybody; they seem to have but one desire: to get through with this painful<l> trial & go free again<,>.

No. 1205 <#8> —8 fellows with bows, & dressed in the gaudiest costumes of the 13th C (½ <leg> leg one color, other half another —tights<)> clear to waist) have got Sebastian up a tree & practising on him, with the Deity & a company of angels just above on a cloud for audience.[37] [#]

---

[36] No evidence survives of Clemens' using Cellini's account of the creation of his famous masterpiece: a large gold button made for the vestments of Pope Clement VII which displayed "God the Father sitting in a sort of a free, easy attitude" above a magnificent diamond supported from below by the upraised arms of three boys and surrounded by "several figures of boys placed amongst other glittering jewels" (*Memoirs of Benvenuto Cellini*, trans. Roscoe, p. 104).

[37] "Martyrdom of St. Sebastian" by Girolamo Genga.

1155 (Tuscan School) by by Bronzino Angiola, a baby son of Cosmo I[38]—very much the best baby I have seen in these acres of pictures. This is a *real* child, with fat face without having an apple in each cheek, has a <w>most silly, winning, chuckleheaded childlike gleeful smile, 2 little teeth just showing in lower jaw—oh, he is perfect! with his well fed body & his uncomfortable little bird grasped in his chubby hand. If he were a Jesus in a Holy Family every woman would want to bite him, & that picture would be the most famous in all the world. Where did they get all those <scrawny sick> unchildlike infants one finds in the <holy>Holy Families?

Ask the money-value of some of the most celebrated pictures.

Tuesday, Oct. 28—From Florence to Rome[39]—8 hrs—arr. 4.30 PM.

Oct. 29—It is the most ridiculous spectacle to see a Virgin or a copper Apostle stuck on top of every stately monument of the grand old "pagan" days of Rome.

The Immaculate Conception has ceased to be a wearying & worrisome question—it is decided by an Ecumenical Council once & for all & everybody is at rest on that subject & there's a monument erected with a boiler-iron Virgin on top of it to commemorate the event.[40] Now these E. Councils are valuable beyond expression or conception. There are several similarly <knotte>knotty questions that need settlement—& like the conception business they can be settled by no tribunal *but* an E.C. for no other is competent. <T>Let us have an E C called, to decide once & forever upon the following questions—who it was that struck Billy Patterson,[41] &c &c.

---

[38] Bronzino's "Portrait of Prince Don Garzia."

[39] The Clemens family took rooms in the Hotel d'Allemagne where they stayed until 11 November. Clemens claimed to realize a substantial saving over the other first-class hotels near the Piazza di Spagna (see pp. 242–243 for his comparison of rates).

[40] The Column of the Immacolata surmounted by a bronze statue of the Virgin Mary was erected in 1857 by Pius IX in the Piazza di Spagna to commemorate the establishment of the dogma of the Immaculate Conception. The column itself was ancient and had been unearthed in 1778.

[41] A "Letter From Billy Patterson Himself," alluding to "a vilent blo reseaved

The next most offensive thing is the staring white dry-goods-box new houses that are springing up here & there in harsh & hideous contrast with the rich old colors & crumbling stateliness about them.

Bought about a peck of wonderfully big & luscious grapes for 2.50 f. (50 cents)

At the fruit shop a man flew at a meek fellow with a basket on his arm—shook fist in his face, jawing in a loud & furious voice—flew at some paper, rattled it—danced around frantic & raging—the meek man could not get in a word—but we have found that in Italy this does not mean bloodshed, so the young lady went in & calmly laid in our grape supplies in the midst of it all without discomposure or apprehension. If they had been Irish there would have been material for the undertaker in ¾ of a minute.

"I have expectorated in this beer." "Ich auch."[42]

Joe would say to the sweet young girl of 14 at Baden, "Now fire up!" to see her blush so prettily.

Oct. 29—Visited the Church of St Peter's & the Pantheon. Bay & the mottled cat & little gray.

Oct. 30.—Sistine Chapel, Raphael's Stanza & *Loggie*—2 pictures by the wonderful modern Raphael who died in his 28th year[43] [#]

---

long sense by some anonymus person," is included in William T. Porter's collection, *The Big Bear of Arkansas and Other Sketches* (Philadelphia: T. B. Peterson and Brothers, 1843).

[42] "With infinite difficulty," Clemens translated the following story from a Mannheim newspaper: "A thirsty man called for beer. Just as the foaming mug was placed before him, some one sent in for him. The place was crowded.—Could he trust his beer there? A bright idea flashes through his brain. He writes on a card, 'I have expectorated in this beer'—fastens the card to the mug & retires with triumph in his eye to see what is wanted. He returns presently & finds his card reversed & this written on it: *'Ich auch,'* (I also!)" (SLC to William A. Seaver, 28 June 1878).

[43] Clemens' reference may be to the figures of Justitia and Fides in the Sala of Constantine of Raphael's Vatican Stanze. These were the only subjects in this final chamber of the Stanze which Raphael painted before his death in his thirty-eighth year, leaving the unfinished work to be completed by his students.

25 court yards in the Vatican.

Cardinals have simply a touch of red—say a mere binding—& a bishop the same in purple—they no longer use the gorgeous robes, servants & gilded coaches—all plain black & utterly simple—mourning for lost temporal power, the guide thought.

They started to erect a monument to the Infallibility edict—& as usual they dug up a pagan column to roost an apostle on, but the annexation came & they quit.[44]

That hateful Beatrice<,> Cenci, the ugliest creation of human ingenuity, stares up at us from the picture-shop window opposite.[45]

The two cherubs of Raphael <i>are the next most worn out & exasperating.

I actually saw a man lazily *sweeping* a corridor of the Coliseum! What a mighty job!

Tomb of Virgin—How she would draw in N.Y.

Oct. 31—Keep the letters received from Will Sage & Joe to-day & do a chapter on this most scoundrelly & infernal custom house system.[46] [#]

---

[44] On 18 July 1870, in a context of political challenges to the church's temporal power, particularly from the popular movement for Italian unification, Pope Pius IX secured from a Vatican Council acceptance of the controversial doctrine of papal infallibility. Just two months later, on 20 September, after the pope had rejected King Victor Emmanuel's requests that he make Rome the capital of a unified Italy and yield its government to the Italian throne, the king's forces easily captured the city. An October plebiscite and a royal decree affirmed the annexation and officially terminated the pope's temporal authority.

[45] Clemens saw numerous copies of this famous portrait—said to have been painted the night before its subject's execution—before he saw the original on 3 November (see p. 240). Among his working notes for *A Tramp Abroad* is the comment: "Beatrice Cenci, the disagreeable creature, is everywhere, with her head in her flour sack."

[46] Clemens' exasperation was in response to a 14 October letter Twichell had received from William H. Sage and forwarded to Rome. Sage reported that in order to get "two Boxes of Clocks" through customs he had to pay eighty dollars and "was obliged to give a bond for $100—to produce, *within three months*, a new

Not a picture in St Peters w^h is not mosaic.

Went down stairs into a depression beautifully walled in colored marbles with designs in Florentine mosaic fashion—custodian opened an ornate golden door & held in a taper in a hole & showed me a gold box, pretty ornamental, made by Benvenuto containing a piece of true cross. Over it was a very ancient box (the coffin in which St Peter had originaly been buried (it had been sawed to fit over & accommodate itself to the arched doorway. *Under* the true cross <[-]>box was the top of the present coffin in which Peter is. We paid the old man 5 cents (25^cta) apiece & he was entirely satisfied. As an investment St Charles Borromeo is superior to Peter—it costs 5 f to see him.

I supposed they would charge me 10 f to see St Peter.

Castellani[47] to-day showed us a bracelet took a man 16 monts to engrave. allowed us to walk off with jewelry worth 1500 f & never even asked our names or hotel—insisted on our taking it home & examining it at our leisure—Said "To-morrow is a festa—no shops open—bring it back Saturday—no hurry."

Italians & Swiss seem to trust to the honesty strangers readily. We have noticed this very often. [#]

---

invoice from the parties Clemens bought the clocks of, certified to before an U.S. Consul; & Clemens own oath, also before an U.S. Consul." On 3 November, Clemens informed Twichell:

> I am disgusted with myself for having put all that work & vexation upon you & Will Sage, but you know we couldn't foresee it. . . . the thing that mainly hurts *me* is, that after I had fortified you and those boxes with a written oath sworn in the presence of the Holy Trinity, my country should deem that group not august enough without the addition of a U. S. Consul. I am sensitive about these things. However, it is all right, now. I have sent to Geneva for the clockmaker's certificate, & as soon as I get to Munich, (Nov. 18 or 20,) I shall swear once more by the Trinity, adding the Fourth Personage, & immediately transmit the document, thus sublimely freighted, to Will Sage.—And at the same time I will thank Sage for taking the trouble this matter has cost him. (Yale)

[47] Augusto Castellani was a celebrated Roman goldsmith and dealer in antiquities. Livy's list of purchases indicates that Clemens purchased a "Necklace made by Castellani after the antique" for $165 and "a Japanesse coin set by Castelani" which cost $30 (see p. 254).

Oct 31—Evening—Wood fire in Mr. Chamberlain's room—C sketched, Mrs. C darned, Livy & Clara crotched, & I read Julius Caesar aloud.

<O> Nov. 1—Great festa-day—shops all closed. Attended High Mass in a chapel of St Peters. Heaps of people of all ages sexes & professions kissing (& scrubbing) St Peter Jupiter's toe.[48] He looks like a black negro & has short crisp hair.

Table d'hote in your own parlor for 5 f each, in Florence & leave out soup & the entreé. <Table> In Rome all the <di> courses, but a franc extra to each person.

Soup—fish—roast—entree,—a vegetable—then roast chicken with a salad—dessert—fruit.

This is the usual Italian table d'hote—8 courses.

In the Transfiguration,[49] the boy<, & the woman near him are> has monstrous arms, packed full of great muscles,<—>as if they were stuffed with kidneys. That boy ought to be able to throw a bull over his shoulder. The woman near him is similarly muscled, & could toss/pitch the bull back.

The people in the ugly & exasperating cartoons of Raphael are similarly muscled. A begging cripple there <is a> is a Hercules.

Michelangelo has built his people in the Sistine Chapel in the same way.

Castellani showed us a small but most exquisitely & elaborately engraved bracelet which it took one of his men 16 months to engrave. <or>—it was *raised work.* [#]

---

[48] "On the rt. side of the nave, placed against the last pier, is the well-known bronze *Statue of St. Peter,* on a marble chair, with the foot extended. On entering the basilica, devotees kiss the toe of this foot, pressing their forehead against it after each salutation. . . . The rude execution of the figure conclusively proves that it is not a work of classical times; and it seems much more likely to belong to the early ages of Christianity, when sculpture, like architecture, was copied from heathen models" (*A Handbook of Rome and Its Environs,* 13th ed. [London: John Murray, 1881], p. 201).

[49] Raphael's "Transfiguration" in the Vatican Pinacoteca. Mark Twain took a consistently satirical stance toward the liberties taken by the Old Masters to achieve ideal form (see pp. 241–242).

Nov. 3

Went to Barberini Palace to-day & saw my pet detestation, Beatrice Cenci, by Guido.

It is not anything in the picture itself, but the awful <tired>tiresomeness of the 100,00,0,00,0,0,0 copies that overlay the earth & confront one even under the poles. "Grandfather's Clock" & "The Sweet By & By" were sweet & pretty & were able to move one —at first; but when everybody & every*thing* persecuted you with them you learned to loathe the originals as well as the copies.

Leo XIII's permanent Colfaxian smile.[50]

Pretend that our hazing is much more manly than college dueling.

"Picture/Vision of St John on Patterson's Island"—Wakeman.[51]

Temple of Marie d'Medici—Materia Medica.

Graham on the ass plunges through the crowds & over the bridge & into the grocery, scattering the customers—& holding out his hand blandly says "A pound of sugar if you please."—The astounded shopman wonders if this is a duke or a bandit that comes in such marvelous style—hands him the sugar—he drives the spurs in, flies across again to the boys & says "Here's your sugar, now where's your whisky & lemons?"

One madonna in a church is well enough—that is what they were painted for—but when you come to take them out of their proper

---

[50] Leo XIII acceded to the papacy in March 1878 and many portraits of him—with his characteristic close-mouthed smile—were reproduced in newspapers and magazines. Clemens was evidently reminded of Schuyler ("Smiler") Colfax' similar expression.

[51] In chapter 16 of *A Tramp Abroad,* Mark Twain noted the peculiar "inscription upon a certain picture in Rome,—to wit: 'Revelations-View. St. John in Patterson's Island.'" The mistranslation of Patmos as Patterson recalled Captain Edgar Wakeman's comical misconstructions of the Bible. Clemens probably considered using it in the story about Wakeman's adventures in heaven which had long engaged him and which, he told Howells on 30 January 1879, he meant to "take up" after completing his travel book (*MTHL,* p. 250). On page 275 of this notebook, Clemens recorded a potential incident for his Wakeman tale.

place & jam a thousand of them together in a gallery, they become tiresom & in the last degree absurd. (Vedder.)[52]

The loose girl said, "You're trying to get St Peter's ham"—St P. has a ham which is to be given to the chaste man or woman in the world—he still has the ham.

I understand good art to be, that way of representing a thing on canvass w^h shall be farthest from resembling anything <on ear>in heaven or on earth or in the waters under the earth.

In good art, a <corr> correct complexion is the color of a lobster, or of a <s>bleached tripe or of a chimney sweep—there are no intermediates or modifications.

In the room with Raphael's Transfiguration is a vast picture of the Last Sacrament of St. Jerome.[53] The withered old man has two distinct knee-joints on the same leg, 4 inches apart. The boy in the Transfig has an arm like Vulcan.

Now that new painter in the vestibule where the umbrellas are, makes men & drapery, complexions, forms & things absolutely as they *are*. They are flesh colored people, of mere ordinary strength.

Over door in next room to umbrella stand—a room full of wretched modern daubs (except the one by Frascatti(?) of hanging the monks.[54] This brutal superstition squeezes & robs the poor of the whole world, on millions annually—& nothing is said—but when <it> a priest gives 15 cents worth of bread to the starving they

---

[52] Elihu Vedder, an American artist who maintained a studio in Rome which Clemens visited on several occasions (see p. 242 and note 60).

[53] Clemens saw the "Communion of St. Jerome" by Domenico Zampieri (Il Domenichino)—"generally considered second only to the Transfiguration of Raphael, opposite to which it stands" (Murray's *Rome and Its Environs,* p. 314)—in the Vatican Pinacoteca.

[54] Clemens is referring to the collection of modern works on the upper floor of the Vatican Palace. Murray's guidebook describes the collection as "two rooms hung with modern pictures of sacred subjects, and especially martyrdoms, of which some by [Cesare] Fracassini, although talented in other respects, are most ghastly compositions" (Murray's *Rome and Its Environs,* p. 304). Cesare Fracassini's painting depicts the nineteen "Martyrs of Gorkum," hanged by the Calvinists in Holland in 1572.

make a five thousand dollar picture of it & put a dab of white wash around his head to stand for a "glory." He turns a <c>fat face full of sappy ecstacy heavenward, with a tuppenny loaf in each hand while the citizens kneel with outstretched hands, perfectly overcome by the Church astounding charity—& the remark in his face is, "O God, suffer this 15 cents to be remembered to the credit of the Church through all Eternity, for Thou knowest we could have allowed this scum to starve, <to>—& spent the money for a

Or, O, <God>Father, sustain me, for this is a new office."

Perhaps it was permissable for the Middle Age artists to represent an earthly scene & a heavenly scene with from 2 to ten feet of cloud between—or a cloud or procession of down-coming cherubs who are life size at a point where they should be no bigger than mosquitoes —but these modern artists are keeping up this absurdity.

New American artist goes to little Italian squalid village, sits down to sketch on a 3-legged camp stool—peasant brings oxen & addresses him—American abuses & curses him & finally appeals to his comrade (Vedder) "What is this devil saying & why does the scoundrel bring his oxen here?"

"He was saying that he has brought his oxen, at the usual hour & place to water them, but if they are an interruption he will take them away & wait—& he added that your camp chair seems uncomfortable & he will go to his house & bring you a chair if you desire it.

Vedder made friends with a whole village with a handful of sugar plums & they manned the walls to Godspeed him when he went.

Nov. 5—Spent all day in Vedder's lofty studio & the evening with him & another artist spining <cards>yarns & drinking beer in a quiet saloon.

Big row in the street but no bloodshed.

Mrs. Ch. crossed the street to look at rooms in the Hotel de Londres, (3^{d} floor): Prices<:> <pr day> per day:
2 rooms & a parlor .... fr. 45.
Service. (for 2 persons) 3

2 dinners served in room, ... 20
Service extra 1
Baths 5
Wood 5

Both these hotels are on Piazza di Spagna.

Here in the Albergo d'Allemagne we pay per day: (on 2^{d} floor):

3 rooms & a parlor 22
Service (for 6 persons) 3
3 dinners in our parlor 18
Baths 3
Wood 3.50

Our daily expense averages 83 francs, against 70 at the New York <hotel>Hotel in Florence. Can's average Venice (say 60 f per day) but then we hardly ever ate in the house.

Speaking of the Hair Trunk, refer to Titian or some other old master with the remark "He is well enough, but he scatters too much."

Now & then make a learned quotation from the Choctaw without translating it, to take off Story & others who pepper us with Italian & Latin without translating.[55]

Nov. 6—Visited the Catacombs. One mummy (shapeless) & one slender young girl's long hair & decaying bones—both in stone coffins & both between 15 & 1600 years old.

---

[55] Mark Twain used this idea in chapter 30 of *A Tramp Abroad* in which he reproduced Harris' "Official Report of a Visit to the Furka Region." The report was studded with words in obscure languages (Fiji, Eskimo, Zulu, Choctaw)—all Mark Twain's inventions—which Harris included to "adorn" his page. The report is followed by Mark Twain's scathing remarks on authors who "pepper" their books with "insolent odds and ends smouched from half a dozen learned tongues whose *a-b abs* they don't even know." On 15 April 1879, apparently while at work on chapter 30, Clemens would write in a similar vein to Howells regarding Bret Harte: "He rings in *Strasse* when street would answer every purpose, and *Bahnhof* when it carries no sharper significance to the reader than 'station' would; he peppers in his seven little French words (you can find them in all his sketches, for he learned them in California 14 years ago)" (*MTHL*, p. 261).

Conversation between 2 women "I've got part of an Early Christian"

"Can you spare me a piece," &c

"Will ask Castellani what he will charge to set an Early <E>Christian"

Church erected over the spot where St Sebastian was martyred[56]

Tomb of <E>Cecilia Metella.

Small church where the Savior appeared to St Peter <&[tu]> who was leaving Rome—turned him back & he was martyred.

See death of Aexander VI in vol 3 of <history>History of Popes. 1st chap Appen[57]

The greatest charm we have found in Europe, by all odds, are the open fire places in Florence & Rome.

Wm Blake, poet & painter.[58]

<To>Turganieff's Visions.[59]

Sorceress, standing with moon behind her £40.

Medusa, with green snake, $250.

Tall poppy woman, $1000.

---

[56] The entrance to the catacombs visited by Clemens is located in the basilica of San Sebastiano on the Appian Way. The tomb of Caecilia Metella and the small church of Domine quo vadis, mentioned in the next two entries, are situated nearby.

[57] The reference is to Leopold von Ranke, *The History of the Popes*, trans. Mrs. E. Foster, 3 vols. (London: Henry G. Bohn, 1876). Section one of the appendix in the third volume contains an account of the intrigue whereby Pope Alexander VI died of the poisoned sweetmeat intended for a cardinal whose property the pope planned to seize. In return for a bribe of 10,000 ducats of gold, the pope's carver revealed how the poison was to be administered, whereupon the cardinal contrived to serve the poisoned confection to the pontiff. Clemens owned a copy of von Ranke's work (*A1911*, item 397).

[58] A note made toward the end of the notebook (p. 281) suggests that Clemens was reading Alexander Gilchrist's *Life of William Blake*, originally published in 1863.

[59] Turgenev's story "Visions—A Phantasy," also noted on page 247, had been published in the July 1872 *Galaxy*. Clemens would meet Turgenev in Paris in May 1879 (see Notebook 18, pp. 308, 309).

Poetess casting away MSS—$100.
Small mermaid captured by fisherman, $150.
Birth of Spring—$1000.[60]

Avoid the Golden Dove in Verona. The best is a German name beginning with (H?)

Die Goldener Sonne, Innsbruck is *good*.

Go to the Due Torre in Verona.

Leave Rome 10.50,
arr. Florence, 6.50.
Leave " 7.50 am
arrive Padua 3.50 p.m.

Get to Venice about 6 PM. Leave V. in the afternoon by boat. Leave Trieste next morning at 6.45 a.m. reach Vienna 9 p.m. Or stop <at> at Gratz at 4 pm; next day <at 11 am & reach> at 11 a.m. & reach Vienna at 6 p.m. Leave Vienna at 7.20 am, reach Salzburg 2.47 pm <Le>Lv. Salzburg 3. pm & reach 6.30, Central station, Munich.

The night was cold, there were no blankets, but God be thanked I had a couple of fifty-frank (or 500?) notes, so I got between them & slept comfortably.

Sketch of the Interrupter.
do do Susan.

Text "Now we've bought that ugly <R>yellow Roman scarf, whatever shall we do with it?" "Give it to Susan." Poor Susan! There are many Susans in this world. Get her address & view her collection. [#]

---

[60] A list of the paintings by Elihu Vedder which the Clemenses considered purchasing. After a visit to Vedder, Livy informed her mother: "Yesterday morning we went to Mr Vedder's studio, he certainly has immense genius, he had such a large amount of pictures and such an infinate variety of subjects—we did enjoy the morning so very much—I felt as if I could spend two thousand dollars there if I had it to spend" (10 November 1878, MTM). Before leaving Rome, the Clemenses bought Vedder's "Head of Medusa" for $250.

A horror—the anticipation of the journey from Rome to Munich.

<O>
Oct. 8—the Bambino at Ara Coeli.[61]

Colossal feet (marble) at Capitol,[62] <s>indicating a statue 54 ft high<t>—the rest probably burned for lime in the Middle Ages.

The original brazen wolf mentioned by (the Eternal Pliny?) as having been struck by lightning. Its hind leg is torn.

It is always safe to say a thing was mentioned by Pliny. He was the father of reporters—he mentioned everything.

Suit of clothes in Heidelberg, $18; in Milan (slop-shop) $9; in Rome (fancy tailor, $25 & $38—both very fine—the latter half dress. At home, $65 to 90.

Cook's agent gone off junketing—<cant> for a few days (Oct 9) —can't get any tickets.

<P>Fresco in Vatican Library of raising the Obelisk in front of St. Peters in 16th cent. Pope Sixtus V (?) said if the crowd uttered a cry it would be on pain of death. A sailor in the foreground saw the ropes fraying & sang <">Out, "Throw water on the ropes!" which was done—but he was arrested & led away to be condemned by the Pope, who set him free & granted him a request. He asked for the monopoly of making the straw things used on Palm Sunday—granted, & his descendants enjoy it yet.[63] [#]

---

[61] Here and below (p. 246.13), Clemens inadvertently dated his entry October instead of November. He was now viewing the Bambino he had read about in William W. Story's *Roba di Roma* (see note 27).

[62] In the court of the Palace of the Conservators are found "the feet and hand of 2 colossal statues, in marble, interesting fragments; they are supposed to have belonged to the statue raised on the Capitoline by Lucullus to Apollo, and to a second effigy of the same god, 30 cubits high." Continuing the tour through the palace, Clemens next notes the "Wolf of the Capitol" in the Hall of Bronzes of the New Capitoline Museum, believed by some authorities to be the wolf "mentioned by Cicero, both in the Catiline orations and in his poem on the Consulate, as a small gilt figure of Romulus sucking the teat of a wolf which was struck with lightning" (Murray's *Rome and Its Environs*, pp. 358, 364).

[63] This anecdote appears in both Murray's and Baedeker's guidebooks.

Saw the Vatican Bible, but could not read it.[64]

Visited Catacombs & got part of an Early Christian, intending to have him set in a pin—but he crumbled to fine dust in a few hours.

Story of the man or party lost in the Catacombs because the guide died of apoplexy—wandered many days & several hundred miles & came out of a hole in the campagna 15 or 20 m from Rome.—

These passages are 50 to 70 ft under ground, & generally not wide enough for 2 persons to walk abreast—very crooked & dark.—

Two corpses of 4th century in glass coffins. One a young girl, bones white & crumbled, but with long hair—the other wrapped like a mummy & shapeless.

No smoke without some fir[e]
Take care of the pounds
Penny wise & p foolish
You can't make

"Life & Habit" by Butler.[65]

"Visions, a <F>Phantasy," by Tourganieff—in the Galaxy.

Stop at Botzen after leaving Padua.

<W>Had several books—wrote Quanto firmato in one—train always left before I could find it[66]

Of all countries America is the most comfortable.

Palace cars, with water, food, liquors, fruit, attendance, water

---

64 "The celebrated *Codex Vaticanus* or *Bible of the early part of the 4th century,* in Greek, containing the oldest of the Septuagint versions of the Scriptures, and the first Greek one of the New Testament" (Murray's *Rome and Its Environs,* p. 352).

65 Samuel Butler's attack on Darwinian theory was published in 1878.

66 Clemens' attempt at *Quánto fermato?* is recorded so illegibly as to suggest he wrote it on a moving train. He had originally noted the phrase as "Quanto fia*ma*to? How long do we stop?" on the flyleaf of his copy of Suetonius' *The Lives of the Twelve Caesars* (trans. Alexander Thomson, revised by T. Forester [London: George Bell and Sons, 1876]). Still another version of the phrase appears on the back endpaper of this notebook (p. 282).

closets, space to walk about, heating apparatus, & a *seat secured beforehand* of wh no one can deprive you. Plenty of trains, reasonably fast, on great trunk lines, *sleeping cars*—& not obliged to start or arrive at horrid hours of the night.

Clean closets in hotels—a thing rare in Germany, Switzerland & Italy.

They *serve* a dinner better in Europe; & outside the great cities they cook it infinitely better than in our minor cities.

Their servants are politer & far more efficient than ours.

They do not know what coffee *is*—nor cream—the <same> former is the case with all <our> European hotels, without exception—but in ours one finds something which at least vaguely *resembles* cream.

Poor lamps—no gas.[67]

Nov. 11—Returned to Florence from Rome.

Took quarters again in N.Y. Hotel & saw splendid torchlight processions crossing the 2 Arno bridges to see the King, at the Pitti palace.

Saw the Smiths & Launt Thompson.[68]

Nov. 13.—Left at 10.45 for Bologna, & tried being courier for the first time.[69] Gave the omnibus driver a franc <&> <[-]> to bring

---

[67] Later in this notebook and again in Notebook 18 Clemens continued the comparison of European and American comforts. He developed a lengthy discussion of the subject, but eventually omitted it from chapter 18 of A *Tramp Abroad*.

[68] Edward M. Smith was the United States consul at Mannheim. The Clemenses had met Smith and his wife during their stay in Heidelberg. The Smiths were currently on a vacation in Italy and upon its conclusion traveled to Munich to spend the Christmas holidays with the Clemens family. Launt Thompson was an American sculptor living in Florence who had called on the Clemenses there in October; Clemens recorded his address on the back endpaper of this notebook.

[69] Clemens' determination to be his own courier arose out of his disgust with the performance of George Burk, the courier whom he had discharged in Venice (see Notebook 16, p. 197). On 17 November he wrote to Howells describing the arduous journey to Munich:

> We arrived here night before last, pretty well fagged: an 8-hour pull from Rome to Florence; a rest there of a day & two nights; then 5½ hours to Bologna;

the conductor of the train out there to me. Made him understand I wanted a 1st cl. compartment to myself & had 5 in my party—for future cash. All right. Omnibus driver also took my luggage into waiting room & brought the ticket-taker to me. Gave *him* 2 francs & he flew around, with many winks & brought the conductor again & both winked that all was right. The former took my 5 through tickets & sent a fat porter to get them visèd—then allowed our tribe to pass through to the train without <sho> tickets. Found the <guard> conductor right outside on the qui vive, who helped me carry my luggage, put us into a compartment & fastened the door. Presently the fat porter came with my tickets & I gave *him* a franc. The conductor allowed nobody to look in, all the way,—not even a ticket-puncher. Had a mighty smooth trip of it. Gave the conductor 5 francs. Total cost, 9 francs. If I had had a courier, I would have had to take care of him, pay him 10 f. wages & 12 f fare.

From Rome to Florence I paid the conductor 5 f & had heaps of attention. Once he kept the train waiting a minute for me at a station.

We find in Florence, Rome, Bologna, &c, the cloak of 30 years ago —reaching below knee, & a corner cast over left shoulder.

Arrived at Bologna at 4.15 pm, stopped at Hotel Brun, & left on 14th for Trento, via<,> Modena, Mantua & Verona, at 12.25 pm.

Am a shining success as a courier, so far, by the use of francs.

Have learned how to handle the railway guide intelligently & with confidence. [#]

---

one night's rest; then from noon to 10.30 pm carried us to Trent, in the Austrian Tyrol, where the confounded hotel had not received our message, & so at that miserable hour, in that snowy region, the tribe had to shiver together in fireless rooms while beds were prepared & warmed; then up at 6 in the morning & a noble view of snow-peaks glittering in the rich light of a full moon while the hotel-devils lazily deranged a breakfast for us in the dreary gloom of blinking candles; then a solid 12-hour pull through the loveliest snow-ranges & snow-draped forests—& at 7 pm we hauled up, in drizzle & fog at the domicil which had been engaged for us ten months before. (*MTHL*, pp. 239–240)

The roast duck was delicious—you couldn't tell it from a piece of angel.

"Now I *tell* you!" "Now look *here!*"—Our <darling> Roman guide.

I judge that the first thing a <new> statue dug up in the Campagna does is to go shopping & buy <the> an offensive & obscene fig leaf.

Imagine him cheapening the article at the counter & contriving how to take the innocence out of his nakedness & make the latter most offensive & conspicuous. Animals with fig leaf under tail.

Make some pictures after the old masters of St Mark's & apply for membership in the Artist's Club as an Amateur. Call them "Works."

There are artists & artists—I am one of the latter kind.

If <hereafter,> hereafter, the mightier the Empire the grander the ruler, the the Devil and the Deity will contrast like the Czar of Russia & the Governor of Rhode Island.

1878

Nov. 30 (Munich) Farewell blow-out at the Artist's Club (American) to Toby Rosenthal, who sails for California.[70] Horstmann, (consul,) read a mighty bright speech, <the> with new & exceedingly funny feature of dropping frequenty into rhyming doggerel—every line rhyming with *tall* & every <verse> stanza ending with "Toby Rosenthal." I mean to borrow & use that happy idea someday.[71]

The oil travesty of Rosenthal's Fright in a Boarding School was a charming bit of broad burlesque. There were some realistic features

---

[70] By 1878 the number of American art students in Munich had grown to over a hundred. Toby Rosenthal, whose "Girls' Boarding-School Alarmed" is described by Clemens in the next entry, was primarily a genre and portrait painter whose training, before going to Munich, had been in San Francisco during the early 1860s.

[71] Clemens' feeble attempt at American Consul G. Henry Horstmann's style of "rhyming doggerel" appears on page 278.

in it—a piece of real bread glued to the canvas, real stockings on a real clothes line, &c.

How to kill your man in a duel.—Take a rusty old gun which <has apparently> you think is not loaded—let it go off accidentally in the direction of the other man with the distinct intion & desire to miss him. This will fetch him, sure.

Lamentations of Cantharides.
Two catastrophes & four Pterodactyls to the measure.

The old masters never dreamed of women as beautiful as those of Kaulbach and Liezen-Mayer.[72]

Make no mention *ever* of suspecting Haggerty.[73]—at end of book or elsewhere. His palpable stealings are sufficient. But when he tries to play "30 days hath Sept" on me for an <original & not only> impromptu, I rebel & then he praises me for knowing literature so widely it would be a dangerous experiment for anybody to try to <fo>deceive me. This flattery pleases me to death.

I detailed a detachment from my corps of observers to go & watch the habits of the people of Venice & report. They mix their reports & apply Chamonix or some other place to Venice. [#]

---

[72] Wilhelm von Kaulbach, director of the Munich Academy until his death in 1874, was regarded as one of the greatest contemporary German artists. He and Alexander Liezen-Mayer were painters of historical subjects and portraits. Kaulbach had also illustrated a number of literary works, among them Goethe's *Faust*. Mrs. Jervis Langdon's Christmas gift to Clara Spaulding, purchased by Livy in Munich, was "a photograph of one of Kaulbach cartoons of the Goethe Gallery it looks almost exactly like a pencil sketch—it makes a picture as large as your Sistine Madonna" (OLC to Mrs. Langdon, 7 December 1878, MTM). According to Livy's list of purchases this was "Kaulbach's Margaret going to church" which cost nine dollars.

[73] Shortly after his arrival in Munich, Clemens rented a "workroom" about a mile from the family's lodgings (see p. 282) where he began writing his travel book. Instructions such as this one appear with increasing frequency through the rest of this notebook and are often concerned with the development of Harris—here called Haggerty (see p. 259)—the fictional travel companion largely based on Twichell.

A Munich friend tells me a pathetic story of <a>the destruction of a lunatic who was ruined by vast speculations. He was always getting new maggots into his head—at last imagined he had bought a comet & it cost so much to keep it—could get no insurance on it &c.

Dec. 18.

"On some of the large ocean steamers the old-fashioned settees have been replaced by revolving arm chairs—Harper's Weekly gravely makes this preposterous statement. Who could stay in one in a storm?

My historical biographical game.[74] Ages & deaths of great men—dates of great events.

My note-book invention.[75]

Abreisen—
<reisee>reiste ....ab.[76]

All humanitarians raised a shout of pride & gratitude when der Schweiz annulled the death penalty. All the world has watched the experiment—one-half wanting it to fail, the other half to succeed. So when it was lately announced that the new Legislature comes

---

[74] A number of schemes for memorizing historical dates preoccupied Clemens until 1883 when he developed an outdoor history game, using pegs along his driveway to mark the reigns of the English kings. He also developed a version of the game using a cribbage board, but advised Howells in a letter on 22 August 1883: "If you haven't ever tried to invent an indoor historical game, *don't*. I've got the thing at last so it will work, I guess, but I don't want any more tasks of that kind" (*MTHL*, p. 439). The game, with a printed board, was eventually patented in 1885, although it was never offered for sale.

[75] Clemens' notebook with tabbed pages, which he was now using, is discussed in Notebook 15, note 45.

[76] "The Germans have another kind of parenthesis, which they make by splitting a verb in two and putting half of it at the beginning of an exciting chapter and the *other half* at the end of it. Can any one conceive of anything more confusing than that? These things are called 'separable verbs.' The German grammar is blistered all over with separable verbs; and the wider the two portions of one of them are spread apart, the better the author of the crime is pleased with his performance. A favorite one is *reiste ab*,—which means, *departed*" (*A Tramp Abroad*, Appendix D, "The Awful German Language").

together instructed to re-instate the death penalty,[77] the one party in the world will shout "We told you so! <without this>with no penalty but imprisonment, homicide increases!" No, just wait a moment. The canny Switzer explains his action—thus: Homicide has *not* increased, but is *cheaper to hang a criminal than feed him in these hard times.*

Go 'way with your monarchical statesmanship—only Republics have real statesmanship.

German language is a dozen fragments of words flung into an octagonal cylinder—take a good look at them before you begin to turn the machine, for you will never see them in their simplicity again—never never any more. TURN!—<up flashes> up spring your fragmental elements with Ver's & Be's & Ge's & Er's & lein's & schen's & gung's & heits & keits & zu's & a thousand other flashing & blazing prefixes, affixes & interjections broidered <in>on them or hung to them.—Turn & turn! the combinations will be infinite, & bewilwilderingly enchanting & magnificent—but *these*, also, like the original fragments you shall see but once, then lose them forever. The patterns in this linguistic kaleidoscope are never repeated.

After this German chapter[78] I will now put the remnants of my mind on other things.

Mutineer Adams's Bible, rebound.[79] [#]

---

[77] Switzerland had abolished capital punishment in 1874. In March of 1879, after an initial rejection, the National Council approved a bill allowing the individual cantons to restore the death penalty.

[78] Clemens' discussion of the German language, described to Howells as encompassing "two or three chapters" (30 January 1879, *MTHL*, p. 249), eventually became Appendix D of *A Tramp Abroad*.

[79] It was at about this time that Mark Twain was writing "The Great Revolution in Pitcairn" as a chapter for *A Tramp Abroad*. In that piece Mark Twain noted that John Adams, the longest surviving mutineer from HMS *Bounty*, "turned Christian and teacher" and became "governor and patriarch" of Pitcairn's Island, but he did not mention this Bible and a prayer-book which were Adams' only means of teaching the islanders to read. "The Great Revolution in Pitcairn" was omitted from *A Tramp Abroad* and was published instead in the March 1879 *Atlantic Monthly*.

The government's placard of law for the ordering of dwellings.

The blank which I filled out for the information of the police.[80]

Almost the interestingest thing in Rome was Castellani's old & reproductions of old, goldsmith's work,—a mighty curious museum. Got a great Jap gold coin set there for 150 fr gold.

I think the higher classes of Europe do not know what comfortable dwellings are. The lower class here & the governing class in America are about on a par.

A paragraph about the woman, fishwife Englishwoman, &c, to show the effect of idiotic genders.

With prayer & a dictionary one may wade through most any sentence

Munich, Dec. 20—To-day, by telegraph in the papers, comes the sad news of Bayard Taylor's death yesterday afternoon in Berlin, from Dropsy.

I wrote him 3 or 4 days ago congratulating him on his recovery. He was a very lovable man.[81]

Annoyance of a good example.

Der Mann ass, trank dann wieder<,> dazwischen, und ass dann wieder.—Briefer, The man ate & drank alternately. [#]

---

[80] Visitors to Munich as well as citizens were required to fill out extensive identification forms. This entry is a note for a chapter omitted from *A Tramp Abroad* in which, weighing the merit of the law requiring police registration, Mark Twain concluded: "Plainly it was simply a law against possible rascals, & we are all possible rascals; any law against possible rascals is likely to be a good law . . . a law for the obstruction of proposed rascality is better than a law for the punishment of accomplished rascality, therefore this was doubtless one of the best sort of laws."

[81] Taylor, then on his way to Berlin as United States minister to Germany, had sailed with the Clemens party in April 1878. On 14 December Clemens wrote to him: "We three folks are most heartily sorry to know that you have been ill at all, but as heartily glad to hear that you are coming happily out of it; & we are venturing to hope that by this time you are wholly restored." Clemens remarked in closing: "We are going to try to run over to Berlin in the spring" (Cornell University Library, Ithaca, N.Y.).

Munich, Dec 21—On scores of street corners, in the snow, are groves of <x>Xmas trees for sale—and the toy & other shops are crowded and driving a tremendous trade.

Reading German books shows in what a narrow groove of vocabulary authors travel—they use the same words all the time. Read a book of one & you can fluently read his others. Take up a book by *another* author & you've got to go for the dictionary—his vocabulary is all different.

A little learning makes the whole world kin—or makes us wondrous kind.[82]

Dickens, Howitt Burns!
Jesus " "

Erlkönig.

<Last> 2 line of last stanza—
Er hält in den Armen das ächzende Kind.[83]

Christmas in Germany.
In the week, a prodigious audience of parents & children in the big theatre. <The> A curtain hung across middle of stage from right to left. In front, a lady <&>with a lot of eager children around her on stools. She asks what familiar story from folk lore she shall read. They clap their eager hands & name a story. She reads, they applaud, or laugh or are grieved—all well drilled & natural—& as she finishes the curtain slowly rises & displays in tableau an exquisite picture from the story. The children in the audience get so carried away that they applaud, shout, cry & make comments aloud. My agent saw this.

Sent agent to visit great picture or mountain, but it was a failure because he had not had time to "put up his emotions". How? "Not

---

82 Clemens is employing the pun from the first line spoken by Hamlet and echoing the famous line from Pope as well as David Garrick's "A fellow-feeling makes one wondrous kind." The first part of this aphorism appears as the epigraph to Appendix D of *A Tramp Abroad,* where it is given a spurious biblical authority and identified as "Proverbs xxxii, 7."

83 Clemens slightly misquotes this line from Goethe's poem.

time, before starting, to select the emotions." How? Hadn't read up; didn't know what style of emotions the best authorities required <there> for that subject.

Mention fires caused by mill-dust in Heilbronn trip.

How to harness a horse.

Frog on man's raft.

Jan. 4/79—Went to Grossen Kirschof & saw 15 or 20 dead.[84]

Smith[85] took me to 3 antiquarian shops—my pet detestation—& examined 3 brass beer mugs (crippled) & 5 ancient & hideously ugly & elaborately figured & ornamented (noseless) Nuremberg earthen ware ones. Price, brass, from 250 to 650 M each—the others from 550 to 1100 marks each. I wouldn't have such rubbish in the house. I do hate this antiquarian rot, sham, humbug; cannot keep my temper in such a place—& *never* voluntarily enter one.

At the Art Union pretty modern brass mugs for 78 M three times as pretty (& uncrippled) as the ancient ones.

Hirschhorn church—hole under edge of old stone alter—make legend, hide hero in there & to sleep & feed—could come out at night & play ghost—no dogs allowed, <[-]> else they would discover him.[86]

<Too pompous> Too much pomp for the occasion—Overdone—like <killing> hunting <cr> clams with a harpoon. game too small for the weapon. [#]

---

[84] The vast Southern Cemetery of Munich had a Leichenhaus or "deadhouse, where the bodies of all the persons who die are exposed to public view" (*A Handbook for Travellers in Southern Germany* [London: John Murray, 1871], p. 81).

[85] Edward M. Smith, United States consul at Mannheim (see note 68).

[86] Mark Twain abandoned the idea noted here, contenting himself in chapter 18 of *A Tramp Abroad* with the observation: "In the chancel was a twisted stone column, and the captain told us a legend about it . . . but I do not repeat his tale because there was nothing plausible about it except that the Hero wrenched this column into its present screw-shape with his hands,—just one single wrench."

That statue which was just projecting from the Marble at the place where we saw the David in Florence.[87]

Make some copies of well known pictures because an artist w^{d} have charged me too much.

Speech at art club—Draw cork, blank in lottery, <check,> all sorts of things—took me so long to learn to draw a check so they would honor it I got discouraged & quit. <White> Boot blacking clear up to whitewashing (water color) Throw in some oil (Pennsylvania coal oil)

Said he was member of Society for Extension (Extinction—Prevention) of Art.

Say, I made a little sketch, &c.
Washington Xing Delaware

[87] Michelangelo's unfinished statue of Saint Matthew in the Accademia di Belle Arti.

Heidelberg Castle.

Grand Canal, Venice
San Marco & Square

Miss Benfey said:

Niemann "is our best singer but he has no voice" (Trouble with all of 'em here—ie is a splendid actor & once *had* a noble voice.[88]

"Very great singer,—one of our greatest—but hasn't any voice these last 10 yrs—but he *must* sing once a year to keep his pension" "He not sing, he cry"[89] [#]

---

[88] Livy described Miss Benfey, her German teacher, in a letter to her mother on 16 February: "She is very fond of literature, a translator and some thing of a poetess–I enjoy my lessons with her very much" (MTM). Albert Niemann, German opera and court singer, was in the production of *Lohengrin* which the Clemenses attended in May 1878. Clemens drafted a disparaging account of that performance in Notebook 14 (pp. 92–94).

[89] Clemens copied the foregoing sentence from Notebook 14 (p. 74) and then used it in chapter 10 of *A Tramp Abroad*. In the book he tells how he was persuaded by a friend to attend the opera in Hanover to hear a celebrated tenor. The singer "was an astonishing disappointment." "If he had been behind a screen I should have supposed they were performing a surgical operation on him. I looked at my friend,–to my great surprise he seemed intoxicated with pleasure, his eyes were dancing with eager delight. . . . I said:–'I don't mean the least harm, but really, now, do you think he can sing?' 'Him? *No! Gott im Himmel, aber,* how he

Harris said he was a member of the Society for the Extension of Art—or the Prevention of Art, I forget which. Extinction of Art.

One often finds notes in his book which no longer convey a meaning—they were texts, but you forget what you were going to say under them—like Blanche found D's hair in the butter &c.[90]

Change Haggerty to Harris.

Germans comb their hair in public & have some other little peculiarities, but they are not the way of the whole nation—but there is one thing which you can charge the entire nation with—ask *any* German a question & you will get a civil answer.

Clara & the three men who helped her get into a closed store & buy a pencil

How the Virgin's Tomb would draw in N.Y!

Why do chimney sweeps wear stove pipe or chimney pot hats?

After the naked model was dressed (in Rome) she showed a touch of nature—for as she climbed down from the platform she exposed too much of her <stocking> ancle & rectified it.[91] [#]

---

has been able to sing twenty-five years ago?' [Then pensively.] '*Ach*, no, *now* he not sing any more, he only cry. When he think he sing . . he only make like a cat which is unwell.' "

[90] By this time Clemens had begun to gather material from his previous notebooks for possible use in *A Tramp Abroad*. His puzzlement here is over a note made in May 1878 "to be inserted in a German novel with pathetic effect" (see Notebook 14, p. 85).

[91] This incident occurred at the end of an art lesson described in a chapter on Rome eventually omitted from *A Tramp Abroad*:

> All the pupils faced toward a platform four feet high, & on this stood a naked girl of twenty-five in a very strong glare of light. . . . This girl was on the platform an hour & a half. The instant her time was up she was set free. . . . And now followed a curious touch of nature—the most curious I think I ever observed. Being dressed, the girl sat down on the front edge of the platform, & started to slide to the floor, but noticing that this process was exposing her leg halfway to the knee, her modesty was shocked & she drew back in quite apparent confusion & retired by the other side of the platform, where there was a step! . . . So it is not nakedness that gives the sense of immodesty, the modifying the nakedness is what does it. (DV 4, MTP)

Jan. 13—79—Munich

<G>

Card sent up, "G. Stitt Anthony" & I expected a fraud.—Not disappointed.

He had been to the Consul. The consulates are constantly infested with tramps bearing naturalization or other evidences of citizenship —wanting help. Mention the number wh have been victimized

This one "came over to Paris to get something to do (he was 23 or 4 & a chemist!—a good place to come,—to a country where chemists are educated to their business & do not pick it up in village drug-shops.)—Got nothing to do—Went with a man to Vienna "as a kind of a *cur*rier"—they both fell sick & the man didn't need him any longer since he didn't know the German language (valuable currier, truly)—lay in hospital—consul wouldn't help him, didn't seem to care tuppence what became of him (these tramps seem to think it a consul's business to take care of them)—the artists & students from America clubbed together & sent him as far as Munich—now he was "what 's called busted, you know." Rich uncle in Phila—blackguarded the consul—"Mighty curious man, anyway—didn't seem to care whether &c &c—gave me some names— Americans—they might help me, maybe—couldn't find any—don't live at the addresses—don't believe there are any such people—gave me your name &c.[92] [#]

---

[92] This unwelcome visit, along with a clipping from the Hartford *Daily Courant* of 4 January describing the recent experiment in Hartford of jailing tramps who refused the city's offer of work, prompted the writing, on February 2, 1879, of a long unmailed letter to the editor of the *Courant* in which Mark Twain described with approval the solution instituted in Munich:

> You are aware that when our ingenious Massachusetts nobleman, Count Rumford, took high office here under the Bavarian crown in the last quarter of the last century, he found Bavaria just what Hartford has been for years,—the Tramp's paradise. Bavaria swarmed with beggars. Count Rumford applied the same remedy which you have lately found so effectual: he provided work for all comers, & then shut square down on all forms of begging. His system has remained in force here ever since. Therefore, for three-quarters of a century Bavaria has had the reputation of being the only country in Europe uncursed by tramps. I have lived here two months & a half. . . . I have been visited at my lodgings only twice by tramps,—one an American, the other a Frenchman.

Count Rumford is discussed in note 97.

Jan. 14—Went to the Opera of Die Weisse Frau. This is not noise, but music.[93]

Describe a little German newspaper in detail.

How would a triple diary do?—a man of 70 (complaining) a <youn>youth of 19 (gushing) & a boy of 10, matter-of-fact.[94]

Shan't I keep a diary instead of reading German?

Keep watching to see one of these wood-splitters <slice> chop off his finger—but am always disappointed. Saw one fellow who *had* done it, some time or other.—Watched men on Hamburg & Heidelberg steeples, to see them fall, but they didn't

Lass mich gebrennt sein.

Drat die Kirchen Glöcken!

Sah ein Weib ein Pferd tragend.[95]

Try Hamlet again, & make free with Shakspere—let Hamlet & everybody else talk with the fellow & wish he was in Hölle as the G's say.[96]

Mention the great American Count Rumford.[97] [#]

---

93 Clemens saw a Munich production of François Adrien Boieldieu's *La dame blanche,* a popular light opera whose libretto was based on Sir Walter Scott's novels *The Monastery* and *Guy Mannering.*

94 An extension of the idea recorded by Clemens in Notebook 15 (pp. 118, 124) of attributing notebook entries, his own as well as invented ones, to diaries kept by foreigners twenty and sixty years old.

95 Clemens' three German entries may be rendered: *Let me be burned; Drat the church bells!; I saw a horse carrying a woman.*

96 Mark Twain first conceived of writing a burlesque of *Hamlet* from the point of view of an added character, Hamlet's country cousin, in the early 1870s, but was dissatisfied with this attempt and destroyed it. The idea continued to fascinate him, however, and he was to take it up again in August 1881. The surviving portion of this second version is in *Mark Twain's Satires & Burlesques,* ed. Franklin R. Rogers (Berkeley and Los Angeles: University of California Press, 1967).

97 Benjamin Thompson was an expatriate American scientist, inventor, and administrator who entered the service of the elector of Bavaria in 1784. As minister of war, minister of police, and chamberlain, he reorganized the army, intro-

Scrhreiben das Französche Trauerspiel wo Jederman hat ---- mit Jederman.[98]

26 columns of Über in the dictionary—

A column of an average city paper in America contains from 1800 to 2500 words. Can't average the whole contents because so many sizes; but Times usually contains about 200,000 words in its reading matter. Have counted the reading matter in Münchener Tages-Anzeiger of Jan 25, '79 & find it is just 1900 words altogether. The paper is a little <quarto> 8-page thing, each the size of a foolscap page; 2 columns on a page. <T>One-quarter of 1st page is taken up with the papers head—this makes it top-heavy. Table of contents: A little sermon of 4 lines, urging mankind to remember that although they are pilgrims here below, they are yet heirs of heaven. Then <come> under the head of "Telegrams," <15> 14⅔ lines from Berlin, <16>15 from Vienna, & & <2½>2⅝ lines from Kalkutta. Then comes the heading "News of the Day." Prince Leopold is going on a visit to Vienna, 6 lines; Prince Arnulph is coming back from Russia, 2 lines; the Landtag will meet at 10 to-day & consider an election-law, 3 lines & one word over; a city government item, 5½ lines; prices of tickets to the Charity Ball, 23 lines (as there are only 80 lines on the 1st page, this ball occupies nearly a third of the page—think of taking up a third of a newspaper page with ticket-prices for a ball); Going to be a Wagner concert in Frankfurt with an orchestra of 108 instruments! oh horror!—7½ lines—<[thi]>Such are contents of 1st page. "Death-Notices," 10 lines, & an opera-criticism, 53 lines, make just half of 2d page.—The other half is occupied with "General News," 2 items, one about a row between the <Z>Czar & his eldest son, of 21½ lines, & an item about the atrocious destruction of a peasant child, 41 lines—& that page is completed, & so is *all* of the reading matter—the rest is advertisements. <4> There are 180 lines of

---

duced reforms in agriculture, suppressed mendicancy by establishing workshops for vagabonds and the unemployed, set up a system of relief for those unable to work, and designed the English Garden in Munich. In 1791 he was made a count of the Holy Roman Empire.

[98] *Write the French tragedy where Everyman has ---- with Everyman.*

reading matter—so the child-murder takes up <in the nei> between ¼ & <⅓> ⅕ of the entire reading matter of the paper. To show how little this is I will translate this ¼ or ⅕ of this German paper & show how little it is.[99]

Jan 25—The mother of the King, 55 or 60, was out walking in the street, to-day, a maid of honor walking beside her, the two talking zealously, 2 vast footmen in blue liveries walking behind them—everybody, who came along, either in the street or on the sidewalk, took off hats & bowed—little boys, gentlemen, ladies, soldiers, cabmen —everybody—& the queen saw every bow & bowed in return, & still kept her end of the conversation.

Have learned to remove my hat when a funeral passes

The noises at Heilbronn.[100]

How *does* a burglar ever get <up> around without waking the block? I sh^{d} make a poor burglar. Burglars entered house of a friend of mine, in stockings, & utterly stripped it—his bedroom & all, & woke nobody—he, wife, a large stock of children & some servants.

But I got up to hunt for the bedclothes, in Heilbronn, then thought I would get a drink of water—got lost in that huge room & wandered about swearing—now & then touching something which <all>always made 35 or 36 times more noise than it would have done in the daytime—then I stopped & held my breath & gritted my teeth muffled, & commented internally—Joe would nestle, & when he got into the swing of his snore again, I would creep on again,

---

[99] The information in this entry appears in "German Journals," Appendix F of *A Tramp Abroad.*

[100] This long entry—one of the few instances in Europe when Clemens used his pocket notebook for extended composition—is based on his hunt for a lost sock in his Munich bedroom. In a letter to Twichell on 26 January 1879, the morning after his nocturnal adventure, he explained that afterward: "I went in the parlor and lit the lamp, and gradually the fury subsided and the ridiculous features of the thing began to suggest themselves. So I lay on the sofa, with note-book and pencil, and transferred the adventure to our big room in the hotel at Heilbronn, and got it on paper a good deal to my satisfaction" (*MTL*, p. 348). After revision and expansion this passage became chapter 13 of *A Tramp Abroad.*

lifting foot with awful caution in 1½ minutes, then the other—creak! creak!—with hands abroad & fingers spread to balance myself—always knocking something down—where in the very nation is that <p>water-pitcher—confronted my dim white self in the mirror—took my breath—stood there & cursed the figure—what made me the maddest was that the windows had changed away from where they were when I went to bed—I <could> could tell by where I had started from & the direction I had come, that they were in an entirely different part of the room from where they belonged—so it was no use trying to use them as a guide. Did not seem to be much furniture when I went to bed—place was full of it, now—especially chairs—chairs everywhere—somebody must have moved in since I went to bed—& I never could seem to glance on one, but always struck it full & square with my shin—I wished I had been brought up differently & had learned to swear when I was young—<s>found a wall & started to feel along it to find a door & use it as a base of <oper> departure on new explorations, knocked down a picture—Joe nestled, I waited—remembered there were doors on <3> 3 sides of the room, so I should not know where I was when I found one—gave up the doors. Got an idea—knew there was only 1 centre table, that vast round massive thing—would use it as a base—had brought up against it several times already—would hunt it up again—got down on my hands & knees—could go quicker & with more confidence, & not knock things off of places—went along very nicely—found the table—with my head—rubbed the bruise a while, then started again using table as base—found a chair—then the wall, then another chair, then a sofa, then an alpenstock, but did not know whose, then another sofa—this confused me—had thought there was only one sofa—hunted up the table, <&>got another bump & started fresh—found some more chairs—it occurred to me that the table was round & was therefore useless as a base to aim from—sat down on floor & took a rest—moved once more among the wilderness of chairs—wandered off into unfamiliar regions, rose up to try erectness again & knocked a candlestick off mantel piece—grabbed at it in the dark & knocked off water pitcher with tremendous crash

—found you at last, knew I must be close upon you—Joe shouted, Murder! thieves!—I'm drowned! <Is it *you*? said I.> It's *you*, is it? said I, in a rage, What in the nation are you doing here?—why in thunder don't you stay where you belong? what are you lying around all over the house for in this idiotic way? "*I*? what are *you* doing here?—I'm in my bed—& I'm *not* lying all over the house—<if> what the mischief do you want here? I wanted some water. Well I didnt—but I seem to have got a whole Heidelberg Tun of it. That crash had roused the house. The consul pranced in, in his long night shirt, bearing a candle—young Smith after him with a candle—a procession swept in at another door with candles & lanterns—the landlord & two German guests in the night shirts, & a chambermaid in hers. I said to the latter, Get a blanket, or some more clothes. She said I am not cold. Cold— —the thermometer stood at 116. Now I looked around—I was at Joe's bed, ¾ of a mile from my own. Joe was half drowned—the wreck of the pitcher was distributed over the bed & the floor, with the candle & candlestick. There was only one sofa—it was against the wall. There was only one chair where a body could get at it—I had been revolving around it like a planet & colliding with it like a comet for an hour. I explained what <I>had been my purpose, to the consul & the procession. The consul said You don't mean to say you wanted *more* water? Joe said, Next time you want a drink, <don't mind disturbing me> do tie yourself to your bed with something, & revolve around your own region. Then we all retired once more.

Enter myself on police records as "Philologist & artist."[101]

Munich church manners are as bad as their theatre manners are good.

The everlasting saluting of the military is very fascinating—keep

---

[101] In his 26 January letter to Twichell, Clemens noted that two of his purposes in coming to Europe were "to study *Art*" and "to acquire a critical knowledge of the German language. My MS already shows that the two . . . objects are accomplished. It shows that I am moving about as an Artist and a Philologist, and unaware that there is any immodesty in assuming these titles" (*MTL*, p. 350).

hand up some time—present arms, (without any) when a general passes.

Royal house up yonder—the two sentinels always salute passing officers.

Bavarians are great big splendid looking men.

The army still wear the helmet instituted by our countryman Count Rumford.

Saw them bring the colors.

Music at the Loggia—the finest military music ever heard.

Drink barrels of Appolonaris water—it costs almost nothing—the physicians recommend it—it is mighty refreshing, whereas the local water is utterly flat tasteless & unrefreshing. Is said to be full of fever.

Either America is the healthiest of countries or our statistics are loosely made—but if they were, would they keep up such a neat & hardly varying average?

I have been carefully/strictly <b>reared, but if it hadn't been so dark & solemn & awful there, I do belive I should have said something then which not be into a S. S. book without injuring the sale of it. (Umbrella falls twice).[102]

Pitcairn procession <set> steps out of line to look at itself.

Stopped at Mezzofanti mainly to see (Bologna) because he knew 111 languages, <(or 5> but he was dead.[103] Wrote to Max Müller & Prof Whitney & J H Trumbull or Phitological matters but only got offensive answers or silence.[104]

---

[102] This paragraph was an addition to Clemens' account of his night crawl in the Munich bedroom and it appears in chapter 13 of *A Tramp Abroad* with only minor alteration. "S. S." is an abbreviation for "Sunday School."

[103] Giuseppe Mezzofanti (d. 1849), cardinal and linguist at the University of Bologna was reputed to have spoken fifty-eight languages. The confused word order in this sentence is the result of Clemens' haste in writing the entry.

[104] Mark Twain's working notes for *A Tramp Abroad* indicate he planned a burlesque correspondence with several great philologists who were to respond either with silence or abuse to his theories on German grammar.

Tried to join several learned bodies & Art (National) Societies, but Jealousy kept me out.

Sent Ill of Heidel^{g} Castle to Paris Exposition—vile notices in L'Art—probably simply because I was a foreigner. Meissonier sold a picture for <5>375,000 fr—I offered mine for less money—larger pictures, too—no sale.

Tell about water color artist who began with fences

Tell about my game of dates

Dew on the raft

List of chambermaids duties.

Mention dew, & how early men & women appeared in fields, what they were doing (especially women)—then say, as our teacher said, they work 18 & 20 hours—then fetch in chambermaid.

Death Notice.

Looked in Eng side for Florin: definition, *Gulden*. Looked in <D>German side for Gulden: def. *Florin*. Now I will state, once for all, that a Mark is a quarter.

Germans themselves say the motto should be Billig & Schlect.

Dienstman—excellent institution. Pay him 3 or 5 or 12½ cents (50 pf) for errand.

"Nasty—Bloody"[105]
"Funny"—Beastly
Damp fog (d—d fog)
We teach children not to say nasty.

Faggot gatherers keep forests clean & beautiful—the *absence of*

---

[105] Notes for a chapter comparing English and American usages "which was crowded out of *A Tramp Abroad*" and later published under the title "Concerning the American Language" in *The Stolen White Elephant* (1882). Additional specimens are recorded in Notebook 16, page 175 and Notebook 18, pages 295 through 297.

underbrush here makes all difference in world. Think there's none in Egland either.

Small chapter from my little (& big) German dictionary (assuefaction)

ut de Dör. Sprung up.

Taylor said the plates of Faust cost him (I think) $1000, & he had received $1005—clearing $5 for 2 yrs work.[106]

He said "Go among people—<if you> it is a duty, if you don't enjoy it—don't keep to yourself.

How patiently he groaned under the lecture-burden in the cars—that <it>is, the long trips, & having to go back over the same piece of road.

He repeated the Lorelei & a German sang it on ship—first time I heard it.

Asked him to help me—gave him one line of a poem—he reflected a few moments—asked for time—then rattled it all off.

Repeated a lot of poetry found of <rh>sound, but wholly meaningless—never tripped.

Repeated Russian poetry & showed how musical it was.

Repeated Arabic, Hungarian, & other poetry.

Spoke of the bear & the great Panjandrum &c—it was made on a wager—Sheridan was to learn it in 15 m—he did it—<Tay in>Taylor in 7.

Was his memory indestructible? *No*—he practiced it as an acrobat does his muscle & a swordsman—said he kept it in tasks purposely to keep it in good condition.

He repeated a short poem which he had read somewhere as a boy—this was the first time he had thought of it in 30 years.

Educated Germans in smoking cabin <dis> submitted disputes to him about German words & accepted his decisions.

---

[106] Bayard Taylor's two-volume translation of Goethe's *Faust*, published in 1871, was much praised by his contemporaries but is today generally considered mediocre. The following reminiscences are perhaps notes for a memorial essay about Taylor who had recently died (see p. 254).

Comforted little Spanish boy in his own tongue—no, wanted to,—little chap wouldn't allow it.

<But> The sign to go below to Capt's room, with Halstead.[107]

Taylor was a good man—it shone forth all the time.

At our house once he told some more anecdotes about animals.

His death was sad, but let us believe it had its part to do in securing his perpetual fame.

Special Providences?

At that dinner piecing out with old stories—"An Andover student started to go to see his parents at New Haven &c—somebody sure to interrupt.

Jim Gillis & the plums.[108]

At that dinner of election I invented a new form of entertainment without intending it. Piecing out a forgotten story. with a remembered one. Somebody is sure to interrupt, "Do you know the story?—An Andover student started to go to New Haven &c."—

Triangular duels between Taylor Fitz James OBrien & R H Stoddard[109]

Mary M^c^Dowlin (Magda [#]

---

107 In an Autobiographical Dictation of 7 July 1908, Mark Twain recalled at length his experiences with Taylor and Murat Halstead, editor of the Cincinnati *Commercial*, aboard the *Holsatia* in April 1878 (see *MTE*, pp. 305–309).

108 Clemens was remembering an incident that occurred in 1865 during his three months' retreat in Jim Gillis' cabin on Jackass Hill; see Notebook 4, note 10, in volume 1.

109 Richard H. Stoddard recalled these informal poetry competitions in his "Reminiscences of Bayard Taylor" which appeared in the February 1879 *Atlantic Monthly*:

> We sat around a table, and whenever the whim seized us, which was often enough, we each wrote down themes on little pieces of paper, and putting them into a hat or a box we drew out one at random, and then scribbled away for dear life. We put no restriction upon ourselves: we could be grave, or gay, or idiotic even; but we must be rapid, for half the fun was in noting who first sang out, "Finished!" It was a neck-and-neck race between Bayard Taylor and Fitz James O'Brien, who divided the honors pretty equally, and whose verses, I am compelled to admit, were generally better than my own. (pp. 247–248)

Why is a man particularly & progressively reliable who never speaks the truth? Because he is a person who lies & re-lies & keeps on re-lying; & so the more he re-lies the more re-liable he <at last> becomes<.>, <at> at last, as a necessary consequence.

Entsprechen, Versohnen, &c—can't ever remember the meanings of these—some English words will never come to me—stimulate, clumsy, &c—have hardly ever written these words.

Lived with Disraeli to consult on public affairs <first time> second time I was in England—<four> twice as expensive as similar lodgings at home but not so many conveniences.[110]

Our $5000 have them.

Flat lodgings are *perfect* in Hd.

London great hotels pretty dark & dreary—Ordinary lodgings are unendurable—tried one for one night.

Had gas at Schloss in bedroom—only case I remember in Europe.

Veitch's Edinburgh

Imperial, Belfast

Good h in Dublin

More I think of it the more I think the mere ordinary mortal with income of 2 or 3000 has no idea of comfort in Europe.

New dwelling at Stratford

I can't exactly define what it is, but there is something very cheerless & depressing about the inside of Euro houses & English—outside is another matter—beautiful England.

Little bits of clams, raw

England gives us copyright in books, we give her copyright or rather absolute protection in plays.[111]

---

110 This peculiar joke, apparently drafted for a discussion of European accommodations, was not used in *A Tramp Abroad*.

111 Clemens was reading Arthur G. Sedgwick's "International Copyright by Judicial Decision" in the *Atlantic Monthly* for February 1879. Sedgwick discussed the superiority of judicially established "stage-right" to statutory copyright and noted that "perpetual and universal" protection against the unauthorized production

I won a suit on uncopyrighted matter by pleading my nom de plume as trade mark[112]

The Dienstman

He & hackman always touch hat to you. First thing they seem to learn with us is to forget their manners—this leaves their ignorance total.

The dark court in Munich houses

"Visitors" & "Servants" on door bells in London.

<R. G.> R G. White mentions "Please do not ring if no answer is required.[113]

English railway comfort.

Difficulty of finding the shop door in Munich—smallness of the shops.

Absurd English colors in dress—false lace.

In London & they send home your purchase before getting the money.

Never heard *real* military music till in Munich.

Germans take off hat to men.

In Switzerland the roar of the torrents tired the head like trains, & get up kind of unrefreshed.

Europe is the hungriest place in the world for an *American* to live

---

of plays—"restricted by the limits of no country, and impaired by no lapse of time" —had been initiated by English and perfected by American courts (pp. 217–230).

[112] In *Clemens* v. *Such*, the New York Supreme Court prohibited the defendant, Benjamin J. Such, from unauthorized publication of essays by Mark Twain. In *A Book for an Hour*, an 1873 advertising pamphlet, Such had published five essays by Mark Twain and one falsely attributed to him after receiving permission to publish a single piece. This was Mark Twain's only successful use of trademark as a deterrent against literary piracy.

[113] Except for the comment about English dress, the information in this entry is from Richard Grant White's article "London Streets" in the February 1879 *Atlantic Monthly*. Clemens' remark about Munich was probably stimulated by White's comment that in London: "I never had the least difficulty in finding any shop to which I wished to go, but once; and in that case the fault was my own" (p. 235).

in. The food is trifling in variety (at least the vegetables are,) & villainously cooked.

English toast! Execrable

" Muffins. good, but indigestible In Europe they don't give you hot bread.

OYSTERS.

Blue points

Ah for a hot biscuit—& coffee, *real* coffee, with *real* cream.—& *real* potatoes. Fried chicken, corn bread, *real* butter, *real* beefsteak, *good* roast beef with *taste* to it.

But the English have whitebait sole (shad)—German trout good, ours *not*. Catfish. Good English butter but poor coffee in hotels. Ah, & the turtle soup! English mutton *good*.

Now I don't know—had good bill of fare at Hotel Brittania, also Lake Como, Hotel New York, & Allemagne.—

My man in Milan who cut a peach in his claret at breakfast.

Pussy wants a Corner

I remember but two places where the food was perfection—Florence & Hamburg,—that is, where you dive into a dish with confidence, without caring to know the name of it.

The continental "breakfast"—honey & coffee—belly aches.

Biscuits & wheatbread prodded with a fork—bacon & greens—corn pone with chitlings hot eggs, bread.—breakfast bacon, corn-cake, —boiled corn—Butter milk. succotash Iced milk—Ice water. cabbage boiled with pork—pot liquor—corn-pone—buckwheat cakes—radishes —fried onions—celery lettuce—sweet potatoes—*mussels* in S.F. baked apples with cream—strawberries—roast turkey—oyster fried & scalloped & *roasted!!!* (Describe) & *steamed* in Wash^{n} The eternal sameness of a bill table d'hote.[114]

---

[114] A number of words and phrases in this paragraph have been crossed through, probably after use rather than for cancellation, since most of them appear, with revision, in the "bill of fare" Mark Twain included in chapter 49 of *A Tramp Abroad*.

In Germany, apples, peaches, cherries, strawberries, raspberries, cherries, pears, plums, broiled salmon—splendid trout from Wolfsbrunnen—Duck—

Canvas back duck—terrapin—perch in Baltimore. *Frogs.* "Light rolls"—*hot.*

Sturgeon, tom-cod & smelts (London & SF) Black bass in Missouri (catfish)

Hard boiled eggs & chickens in Palestine—raisins & figs in Smyrna —dates & pomegranates in Egypt.

Crabs, soft & hard, lobsters, & deviled, potato salad, celery salad, peas, baked & boiled beans, carrots, turnips, pumpkin, squash, lima beans, asparagus, Roquefort cheese, quail, partridge, squirrel, rabbit, coon, possum, rib of beef, shrimps.

(German sausage)

We have no turtle soup—but a sham.

Turtle steak.

Pine nuts.

Flying fish—S. Islands.

Baroness—God-dam is swearing in English—Baron—Yes, God dam, god-dam. (Baron prides himself on knowing this one English word.

German swearin

Jan. 23 Frank Bliss wrote to inquire what progress I am making in the book. *Of course* I sat down in Munich as soon as he took up his pen in New England—& by the time he <g>had got his brief inquiry on paper I was well under way with my long answer to it. Had not heard from him since last June.[115] [#]

---

[115] Clemens' reply to Bliss, inspired by "mental telegraphy" (see Notebook 14, note 101) and sent through Twichell, states: "I have torn up 400 pages of MS, but I've still got about 900 which need no tearing. They suit me very well. So the book is half finished. If anybody will tell me how long it will take me to write the other 900 in a way which shall satisfy me, I shall be under many obligations to him. I know *one* thing,—*I* shall fool away no time—*I* want to get through" (23 January 1879, *MTLP*, p. 110).

Chapter "Not to be read Aloud"—about German Water Closets.

Orion's 3 famous adventures—

1. Getting into bed between 2 old maids when he was 21.[116]
2. Calling on a young lady at 3. AM & being received by her father in long night shirt <& inv> entertained an hour in a freezing parlor by the old man, then invited to stop to breakfast.[117] 3. Taking bath in Hartford boarding house without locking door.[118]

Socratic catch:

You believe they have the best form of government in heaven that could be devised. Of course

Then of course you believe that the Lord & his Judiciary &c are elected by universal suffrage?

N-no. <no.> I don't.[119]

What are we as a nation? Snobs? Frauds?

Article on Lying.[120] [#]

---

116 Recounted at length in Mark Twain's Autobiographical Dictation of 28 March 1906 (*MTA*, 2:272–274).

117 This incident was not as cordial as the notebook entry suggests. In a section of his 28 March 1906 Autobiographical Dictation published in the *North American Review* of 18 January 1907, Mark Twain explained that Orion—oblivious to the old man's "expression of unwelcome which was so thick and so large that it extended all down his front to his instep and nearly obliterated the dressing-gown"—"talked and talked and went on talking—that old man looking at him vindictively and waiting for his chance. . . . At last Orion got up and made some remark to the effect that probably the young lady was busy and he would go now and call again. That was the old man's chance, and he said with fervency 'Why good land, aren't you going to stop to breakfast?' " (pp. 117–118).

118 A description of this bath may be found in Notebook 15, note 20.

119 Clemens' "catch" was prompted in part by "Limited Sovereignty in the United States," an unsigned article in the February 1879 *Atlantic Monthly* which examined defects in the American elective system and called for modifications of universal suffrage, including a reduction in the number of offices open to election. In Notebook 14 (p. 68) Clemens also commented on celestial government, in a note for "Captain Stormfield's Visit to Heaven."

120 "On the Decay of the Art of Lying" was first published in 1882 in *The Stolen White Elephant*.

Pontius Pilate, wandering around with heavy conscience, drowned himself in Lake Lucerne—hence Mt. Pilatus.

Going to Interlaken, we drove by the place where St Niklaus lived & died & performed that odd miracle.[121]

Write the history of two young men—one modest, diligent, temperate, possessed of all the virtues, even poverty—is allowed by the community to hoe his own row & die a pauper.

The other drinks, &c, & the community bands itself together to get situations for him—the prisoner's aid society looks out that he gets a place as soon as he is out of prison—the other young fellows girl marries the rascal because she thinks she can reform him—when he murders her the court is full of weepers at his trial, the women sing & pray with him in prison, besiege the governor for his pardon, & when he is hanged, they support him on the gallows, cry over him, clothe him in flowers &c. <He>His last words are,—"The successful life is the life of a rascal."

The other dying, says, "The honest life is the failure.[122]

Wakeman—You talk about happy creatures—did you ever notice a porpoise?—well there ain't anything in heaven here superior to that happiness.

---

[121] In chapter 31 of *A Tramp Abroad*, Mark Twain recounts the legends noted here. The "odd miracle" of Saint Nicholas, who became a hermit at the age of fifty, leaving his family of ten children, consisted of living solely on the bread and wine of communion which he took only once a month.

[122] Mark Twain's notebook entry may have been inspired by an undated newspaper clipping in Clemens' 1878/1879 scrapbook. After discussing a murderer who "died sermonizing and rejoicing on the scaffold" and noting that "the newspapers are overflowing with [his] sentimental and pious effusions," the clipping comments: "It strikes us that a little more penitence and humility on the part of these gallows saints, and a little less ostentatious assurance of a heavenly welcome would be more becoming and more in accordance with 'the eternal fitness of things.' " "Edward Mills and George Benton: A Tale" which emerged from these notes was published in the August 1880 *Atlantic Monthly*. Clemens had used variations on this theme for at least three earlier pieces: "Story of the Bad Little Boy," "Story of the Good Little Boy," and "Lionizing Murderers," all collected in *Mark Twain's Sketches, New and Old* (1875).

Put the Early Christian into the mouth of a poor fellow who is pathetic over his loss of it.

Mention the zither.

Describe <cou>France as a country of dates:[123] 16th May, 18th March, 2^{d} December, 18th Brumaire, <2^{d} of> 10th August, <& 5th (or 10th?)> 2^{d} Sept. (9th Thermidor) <(10 Aug> Write a bombastic & senseless paragraph ringing them in—or say it was a speech in Paris & they applauded to such an extent that I supposed it was only *figures* that delighted them, & therefore went wildly on, *inventing* dates, whereat the enthusiasm subsided. Or I heard another man stir them with dates, & judged 2 could play at that game, so sailed in.

"The men of the 18th March" & "the men of the 16th May" &c.

(Orator might say—

The man who causes 2 dates to grow in French history where only one date grew before, is his country's benefactor.

Playing 11½ at the Artist Club—paying for the cards by 1, 2, hup! 4, 5, <6>hup! 7, 8, <hup!!>hupp! 10, 11, <hup!!>hupp! <hup!!>hupp! 14, hup! 16, 17, hup! 19, 20, hup! 22, hup! hup! 25, 26, hup! 28 29, hup! hup! hup! hup! hup hup! hup! hup! hup! hup! 40.

One pfennig fine for an error or for mis-correcting anybody. Cards cost 30 pf. <or ther>

11½—ace is 1 or 11, as you choose—face cards are ½

Have 2 rich benevolent brothers attend the auction of a poor scholar's library in disguise, & <with> bidding with disguised voices, each, unknown to the other resolved to buy the library & secretly return it to the scholar. They run each other up to a tremendous figure, there is mighty excitement in the crowd, one bidder forgets for a moment & bids $50,000 in his natural voice.

---

123 The entries developing this idea were the basis for part of a chapter omitted from A *Tramp Abroad* and published under the title "Paris Notes" in *The Stolen White Elephant* (1882).

Tother says, "Aha! you're there, are you? Take the books, I know what you want to do with them!"[124]

Roman's time in the grave with corpse.[125]

Man sitting up with corpse in thunderstorm—in a vivid flash, the electricity-charged corpse rose to a sitting posture &—"& *what?*—what did it do?" "You d - - fool <[y]>do you suppose I waited to see?"

30th Jan, resignation of McMahon[126]—5th Jan Senatorial elections —5 Oct, elections for Deputies—the "July Monarchy" Louis Philippe's Govt or "Revolution of July" (1830)—"Revolution of February" (1848) (overthrow of L. Philippe)—<M> 16 May McMahon dismissed his Ministry against the will of the Chamber—"the 30th Jan avenges the 16th May"—18th March (What does it refer to?—must inquire)—18th Brumaire, Napoleon overthrows the Directory—2^{d} December is the "counterpart" of this.—10th Aug, Massacre of Swiss Guard—2^{d} Sept, massacre of Princess Lamballe

---

124 The story outlined here was included as Appendix E in *A Tramp Abroad* and may in part have been suggested by a newspaper clipping which Mark Twain dated "End of Feb. 1879." and pinned to the back endpaper of the notebook:

> Dr. William Dindorf, the well-known scholar, is forced by misfortune to part with his library, which will be sold by auction at Leipzig in two or three weeks. The catalogue contains 4,700 entries, of which the Greek dramatists form a large proportion, says the *Augsburger Allgemeine Zeitung*. Sophocles alone is represented by 116 works and 101 dissertations, Æschylus by 124 works and 165 tracts.

Five other clippings were also attached to the endpaper. Only one of these, a long extract from "The Growth of London" in the *Cornhill Magazine*, bears Mark Twain's annotation. After underlining some of the article's curious statistics—for example, "London has seven thousand miles of streets. . . . Its beershops and gin palaces . . . would stretch . . . a distance of sixty-two miles. . . . sixty miles of shops are open every Sunday"—Mark Twain wrote at the top of this clipping: "Observe the absurdity of these figures."

125 From Mark Twain's working notes: "Roman's adventure in grave with corpse.—very huge corpse—finally fell on him & kept there far into night."

126 Here Clemens adapted a current news item to his plan to "describe France as a country of dates" (p. 276): the resignation of Comte Marie Edmé Patrice Maurice de MacMahon as president of the Third Republic.

& other stacks of prisoners.—9th Thermidor, fall of Robespierre's power in the Convention.

There was a little clam,
& his given name was Sam
& he owned a Spanish ram
who was very fond of jam
which he swallowed just as ca'm
'zif he didn't care a cent
If a *nation* saw him cram
—for he <ha[te]d> <[--]>never was a sham
—& he wouldn't give a dram
for a man 'at couldn't slam
his hide outside a ham
but considered him a nam-
by-<p>what you call <a> it pam-
by chuckle-headed cham-
paign bottle full of Psalm-
singing miserable dam-
aged sable sons of Ham.[127]

There isn't *any*thing in the whole wide world that a body can't buy in London except a good potato.

Swearing.

"Herre Gott, Dürten, ik hadd de Kurage nich, em so weg taü schicken."—Fritz Reuter, "*Dörchläuchting.*"[128] (Stining, a blooming, sweet young girl, says that to her <sh> sister Dürten.)

---

127 Clemens' attempt at the "rhyming doggerel" he had found "exceedingly funny" in Munich (see p. 250).

128 The sixth and final volume of Fritz Reuter's series of stories titled *Olle Kamellen* [Old stories of bygone days]. Reuter was a popular author who wrote in a Low German dialect. He was particularly successful in realistic and humorous tales and poems about the rural people he had known in Mecklenburg, the region of his birth. On 2 February 1879, Livy informed her mother that she would be bringing home "a translation of one of Fritz Reuter's books I intend not to read until I can read it with you." Clemens' quotations from "Dörchläuchting" may be translated: *"God Almighty, Dürten, I didn't have the courage to send him on his way." "God in high Heaven! now he is composing once again."*

“Gott in den hogen Himmel! <”> nu dicht’t hei all wedder.”—*Ibid*

The Burning Shame.[129]
Southern Courting—Making a gelding.
Twichell & the Ostler.
An’ I don’t care a d—n if I *never* git to Texas!
How Irish were made.
He could ’a’ heard his ----- jar!
W. C.—Wesleyan Chapel, seats for 400—never less than 250 present—“too public”
O, I *am* so dry!—O I *was* so dry!

<Small chapter>

Strifenhofer,
Augsburgerhof.

trockneschröpfkopf

You go to bed & let the other man do the walking.

If all one dog, mighty long dog. Moncoon.

Now if you fool with me I’ll shove this umbrella up your --- & *open* it!
Sitting on that cold rock just married!

I like my whisky in the morning.
I like my country pumpkin pie

The Adam-calf of the universe! seed calf of
“Original Jacobs.”
How the Virgin’s Tomb would draw in New York.
I copper that.

Rev. Knight’s Jersey man & coffin plates.
Whistling & stuttering yarn.

---

129 The following list is the product of Clemens’ habit of intermittently recording cryptic memoranda for jokes and anecdotes in the back pages of his notebook.

Stomach's gone to the chemists.
Other funeral yarns.

John & Sally up stairs in back room with door locked "Don't jump to Conclusions on mere circumstantial evidence."

Man in ox wagon over stumpy road.
Joe & the ostler.
Man on ladder says, "Er ist in ihr aftern."

JOHN BROWN
RISE & SHINE

Bayerische bank[130]
Get Consul's address
" Duverneck's "
" 107 f paper changed.
Draw on Koester for balance. (11 or 1200 M.)

G. Henry Horstmann
15 Otto st
10 to 3.
Nymphenburger st 43/2
Frau Kratz.

Boyesen,[131] <78 Theresiens st>
Vier Jahreszeiten

Douvernak
<Toby Rosenthal.>

---

[130] This group of notes inscribed near the back of the notebook reflects Clemens' efforts to establish himself in Munich.

[131] Hjalmar H. Boyesen, novelist, critic, and professor of German at Cornell University. On 20 November Clemens had written to Twichell: "The Boyesens have been in Munich ten days. I saw their names on the banker's books, & that they were to leave today for Italy; so Livy & I drove to their lodgings yesterday afternoon; by my translation, the landlady said they had left town. But after we had returned home the German sediment gradually settled to the bottom & the correct translation was revealed—to-wit: the Boyesens were simply *nicht zu hause*. However, it was too late to try again." Clemens was to see Boyesen in Paris, where they called on Turgenev together.

J. Eglinton Montgomery
Consul, Geneva.

180

Oct. 28—5 PM.—Hotel d'Allemania, Rome.
Rooms, 22 f.

3 caffeés complet,	6 f.
1 beefsteak,	2.25
3 table d'hotes,	18.
	26.25
Rooms	22
	48.25

Little Pedlington
Hotel bill
R'way tickets & trunks.
Sell paper, buy gold.
50 cigars.
2. Telegraph Smith & hotel[132]
Return "Silverland."
"Life of Blake."[133]

Marienbad

Scotch Whisky—	lemons
Metal pitcher—	tobacco box
Blotting paper—	envelops
Postage stamps—	Purple ink
Warm slippers 2	Drawers.
Letters from P.O.	Money order. [#]

---

132 Clemens' telegram was probably directed to Edward M. Smith, United States consul at Mannheim (see note 68). The entries from "Little Pedlington" (conceivably a reference to John Poole's 1839 satire *Little Pedlington and the Pedlingtonians*) to "Vincenzo . . . Piano" were written on the back flyleaf; all of the remaining entries in the notebook were written on the back endpaper on various occasions.

133 George Lawrence's *Silverland* (1873), a descriptive travel book on the Pacific coast states; Alexander Gilchrist's *Life of William Blake* (1863).

Nov. 19/78, took a workroom at 45 Nymphenstrasse—Frau Kratz.

Quanto tempio (ci) fermiamo?

Tobacco shop on corner under Hotel Bellevue, opp. Karls Thor.

180
1440

181
8
———
1448

Swanee River

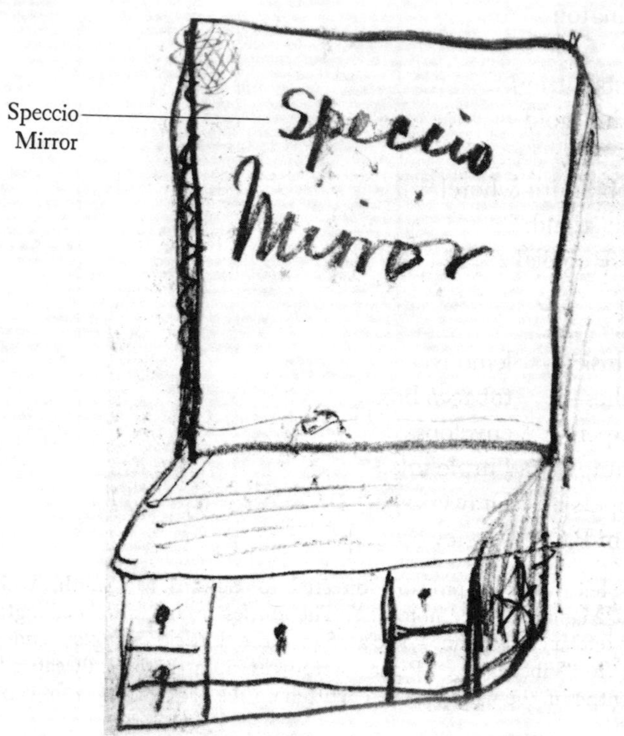

D^r^. Ranke[134]
Sophienstrasse
3—2^d^ floor.

Vincenzo Malaspina
Via della Penna. N° 137
3° Piano

Continental Hotel, Paris.
La Lolita .... 15 f
Esquisitos de Cuba 15.
(small
Miss Ellis, Pension, Paris.
<Hanfstaegel
Hof Photographer,
Munich.>

Racinets "Le Costume Historique" $100 Paris, Didot[135]

<Launt Thompson>
109 Via dei Serragli
Florence.

John Dawson
Oakleigh
Clapham Park
London
Mary Ellen, Kate and Judy.[136]

Florence to Rome
3 trunks. No. 185—paid f20.40^c^ [#]

---

134 The Clemenses' doctor during their winter in Munich, "a trustworthy, well-instructed, and obliging man, speaks English" (Murray's *Southern Germany,* p. 45).

135 The lavishly illustrated work by Albert Charles Auguste Racinet was being published in Paris by Firmin-Didot et Cie. Each of its twenty numbers cost $4.50.

136 The English family whom the Clemenses met in Switzerland (see Notebook 15, note 67).

National Anthem—(Infant musical exercise)
<The Great Duel—>
Extracts from Notes. Student Duel.
The loss of the girls' jewels.
Learning German. Cook-book[137]
Artists

---

[137] Clemens noted here some subjects to be included in his manuscript. The sketches designated as "National Anthem—(Infant musical exercise)" and "Artists" do not survive in *A Tramp Abroad*, nor did he use the sixteen-page manuscript about the "loss of the girls' jewels," "The Lost Ear-ring" (*Mark Twain's Fables of Man*, ed. John S. Tuckey [Berkeley, Los Angeles, London: University of California Press, 1972], pp. 145–148). The other subjects in this list were incorporated into chapters 8 ("The Great Duel"), 21 ("Extracts from Notes"), 5 and 6 ("Student Duel"), Appendix D ("Learning German"), and chapter 49 ("Cook-book").

XVIII

"Neither Winter Nor Summer Nor Morals"

(February–September 1879)

Notebook 18 covers the balance of the Clemenses' stay in Europe—from their arrival in Paris on 28 February 1879, through the whirlwind tour of Belgium and Holland and the month-long stay in England, to the departure of the S.S. *Gallia* from Liverpool on 23 August, bound for New York. There are a few final entries written after Clemens' return. Most of the notebook deals with the Clemens party's four-and-a-half-month Paris residence during a cold and rainy spring and summer.

After months of tedious work on the manuscript of *A Tramp Abroad*, Clemens at last had been able to write triumphantly to Mrs. Langdon, to Twichell, and to Howells at the end of January 1879 that the book was half done. With the worrisome book finally taking shape, the Clemenses could make plans, early in February, to leave their comfortable Munich quarters. Livy wrote to her mother on 16 February: "We expect to leave here a week from this week Thursday (Feb. 27th) going to Paris where we shall remain until Mr Clemens has finished his book, we hope not more than three months but it may be more than four—he is working very hard now and it is bad for him to be interupted but we don't like to spend the spring months here." But it was just at this time that Clemens made a dismaying discovery, as he explained to Mrs. Fairbanks on 6 March: "By George I had a rattling set-back in Munich 2 or 3 weeks ago. When I struck page 900 I wrote home jubilantly, that my book was just half done —& I treated myself to several hours' genuine happiness, too; & *then* I counted up & found that I had written only 65 to 70 words on a page, instead of 100! Consequently I was only ⅓ done. I had been writing 30 pages a day, & allowing myself Saturdays for holiday. However, I had 8 clear days left before leaving Munich—so I buckled in & wrote 400 pages in those 8 days & so brought my work close up to half-way" (*MTMF*, pp. 225–226). The manuscript that Clemens added hastily at the end of his Munich stay roughly corresponds to chapters 20 through 25 of *A Tramp Abroad*—leaving him with the longest section of the book, the chapters on Switzerland, still to be written.

Clemens' mood of triumph had disappeared by the time the party set out for France—and his first view of Paris, suffering from one of the iciest winters on record, did not add to his disposition to enjoy the French capital. His displeasure soon extended to all of France, a country, he noted, which had "neither winter nor summer nor morals."

Clemens' attitude toward the French had been indulgent on his 1867 trip with the *Quaker City* pilgrims. The scene on his first night in "magnificent Paris" struck him then as delightfully foreign and exciting, the crowds were "so moustached, so frisky, so affable, so fearfully and wonderfully Frenchy!" (*The Innocents Abroad*, chapter 12). Clemens' satire was reserved for the American visitor in France who snobbishly aped the French, "making of himself a thing that is neither male nor female, neither fish, flesh, nor fowl—a poor, miserable, hermaphrodite Frenchman!" (*The Innocents Abroad*, chapter 23). In *The Gilded Age*, Clemens blasted the pretentiousness of the Patrick O'Rileys who, aspiring to Washington's "Aristocracy of the Parvenus," established themselves for a time in Paris, "that Paradise of Americans of their sort," and shortly afterward "landed here as the Hon. Patrique Oreillé and family," acknowledged "ultra fashionables," having acquired a veneer of French manners and French phrases (chapter 33). Notebook 18 reveals Clemens' emergent contempt for what he saw as the trivial and barbarous social and political customs of the French themselves.

The notebook comments about the French were further developed in more than 140 pages of manuscript written concurrently with the manuscript for *A Tramp Abroad.* Here Clemens attacked French morality, political history, habits of courtship and marriage and other customs, and provided a long description of the 1879 Grand Prix. This manuscript was not numbered for inclusion in the manuscript of *A Tramp Abroad;* it is likely that even as he worked on it Clemens realized that its biting personal tone would not blend happily with the lighter humorous vein of his travel book. In fact, *A Tramp Abroad* records only the first half of Clemens' trip, ending with the travelers in Italy. Munich, Holland, and Belgium, as well as Paris, are only briefly mentioned on the last page of the book; the stay in England is not mentioned at all.

Clemens made no progress on *A Tramp Abroad* for several weeks after arriving in Paris. He wrote to Frank Bliss on 15 April: "I have been sick—sick—and sick again—with rheumatism and dysentery. I have spent four-fifths of my six weeks' residence in Paris in bed. This is an awful set-back. I hired a den a mile from the hotel and went to work as soon as I reached Paris, but my fire went out and I was laid up the very first day. I only got fairly and squarely to work again a week ago. . . . I am working, every chance I get, and that's the best I can do. I am hoping to be able to go right along, now" (*MTLP*, p. 111). In fact, once he began work again, Clemens made a great deal of progress on his manuscript, adding about 800 pages to it by the end of May when he wrote to his mother and sister that he had reached manuscript page 2041 (*MTBus*, p. 137)—which brought his book up to what is now chapter 47. Clemens presumably continued his work through June. On 6 July Livy wrote to her mother: "We are taking particular comfort now because Mr Clemens is not going to work any more until he gets home, and it is so nice to feel that he is at leisure" (MTM).

Despite Clemens' grumblings, the stay in Paris had not been without its amusements. There were a number of Americans either living in or traveling through the city with whom the Clemens party visited; Livy's letters to her mother are full of accounts of social excursions. General Lucius Fairchild, the American consul in Paris, and his family were frequent companions, as was Moncure Conway, Clemens' English agent. Hjalmar Boyesen and his young wife improved their acquaintance with the Clemenses. Thomas Bailey Aldrich and his wife visited with them. Mrs. Aldrich later recalled: "[Mr. Clemens] had most comfortably ensconced his family at the Hotel Normandy, and was himself very busily engaged in wrestling with the French language, which he said was illiterate, untenable, unscrupulous, for if the Frenchman knew how to spell he did not know how to pronounce—and if he knew how to pronounce he certainly did not know how to spell. How it all comes back and springs to memory—the wit, the chaff, the merry dinners in the rue de l'Eschelle, the gaiety and laughter! Mr. Clemens said, 'When Aldrich speaks it seems to me he is the bright face of the moon, and I feel like the other side' " (Lilian Aldrich, *Crowding Memories* [Boston: Houghton Mifflin Co., 1920], pp. 229–230). Through Aldrich Clemens met Mme Thérèse Blanc ("Th. Bentzon") of the *Revue des deux mondes*, the translator of Clemens' "Jumping Frog" sketch and an exponent of American writers. Clemens found a congenial group in the artists and literary men of the Stomach Club, meeting there Edwin Austin Abbey and Augustus Saint-Gaudens. Saint-Gaudens' studio was a gathering place for the artists and Clemens became a welcome guest: "After supper Samuel Clemens (Mark Twain) whom they had come to know, would sometimes drop in to discuss his dyspepsia. It was their pleasure and privilege to count and record the number of black cigars he smoked—so vast a number that, towards midnight, he would be overcome by the perplexities of an artist's life and insist upon knowing: What is art?—Whereupon they would bundle him off home" (Charles C. Baldwin, *Stanford White* [New York: Dodd, Mead & Co., 1931], pp. 95–96). Artist William Gedney Bunce, cousin of the Clemenses' Hartford friend Edward Bunce, entertained Livy and Clara Spaulding at a lunch of radishes, homemade corned beef hash, and pickles, and was their companion on a number of occasions. The Clemenses attended the wedding of their friend, artist and reporter Frank D. Millet, Clemens acting as the witness. In May, Clemens' nephew Sam Moffett arrived from Munich. For Livy and Clara Spaulding there were also shopping and sightseeing expeditions and French lessons. Livy wrote to her mother on 13 May, sounding a little weary: "We live in such a perfect whirl of people these days, that it seems utterly impossible to do anything, I wish that I had put down the names of the people that have been here for the last two months, but I think every day, well this will be the last we shant have as many again" (MTM).

On 10 July the Clemens party left Paris and spent nine days on a hurried tour of Brussels, Antwerp, Rotterdam, Amsterdam, and The Hague. By 20 July they were in London and Livy wrote to her mother from the Brunswick House Hotel: "Doesn't that address sound (or look) as if we were nearing home? We reached here this morning having crossed the channel in the night" (MTM). The month-long stay in England included a six-day visit to Reginald Cholmondeley's Condover Hall, a trip to Oxford, and a three-day visit to the Lake District. The Clemenses undoubtedly had a warm reception in England and renewed many of the acquaintances made on their previous trips. Clemens' entries at the end of Notebook 18, however, indicate a tempering of his earlier enthusiasm for England. He criticizes the growing practice among English newspapers of scoffing at America and notes American advances in technology and literature, predicting that "we shall presently be indifferent to being looked down upon by a nation no bigger & no better than our own" (p. 348). Clemens' remarks echo Livy's in a letter to her mother written on 3 August from Oxford: "We are very glad that the time is getting so near for us to go home. . . . I am *desperately* glad that we live in America" (MTM).

On 23 August the S.S. *Gallia* left Liverpool, arriving at New York on 3 September. The Hartford *Courant* interviewed Clemens while "twenty-two freight packages and twelve trunks" were cleared through customs. The reporter noted: "He looks older than when he went to Germany, and his hair has turned quite gray." Clemens stated that his new book would be published in November, adding: "I don't know what the name of it is, but I know what it's about. It's about this trip I've taken. No, it isn't fiction–it's about my journey, like the 'Innocents Abroad,' all serious –all facts and wisdom. . . . The first half is done, but I've got to go through the last half and throw whole rafts of it away. After that I may run through the first half and throw away lots of that; then it will be ready for the printer" (Hartford *Courant*, 4 September 1879).

The family went directly to Quarry Farm, where on 8 September Clemens wrote to Frank Bliss to whom he had sent the manuscript of *A Tramp Abroad*: "You will perceive that my book is not finished. I shall finish it here, after the M.S. comes back to me. There is nearly matter enough but I shall probably *strike out* as well as *add*" (*MTLP*, p. 119). Clemens' prediction of a November publication date for *A Tramp Abroad* proved to be optimistic. By 19 November all that had appeared was a bound prospectus of selected pages for the use of the subscription agents (Hamlin Hill, *Mark Twain and Elisha Bliss* [Columbia: University of Missouri Press, 1964], pp. 146–148). *A Tramp Abroad* was finally published in March 1880.

Notebook 18 is the third of Clemens' notebooks to be made with page tabs according to his design. The cover—of pliable, brown, grained leather with blind stamped borders on the front and back—is, except for its color, identical to those of Notebooks 16 and 17. The pages are the same size as those of Notebooks 16 and 17, and like them their edges are tinted red. Notebook 18 now contains 182 pages, 1 of them blank. Five and one-half leaves have been torn out and are missing. The pages are ruled with twenty faint gray horizontal lines. The endpapers and the sides of the flyleaves that face them are of a shiny light blue paper. The inner sides of the flyleaves are white. With the exception of an entry in black ink (p. 296.11), all of the writing is in pencil. Paine's use marks and various forms of Clemens' use marks, all in pencil, appear throughout the notebook. Notebook 18 is heavily worn with use, and some gatherings and single leaves are loose.

100,000 words of *reading* matter in a 20-page copy of the London Times.[1]

<19 Boulevard Montmartre>[2]

<B>Name of boat from Antwerp to London bridge—"Baron Osy" is the best.

Send books to—
Edward Wyndham,[3]
New University Club
St James's st. W. [#]

---

1 Clemens entered this word count of the "bulkiest daily newspaper in the world" on the front endpaper. He used the information in Appendix F, "German Journals," of *A Tramp Abroad*—contrasting English and American dailies with the Munich *Tages-Anzeiger* which, he wrote, contained in its 25 January 1879 issue just 1,654 words. (See also Notebook 17, pp. 262–263.)

2 This address for Goupil & Compagnie, internationally known dealers in art and engravings, and the two subsequent entries were all written on the front flyleaf at various times between February and August 1879.

3 Edward Wyndham was the Clemenses' host during their visit to Oxford in August (see p. 337).

<REMEMBER—The present book is to satisfy the Riley contract —Frank Bliss must wait for the next one.>[4]

Feb. 26/79

Shipped from Munich to Cunard Co, Liverpool marked Clemens &c

1 large box, R. N. 3947
1 smaller " R. N. 3948.

Shipped from Heidelberg June 9, Case "M. C. <con> 346 gross 204 pounds, containing 1 table and carved works."

Shipped from Frankfort June 20, case marked B & C, containing crockery.

The neglected but sober young man marries, raises a family in hard lines, is cashier of a bank, is handcuffed, gagged & murdered because he will not give up the safe combination to the other hero & his pals (the one that goes to thc gallows wreathed in flowers.) A

---

[4] In November 1870 Clemens persuaded his old friend, the journalist J. H. Riley, to travel to the South African diamond fields to gather material for Clemens' next book (*MTLP*, pp. 42–44). Elisha Bliss provided an advance to finance Riley's trip and Clemens signed a contract with the American Publishing Company to write a book on the diamond mines or "upon some other subject which shall be mutually agreed upon" (Hill, *Mark Twain and Elisha Bliss*, p. 129). Riley contracted blood poisoning during the trip and his death in 1872 ended all plans for the book, although Clemens did not return the advance. Bliss did not remind Clemens of the contract and the debt until 13 February 1879, when he wrote to propose that Clemens repay the advance and draw up a new contract with the American Publishing Company for his next book. The entry here indicates that Clemens intended, at least temporarily, to supply *A Tramp Abroad* to Elisha Bliss in fulfillment of the old contract, despite a secret agreement he had made in March 1878 with Frank Bliss, Elisha's son, to publish the European travel book through another company Frank had recently formed. The entry was later canceled, however, perhaps by 15 April 1879 when Clemens wrote Frank Bliss that he planned to tell Charles Perkins, his lawyer in Hartford, "to let the Co pay themselves the $2000 out of my copyright money, and take a written release from the contract to write another book" (*MTLP*, p. 112). After further negotiation, Clemens and Elisha Bliss agreed that the publication of *Tom Sawyer* in 1876 fulfilled the terms of the 1870 contract and that the outstanding advance should be repaid from royalties due Clemens. In the end, Frank Bliss rejoined the American Publishing Company, and *A Tramp Abroad* was issued by that firm.

subscription for the family of the noble fellow fails, & they go to the poor house but a *memorial church* is built to the memory of his heroism.[5]

Send a book to Dr. H. Ranke, 3 Sophienstrasse, Munich.[6]

German books fall to pieces when you open them.

Feb. 27, at Strasburg.

Feb. 28/79—Arrived at Paris at <P> 5 P.M.[7]

That bright fellow, No. 2512, who took full charge of us, said we had 9 trunks & that they arrived in the <evening> morning. Shipped us to St James Hotel—gave him 5 fr.

Madame Thierry
44 rue de Clichy

American Embassy cor. Avenue Josephine & rue Chaillot

Hotel de Normandie
place du theatre français

Mme. Freeman, near Parc Manceau

<Hotel d'Oxford et Cambridge cor St Honorè & d'Alger.>

Hotel de Fleurus
No 3 Rue de Fleurus
near Luxembourg gardens
other side of the city [#]

---

[5] Mark Twain followed this plan in writing the conclusion to "Edward Mills and George Benton: A Tale" (see Notebook 17, note 122).

[6] Dr. Ranke was the Clemenses' physician during their winter in Munich.

[7] On arriving in Paris, the Clemens party stayed at the Grand Hotel St. James in the rue Saint-Honoré only until 4 March, when they removed to the more comfortable Hotel Normandy on the rue de l'Echelle. On 9 March Livy wrote to young Sam Moffett, who was in Germany, about their accommodations at the Hotel Normandy: "We are very nicely situated here, but it is a much more expensive place than we intended to stop in, but we could not suit ourselves better although we looked about a good deal."

Hotel des Saints Peres
rue de Sts. Pères
other side of city also

In ungraciousness of stranger to stranger we are exactly like the French—mannerless.

The cabman of Paris is exactly like the <cabm> Irish hackman of New York—mannerless. The French cabman never treats you to a civility—never leaves his seat to assist a lady—receives his fare without even a grunt, whether it be too much or two little.

42 rue Labruyére
<Huntingdon>Huntington.[8]

St James parlor.

Two marble-topped brass-inlaid (very handsome) <low> cupboards, with a tub of the same about the shape & size of a foot bath <but n[o]> on each, filled with a peck of great coarse artificial flowers, once glaring & gaudy but now they <reds & blues & greens are> are *so* faded & shabby, & so filthy with the gathered dirt of ages. In fact they have gathered so rich <I>a soil, I wonder they don't grow.—

In the centre a fanciful table of the same, (handsome.) Four other tables of differing patterns & degrees of ugliness. 10 squatty, ugly arm-chairs upholstered in the ugliest & coarsest conceivable scarlet plush—2 hideous sofas of the same—7 armless chairs ditto. <4> 5 "ornamental" chairs, seats covered with a coarse rag embroidered in a flat expanse & confusion of leaves such as no tree ever bore, six or seven a dirty white & the rest a faded red—how those hideous chairs do swear at the hideous sofa near them! A sham Persian carpet, full of strong splotches of red, <&>green & pale blue—& how these colors do swear at the hideous scarlet chairs &

---

[8] William Henry Huntington, an American newspaper correspondent and collector of Frankliniana. A resident of Paris since 1858, he "sought and won the heart of every American of interest that came to Paris" (John Bigelow, *Retrospections of an Active Life*, 5 vols. [New York: Baker & Taylor Co. and Doubleday, Page & Co., 1909–1913], 4:9).

sofas! Over 2 of the tables are spread coarse, & exceedingly soiled covers with still yelling figures in black, green & yellow—& one must see *this* green to comprehend how it swears at the far different shade of green in the carpet. These covers unquestionably did not cost 2 francs apiece. 8 chandeliers of 8 burners each—64; a great ugly central ditto of <28>26 burners—90 gas burners & no gas!—4 vast mirrrors let into the walls, each 6 ft wide & 15 high, made each of 3 great sheets of glass, one above the other & showing the divisions most unpleasantly. 2 oil pic—poor. Room 30 × 25—3 mighty windows 18 × 7 ft.—with very dirty & aged lawn <curtains> shades & heavy dark red curtains.—walls & ceilings formerly white stucco work—elaborate birds, cupids, wreaths, &c—yellow & very dirty, now. Discolored shabby marble clock—We used a lamp.

The wood floor sags toward the centre & warps & yields everywhere under your step—afraid you'll go through.—& how horribly it screaked & sunk—& how pallid & sick the carpet's blues & greens & reds were by the windows where the light had struck it. This is the very hatefulest room I have seen in Europ.

O how *cold*, & raw & unwarmable it was!

Here insert parlor of Normandy Hotel.

Been reading that disgusting Tom Jones—the same old paltry stuff & poverty of invention—a poor devil with no father, in love with a girl far above him—he goes through the round of gambling & whoring & beggary & enlisting & fighting, & finally his magnificent father turns up—Roderick Random over again. <Old> The characters are mighty well drawn, but not all prigs or humbugs or sentimental gas-bags except one—only one character in the whole book that you always welcome, especially if he is particularly drunk profane & obscene—Squire Western—he is the only man whose violent death one does not <yearn f>hunger for.

The English ought not to patronize the Zulus,[9] <&>the

---

[9] The attempts of the Zulus to occupy disputed territories in the Transvaal and

Livingstone River Cannibals & say <hol> piously we are <ho> <finer> better than thou, for <is>it is very plain that haven't been better more than a hundred years. They are a <f>very fine & pure & elevated people now, but what they were between the Roman invasion & a time within the memory of a centenarian was but small improvement upon the Shoshone Indians—I select the Shoshones because they have certain peculiar vices & also certain peculiar conspicuous virtues.

I do not speak English but American.—The main difference is that the main body of the English talk through their noses—which accounts for a scattering few of the people in the 6 New England States doing the same—but we have 32 States whose people do *not* say käow & you näo<w>, like many Englishmen & a scattering few country people in the back regions of the 6 little N. E. States. The English all say <Wawtah> & glahs/gloss and grahs, und bahsket/bosket, & this peculiarity they have planted so firmly in the 6 little N. E. S. that <*all*> nearly *all* the natives pronounce those words in that way—4 or 5 000,000—but there are 32 States & 40 or 45 000 000 who *never* use that foreign form, but use the flat <american>American form, like flash, clash, rash, dash, mash.

<English> Italian boy in Venice—"I have it not"—'is that right?"

And American would have said *yes*—but an English lady said, "It is right enough, but it is better to say I have not *got* it.—

Now we all know that that answer could never have been given by an American, because not good American, & we also know, by English books newspapers & conversation that it was the right correction for that English lady to make, because it is perfectly good English—<she made> Mr. Longfellow could use that form in a London periodical, but the American editor would kindly but firmly strike out the "got."

In words & their meanings, the English & American languages are

---

Natal had prompted the British government to send troops into Zululand in January 1879.

essentially the same, but of our 50 000 000, 47,000 000 pronounce after Am fashion & only 3 000 000 after Eng^{h}

Eng say *o*ful nice

″ nahsty

″ won't say bloody.

See 3 leaves ahead.[10]

Eng ladies say don't—you—<know>—Ams say dontchu—<know>

Toole's broad English a's the N. Y's couldn't stand—nor his broad fun either.[11]

four—*for* hundrd &c

Directly—means delay.

Clever—means kind.

An humble

From a murder trial—English witness says, "It would be soon after 7"—meaning "It was (probably) soon after 7."

"He will be about 40 years old."

"Out of window."

From the trial "This would be in the evening part of Friday."

English—A ukase—an hotel.

An hospital—This suggests that formerly educated people dropped the H.

o is pron. ahn and awn (on)

an hospital }
an hotel } English, not American.

---

[10] A reference to the entry on page 298 beginning "Funny is American," which is circled in the notebook. These notes and related entries elsewhere in the notebook formed the basis of "Concerning the American Language," published in *The Stolen White Elephant* (1882), with the explanation that the piece was originally "part of a chapter which was crowded out of 'A Tramp Abroad.' "

[11] John Lawrence Toole was a popular English comedian whom Clemens met in London in 1872 (*MTL*, p. 199). He first appeared before the American public in 1874. George C. D. Odell mentions the reception of Toole in New York: "As a matter of fact, Toole was at first a great failure; American play-goers did not care for his style of humour, and they are reputed not to have understood the extreme Briticism of some of his plays" (*Annals of the New York Stage*, 15 vols. [New York: Columbia University Press, 1927–1949], 9:519).

English make Jewellery 4 syllables—we three.
lash, trash, cash, &c Hong Kong God Hog.

French, a <lan>literature confined to the two great branches/divisions/specialties of modern F thought—science & adultery.

Every other man <wea[thes]>wears the button or the ribbon of an officer or "private" in the legion of honor.

Cabman—"Well then, why don't you get in, — — you."

Wood 3 f per basket of 6 sticks—8 baskets a day for 2 fires—total 24 fr.

<Describe parlor at Hotel Normandy.>

Speech—literature devoted & confined to the two great branches of Fr thought, Science &—&—adultery.

Cabs over No. 6000 are drivers who have been discharged by the best cab companies.

Case of a tramp who was loaned a £1000,000 note for 30 days & he got rich on it because nobody could change it.[12]

Burglars after the wood. Miser counting up his wood.

In Munich they destroyed our clothes with acids which rotted them & took all color out.

Beggarly goverment to pay but <$7>$17,500 at Berlin, Paris can't *board* for that. Bayard Taylor could not get a decent house had to *furnish* one—took all his advance—then he died.[13] [#]

---

[12] Clemens completed the story of "The £1,000,000 Bank-Note" in Florence in 1892, although, according to Paine, it had been "planned many years before" (*MTB*, p. 957). It was first published in the January 1893 *Century*, and appeared as the title piece in a collection of Mark Twain's stories published the same year.

[13] For several months before his death (see Notebook 17, p. 254), recently appointed United States minister to Germany Bayard Taylor had been concerned about finding suitable housing for himself and his family. He finally located a residence large enough to accommodate ministerial functions, but then was forced to spend considerable sums of money to furnish it (*Life and Letters of Bayard*

Before door of the Mairie, where every body must go to get married is a sign which nobody can overlook, in big letters, "Sage-femme."

Make some pictures out of stiff fashion plates to illustrate book. Call it a party.

Have studied art straight through from — — to Benvenuto Cellini's great picture of Nap Xing the Alleghenies.

Abuse the idiots who laugh at foreigners because they make such wild blunders about American geography.

Lavishly praise (& copy) the masterpiece of a modern master & contrast it with naked old Masters—<cant make out subject of picture because> subject Les Modes Parisiennes de l'annè 1879. (fashion plate.)—or—<dress a> "Susannah & the 4 & 20 Elders. (Harris trans)

Harris buys his trousseau to go on foot through Europe with.

No drearier reading <that>than Tom Jones by Fielding.

Funny is American, & Nahsty & awful are English. They are equivalents of *very*, or uncommonly, or xtrordnry.

Can't speak—lowspirited.

Thank you much. Have just got back from England, where I went to attend D of C's wedding.[14] But it was a great disappointment—neither our minister nor I was invited. And why<?> wasn't our min. invited? Because he could not get a free pass over the road to Windsor & his salary is so pitiful that neither he nor any other Amer

---

Taylor, ed. Marie Hansen-Taylor and Horace E. Scudder, 2 vols. [Boston: Houghton, Mifflin and Co., 1884], 2:754, 757). Clemens' indignation about the meager support of American diplomatic representatives, recorded recurrently in this notebook, finally was expressed in "Diplomatic Pay and Clothes" (*Forum*, March 1899).

[14] Queen Victoria's third son, Prince Arthur, duke of Connaught, was married on 13 March 1879 to Princess Louise of Prussia at Windsor.

rep abroad can afford to buy such a thing as a RR ticket. Therefore he declined to be invited.—

<well> I will tell you, in order to clear up this torturing & tantalizing mystery, but I don't want it to go any further. <You've heard a good many reasons given for that curious omission, but they> <You know what an Amer> It was because he couldn't get a free pass over the road to Windsor. You know what the salary of an Ambassador of the US of A is. It pays his board, <but> & that is all. <That is all> that is necessary, <too;> because out of courtesy to the great country he represents, he can lodge on <any> the benches in the parks by showing his credentials. In most foreign cities the Amer minister must <sn> take his chances with the rabble & snatch a bench, but England always anxious to show us courtesies, has a bench set apart in each of her parks for our Rep.—It is labeled, "Bunk of the Am Min—no other tramp allowed." <to sleep>

Doug. Straight[15]

Mi-Careme, Mid-Lent, 21st March. Went to President Grévy's reception with Conway & General Noyes, American Minister, at 10 PM,—Mr. Hitt, first Secretary drove Conway & I to the New Opera House at 11.30—waited outside till doors opened at midnight—vaste horde of maskers.[16]

---

[15] Clemens met Douglas Straight in London in 1872, when Straight was a member of Parliament. In 1879, Straight was appointed judge of the Allahabad High Court where he served until 1892 (see p. 301).

[16] Moncure Conway, Clemens' literary agent in England, was in Paris at this time. He reminisced in his autobiography: "Mark was working steadily—indeed hard—on 'A Tramp Abroad,' and I had the happiness of making myself useful to his wife in seeing Paris. . . . He worked in the evening and could not go with us to theatres; but on Mardigras about midnight he and I started out in a voiture and looked in on a dozen fancy balls" (*Autobiography: Memories and Experiences*, 2 vols. [Boston: Houghton, Mifflin and Co., 1904], 2:146). The other people Clemens mentions in his entry are Jules Grévy, the newly elected president of France; General Edward Noyes, United States minister to France; Robert R. Hitt, first secretary of the American legation at Paris; Léon Gambetta, the newly elected president of the Chamber of Deputies; Prince Chlodwic of Hohenlohe-Schillings-

Gambetti, Prince Hohenlohe, <Min> <Wa> Mr. Waddington, Minister of Foreign Affairs, the Turkish minister, &c &c were at Grevy's—also the brother of Grevy's mistress. At 1 a.m. left the Opera & went to a mask ball at the American circus, to another at the Tivoli —to the Opera till 4 a.m. then saw wind-up dance at another mask ball & got home at 5 or 5.30. Opera ball, 20 fr each; Circus, 2 f Tivoli 3 fr & nothing at the final ball as it was about to close.

Dandy angels with variegated wings among old masters.

<8> 52 Devonshire st.
Portland Place W.

Anderson 16 rue de la Tour d'Auverne

French women poke your eye with umbrella.

Roman's time in grave with corpse.

Sermon on Mount in third person.

French speech in dates—should have built one if I had not had rheumatism.—a perplexing thing, for they only mention the date & not the occurrence.

I'm for cremation. It would shock people to burn an abandoned sinner whom they believed was going straight to eternal cremation.

I disfavor capital punishment.

Speech in 3^{d} person is detestable—only the exact word has point— Could you 3^{d} person Josh Billings', or Robert Burdette's or the Danbury News' happy remarks—<Difference between Genius & talent is the difference>

Angle-worm too much tail. Man stepped on orange peel—reason he didn't miss the train. [#]

---

fürst, German ambassador to France; and William H. Waddington, the French minister of foreign affairs.

See scrap book for Am & English humor.[17]

Baptised milk is Christian.

Liberty (to rob <& murder> burn & butcher)—Eqality (in bestiality)—Fraternity <(in> <(the> (of Devils.)

Miserly government pays Minister $17,500—ought to pay him nothing or <$75> or $100,000.

When I was a bachelor, had chance to be minister to China[18]—was not competent—if I had been I could not have afforded it—I wouldn't *give* my services to a gov. too stingy to pay me for them—but that is what all our ministers (who are generous men) do. They can't pocket one penny.

A friend of mine, Douglas Straight has gone judge in India—salary $22,500. Our Supreme Judges do not get half as much. Physican takes years to learn to cure or kill, then he gets big pay—judge ought to, also.

Unrestricted suffrage—why don't banks let each stockholder have equal vote? Why don't

My dream—talk with the Devil. [#]

---

17 Clemens' 1878/1879 scrapbook contains a clipping from the London *Daily News* offering an analysis of American humor:

> The humourists are Puritans at bottom, as well as rustics. They have an amazing familiarity with certain religious ideas and certain Biblical terms. There is a kind of audacity in their use of the Scriptures, which reminds one of the freedom of mediæval mystery-plays. Probably this boldness began, not in scepticism or in irreverence, but in honest familiar faith. It is certainly very odd to us in England, and probably expressions often get a laugh which would pass unnoticed in America. An astounding coolness and freedom of manners probably go for something in the effect produced by American humour. There is nothing of the social flunkeyism in it which too often marks our own satirists.

18 In a letter published by the *Alta California* on 3 March 1868, Mark Twain claimed that John Ross Browne, Anson Burlingame's successor as United States minister to China, had offered him "a lucrative position on his staff in case he goes to China."

The time I read that dreadful verse in <old>Old Bible during family Worship.—[19]

Make myself a hero by saving that young girl.[20]

Samson was a Jew—therefore not a fool. The Jews have the best average brain of any people in the world. The Jews are the only race in the world who work wholly with their brains & never with their hands. There are no Jew beggars, no Jew tramps, no Jew ditchers, hod-carriers day laborers or followers of toilsome mechanical trades. They are <the> peculiarly & conspicuously the world's intellectual aristocracy.

"That reminds me that 700 years of English oppression is said to be the reason that the South of Ireland furnishes mainly people so deficient in intellect that they are obliged to earn their living by callings that require <no brains, but only> muscle<.>, not brains. The Jews have suffered far severrer deprivations, <oppo>oppressions <& persecutions to which those suffered by> & persecutions than the Irish; <are trifling.> <The Jews>They have endured these oppressions about 2,000 years—& yet, as I have said, they are the world's intellectual aristocracy. <They>There are some things which oppression won't account for

In 3 year he will have the experience & I'll have the capital.

Communism is idiotcy. They want to divide up the property. Suppose they did it—it requires brains to keep money as well as make it. In a precious little while the money would be back in the former owner's hands & the Communist would be poor again. The division would have to be re-made every three years or it would do the communist no good. [#]

---

[19] The verse is evidently identified on page 303 as 2 Kings 18:27: "But Rabshakeh said unto them, Hath my master sent me to thy master, and to thee, to speak these words? *hath he* not *sent me* to the men which sit on the wall, that they may eat their own dung, and drink their own piss with you?"

[20] Clemens described this incident at greater length in Notebook 16 (p. 160) and in chapter 36 of *A Tramp Abroad*.

2 or 3 yarns of Artemus Ward.

It takes a heap of sense to write good nonsense

2 Kings, <VI> 18 ch & 27 v.

People praise Tom Jones & Rod. Random (beastly witless, poverty) & dispraise Mystery of Mechanicsville"[21] whereas their argument fits both—"the memory of such a society should not be preserved—it has no right to a place in literature"—it defiles literature. It depends on who writes a thing whether it is coarse or not. Rabelais. I once wrote a conversation between Elizabeth, Shaks, Ben Jonson, Beaumont, Sir W. Raleigh, <4 maids of honor,> Lord Bacon Sir Nicholas Throckmorton, & a stupid old nobleman—this latter being cup-bearer to the queen & ostensible reporter of the talk. There were 4 maids of honor present, & a sweet young girl 2 years younger than the boy Beaumont. <I used> I built a conversation which *could* have happened—I used words such as *were* used at that time—1601. I sent it anonymously to a magazine—& how the editor abused it & the sender. But that man was a praiser of Rabelais, & had been *saying*, O that we had a Rabelais—I judged I could furnish him one.

Then I took it to one of the greatest & best <o>& most learned of divines & read it to him. He came in an ace of killing himself with laughter (for between you & me <it [w]>the thing *was* dreadfully funny; I don't often write anything that I laugh at myself, but I can hardly think of that thing without laughing.) That old divine thot that was a piece of the finest kind of literary art—& David Gray of the Buffalo Courier said it ought to be printed privately & left behind me when I died, & then my fame as a literary artist would last.[22] [#]

---

[21] Edward Eggleston's *Mystery of Metropolisville* (New York: Orange Judd and Co., 1873) is a realistic depiction of life in a Minnesota prairie town during a land speculation boom in 1856. Bryant M. French has pointed out the parallels between Eggleston's book and *The Gilded Age* (*Mark Twain and "The Gilded Age"* [Dallas: Southern Methodist University Press, 1965], pp. 231–232).

[22] In his Autobiographical Dictation of 31 July 1906 Clemens recalled that 1601 or *Conversation, As It Was By the Social Fireside, in the Time of the Tudors* was

The funniest things are the forbidden. Do you know T? When I have a pure audience I tell about the hostler.

Stanley is <the> almost the only man alive to-day whose name & work will be familiar 100 yrs hence.[23]

Copyright.

You can't put in the pauses—& they are the main thing. Did you ever hear a clergyman do the Lord's prayer? He doesn't know the value of pauses.

When I spoke against Gen. Mott's RR I was interested.[24]

Mch 28/79—Went to see pictures rushed into Palais d'Industrie[25] end of afternoon—last chance to get them in. Stair ways crowded—street full of vans & the vans full of pictures. Every time a poor picture came in, everybody groaned. Perfect howl went up, sometimes when particularly poor one came—it was snatched & passed from hand to hand. Picture of wood-sawing—everybody made a sound like sawing. Picture of St Jerome & skull—lot of students followed

---

written as a letter to Twichell in the summer of 1876. David Gray, newspaper writer and poet, told Clemens: "Put your name to it. Don't be ashamed of it. It is a great and fine piece of literature and deserves to live, and will live. Your *Innocents Abroad* will presently be forgotten, but this will survive. Don't be ashamed; don't be afraid. Leave the command in your will that your heirs shall put on your tombstone these words, and these alone: '*He wrote the immortal* 1601'" (*MTE*, p. 209). The earliest edition of 1601, instigated surreptitiously by John Hay, was the 1880 printing by Alexander Gunn of four pamphlet copies. Clemens authorized a limited edition of 50 copies in 1882 from the West Point Academy press. A full discussion of the book's history is in Franklin J. Meine's 1939 edition printed for the Mark Twain Society of Chicago.

[23] Henry M. Stanley's *Through the Dark Continent*, an account of his adventures during his 1874–1877 expedition to the interior of Africa, was published in 1878.

[24] General Gershom Mott resigned his commission in the United States Army in 1866 to become paymaster of New Jersey's Camden & Amboy Railroad, a position he held until 1875 when he became treasurer of New Jersey. The nature and the occasion of Clemens' attack on the railroad is unknown.

[25] The Palais de l'Industrie on the Champs-Elysées was used for various exhibits, the most famous of which was the Salon, the great annual exhibit of modern art held from May through June.

it weeping on each other's shoulders. Was a row last year, so it was announced that this year only people bearing pictures would be admitted—so there came 50 students, each carrying a 10-cent chromo very carefully.—There were acres of pictures. Any artist may send two. or three but not more. I think they said 2 was the limit. A jury of the first artists of France (elected by the exhibitors) will examine these 6 or 7000 pictures between now & May 11, & retain about 2000 & reject the rest. They can tell a good picture or a bad one at a single glance—these are at once set aside & the real work begins, the culling the best from among those that lie somewhere between the perfectly good & the perfectly bad. And a tough job it is.—An artist can't vote for the jury till he has exhibited more than twice. Pictures are <s>often rejected for want of room. These can be offered again next year. Among the acres we saw one which had been rejected twice already. It would take a plucky man to carry his own picture up those stairs. Sometimes a fine picture is applauded.

Take a ride on the steam roller to the Bois de Boulogne, from Place de la Concorde to avoid carriages.

Religion consists in a set of things which <a man> the average man thinks he believes, & wishes he was certain.

<Some things are impossible:>

White,[26] now of Berlin—Yes, G *is* a d—d old *nepot!*

Amer. authors.

Susie's bears.[27] [#]

[26] Andrew Dickson White, first president of Cornell University, succeeded Bayard Taylor as United States minister to Germany. Clemens wrote Howells of his approval of White's appointment on 15 April 1879 (*MTHL*, p. 260).

[27] In a 17 November 1878 letter to Howells, Clemens described his daughter's complaint: "She is sorely badgered with dreams; & her stock dream is that she is being eaten up by bears. She is a grave & thoughtful child, as you will remember. Last night she had the usual dream. This morning she stood apart (after telling it,) for some time, looking vacantly at the floor, & absorbed in meditation. At last she looked up, & with the pathos of one who feels he has not been dealt by with even-handed fairness, said, 'But mamma, the trouble is, that I am never the *bear*, but always the PERSON' " (*MTHL*, pp. 241–242).

Tell how Riley being stopped in a driving snow storm by applicant for S F Post office, calmly buttonholed him & told him about that man that stopped at Gadsby's hotel, when going to collect a Govt claim. Man left next day for San F.[28]

Dined with the Earl of Dunraven. D. D. Home (pronounced *Hume,*) the spiritualist miracle-worker, was present. An Austrian prince Wrede, brother of the great diplomatist, came in—a fascinating man, simple-hearted, unpretending, & a fine mind—more than 6 feet high<t> & exceedingly handsome—about 30 yrs old. Home is 45, but only looks 35. Resembles me in the face. He is a very fine fellow & makes warm & everlasting friendships with all sorts of people.[29]

The girl from Indiana, who so signed herself in her report to the Munich police—& everybody crowded forward to see the Indiana (Indian)—& remarked "Why she's white!")

Wonderful French artificial flowers.

Early morning (if quiet) in Paris, is like <a sum> dozing in country in summer,—with the strange & plaintive cries of the hucksters for grasshoppers—How rich & strong & musical these voices

---

[28] Clemens had related some of J. H. Riley's anecdotes in the article "Riley—Newspaper Correspondent" published in the November 1870 *Galaxy*. Riley's story of "The Man Who Put Up at Gadsby's" is told by Mark Twain in chapter 26 of *A Tramp Abroad*. See note 4 for further information about Clemens' involvement with Riley.

[29] "Last evening we had calls from eight o'clock until a few minutes after twelve," Livy wrote to her mother on 28 April. "We had an exceedingly interesting evening because we got on the topic of spiritual & mesmeric influences &c—ghost stories & the like—Mr & Mrs Chamberlain and a very bright Englishman were of the company so there was plenty of bright talk—Mr Home the man who floats out of third story windows and does other marvelous things has been here a number of times—the man does not impress me very pleasantly—I should not feel inclined to trust him unreservedly—oh we do see such queer people." An eye-witness account of Home's third story feat is provided in the Earl of Dunraven's *Experiences in Spiritualism with D. D. Home* (Glasgow: Robert MacLehose & Co., 1924), p. 156. Home died in 1886, the authenticity of his "miracles" having been cast very much in doubt in the later years of his life.

are—& how some bore into your head & *through* it—& <h>what long distances they can be heard. What *vast* sounds some of them are!

When I was 5 prayed for ginger snaps & assisted <by> Providence by helping myself.[30]

12th Apl—Paris—While writing an "interview" for Mr. Richard Whiteing, representative of N. Y. World, I was about to say something about International Copyright, when it occurred to me that a trade-mark case decided in my favor by Judge Lawrence in New York (about 1873) *really established international copyright* with need of new legislation. I altered the interview to that complexion. I make this note while waiting to see what the upshot will be.[31] [#]

---

30 In his Autobiographical Dictation of 15 August 1906 Clemens recalled this incident from his early school days in Missouri. The schoolteacher, Mrs. Horr,

> always opened school with prayer and a chapter from the New Testament; also she explained the chapter with a brief talk. In one of these talks she dwelt upon the text, "Ask and ye shall receive," and said that whosoever prayed for a thing with earnestness and strong desire need not doubt that his prayer would be answered. . . . I believed in Mrs. Horr thoroughly and I had no doubts as to the result. I prayed for gingerbread. Margaret Kooneman, who was the baker's daughter, brought a slab of gingerbread to school every morning; she had always kept it out of sight before but when I finished my prayer and glanced up, there it was in easy reach and she was looking the other way. In all my life I believe I never enjoyed an answer to prayer more than I enjoyed that one; and I was a convert, too. (*MTE*, pp. 108–109)

31 Richard Whiteing, an English journalist, was the Paris correspondent for the New York *World*. His interview with Clemens was published in the *World* of 11 May 1879 and partially reprinted in the Hartford *Courant* of 14 May 1879. The "trade-mark case" to which Clemens refers is the 1873 case of *Clemens* v. *Such* described in Notebook 17, note 112. On 15 April 1879 Clemens wrote to Frank Bliss: "Been interviewed by the 'World' representative. . . . He is an old lawyer—does me the honor to think I may possibly have solved the problem of International Copyright, and I,—who am no lawyer,—am of his opinion. I'm going to lay the matter before some experts, before I take on any airs in the matter" (*MTLP*, pp. 111–112). Clemens' "experts" were evidently dubious about his solution, for the published interview did not mention the case, although it included a long discussion of international copyright. While American authors, Clemens stated, did not presently have a great pecuniary interest in the success of international copyright, they certainly should fight for its acceptance on moral grounds.

Yes, I <know Fr> speak Fr just well enough to call for hairs when I want horses. (cheveux chevaux)[32]

To Harris at Paris fair—Where are you going?
To hell!
Yes,—but I mean *now?*
I'm going now (a show)

Frenchman speaking admiringly of a little girl—"What! <7> seven years old & still virtuous? The little angel!"

Paris, 7th May. I wish this eternal winter would come to an end. Snow flakes fell to-day, & also about a week ago. Have had rain *almost without intermission* for 2 months & one week. Have had a fire every day since Sept. 10, & have now just lighted one.

"He boards at the Bon Marchè"[33]

May 8—Called on Tourgènieff <&> with Boyesen & had cup of tea out of his Samovar.[34]

<At> May 11. Attended <p>the "private View" of the Salon.[35] [#]

---

[32] Clemens used this play on words in a chapter about French customs which was not included in *A Tramp Abroad*. In the unpublished manuscript, Clemens explains the impossibility of the existence of poetry in France: "Poesy cannot thrive at its best except on higher levels. Besides, a language which is so blurry & undecided that it cannot make any palpable distinction between hairs & horses (*cheveux* and *chevaux*), is not favorable to Poetic expression."

[33] Clemens contemplated writing a chapter about the famous Parisian department store, Au Bon Marché (see p. 311), founded in 1852 by Aristide Boucicaut.

[34] Norwegian writer Hjalmar Hjorth Boyesen and his wife visited frequently with the Clemenses in Paris. Clemens wrote to Howells on 15 April 1879: "We like Boyesen & his wife, heartily. Poor fellow, there are 12 Orions in his family. That's enough to make anybody warm to him" (*MTHL*, p. 260). Boyesen had first met Turgenev in Paris in 1873 and had published his conversations with the Russian novelist in an article in the April 1874 *Galaxy*.

[35] In some pages from his discarded *Tramp Abroad* chapters, Clemens mentioned the preview and his new acquaintance, Turgenev: "'Varnishing day' is sacred to the artists & their invited friends. This is the day before the public opening, & is called the 'private view.' . . . Evidently there are many artists, & they have many friends, for the mighty building was pretty full that day. It was a good time to see

May 12. Tourgènieff called & spent evening. Brought me one of his books. Gave him Tom Sawyer.[36]

'Tis a wise Frenchman that knows his own father.

Conversation with one of those curious (& very frequent) persons who speak English but cannot understand it:

I—These are very fine oranges—where are they grown?

He—More? Yes, I will bring them.

I—No, do not bring any more—I only want to know where they come from—where they are raised?

He—Yes! (rising inflec)

I—Yes—can you tell me <where>what country they are from?

He—Yes—(ris. infl).

I (disheartened)—They are very nice

He—Good-<night>nice.[37]

The Autobiography of a Coward. Make him hideously but unconsciously base & pitiful & contemptible.

French story.—<Pat> To close with a pathetic deathbed scene where she takes pious leave of her <husban> childless husband, her 9 children, & their 9 fathers, <receive> <gets> mind wanders a little, gets some children & fathers mixed, <received>receives absolution, & dies amid showers of tears. [#]

---

celebrities of all sorts, for they were all there. The one that interested me most, was the illustrious Tourguenef, great in literature & equally great in brave & self-sacrificing patriotism. It was not easy to get interested in the pictures while this grand presence was there to draw away the eye & stir the imagination."

[36] In addition to the copy of *Tom Sawyer,* Clemens had Chatto & Windus forward Turgenev a copy of *Roughing It* (Justin Kaplan, *Mr. Clemens and Mark Twain: A Biography* [New York: Simon and Schuster, 1966], p. 221) and inscribed a copy of the 1879 Tauchnitz edition of *The Innocents Abroad:* "To M^r. Ivan Tourguèneff With the affectionate regards of The Author. Paris, May, 1879." Clemens explained in a note added below the inscription: "Tourgueneff asked me to autograph this book for him. Apparently I forgot to return it to him. SLC May, 1908."

[37] This entry and the entries about the "Church of the '*Gratis French Lesson*'" on pages 314 and 316 were used in a chapter omitted from A *Tramp Abroad,* later published as "Paris Notes" in *The Stolen White Elephant.*

Write book on Etique & Complete Letter Writer.[38]
How to enter the presence of a debtor.
Of a creditor—
Of a fiancée
Of a beautiful girl &c

When I get beyond 6 times 7 is 35 I'm done.[39]

Horror: Young lady in hotel in Trent wanted a "priest in bed" with her—turned out to be a warming pan.

That dear sweet old German baroness who loved to find similarities between G & E—'Ah the 2 languages are so alike—we say Ach Gott, you say Goddam." To laugh when peop[le] are serious is not a fault of mine, but this "fetched" me.[40]

A Talk with the departed.
To Henry, (through medium Mansfield)—Pray <move to> try the the other place; <it [-] is better to be less comfortable> you don't seem to have much intellect left, but even that is worth saving, & a change might help."[41] [#]

---

[38] An entry about visiting cards on page 342 is the only other reference in this notebook to Clemens' projected burlesque of etiquette books. Clemens apparently did not begin work on the project until the spring of 1881, when Howells' enthusiasm for the idea revived his interest in it (*MTHL*, pp. 359–360). Portions of the unfinished work appear in Paine's biography (*MTB*, pp. 705–706) and in *Letters from the Earth* (pp. 191–208).

[39] "I had been to school most all the time, and could spell, and read, and write just a little, and could say the multiplication table up to six times seven is thirty-five, and I don't reckon I could ever get any further than that if I was to live forever. I don't take no stock in mathematics, anyway" (*Huckleberry Finn*, chapter 4).

[40] In "A Family Sketch" (Edward L. Doheny Library, Saint John's Seminary, Camarillo, Calif.) written in 1906, Mark Twain confesses: "One is obliged to like the German profanity, after the ear has grown used to it, because it is so guileless & picturesque & alluring. As winning a swearer as we have known was a Baroness in Munich of blameless life, sweet & lovely in her nature, and deeply religious. During the four months we spent there in the winter of 1878–9, our traveling comrade, Miss Clara Spaulding, spent a good deal of time in her house, & the two became intimate friends. The Baroness was fond of believing that in many pleasant ways the Germans & the Americans were alike, & once she hit upon this happy resemblance: 'Why, if you notice, we even talk alike. We say Ach Gott, & you say goddam!' "

[41] James Vincent Mansfield, the "spirit postmaster," had begun his lucrative

I hate discussions. I was present at one where it took fully a ¼ hour to settle a point of the most trifling nature—yet both were men of unusual capacity & practiced in debate. I made up my mind then that <revolvers are> revolvers waste much more time than bowies.

I drew a nice picture but he drew a check for $500—his sold for most.

Wakeman says—it seemed an odd thing to me <the[-]>that we never received spirit communications from spirits born in the other stars."[42]

Make full Chapter about Bon Marché.

Thought I wd go to picture gallery—changed mind & went to B. M.

He boards at the B. M.

Paris, May 28/79—This is one of the coldest days of this most damnable & interminable winter.

Indignation meeting of Bret Harte's characters for being so misrepresented & required to talk impossible & non-existent "dialects" & change them every ten minutes. Till at last some of the whores & burglars said, "We owe him *one* grace, anyway. We have been the

---

business in New York as a "mail-order medium" during the spiritualist craze of the 1850s (Howard Kerr, *Mediums, and Spirit-Rappers, and Roaring Radicals* [Urbana: University of Illinois Press, 1972], pp. 110, 166). A few years after this entry was written, Clemens described a séance, conducted by a medium he called Manchester, in chapter 48 of *Life on the Mississippi*. In a draft of the chapter he wrote, "I called on him once, ten years ago, with a couple of friends to inquire after my brother, lost in the Pennsylvania" (Pierpont Morgan Library, New York, N.Y.). In the published version the séance is conducted for a "friend" of Clemens who wishes to "inquire after a deceased uncle." Speaking through Manchester, the "late uncle" provides only "sloppy twaddle in the way of answers" and cannot answer specific factual questions at all. Clemens' disgust at having the responses of a "beatified vegetable" represented to him as Henry's spirit voice is evident in the original manuscript and in this notebook entry.

42 Clemens had written to Howells from Munich on 30 January 1879 that as soon as he completed his work on A *Tramp Abroad* he intended to "take up Wakeman & Heaven at once" (*MTHL*, p. 250); he did not, however, return to the project until late 1881 (*MTHL*, p. 376).

filthiest lot of heartless villains all our lives that ever went unhung—now instead of using the sufferings of the really good & worthy people whom we have robbed & ruined as the basis of his pathos, he hunts out (no, not that,)—he *manfactures* the one good deed possible to each of us, & in this way he has set the whole world to snuffling over us & wanting to hug us. We owe Harte a deep debt of gratitude—the reverence in which gamblers, burglars & whores <are> are held in the upper classes to-day is all due to him, & to him only—for the dime novel circulates only among the lower ranks.[43]

Accused of beating my wife when I hadn't one!

At Salon—I like French battle-pieces<—>. < because>Because the French fight so well in them.

Salon is the most fascinating place.

Salon

Criticism is a queer thing. If I print "She was stark naked"—& then proceeded to describe her person in detail<s>, <who could> what critic would not howl?—who would venture to leave the book on a parlor table.—but the artist does this & all ages gather around & look & talk & point. I can't say, "They cut his head off, or stabbed him, &c" <&>describe the blood & the agony in his face.

Paris, June 1, 1879. Still this vindictive winter continues. Had a raw cold rain to-day; to-night we sit around a rousing wood fire.

---

[43] Clemens had elaborated on his criticism of Harte's style in a 15 April letter to Howells, prompted by his reading of Harte's new book of sketches, *An Heiress of Red Dog and Other Tales*. He blasted Harte's ridiculously pathetic characters and situations, his inconsistent dialects, and his literary mannerisms, concluding: "If I ever get my tedious book finished, I mean to weed out some of my prejudices & write an article on 'Bret Harte as an Artist'—& print it if it will not be unfair to print it without a signature" (*MTHL*, pp. 261–262). In June 1880 Clemens did publish a somewhat milder commentary on Harte in a long anonymous article in the *Atlantic's* "Contributors' Club," remarking that "no human being, living or dead, ever had experience of the dialect which he puts into his people's mouths. Mr. Harte's originality is not questioned; but if it ever shall be, the caviler will have to keep his hands off that dialect, for that *is* original" (pp. 850–851).

Drove to Nanterre (about an hour from Paris) & saw the Rosiére[44] crowned. The last year's Rosière led the procession <&> (the sweetest face in France,) the new Rosière, (with a pretty maid of honor in blue sash) followed—then came a double file of wee girls, then bigger ones, all in white & blue—future Rosières? The band banged, the trumpets blared, the strong choir sang, the packed church watched the crowning & enthroning of the Rosière—then the ex-Rosière took off *her* crown & wore it on her arm the rest of the time. The new R is an orphan & <suppote>supports 3 brothers taking in washing. She gets 300 fr now—& 200 by & by, or if she marries, gets wedding <dre> apparel in place of it. It once prevailed all around France; but one marked effect of the leveling work of a republic is to destroy aristocratic exclusiveness by making everybody aristocrats. Aristocrat<s> with a tinker's trade & income won't do these things any more than Dukes & *other* aristocrats formerly would.

Gentleman & lady are terms invented expressly to describe aristocrats. You can insult a Republican by calling him an aristocrat, but <eve> you can't insult him by calling him the the same thing in that other form 'gentleman.' You can insult a tinker, with us if you intimate that he is *not* a gentleman. We make it a title of honor instead of a simply descriptive title—hence everybody is entitled to it<.>, tinker & all.

No good smoking tobacco in Europe—no Durham, Vanity F, Lone Jack—but I brought mine with me—been over before.

Washing 12 disciples' feet in palace at Munich—military man to represent the Savior & the King, poured a little water on each's 1 foot & priest gave it a rub—<Dis> Dis. 90 yrs old—fare & keep paid, & purse of 30 2-mark pieces hung round each's next.—oldest & poorest in Bavaria—these are the requirements for the position of Disciple.

---

[44] An annual village ceremony begun in the sixth century by Saint Médard, the bishop of Noyon, who chose his sister as the first Rosière. The ceremony included the coronation of a young virgin renowned for purity and wisdom with a crown of roses.

Let a young American call them the 12 Scribes & Pharisees & describe—& the humiliating thing was that this climax of ignorance was studying for ministry

Presbyterian Young clergyman who sat among catholic worshipers & examined Badeker's map—said he forgot himself. These acts of brutality make religion pleasant <[to]>and give people confidence in it, because they see how it builds up the humanities in the devotee.

<Write chapter> "Quaint Customs."

1. Rosière. June 1.
2. Disciples.
3. Shefflers.[45]

Recount how marriage presents made a man poor.[46]

You can <take> study Bellows' dictionary in Church without scandal, for it is the counterpart of a morrocco covered pocket Testament.

Church of the "*Gratis French Lesson.*"

French story[47]
English speakers
English lady "I have not *got* it.[")]
Graham's Mule Trip.
Hair Trunk.

---

[45] In a chapter omitted from *A Tramp Abroad* Mark Twain tells the legend of the Schefflers, a band of "bold coopers" who helped deliver Munich from a twelfth-century plague, and describes the parade that takes place every seven years to commemorate the event.

[46] A forty-nine page chapter on French courtship and marriage customs dropped from *A Tramp Abroad* was elaborately serious, with footnotes and documentation from such sources as J. G. Wood's *The Uncivilized Races of Men* and H. H. Bancroft's *The Native Races of the Pacific States*. Clemens' intention, however, was satirical. He pretended to show that French "civilization" was no greater than that of primitive tribes and that French etiquette merely formalized that nation's ignoble customs. Clemens drew heavily upon a manual of French etiquette, translating and mistranslating long passages.

[47] Most of the notes in this list refer to entries made at greater length in Notebooks 16 and 17.

Fellow that robbed <St>San Marco.
Discharged George.

India shawl $700 in war time worth $20 now & still falling—$80 & $100 gets a fine one.

In American hotels <c>hall carpets differ in color on each floor—in Europe you never know which is your floor.

English say, "She threw herself on the *ground*" meaning the floor.

No gas in Europe—the dingy lamps make life utterly wretched.

First class hotels all seem to use poor cheap 2^{d} hand meats & veg because cheap.

They begin to have strawberries when they have been 2 full months in market—then they buy <&>*old* & poor ones.

New potatoes *one single day*—it was never repeated.

Sunday June 8—We went with Clara & Gen. Fairchild[48] to the Grand Prix & saw Nubienne win the $20,000 given half by City Govt & ½ by RR's—12 horses in that race.

De Lesseps gave the Rosière stock certificate No. 1 in the Isthmus Interoceanic Canal ($100.)[49]

Cream-colored slippers—
Some toilettes.

Ticket given to legations to break through any procession except funeral & soldiers.

I lost 100 fr & won some trifles—part of loss was six balloon tickets (60 fr.)[50] [#]

---

48 A former governor of Wisconsin, General Lucius Fairchild was the American consul-general in Paris.

49 Ferdinand de Lesseps had been elected president of the international congress on the Interoceanic Canal which met in Paris from 15 to 19 May 1879 to consider reports on the cost, location, and commercial significance of the projected canal. Work on the Panama Canal began in February 1881.

50 One of the greatest attractions of the 1878 Paris Exposition was Henry Gif-

Of girls who rode alone in superb carriages. Little E thought they must be duchesses. They were not town-women. It appears per last census that every man in France over 16 years of age & under 116, has at least 1 wife to whom he has never been married. French novels, talk, drama & newspaper bring daily & overwhelming proofs that the most of the married ladies have paramours. (Put that before the former sentence.) This <oc>causes/makes a good deal of what we <should> call crime, <but which> and the French call sociability.

"Church of the Gratis French Lesson."[51]

Church of the Holy Mary &c. He pointed & said "This is the Arc de Triomphe—this is the French Protestant Church, *alias* the <&cc>&c &c—the French can't get into it—always full of Yanks & Eng with F. <book bound like> Testaments & Bellows's admirable dictionary which is always bound like a Testament in dark morocco, has a flap, &c.

The Moses.[52]

Put in my duel with Laird?[53] [#]

---

fard's captive balloon in the courtyard of the Tuileries. The balloon, which could accommodate 38 persons, was permanently installed at the Tuileries in 1879, making its first ascension on 16 June 1879. An entry of 23 June in General Lucius Fairchild's diary (Wisconsin State Historical Society, Madison) indicates that Clemens, Livy, and Clara Spaulding were to make the excursion with Fairchild on that date.

[51] In "Paris Notes" (*The Stolen White Elephant*, 1882) Clemens claimed that in a church "nicknamed 'The Church of the Gratis French Lesson'" "devout foreigners" pretended to read the Bible when in fact they were studying John Bellows' *Dictionary for the Pocket: French and English, English and French*. Bellows' dictionary, he noted, was "in look and binding and size . . . just like a Testament." On 5 March 1883 Bellows wrote thanking Clemens "heartily for the kind and humorous notice . . . of my little dictionary."

[52] On 10 June 1879 Clemens wrote to Frank Bliss regarding the illustrations for *A Tramp Abroad*: "I shall have one full page made here by a fine wood-engraver if he will cut it for anything under $100. . . . It is a thing which I *manufactured* by pasting a popular comic picture into the middle of a celebrated Biblical one—shall attribute it to Titian. It needs to be engraved by a master" (*MTLP*, pp. 116–117). The composite illustration appears as the frontispiece to *A Tramp Abroad*.

[53] In the Autobiographical Dictation of 19 January 1906, Clemens told of his

Drawing from the nude in Rome

A French marriage & funeral.

Stupid fashion of European physicians in sending in no bill.

Rotten strawberries for dinner.

With French dressmaker always take a sample or they use cheaper material.

Louis XIV destroyed the Palatinate in mere spite & Frenchmen destroyed St Clou merely to keep Germans from doing it—& *they* would not have done it.

Put this with D'Aiguillon[54]

No Frenchman big enough to see greatness in Germany or a Ger

Don't know the rules of art—but no matter—at a public <dinner> table I may criticise the dinner without being a cook.

Tell Brown[55] to make stiff fashion-plate pictures.—no send them home to be processed. Subject Les Modes Parisiennes de l'annè 1879 —the Moods of the Parisians at an Annual in 1879. (Harris's trans.)

Thinking Tiffany would give honest measure, went there & ordered 15 sticks of wood. He said he had none in stock—said <he>his license allowed him to deal only in such jewelry as comes

duel in 1864 with James L. Laird, the proprietor of the Virginia City *Union* (*MTA*, 1:355–359). Henry Nash Smith gives a more impartial account of the affair in *Mark Twain of the "Enterprise"* (Berkeley and Los Angeles: University of California Press, 1957), pp. 24–29.

[54] In 1688/1689 Louis XIV invaded the Protestant Palatinate territories, destroying Mannheim, Heidelberg, Spires, Worms, and Bingen. The destruction of the palace of Saint Cloud occurred on 13 October 1870 during the Franco-Prussian war. Clemens evidently intended to add these two episodes to "The French and the Comanches," a chapter dropped from *A Tramp Abroad* (published in *Letters from the Earth*, pp. 183–189). Only an account of D'Aiguillon, minister of foreign affairs and minister of war under Louis XV, appears in that sketch.

[55] The illustrator chosen by Clemens for *A Tramp Abroad*: "I've got an artist, here, to my mind,—young Walter F. Brown; you have seen pictures of his occasionally in St. Nicholas and Harper's Weekly. He is a pupil of the painter Gerome, here, and has greatly improved, of late" (SLC to Frank Bliss, 10 May 1879, *MTLP*, p. 114).

under the head of "wearing apparel." Said a great jeweler here once attempted to evade or ignore this, but the moment he displayed a wood-pile in his show-case the regular wood dealers mutinied in a body & began to sell diamonds in their woodyards at ruinous rates. This brought about an immediate compromise, & the two trades have never encroached upon each other's domains since.

France has usually been governed by prostitutes.

Looking back over history, one is comforted. Bad as our gov't is, it is a mighty improvement on old times.

France has neither winter nor summer nor morals—apart from these drawbacks it is a fine country.

You perceive I generalize with intrepidity from single instances. It is the tourist's custom. When I see a man jump from the Vendome column, I say "They like to do that in France."

Gave away all my Durham & kept the worst brand in America—still it was of course better than any in Europe—Latakie is almost as good—

Frauenkirche—cow-teats.[56]

The French are fuller of greatnesses & fuller of littlenesses or childishnesses than any other nation. When d'Aiguillon sent to require the Parliament of Paris to resume duty, out of near 200, (at midnight) only 40 agreed, & these retracted next day.

Corsica became a French possession only just in time to make Napoleon a Frenchman—he was born the year after the annexation.

Don't forget to tell Abbey's joke on the Stomach Club—couldn't make a speech but would tell a story—talked everybody out of the place & then pretended he could not remember the end of the tale & hoped they would excuse him from proceeding with it—[57]

---

[56] Clemens' association was suggested by the shape of the two towers of the Frauenkirche, the fifteenth-century cathedral in Munich.

[57] Edwin Austin Abbey delivered his burlesque speech at a Paris Stomach Club

He is a fine artist in more ways than one.

Stomach Club has good times.

Titian's Venus in the Tribune is grossly obscene—it is wholly sensual—the <ex>face, the expression, the attitude—not a relieving refinement about it anywhere—she is purely the Goddess of the Beastly (Bestial)—(One can't describe in print what an artist is permitted to display to the eye unmasked) In the Salon is nude beauty going to the bath who is just the reverse—while she is much more lovely than V, she <excites> is as pure in her thoughts & her heart & spirit as she could be with all her clothes on. She is thinking nothing that can soil her or the spectator—V is thinking bestialities. She inflames & disgusts at the same moment. The S. girl excites <n[--]>no base reflection—you only think "How sweet & beautiful she is"—you hardly think about whether she is <nude> naked or not. Young girls <m>can be defiled by looking at V but not at S.

Drawing from nude in Rome—can't even say naked, but a painter can paint it as much as he wants to.

The woman dressed on the platform.

If she is a specimen the average woman is but ill formed.

When you are in Europe it is such a rest from care. At home every funeral is a personal matter & you sigh or even cry. Here you look on & are cheerful<ly> & able to say say "I'm glad you're gone."

French is the artificial nation.

<The glory of>*Glory* is the essential thing. French glory is

---

dinner. The joke is explained in Abbey's biography: "Although [Abbey's] conception of a chestnut was different from that of the majority of us to-day, he it was who led up to its present sense. Abbey's chestnut was a 'spoof' story—a story, that is, which went nowhere and never finished. It had something to do with the number of chestnuts on a tree, and could be carried on indefinitely, with endless ramifications, and was told with a face of profound gravity, until at last the purpose of the narrator broke on the baffled and patiently expectant audience and they burst into laughter" (E. V. Lucas, *Edwin Austin Abbey, Royal Academician: The Record of His Life and Work*, 2 vols. [New York: Charles Scribner's Sons, 1921], 1:52–53). According to Albert Bigelow Paine, Clemens delivered his speech "Some Thoughts on the Science of Onanism" at this same Stomach Club dinner (DV 200; *MTB*, p. 643).

different from other glory—for French <glories>glory can be won in <the> very inglorious ways—in unjust wars, in silly wars, in petty victories over pitiful numbers.

French are the connecting link between man & the monkey.

<A><Disciples>

Devotees of the trivial.

<Prove> Whatever is trivial to another man is important to a Frenchman. It is this that makes the French the most (artificially) polite nation.

Trivial Americans go to Paris when they die.[58]

They have no poetry else we should have some in translations. Bayard Taylor said the F. language was an inadequate vehicle for the conveyance of poetic thought.

The language is right for the people—it is a mess of trivial sounds—words which <mi> run into each other (by law)—<w> & words which never end, but fade away. If one tried to be in earnest in such a language he could only be sophomoric & theatrical—& that is what an F usually is when <serious> earnest—or what *he* thinks is in earnest.—& a F can be in earnest for a little while at a time, but he cant stay so, he is too light, too fickle, too frivolous.

It is the language for lying compliment, <&> for illicit love & for the conveying of exquisitely nice shades of meaning in bright graceful & trivial conversations—the conveying, <of> especially, of <indecencies> double-meanings, a decent & indecent one so blended as—nudity thinly veiled, but gauzily & lovelily.[59]

Foreignly speaking, they <were>have been more accustomed to be licked than to lick, before <the>and since the

---

[58] Clemens is recalling Thomas Gold Appleton's aphorism "Good Americans, when they die, go to Paris."

[59] Seven clippings from French newspapers were pinned to the notebook at this point. One clipping is a factual account of a recent duel; another, which Clemens noted as being from *L'Evénement,* is a strongly worded attack on the charity bazaar, an institution which, the paragraph stated, offended the nation's "moral sense of smell." The five remaining clippings illustrate the slightly salacious flavor of French journalistic humor. Clemens retained the clippings in support of his statement that the French language was best suited to the expression of indecencies "thinly veiled."

<<victories>victorious time> day of that great foreigner the 1st Napoleon.

Foreigners still run the important offices.

Spent <a>more time fighting among themselves than any other nation except the Fiji Islanders, <&> the Digger Indians & the Kilkenny cats.

The nation as a nation, <is> was a nation of savages up to within the memory of men—I don't mean the lower classes, for that goes without saying,—but the uppers. It was the uppers who invented, those bridal & feet-warming privileges,[60] some centuries ago—They were savages at heart, no matter how cultivated <the> & polite they were. Only savages <[w]>could <maintain>tain & preserve & transmit those atrocious privileges from father to son through the ages—F. was able to furnish those savages. England could not have done it.

For 1000 years the savage nation indulged itself in massacers—every now & then a big massacre or a little one. <Two chief traits—love> <F.'s chief> <I>The massacring spirit is peculiar to F—I mean in Xdom—no other state has had it. In this, F has always walked abreast kept her end up with her brethren the Turks & the Burmese.

Bastile

Two chief traits—love of glory & massacre.

Childish race & great.

The Reign of Terror showed that without distinction of rank the people were savages—marquises, dukes, lawyers, blacksmiths, they <al> each figure there in due proportion to their craft's numbers—fewer marquises than blacksmiths merely because there were fewer

---

[60] Clemens discussed "several striking and remarkable customs" of the French nobility in "The French and the Comanches," among others "the lord's right to make the peasants, after working all day, sit up and whip the ponds all night with boughs, to prevent the frogs' music from disturbing my lord's slumbers; the lord's right to cut open a peasant and warm his feet in him, as in a foot muff, when the chase had wearied my lord and made him cold; and, finally, comes *le droit du seigneur*—let it go in French, it would soil the English language to describe it in that tongue" (*LE*, pp. 183, 184).

Marquises than b. There was no difference between the city exquisites & the country clods—in savagery <both> they were equal & it was the equality of perfection. Paris was not able to teach the back settlements anything in the way of atrocities—but <the two together> either of them could have taught our Indians a trick or two. To strip men & women & youths & girls naked & tie them together in couples—a male to a female—& usually without introducing them to each other—& then throw them into the river to drown, was a touch above the invention of our Indians.[61]

One gets his notion of the F from their books & their history.

Chastity

Lying—*constant* in books

<Honor>

—plainly it is *no* shame to lie in F. If one may judge by books & history, a F. does not know what it is to tell the truth for its own sake; he cannot conceive of telling truth merely to preserve his self-respect—no, truth, to him, is a thing to be told when it will answer the purpose as well as a lie.

It is a country which has been governed by concubines for 1000 years. <I am not referring <to> alone to the <despots> conspicuous despots> Its <kings> bachelors & its husbands have been ruled by their concubines, from the king all the way down though <the> every rank & subdivision of society to the scavenger, the rat catcher & the street beggar. While the Pompadour was directing the armies in the field, or while Madame Du Barry was destroying the Parliament of Paris, the concubines of the inconspicuous millions have been attending to directing the minor details of the government of the country; while the throned concubines have managed matters of state, their myriad sisters have managed those beneath the state crust. <Wh> In countries where wives hold the first place in the husbands' hearts, the men govern the country—they govern it, receiving wise & <r>unselfish counsel

---

[61] Clemens is remembering Carlyle's description in *The French Revolution* of the *noyades* (in Carlyle's language, the "Drownages") of December 1793 in Nantes.

from the wives. The wives do not *govern* the country, for they do not govern its men. But concubines do govern the men, & in the very nature of things they govern them with selfish ends in view. A <country> nation governed in all its big & little details by foul & selfish & trivial-minded prostitutes is not likely to have much largeness or dignity of character. As for purity, & real refinement, they are impossible under such a system—plenty of sham refinement, though.

A Frenchman's home is where another man's wife is.[62]

The nation of the filthy-minded.

Their match-boxes go into the family & are foul; their *daily* papers reek with <smutty> indelicate witticisms; their novels

Let us not underestimate the humble match-box as an indicator of national character. It goes into the bedchambers of the girls & the boys the men & the women of the lower classes, the middle classes, the top crust & all.—& to all it carries its indelicate allusion & its immodest (& often obscene) picture.

<He put me on the sofa, & put his hand on my ancle & pushed it up above my stocking & then up between my naked thighs & then>

All children are <led> guarded to school—even great louts of boys<.>—this latter <fact is suggestive in so loathesome a society as this.> protection would be wise in Turkey—& between Turkey & France the difference in some things is not perceptible. (Don't use that insinuation if it is erroneous.)

They have bestialities which are unknown in civilized lands.

I might gloss over things & speak of F as one of the civilized nations, but that wd be F politeness—which consists in the avoidance of uncomfortable things by the medium of a lie.

<D>In F romances, *all* the characters lie, & in the most indifferent way, from the King & the Archbishop down. They don't know what truth is.

---

[62] Most of the notes on the following pages (through p. 326) were used in a discarded chapter on French morality and customs which was intended to precede the "French and the Comanches" manuscript.

Nor honor. The generals decided "for the honor" of France<"> to resist an impossible siege by the Germans. Silly.—

They fight duels to mend their injured honor, & the F duel indicates the size of F honor very exactly.

The shopkeepers <all> are given to cheating in small irritating ways. Sell you one quality & make the clothes of another. Sell you 10 yards & only use 8.

A F. lady said, "I have no shoemaker—I change every time—they always try to please, the first time & get one's custom."

Compulsory chastity in F till marriage—no restrait required after that, apparently.

Scratch an F & you find a gorilla.

Take America by & large & it is the most civilized of all nations. Pure-minded women are the rule, in every rank of life of the *native-born.* The men are clean-minded, too, beyond the world's average.

The <popular> common & popular F novel is as easy to buy or borrow as is the box of matches, & doubtless the young girl reads them—she can read the papers, too. She is reared in an atmosphere which is suffocating with nastiness <& because she is watched over by a <foul<d>> nurse & never allowed to go out alone, perhaps she is consi> & the absolutely necessary consequence is that she is nasty-minded. Perhaps the reason English & Am girls look so <pure> clean & sweet & wholesome over here is because we know their <thoughts> minds are not acquainted with unclean thoughts —in view of F history & literature a man must be a fool who can believe in the cleanliness of the average F girl's mind.—

<He believes in her body's chastity>

The body's chastity is manifestly all that the F value—the mind's <unchastity>chastity is a thing they certainly cannot value.

The F is the connecting link between monkey & human being.

It is a race of libertines &

<His> A F.'s home is where another <woman's> man's wife is. [#]

Country of incomplete civilization

Liberte, Equalite, Fraternité

Never been but one great era in F & that was under the <great>Great Foreigner, Nap. ?

They probably have an idea of decency, but it is not easy to imagine what it can be. It is about what a scavenger's idea of cleanliness is.

<Untran>Unrepeatable dirt in every daily paper—put in the suggestion about p—ing & praying at the same time.

I don't approve of putting in untranslated foreign stuff, but <you> as to pp's from F papers, we must draw the line somewhere.

The head of the X^n religion in F. <r[-]>is Paul de Cassagnac.[63] This pious man fights for religion & the empire.

Scratch a F & you find a savage . . . a Fw & you find a harlot. I think my overstates this.

The language is seldom called upon to do the pathetic, but sometimes a pathetic thing does occur there:

Dying lady takes affectionate leave of her <11>12 children & their 10 fathers—has forgotten name of the other father—commends all to God & wants them to be always pious & worthy of her. Takes tearful leave of her husband, & says, "My <darlin> dear spouse, you must lose me, but I leave you these my <<chi>darling> children for your solace—& you are not childless *yourself*, is it not so?"

"I have 3 <ch>sweet cherubs by our friend's wife next door."

"The good God has bountifully blessed us, praised be His name."

This nation is not wholly savage—it has a surface humanity which crops out in hospitals, asylums, places for succor of wounded <or>&

---

[63] Described in chapter 8 of *A Tramp Abroad* as "the most inveterate of the French duelists," Paul de Cassagnac edited the Conservative paper *Le Pays* and served in the Chamber of Deputies. He figured in several political duels defending the Bonapartist cause against the Republicans. On 3 July 1879 Cassagnac was tried and acquitted of "inciting hatred and contempt of the Government" (London *Times*, 4 July 1879).

drowned people. It is capable of being raised to quite a fair sort of civilization by the right sort of Am & Eng missionaries. The Ams we have established there are *not* the right sort, for they ape & admire the natives.

They doff hats when a hearse passes—that shows a possibility of civilization.

But a great drawback is the fact that many of <the [r]a>them think it *already* a <civilizati>civilized nation! I am not jesting. I have seen it repeatedly in print. Victor Hugo has even spoken of France as the sun of intelligence whence the rest of the world is lighted & hence civilized. I think he was in earnest, though of course he may have been speaking ironically.

Speak in these ch. of Munich & other dwellings & cookery.[64]

Venice—here I appointed agents to do the rest of the walking (all over Europe) & then we used trains afterward.

Get copy of L'Assomoir<.>illustrated—[65]

They lash & beat their horses—German's don't. When they pick up the reins the horse is all of a tremble, <& he is no>in dread of the lash & he is not disappointed Down it comes, the moment his head is in right direction. G's *crack* <[w]>the whip, only.

The colony has its feeble newspaper to glorify its movements, court-journal fashion

Another was started by an escaped convict, a Scotchman named John Hanlon (a "society" journal in such hands!) but it died.[66] [#]

---

[64] Clemens drafted eleven pages of a chapter comparing the comforts of life in Munich and elsewhere in Europe with those in America. The final page of the incomplete manuscript contains part of the first paragraph of the discussion of European and American cooking which appears in chapter 49 of *A Tramp Abroad*.

[65] Emile Zola's novel about the effects of drunkenness in a working class family appeared in 1876, and soon became the focus of a controversy over naturalism in literature and in the theater. Only one illustrated edition of the novel was published (Paris: C. Marpon & E. Flammarion, [187?]).

[66] On 6 April 1879 John Hanlon wrote to Clemens soliciting a contribution

Idiotic fashion of living in flats & putting no name on door. Concierge can never explain your location intelligently. You always go a flight too high & come down a flight too low & you ring the bells of all the floors before you get through. The name or even the initials (if you fear frauds) on the door would save much climbing & profanity.

Paris papers small & dirty are dated a day ahead & contain last week's news.

1 or 200 years from now we shall have a pop of 150 or 200,000,000 & then we shall lead the fashions & be the centre of intelligence.

Joseph Verey,[67] courier, from Paris through Holland to London. —As he has to go to London anyhow, he makes the short trip at his customary wages for longer ones—i.e. at the rate of £12 a month, $2 a day.

Wages to begin July 8.

Knock Mr. Carrall's invention in the head by describing this note-book[68]

To be witty in France is very simple—one <only> merely needs to be dirty.

---

to "the new paper the *Boulevard*, to be published immediately, by means of which we intend to provide a high-class original literary journal for all the English-speaking peoples on the Continent of Europe, adopting, to some extent, the features of the society journals of England." A prospectus was enclosed, on the back of which Clemens wrote: "Letter from that thief John Hanlon." The reason for Clemens' dislike of Hanlon remains obscure.

[67] Recalling his displeasure with George Burk—whom he had discharged in Venice for incompetence—and the difficulty of traveling without expert assistance, in *A Tramp Abroad* Mark Twain praised one courier "who might fairly be called perfection." This was the "young Polander" Joseph N. Verey who "spoke eight languages, and seemed to be equally at home in all of them; he was shrewd, prompt, posted, and punctual" (chapter 32). Livy also praised Verey in a letter of 20 July to her mother: "Our currier proved to be *perfect* we had no care whatever he managed everything so splendidly—we have wished during all these days that we had had him last Fall we should have had so much more pleasure in our Switzerland and Italian trip" (MTM).

[68] Clemens' notebook invention is described in Notebook 15, note 45. "Mr. Carrall's invention" has not been identified.

Hence there are plenty of <w> humorous papers in Paris.

July 10 Left Paris at 7.20 a.m., arrived at Brussels, a dirty, beauful (architecturally) <town> interesting town)—& remained till afternoon<s> of 12th.

Wiertz <g> Museum

He did so & so in Amsterdam—it was evident that he was an Amsterdam fool.

No man in a splendid uniform can do a trivial thing.
No judge in a wig can descend from his proper dignity.

<D>Some fool put our ministers & consuls in plain clothes—he had never been abroad, probably, & did not know the value of clothes.

The Dutch painters, like <Se>Saftleven, Griffier, D. Teniers, Jr., [*blank*] must have used a single hair for a brush & trimmed it to a point.

Afternoon of 12th July went to Antwerp.
13th, Sunday, went on board flag-ship Trenton.
Dined that evening with Consul Stewart & some officers of the Trenton & the Alliance.[69]
Took the family & breakfasted on board Trenton 14th (Monday.) Admiral Rowan arrived during the meal.
I smoked on the Admiral's side of the deck, not knowing it <was unlawful> was sacred by naval etiquette.
We were still freezing, these days & it was still raining constantly. We had 4 steady months of rain & cold weather in Paris, & now it still continued. We could get only one room with a fire in it, so we gave that to the children.
Attended high mass, Sunday, in Cathedral of Antwerp. There is nothing solemn or impressive about this exasperating mummery.

---

[69] John H. Steuart was the United States consul at Antwerp. The flagship *Trenton* and the *Alliance* were under the command of Vice-Admiral Stephen Clegg Rowan, a hero of the Mexican and Civil Wars.

Rubens masterpiece, the Ascent of the Cross—Christ seems to be an acrobat.[70]

In Brussels Cathedral heard the most majestic organ music & men's voices, ever listened to. Never have heard anything that rose to the sublimity of those sounds. The jingling of a little bell occasionally, the distant booming of the great bells in the steeple, the <dis> remote priests bowing & mumming, the faint clouds & puffs of incense rising from swinging censers, the dim distances, the pictured windows, the going & coming kneelers, the high (miraculously made & miracle-working Virgin), the old women selling candles to burn in a rack before her (if the devotee burns a candle & makes a prayer 9 successive days, it will help the sick or produce a child or other desired advantage—& is worth double the penny the candle costs.) The old women save the refuse wax.

Saw a funeral of a baker—his 17 sons & 3 daughters all present—only one married (a daughter.) About 500 candles were devoted by the friends who marched around the coffin. These people bore marks of the hardest possible hard-working lives & poor nourishment—how poorly dressed & old & ugly they were—an astonishing spectacle. Foreigners poking around among the solemnities, red guide-book in hand, & beadle chasing them.

Bought silk (black, 36 yards at $4.50—802 fr.)

Admiral bought his wife a dress there 10 yrs ago & she wears it yet. He now bought 4 yds to renew the sleeves. The silk washes, & may be packed like rags & will not take wrinkles. This man is about 60 & his father & grandfather made & sold this same silk in the same house.

14th (Monday) went to Rotterdam—Victoria Hotel. How very pretty & fresh & amiable & intelligent the middle-class Dutch girls are. Wish they would come over to us instead of Irish.

Curious head-dresses.

Saw only 4 people with spectacles in a drive of 2 hours.

---

70 Clemens is probably referring to Rubens' "Descent from the Cross" in the cathedral at Antwerp. This entry is written across the previous one.

The whole family live on the canal boats.
Stoops washed with soap & soda every Saturday.

Tuesday, 15th, in afternoon, went to Amsterdam. Hotel Doelen with canal behind it.

A bricked square filled with cheap trash (Jews)—could have bought the whole thing for $300 & lost money.

Orphans of both sexes, dress half red, the other half black. Girls wear white turban & pins, & gloves to elbow, white apron, white cape coming to point at waist behind.

Went to Museum & saw Rembrandt's Night Watch[71] & his portraits of some burghers. or burglars, have forgotten which.
A Gaye's[72] tribe of 72 Americans arrived.

Left Amsterdam Thursday afternoon 17th & went to the Hague, stopping off 2 or 3 hours at Harlaam & visiting farm house, dairy, & beautiful country seat.
Cleanliness of the dairy.
Round cheeses.
Everything scoured & shining.
Names of cows & horses over racks.
Hog pen which did not stink. smelt like
Dutch milk & cream.
Turf extinguisher.
Old blue Dutch china.
Handsome youth & young girl[73] who spoke German, English,

---

[71] During their visit to The Hague, the Clemenses purchased an etching of "The Night Watch" (OLC to Mrs. Langdon, 20 July 1879, MTM).

[72] Gay & Son, tour directors based in London, were the employers of Joseph Verey.

[73] Livy described the Dutch farm in her letter of 20 July to her mother and mentioned young Fräulein Korthals: "She was a wholesome hearty girl of fifteen. She rolled the children on the hay, talked German with them, English with us, Dutch with the dairy woman and also spoke French and a little Italian" (*S&MT*, p. 106). In a later entry made in London Clemens reminded himself to send Fräulein Korthals one of his books (p. 334).

French, Italian & some other tongues <& wanted to be considered German & not Dutch.>

Aviary, boats, fine horses & carriages—in old times a monastery. In winter they live in Amsterdam.

Drove through Blumen-something & saw lovely country seats.[74]

No wonder W^{m} III pined for Holland, the country is so green & lovely, & quiet & pastoral & homelike. Boats sailing through the prairies, & fat cows & <w>quaint windmills everywhere.

Staid at the Hague till Saturday July 19 & left at 6 PM for Flushing & thence to England by night boat.

It did not rain in The Hague & the sun actually shone half the time, but the evenings & nights were <c>raw & cold. Everywhere else we had rain.

At the Hague visited Museum & saw Rembrandt's School of Anatomy & Potter's bull[75] (flies visible under the hairs.) This is absolute nature—in some other pictures too close a copy of nature is called a fault.

Drove out to a country palace where Motley used to visit long at a time with the royal family. Good portrait of him there. Also some frescos which can't be told from stone, <bas-re> high-reliefs, across the room. Drove there through about the noblest woods I ever saw.[76] [#]

---

[74] "The most attractive place in the *Environs* of Haarlem, . . . which are much admired by the Dutch, is the beautiful village of Bloemendaal, with its numerous country-residences and park-like grounds" (*Belgium and Holland* [Leipzig: Karl Baedeker, 1885], pp. 257–258).

[75] The "School of Anatomy" and Paul Potter's "The Young Bull" are in the picture gallery of the Mauritshuis in The Hague.

[76] John Lothrop Motley, in an 1876 letter to Oliver Wendell Holmes, described the Huis ten Bosch, or House in the Wood, which Clemens visited: "The Huis ten Bosch, where we are staying, is the summer palace or villa of the Queen of this country. . . . This house is swallowed up, literally embowered, in the beechen forest which surrounds the Hague" (*The Correspondence of John Lothrop Motley*, ed. George William Curtis, 2d ed., 2 vols. [London: John Murray, 1889], 2:391–392). The portrait which Clemens mentions is reproduced as the frontispiece of *John Lothrop Motley and His Family*, ed. Susan and Herbert Mildmay (London: John

Let us so live as to go to heaven—where the Irish are all going.

We have been obliged to keep fires going constantly 10 months steadily—from 10th September to 15th July. In Italy, Bavaria, France, Holland & Belgium.

"Es gibt Leute" as the Baroness used to say—"There are people" . . . . finish the sentence as you please—*she* never finished it. It might usually be finished thus—"who are <en> fool enough so that one need not be surprised at anything they do."

2 plans for after-dinner speeches:

Have a toast—to literature, for instance; Moon along, about Indians, & religion, & guano, & cats, & safety parlor matches, & original sin, & lockjaw, <attributing things to> illustrating & backing up remarks by quotations from Shakspeare <etc> et al which they never uttered, & which do not <in> <re> apply, anyhow—& occasionally fetching in an "Again"—& occasionally making a chance reference to my text, but managing to get through, after all, without having said anything about literature.

But I wander from my subject.

2—<T>Attribute all sorts of absurdities to persons present & combatting them earnestly, attributing unworthy & malicious motives to the utterers.

Report of the Debate had at Huckleberry Hollow, S. C., on the proposition to organize & institute The Society for the Propagation of <Moral> Esthetic & Intellectual Culture. Let the dispute arise on the *name*—& break up in a row & bloodshed without getting further. Let it begin in a lofty & courtly parliamentary style of dignity, with some chief person, say the Methodist deacon, who <w>simply wants "Religious" substituted for "Aesthetic," & supports his motion by a dignified but sophomoric speech. Two parties spring up—one for Religious, the other for Aesthetic—& as the debate gradually warms up, the drop into the most magnificent profanity & the most

---

Lane, 1910), and identified as "a portrait by Bisschop, noted Dutch Artist, painted for Queen Sophie of the Netherlands. Now hangs in the Huis ten Bosch" (p. xi).

opulent & imaginative obscenity & finally have a fight. Send it to Dean Sage.[77]

Make a collection of my profane works to be privately printed.

Communists bought island—divided it up equally—government must support them—so government kept an immense grocery—$10,000 in paper money given to each male citizen—all wealthy alike—now show how the smart ones kept up their farms & the loafers didn't—loafers spent their $10,000, then sold their farms bit by bit to the smart ones—then became their laborers at wages.

The government shop is first started by robbing <those> rich men at home & buying the big stock to carry to the island.

At end of 10 years the smarts have got all the property.

Then they have a re-division.

After 10 years another re-division.

The same old smarts <all>always turn up ahead & the same old loafers do the other thing—showing the fallacy of community of "start" where there isn't community (equality) of brains.

London. July 20, 1879. Arrived here at 8 A.M.—Rainy & cold. Have had a rousing big cannel-coal fire blazing away in the grate all day.[78] A remarkable summer, truly.

Boyesen

Tourgueneff

Girl near Haarlem (book.) (write in it.

Ask Chatto what terms he gives for new book.

Ask him about Harte's copyright to be turned over to me.[79]

---

[77] A Yale classmate of Twichell's who was an executive in his father's lumber business in New York, Dean Sage contributed articles on hunting and fishing to the *Atlantic*, the *Century*, and the *Nation*.

[78] Livy wrote to her mother this same day: "We find ourselves so *very comfortably* housed here 'The Brunswick House Hotel' Hanover Square . . . for real comfort there is nothing better than a family London Hotel" (MTM).

[79] The copyright was for the play *Ah Sin*, an 1877 collaboration by Clemens and Bret Harte. An account of the history of this unhappy venture is in the preface to "*Ah Sin*," ed. Frederick Anderson (San Francisco: Book Club of California, 1961).

Ask if Conway's in town.[80]
Am engaged to dine (but not on set days,) till go to Condover.)[81]
Go tailor shop.
Bank.
Write Dr Jno Brown.[82]
Note to Bierstadt (Langham).[83]
Go to Conway's.
Cigars
Whisky.
Umbrella.

Fräulein Korthals[84]
Het Klooster
(On the Alkmaar road)
Haarlem
Holland. [#]

[80] Livy had written to her mother from Paris on 30 March 1879 (MTM) that the Moncure Conways had extended an "urgent invitation" to the Clemenses to visit them. Conway recalled: "At a dinner company given to these dear friends at Inglewood, our house in London, Mrs. Crawshay [a friend of the Conways] brought out a toy 'leaping frog' which she had found in Paris. Mark was more amused than I had ever seen him. He got down on his hands and knees and followed the leaping automaton all about the room" (Conway, *Autobiography*, 2:145).

[81] Condover Hall in Shropshire was the home of an eccentric ornithologist, Reginald Cholmondeley, whom the Clemenses had visited in 1873. The Clemenses visited Cholmondeley again on 28 July (see p. 336). Condover Hall was a local landmark, an Elizabethan structure of pink stone, "looking over a tree-dotted landscape: gables, mullions, chimneys. Fancy-clipped box-tree gardens" (John Piper and John Betjeman, *Shropshire* [London: Faber and Faber, 1951], p. 26).

[82] Clemens finally wrote to Brown, the Edinburgh physician and author he had met in 1873, on 21 August from Liverpool. The Clemens party was to sail for New York on the following day: "My wife and Miss Spaulding are along, and you may imagine how they take to heart this failure of our long promised Edinburgh trip. We never even wrote you, because we were always so sure, from day to day, that our affairs would finally so shape themselves as to let us get to Scotland. But no,—everything went wrong—we had only flying trips here and there in place of the leisurely ones which we had planned" (*MTL*, p. 360).

[83] The American landscape painter, Albert Bierstadt, was evidently staying at the Langham Hotel in London.

[84] See note 73.

Conway's professional hat stealer of the picture galleries, who stole only hats of foreigners who could not remain to prosecute—a profession which may be said to have been created by the law, since in a country where there was no law, a <p>man would be promptly punished (on the spot) who stole a hat.

Aldrich gives his seat in the horse car to a crutched cripple, & discovers that what he took for a crutch is only a length of walnut beading & the man ain't lame—whereupon Aldrich uses the only profanity which ever escaped his lips: "Dam a dam'd man who would carry a dam'd piece of beading under his dam'd arm."

Bierstadt
Hat.
Go Smalley (Lords)[85]
Get cards printed.
Deposit money.
Pinafore
Overcoat
Money from Madam.[86]
Speak of the Silks
Dean Stanley.[87]

Burns's Merry Muses.[88]

Unexpurgated Sir John Suckling.[89]

Chaucer for Children[90]

---

[85] George Washburn Smalley went to England in 1867 to organize the New York *Tribune's* European bureau and remained in London as its director until 1895. Clemens had met Smalley during his 1873 stay in London.

[86] Clemens occasionally referred to his wife as "the Madam."

[87] Arthur Penrhyn Stanley, dean of Westminster.

[88] Robert Burns's collection of bawdy Scottish songs had been privately printed on two occasions, first around 1800 and again in 1827. Clemens is not known to have owned a copy.

[89] The first scholarly edition of Suckling, edited by William Carew Hazlitt, was published in 1874.

[90] Mrs. H. R. Haweis' *Chaucer for Children: A Golden Key* was published by Chatto & Windus in 1877.

H'yarro (hero)

Sarah Bernhard preceded 4 English dukes' daughters to dinner.[91]

yer (year)
yer (ear) yerz (ears)
<yea>

Peculiar lease-hold requirements—book about it.—Order it.

Dropping the g's—everybody.

Monday July 28, went to Condover Hall, near Shrewsbury, to visit Mr. Reginald Cholmondeley. Present, visitors: Hon. Mr. Egerton, & Hon. Miss Egerton; Col. Cholmondeley, young Tom Cholmondeley (heir to Condover Hall) Mr. & Mrs. Drummond & two children; Millais the artist, wife & 2 daughters & one remarkable son aged 13 (Jack); 2 Misses Wade, etc, etc.[92]

---

[91] Sarah Bernhardt first appeared in London on 2 June 1879 in a performance of *Phèdre*. The flattering reception accorded Miss Bernhardt and the Comédie-Française troupe prompted some sarcastic remarks from Clemens. In his working notes for his discarded chapter on French morality, Clemens noted—erroneously—"Sarah B. (Miss) has 3 children" and in the manuscript itself he wrote: "In times past, whenever a child was born to an unmarried French actress, the fact was always announced in the Parisian daily journals the next day. This custom is going out. At present one hardly sees such a thing published three times a month. . . England has nobly come forward, of late years, & assisted the uplifting of France by wise & judicious encouragement. Her very highest & purest have received at their sacred firesides these actresses & their little ones, & paid them the same exalted honors & served them with the same loving devotion which Florence Nightingale had won from them by *her* noble works. This is an example which we should follow—& will, when the opportunity comes."

[92] In a draft of a response to Matthew Arnold's *Civilization in the United States* (1888), Clemens recalled the visit to Condover and the discomfort of his small party amidst the "menagerie" of ill-bred guests visiting there:

> We remained a week in that house—& learned much. Sometimes there were a dozen guests, sometimes two dozen. At first there were no nobilities, but there were several persons who were but little better. Among these I recal five women whose conduct & breeding entitled them to high places in the peerage, but they had been overlooked; on account of a glut in the market, perhaps. It was their custom to assemble in the drawing-room in the evening & discuss wills & other family matters for three hours; & into their conversation they introduced nothing which was not of this private nature. This, when two American ladies were

Remained through the week & came to Oxford Saturday.— <Saturday> Sunday Aug 3, visited all the colleges with Mr. Edward Wyndham.[93]

Room
19 & 20 Saloon or upper deck.

Trelawney's Adventures of a Younger Son & Reminiscences of Shelley & Byron.[94]

Galleries of pictures where there is much splendid conflagrations of color have the effect of nauseating the spectator. Turner soon makes one sick at the stomach—it is partly intense admiration & partly the color.

10th August, London—We still have to have fires every few days—had one to-night. We have had fires almost all the time, in Rome, Munich, Paris, Belgium, Holland, <&> Condover Hall & London, from the <10th> 1st of last September <(Ro[m]> (Florence) till the present time—*nearly 12 months.* [#]

---

present—& by consequence dumb. Was this better manners than talking in whispers or in a foreign tongue would have been? The two American ladies had to sit silent every evening that week, or talk exclusively to each other. (DV 16, MTP)

The guests that Clemens mentions in his notebook entry were mostly members of Cholmondeley's family. Artist John Everett Millais had married John Ruskin's former wife; John Guille Millais later wrote his father's biography.

Cholmondeley had sent the Clemenses several invitations to Condover, usually scrawled on ragged scraps of stationery, naming dates several months in advance. An amusing account of Cholmondeley's acquaintance and correspondence with Clemens is in chapter 15 of *Following the Equator*.

93 Livy's letter to her mother from Oxford on 3 August states: "We arrived here yesterday from Condover, about six o'clock, we sent the children on to London with Rosa. . . . Mr Wyndham met us here and has been with us all day today showing us about Oxford—he was educated here so he knew just what to show us—We return to London tomorrow" (MTM). A memento of the Oxford visit, a three-handled loving cup of cream and brown pottery given to Clemens by Wyndham, is now at the Mark Twain Memorial in Hartford.

94 Edward John Trelawny's *Records of Shelley, Byron, and the Author*, an enlarged version of his *Recollections of the Last Days of Shelley and Byron*, was published in 1878. His autobiographical *Adventures of a Younger Son* first appeared in 1831.

One must have a play-book at English play—the English accent is so different one cannot understand or follow the actors. The same in ordinary conversations which one tries to overhear.

Rellwy (railway)
Wy—(way)
Is that *o*ll, (all)?

Thursday Aug 14

Before going to the Royal Aquarium with Rosa, J & the ch^{n}, I owed J. 15$^{s.}$ 8^{d}—gave him £6 which is equivalent to starting square & fresh, he owing me——(capital) £5. 4. 4.

Saturday Aug 16. Gave Joseph—£5.
Monday 18 10
Windermere 19th . . . .£10.—
Grasmere 20th . . . . 5.—
Coniston, Thur. 21st . . . . 20—

Sunday Aug 17/79. Raw & cold, & a drenching rain. Went over to the Tabernacle & heard Mr. Spurgeon.[95] House ¾ full—say 3000 people. 1st hour, lacking 1 minute, taken up with two prayers, two ugly hymns, & Scripture-reading. Sermon ¾ of an hour long. A fluent talk. Good sonorous voice. Topic treated in the unpleasant old fashion—man a mighty bad child, God working at him in forty ways & having a world of trouble about him.

A wooden-faced congregation—just the sort to see no <improp> incongruity in the Majesty of Heaven stooping to beg & plead & sentimentalize over such, & see in their salvation an important matter.

English sacred music seems to be always the perfection of the ugly—the music to-day could not be worsted. It neither touched nor pleased. It is a slander to suppose that God can enjoy *any* congregational singing.

---

[95] Minister Charles Haddon Spurgeon preached at the huge Metropolitan Tabernacle in London.

Spurgeon was not at his best, to-day, I judge—he was probably even at his worst.

It was so cold I was freezing—the pouring rain made everything gloomy—the wooden congregation was not an inspiration—the music was depressing—<how> so the man *couldn't* preach well.

London shops are not open for business till 10 AM

Monday Aug 18—Left London at 10.30 AM for Windermere—changed cars all day. Too much variety.

Box keeper at a London <keeper> theatre said, "I am sorry, but I am only a servant—if you would speak to the Manager," &c.—In America he would have described himself by a more pompous term, but he would have been <">a servant, after all.

Tuesday Aug 19—Went up Windermere Lake in the steamer.—Talked with the great Darwin.[96]

R-way station <Askem> Askem—Bay spelt it out & said "In German, '*Frag' ihn.*'"

"Our Old Nobility" (from Echo)[97]

New Pepy's Diary[98]

1 box from Frankfort
1 " " Heidelberg
2 boxes from <Sw>Geneva
1 box from Florence
2 boxes " Munich—

---

[96] Darwin and his wife were spending the month of August at Coniston in England's Lake District and made a trip to nearby Grasmere, where the meeting with Clemens took place.

[97] A scathing look at the history of England's oldest and most influential families, denouncing the "palpable absurdity" of the "hereditary principle," written by Howard Evans under the pseudonym of "Noblesse Oblige." It was published in 1879 by the Political Tract Society and was a "reprint with a few corrections and additions, of a series of articles which have appeared in the Echo."

[98] Mynors Bright's six-volume edition of the *Diary*, considerably expanded from previous editions, was published from 1875 to 1879.

roll of rugs from Paris—
1 box from London—

Venice

1 box Glass Salviattis

Rietti

1 box with bellows &c—

Besarel—

12 *Trunks.*

Geneva—600

2 leather
3 *willow*—smallest, *statero[om]*
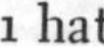
1 hat
1 ship—stateroom
<2 new>
1 Dan Slote
1 Paris black wooden trunk

3 Spaulding

Clara's small old banged-up willow, marked C. A. S.—the smallest of her 3—*stateroom.*

Recapit—Stateroom

Clara's smallest—C A S.
Our smallest willow 
Our ship trunk.

Aug. 31—At sea in the "Gallia," approaching New York (left Liverpool 23^{d})—about 9 PM brilliant moon, a calm sea, & a magnificent lunar rainbow—a complete arch, the colors part of the time as brilliant as if it were noonday—some said not *quite* as brilliant, softened with a degree of vagueness, but to me it was not different from a daylight rainbow. One cannot see this wonder twice in his life. <12> 15 years ago I saw a lunar rainbow (a complete arch) in California, but it was silver white—perfectly colorless.

The <colorado>Colorado miner on board who hates English & won't allow them to pass things to him at table.—Loathes his 3

English roommates because of their effeminate affectation of wearing night shirts.

The dead passenger lies in ice in life-boat No. 6, port side abaft the smoking cabin (the people don't know it) & the hilarious passengers sing & laugh & joke under him & the melting ice drips on them<,>. Grisly.

Sailor in the Xtrees had apoplectic fit but comrades saved him when about to fall to the deck yesterday.

"Several of the daily papers have announced the appointment, by United States Commissioner of Education Eaton"—*Nation* of Aug 28/79.[99]

The nasty French civilization.

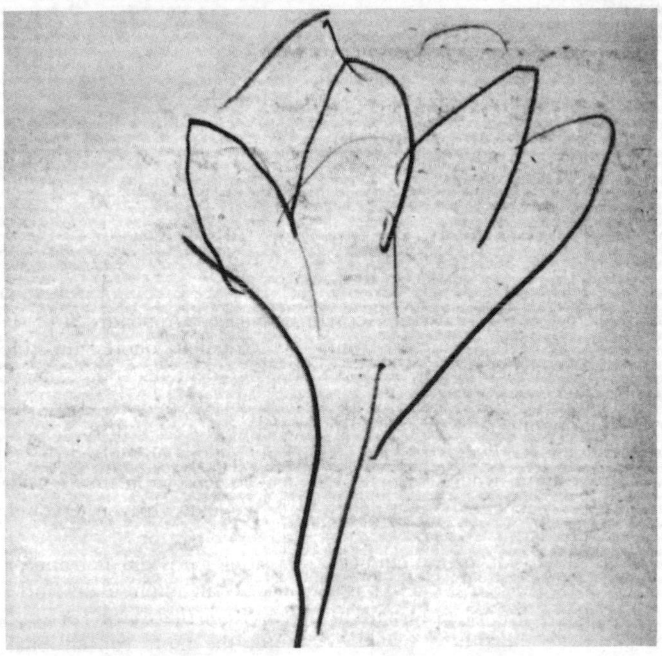

[99] Clemens was struck by the *Nation's* ponderous rendering of Eaton's title, an example of the "compounding-disease" evident in American newspapers and the

Random Memoranda (separate the subjects with stars x x x

1—from Leghorn
2— " Antwerp
5— " Havre
2 " " London
<4> 5 " Venice
<1>2 " Rotterdam

6 trunks & } London
<1 pk> }

6 trunks } Paris
1 <pc>pkg }

John Pyne
Nassau street

Second-hand Books.

Brown.

Wrote Howells about noon, Sept. 8.[100]

Con. Club—Formal visiting—substitute *cards.*[101]

Bret's saintly wh's & self-sacrificing sons of b's.[102] [#]

German language (see "The Awful German Language," Appendix D of *A Tramp Abroad*). The rest of the sentence from which Clemens quotes announced the appointment of Henry Hurlbert, the son of the president of Middlebury College, as a traveling commissioner to examine systems of education in Europe. The *Nation* condemned the appointment as an "outrageous piece of favoritism."

100 Following the *Gallia's* arrival in New York on 3 September, the Clemens family went to Elmira, where on 8 September Clemens wrote to Howells: "Are you *dead*—or only sleepeth? We are all well, & send love to you & yours by the hand of Yrs Ever Mark" (*MTHL*, p. 268).

101 Clemens' discussion of the etiquette of visiting cards did not appear in the *Atlantic*'s "Contributors' Club." It was included in an unfinished "Burlesque of Books on Etiquette" published in part in *Letters from the Earth* (pp. 200–207). Clemens' burlesque substituted playing cards for the more conventional article and included careful instructions on how to play one's hand for social advantage.

102 The last pages of this notebook are filled with "snappers" for jokes and anecdotes, names and addresses, and random entries made at various times through-

Joe Twichell's Decoration-day prayer—"G - d d—n that dog."

I'd a stole that calf if it was the last relic of redeemed creation, the Adam calf of the world.

"You lay your heft on the *corpse*—*I* can stand it.

Twichell's children's dramatic performances

If I ever go to — I want to go in an ox wagon &c.

Bissell making love—"hooray for the old rail-splitter." (Enters a prayer-meeting drunk thinking it is a primary.)

"Say what you d— please—you can't turn *my* stomach."

"It's d— seldom what's become o' that carpet sack."

<"Say what you darn please—You can't turn *my* stomach.">

"In the last great day, when the Archangel &c &c some flannel-mouth from Buffalo, &c &c."

"*There's* sap for your pine-apple."

"*Agreed* with him?—Got him downstairs on the ice!" [#]

---

out the period of the notebook's use. Clemens incorporated many of the anecdotes, with occasional modifications, into his published work. Some of the stories appear in fuller form in earlier notebooks or can be conjectured from the punch lines; some others are now obscure. Several of the characters mentioned in this list are familiar; others require additional identification: George Bissell, Hartford banker and stockbroker; Solomon Lewis Gillett, prominent Elmira merchant and banker; possibly journalist Moses Sperry Beach, proprietor of the New York *Sun* from 1848 until 1868; Joseph Lawrence, former editor of San Francisco's *Golden Era*; Charles Flower, mayor of Stratford-on-Avon; New York wit and financier William R. Travers; New York department store magnate Alexander T. Stewart; Boston publisher James R. Osgood; Captain James Smith, discussed in Notebooks 5 and 6, the prototype for the "old Admiral" in chapter 62 of *Roughing It;* John Shoot, a Hannibal acquaintance of Clemens; F. A. Oudinot, the extraordinary liar Clemens met in Maui, depicted as Markiss in chapter 77 of *Roughing It*; Hector J. Kingman, Clemens' fellow traveler on the long trip from San Francisco to New York in 1866/1867; John Phoenix, the pseudonym of American humorist George Derby.

"Go on with the play—I'll be the wolf."

["]Mighty rich folks here—eat butter on sausage."

"What wi' bringen on 'em in & takkin on 'em oot again, there're nae muckle <paw>prawfut in 't after aw'."

"I hae my doots aboot John."

"Is Tim O'Shaughness in the ranks?" "Here,<"> <s>yer anner," says I. "Then let the engagement begin," says he.

It had effect 34 <fo> times before he [lied] & 48 after it.

The Moncoon.

Mary McDowling.

— — have I got to kill one of my own species.

Disgorge!

<— — —>Go-to-h— do you understand *that!* (Lisper.)

Is Sol Gillette, & Beach, & old Moses going to heaven?—Well, I'll go 'long with *you*, Col. (To h—l.)

"I most busted out a laffin in meetin when you told some of them funny tales."

He calls it a deestrict. I can stand in the middle of it & all over it—when I'm in order.—You're out of order now. How'd *you* know it.

I always do that when I drink claret.

Free fight? Count me out!

Jo Lawrence & Mr. Flower.

Bret Harte—"conspicuous even [i]n *this* town, for her chastity."
"*You* wrote Luck of R.C?—*son* of a b.

Bissell addresses the prayer meeting. [#]

The lecturer interrupted by call for lady in audience named Jones.

Traverse<—>& wife—Why do you come home at this time in the morning? All the other places shut up.

Fisk & Gould—Where is the Savior?

Buy the Rat. Ornament to the bar.

Stewart raps on table. Traverse sings out "Cash!"

How Irishmen came to be made.

Nothin' but a couple o' old people on my han's. (no fader nor mudder.

<Oxen running away on stumpy road.>

Whistling & stammering.

I *did* eat some corn, but derned if I et <all> the half of *that*.

Kenyon—teeth pulled—suicides & it is found the other corpse had the money.

What you done with your other wife? Me *eat* her.

History of Andover student's adventures—Osgood & Bayard Taylor dinner.

A. E. Abbey tells a story to the Stomach club.

Admiral Smith's short tail cow—sun shines & sours the milk.

Fellow invited his girl in vain to ride. He said, "Its entirely amphibious to me, whether you do or not.

<It's d—d seldom what's become o' that carpet sack.>

<Say what you d—d please, you can't turn my stomach.>

Got to run all over hell to find you & get that receipt.

St Petter "You're the first man ever came here from Chicago.

Devil (when Petter threw 7^{s})—Come, play fair, none of your miracles.—Organize! &

Pay James A. Heady $6.75, for I've ketched you all together *axidently*.

Drunk man—Is that the moon? 2^{d} D M—Don't know—I don't live around here.

Lady to Capt—Is it always foggy here? Don't know, m'm—I don't live here.

Your d—d old house ain't *plumb*.

Never mind, if you know your way in the dark I think I can follow that.

Mr. Jones won't have that.

John Shoot—Never mind, Capt. You blow while I pray.

The Lord will provide—(under tuble) "Blow here & wait for an answer." (How long such a thing go without being noticed.

(Traverse.)

3 biggest liars in the world. Ferguson is one, & you are the other two.

I've been here but fufteen minutes, & twa o' them's had their hands on aready—it'll be a sterom' braw <knecht>necht to-necht.

Used to eat apples & — & be so sociable.

Gov. Preston—Inside of 10^{m} he had borrowed all my tobacco, had his feet in my lap & had spit all over me—a very sociable man.

Dalton tunnel—Old Sherman bring another with him.

Jim <Tho>Townsend—I wouldn't <spit> in her if her soul was on fire.

Couldn't tell whether the short man had sore throat or piles.

Hot journal—Old Admiral: *hot*—its froze!

Steamboat loafers & the dilberry.

Gov. Fuller & the bit of leather—while he talked of diamonds.

"This bit of country reminds <one>me of South of France."

Little girls to Dan de Quille. "O them fellers are allways down there a-them squaws.

Jim Gillis & the plums.

3 coincidences (taken for great men) "My *God* how do you do?"

Preacher—That dog's been after those sausages in my tail-pocket all day.

In Beer-mill—"Ich auch."

I'm the fust that's riz." (old)

Oudinot's fast horse, blaster, &c.

Artemus's Lone hand—

"Adam? What's his other name?"

Kingman's rare bird—his Queen Anne musket—

<Moon> Moncoon.

Isaac & prophets of Baal.

Wakeman first sees his wife.

Monkey on top of sounding board mimics the preacher.

Old maid newly wedded—I never *could* worth a dam on a steamboat.

Our John just slaps it in dry. Well have *you* noticed that wart?—you're the millionth man.

Across the bride's stomach was legend stenciled—Try Helmbold's Balsam Coperia.

Col. Gift's sifting motion. Fats *thim?* You wouldn't take advantage of a poor blind girl?

Dentist been here & pulled a tooth from mother that long.

When the Shah of Persia was invited to attend the Derby, he replied, "It is already known to me that one horse will run faster than another."

"Didn't run average."

John Phenix & the besieged fort."

Asked man to punch another in theatre with cane.

You had a miscarriage. I did. "I am that miscarriage.—Come to my arms."

Jo Lawrence

Political parties who accuse the one in power of gobbling the spoils, &c, are like the wolf who looked in at the door & saw the shepherds eating mutton, & said, "Oh, certainly—it's all right as long as it's *you*—but there'd be hell to pay if I was to do that."

Bad Boy—Mother had two good sons—didn't see why she couldn't be satisfied.

Crying because you didn't die when the old chief died.

Eat personal property—real estate.

About Cassaignac— P—ing & praying at the same time. [#]

Monuments to André—one proposed to Benedict Arnold—[103]

All English individuals are kind & likeable—the newspapers are snobbish, pretentious, & they scoff at America or contemptuously ignore her. English speeches & statesmen try to draw the two nations together in friendship & mutual respect—the newspapers, with what seems a steady & calculated purpose, discourage this. The newspapers are going to win in this fight. The nations are at their friendliest now —the widening apart has begun—the separation will be complete in a generation.—

For some years a custom has been growing up <at>in our literature to praise everything <el>English, & do it affectionately. This is not met half-way & so it will cease. English individuals like & respect American individuals; but the English nation despises America & the Americans. But this does not sting us as it did when we <ar>were smaller. We shall presently be indifferent to being looked down upon by a nation no bigger & no better than our own. We made the telegraph a practical thing; we invented the fast press, the sewing machine, the sleeping & parlor <car, & hotel> car, the telephone, the iron-clad, we have done our share for the century, we have introduced the foretelling of the weather. Nobody writes a finer & purer English than Motley Howells, Hawthorne & Holmes.

An heroic[104]

---

[103] During a visit to the United States in the fall of 1878, Arthur Stanley, dean of Westminister, encouraged Cyrus W. Field to build a monument on the site of Major John André's execution. Field purchased the land, which was near his home, and a five-ton stone monument, with an inscription by Dean Stanley, was placed on the spot in October 1879. On 4 October 1879 the New York *Times* published a scathing denunciation of Field's action, accusing him of erecting the André monument for his own self-aggrandizement:

> The monument is not only intended to perpetuate the memory of Mr. Field . . . but it will specifically commemorate the fact that Mr. Field . . . has extended his patronage to Dean Stanley, and permitted the latter to associate with him almost upon terms of equality. . . . There is no reason why Mr. Cyrus W. Field should content himself with a single monument. . . . He would do well to erect his next monument in the guise of a monument to Gen. Benedict Arnold.

[104] This and the following entries were recorded on the back flyleaf.

hospital
humble
historic
hotel.

This shows that formerly the *educated* dropped their h's, too. Here is the rudimentary n, proving the presence of the former h, as Mr. Darwin would say.

u
Yank root, <boot—> boot.
clever.
stout—(strong.)
quite
Gentleman & lady—Eng & Am definitions.
Nasty
beastly
female (woman)
Hear, h'yaah! h'yaah! (negro. & Eng.
(Amer is heer, h'*yer*, & *hee*-er & N. h'*yaah*
Knocked up.

He hadn't *got* any socks <En>in English, it is to possess, in American to *procure*.

American, *dontchu*, English *don't-you*.

Joseph N. Very, 142 Strand, Gaye & Son.

Robt Allen
59 rue Neuve des Mathurins

Leave Paris 11.40 get to Calais 7—stop Meurice's[105]

Leave Calais <1.10>1.20 P.M.

Check baggage to <X>Charing X.

For books, Sotheran, 136 Strand—ask for Mr. Edwards.
For tailor (very excellent), Freeman 134 <B>Regent st.

---

105 That is, stay at the Hôtel Meurice in Calais.

Stained glass panels 64 Charlotte st W (Gibbs & Howard) lady-decorators Agnes & Rhoda Garrett.

Cunard reading room 29 Pall Mall

Bible House (Hotel) Amsterdam.[106]

St Gaudens
49 Notre Dame des Champs

Mr. Dubois.[107]
54 rue de Saints Perès

W F. Brown
27 rue Jacob

---

[106] The remaining entries appear on the back endpaper.

[107] The American painter Charles Edward Dubois whom Clemens had met at the Paris Stomach Club.

XIX

"Ask Charley"

(July 1880–January 1882)

THERE IS a lapse of nearly a year between the conclusion of Notebook 18 in September 1879 and the beginning of Notebook 19 on July 26, 1880, the day Jean Clemens was born. During that time the Clemens "tribe" completed its European tour. Landing in New York on 3 September 1879, the family went directly to Quarry Farm where Clemens spent his time hard at work on the manuscript of *A Tramp Abroad*. He hoped to complete the book before leaving Elmira, but continuous revisions were necessary and the book was still unfinished when the Clemens family returned to Hartford in late October 1879. In the midst of his literary efforts Clemens was faced with the turmoil of setting up housekeeping again, resuming the task of answering his extensive correspondence, and meeting his varied social obligations.

Two of his public appearances in the winter of 1879 were conspicuous triumphs for him, firmly establishing his place in the political and literary community. His speech honoring General Grant at the reunion of the Army of the Tennessee in Chicago was greeted by "a tornado of applause and laughter" (SLC to OLC, 14 November 1879); and his address at the *Atlantic* breakfast honoring Oliver Wendell Holmes was so well received that for Clemens it somewhat mitigated the "disgrace" of his Whittier dinner speech of December 1877.

On 23 November 1879 Clemens wrote to Howells: "My book is really finished at last—every care is off my mind, everything is out of my way" (*MTHL*, p. 281). However it was not until January 1880 that Clemens finally gave up his "life-&-death battle" with the manuscript of *A Tramp Abroad* and delivered the closing chapters to Elisha Bliss of the American Publishing Company, determined that he had written the "very last line" of "a book which required 2600 pages, of MS," and for which he wrote "nearer four thousand, first & last" (SLC to Howells, 8 January 1880, *MTHL*, pp. 286–287).

Having at last completed *A Tramp Abroad*, Clemens turned, early in 1880, to a number of other projects—chief among them the unfinished manuscript of *The Prince and the Pauper* and the Kaolatype company.

Encouraged by the moderate success of "Mark Twain's Self-Pasting Scrap Book," Clemens had been casting around for a new and larger profit-making enterprise for some time. In February 1880 he bought the patent for the Kaolatype engraving process from Dan Slote. A company was formed with Clemens as president holding four-fifths of the stock and providing most of the working capital; Slote and Hartford attorney Charles Perkins were the other partners.

Clemens, with his customary enthusiasm, believed Kaolatype would supersede engraving in the printing industry. He told Orion on 27 November 1880:

> I wrote you last March that I believed I had invented an idea that would increase the value of Kaolatype a hundred fold. It was to apply it to the *moulding* of bookbinders' brass stamps, in place of *engraving* them. Ever since then I have been trying to find somebody who could invent a flux that would enable a body to mould hard brass with sharp-cut lines & perfect surfaces. . . . At last I struck a young German [Slote's friend Charles Sneider] who believed he could do it. . . & at last he has worked the miracle. In the rough, it is true; but all new things are in the rough. . . . He & Slote came up yesterday, bringing six specimens of moulded brass stamps, & I contracted to pay him $5,000 when he is able to put his patents into my hands . . . & pay him $150 a month to go on & perfect his methods, & also the attendant expenses. I never saw people so wild over anything. (*MTBus*, p. 148)

For one year Clemens poured money into the Kaolatype business, anxiously awaiting word of the perfection of Charles Sneider's "miracle" process. By March 1881 Clemens was angry and disillusioned with Slote's management and with Sneider's expensive and unsuccessful experimentation. He wrote to Slote on 31 March 1881: "I hope that before April is over we shall see palpable & demonstrable (not theoretic & imaginative) reasons for going on; but my hopes are not high—they have had a heavy jolt. I feel pretty sore & humiliated when I think over the history of the past few months" (*MTBus*, p. 152). In fact, Clemens had initiated his own investigation of the Kaolatype business. His nephew by marriage, Charles L. Webster, a real estate and insurance salesman in Fredonia, New York, had come to see Clemens to encourage him to invest in stock of the Independent Watch Company at the end of March and Clemens persuaded him to stay and investigate Slote and Sneider's management of Kaolatype. Within a few weeks, Webster was able to prove, at least to Clemens' satisfaction, that Slote was "either a knave or a fool" and that he was undoubtedly conspiring with Sneider to "bleed" Clemens (Webster to SLC, 5 May 1881). Clemens' long-standing friendship with Slote was ended and Webster became Clemens' business manager, with full control over Kaolatype.

Early in 1880, Mark Twain returned to the manuscript of *The Prince and the Pauper*, which he had begun in 1877 and for which he had been doing extensive background reading. Work on the manuscript proceeded well and he took a "jubilant delight in writing it" (SLC to Howells, 5 March 1880, *MTHL*, p. 290). As each chapter was completed it was read aloud to an enthusiastic family audience. The conventional taste of such critics as Livy and "Mother" Fairbanks was especially well satisfied. The extraordinarily long list of people to whom Clemens planned to send complimentary copies of the book reflects his determination to receive the approval of the polite audience which he craved.

Clemens, who was disappointed in Elisha Bliss's management of his books, was determined to publish *The Prince and the Pauper* according to his own specifications, and to reap a larger portion of the book's profits. Therefore, shortly after the death of Bliss on 28 September 1880, Clemens contracted with James R. Osgood and Company to produce and distribute his new book. Osgood and Clemens had discussed joint publishing schemes as early as 1872, and in 1877 Osgood had issued a small volume of two of Clemens' stories, *A True Story and the Recent Carnival of Crime*. Clemens was to supply the capital for the production of *The Prince and the Pauper*; Osgood was to handle subscription sales and act as Clemens' agent in all book matters. It shortly became clear, however, that Osgood knew very little about subscription-book publishing and Clemens found himself becoming more and more involved in the eventually disastrous business of publishing books himself. (See Frederick Anderson and Hamlin Hill, "How Samuel Clemens Became Mark Twain's Publisher: A Study of the James R. Osgood Contracts," *Proof* 2 [1972]: 117–143.)

Notebook 19 includes appointments, shopping reminders, family anecdotes, household accounts, notes about the renovation and redecoration of the Hartford house, and entries about Kaolatype and other business affairs. There are several pages of notes made during Clemens' two-week stay in Canada with Osgood, and three clumsy attempts at poetry. There are also numerous references to books which Clemens planned to buy or was reading at the time. Literary ideas are sketched out which were in fact the germ of later work—for example, the references to themes which were developed in "Three Thousand Years Among the Microbes" and "Captain Stormfield's Visit to Heaven." The notebook has surprisingly few references to the actual writing of *The Prince and the Pauper*. Clemens' burlesque etiquette manual and his burlesque *Hamlet*, which he worked on in the spring and summer of 1881, are not mentioned directly. Walter Blair has provided evidence that Clemens was working on chapters 19 through 21 of *Huckleberry Finn* during the summer of 1880; however, no material relating to the book appears in Notebook 19, nor is there any mention of Clemens' long-planned Mississippi River trip of 1882.

This notebook contains three drafts of Clemens' 16 October 1880 speech welcoming General Grant to Hartford. Two of the drafts (on pages 373–374 and 425) are substantially the same speech, and were both superseded by the longer, much reworked draft on pages 375–377. Grant's visit was part of a campaign tour in support of Garfield. Clemens joined the welcoming party which escorted Grant from Boston to Hartford on a special train. Clemens' speech, delivered at Hartford's Bushnell Park, was enthusiastically received. Clemens wrote to Howells on 19 October: "Gen. Grant came near laughing his entire head off. . . . The words 'in every conceivable . . . . inexpensive way' invoked the loudest shout, & the longest, & the most full-hearted that was heard in Hartford that day. It started in laughter but ended in a thunder of endorsement" (*MTHL*, p. 332). The transcript of the speech in the New York *Tribune* of 17 October reveals Clemens' revision of the drafts in this notebook:

I also am deputized to welcome you to the sincere and cordial hospitalities of Hartford, the city of the historic and revered Charter Oak, of which the most of this town is built. [Laughter.] At first it was proposed to have only one speaker to welcome you, but this was changed, because it was feared that, considering the shortness of the crop of speeches this year, if anything occurred to prevent that speaker from delivering his speech you would feel disappointed. [Laughter and applause.]

I desire, at this point, to refer to your past history. By years of colossal labor and colossal achievement, you at last beat down a gigantic rebellion and saved your country from destruction. Then the country commanded you to take the helm of State. You preferred your great office of General of the Army and the rest and comfort which it afforded, but you loyally obeyed, and relinquished permanently the ample and well-earned salary of the Generalship, and resigned your accumulating years to the chance mercies of a precarious existence. [Applause.] By this present fatiguing progress through the land you are contributing mightily toward saving your country once more—this time from dishonor and shame, and from commercial disaster. [Applause.] You are now a private citizen, but private employment is closed against you because your name would be used for speculative purposes, and you have refused to permit that. But your country will reward you, never fear. [Loud applause.]

When Wellington won Waterloo, a battle about on a level with some dozen of your victories, sordid England tried to pay him for that service with wealth and grandeur; she made him a Duke and gave him $4,000,000. If you had done and suffered for any other country what you have done and suffered for your own, you would have been affronted in the same sordid way. But thank God, this vast and rich and mighty Republic is imbued to the core with a delicacy which will forever preserve her from so degrading a deserving son. Your country loves you, your country is proud of you, your country is grateful to you. [Applause.] Her applauses, which have been thundering in your ears all these weeks and months, will never cease while the flag you saved continues to wave. [Great applause.] Your country stands ready from this day forth to testify her measureless love and pride and gratitude toward you in every conceivable inexpensive way. Welcome to Hartford, great soldier, honored statesman, unselfish citizen. [Loud and long-continued applause.]

The notebook contains extensive working notes for Clemens' biography of New York *Tribune* editor Whitelaw Reid, a project into which Clemens plunged in order to "revenge" himself for some reported attacks on him in Reid's newspaper. Clemens' suspicions had first been aroused, evidently early in January 1882, by a "sensitive friend" whom Howells identifies in chapter 17 of *My Mark Twain* as "Warner." Charles Dudley Warner was in Europe at this time, and it is possible that the reference is to his brother George Warner, a Nook Farm neighbor. Clemens' wrath was undoubtedly fed by his houseguest, Edward H. House, and by John Russell Young of the *Herald* who visited Clemens in Hartford and supplied him with some damning comments on Reid's character. On 21 January Clemens asked Charles Webster to check the files of the *Tribune* for the supposedly damaging paragraphs written about him. Webster's investigation turned up no evidence of a "crusade" of "sneers & brutalities" and Clemens relegated his three weeks' accumulation of notes to "the ignominious pigeon-hole," writing an exasperated, apologetic description of the episode to Howells on 28 January 1882 (*MTHL*, pp. 386–389). Clemens' dislike of Reid, however, persisted even into old age. The Autobiographical Dictation of 27 August 1907 characterizes Reid as "narrow, and hard, cold, calculating, unaffectionate."

There are several pages of notes referring to another project which captured Clemens' enthusiasm in 1880. In July 1880 he received a proposal from George Gebbie, a Philadelphia subscription publisher, to edit an anthology of humorous writings. Clemens' other literary commitments prevented him from immediately undertaking the project, but his enthusiasm for the idea grew over the next few months. Clemens interested Howells in the anthology during his visit to Belmont in mid-October 1880 and the two had high hopes for a collaboration. Clemens informed Howells shortly after the visit: "I'm a laying for that Encyclopediacal Scotchman; & . . . when he hears my proposed tariff his skin will probably crawl away with him. . . . The proposed work is growing, mightily, in my estimation, day by day" (24 October 1880, *MTHL*, p. 333). By February 1881 Clemens' enthusiasm had cooled—he refused to continue in person his faltering negotiations with the unreliable Gebbie and impressed James R. Osgood into working out the contract for that "big, stupid, laborious piece of work" (SLC to Osgood, 12 February 1881, *MTLP*, p. 132). No contract with Gebbie was ever signed despite Gebbie's belated attempt to revive the proposal in 1884 (Gebbie to SLC, 7 August 1884). Clemens, collaborating with Howells and Charles Hopkins Clark of the Hartford *Courant*, eventually produced an anthology inspired by Gebbie's original proposal. The volume was published by Clemens' own publishing company in 1888 as *Mark Twain's Library of Humor*.

The notebook's greatest interest lies in the diversity and range of the entries, permitting glimpses of Clemens in many roles—as author, family man, entrepreneur, and public figure. There are also disturbing presages of Clemens' coming financial crisis evidenced by the accelerating demands of the Clemenses' style of living in Hartford, and by Clemens' growing involvement in business speculations.

Notebook 19 now contains 156 pages, 22 of them blank. It is identical in design and format to Notebook 18. Notebook 19 is heavily worn with use; the first gathering of leaves and a number of single leaves throughout are loose; both flyleaves, eighteen ruled leaves, and portions of eight others have been torn out and are missing. Most of the notebook is written in blue ink using a stylographic pen (see note 138). A few entries are in pencil and two are in black ink. There are occasional use marks in both ink and pencil, most of them probably Paine's.

W[--]dens[1]
Bank

Send 2 books to Frank Wilkie,[2] Chicago Times.
[One] to D^r. Jackson, 785 Mich Ave

C. F. <Kipp> Knapp
510 Arch st Phila.
Combined Violet Ink.[3] [#]

---

[1] The entries through "Walkers . . . Corn[wall.]" were written in pencil on the front endpaper of the notebook. The next five entries (through "Aug. St. Gaudens . . . New York.") were written in ink over the penciled entries.

[2] Clemens met Franc B. Wilkie, editorial writer for the Chicago *Times*, at the Reunion of the Army of the Tennessee in Chicago in November 1879. Clemens, Dr. A. Reeves Jackson, the "Doctor" of *The Innocents Abroad*, and several journalists breakfasted at Wilkie's home during the reunion (Chicago *Times*, 15 November 1879). The books which Clemens meant to send were probably copies of *A Tramp Abroad*, published in March 1880.

[3] Clemens must have meant to renew his supply of the violet ink he used from 1876 through mid-June 1880. Apparently he did not; Walter Blair reports that "no scrap of writing in letters, datable manuscripts, or notebooks written between June 15, 1880, and the end of December, 1884 . . . is in violet ink" (*Mark Twain & Huck Finn* [Berkeley and Los Angeles: University of California Press, 1960], p. 201).

Walkers new [*one or two words*] stor[e]
Corn[wall.]

A. St. Gaudens[4]
Sherwood Building
<5^{s}> 57st & 6 Ave.
Ellisworth[5]

Miss A. Bailey[6]
128 W. 12th st
Bet. 6th & 7th Aves.

Conway—[7]
Inglewood,
Bedford Park
Turnham Green
London
care Prof March[8]
Lafayette College
Easton, Pa. [#]

---

[4] After meeting the self-trained sculptor Karl Gerhardt in Hartford in February 1881 and obtaining enthusiastic opinions of his work from several prominent artists, the Clemenses arranged to subsidize Gerhardt's study in Paris. Shortly before Gerhardt departed for Europe on 5 March, he called on Augustus Saint-Gaudens at his New York studio, apparently at Clemens' suggestion.

This entry and those through "Charley, 412 W 57th st." (p. 360.1–2) were written on the front endpaper and first page of the notebook (the front flyleaf is missing) at various dates throughout the period of Clemens' use of the notebook. The footnotes provide approximate dating; more specific information about the inscription and position of entries is recorded in Details of Inscription.

[5] Probably William Webster Ellsworth whom Clemens was hoping to interest in the Kaolatype engraving process (SLC to Charles Webster, 2 October 1881). After 1881 Ellsworth assumed a leading role in the management of the *Century*. His memories of Mark Twain are included in *A Golden Age of Authors* (Boston: Houghton Mifflin Co., 1919).

[6] A receipt of 22 October 1880 indicates that Livy purchased five hats and a pair of stockings from Annie Bailey.

[7] Clemens wrote to Moncure Conway on 19 January 1880 praising Conway's choice of the name "Inglewood" for his new house.

[8] Francis A. March, a professor of philology at Lafayette College, married Moncure Conway's sister. Conway's letter of 12 August 1880 informed Clemens that he was visiting the couple in Easton.

W. D. Howells
Belmont[9] (via Arlington)
(Telegraphic address.)

Aug. St. Gaudens
58 W. 57th
New York.

Chas. Sneider,[10] 167 E. $123^{d.}$
23 Stuyvesant st—off 3^{d} av. on 9th st.
3^{d} ave Elevated road, 9th st station

Running a church choir.

Don Quixotte is defended against Arabian Nights Supernaturals <[-]> by Telephone Telegraph &c & successfully.

The principle of truth may itself be carried into absurdity.—Parkman.

The saying is old that truth should not be spoken at all times; & those whom a sick conscience worries into *habitual* (I have it not!) violation of the maxim are imbeciles & nuisances—Ib

Children & fools <spea> *always* speak truth.[11]

Miss Marian P. Whitney,[12] 246 Church st. New Haven, Oct. 22.—12 to 1 PM [#]

---

[9] The Howells family had moved into the Belmont house, which was designed by Elinor Howells' brother William Rutherford Mead, in July 1878.

[10] On 27 November 1880 Clemens wrote Orion that Charles Sneider had been on his payroll for three months, adapting the Kaolatype process to mold bookbinders' brass stamps (*MTBus*, pp. 147–148).

[11] "On the Decay of the Art of Lying," a speech Clemens delivered on 5 April 1880 at the Hartford Monday Evening Club and published in *The Stolen White Elephant* in 1882, includes the two quotations about truth attributed to Parkman and the reference to "Children & fools." There are several references in this notebook to Clemens' reading of Francis Parkman's works. The two had met in December 1879 at the *Atlantic* breakfast in honor of Oliver Wendell Holmes.

[12] Twenty-year-old daughter of William Dwight Whitney, professor of Sanskrit at Yale. Clemens was the Whitneys' guest in New Haven in October 1881, when he spoke on "mental telegraphy" at a meeting of that city's Saturday Morning

Charley,[13]
412 W 57th st.

F. Hopkinson Smith[14]

Mrs Colt—C
$25.[15]

A—autographs

4 mats & pincushion

8 or 10 ounces single zephyr bright red worsted.

Licorice drops.

8000
100
800000

Sirius is 1500 times our diam.
A man w^d be 9,000 ft high.

Beefsteak for 1
Stewed potatoes 1
Coffee 2

Apollonaris Oleomargarine[16]

Club. The club was evidently a young ladies' social and cultural group similar to the Hartford Saturday Morning Club (SLC to Whitney, 24 October 1881, Vassar College Library, Poughkeepsie, N.Y.; clipping in MTP from the New York *Independent* [1881?]).

[13] Charles L. Webster, husband of Clemens' niece, Annie Moffett Webster, came to New York from Fredonia in April 1881 to manage the Kaolatype company. He wrote Clemens on 23 November 1881, giving his new address in the city.

[14] Clemens first met F. Hopkinson Smith, author, engineer, and painter, at a Tile Club dinner in New York on 20 December 1880 (*MTHL*, p. 340, n. 2).

[15] Conceivably a contribution by Clemens for a charity sponsored by Mrs. Samuel Colt, the widow of the Hartford arms manufacturer.

[16] Two of the names on this list, Apollinaris and Blatherskite, were eventually given to Quarry Farm cats (*Concerning Cats*, ed. Frederick Anderson [San Francisco: Book Club of California, 1959], p. viii).

The Compound Extract of Buchu & the Extractess.
Lord Bilk
" Hell(va)bore.
Whoopjamboreehoo
Blatherskite
Flapdoodle High-daddy

Burton's Cyclopédia D. Appleton, 1858.[17]
Bill Arp.
Brownell (funny poems.)[18]
Examine Newspapers.
"Library of Humor."
C D Warner
Simon Suggs
Flush Times
Max Adler
Trowbridge—Darius Green.
The Alarmèd Skipper, by James T. Fields.

---

[17] The reference is to William Evans Burton's *Cyclopædia of Wit and Humor; Containing Choice and Characteristic Selections from the Writings of the Most Eminent Humorists of America, Ireland, Scotland, and England* (New York: D. Appleton and Co., 1858). In July 1880 Clemens was approached by a Philadelphia subscription publisher, George Gebbie, with the suggestion that he compile an anthology of humor "similar to Burtons Encyclopaedia" (Gebbie to SLC, 14 July 1880). Clemens was sufficiently interested in Gebbie's proposal to draw up the following list of humorists for the anthology. The chaotic order of the notebook list and the numerous marginal additions (see Details of Inscription for interlined items) suggest that Clemens returned to the list more than once, possibly adding Howells' suggestions to it during a visit to Belmont in October 1880. Notebook 20 contains further notes about selections for the anthology. Clemens' list of authors and titles has been selectively annotated since biographical and background information about many of them is readily available in such works as *Mark Twain's Library of Humor* (New York: Charles L. Webster & Co., 1888; reprint ed., New York: Garrett Press, 1969) and Walter Blair's *Native American Humor (1800–1900)* (New York: American Book Co., 1937).

[18] Probably Henry Howard Brownell whom Oliver Wendell Holmes dubbed "Our Battle Laureate" for his serious Civil War poetry. Brownell also wrote lighter verse, such as "Lines Kimposed a Bored of a Californy Male-Steemer," for newspapers.

Talmage's Sermons.[19]

1 Sut Lovengood—Dick & Fitzgerald.[20]
2 <Old Si> (?) Uncle Remus writer of colored yarns[21]
3 Gnaw a file & flee to the mountains of Hepsidam.[22]
4. Burdette.
Danbury News
Nasby
Georgia Scenes.

---

[19] An ironic reference to the pious and platitudinous sermons of the Reverend T. DeWitt Talmage, pastor of Brooklyn's Central Presbyterian Church, whom Clemens attacked in "About Smells" (*Galaxy*, May 1870; *What Is Man? and Other Philosophical Essays*, ed. Paul Baender [Berkeley, Los Angeles, London: University of California Press, 1973], pp. 48–50).

[20] George W. Harris' *Sut Lovingood: Yarns Spun by a "Nat'ral Born Durn'd Fool"* was published by Dick & Fitzgerald, a New York firm, in 1867. Clemens' comments on the book appear in his letter of 14 July 1867 to the *Alta California* (*Mark Twain's Travels with Mr. Brown*, ed. Franklin Walker and G. Ezra Dane [New York: Alfred A. Knopf, 1940], p. 221).

[21] Joel Chandler Harris' Uncle Remus stories had been introduced into the Atlanta *Constitution* in 1878 to replace Samuel White Small's column of anecdotes and sketches which featured another Negro raconteur, Old Si. Harris' dialect tales were immediately popular and were regularly reprinted in the New York *Evening Post* where Clemens probably saw them. His questioned cancellation of "Old Si" and addition of "Uncle Remus" suggest that his acquaintance with Harris' work was new. Clemens was delighted with Harris' stories and he adopted the idiom of Harris' tales in letters to "Brer Osgood" and "Brer Whitmo'." Clemens would write to Fields, Osgood & Co. on 28 November 1880 (quoted in "Mark Twain, a Collection of First Editions . . . and Books from His Library," Maxwell Hunley Auction Catalogue, item 161) requesting a copy of Harris' first collection, *Uncle Remus: His Songs and His Sayings*.

[22] The refrain from a burlesque "Hard-shell Baptist" sermon, "Where the Lion Roareth and the Wang-Doodle Mourneth," collected in Samuel P. Avery's anthology of American humor, *The Harp of a Thousand Strings* (New York: Dick & Fitzgerald, 1858), pp. 224–226. The author of the sermon appears to have been William P. Brannan of Ohio, a journalist and portrait artist. According to the preacher, to gnaw a file "means going it alone and getting ukered." Moreover, "thar's more dams than Hepsidam. Thar's Rotter-dam, Had-dam, Amster-dam, and 'Don't-care-a-dam.' " George William Bagby made use of the refrain in his political satire *A Week in Hepsidam; Being the First and Only True Account of the Mountains, Men, Manners and Morals Thereof* (Richmond, Va.: G. W. Gary, 1879).

Sam Slick
Maj. Jones Courtship
Flush Times in Alabama
The man who "went in on nary pair" (at camp meeting.)[23]
Maj. Jack Downing.
Doesticks
John Phoenix
Josh Billings
Artemus Ward.
Lamb's Origin of Roast pig.
Lowell
Harte
Howells
Holmes
Hall (Georgia Scenes.[24]
Arthur Rose ("Mrs. Brown") (rot)[25]
Cousin Sally Dillard[26]
Widow Bedott.
Neal, Charcoal sketches.
The South has contributed more humorists than poets &c.
Look out for Canadian Pirates.[27]

---

[23] The reference is to Johnson J. Hooper's "Simon Suggs Attends a Camp Meeting" in *Some Adventures of Captain Simon Suggs* (1845).

[24] "Hall" was the pseudonym of Augustus Baldwin Longstreet. Clemens owned a copy of Longstreet's *Georgia Scenes* (A1911, item 298).

[25] Collections of "Mrs. Brown" monologues, the topical comments of a garrulous and opinionated old woman, by George Rose ("Arthur Sketchley"), were published from 1866 to 1882.

[26] "Cousin Sally Dilliard" by Hamilton C. Jones, a short burlesque piece about a witness at a court trial, appeared in the *Spirit of the Times* in May 1844. It is included in Franklin J. Meine's collection *Tall Tales of the Southwest* (New York: Alfred A. Knopf, 1930).

[27] Belford Brothers had taken advantage of the nebulous copyright laws of the time to issue unauthorized editions of Mark Twain's "Old Times on the Mississippi," *Tom Sawyer*, and A *Tramp Abroad*. Clemens had recently attempted to interest Congress in a bill "making the selling of <Cana> pirated books a penal offence, punishable by fine & imprisonment, like dealing in any other kind of stolen goods" (SLC to Howells, 24 March 1880, *MTHL*, p. 295).

Der Engländer (German)
Irving
Widow Bedott.
French (none)
Mr. Lincoln (a yarn or two)
Orpheus C. Kerr.
See Burton's Cyclopedia for some English rubbish.
Make it an Encyclopedia of *American* Humor.[28]
John G. Saxe.
—Josh Billings
Josiah Allen's Wife.
(Examine Drake's & Allibone's <Dictionary>Dictionaries of Authors to see who *have* been humorists.[29]
(Nothing from Sunset Cox or Proctor Knott.)
Sydney Smith (Dn the Equator)
(Greville, page 265[30]

---

[28] The original idea as proposed by publisher George Gebbie was for an encyclopedia of American and European humor. Clemens here rejects that plan but, after a visit to Howells, Clemens wrote to him on 24 October 1880: "If I make a contract with the canny Scot, I will tell him the plan which you & I have devised (that of taking in the humor of *all* countries)" (*MTHL*, p. 333). After negotiations with Clemens lapsed, Gebbie himself published a five-volume "comprehensive" anthology including "the Masterpieces of Wit and Humor, from the 'Attic Salt' of the Greeks, to the 'Cakes and Ale' of the present day; from Aristophanes . . . to Mark Twain, the model Humorist of the Nineteenth Century" (prospectus for A. R. Spofford and Rufus E. Shapley, eds., *The Library of Wit and Humor* [Philadelphia: Gebbie & Co., 1884–1894] in MTP).

[29] Francis S. Drake, *Dictionary of American Biography* (1872); S. Austin Allibone, *A Critical Dictionary of English Literature and British and American Authors* (1858–1871).

[30] "In the evening dined with Moore at the Poodle's. He told a good story of Sydney Smith and Leslie the professor. Leslie had written upon the North Pole; something he had said had been attacked in the 'Edinburgh Review'. . . . He called on Jeffrey [who founded the *Edinburgh Review* with Sydney Smith] just as he was getting on horseback, and in a great hurry. Leslie began with a grave complaint on the subject, which Jeffrey interrupted with 'O damn the North Pole.' Leslie went off in high dudgeon, and soon after met Sydney. . . . He told him what he had been to Jeffrey about. . . . 'It was very bad,' said Sydney; 'but do you know, I am not surprised at it, for I have heard him speak very disrespectfully

Ahkood of Swat
World Fables.[31]

Don't our ways seem queer to them, mama?[32]

No, mama I did not miss you—I had Aunt Sue & Rosa[33] & Papa—& papa read to me—no I did not miss you.

Livy—It broke my heart a little, but I admired her for sticking so steadily to the simple truth

Bay—(sitting up in crib) Well—sometime *I* go down town <in> come back & throw up.

Susie sick <to-day>—B. envious of attentions shown.

Susie has 2 loose teeth, B only 1, & it not movable—she finds it no use to buck against suc[h] odds.

"Numbered by days." "this afternoon (July 26)[34] it was <s> still numbered by <d>hours."——365 days—O, then in 2 yrs it will get its teeth—then learn to walk—& by & by it will be 7 or 8 & we'll be big & it will have to mind us. [#]

---

of the Equator'" (Charles C. F. Greville, *The Greville Memoirs*, ed. Richard Henry Stoddard [New York: Scribner, Armstrong & Co., 1875], p. 265). Clemens refers to a page in Stoddard's abridgment, although he owned a copy of the three-volume 1874 edition edited by Henry Reeve (A1911, item 210).

[31] Clemens would include eight selections from George T. Lanigan's *Fables by G. Washington Æsop, Taken "Anywhere, Anywhere, Out of the World"* (New York: The World, 1878) in *Mark Twain's Library of Humor*. Although he mentioned it several times in Notebooks 19 and 20, Clemens did not include Lanigan's popular "Threnody," a comic dirge inspired by news of the death in January 1878 of Abdul-Ghafur, the Akhoond of the territory of Swat on the northwest border of India.

[32] Clemens had begun compiling "A Record of the Small Foolishnesses of Susie & 'Bay' [Clara] Clemens (Infants)" at Quarry Farm in August 1876 and added to the manuscript over a period of nine years, particularly during July and August of 1880 (see *S&MT*, pp. 98, 120, 121).

[33] Rosina Hay was the German nursemaid who had cared for the children since March 1874.

[34] Jean, the Clemenses' youngest daughter, was born on 26 July 1880 at Quarry Farm.

If it gets too much it can put it out (throw up)—babies do that. (Susie.)

Dr. Geo. H. Taylor
fash & not so good for invalids
Mrs. Z. says he's just as enthusiastic as ever.[35]

Bierce's Fables[36]
The World's Fables
Town Crier, S. F.[37]
Ahkoond of Swat
Prentice Mulford[38]
N. Y. Times funy Man—little girl who <gur>got up drama of Robinson Crusoe.[39] [#]

---

[35] Mrs. W. D. Howells, who was suffering from a painful back, wrote to Livy on 13 August 1880 inquiring about Taylor, a New York physician. Clemens' reply of 17 August said that Livy, whom the doctor had treated some years before, had the impression that Taylor's "place has become a resort for fashionables . . . & that its efficiency had rather fallen off," but for a more professional opinion they had applied to Livy's physician, Mrs. Zippie Brooks of Elmira, who reported that the doctor was "as full of enthusiasm as ever" (*MTHL*, pp. 323–324). The appearance of the notebook entry suggests that Clemens noted Dr. Taylor's name and later filled in the two lines about Taylor to be used in the reply to Mrs. Howells' query.

[36] Ambrose Bierce contributed a series of humorous sketches called "Fables of Zambri the Parsee" to the English journal *Fun* from July 1872 to March 1873. In 1874 they were included in Bierce's *Cobwebs from an Empty Skull*.

[37] From 1868 to 1872 Bierce contributed to the "Town Crier," a page of satirical editorials in the San Francisco *News Letter*.

[38] Clemens had known Prentice Mulford in San Francisco in the 1860s when both were contributing humorous articles to the *Golden Era*. Mulford's varied career was marked by failures and disappointments in a number of callings. In 1873 when the paths of the two writers again crossed in England, he had written despondently to Clemens asking for help in his flagging literary career. A few years later Mulford accepted a position on the New York *Daily Graphic*, continuing his column, "The History of a Day," until 1883. Mulford's later works were primarily autobiographical and meditative rather than humorous.

[39] William Livingstone Alden had written editorials for the New York *Times*, the New York *World*, and the New York *Graphic*. He gained a reputation as a humorist with a *Times* column, later collected in *Shooting Stars* (New York: G. P. Putnam's Sons, 1878). The piece Clemens refers to, "Carrie's Comedy," was included in *Shooting Stars*, and in *Mark Twain's Library of Humor*.

Well, one can't really ever get anything sober out of uncle Theodore. (Susie)

(Aug. <2>1, 1880.) Talking, last night, about home matters, I said, "I wish I had said to George (colored butler) when we were leaving home, 'Now George, I wish you would take advantage of these 3 or 4 months idle time while we are away—' " "to learn to let my matches alone!" interrupted Livy. They were the very words I was going to use. Yet George had not been mentioned before, nor his peculiarities.[40]

Several years ago, I said, "Suppose <the Earl of Durham &> I should live to be 92, & just as I was dying, a messenger should enter & <say 'You<r>> say—" "You are become Earl of Durham!" interrupted Livy. The very words I was going to utter; yet there had not been a word said about that earl or any other, nor had there been any conversation calculated to suggest any such subject.

The slave is getting breakfast (Johnny Howells.)[41]

Bay periling her life on the stairs at Baden Baden[42]

Please God forgive Susie for interrupting when I'm praying. [#]

---

[40] Clemens had first collected instances of thought transference while in Heidelberg in June 1878, intending for a time to include them as a chapter of *A Tramp Abroad*. Clemens apparently unearthed the 1878 manuscript in September 1881 and added this and the following episode, planning to publish the revised article in the *North American Review* (*MTHL*, pp. 369–370; *MTLP*, p. 142). The article was finally published, with further additions, in the December 1891 issue of *Harper's New Monthly Magazine*. A sequel to it, "Mental Telegraphy Again," appeared in the same magazine in September 1895.

[41] William Dean Howells wrote to his father after a visit to the Clemens house with his eight-year-old son in 1876: "When he found the black serving-man getting ready for breakfast, he came and woke me. 'Better get up, papa. The slave is setting the table' " (*MTHL*, p. 127, n. 2).

[42] Clara was saved by her nurse, Rosina Hay, from a possible fall in 1878 (*MTB*, p. 699n.). Clara later recalled the incident: "At the age of four I was discovered on the sixth story, crawling around the inside of the banister of a hotel corridor, with a marble floor far below" (Clara Clemens, *My Father Mark Twain* [New York: Harper & Brothers, 1931], p. 6).

Write Dr John Brown[43]

Get some fashion-plates (both sexes—& children) & fit a deep[ly] romantic story to them for Scribner or St. Nicholas. Have the plates *fac-similied* (not *altered*) with descriptive legends below—viz "He gazed mutely upon the stupefied Assemblage, with curling lip & flashing eye."

A boy was washed into the ungrated opening into a sewer, during a tremendous rainstorm & was carried half a mile through the dark way, pretty roughly buffeted (catching flashes of light through similar openings every block) & was shot safely out into the river. In a story a man might use that.

Tight Man who had swallowed a small ball of thread & stood pulling it out, yard after yard & swearing to himself.[44]

<Who> <Well, who> Who was there?

Well there was a gentleman from Alabama, <feller> couple of chaps from Cincinnati, feller from New York & a son of a b— from Boston.

<There is <not a single> hardly a/not a single celebrated Southern name in any of the departments of human industry except those of war, <assassination, lynching,> murder, the duel, repudiation, & massacre.>

There is not a living Southern celebrity in art, to-day; nor science &c

Early, in heaven Stormfield is delighted with the social equalities —a nigger, a <Chinaman,> Digger, an Esquimaux, & a <nasty Frenchman> Fejeean invite themselves to dinner with him—"if we had another animal or two, we could start a menagerie." Next time,

---

[43] The Clemens family first met and grew fond of Edinburgh physician Dr. John Brown when they visited Scotland in 1873. Clemens probably intended to inform Dr. Brown of the birth of Jean, although no letter survives.

[44] Mark Twain used this grotesque situation in his burlesque *Hamlet* a year later (*Mark Twain's Satires & Burlesques*, ed. Franklin R. Rogers [Berkeley and Los Angeles: University of California Press, 1967], pp. 78–79).

they bring also an orang-outang. "The <mag> menag. progresses." Next time they bring also a Frenchman. "The menagerie is complete" says Stormy. But next time they brought also a French married lady. "This is carrying it too far; this will not answer; I have read enough French novels to know that a French married lady cannot enter even a menagerie without bringing the purity of that menagerie under suspicion." It was proposed to <bring> substitute a French maiden of 12, or one of 75. "No, it would not be best for the menagerie. The French confess, by the strict guard they keep <of> over their maidens of all ages, <& all stages of> that they cannot be trusted. Their novels are everywhere—nothing could prevent their girls from reading them; they do read them; consequently, whilst they are chaste in body, through compulsion, they are unchaste in mind. Let us keep the menagerie pure, from the American point of view, not the French. <No, we will have no> That is to say, let us have real, not sham, purity."

The menag. continued to grow, till it had in it cannibals, Presbyterians, pariahs, politicians, <teetotalers,> Turks, tramps,—indeed, all sorts of disagreeable people; & they all called him "Brother Stormfield" & kept falling on his neck & weeping down his back in pious joy. Finally he said "Heaven is a most unpleasant place; there is no privacy in it. I must move."[45]

page 51.

Old Sir Humphrey was yeoman-harbinger to the King.

W$^{m.}$ Armorer, cloth-worker, <G>Esq., governor of the pages of honor, under H. VIII, Ed VI & Mary. (or henchmen).

---

[45] Clemens had worked intermittently on the story of "Captain Stormfield's Visit to Heaven" since 1868 when Captain Edgar Wakeman first told him of his dream of a journey to heaven. The picture of heaven as a mixed community—and Stormfield's uneasiness in the heterogenous society—appears in a discussion between the angel Sandy and the captain (*Report from Paradise,* ed. Dixon Wecter [New York: Harper & Brothers, 1952], pp. 75–79). There Sandy concludes: "'*What a man mostly misses, in heaven, is company*—company of his own sort and color and language.'" The venomous attacks on the French echo Clemens' notebook entries during his 1878/1879 trip abroad (see Notebook 18).

Henchmen were pages of honor & always walked beside the King's horse in procession—they were gentlemen's sons. P. 50.[46]

Charlotte . . <$12> . . . . $12.
William . . . . <15>10.
A C 7
S L. . . . . 1[47]

XXU8 . . . .<X> X10U8

Slote 10 AM[48]
St Gaudens 11 to 12
Tiffany 12? (telephone them.)[49] [#]

---

[46] Clemens did extensive reading in order to establish the historical and social background for *The Prince and the Pauper*, on which he had been working steadily since the first months of 1880. The source for these notes has not been found, but similar information about the royal household, including William Armorer and the henchmen, can be found in the "Biographical Memoir" (particularly 1:lxxiv–lxxvi) of *Literary Remains of King Edward VI*, ed. John Gough Nichols, 2 vols. (London: J. B. Nichols and sons, 1857). Mark Twain mentions "Old Sir Humphrey Marlow" briefly in his novel as the father of the whipping boy; *Literary Remains* denies the historical existence of the office, but notes that tradition named Barnaby Fitzpatrick as the whipping or "breeching" boy.

[47] This list was probably made shortly before the Clemens family left Quarry Farm at the end of September 1880 to return to Hartford. The Clemens and Crane families shared household expenses during the summer months and Clemens was doubtless reminding himself to make payments to the Quarry Farm servants, including Charlotte, the laundress; Aunty Cord, the cook; and Susan Lewis, the young daughter of the Cranes' tenant farmer, John Lewis.

[48] Clemens and his family stopped for three days at the Gilsey House in New York on their way home. He evidently planned to see Dan Slote, his partner in both the scrapbook and the Kaolatype venture. Clemens' repeated memorandum to "ask what my scrap royalty averages per book" suggests concern about Slote's management of the scrapbook. A letter from attorney Charles Perkins may have aroused Clemens' suspicions about Slote: "I have written over & over again to Slote but he does not send any account, or money—perhaps a letter from you to him might have some effect" (17 September 1880). The business meeting with Slote appears to have satisfied Clemens' doubts about his scrapbook royalties. However, several months later, when his disenchantment with Slote was complete, he wrote to Charles Webster: "The Scrapbook gravels me because while they have been paying me about $1800 or $2000 a year, I judge it ought to have been 3 times as much" (5 June 1881, *MTBus*, p. 160).

[49] Clemens' appointment with Tiffany & Company probably concerned the set

Send Music box man.[50]
Ask Dan make detailed statements.
Ask what my scrap royalty aver p. book.

The quality of Mercy . . . . . is twice bless'd;
It blesseth him that gives & him that takes;
'Tis mightiest in the mightiest: it becomes
The thronèd monarch better than his crown.
—SHAKSPEARE, *Merchant of Venice*.[51]

Read Homer once, & you can read no more;
For all books else appear so mean, so poor;
Verse will seem prose; but still persist to read,
And Homer will be all the books you need.
—SHEFFIELD, *Duke of Buckingham*

<Su>Mrs. Hall—He doesn't mind—you <have> mind better, don't you?

Susie—We *have* to.[52] [#]

---

of nineteen membership "badges" which he had ordered from the New York firm in August. The pins were for the young ladies of the Hartford Saturday Morning Club which met from October through June, assembling once a year at the Clemens house. Helen Post Chapman writes: "On one of these occasions he presented each one of us with a beautiful pin. . . . These pins were designed by Tiffany, a bunch of lilies embossed and enameled in the centers, a ribbon band making an oval setting in gold on which was inscribed in blue enamel 'Saturday Morning Club of Hartford.' On the back was engraved the name of the owner" (Helen Post Chapman, *My Hartford of the Nineteenth Century* [Hartford: Edwin Valentine Mitchell, 1928], p. 61).

[50] The music box which the Clemenses had bought in Geneva in 1878 had been damaged in shipment to Hartford. Clemens had been trying to find a music box "expert" who could come to Hartford and repair the instrument since October 1879. The music box references in this notebook, written in late September 1880, indicate that the repairs were still not complete.

[51] This passage, identically abridged, appears as the epigraph of *The Prince and the Pauper*. About the time this entry was written, Clemens wrote to Thomas Bailey Aldrich that he had just completed the book (15 September 1880, *MTL*, p. 386), but revision of the manuscript actually continued for several weeks.

[52] A similar anecdote concerning the Clemens children's sense of obedience appears in "A Record of the Small Foolishnesses of Susie & 'Bay' Clemens (Infants)" (*S&MT*, p. 114).

Send Music box man.

Ask Dan to make detailed statements.

Ask what my scrap royalty averages per book.

Holmes, Burglar Alarm Co, N.Y.

Why don't you state K. prices in circular?—afraid?[53]

Abou Ben Butler—(may his tribe decrease/surcease!)[54]
Awoke one night from a deep dream of peace,
And saw within the moonlight in his room,
Making it rich & like a lily in bloom,
An angel writing in a book of gold.
Exceeding cheek had made B. Butler bold,
And to the presence in the room he said,
"What writest thou?"—The vision raised its head,
And, with a look made of all sweet accord,
Answered, "The names of those who <love> serve the
<lord>Lord."

"And is mine one?" said Abou. "Nay, not<,> so,"
Replied the angel.—Abou spoke more low,
But cheerly still; & said "I pray thee, then,
Write me as one <that loves> <'t adores> serves his
fellow-men."
The angel wrote, & vanished. The next night

[53] This query about Kaolatype is addressed to Dan Slote and reflects Clemens' growing concern over the cost of the Kaolatype engraving process.

[54] As commander of the Union forces occupying New Orleans during the Civil War General Benjamin F. Butler had incurred charges of despotism and corruption for his high-handed administration. He became the subject of a number of satirical poems, including Charles H. Webb's "Aboo Ben Butler" published in *John Paul's Book* (Hartford: Columbian Book Co., 1874). Formerly a radical Republican who had led the floor fight in the House of Representatives to impeach Andrew Johnson, on 28 August 1880 Butler announced his support for Winfield S. Hancock, the Democratic presidential candidate (New York *Times,* 29 August 1880). Clemens' pastiche, written sometime in September, was probably prompted by the widely-discussed endorsement speech.

It came again, with a great wakening light,
And showed the names whom God's dear/firm/high
love/trust had blessed,—
And lo! Ben Butler's name was left out intirely.—/had "got
left."/it was distinctly manifest that Abou Ben B. had "got
left."

<W>Gilsey House—[55]

Avoid 5, 3 & 1, First floor.

6 & 8 are large & good, First floor.

96, Fourth floor, is good—alcove-parlor & fine clean air on 29th st. with bath-room.

86 & 88 (4th floor) communicate, & are large enough, & choice. They are on 29th st, & both have baths.

Always call for rooms on 29th st & *not elsewhere.*

Paid Rapelyea on ac/—16 <^{c}/ct[-]s>
Sept. 28/80.

Rosa Conchas $12[56]
Park & Tilford.

<You have taught your century (generation) the value of short speeches.>[57] [#]

---

[55] Clemens booked accommodations in advance of his trip to New York at the Gilsey House on Broadway and Twenty-ninth Street. The Gilsey House proprietors wrote Clemens at Quarry Farm confirming his reservation: "To a moral certainty you shall have as you ask viz—2 double rooms, adjoining with cots &c &c" (20 September 1880).

[56] In May 1880 Clemens had purchased from James Lidgerwood & Company, a New York establishment specializing in imported delicacies, wines, and "segars," 100 Rosa Concha cigars. Clemens, despite his purported preference for cheap cigars, apparently planned to buy more of this more expensive brand. The Clemenses usually shopped at Park & Tilford's, fashionable grocers, on their trips to New York. "Rapelyea" has not been identified.

[57] This is the beginning of the first of three drafts of Clemens' 16 October speech in this notebook. The relationships between the three one-sentence paragraphs that begin this draft are uncertain. Apparently Clemens wrote "You have . . . speeches" first, and he must have canceled that sentence just before continuing the draft of

<—& I>My fel cits have paid me the high comp—& I hope it was not misplaced—of de

I am deputed <to>by my fellow cc to welcome you to the <hearty> cordial hospitalities of Hartford—the city of the <historic> Charter Oak—of which the main part of this town is built.

By your example you have killed the hoary <& foolish> fashion of long speeches; & for this you deserve immortal/imperishable gratitude. <Let us> We shall best honor you in honoring the lesson you have taught. <P>As a soldier you proved yourself without a peer—& so we welcome you as the first soldier of the Republic; as President you inaugurated international arbitration—& so we welcome you as the first to lay the axe to the root of the trade of war, & as the pioneer in the march of the nations toward the last perfection of enlightened government, the substitution of reason for <the> <rude> <savage> force in the settlement of controversies; & finally, as one who, being almost called—& yet not quite—to carry the standard of a great party for the third time, in a Presidential campaign, has sunk the hero in the patriot, has cast aside all considerations of self, all pique, all narrow feeling, & has devoted his whole heart & the might of his great name to the cause of that party, and through it to the highest & best interest of his country, its progress & its civilization, we welcome you by the noblest of all the titles you have earned, that of First Citizen of the Republic!

Oct. 10.<—>1880.—Told Susie Gen. Grant's military history.

---

the speech with the sentence beginning "By your example." At the same time or later, he inserted at least part of the sentence beginning "I am deputed" as a new opening for the speech. (The new opening may originally have ended with "Hartford" or perhaps with "Oak"; if so, its latter part could have been added at any later time.) The false start "—& I" was probably intended to follow "Hartford"; Clemens canceled the false start with a sentence ("My fel cits . . . of de") which both includes the language of the false start and serves as an alternative to the opening "I am deputed."

The other two drafts appear on pages 375–377 and on page 425. The speech is discussed in the headnote to this notebook; additional textual information appears in Details of Inscription.

"What a wonderful man, to fight five years—he must be scratched up a good deal, isn't he?"

"He must have had a great many swords & guns." "Yes—they would reach to Elmira." "How did he ever get rid of them."

<After> Through/By years of colossal labor & colossal achievement, you <at last> at last beat down a gigantic rebellion & saved your country from destruction. Then the country commanded you to take the helm of State. You <wanted to> <wanted to> preferred your great office of General of the armies, & the rest & comfort which it afforded; but you loyally obeyed, & <gave up the> relinquished permanently the ample & well-earned salary of the generalship. <which had assured your remaining years against any possible> <—you exchanged an assured living for> & resigned your approaching age/accumulating years to <a>the chance mercies of a precarious existence.[58]

<By this present tedious & exhausting progress through the land; <&> by the sight of your honored face; by the wisdom of your words; & by the magic of your name, you <c>are contributing a share whose magnitude cannot be overestimated, toward saving your country <a>once more—not from destruction, but from dishonor & shame, & from industrial disaster.

Rest assured that your country is grateful for these high services & heavy sacrifices—& in no sordid way.>[59]

---

[58] Clemens recorded the word count of his speech in five places throughout this draft. The first figure, "80," appears on the otherwise blank left-hand page facing the first page of the speech, and records the count up to the end of the first paragraph. Clemens evidently made the word count after completing his revisions of the draft since the count refers only to uncanceled material.

[59] The manuscript is complicated by the fact that Clemens initially planned to write this draft of the speech only on the right-hand pages of the notebook—leaving the facing pages blank for possible revisions. Where the left-hand pages have been used for revision, the intended order of paragraphs of the speech has become uncertain. Here, two paragraphs ("By this present . . . disaster" and "Rest assured . . . way") were written on the left-hand page, and subsequently canceled. However, there is no indication whether these two paragraphs were intended to precede or to follow the paragraph on the facing right-hand page ("You are now . . . permit

You are now a private citizen, but <you are> private employments are closed <against> <upon> against you—<the doors of all industries are shut against you>—<but>because your name would be used for speculative purposes, & you have refused to permit that.

You are doing this generous work—you who have earned repose if ever a man earned them.[60]

When Wellington won Waterloo, <grateful England made him a duke, loaded him with minor & yet great & shining dignities, & gave him a sum of money equivalent, at present values, to $5,000,000<,>. <besides> <& also a long list of>>—a battle about on a level with some dozen of your victories—sordid England tried to *pay* him <in> for that service—in money & grandeurs! She made him a duke, & <loaded him> gave him $4000 000

If you had done & suffered for any other country what you have done & suffered for your own, you would have been affronted in the same sordid way; but thank God this vast & rich & mighty Republic is imbued to the core with a delicacy which will forever <keep her> preserve her from so degrading a deserving son. Your country loves you, your country is proud of you, your country is grateful to you. Her praises, which have been ringing in your ears all these weeks & months will never cease while her flag continues to wave. <& this the noblest & best of governments continues to exist.> Your country stands ready, from this day forth, to testify her measureless love, <her> & pride & <her> gratitude toward you, in every conceivable —inexpensive way. Welcome to Hartford<!>, great soldier, honored <sol> statesman, <patient,> unselfish citizen!

By this present laborious progress through the land, you are

---

that"). The sequence presented in this text, for want of more substantial evidence, is based on the sequence of the speech as published in the New York *Tribune*. There the two canceled paragraphs are represented by the shortened and revised version which Clemens added at the end of this draft ("By this present . . . disaster" on pages 376–377). This revised version, in the published speech, precedes the paragraph "You are now . . . permit that."

[60] This sentence is not included in Clemens' word count nor does it appear in the New York *Tribune* report of the Grant speech.

mightily contributing toward saving your country once more—this time from dishonor & shame & from industrial disaster.[61]

Mrs. Taft[62] was going to have a tin cradle, full of roses, awaiting Jean's arrival in Hartford; but it failed because we arrived unexpectedly.

<Our division of the procession finished passing at 6 o'clock.> Figures at hand now, (10 p.m.) warrant the conviction that a <republican> Conn. majority of [*blank*] attended the Dem funeral to-day.[63]

Extract of Gluten & Barley
Health Food Co.

The Universal Food.[64]

(In Methodist Class-meeting.)

He—What was your first notable Christian experience, after you became reconciled to God?
She—I had a miscarriage.
(Pretend this happened somewhere.)

Burlington Letter & Postal Card file.
Theo. L. Pilger[65]
Box 750 Burlington Iowa [#]

---

[61] This paragraph, added at the end of the speech draft, is a revised and shortened version of the canceled paragraph "By this present . . . disaster" (p. 375.16–21). The canceled paragraph appeared on page two of the draft; Clemens wrote the number "2" above the new version of the paragraph to indicate that it was to replace material on that page.

[62] The wife of Dr. Cincinnatus A. Taft, the Clemens family physician in Hartford.

[63] Clemens delivered his ironically lugubrious speech, entitled "Funeral Oration Over the Grave of the Democratic Party," at the "Republican jollification" in the Hartford Opera House on Election Day, 2 November 1880. The text of the speech was published in the Chicago *Tribune* of 4 November 1880.

[64] The preceding entries probably reflect a recent meeting with Frank Fuller, an old friend and business associate of Clemens, who was president of the Health Food Company in New York.

[65] A receipt from Pilger dated 12 November 1880 indicates that Clemens pur-

Piper's Son —Mr. Carter[66]
Dame Trot Anne Trumbull
Where You Going Miss Wheeler
Old Bean Prof. Holbrook.
Simple Simon—Berguin
Mistress Mary Quite Contrary (Robinson)
Blue Beard & wife Mr. <B>Adams & Miss Trobridge
Miss Muffett—Miss Barnard
Little Boy Blue—Mr. Carpenter
<Peter Piper>

Emily Mother Goose

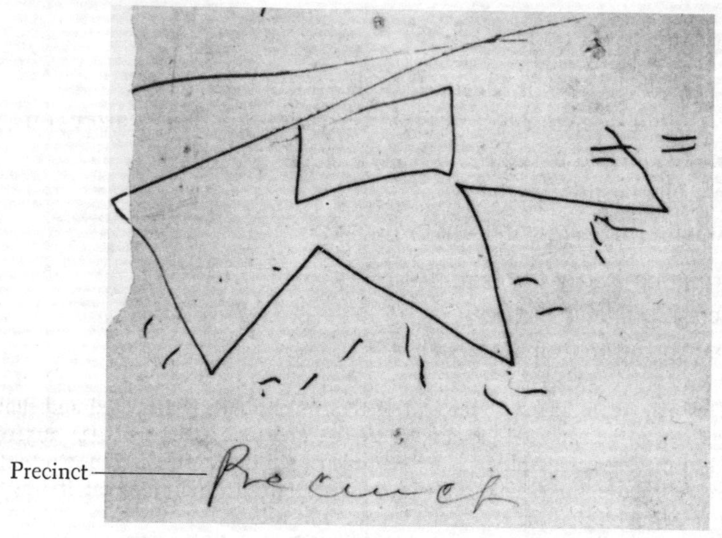

Precinct———

chased ten letter files. Albert Bigelow Paine discusses Clemens' delight in inventions "that would provide physical or mental easement for his species" and notes that "once he was going to save the human race with accordion letter-files—the system of order which would grow out of this useful device being of such nerve and labor saving proportions as to insure long life and happiness to all" (*MTB*, p. 688).

66 Moncure Conway wrote to Clemens on 20 December 1880: "Nor shall I forget the Mother Goose Party. The ambition of my life is to get one of the same kind up here at Bedford Park." Evidently the Mother Goose party was modeled

Dean Sage, Joe, & the innkeeper—"*You* bring a G— d— tapeworm like *that*, here & then dispute my bill, will you, G— d— you!"[67]

<Dec. 10/80—Remember to add $5,000 to list of investments through Bissell—7 per cent.>[68]

Write story for boys about a *small* man with (unsuspected) gigantic strength—always suprising people with it.

To satirize the world in petto—write private journal of a Pitcairn Islander[69] [#]

---

after the birthday ball for Caldwell H. Colt which the Clemenses had attended on 24 November 1879 at Mrs. Samuel Colt's mansion. The ball was "one of the most brilliant parties which has ever been given in Hartford" (Hartford *Courant*, 25 November 1879). Livy described the scene in a letter to her mother: "I enjoyed it and Mr. Clemens enjoyed it *exceedingly*. . . . Sixteen young ladies and gentlemen dressed in fancy costume, with powdered hair formed two quadrilles dancing to their own singing which was the Mother Goose melodies–'Where are you going to my pretty maid,' 'How does my lady's garden grow,' 'Bo-Peep,' 'Sing a Song of Sixpence,' 'Little Mary quite Contrary' etc. etc.–it was exceedingly pretty to see them" (30 November 1879, *S&MT*, p. 112). In this notebook entry, Clemens first listed the characters and later added the names of those who assumed the roles.

67 Clemens described Dean Sage's practical joke on Twichell in the Autobiographical Dictation of 10 October 1906. The two friends had been tramping about in the Adirondacks when they were forced to put up for the night at a cabin in the woods which advertised food and lodging. Twichell ate ravenously of the "odious" dinner and breakfast their host provided. Sage, as a joke, persuaded the innkeeper to present an outrageous bill of thirteen dollars, then pretended to dispute it with much profanity, while Twichell tried unavailingly to prevent a fracas. The anecdote concludes with the landlord saying " 'when a man brings a hellfired Famine here that eats a barrel of pork and four barrels of beans at two sittings–' " and Sage replying " 'I never thought of that, and I ask your pardon.' " Clemens delighted in anecdotes connecting Twichell with profanity. Another example is published in *Mark Twain in Eruption* (pp. 366–372).

68 George P. Bissell & Company were Hartford bankers and stockbrokers with whom Clemens had an account. On 9 December 1880 Clemens' lawyer and business agent, Charles Perkins, wrote to him: "Mr Bissell tells me he has a very choice 7 p[ercent] loan of $5000–if you wish to make an investment." Bissell & Company sent Clemens confirmation of their purchase of 500 shares of the "American Exchange in Europe" for $5,000.

69 Clemens apparently planned an extension of his "Great Revolution in Pitcairn" which had appeared in the March 1879 *Atlantic*.

Go first to Mad. Fogarty's[70] from Gilsey—8 blocks below.

Send a word to Ned House,[71] Union Square Hotel.

See Will Gillette<.>—show Howells letter.[72]

Man with a joke trying to lead up to it—constant failure.

Caswell's beef, wine & iron (bottle)
Arnica plaster

De Casey Yrugy Moore.[73]
Don Cervantes Peck
Calvary
Don Alonzo Stanley.
Marquis de Lafayette
Earl Douglas

---

[70] Madame Fogarty was the New York dressmaker who had made Livy's wedding dress and from whom she often purchased clothing (*S&MT*, p. 192). Several years later Grace King, a friend of the Clemens family, would describe a visit to Madame Fogarty's shop with Livy: "She is . . . a 'swell' dressmaker—Mrs Clemens asked to see her pretty things—and you never in your life beheld a more superb collection of gowns and cloaks—The cheapest dress was about $250!" (Grace King to her sister, Mrs. McDowell, 22 November 1888, Grace King Papers, Louisiana State University, Baton Rouge)

This and the following entries were probably memoranda for Clemens' short trip to New York with Twichell on 20 December 1880. The two stayed at the Gilsey House where they jokingly registered as "Jno Smith & Son" (Gilsey House bill in MTP). Clemens' short visit seems to have been made on two accounts—an invitation to attend a meeting of the Tile Club, an informal society of artists, and a meeting, in Twichell's company, with General Grant to discuss the Chinese Educational Mission (see note 109).

[71] Edward House had recently returned to the United States after nearly ten years in Japan, and was traveling, as correspondent for the *Tribune*, with Grant's party. A letter of 13 September 1880 from House to Clemens indicates that they had renewed their friendship by that date.

[72] William Gillette's theatrical career began in 1874 when Clemens loaned him three thousand dollars and arranged a small role for him in the 1875 Hartford production of *Colonel Sellers*. The letter to which Clemens refers in this note is unidentified.

[73] None of these fanciful names is included in Mark Twain's numerous literary projects in 1880 or 1881.

Valet de chambre <Holco> Utterback (chief machinist, now, & called VALLETT <de>D. Utterback.

Susan Sarepta

Loranda
Diantha
Lodema
Sabra
Loammi

Stephania cigarettes—glass mouthpece attached.

Cohn & Co
15 Wabash ave
Chicago.

[M]ind telegraphing—Barnum Jan 25/81—I thought of his letters in night got his letter on the same subject that morning or afternoon[74]

Swinge him wid de gospel wrath
& <boost> <shove> <highst> yank him into de gospel path

<Knock him down wid de good ole Book
An <pull him out> <drag/snake> yank him home wid <de>dat Shepherd' Crook.>

Yank him home

O take dat sinner by de neck
& break his heart wid a Bible tex'

Dey ain't no chance for him no mo'
Onless he break for de hebenly sho' [#]

---

[74] P. T. Barnum's letter of 24 January 1881 enclosed a clipping from the New York *Sun* about the importunate letters he frequently received from job-seekers and beggars. Clemens' entry, written on a torn half-leaf of the notebook, may have been added at a later date than the entries on the preceding and following pages to accompany the other instances of "mind telegraphing" noted earlier in this notebook.

The point made was that conscience was above logic in treating of morals.

Jehovah Gap.[75]

House fed Seidlitz powder to a costive dog, in meat—had kept him without water a day—then filled him up with water.—Imagine the result.

Ned Bunce[76]
<Send Prince to Tauchnitz.>[77]
<Jo. Goodman, Fresno, Cal.>
<Mother Fairbanks>
<Twichell,> <Parker,>[78] Warner

---

[75] Edwin Pond Parker recalled an anecdote which Clemens told in the 1860s on a visit to Hartford. The story concerned "a minister in a mining camp who won the hearts of the men. Suggesting that the name of the camp should be changed, the minister was not sure that he had accomplished what he wanted to, when the men did change the name–from Devil's Gulch to Jehovah Gap" (Leah Strong, *Joseph Hopkins Twichell* [Athens: University of Georgia Press, 1966], p. 97). An expanded version of the story was to have been part of chapter 25 of *Life on the Mississippi*. The suppressed passage was published in the 1944 Heritage Press edition of *Life on the Mississippi* (pp. 390–391).

[76] Edward M. Bunce, cashier of the Phoenix National Bank in Hartford, heads the list of people, many of them well known, to whom Clemens planned to send complimentary copies of *The Prince and the Pauper*. The list was probably begun in December 1880, shortly after Clemens and Osgood concluded an informal agreement to publish the book (SLC to Orion Clemens, 27 November 1880, *MTBus*, p. 147). Howells read and criticized the manuscript in mid-December (Howells to SLC, 13 December 1880, *MTHL*, p. 338) and on 1 February 1881 Clemens suggested that Osgood bring the formal contract to Hartford "& lug off the MS—which I finished *once more* to-day" (PH in MTP). The contract was signed on 9 February. Clemens continued to add names to his list at various times during 1881 (see Details of Inscription for interlined names). *The Prince and the Pauper* was issued in December 1881.

[77] *The Prince and the Pauper* was published in Germany by Tauchnitz early in December 1881.

[78] Edwin Pond Parker, Congregational minister of Hartford and member of the Monday Evening Club, wrote to Clemens on 22 December 1880 praising him as the only American writer of the generation "capable of writing such forcible,

Kinney,[79] Charly Clark

<Mrs. Whitmore.>

<Station Master Collins>[80]

David Gray.

John Hay

H. H. Boyesen.

<Charley Stoddard, Honolulu.>[81]

Howells.

<Clara Spaulding.>

<Mother,>[82] <Charley,> Julia[83] Sue.[84]

<Ma,> Orion.

Dr. O. W. Holmes.

Ed. C. Stedman.

Lilly Warner.

<Dan Slote.>

Montgomery Schuyler, "World."

Noah Brooks.

---

sinewy, racy English" and urging him to undertake some work "that shall bear the stamp of your individuality plainly enough, and at the same time have a sober character and a solid worth & a permanent value." Clemens replied on Christmas Eve: "I thank you most sincerely for those pleasant words. They come most opportunely, too, at a time when I was wavering between launching a book of the sort you mention, with my name to it, and smuggling it into publicity with my name suppressed. Well, I'll put my name to it. . . . Will you . . . take the manuscript and read it, either to yourself, or, still better, aloud to your family?" (Hartford *Courant*, 21 June 1912). Parker's favorable review of *The Prince and the Pauper* appeared in the Hartford *Courant* in December 1881.

[79] John C. Kinney and Charles Hopkins Clark were assistant editor and managing editor, respectively, of the Hartford *Courant*. Clemens hired Clark to do some of the preliminary work on *Mark Twain's Library of Humor*.

[80] William H. Collins was the railway stationmaster in Hartford.

[81] Clemens inscribed a presentation copy of *The Prince and the Pauper* to Stoddard, the writer who had served as his secretary and companion in London in 1873/1874, "With the love of The Author. Hartford, Dec. 20, 1881." Stoddard had written Clemens of his decision to move to Hawaii in October 1881 (see SLC to Howells, 26 October 1881, *MTHL*, p. 378).

[82] Mrs. Jervis Langdon, Livy's mother.

[83] Julia Langdon, daughter of Livy's brother Charles.

[84] Susan Crane.

John Russell Young.[85]
<Gen. U.>[86]
<M. H. Bartlett[87]
Avon Conn>
Dr. Burton.[88]
D^{r}. John Brown.
<"Hawkeye" R. J. Burdette.>[89]
<Wattie Bowser.>[90]
T. W. Crane & Mother. & Chas.
<Gen. Garfield.>
G. W. Curtis.
J. R. Lowell.
Elihu Vedder.
Willie Winter.[91]
Rose Terry Cooke.[92]
Ned House.

---

[85] Schuyler, Brooks, and Young were journalists associated at this time with the New York *World*, *Times*, and *Herald* respectively.

[86] Presumably U. S. Grant.

[87] Matthew H. Bartlett was the publisher of the Hartford *Republican*. In 1867 he constructed Bartlett Tower on Talcott Mountain, five miles from Hartford, a favorite destination for Clemens and Twichell on their walking excursions.

[88] Nathaniel J. Burton was the minister of Park Congregational Church in Hartford.

[89] Clemens' inscription in the copy of *The Prince and the Pauper* sent to Burdette reads, "With the kindest regards of The Author, Hartford, Dec. 20, 1881" (MTM).

[90] A twelve-year-old Dallas schoolboy, David Watt ("Wattie") Bowser, first wrote to Clemens on 16 March 1880, enclosing his report card and a composition about Mark Twain, explaining: "At school we were required to select some man among the living great ones . . . with whom we would exchange places, and I selected you." Clemens replied at length on 20 March 1880 and the correspondence between author and schoolboy continued until 1882. Bowser's letter of 4 January 1882 thanks Clemens for having sent him a copy of *The Prince and the Pauper* (Pascal Covici, Jr., "Dear Master Wattie: The Mark Twain-David Watt Bowser Letters," *Southwest Review* 45 [Spring 1960]: 106–109, 114).

[91] William Winter, poet, essayist, and drama critic for the New York *Tribune*.

[92] Rose Terry Cooke frequently contributed poems and short stories to the *Atlantic*.

Lt. C. E. S. Wood, West Point.[93]
Frances H. Burnett.[94]
Ed. Everett Hale.
Press Club, N. Y.
" " Chicago.
Thos. Bailey Aldrich
Smith, of Tile Club.
<Dean Sage.>
Miss Yonge, (through Conway.)[95]
Moulton[96] " "
Mrs. Beecher[97]
<Susie & Bay (special binding.)>[98]
Mrs. Knight Cheney?[99]
Mrs. Chas. Perkins.
<Mrs. Karl Gerhardt>

---

[93] Charles Erskine Scott Wood, whom Clemens met when he read at West Point in February 1881, would print *1601* on a small press at the Academy in 1882. The name has been squeezed in between the entries preceding and following it and undoubtedly was added at a later date.

[94] Several years later, Clemens recalled having sent Mrs. Burnett a copy of his book: "I doubt if Mrs. Burnett knows whence came to her the suggestion to write 'Little Lord Fauntleroy,' but I know; it came to her from reading 'The Prince and the Pauper' " (SLC to Rev. F. V. Christ, August 1908, *MTL*, p. 814).

[95] Charlotte M. Yonge was the English author of *The Prince and the Page* which may well have influenced the title of *The Prince and the Pauper*. Clemens later claimed that the book itself had been "suggested by that pleasant and picturesque little history-book, Charlotte M. Yonge's 'Little Duke' " (SLC to Rev. F. V. Christ, August 1908, *MTL*, p. 814).

[96] Possibly John Fletcher Moulton, a friend of Moncure Conway whom Clemens may have met on one of his visits to England.

[97] Julia Beecher, wife of Thomas K. Beecher, the Elmira minister.

[98] The special binding was white cloth stamped in gold (Merle Johnson, *A Bibliography of the Works of Mark Twain*, rev. ed. [New York: Harper & Brothers, 1935], p. 40). Clemens wrote to Edward House: "I had half a dozen of my books printed on China paper for Susy and Bay and Koto and two or three other especial friends" (27 December 1881, *S&MT*, p. 145). Koto was House's adopted Japanese daughter.

[99] The brothers Knight and Frank Cheney headed the Cheney Silk Mills in Manchester, Connecticut.

Will Bunce.[100]
George MacDonald.[101]
Seaver.[102]
W. P. Hanscom, Chicago News (Washington office)
Frank Wilkie, Chicago.
<Wattie Bowser,
Dallas, Texas.
care Bowser & Lemon.>

As <I> a boy, I supposed a word had been left out; so I added it, to make sense:

Ye shall bring forth fruits *and* meet (meat) for repentance.

F. Hopkinson Smith
"Templeton"[103]
Holmes, Emerson, Whittier
Longfellow.
E. H. House—Geo Wm Curtis

<D[i]> Liver poem

Gaily the Osgood*ar*[104]
Smoked his cigar,

---

100 The painter William Gedney Bunce, cousin of Edward Bunce, had been a frequent visitor during the Clemenses' stay in Paris in 1879.

101 Clergyman, poet, and author of many popular children's books whom Clemens had met in Scotland in 1873 (*MTA*, 2:231).

102 William A. Seaver was in charge of the "Editor's Drawer," a department of *Harper's New Monthly Magazine*.

103 For many years, George H. Munroe wrote a popular weekly series of letters from Boston for the Hartford *Courant* under the pseudonym of "Templeton" (John Bard McNulty, *Older than the Nation, the Story of the Hartford Courant* [Stonington, Conn.: Pequot Press, 1964], p. 109).

104 Clemens' doggerel is an adaptation of T. H. Bayly's "Welcome Me Home," a song which Clemens often heard in his Hannibal days (*HH&T*, p. 34). The first stanza of Bayly's version reads: "Gaily the Troubadour/ Touch'd his guitar,/ When he was hastening/ Home from the war./ Singing 'From Palestine/ Hither I come,/ Lady Love! Lady Love!/ Welcome me home' " (Thomas Haynes Bayly,

When he was contempla-
Ting his depar-*

Singing When I get thar
<'F I know myself,>
'Rah!—'rah!—'rah!
Mac-cass*ar*, Mac-cass*ar*,
You'll restore my har.

Then <gathered all> <came>swarmed the joyful boys
And gave him a send-off,
<Costing a rattling sum>
But without going, he de*cei*ved them WITH
Rep.

Now when he goes again
You bet he *will* go
Or, most Inj*uni*ously
He'll *lose* his har.

Singing O never more
Never, *nev*er more,
I didn't have *time* to-<com>-write-the-rest-of-that-
<verse>*ver*-her-her<se>-rr-se, & so I won't try for to
sing it.

Write Mrs. Swisslielm[105]

---

*—*ture to Europe* is necessary to complete the sense, but that would disorder the rhyme<,>. <which> [*Clemens' footnote*]

Songs, Ballads and Other Poems, 2 vols. [London: Richard Bentley, 1844], 1:192). "Osgoodar" is publisher James R. Osgood, who did eventually sail for Liverpool in June 1881 (Carl J. Weber, *The Rise and Fall of James Ripley Osgood* [Waterville, Me.: Colby College Press, 1959], p. 185).

[105] Mrs. Jane Grey Swisshelm, abolitionist and women's rights reformer, wrote to Clemens on 19 January 1881 apologizing to him for allowing a portion of his letter of praise to appear in the advertisements for the third edition of her memoirs, *Half A Century* (Chicago: Jansen, McClurg, 1880).

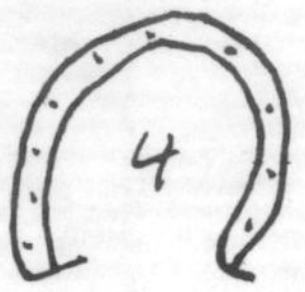

1	1	11	30
2	3	12	90
3	7	13	310
4	15	14	550
5	31	15	1330
6	63	16	2330
7	1.27	17	4,330
8	1.90	18	8,700
9	6.	19	17,000
10	14.	20.	34,000

1	1	17	64000
2	2	18	124,000
3	4	19	256,000
4	8	20	512,000
5	16	21	1,024,000
6	32	21	2,048,000
7	64	21	4,100,000
8	128	22	8,200,000
9	256	23	16,400,000
10	512	24	32,800,000
11	1024	25	<66,000,000>65,000,000
12	2048	26	130,000,000
13	4096	27	260,000,000
14	8,000	28	520,000 000
15	16000	29	1,040,000 000
16	32000	30	2,080,000 000[106]

[#]

[106] Clemens' numerical progressions may derive from the martingale system of gambling, in which one doubles the stakes after each loss.

Kelsey & Hitchcock.[107]

P.	30	G.	<50>40
G.	25	M	50
L	10	O	75
D	20		476
K.	16		506
R	15		
J	20	Gil	30
P	50	Mus.	20
T	35	Danc.	6
S	150		562[108]

Jno Stokes

43 Hammond st.
Boston Highlands
Boston, Mass.

$25 unframed.

Recommend Y. W.[109] for Robt. Hart's[110] place—inspector General

[107] Hartford "Merchant Tailors."

[108] This seems to be a list of expenses, possibly monthly wages or Christmas bonuses, for the Clemens servants—Patrick, George, Lizzie, Delia, the cook, Katy Leary, and Rosa. The remaining notations may refer to Christmas gifts for family members (Theodore and Sue Crane, Mollie and Orion Clemens, etc.). "Mus." and "Danc." probably refer to the Clemens' children's music and dancing lessons; "Gil" may be a bill due to the Gilsey House in New York.

[109] Yung Wing, a naturalized United States citizen, was the director of the Chinese Educational Mission in Hartford from 1872 to 1881. Clemens had been asked by Twichell to arrange a meeting with General Grant in New York in order to secure his intercession on behalf of Yung Wing to forestall the closing of the mission. Twichell and Clemens saw General Grant at the Fifth Avenue Hotel on 21 December 1880. Clemens described the interview in a letter to Howells: "Grant took in the whole situation in a jiffy, & before Joe had more than fairly started, the old man said: '*I'll write the Viceroy a letter*—a separate letter—& bring strong reasons to bear upon him . . . I shall be *glad* to do it—it will be a labor of love' " (*MTHL*, p. 340). The mission, which provided for the education of about one hundred Chinese students in America, was closed by the Chinese in 1881 and the pupils sent home despite petitions from Grant, Clemens, Joseph Twichell, and others to Viceroy Li Hung-chang.

[110] In 1881 Hart had been inspector-general of customs in China for eighteen

of Customs—been there 10 yrs & resigned several times & not accepted because nobody to take the place. Hart is an Irishman—was British Consul.

Y. W.^s salary is $15,000. He is well fitted for present position but could do 10 times more for China *in* China than here.

Russell Young[111] ought to change & go to China.

Y. W. has prospect of being Chief Minister with emoluments of $20 to $25,000 a year—& is building house & has American family.

Gen. G. to negociate loan here or in Europe.

Y. W. being there could throw the building of the roads into American hands.

Remember, Li-hung Chang *knows* Y. W. *personally*, & is his puissant friend.

They were to come to me patented?[112] Then that cost should fall on him. [#]

---

years. He continued in that position actively until 1906 and nominally until his death in 1911. His achievement as the architect of the imperial maritime customs service earned him a baronetcy and was lauded by the London *Times* as "one of the most striking monuments ever produced by the genius and labor of any individual Englishman" (10 January 1899). Hart began his career in China at the age of nineteen in the consular service, but never held the rank of consul.

[111] John Russell Young accompanied Grant on his world tour of 1877/1878 as the representative of the New York *Herald*, and met both Hart and Li Hung-chang. He described Hart as "perhaps one of the best-informed Europeans living as to the resources of the Chinese Empire, and the manners and customs of the Chinese people." Young was equally impressed with Li Hung-chang, "the most eminent man in China . . . the Bismarck of the East" (John Russell Young, *Around the World with General Grant*, 2 vols. [New York: American News Co., 1879], 2:286, 371). Young became United States minister to China in 1882.

[112] This query begins a series of entries about Kaolatype, in which Clemens first invested in February 1880. Albert Bigelow Paine described the Kaolatype process: "A sheet of perfectly smooth steel was coated with a preparation of kaolin (or china clay), and a picture was engraved through the coating down to the steel surface. This formed the matrix into which the molten metal was poured to make the stereotype plate, or die, for printing" (*MTB*, p. 727). Clemens' angry notes here, probably written at the end of March 1881 for Webster's information, mark the first of a complicated series of bitter accusations and denials and threatened

Experimenting would take but a month or two.

Could make book stamps. Didn't.
Ditto cylinders.[113] Ditto.
Could electrotype K. Ditto.
Could improve K mud. Ditto.

Been working chiefly at ice & pencil?

Nobody else could cast a plate. Not so. Casts plates with glass base—told W.[114] so. Is not true.

Wherever glass is used infringes K.

Been 4 months making 4 plates.

Said B.[115] considered them wonderful & was delighted. Not so
Hinted he would give 10 to $20,000 for a "piece." Not so.

Pay wages a month longer, but no expenses.

Get K base & clay & have Page[116] experiment. [#]

---

lawsuits which would see Charles Webster brought into the company and Sneider and Slote forced out.

[113] The cylinders were to be used to print or emboss wallpaper (see SLC to Webster, 7 September 1881).

[114] Charles L. Webster made his appearance in Clemens' business affairs in March of 1881. After a brief stay in Fredonia in mid-April, Webster returned to manage Clemens' affairs in an official capacity. A note from Clemens to Webster dated 29 April 1881 (*MTBus,* p. 152) confirmed Webster's "complete authority over Kaolatype & its concerns," thus installing him in actual power over Slote, whom he eventually supplanted. Webster was soon able to prove that all the models which Sneider had provided "were cast the old fashioned way viz; Sneider brought a plaster cast of the design which he moulded in sand the ordinary way & then cast them. No glass about it" (Webster to SLC, 13 May 1881).

[115] Beck, a manufacturer of wallpaper and a potential customer for Kaolatype cylinders. Clemens' first suspicions about Sneider's "miracle" process had evidently been stirred by an interview with Beck, who doubted that a process such as Sneider claimed to have invented was possible (see SLC to Slote, 31 March 1881).

[116] James W. Paige (Clemens consistently misspelled the name) was the inventor of the typesetting machine in which Clemens first invested in the fall of 1881. No evidence has been discovered to indicate that Paige became involved with Kaolatype.

Have W. ask B. if he will give remunerative orders for plates.

B. says his plates not as good as his own—never required chaser & finisher before. If they <are> require it now, is it because it will *pay* to finish them? Looks like it. Ask him.

Said B's got a great stock of patterns, <w>and is impatient for him to get shop ready—give him all of them to cast. Not proven.

Said they'd be worth $300 or $400 apiece. Not so.

B. keeping out of the way. Playing indifferent. Not true.

Two shops burned down.[117]

Going to use photography.

Mr. Koch[118] excited. Biggest thing in the world. H—possessed to get Germany—wants to pay big money for it. Not proven.

Said his plates required no doctoring—ready for press at once.

Instead of working at our affairs (being under our pay,) uses our time to invent & patent figured gas-fixtures. Ask about this.

Who owns K. in England? Was this the consideration for—what? Or did that happen before I got in? Think it did.

Borrowed of me & then failed in a month or two.[119] [#]

---

[117] Clemens later recalled in a letter to Howells that Sneider "had a very ingenious way of keeping me from seeing him *apply* his invention: the first appointment was spoiled by his burning down the man's shop in which it was to be done, the night before; the second was spoiled by his burning down his own shop the night before" (15 February 1887, *MTHL*, p. 586).

[118] Webster's letter of 5 September 1881 to Clemens mentions Koch & Son, Printers, as potential purchasers of Kaolatype book stamps.

[119] Clemens recalled this incident in his Autobiographical Dictation of 24 May 1906: "One day he [Slote] asked me to lend the firm five thousand dollars and said he was willing to pay 7 per cent. As security he offered the firm's note . . . so I gave him the five thousand dollars. They failed inside of three days." Slote, Woodman & Company failed in July 1878 (*Publishers' Weekly*, 27 July 1878, p. 633); after its creditors agreed to accept thirty cents on the dollar to settle their claims, the firm was reorganized as Daniel Slote & Company. In his letter of 1 May 1881 to Webster, Clemens explained that he considered the 1878 loan a debt of

Either can sell or work the thing alone. <I>Go it.

The *only* thing to work at, now, is the book stamp.

The only thing worth trying, later, is the cylinder.

Must have a voucher for every item of expense I have paid. Got none? Been taking his word for *that*, too?

Bring criminal action.[120] <[- - - - -]>

Told me (at first), the colors were caused by dash of cold water while hot. Forgot that, & told me he created them by alloys of metals. Also that he could *regulate* them & make each leaf a different color. <& confining & any color>

I think plates for walls will be handsome—but exclusive; anybody can cast them.[121]

Ask B if he printed from one of the plates, *really*.

End of March—he is going to make book-stamp, now, but must use coarse sand—all fine sand burnt up at Haggerty's.[122] (There's a barrel of it in his own back yard.)

Wreck of the Grosvenor.[123] [#]

---

honor and that Slote should have antedated the firm's note to the beginning of 1878 so that Clemens could get full payment of the debt.

120 On 18 May 1881 Webster reported: "The bubble has burst. Sneider has confessed . . . that the whole thing was a swindle from the beginning. . . . Sneider says he's going to commit suicide." After Slote's death, a year later, Clemens wrote to Mrs. Fairbanks: "If Dan had died thirteen months earlier, I should have been at the funeral, and squandered many tears; but as it is, I did not go and saved my tears. . . . Under the protection afforded by a trusting friendship, Dan stole from me, during at least seven years unsuspected by me. I never found him out, until twelve months ago. . . . I came very near sending him to the penitentiary" (21 February 1882, *MTMF*, p. 247).

121 In a letter to Dan Slote, Clemens mentioned a plan to sheathe his library walls and ceiling with "the elegant brass [Kaolatype] plates" (SLC to Slote, Saturday, n.d., [between January and March 1881]).

122 The shop in which Sneider cast his plates (Webster to SLC, 13 May 1881).

123 The novel by William Clark Russell about the British merchant marine was first published in 1878. In 1893 or 1894, Clemens began but never finished a

Wm. Lee Howard.[124]

Samson & foxes humorous.[125]

Iron Mountain[126]

Guide me, O thou Great Jehovah by J N. Pattison, (Wm A Pond & Co[127]

Mother Goose—W A Elliott.[128]

The Slave Songs of the South—advertised in the South.[129]

15
13
30
390 [#]

---

criticism of Russell's novel which was to be one of a series of "Studies in Literary Criticism" along with "Fenimore Cooper's Literary Offenses" and "Cooper's Prose Style" (see *LE*, p. 290).

[124] William Lee Howard (1860–1918), son of prominent Hartford Republican Mark Howard, had traveled extensively before the age of twenty, spending two years as a practical seaman on a whaling voyage. In 1880, as correspondent for the *Herald*, he accompanied an attempted rescue of the ill-fated *Jeannette* expedition to the North Pole. The same year Howard was elected to the American Geographical Society. Howard later was a writer and physician, doing pioneer research in the use of hypnotic suggestion for the treatment of nervous diseases and championing the cause of sex education.

[125] Mark Twain made comic use of this biblical episode (Judges 15:4–5) in the 15 November 1863 *Territorial Enterprise* and in a portion of "The Chronicle of Young Satan" written in 1897/1898 (*Mark Twain of the "Enterprise,"* ed. Henry Nash Smith [Berkeley and Los Angeles: University of California Press, 1957], pp. 90–91; *Mark Twain's Mysterious Stranger Manuscripts*, ed. William M. Gibson [Berkeley and Los Angeles: University of California Press, 1969], pp. 55–56).

[126] Dean Sage, who often advised Clemens on business investments, wrote on 10 May 1881: "I hear that Iron Mountain *incomes* are good as an investment & will yield a '*sure profit.*' "

[127] John Nelson Pattison published a new arrangement of this traditional hymn in 1863.

[128] Perhaps James W. Elliott's collection of Mother Goose nursery rhymes set to music, published under various titles between 1870 and 1874.

[129] Clemens may be referring to William Francis Allen, Charles Pickard Ware, and Lucy McKim Garrison's *Slave Songs of the United States* (1867).

Tear-drop<s> containing <3,000> <2 to 2500> 1,500 barrels.—⅛ inch in diam.

Sheldon & Co }
N. Y. Herald } collect[130]

Green Hand 68 (No.)
Sailor's Sweetheart 142[131]

W H Smith, Treas.
Indepen^{t} Watch Co.[132]

Dunnigan
115 Wall st. New Haven
(new carriage.)[133] [#]

---

130 This reminder to collect payments due Clemens was included in a letter to Charles Webster on 30 May 1881 (*MTBus*, pp. 158–159). Sheldon & Company were the publishers of the *Galaxy*, a magazine for which Clemens wrote a monthly "Memoranda" column in 1870 and 1871. The magazine ceased publication in 1878 because of financial difficulties. The same company published *Mark Twain's Burlesque Autobiography and First Romance* in 1871. As late as September 1882 Clemens was still attempting to collect the disputed royalties for that book (*MTBus*, p. 201). The particulars of Clemens' difficulties with the New York *Herald* are nowhere discussed—Webster mentioned in a letter to his wife Annie Moffett Webster merely that he had "to see the N. Y. Herald about an old bill" of his uncle's (1 August 1881).

131 Clemens' letter of 23 May 1881 to Osgood orders two novels, "No's 68 and 142 of Harper's Franklin Square Library (Green Hand and Sailor's Sweetheart)" (*MTLP*, p. 136). A *Sailor's Sweetheart* (1880) was written by William Clark Russell, author of *The Wreck of the Grosvenor*; *Green Hand* (1879) is by George Cupples.

132 In March 1881, Clemens had been persuaded by Charles Webster to buy $5,000 worth of stock in the Independent Watch Company owned by the Howard Brothers of Fredonia, New York. The Howards were "quite anxious that Mark Twain should become a stockholder. . . . So they pay Charley's expenses to go & see him & lay before him a statement of the affairs & prospects of the company . . . & see if he could get him to take ever so small an interest;—and ask his consent to one of their 'movements' being named for him, the Mark Twain movement" (Pamela Moffett to Samuel Moffett, 20 March 1881). The Howards' company proved to be fraudulent and by September 1882 Clemens was wrathfully threatening an action against the "watch thieves." Charles Webster, more and more embroiled in Clemens' affairs, finally cleared up the matter of the watch stock, bringing it off "miraculously" according to Clemens (*MTBus*, pp. 198–199).

133 During this period, Clemens was preoccupied with plans for buying a new

12
14
16

Webster
178 Clifford st
Providence[134]

Get all the Gerhardt letters to read to Sue.[135]
<Get <S>baby clothes from Katy.[136]
July Scribner[137]
Fill pens.[138]

---

carriage which he eventually had built to his own specifications by Hooker & Company of New Haven.

[134] Charles Webster was in Providence in March and April 1881 on Kaolatype business. The address is written lengthwise on the notebook page in pencil and was probably recorded at an earlier date than the surrounding entries.

[135] The Clemenses initially agreed to underwrite the expense of a five-year course of study in Paris for the young sculptor Karl Gerhardt. The Gerhardts sailed for Europe on 5 March 1881 and corresponded frequently with the Clemens family; Clemens particularly enjoyed the amusingly misspelt letters of Mrs. Gerhardt.

The Clemens family left for Montowese House, Branford, Connecticut, on 4 June and remained there until 4 August, when they journeyed to Quarry Farm, with a stop in Hartford to do the errands listed here.

[136] In October 1880 Katy Leary of Elmira was hired as Mrs. Clemens' personal maid. She remained with the family until 1910.

[137] The July 1881 issue of *Scribner's Monthly* printed the second installment of Howells' A *Fearful Responsibility* and the last installment of George Washington Cable's *Madame Delphine*. Clemens met Cable for the first time in mid-June 1881, interrupting his vacation at Montowese House in order to lunch with Cable at the home of Charles Dudley Warner in Hartford.

[138] One of Clemens' current fascinations was the "stylographic" pen which he enthusiastically endorsed in a letter to Elinor Howells on 17 August 1880: "And speaking of Howells, he ought to use the stylographic pen, the best fountain-pen yet invented" (*MTHL*, p. 324). Clemens managed to press the experimental pen on Howells, Twichell, and Dr. John Brown, but none of the three seems to have adopted it for very long (*MTB*, pp. 688–689). Clemens was still enthusiastic in January 1881 when he urged an admirer to "get one of these American pens—the 'Stylographic' or 'Mackinnan.' The shaft of it holds ink enough to last for three weeks. We've thrown all our ink stands away" (SLC to Annie Lucas, 31 January 1881, TS in MTP). Unlike the previous notebooks, which are written almost

Croquet
Money
The Colonel's Opera Cloak>[139]
Claude Lorraine glass.[140]
Sinopisms
Borax
Bathing suit
Sugar
<Telegraph Miss Bartlett>[141]

Mrs Warner
c/ Prof Willard Fiske[142]
Hotel du Rhin
4 Place Vendome
Paris

1—10	11	21
2 17	12	22
3 20	13	23
4 30	14	24
5 40	15	25
6 50	16	26
7	17	27
8	18	28
9	19	29
10	20	30 [#]

entirely in pencil, Notebooks 19 and 20 are largely written in medium-blue ink and have the uniform and clean appearance attributable to the stylographic pen.

139 A novel by Mrs. Christine Chaplin Brush published in 1879.

140 A slightly convex mirror of black or colored glass for viewing the reflected landscape. Clemens had purchased a Lorraine mirror in Venice in 1878 (see Notebook 17, p. 221).

141 Mary L. Bartlett of Hartford was Susy's piano teacher.

142 Mrs. Charles Dudley Warner was in Paris at this time at the bedside of the dying Mrs. Daniel Willard Fiske. The tale of Cornell professor Fiske's long-term romance with heiress Jennie McGraw, their marriage, and the battle between Professor Fiske and Cornell University over the terms of Mrs. Fiske's will is told by Clemens in his autobiography (*MTA*, 2:341–348).

Sus.	Bay.
18	14
<24>	20
22	27
29	
32	
35	
45 strike	
46	
47	
57 strike[143]	

Major John B. Downing, Middleport, O.[144]

Etiquette.[145]

Wedding Presents.
Birthday do.
Presents to name-child.

---

[143] During his summer vacation at Montowese House in July 1881, Clemens wrote a description of a game, "Tenpins in Verse" (Howard S. Mott, Inc. catalog no. 16, n.d., item 52). The numbers listed here appear to be scores for the game.

[144] On the envelope of a letter from Downing of 15 August 1881, Clemens identifies him as "a former fellow-pilot." Downing had written asking Clemens for the story of the origin of his pen name, mentioning that he had heard a version of the story from another piloting acquaintance, Bart Bowen. "If I am correct," wrote Downing, "you were in the pilot house with Bart, and had written an answer to some wonderful story that old Capt Sellers had published on the former channel of the river at some given point, and you had just remarked, 'Bart?' how shall I sign it, when the deck hand, who was 'heaving the lead,' cried out '*Mark Twain*,' which then you accepted, Am I right?" The account of the origin of Clemens' pseudonym is told in Paine's biography and differs considerably from Downing's version (*MTB*, pp. 149–150, 221–222).

[145] Clemens had first become interested in writing a burlesque etiquette manual in 1879 and evidently revived the project in March 1881 because of Howells' praise of it (*MTHL*, pp. 359–360). Clemens wrote nearly a hundred pages of the burlesque before abandoning it. On 3 September 1881 he wrote to Howells that his recent visit to Belmont had provided him with the impetus to write a "chapter on international etiquette" (*MTHL*, p. 370). Excerpts from the manuscript were published by Paine (*MTB*, pp. 705–706) and Bernard DeVoto (*LE*, pp. 193–208).

Xmas Presents.

New Year ditto.

"Tiffin" bill of fare.

German & French.

Col. Valentine Baker[146] & the Army & Navy Club.

The hostler's criticism on "Matrimony."

Sirius—You say you have dignities—that Smooks have earls & kings! & a religion![147]

Get rooms on 4th floor at Gilsey.[148]

Get Tiffany or Mrs. Wheeler to go to Hartford with me.[149] [#]

146 English cavalry officer, called Baker Pacha because of his career in the military service of Egypt and Turkey. In 1875 Baker was charged in London with "indecent assault" upon a young woman in a railway car (New York *Times*, 9 August 1875) and convicted. Clemens may have intended to use the incident in his burlesque etiquette book; he made satirical reference to Colonel Baker's case, as an instance of the deficiency of European manners, in chapter 47 of *A Tramp Abroad*.

147 Clemens' preoccupation with parallel communities of radically different magnitude did not receive its fullest expression until 1905 when he explored the microscopic world of the "swinks" in "Three Thousand Years Among the Microbes" (*Mark Twain's Which Was the Dream? and Other Symbolic Writings of the Later Years*, ed. John S. Tuckey [Berkeley and Los Angeles: University of California Press, 1967], pp. 433–553).

148 As was their custom at the end of the summer stay at Quarry Farm, the Clemens family stopped in New York before returning to Hartford. They arrived at the Gilsey House on 20 September 1881, planning to "remain a day or two for Mrs. Clemens to do some shopping before proceeding to Hartford" (SLC to Webster, 17 September 1881, TS in MTP). Clemens' New York stay was spent attending to Kaolatype business and arranging for the redecoration of the Hartford house, which had been in the process of renovation since March. Clemens described the turmoil which the family found on their return to Hartford in a letter to Mr. and Mrs. Gerhardt: "We are in our carpetless & dismantled home, living like a gang of tramps on the second floor, the rest of the house in the hands of mechanics & decorators. We have pulled down the kitchen & rebuilt it, adding twenty feet to it, & have lowered the ground in front of the greenhouse, & also carried the driveway a hundred feet further to the east" (9 October 1881, PH in MTP).

149 In August, decorator Herbert M. Lawrence had recommended the firm of Louis C. Tiffany & Company for the work in the Hartford house (Lawrence to

If succeed in getting a decorator, have George[150] put the dining room carpet in the nursery.

Get White or Lathrop if can't get Tiffany.[151]

Or get Tiffany to recommend somebody.

Maitland Armstrong.[152]
25th st & 4th ave. Tiffany's.

Nursery—<|||> 3 (2 facets & door)
Mother's—2 loose facets, *door* & *bath* plug fast, & no chain.—<5.> & a facet misplaced—6
N.E. room—*door*.
Pink—*Door*. Closet often out of order, G. says.
Mahog—Hole in bath, bad. Left facet drips.—<2> Sitz hole shabby. Two things gone. <2> Drawers out of shape. 2 doors lacking. 9.
Laundry—2 fascets & 2 overhead.—4. Pipe broken down over door.
Kitchen—Pipe to boiler leaks.

Irish setter (red)

Ask Charley if Ahern was to gas the kitchen & move library chandelier.[153] [#]

SLC, 26 August 1881). Clemens had sent a note to Tiffany before leaving Elmira in September requesting a meeting in New York. On 24 October 1881 the Tiffany company contracted with Clemens "For the sum of Five Thousand dollars" to do the extensive decorating work which included covering the library walls and ceiling with metal leaf. Mrs. Candace Wheeler was one of Tiffany's Associated Artists and later became a close friend of the Clemens family.

150 George Griffin.

151 Francis A. Lathrop was a New York artist who created stained glass windows and other decorative work. Neither Stanford White nor Lathrop was engaged in the redecoration of the Hartford house.

152 David Maitland Armstrong was the head of a company of decorators and stained glass artists.

153 During the summer of 1881, Charles L. Webster, in addition to managing Kaolatype, supervised the renovation of the Hartford house while the Clemens family was on vacation. James Ahern, "Practical Plumber and Gas Fitter" of Hartford, was engaged in the renovation work (contract dated 26 August 1881 between Clemens and Ahern in MTP; *MTBus*, pp. 162–165).

Suggest sending brass <s>Prince stamps to London.[154]

Fredericks, 770.

W^m^ H Jackson & Co (tiles).[155]

Louis Tiffany & Armory of 7th Regiment.[156]

Chatto's Notes[157]

Depos. with Bissell Oct. 4, '81.

Due Jan	15, '82—£200		
" Mch	15	300	
" Apl	15	374.16.9.	

Oct. 5.—Sent Patrick for Ahern 10 days ago.—He didn't come. Sent for him yesterday by Dr Hooker,[158] to mend up a hot water leak & other things. He didn't come.

---

[154] In a letter of 7 October 1881 to Chatto & Windus, Clemens mentions this suggestion: "I told my nephew, C. L. Webster, to write & ask you if you wanted duplicates of the brass stamps which are to be used in printing the covers of the 'P. & P.' But you need not answer him, for I perceive the time is too short, now. The suggestion was only born of personal vanity, since these stamps were made by a process of my own invention, whose merits are cheapness & celerity of production" (British Museum).

[155] Charles Webster had written to Clemens on 2 September 1881: "Please tell Aunt Livy that the upper part of house is finished if the hearths are not changed" and Clemens replied on 4 September that "those hearths must be changed. I have written to N. Y. for specimens of tiles to be sent to us here" (TS in MTP). Evidently Clemens wrote to the New York firm of Wm. H. Jackson & Company which dealt in "everything pertaining to Grates or Open Fire Places," including a full range of decorative tiles.

[156] Clemens admired Tiffany's elaborate decorative work in the Veterans' Room of the Seventh Regiment Armory in New York. Some of the tiles used for Clemens' fireplaces were duplicates of those in the armory (Robert Koch, *Louis C. Tiffany, Rebel in Glass* [New York: Crown Publishers, 1964], p. 19).

[157] In his letter of 7 October 1881 to Chatto & Windus, Clemens wrote: "Your notes for £874.16.9. have arrived from friend Conway, for which please accept my thanks. The sale has been flatteringly large, & the result correspondingly gratifying" (British Museum). The payments were royalties for *A Tramp Abroad.*

[158] Clemens' neighbor Dr. Edward Beecher Hooker, son of John and Isabella Beecher Hooker, occasionally acted as a consultant for the plumbing renovations being completed in the Hartford house (see *MTBus*, pp. 163–164). Charles Webster would write Clemens on 9 September 1881: "Dr. Hooker handed me his bill

Sent for Robt. Garvie this morning, the necessity being pressing. He came, & did the work.[159]

13th.

7.30 p.m., *black* shows. (This is wrong.)[160]

Turned it 12 hours, at 11 p.m., & made black *continue* to show—(this is right & puts the alarm on.)

14th

It was right in the morning & wrong in the afternoon

Behave & you will be happy.

Spoke of Louise Messina (in bed in morning Nov. 12) first time in 3 years. Two days later got a letter from Andrew Langdon in Chicago dated 12th, asking indirectly for a contribution <for> of money for <Louise Messina> her.[161]

"Castle Blair" & "Hector" (Roberts Bros.) By Flora L. Shaw.)[162]

St Simon in French.[163] [#]

---

and as I know nothing about it I send it to you. . . . As expert's go it is a reasonable bill if he is an expert."

[159] William and Robert Garvie, Hartford plumbers, contracted to do some of the extensive plumbing work in the Hartford house.

[160] Clemens' entry refers to the performance of the Hartford house's burglar alarm in November 1881. The disorderly burglar alarm was a continuing concern of the Clemens household (*MTA*, 2:75, 78–81).

[161] Livy's cousin was a prominent Buffalo businessman (complete biographical information is in *What Is Man? and Other Philosophical Writings*, pp. 538–539). His letter to Clemens does not survive and the identity of Louise Messina has not been established. Clemens' entry reflects his continuing interest in evidences of "mind telegraphing."

[162] Both *Castle Blair* (Boston: Roberts Bros., 1878) and *Hector* (Boston: Roberts Bros., 1881) are children's stories.

[163] Clemens acquired a copy of Bayle St. John's translation of Saint-Simon's *Memoirs* (London: Bickers & Son, [188?]), which he signed and dated "Hartford, Nov. 1881." The three-volume set, now in the Mark Twain Papers, includes many marginal comments by Clemens who reread the work a number of times. There is no record of Clemens having read the *Memoirs* in French.

A ring at Joe's door—as Joe starts down stairs, the thought flashes through his head, "Dear me, I wonder what <I> ever did become of that old volume of pamphlet sermons I used to have, long ago." Enter <an> a middle aged man, a former college mate, who tells of his mother's recent death, & breaks down & cries; & says "Up to the very day of her death she got comfort & pleasure out of that old volume of pamphlet sermons which you lent her some years ago!"

Lepesium.

Stevia.[164]

Nov. 24—wrong at 11 AM—black showed, & rang alarm. I have set it right for afternoon—brass shows.

Parson Greeley, Oswego—90 yrs old & deaf—revisits his church.

Boston & Lowell Station[165]

Old fool talking statesmanship, Centennial, manufactures & "blow" in large voice.

Younger fool talking French to his 10-yr daughter & glancing around for admiration.—closing most sentences with "comme ça" or "nestcepas." Disobedient girl—had to be told more than once to do a thing, & then didn't.

Met gentleman who had been in the Batavia—it reminded me of how Gen Green & I were each refusing the only seat in the fiddle one night when Wood came in & jocularly remarked that while we did the polite he would reap the advantage of a careful coarser training—

[164] On 16 March 1881 Clemens had written to Pamela Moffett of his purchase of "Mr. Chamberlain's greenhouse & 100 feet of land adjoining our east line" (*MTBus*, p. 150). Lopezia and stevia are semi-tropical plants, no doubt intended for the greenhouse.

[165] Clemens left for Montreal on 26 November 1881, stopping first at Boston on the night of the twenty-fifth. Clemens' residence in Canada for a short time was necessary in order to secure British copyright for *The Prince and the Pauper*, to be published on 1 December in London. The following entries were made on this journey. He returned to the United States on 9 December.

took the seat & got shot in the back by a sea that nearly broke him in two.[166]

Read in Parkman that Champlain suggested the Isthmus canal some 350 yrs ago.[167]

Boot black conversation—had a cold.

At hotel publisher came & told me new developments & intricacies in Canadian copyright, & I let on that I understood—but I didn't. <[Tre]>
<Said he would>
I gave him such a commanding impression (idea) of my incapacity that he said he would come & start me off himself. He also gave me a marked map in the hope that it would help me find my way. Advised me to buy a guide book on train. Asked him "Who will explain it to me." He said reflectively, "I do not see why you keep only one nurse." (Before this, I have remarked that we keep a nurse.)

"Montreal." <">Ticket agent: "Which way you want to go?" Went & brought O[168] & said "*He* knows."

In smoking car man talking oil—use that old incident.[169] [#]

---

[166] C. F. Wood of England and Colton Greene of Tennessee were among the passengers on the S.S. *Batavia* on Clemens' return voyage to America from his first trip to England in 1872. The ship was caught in a storm, her "starboard bulwarks were stove in and the water entered the main saloon," Mark Twain told the Royal Humane Society in urging a medal for the ship's captain (Boston *Daily Advertiser*, 26 November 1872, clipping in MTP).

[167] Clemens wrote to Livy from Montreal on 28 November: "I brought away 3 volumes of Parkman, but by day after to-morrow I shall have finished them" and requested that she mail to him immediately the next two volumes of Parkman's series on New France. The first five volumes of the series were *Pioneers of France in the New World, The Jesuits in North America in the Seventeenth Century, La Salle and the Discovery of the Great West, The Old Régime in Canada,* and *Count Frontenac and New France under Louis XIV*. The passage in Parkman which Clemens refers to in his notebook entry is on page 217 of *Pioneers of France* (Boston: Little, Brown, and Co., 1880).

[168] Osgood, however, did not leave Boston with Clemens. He joined Clemens a few days later at the Windsor Hotel in Montreal.

[169] The detail and the humorous exaggeration of many of these Canadian travel

A subdued aged man whose face I could not see, talked of his faithful efforts to become great, but had failed in all, & now awaited the tomb. He had lived on bread & water, like Franklin but did not become a philosopher of note; ate pebbles like Demosthenes, yet after 2 years of it had worn out his teeth yet couldn't orate worth a d—n. &cc

Manchester, N. H.—Canal st & a number leading out of it marked "Private Way." Was going stop there day or so, but had a delicacy about intruding; but if I had detected a public way I would have got ashore.

The brick blocks were all alike—like St Louis of 25 yrs ago (or Phila)—& they were building a dozen fanciful & very massy new blocks—an entirely new pattern for Manchester; but all *alike*.

Leaving M, traveled along a stream 50 yds wide. Passenger tells me it is the St Lawrence. <I think> Think this is a lie.

Good-natured giant with a kink in his hair & a peculiar ruddiness in his yellow negro face got in with a profane elderly man (smoking car), somewhere out of Concord, & every now & then would break into my "L'Ordre de Bon-Temps" [170] with some wild enthusiasms about a bull-calf which he had sold to the latter. "Dam good bull. All you got to do is to tie a rope on each side of his head & put him in any kind of a wagon, with a little hay, (& some other details which I could not catch) & just cramp him down, & he ain't goin' to jump." By & by (5 minutes later,). "Why he *can't* jump—he ain't got no *chance*." 5 m. later) "Dam good bull." (5 later). "You tie him jess's I told you; he ain't goin' to jump—he ain't got no chance, you see."

At *last* I comprehended he was to be tied *in* the wagon—not hitched in front of it. [#]

---

notes suggest that Clemens intended to use them for a travel sketch. However, no such manuscript survives and only Clemens' Windsor Hotel dinner speech incorporates some of the ideas noted here.

170 Clemens was reading Parkman's account of this convivial group of the fifteen "principal persons" in Champlain's Port Royal colony (Parkman, *Pioneers of France*, p. 243).

Wished the sham Frenchman had been with the real ones whom Menendez beguiled with false oaths & massacred.[171]

Big peanut eating lout who vacated car & left door open.

As I went out, caught that half-soliloquizing remark, "Dam good bull.—you tie him, &c."

Brilliant day, but snow everywhere—when sky overcast, a dreary prospect, which helped me to realize the times of Champlain & others in Canada.

A female (woman dignify her too much) raised a window to make herself comfortable & froze us all to death for an hour. J'était charmé quand un jeun homme raised un autre et refusé l'enfermè après touts persuasions de cette femelle.

Before reaching Essex, Met a military friend who turned the big compartment into a smoking room by force—a thing which I had been trying to do by persuasion all day.

<25>20 m from St Albans x^d^ the line & I prepared to tell a lot of feeble & unsatisfactory lies to account for the preponderance of cigars & Scotch whisky over clothes & theology in my baggage (2 satchels), but the official merely glanced at the giddy array & offered no objections.

<About>

Railroad man told me good many things—he lived at St John's & got off there. He has lived 25 yrs in Canada & thinks if it were annexed its wasted water powers would soon be occupied by factories.

After St John's a nice train boy sold me some photo views, & tried to sell me a pirated Tom Sawyer, but I told him that this very day a mighty fine man recognized me by my portrait & wouldn't let me pay for my supper—said the author of Tom Sawyer couldn't pay for

171 Pedro Menéndez de Avilés led a Spanish expedition to Florida in 1565. Parkman tells of his treachery to a group of shipwrecked Frenchmen who had surrendered to him in the belief that they would be treated mercifully (Parkman, *Pioneers of France*, pp. 121–127). For the sham Frenchman see page 403.

anything at *his* board—& now here are you trying to deplete my store with a pirated edition. He asked my pardon.

Reached Windsor about 9.15. pm

Describe Vennor,[172] <& have my friend> say What will you take for a snowstorm?—& what discount will you allow if I take a gross?—& what if I take a full line of your goods? Vennor replies. It turns out that it is not Vennor—<a joker or> a fraud has fooled me & got my money for a lot of weather which he can't deliver. My idea is getting up this weather is so I can see Canada in its wintriest aspect <s> a month before the right time.

Monday Nov. 28—Mild yesterday & sifted snow<ed> all day. That was according to Vennor's prediction made Sept. 1. This morning it is mighty cold, with yesterday's one inch of snow crunching & grinding under the cart wheels in a shrill metallic way. Vennor says, "a very sudden & severe fall of temperature will occur generally through Canada in the last week of Nov., with but little snow, if any, on the ground."

There has been mild weather for <a week> some time, before this—Vennor spotted it right.

Abrahams, Fortescue, Dalhousie

"Sir, I think I am lost, but I am not acquainted with the city, & so I cannot really tell. If you will be so kind as to give me an idea of the direction of the W/Windsor Hotel, God will reward you.—Of course I may *not* be lost, after all; I cannot by any means swear that I *am*, for there is nothing here to swear by—I mean nothing I can recognize, nothing I ever saw before; but if I could see something which I have

---

[172] Henry George Vennor, the Canadian naturalist, published a popular almanac between the years 1877 and 1884 which contained astonishingly accurate weather predictions. Clemens evidently visited Vennor at his Montreal residence "The Towers" (see p. 411 of this notebook). In the Windsor Hotel dinner speech, Clemens mentioned Vennor: "Canada has a reputation for magnificent Winter weather, and has a prophet who is bound . . . to furnish it" (New York *Times*, 10 December 1881).

seen before, I could tell in a minute, by its position, whether I am lost or not: that is, I could tell by comparing its position with mine, whether *it* was lost, or whether it was *me*; & I could then know *which* of us was lost, & act accordingly: that is to say, if it turned out to be <*it*> *me* that was lost, I shouldn't do anything, at least at the moment, preferring to wait & sue the city; but if it turned out to be *it*, I should of course call assistance; for I hold that a humane man—

Gilbert White, bees & idiots.[173]

Do I go by the Bastille yonder?
It isn't the B.
Windsor Castle, then?
It isn't WC—it is St. Peter's Cath.[174]

Tupper[175] called in England Solomon-&-Water. <Brandy & soda.>

28th—It is a great & beautiful city from Royal Mount.—the great St Law stretching in both directions, & the wide plains on other side with groves & meadows & with mountains beyond.

Monday *night* 4° below zero here, & 15° below in Quebec. Sharp & sudden change, you see.

(Gilbert White's bees & idiots.)

The children of Israel here call it the Pork Pie-Passover.

That is the Immac—oh, yonder's Jones!
<Mince—> Irish stew—or Congregational.
<Old> Hard-shell Baptist—<another> kind of mince; they

---

[173] In *The Natural History and Antiquities of Selborne*, Gilbert White tells of an idiot boy who regarded bees as "his food, his amusement, his sole object" (letter 27 to the Honourable Daines Barrington). Clemens owned a copy of an 1875 edition of White's book (*A1911*, item 483).

[174] Under construction on Montreal's Dominion Square, the cathedral was "designed to reproduce, on a smaller scale, all those features of St. Peter's at Rome which are suited to the climate" (S. E. Dawson, *Handbook for the Dominion of Canada* [Montreal: Dawson Brothers, 1884], pp. 179–180).

[175] Martin Farquhar Tupper was the English author of the popular but fatuous *Proverbial Philosophy* (1838).

don't cook it, they petrify it.—The ungodly call <them> 'em ironclads. The soldiers wear <'em>'m under their clothes in war-time; the artillery use 'm for targets in time of peace. They used to pave with <'em>'m, but they hurt the horses' feet & gov'ment <put> shet down on it. The lightning struck one of 'm once. (Pause.)

Well?—do any harm?

To the pie?—no; to the lightning?—yes. She was as straight as the equator, when she struck; & the next second <tha>there she laid, in a <po>pile, all squirmed up like a basket of fishing-worms.

Reformed Catholic—cream puffs with the stuffing left out.

Presbyterian Hereafter—a pudding; main thing about it is the juice—the sauce. Some thinks it's made out of brimstone & blue vitriol; some says dog-bites & aqua fortis.

French market & market people—good-faced man with thin face & bright brown eyes—woman hidden in vast coon skin robe. Two or three pretty girls. Native tobacco; butter; stockings; chewing gum; shoes; slippers; cat taking care of dead poultry;

<church or> chapel of Our Lady of Lourdes—statue of Virgin, from Murillo, under a half dome, standing on rolling clouds, with light pouring luminously upon one side—very striking & effect. Chapel gay with color, bright & new.

The old Bon Secours church—tin ship<?>hanging up? Didn't see it—take on trust.

Notre Dame—huge and gaudy with gilding & vivid & variegated color<.>—<fancy candy & barber-poles.>

Shops for the sale of disciples, saints &c—highly colored images, these, in singles, couples, groups & gangs, ready for altars & niches—& a multitude of sacred wax dolls in evergreen beds, ready for Xmas.

What are the obvious jokes?—for there are such belonging to every town. Does the stranger shout & tell a man he is losing his sleigh-robe out behind?

My man named <e>Edmund Burke. My own names, for puns.

Think of a pile-driver worked by *men*, in *this* end of the century! [#]

Thought I would use the French *construction,* & maybe that would assist the housemaid: What would Monsieur

Monsieur Jacques Cartier, is he with himself?

Je Ne comprend pas.

Is it that he is not yet returned of his house of merchandize?

Ne comprend pas.

He will desolate himself when he learns that his friend Americain was arrived & he not with himself to shake him at the hand.

Comprehend *pas!*

Well, don't get excited<,>. <Pauline.> You see that I remain calm." So I turned to go; but just to show that I *could* <talk the language if I wanted to,> <rip> blast out a French remark or so if I wanted to, I <discharged> delivered the following over my left shoulder with that supple facility which practice only can give:

J'ai le <beau> belle bouton d'or de mon oncle, mais je n'ai pas celui du charpentier; et si vous avez le bas de fil <d> noir de votre sœur, c'est bon: mais si vous ne l'avez pas, le bon Dieu vous garde! A dieu ne plaise que nous <meet> revoir non plus! <Adieu,> <Au revoir, belle domestique."> So-long."

A sharp voice rang out from the gloom of the back hall:

"Qui est donc là!

C'est un fou!—& the door slammed behind me: par derrière, I suppose I ought to say.[176]

This gray limestone makes a stately & oppressively massive & substantial house, but not a pretty one. It refuses to be either graceful or gracious. It is just the thing for churches, though: hence their multiplicity, I suppose. There is an average of one clergymen per sinner here, I judge

---

[176] Clemens used this linguistic burlesque in his speech at the dinner given for him at the Windsor Hotel on 8 December 1881. *The Dominion Annual Register and Review . . . for 1880–1881*, ed. Henry J. Morgan (Montreal: John Lovell & Son, 1882), lists the dinner in its "Journal of Remarkable Occurrences" and notes: "Mr. Clemens, in responding to the toast of the evening, delivers a very humourous and characteristic speech" (p. 275). The full text of the speech was published in the New York *Times*, 10 December 1881.

Have you been out any?

No. Have looked around the Windsor any? No. Well theres 74 churches within a radies of 330 yards, timber measure.[177]

These are facts? You would not deceive me?

He takes me to see Vennor—whose device is 3 owls.

Trace Father <Breboeuf>Brebeuf all through this trip & when I am in a rage & can't endure the mouse, be reading of Brébeuf's marvelous endurances,[178] & be shamed. And finally, after chasing the bright-eyed rascal several days & throwing things & trying to jump on him when in my overshoe, he darts away with those same bright eyes—then straightway I read Brèbeuf's magnificent martyrdom, & turn in subdued & <a>wondering. By & by the thought occurs to me, <Compared with great Brebeuf I am as a mouse> Brebeuf with his good great heart would spare even that poor humble mousie —& for his sake so will I—<[hun]>I will throw the trap in the fire— jump out of bed, reach under, fetch out the trap, & find him throttled there, & not two minutes dead. [#]

---

[177] Clemens remarked in his Windsor Hotel dinner speech: "This is the first time I was ever in a city where you couldn't throw a brick without breaking a church window" (New York *Times,* 10 December 1881). In a letter to Livy from Montreal, Clemens' remarks are less humorous: "I have . . . inspected a lot of Catholic churches, French markets, shop windows, &c. But for the shame of it, the indignity to my pride, I would like to be a priest's slave, & glide in with my basket or my bundle, & duck my head & crook my knee at a painted image, & glide out again with my immortal part refreshed & strengthened for my day's burdens. But—I am not a priest's slave, & so it hurts me, hurts me all through, to recognize, by these exhibitions, what poor animals we are, what children, how easily fooled, beguiled, & by what cheap & trivial devices, by what thin & paltry lies" (29 November 1881, *LLMT*, p. 205).

[178] Clemens had been reading Parkman's account of Father Brébeuf's extraordinary sufferings and death: "After a succession of other revolting tortures, they scalped him; when, seeing him nearly dead, they laid open his breast, and came in a crowd to drink the blood of so valiant an enemy, thinking to imbibe with it some portion of his courage. A chief then tore out his heart, and devoured it" (*The Jesuits in North America* [Boston: Little, Brown, and Co., 1880], p. 389). Clemens' attitude toward such missionaries was divided. He wrote to Livy from Canada: "In endurance & performance they were gods; in credulity, & in obedience to their ecclesiastical chiefs, they were swine" (29 November 1881, *LLMT*, p. 206).

City of Burglars.

If there is a man in Hartford who is not a burglar, I am not aware of it, & I am not acquainted with him.

<(Include *yourself*, do you?)>

The most gaudy joke of the century was the Irishman's <interlarding> taking Rev ——s lecture down in shorthand, & then wherever Cromwell &c speak, make him utter a wild eulogium upon one of the patent medicines which this Irishman had for sale. Lecture was not copyrighted; however the Court enjoined it & fined Irishman $500.

Two tramps with but a single shirt,
Two beats that bilk as one.[179]

Man buried in stone & cement—much rioting.

Dec. 2—election day in the Dominion. Gazette has in block type: "What has Stephens ever done save blow his own trumpet & hoard his ducats?"

"The elector who votes for McShane proclaims his preference <over> for hypocritical corruption <(> over intelligent manliness." (What *is* hypocritical corruption?—& how does intelligent manliness differ from other kinds of manliness?—that writer's kind, for instance?)

(McShane is not fictitious—it is the real name.

"A precious trio<;>: McShane the Boss Tweed; Stephens the barking Watch Dog; & Perrault, the Revolutionist."

In block type in Gazette.[180] [#]

---

[179] Clemens was recalling the closing lines of the play *Ingomar, the Barbarian* which he had reviewed for the *Territorial Enterprise* in 1863. The review was reprinted as "'Ingomar' Over the Mountains," in the *Golden Era* of 29 November 1863. The original lines from the play were: "Two souls with but a single thought,/ Two hearts that beat as one" (Edgar M. Branch, *The Literary Apprenticeship of Mark Twain* [Urbana: University of Illinois Press, 1950], p. 288, n. 96).

[180] Clemens joked about the election in his Windsor Hotel dinner speech. "I have meddled nowhere but in the election. But I am used to voting, for I live in a town where, if you may judge by the local prints, there are only two conspicuous

Sexton—Care-taker.

Sent to Lachine rapids for some of the water.
Then went & saw where it flowed past the city.

Dec. 3. McShane & Stephens were both elected.

Russell Hotel Museum of Antiquities. Kept first by Jacques Cartier, <af> in later centuries by Samuel de Chamberlain &c. This was the first house built by the Indians on the bluff. It was then called the Stadaconé & was kep by <Doncona>Donnacona the King.[181]

Snowing lightly—girls slipping down everywhere, sidewalks so icy. —on their way to school.

Must have colored swinging inside windows.

This is the foulest hotel in some respects in Am.

On a great blackboard at head of stairs a big yellow disk: meaning, I suppose, St George harpooning the dragon for breakfast.

Hours of meals — Hours of meals.

So *many* pretty girls—never so many in one town before— beauty of girls, & of little children of both sexes so common as to be almost monotonous—but then one has the occasional relief of the other

---

industries—committing burglaries and holding elections—and I like to keep my hand in, so I voted a great deal here" (New York *Times*, 10 December 1881). George Washington Stephens, James McShane and Joseph X. Perrault were Liberal party members running for the Dominion legislature in the 1881 election. The Montreal *Gazette* was a Conservative newspaper.

[181] Clemens and Osgood made a three-day excursion to Quebec and stayed at the old Russell Hotel. Clemens wrote to Livy on the night of his arrival in Quebec: "Thus far, I don't like Quebec. The hotel is infernal. You couldn't endure these beds. Everything in the hotel is of the date of Champlain, or even of Cartier, & thoroughly worn out. I don't think any town has much interest to me unless the hotels are good" (2 December 1881) Stadacona, the Indian settlement of Chief Donnacona in Cartier's time, became the site of Quebec.

sort—or one can look in the glass. Girl's costume is plain, simple, graceful shapely, & topped with brimless fur cap; often a black fur cape handsomer than seal skin; then there are often fur borders to clothing. The dresses are short.

This nipping air is delicious, & gives everybody splendid ruddy cheeks. The complexions are very fair among the girls, & also darkish —½ & ½—Eng & French.

The French went to church in troops & droves, from 8 till 9, this Sunday morning, <(Dec. 4?)>[182] & the English from 10 till 11.

Drove half way to Falls of Montmorency, then came back & bought a photograph. The wind down on the low ground was mighty cold. The photograph is very satisfactory.

Dejeuner a la Fréchette, probably old.[183]

When I look around me & see the humanity virtue & intelligence of your people, I feel that through piracy I have not lived in vain[184]

The hotel fools landed us at the station 35 minutes before train time—yet the distance was only 3 minutes. We had to put in the time driving around. [#]

---

[182] Clemens had written to Livy from Quebec on 2 December: "Our present plan is to go back to Montreal to-morrow (Saturday) where we have business Monday." But he was still in Quebec on Sunday, 4 December. Clemens decided to remain in Canada a few days longer when the banquet for him at the Windsor Hotel in Montreal was scheduled for Thursday, 8 December.

[183] Louis Fréchette, the French-Canadian poet-laureate, was the brother of Léonard Achille Fréchette, Howells' brother-in-law. His poem, "To Mark Twain," printed in French on the menu card for the banquet at the Windsor Hotel, hails Clemens as "le plus grand des philosophes,/ Puisqu'il est le plus amusant" (MTP). Fréchette was Clemens' guest in Hartford early in 1882.

[184] Clemens had commented on the positive aspect of literary piracy in a letter to Howells a year earlier: "My notions have mightily changed, lately. Under this recent & brand-new system of piracy in New York, this country is being flooded with the best of English literature at prices which make a package of water closet paper seem an 'edition de luxe' in comparison. . . . These things must find their way into the very kitchens & hovels of the country. A generation of this sort of thing ought to make this the most intelligent & the best-read nation in the world. International copyright must becloud this sun & bring on the former darkness and dime-novel reading" (30 October 1880, *MTHL*, p. 334).

Mr. Dawson[185]
258 University st.

Louis Frèchette
629 Ontario st.

L. S. Huntington.[186]
Montreal.

Torry's (rugs)
348 Washington st.

H. Clay Trumbull[187]
4103 Walnut st.

Plane floor by dr. door in din r.
" " in library bay window.
Trim bottom of closet door in hall.

Gas logs in dining room.
do do in billiard "

Rollo & his Uncle Visit the Hotels. Make sketch of it.[188] [#]

---

185 S. E. Dawson was Clemens' Canadian publisher. He served as a member of the committee for the Mark Twain Dinner at the Windsor Hotel, as did Louis Fréchette.

186 Lucius S. Huntington, Liberal party member of Canada's House of Commons, was chairman of the Windsor Dinner Committee.

187 A Congregational clergyman who had invited Clemens to the dinner of the New England Society of Philadelphia held on 22 December 1881 to celebrate the landing of the Pilgrims at Plymouth Rock. Clemens delivered a humorous speech (*Mark Twain's Speeches*, ed. Albert Bigelow Paine [New York: Harper & Brothers, 1923], pp. 86–92). Trumbull was the brother of J. Hammond Trumbull, the Hartford scholar who provided the multi-lingual chapter headings for *The Gilded Age*.

188 Livy read Jacob Abbott's popular, moralistic "Rollo Series" and his *Franconia Stories* with the children, although Clemens was contemptuous of Abbott's work, observing "how harmoniously gigantic language and a microscopic topic go together" (*Concerning Cats*, p. 15). Clemens' entry in this notebook suggests that he considered burlesquing *Rollo's Tour in Europe*, the tedious and didactic account in ten volumes of young Rollo's adventures abroad with his uncle Mr. George.

The Fate of Madame La Tour. (Ford, Howard & Hulbert)[189]

Get up a profound metaphysical essay something like Hamersley's "Does Thought or action exert most influence upon man?"—only let it be all sounding pretense, meaning nothing—but do level best to fool the Club with it, & get them to <conscious>conscientiously go floundering through it, honestly trying to refute it.[190]

D. & R. G.—68.
West^{n} Union 78½ & Mo. Pac. 101.
Lake Shore 117[191]

Men are more compassionate/(nobler)/magnanimous/generous than God; for men forgive the dead, but God does not.

Men are more noble-natured than

Steam printing—
Railway—
Telegraph
Telephone
Stereoscope
Anæsthetics
(Electric light. & motors (future)
Steamship.
Sewing machine
Photography
Wooden legs.
14 photos in a second.
Chromos.

---

[189] A fictional account of the Mormons by Mrs. Cornelia Paddock (New York: Fords, Howard, & Hulbert, 1881).

[190] William T. Hamersley's paper for the Monday Evening Club was entitled "The Relative Power of Thought and Action" and was delivered on 19 December 1881 (*The List of Members of the Monday Evening Club Together with the Record of Papers Read at Their Meetings* [Hartford: privately printed, 1954], p. 36). None of Clemens' papers read to the club follow the proposed plan.

[191] Clemens had invested in the Denver & Rio Grande Railroad, the Missouri & Pacific Railroad, and Western Union Telegraph and was probably considering investing in the Lake Shore & Michigan Southern Railroad.

Geology. Paleontology. destroyed Genesis

There is a difference between invention & application.—The ancients invented; the modern spirit invents & applies.

Destruction of the personal devil.—a great victory.

Destruction of infant damnation.

Pneumatic tubes.

The medical & surgical science.

<Logariths>Logarithms & quarternions.

Compass, 1322. Rotundity of <wor>earth, 132[2]

Sir John Mandeville.[192]

Thomas McWaters (his father is in Custom House).[193]

(Write Tribune).

"Apologia pro vita sua" by Cardinal Newman[194]

W. Reid—"Lotos Leaves"[195] [#]

---

192 Fourteenth-century traveler who compiled a book, written by himself and others, of actual and fantastic accounts of natural phenomena. Mandeville's narrative is included in a book which Clemens owned, *Early Travels in Palestine* (ed. Thomas Wright [London: Henry G. Bohn, 1848], pp. 127–282), now in the Mark Twain Papers. Mandeville's remarks on the rotundity of the earth are on page 219 and were marked by Clemens as an item of special interest.

193 A George S. McWatters was a New York customs inspector in 1881 (U.S. Civil Service Commission, *Official Register of the United States*, vol. 1, *Legislative, Executive, Judicial* [Washington, D.C.: Government Printing Office, 1881], p. 188). Clemens' connection with the family is not known.

194 The following pages contain notes for Clemens' "revenge" on Whitelaw Reid, editor of the New York *Tribune*. Cardinal Newman's *Apologia* may have suggested the mode for Clemens' attack. This entry appears to have been written by John Russell Young of the *Herald*, who was involved in Clemens' proposed biography of Whitelaw Reid from its inception. "The more I think of the life," he wrote Clemens on 11 January 1882, "the more it amuses me—He is such a gigantic donkey—with none of the donkey's redeeming qualities."

195 *Lotos Leaves* (Boston: William F. Gill & Co., 1875) was a collection of "Original Stories, Essays, and Poems" by members of the Lotos Club, including Reid and Clemens, edited by John Brougham and John Elderkin. Reid's contribution, "Some Southern Reminiscences," is the first selection in the book.

House & Reid—"Gilded Age"[196]

Dinner at Bennett's.[197]

Essay on Journalism.[198]

Pendleton ought to have married you & made an honest woman of you.

Cunard Co.
Appleton & Co.

Pres. Lotos Club.[199]

Grant at Lotos Club. ask Grant.[200] [#]

---

196 The rift in Clemens' friendship with Reid initially occurred in 1873 when Reid refused to allow Edward House to review *The Gilded Age* for the *Tribune*, claiming that House's friendly interest in the book made the proposal dishonorable. Reid was as angry as Clemens about the episode, as evidenced by his letter of 17 July 1873 to journalist Kate Field: "I hear [Mark Twain] says he has a quarrel with 'The Tribune.' If so, it is simply that 'The Tribune' declined to allow him to dictate the person who should review his forthcoming novel. His modest suggestion was that Ned House should do it, he having previously interested House in the success of the book by taking him into partnership in dramatizing it. There is a nice correspondence on a part of the subject which would make pleasant reading; and if Twain gives trouble, I'm very much tempted to make him a more ridiculous object than he has ever made anybody else" (Lilian Whiting, *Kate Field: A Record* [Boston: Little, Brown, and Co., 1900], pp. 307–308). In later years, Clemens' anger at Reid's part in the quarrel was mitigated by his then greater animosity toward House.

197 James Gordon Bennett, Jr., was editor and publisher of the New York *Herald*, and therefore Reid's competitor. The occasion for the dinner which Clemens mentions here is unknown.

198 In the spring of 1872, Reid lectured on journalism at the City College of New York (Royal Cortissoz, *The Life of Whitelaw Reid*, 2 vols. [New York: Charles Scribner's Sons, 1921], 1:236). His address, "Schools of Journalism," was published in *Scribner's Monthly* for June 1872. He defended journalism but conceded its abuses and sketched a rigorous college program for prospective editors which would reform the trade and raise it to the status of a profession.

199 Reid was president of the Lotos Club from 1872 to 1876 and from 1878 to 1889 when he resigned in order to accept the position of United States minister to France.

200 Grant was given a testimonial dinner in November 1880 by the Lotos Club. Reid, who had openly opposed Grant in the past—supporting Greeley's campaign against him in the presidential election of 1872, for instance, and criticizing Grant's

Don Piatt.

G. A. Townsend.[201]

Changing policy of Tribune frequently.

Get Nast to illustrate.[202]

Noah Brooks[203] (direct ownership of Reid by Jay Gould.[204] [#]

---

attempt in 1880 to capture the Republican nomination for a third time—made the introductory speech. Stephen Fiske in his *Off-Hand Portraits of Prominent New Yorkers* (New York: G. R. Lockwood & Son, 1884) described the scene at the club "when, as President, [Reid] is proposing the health of General Grant, whom he has persistently opposed and abused in the *Tribune*. He is a fluent, pleasing speaker, and has no blushes when Grant looks up at him with a surprised, studious stare" (p. 270). Reid's biographer, Royal Cortissoz, described the Lotos Club speech more positively: "Reid presided, and when he rose to pay a tribute of welcome to the guest sitting at his right hand, there was not a man present who failed to realize the piquancy of the moment and the bristling nature of the hurdles which the speaker faced. He took them with candid directness, pausing only to eulogize the soldier and to recall his own observation of Grant's calm carriage at Pittsburg Landing. . . . There was nothing left for acrimony between the political adversaries of a long period, now breaking bread together in peace and amity" (Cortissoz, *Whitelaw Reid*, 2:27–28).

201 With George Townsend, who used the pen name "Gath," Donn Piatt founded the *Capital*, a Washington weekly devoted to exposing weakness and corruption in members of both political parties. So vigorously did the paper pursue its ends that Piatt was for a short time in 1877 under indictment for inciting rebellion, insurrection, and riot.

202 Nast had no love for Reid and had caricatured him during Greeley's 1872 presidential campaign. The *Tribune's* harsh condemnation of the congressmen involved in the Crédit Mobilier scandal prompted another Nast cartoon. In it a self-righteous Reid is pictured in front of a group of "Saints of the Press" ready to accuse the Crédit Mobilier ring. The caption, spoken by Justice, reads: "Let him that has not betrayed the trust of the People, and is without stain, cast the first stone" (J. Chal Vinson, *Thomas Nast Political Cartoonist* [Athens: University of Georgia Press, 1967], cartoon 87).

203 Brooks wrote for the *Tribune* from 1871 to 1876, then went over to the *Times* after quarreling with Reid. When he resigned he wrote Anna Dickinson that Reid "flew into a rage, sent me an abusive note, and to cap the ridiculous climax, forbade my ever entering the office after my duties in the paper came to an end! Poor child! He had the worst fit" (Giraud Chester, *Embattled Maiden: The Life of Anna Dickinson* [New York: G. P. Putnam's Sons, 1951], p. 162).

204 During the scramble for control of the *Tribune* after Greeley's death in 1872, Reid bought a half-interest in the paper for $500,000 and signed a five-year

Altering stock reports.

Grant after Shiloh—"Agate" of the Gazette.[205]

<Ask> Grant calls him Outlaw Reid

Winter's Dedication to Reid[206]

President of the Esthete Club.

Courting Anna Dickinson—going to educate her—buy Bleak House.[207] [#]

---

contract giving him complete control over the paper's policies. Among his financial backers then was Jay Gould, who later sold his shares to Darius Ogden Mills in 1881, the year Reid married Mills's daughter. Though Gould was apparently not active as a stockholder, the rival New York *Sun* liked to refer to the *Tribune* building as "Gould's office" (Harry W. Baehr, Jr., *The New York Tribune Since the Civil War* [New York: Dodd, Mead & Co., 1936], pp. 121–122).

[205] Reid, as "Agate" of the Cincinnati *Gazette*, wrote an extended account of Shiloh based on personal observation which won him national fame as a war correspondent. He was often severely critical of Union conduct, particularly on the first, nearly disastrous, day of the battle, and also directed his sarcasm at Grant's generalship: "Major-Gen. Grant had indeed said there was great probability of a rebel attack, but there were no appearances of his making any preparation for such an unlooked-for event, and so the matter was dismissed." Shortly afterward "there was a council of war, but if the Major-General commanding developed any plans there beyond the simple arrangement of our line of battle, I am very certain that some of the division commanders didn't find it out" ("Cincinnati 'Gazette' Account," in *The Rebellion Record*, ed. Frank Moore, 12 vols. [New York: G.P. Putnam, 1862], 4:386, 397). At a later meeting of the members of the Society of the Army of the Tennessee in Cincinnati, "Agate's" account of the "surprise" attack at Shiloh was labeled as a fiction and General Sherman, whose conduct at the battle had been called into question by the account, announced publicly that there was "not one word of truth" in it, for "it was written at Cairo and not on the field at all" (New York *Times*, 7 April 1881).

[206] William Winter, drama critic for the *Tribune*, dedicated *The Trip to England*, a collection of travel letters first published in the *Tribune*, to Reid "with esteem for his public career, with honour for his pure character, and with affectionate friendship" (2d ed. rev. [Boston: James R. Osgood and Co., 1881]).

[207] Reid had first met and courted the lecturer in 1863. They visited and corresponded extensively and in 1869 and 1870 newspaper gossip reported their impending marriage. Though rumors about the romance were still appearing in the press, their friendship faltered when Reid began to devote all of his time to the *Tribune* in the early 1870s. By 1881 it had become "common newspaper gossip

Abject appeals to the old boys to stand by the old Tribune.[208]

F. B. Carpenter[209] the artist—death of Greely, & Reids miserable connection with it.[210]

First Smith
Was Chase's dog.[211]
Swinging from tree by tail & hand like monkey—from <Grant> great man <&>to great man.
Attacked Garfield on Credit Mobilier in 73.[212]

---

that Reid was using his paper to strike back at Anna for jilting him" (Chester, *Embattled Maiden*, p. 215). In later years Miss Dickinson venomously denounced Reid from the lecture platform, shocking her audience with her portrait of the eminent journalist as a man with "the tainted blood of his father on the one hand, and with the insane epileptic blood of his mother on the other, himself between, taking as he himself asserted medicines to make a man of himself" (Chester, *Embattled Maiden*, p. 268). Clemens met Anna Dickinson in 1868 when both toured on James Redpath's lecture circuit. No evidence links Miss Dickinson's dramatic ambitions to any production of *Bleak House*.

208 Possibly a reference to the struggle for control of the *Tribune* immediately after Greeley's death.

209 In 1867 Francis Bicknell Carpenter had been commissioned by the *Tribune* Association to paint a portrait of Greeley.

210 After his unsuccessful presidential campaign, Greeley resumed the editorship of the *Tribune* on 7 November 1872. At the same time, J. R. G. Hassard, music critic for the paper, published an editorial entitled "Crumbs of Comfort" expressing relief that the *Tribune* would now be free of the political office-seekers who had been importuning Greeley for favors. When an offended Greeley replied to the editorial, Whitelaw Reid suppressed the reply, asserting that its publication "would have sent every editor out of the staff." Charles A. Dana, editor of the New York *Sun*, charged in his newspaper in 1872 and again in 1879 that Reid's action was the final blow to Greeley's health (Baehr, *The New York Tribune*, pp. 114–118).

211 Reid's efforts in the Cincinnati *Gazette* to vindicate Salmon P. Chase's administration of the treasury department were taken by many as support for Chase's bid to displace Lincoln as the 1864 Republican presidential nominee (Cortissoz, *Whitelaw Reid*, 1:195–196).

212 Following the report of the House committee on the congressmen implicated in the Crédit Mobilier scandal, a *Tribune* editorial scorned "this timid investigation" and commented harshly on each of the "calumniated Congressmen" including Garfield: "James A. Garfield of Ohio had ten shares; never paid a dollar; received $329, which, after the investigation began, he was anxious to have considered a loan from Mr. Oakes Ames to himself" (19 February 1873). Reid and Garfield had been close friends since the Civil War.

Ask Anna Dickinson about Reid.

Soon as Garfield up for President, fawned on him.

J. B. <McCo>McCullough of St Louis Globe Democrat—ask him.[213]

Wm. Black, Paston House Paston Place, Brighton or Reform Club—ask him for his episode with Tribune.
Madcap Violet. £200[214]

Get this story from Jno. Russell Young.

Reid the Esthete.
Smalley the Athlete.

Smalley in White Wings—Smethurst as Smalley— —2d Chap.[215] [#]

[213] According to Walter B. Stevens in his article "Joseph B. McCullagh" (*Missouri Historical Review* 25, no. 3 [April 1931]: 425), the Cincinnati *Gazette* refused to print McCullagh's account of the first day's fighting at Shiloh because it discredited Union forces. The *Gazette* did print Reid's critical dispatch.

[214] Black was a Scottish novelist, author of *Madcap Violet* (1876), *White Wings* (1880), and many other popular romances which had a large following of American readers. He was handsomely welcomed on his trip to America in 1876 by both the press and the public. In 1877 the *Tribune* reviewed two of Black's books, *Madcap Violet* and *Green Pastures and Piccadilly*, rather critically, but there is no evidence of any other source for displeasure with the newspaper or Reid, unless Clemens is referring to the episode described in note 215.

[215] George W. Smalley was the *Tribune's* chief European correspondent and Reid's close friend. William Black's biographer, Wemyss Reid, mentions the unpleasantness occasioned by Black's habit of drawing the characters of his novels from life, notably in his yachting romance, *White Wings*:

> Rightly or wrongly the initiated insisted that this very disagreeable man [Smethurst in *White Wings*] was intended to represent a person well known in certain circles. Black stoutly denied that this was the case, though he was fain to admit that some rather prominent characteristics of the man in question had been introduced into the description of the fictitious personage of the book. Unluckily . . . the artist who illustrated 'White Wings' in the *Cornhill Magazine*, in drawing a picture of this particular character gave him the outward appearance of the supposed original. Black himself had nothing to do with the coincidence, but it is to be feared that the gentleman who believed that he had been described in the story was not easily satisfied as to the author's innocence. (Wemyss Reid, *William Black* [London: Cassell & Co., 1902], p. 224)

The character Smethurst is first mentioned in chapter 4 of *White Wings* and

Gabrielle Greeley "At Chatauqua"—attribute it to Reid.[216]

Consult files of Tribune & attribute all silly gushing editorials to Reid.—Also the Editorial "Poor Tom"—(Tom Nast.)[217]

Appleton's didn't put Reid in the Cyclopedia.

Dedicate the book to <Lotos>

He reads from "Ohio in the War"[218] (which he carries around in his boots) to company.

He was the humblest man in America when he came to Tribune.

Chased after all the rich girls in California.[219]

Reid wrote campaign life of Grant in '68.—Since, abused him.[220] [#]

---

makes his appearance in chapter 6 where he is described in detail: "He had closely-cropped, coarse grey hair; an eagle beak; a certain pink and raw appearance of the face, as if perpetual east winds had chafed the skin; and a most pernicious habit of loudly clearing his husky throat. Then with the aggressive nose went a well-defined pugilist's jaw and a general hang-dog scowl about the mouth. . . . The precision of his costume only gave him the look of a well-dressed groom, or a butler gone on the turf" (*White Wings*, 3 vols. [London: Macmillan and Co., 1880], 1:77).

[216] Gabrielle Greeley was Horace Greeley's youngest daughter. "Chatauqua" is probably Clemens' misrendering of Chappaqua, New York, the location of Greeley's country retreat.

[217] In October 1873, James Gordon Bennett's *Herald* started a collection for the purportedly indigent Nast, and for several weeks a satirical column in that paper recorded contributions to the fund for "Poor Tom." Clemens in this note mistakenly attributes the hoax to Reid.

[218] Reid's second book, a history of Ohio's part in the Civil War, was published in 1868.

[219] Reid made his first trip to California in the summer of 1879. In New York, on 26 April 1881, he married Elisabeth Mills, the daughter of California financier Darius Ogden Mills. Among the wedding guests were Mr. and Mrs. William Dean Howells and Charles Dudley Warner, who did not share Clemens' dislike of Reid (New York *Times*, 27 April 1881).

[220] Royal Cortissoz notes that Greeley and John Russell Young of the *Tribune* in 1868 "persuaded [Reid] to write a life of Grant in a pamphlet of some fourscore pages, to be circulated as a campaign document" (Cortissoz, *Whitelaw Reid*, 1:141).

I do not begin with his boyhood, which is of no consequence—nor with his manhood, which has never existed.

Reid is Guiteau with the courage left out.[221]

'Reid looks as if he was waiting for a vacancy in the Trinity." —Hnry Clapp.[222]

Concerned in whisky ring & the $2-tax on whisky Horace Greeley blushed when it was mentioned, & said "Well, that all occurred before he came to us."[223]

Jacob Whitelaw Reid.[224]

Reid is altered, lately.
No, he has always been so.

Whitlow.

Reid's treatment of A. B. Mullet.[225] [#]

---

[221] Charles J. Guiteau shot President Garfield on 2 July 1881. Garfield died on 19 September 1881.

[222] Henry Clapp, founder of the short-lived *Saturday Press,* was famous for his wit and was the undisputed king of New York "Bohemians." Clapp's witticism was actually directed at the Reverend Dr. Samuel Osgood, a pompous Park Avenue minister. In an earlier reference in one of his letters to the *Alta California* (*Mark Twain's Travels with Mr. Brown,* p. 276), Clemens correctly identified Osgood as Clapp's subject. In the present case, Clemens may have had a confused memory of another of Clapp's remarks—his description of Reid's mentor, Horace Greeley, as "a self-made man that worships his creator" (William Winter, *Old Friends* [New York: Moffat, Yard and Co., 1914], p. 62).

[223] Possibly a reference to the Whiskey Ring scandal of Grant's presidency in 1875 and 1876, when revenue officials and distillers in several cities were shown to have defrauded the government of millions in tax revenues. There is no recorded connection between Reid and the ring. Horace Greeley died in 1872, before the frauds were exposed; if this accusation refers to that scandal, it is a figment of Clemens' anger.

[224] Reid was baptized Whitelaw; his mother decided to call him James Whitelaw and he used that name until he graduated from college (Cortissoz, *Whitelaw Reid,* 1:10).

[225] Alfred B. Mullett, supervising architect for the United States Treasury from 1866 to 1876, had been savagely denounced by the *Tribune* in 1877: "he left the country pitted all over with the pustules of his extraordinary architecture," said the editorial, adding complaints about the large government expenditures for his

Professional pall-bearer.[226]

Geo. E Blackham[227]
S L Clemens

General Grant[228]—I am deputed by my fellow-citizens—by the civilians of the community—to welcome you to the cordial hospitalities of Hartford. By your example you have slain the fashion of long speeches; & for this you deserve immortal gratitude. We shall best honor you in honoring the lesson which you have taught. As a soldier, you proved yourself without a peer—& so we welcome you as the First Soldier of the Republic; as President, you inaugurated international arbitration—& so we welcome you as the first to lay the axe to the root of the trade of war, & as the pioneer in the march of the nations toward the last perfection of enlightened government, the substitution of reason for force in the settlement of controversies; & finally, as one who, being almost called, & yet not quite, to carry the standard of a great party for a third time in a Presidential campaign, has sunk the hero in the patriot, has laid aside all considerations of self, all narrow feeling, & has devoted his whole heart & the might of his great name to the cause of that party, and through it to the best interest of his country, its progress & its civilization, we<l> welcome you by the noblest of all the titles you have earned—that of First Citizen of the Republic! [#]

---

buildings, and the "ornate and polysyllabic" manner of his profane speech, "the flow of it like some overcharged sewer in a storm" (New York *Tribune*, 16 March 1877). The issues of 10 May 1877 and 27 November 1881 also contained attacks on Mullett.

226 Reid acted as pallbearer at the funeral of Salmon P. Chase in 1873 and marched in the procession at Greeley's funeral in 1872. Clemens made a further note in Notebook 20 of Reid's presence at the funeral of wealthy industrialist Webster Wagner. Beginning here, the pages of Notebook 19 have been used haphazardly to record miscellaneous information and do not follow the fairly strict chronology of the rest of the notebook.

227 This name is not in Clemens' hand and is presumably Blackham's signature. It is followed by Clemens' signature.

228 This superseded draft of Clemens' speech occupies three consecutive right-hand pages of the notebook; the facing pages have been left blank. The speech is followed by six blank pages.

130
150
———
280

18
15
———
90
18
———
<190>170
280
———
<470>

Kimmend (command)
Jerus'lim—Islem (a)
werld (o)
unhappy lend (a)
Asha—Persha.
Syriar, Russiar, Juder
Mesopotamier
awr (our)

Whitmore[229] bets (on 75 pts.)
100 cigars. .... lost.
100 " (on 50 pts.) .... lost
200 " .... lost.
400 " .... won. even.
one hug. Whitmore
Whitmore Whitmore
Whitmore Whitmore

---

[229] F. G. Whitmore was one of the regulars of the Friday Evening Club which met in Clemens' billiard room. Other members of the club who assembled to enjoy the billiards, cigars, and whiskey, were Henry C. Robinson, Charles Perkins, and Edward Bunce (Kenneth R. Andrews, *Nook Farm: Mark Twain's Hartford Circle* [Cambridge: Harvard University Press, 1950], pp. 93, 114). The figures may refer to bets placed according to a martingale system, mentioned in note 106, above.

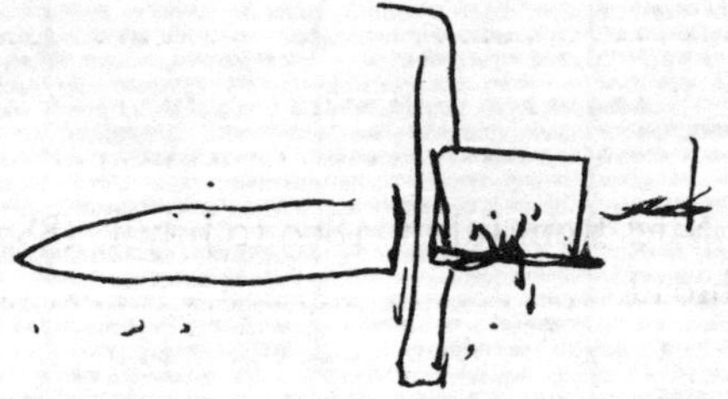

Whitmore bets (on 50 points)

100 cigars .... lost
100 " .... <">lost
100 " .... lost.
200 " .... lost.
200 " .... won.
200 " .... won.
100 " .... won.
200 " .... lost owes 400
200 " .... lost. " 600
200 " .... lost " 800.
400 " .... won. " 400.
400 " .... won. even.

---

100. " .... lost.
100 " .... won.

Mr Clemens bets on 30 pts.

100—" .... lost.
200—" .... lost
400—" .... lost.
800 " .... lost.
1600 " .... lost.
1600— .... won.

100— .... lost.
<200>300— .... lost.
<400>600— .... lost.

1200— ....lost
2400— ....lost—
4800 ....won.

Sales from July 1, 1879 to July 1, 1880.

Innocents Abroad 3,182
Roughing It .... 2,466.
Gilded Age 1,700
Tom Sawyer 3,186
Sketches 1,518
Tramp Abroad, from March 1, 1880, to
July 1, same year .... 47,563.

Poem on the man who killed 10 desperadoes in <Alabama> California—"And Captain Jones of Alabama"—[230]

The Talkative barber in Arabian Nights.[231]

"Hajji" Something—written by Morton.[232]

Happy Thought Burnham[233]

Quote from English funny journals.
Helen's Babies & The Worst Boy in Town—by the ass Habberton.

Gen Grant
" Sherman
Sheridan

---

[230] The following entries refer to *Mark Twain's Library of Humor*. Some names duplicate those listed on pages 361–365 of this notebook.

[231] Clemens owned a copy of the three-volume first edition of Edward Lane's translation of *The Thousand and One Nights* (London: Charles Knight & Co., 1839) ("Books from the Library of Mark Twain . . . ," Zeitlin & Ver Brugge catalogue no. 132, May 1951, item 29). In chapter 5 the Talkative Barber tells his story and the stories of each of his six brothers.

[232] Clemens owned two copies of James J. Morier's *Adventures of Hajji Baba of Ispahan* (A1911, items 340 and 341) including the three-volume first-edition set (London: John Murray, 1824).

[233] George P. Burnham was the author of *Gleanings from the Portfolio of the "Young 'Un"* (1849) and *The History of the Hen Fever, A Humorous Record* (1855).

Dickens
C D Warner
World Fables & that poem of his on that Eastern savage that died.
Bierce's <fan> fables in S. F. News Letter.
Page (Dow Jr)
Dan de Quille
Author of Punch Brothers Punch (now on Tribune).[234]
"Saturday Night" Cincin.
Newspaper paragraphists[235]
Herald P. I. man

Phenix's military problem.
His wheelbarrow

Coan! *I* ain't Coan—he's outside selling tickets
John Phenix
Sut Lovengood
Irving
Georgia Sketches
Haliburton
Widow Bedott
Burdette
Artemus Ward
Danbury News
D R Locke
B. Harte
J R Lowell
O W Holmes
Howells
Aldrich [#]

---

[234] The jingle upon which Clemens based his sketch "Punch, Brothers, Punch" was written in 1875 by Noah Brooks and Isaac Bromley when both were on the staff of the *Tribune*.

[235] Examples of the work of the foremost "paragraphists," or "newspaper wits," George D. Prentice, John E. Hatcher, and Albert Roberts, are collected in Henry Watterson's *Oddities in Southern Life and Character* (Boston: Houghton Mifflin Co., 1882), pp. 446–473.

These are bets of cigars that Geo. Robinson[236] could not place 7 balls to suit himself, play with the eighth, & score <[--]> 30 points on a single inning. Once he owed me 4,000 <cigs>cigars.

S. L. C.

He lost 3 bets—then
G. owes me 13 & bets 20 more.
" " " 33 " " 50 "
" " " 83 " " 100 "
" " " 183 " 200 "
383 " 400 "
783 "1000 "
<2>
He won this 1000

He bets me 217. He lost & we are even.

He bets me 100—he lost.
" " " 100 " "
" " " 200 " won.

" " " 100 " lost.

" " " 200 " won.
" " " 100. " "
" " " 200 " lost even

" " " 200 " lost 200
" " " 300 " lost. 500
" " " 500. " lost 1000
" " "1000. " lost 2000
" " "2000. lost 4000
" " "4000 won—even

---

[236] George M. Robinson of Elmira had signed the petition to erect a monument to Adam in Elmira (*MTB*, p. 1650).

XX

"A Profane & Irritable Man in a Hurry"

(January 1882–February 1883)

"NOBODY KNOWS, better than I," Clemens wrote to Howells on 28 January 1882, "that there are times when swearing cannot meet the emergency" (*MTHL*, p. 386). Yet profanity was better than nothing during a year in which Clemens found himself bedeviled by expensive interior decorations for the Hartford house—"a life of don't-care-a-damn in a boarding house is what I have asked for in many a secret prayer," he confided to Howells (*MTHL*, p. 389)—social engagements, frequent house-guests, children's diseases, personal ailments, public readings, importunate correspondents, irksome stock market decisions, and—heaviest burden of all—the nagging necessity of producing a new travel volume he had committed himself to write. Notebook 20 also continues Clemens' angry assault on Whitelaw Reid and records his attention to the faltering Kaolatype venture, his dealings with James R. Osgood's publishing firm, and his growing reliance on Charles L. Webster's services.

The most significant entries are those which combine commercial interests and literature. Mark Twain had decided that during 1882 he would produce for subscription publication a large volume about the Mississippi River, based on his firsthand knowledge of the subject. A part of the book —describing his own piloting apprenticeship—was already written: a series of sketches, "Old Times on the Mississippi," had been published in the *Atlantic* in 1875. To amplify these he decided to revisit the river which he had not seen since his 1868 trip to Saint Louis.

On 28 January Mark Twain concluded that the report of Reid's "almost daily" insults was unfounded and he shelved his intemperate scheme for retribution. "I could have earned ten thousand dollars with infinitely less trouble," he commented ruefully to William Dean Howells (*MTHL*, p. 389). By this date his "river book" had captured his attention and in February he began a series of notes in preparation for the Mississippi excursion; numerous memories about his piloting years already were logged in the pages of the notebook before he left Hartford. This trip realized a long-deferred desire; upon completing *Roughing It*, Mark Twain had confidently predicted to Livy on 27 November 1871: "When I come to write the Mississippi book, *then* look out! I will spend 2 months on the river & take notes, & I bet you I will make a standard work" (*LLMT*, p. 166).

Originally he had hoped to have Howells' companionship when he returned to New Orleans, and during eight years he periodically tried to persuade his friend to undertake the journey with him. Howells' continuing editorial responsibilities and a sequence of illnesses in his family prevented him from participating, however. In April 1882, shortly before Clemens departed for Saint Louis, he attended a luncheon in Boston at which Howells was present, and then with Howells went to Concord to visit Emerson. Afterward, Howells gave his benediction to the travelers who were making the tour which he had so long anticipated for himself: "I am sorry that Osgood is with you on this Mississippi trip; I foresee that it will be a contemptible half-success instead of the illustrious and colossal failure *we* could have made it," he wrote good-naturedly on 18 April (*MTHL*, p. 403). Howells himself would depart in July with his family for a recuperative year in Europe.

Following a banquet held at the Union League Club on 17 April, Mark Twain left New York City the next morning with Osgood and Roswell Phelps, a Hartford stenographer whom he engaged to transcribe his comments during the tour. Phelps's transcription of these dictations is published as Notebook 21 in this volume. The reporter's eye in Mark Twain noticed the regional differences in the residents' appearance as the train passed through Pennsylvania, Ohio, Indiana, and Illinois. Upon reaching Saint Louis he found the city much expanded, while the wharf district had diminished disappointingly from its former size and activity, providing a melancholy backdrop for Mark Twain's lively memories about the previous grandeur of river commerce. Once he was on board a river vessel, however, dictating his impressions to Phelps, it is evident the majestic Mississippi still possessed its evocative power. A letter Clemens sent to Livy from Vicksburg on 25 April contains a lyrical description of "the luxurious green walls of forest! & the jutting leafy capes! & the paling green of the far stretches! & the remote, shadowy, vanishing distances . . . *and* the riot of the singing birds!" in the dim light preceding dawn (*LLMT*, p. 210).

In spite of all the changes that steamboat piloting had undergone—meticulous navigation charts, mechanical signal systems, electric lights—Clemens discovered with gratification that romance lingered about the boats and their crews. On the *Gold Dust* and elsewhere he sought out veteran pilots to assist him in reviewing yarns about departed captains, pilots, clerks, and engineers. This flowing talk of steamboats and of rivermen was the reason Clemens had returned to the Mississippi Valley. His familiarity with the people and their surroundings produced notebook entries that are more spontaneous, evocative, and constantly interesting than the mechanical, often forced observations that he had set down in Notebooks 14 through 18 during his foreign travel in preparation for writing *A Tramp Abroad*. Notebooks 20 and 21 reflect his pleasure in revisiting "home ground" to obtain literary material.

Not all of the memories were nostalgic nor were his observations all lyrical. As the *Gold Dust* churned southward Clemens passed again the island, the bend, and the city which irrepressibly called to mind his brother Henry's agony and death in Memphis following a steamboat explosion. Now and then, too, he recognized outlines of stunted river villages on the bank, impoverished hamlets ignored by the boisterous American economy following the Civil War. Finally, as well, Clemens learned the local details of the war he had avoided by leaving for the West.

Mark Twain was contemptuous of what he felt to be a peculiarly Southern susceptibility to sham, pretension, ignorance, and squalor. He incorporated many of the criticisms jotted down in Notebook 20 into an early version of *Life on the Mississippi*, but later consented to the deletion of the sharpest passages before the book's publication. Yet his delight in hearing again Southern Negro dialect and in the reunion with his friend and mentor, Horace Bixby, was unalloyed. He also enjoyed his visits with two distinguished Southern writers: before leaving Hartford he had made arrangements for Joel Chandler Harris of Atlanta to join George Washington Cable and himself in New Orleans. Harris originally had hoped that Mark Twain's itinerary would allow him to come to Atlanta, but when that invitation was declined Harris had written on 6 April that he would "gladly" meet Cable and Clemens in New Orleans. There Mark Twain told both writers of the financial advantages of Canadian copyrights and public reading tours; after his trip he would go so far as to propose that the three of them should tackle the lecture circuit together as a grand literary "menagerie."

On Bixby's *City of Baton Rouge* Mark Twain retraced his route up the river to Saint Louis; Bixby later recalled that during the voyage "Sam was ever making notes in his memorandum-book, just as he always did" (*MTB*, p. 739). This trip on Bixby's steamboat proved to be his final view of the river south of Saint Louis. At Saint Louis Osgood took a train to Chicago to attend to business affairs, arranging to rejoin Mark Twain at Davenport, Iowa, on 18 May. Following a one-day layover Mark Twain proceeded north aboard the *Gem City* to Hannibal, where he received a warm reception and stayed at John Garth's spacious summer home. In Hannibal Mark Twain observed that boys now scorned the decaying steamboat lines and prided themselves on knowing the names and routes of nearby railroad systems instead, a disconcerting realization for the man who had achieved "boyhood's ambition" only two decades earlier by becoming a pilot.

The initial joys of this trip were gone. By the time Clemens continued north on board the *Minneapolis* to meet Osgood for the final segment of their river journey he had grown weary and petulant: "I am desperately homesick," he wrote to Livy on 17 May from Quincy, Illinois. "But I have promised Osgood, and must stick it out; otherwise I would take the train at once and break for home" (*MTL*, p. 419). When he reached Saint Paul Mark Twain had satisfied his own requirements for the trip; oppressed by thoughts about the amount of writing that lay before him, he went directly home.

Upon arriving in Hartford on May 24, Mark Twain reluctantly set to work upon his subscription book, while its publisher, Osgood, prepared to spend a pleasant summer in London, Belgium, and Paris. A series of retrospective entries in Notebook 20 concerning Mississippi River scenes and characters documents Mark Twain's efforts to extract every usable item from his recent impressions. In mid-June he constructed a self-contained dialogue between two Negro deckhands which anticipates in technique conversations between Huck and Jim in *Huckleberry Finn.* Evidently he planned to insert this vernacular argument about the Creator's responsibility for man's sinfulness into his travel narrative. The deterministic notion that man's inherently flawed nature effectually exonerates him from blame for his behavior and this colloquy form of discourse would coalesce again in *What Is Man?* and other late writings.

Just when Clemens and his family were about to escape from the social distractions of Hartford to the solitude of Quarry Farm where his literary work thrived, Jean was stricken with scarlet fever. Her sister Susy subsequently became ill with what was feared might be the same disease. His house quarantined, Clemens tried to make the best of a distressing situation—even to the point of recording ideas in his notebook for employing the scarlet fever experiences in a humorous sketch about the McWilliams family.

At last on 13 July the family was well enough to make the journey to New York City, where they stayed overnight before taking a private railway car for the trip to Elmira. At Quarry Farm Clemens set to work immediately on the troublesome book. But now his own health began to betray him, and he was vexed throughout the rest of the year by a sequence of debilitating ailments. In July he suffered an attack of lumbago. Later he complained to Joel Chandler Harris on 5 September about what he termed his "malaria"; on 19 September he wrote Webster that he was "not well yet, & my book drags like the very devil" (*MTBus,* p. 199). This enervating malady kept him bedridden intermittently even after he returned to Hartford on 29 September. Comparatively few notebook entries originated during the subsequent period of intense labor. To Edward H. House he wrote in only slightly exaggerated despair on 2 December that "the book is not done yet, for the powers of heaven and earth and hell are leagued against it, and it may never be finished at all" (Clifton Waller Barrett Library, University of Virginia, Charlottesville). When Osgood's firm sought his decision about awarding premiums to canvassers on 3 January 1883, Mark Twain simply sent the letter to Charles L. Webster along with a peevish declaration: "If there are any instructions to be given, you may give them—I will not interest myself in *any*thing connected with this wretched God-damned book" (*MTBus,* p. 207). Finally on 15

January 1883 he could notify George Washington Cable, "I have just finished my book at last" (Guy A. Cardwell, *Twins of Genius* [East Lansing: Michigan State College Press, 1953], p. 89).

Clemens used Notebook 20 at least until early February 1883 when he recorded the purchase of new shares of American Exchange in Europe stock (p. 491).

Newspapers and city directories of 1882 for Hartford, New York City, Saint Louis, and New Orleans supplied facts about individuals and events mentioned in Notebooks 20 and 21. Annotation in these notebooks is also based in part on replies from Mrs. Goldena Howard of the Reference Library in the State Historical Society of Missouri, Columbia, and on Allan C. Bates's doctoral dissertation, "Mark Twain and the Mississippi River" (University of Chicago, 1968).

Notebook 20 now contains 186 pages, 3 of them blank. It is identical in design and format to Notebook 18. Notebook 20 is heavily worn with use; some gatherings and single leaves are loose; three leaves and portions of six others have been torn out and are missing. Entries are in blue ink, black ink, and pencil. Paine's use marks and various forms of Clemens' use marks, in both pencil and ink, appear throughout the notebook. A clipping, apparently dating from early 1883 and probably from a Springfield, Massachusetts, newspaper, has been inserted near the back of the notebook. It discusses the growth in population and commerce of western cities, including Minneapolis, Chicago, Saint Louis, Kansas City, and Denver.

Mississippi River Tour, April–May 1882

17 April	Attended dinner at Union League Club in New York City.
18	Left New York City by train.
19	Indianapolis (noon); reached Saint Louis (8 P.M.).
20	Departed from Saint Louis aboard *Gold Dust* (5 P.M.).
20	*Gold Dust* delayed at East Saint Louis (10 P.M.).
21	Paused at Menard, Illinois.
21	Stopped at Cairo.
23	Toured Memphis (morning).
24	Passed Napoleon, Arkansas.
26	Visited Vicksburg, Mississippi; boarded *Charles Morgan*.

27 Stopped briefly at Baton Rouge.
28 Arrived in New Orleans (8 A.M.).
6 May Left New Orleans on *City of Baton Rouge* (5 P.M.).
7 Natchez, Mississippi (4:15 P.M.).
8 Vicksburg, Mississippi (8 A.M.).
10 Memphis, Tennessee (morning).
11 Cairo, Illinois (7 A.M.).
12 Arrived in Saint Louis (morning); Osgood left for Chicago.
13 Departed from Saint Louis aboard *Gem City* (4 P.M.).
14 Disembarked at Hannibal (early morning).
17 Left Hannibal on *Minneapolis*; Phelps had returned to Hartford.
17 Stopped at Quincy, Illinois.
17 Saw Keokuk, Iowa.
18 Stopped at Muscatine; Osgood rejoined Clemens at Davenport.
19 Dubuque, Iowa.
20 Lake Pepin, Minnesota (evening).
21 Arrived at Saint Paul (7 A.M.).
22 Departed from Saint Paul by train (1:45 P.M.).
24 Reached New York City; left immediately for Hartford.

Charley's new No—418 W. 57th.[1]

Scribner, $33.50 per page. (13½ pages, $450.)[2] [#]

---

[1] Charles L. Webster had moved from Fredonia to New York City in April 1881 to oversee Clemens' business affairs; when the arrangement seemed permanent Webster sent for his family. He notified Clemens on 23 November 1881 that they had rented a flat at 412 West Fifty-seventh Street, but sometime between 3 January and 24 March 1882 they moved a short distance to the flat at this address.

[2] Mark Twain's "A Curious Experience" had appeared in the November 1881 issue of the *Century Illustrated Monthly Magazine*, until then known as *Scribner's Monthly*. This was Mark Twain's first appearance in the magazine and he received $400 in payment "with the understanding that if it should exceed 13⅓ pages" he would be "paid for such excess at the rate of $30 per page" (James R. Osgood to SLC, 11 May 1881).

<Gerhardt, 78 Boulevard St. Michel.>[3]

uncle Remus.[4]

603 Safe Dep. Box.

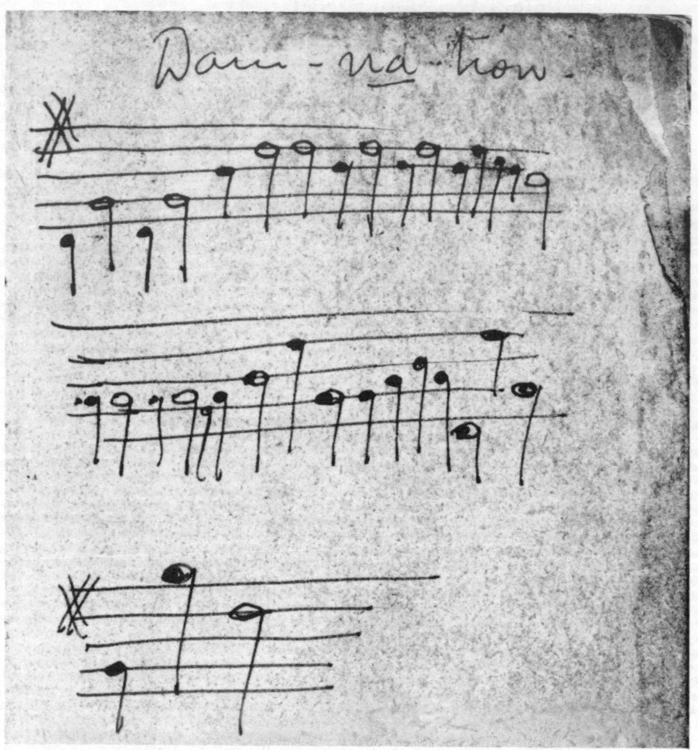

Dam-*na*-tion! I can't remember his name! Just now it clung to the tip of my tongue, But I fear 'twill remain unsung! [#]

---

[3] The Clemenses had dispatched Karl Gerhardt and his wife Hattie to Paris in March 1881 for Karl's art lessons. A 22 January 1882 letter from Hattie Gerhardt is the earliest use of this address.

[4] While comparing versions of a Negro ghost tale with Joel Chandler Harris in a 12 December 1881 letter, Clemens promised to "drop Osgood a hint about your proposed story of slave life." He also suggested to Harris: "When you come north . . . give me a day or two at our house in Hartford" (*Mark Twain to Uncle Remus, 1881–1885*, ed. Thomas H. English [Atlanta: Emory University, 1953], p. 15).

May 206
474
581
420.50
1681.50

Literary people are low.

An isolated & helpless young girl is perfectly safe from insult by a Frenchman, if he is dead.[5]

A dead Frenchman has many good qualities; many things to recommend him; many attractions—even innocencies. Why cannot we have more of these?

<Read> Keep "up" in <light> Fr. novels. There's enough high stylish life to make up for the <heroes>hero's trivial (sham—ridiculous) heroisms & the heroine's nastiness.

Some Frenchwomen are perfectly decent.

Rules for Com[g] Suicide for Love.[6]

Sort of Note to leave behind.

Where both suicide—charcoal preferable.

When the naturalist finds a new kind of animal, he writes him up, in the interest of science. <It> No matter if it is an unpleasant animal—he wrote up the skunk (Latin name.) R.[7] is a new kind of animal—& in the interest of society must be written up. He is the (skunk) of our species.

R applied for foreign mission & wrote his application in Ollendorffian French.[8] [#]

---

[5] This is the first entry in the main part of the notebook. The previous notes were made at various times on the front endpaper and the front flyleaf.

[6] Notebook 19 also contains ideas for a burlesque manual of etiquette.

[7] This entry revives the vituperative onslaught against Whitelaw Reid begun in Notebook 19.

[8] In chapter 30 of *Roughing It* Mark Twain had described Heinrich Ollendorff

In prosperity turned his back upon the man who housed & sheltered him when he came poor to N.Y. Get his name. H. L. Stewart.[9]

He is purely & simply a Guiteau with the courage left out.[10]

First ed Tribune was incorruptible honesty—last one incurable dishonesty.

Draw a full parallel between Greeley & Reed.

Get life of Greeley & notice in Cyclopedias.

19,999 out of 20,000 readers will naturally ask Who is WR? & then Why tell about this unknown person? But would have heard of Kidd, &c if their lives had not been written?

Gould had not merely a mortgage on him, he owned him.

There are men who require in <a> the future wife two qualities, only—money & sex.

He could not lie. He said, "Alas, I have no <stones.> nuts." <Thirty brief years have passd, & how changed!> Pity but he had made those sweet & simple words his motto, through life—his charm

---

as "the party who has inflicted so much suffering on the world with his wretched foreign grammars, with their interminable repetitions of questions which never have occurred and are never likely to occur in any conversation among human beings." Whitelaw Reid was offered—and refused—the ministry to Germany by President Hayes in 1878 and by President Garfield in 1881; later he accepted appointments as United States minister to France (1889) and ambassador to Great Britain (1905).

[9] Clemens' source for this name, which he added later, has not been determined. Stewart is not mentioned in any available biographies of Reid. In the fall of 1868, Reid left his position on the Cincinnati *Gazette*, and joined the staff of Horace Greeley's New York *Tribune* as "first writing editor." Greeley had been importuning him to join the *Tribune* for several years.

[10] On 25 January 1882 a jury convicted Charles J. Guiteau of assassinating President Garfield; Guiteau thereupon declared that "only good has come from Gen. Garfield's removal" and warned that God would punish "the American people if a hair of my head is harmed" (New York *Times*, 27 January 1882). Guiteau was executed in Washington on 30 June 1882.

against sin, his protection against all tamperings with the truth. <Alas,> I have no nuts! How many & many a time they might have saved him from evil doing. In the early days when the tempter began upon him his earliest advances, pity but he had been repulsed with the <quiet> calm retort, Away!—<beg> I have no nuts! &c &c.

temptation

He envied the Stones of Venice.

<Eunuch>

Somebody said his character was unique; by the time it had traveled to him the word was <Eunuch.> one which looks like it & sounds like it, but <has a> isn't it—in fact has a quite different meaning.

selfish organs

so heavy they weigh down back of head & tilt his face upward.

<S>Give Read's phrenology[11] thus, to <avoid> better express it than figured would:

Individuality

<Ideality.>

Constructiveness (lying & slander).

Courage

CAUTION.

Personal Honor (have it too small to read).

&c &c—full chart. [#]

---

[11] The rear position of Self-Esteem and the other "selfish" phrenological organs was the lesson Clemens remembered best from his early study of the pseudoscience. In "Mark Twain, Phrenology and the 'Temperaments': A Study of Pseudoscientific Influence" (*American Quarterly* 24 [March 1972]: 51, 59–61), Alan Gribben points out that Mark Twain also bestowed enlarged selfish organs upon a fictional steamboat captain in chapter 24 of *Life on the Mississippi*. "He had more selfish organs than any seven men in the world—all packed in the stern-sheets of his skull."

Steel portraits of him as a sort of idiot, from infancy up—a dozen scattered through book—all should resemble him. The first should be a baby after the style of my "Moses."[12]

Get name of that (now) friend of his who had his Garfield letters.

By & by write Hay & Halstead[13] seriously to <give> put me on track of some good act of his like sending children west.[14]

(It was reported that these were all his own children<.>; but <there>this was an error—none of them were his. Some authorities think the report was gotten up by enemies to injure him; other authorities believe it was gotten up by <friends> himself to <help him.> repair a defect in his reputation.

The above refers to his one good act—acting as agent for charitable people & sending homeless little Arabs west.

PREFACE.

(Here follow slurs & sneers from Tribune, dating back to '73, & all signed WR. And this is all there is of preface—no comments & no signature. Merely the date Hartford at bottom)

<Dedicate>
<To the <D>Remote Darwinian>
The Missing link is WR.

He is 6 ft <3>2: was intended to be 9 ft high; as is observable by the proportions of his feet. In physiology the tables of proportions are very exact; so exact, indeed, that if a physiologist do but see a

---

[12] Mark Twain had captioned the burlesque frontispiece of *A Tramp Abroad* "Titian's Moses." The sketch depicted a squalling infant Moses among the bulrushes.

[13] Murat Halstead, editor of the Cincinnati *Commercial*, knew Reid through journalistic and Republican political circles. Halstead and his family met the Clemenses when they sailed to Germany on the *Holsatia* in 1878.

[14] With the assistance of the Children's Aid Society, Reid had arranged in 1879 for the transportation of boys from New York slums to farms in Kansas and Iowa (Royal Cortissoz, *The Life of Whitelaw Reid*, 2 vols. [New York: Charles Scribner's Sons, 1921], 2:10).

joint of a person's little finger he will tell you that person's stature to an inch. <It was in this w> A physiologist happened to observe R's feet once; <&> he knew <at a glance> that such such foundations as those are <never> only applied to a tower or a tree, & so he was interested at once, & got a civil engineer to <take> make a survey & a map; & by casting up the figures & proportions thus obtained, it was found, as before stated, that WR was intended to be 9 ft high.

His telegram to Garfield stopped the N.Y. reconciliation & bred Guiteau—*but he* never inspired the letter—must have been Blaine or somebody—he has always done what other men required—never has belonged to himself.[15]

Write series of maudlinly & extravagantly affectionate letters to WR like from mother to child—about his bowel complaint, & don't take cold, darling, & What are you going to name the child.

Sign them "Aunt Sarah" & praise them.

<And> letters in which I drop occasionally into public matters & quote him, vain & sillily.

Erect Monument to Whitelaw Reid—smiling, wise jackass's head —Gerhardt—designer. Bronze—to celebrate (<on>in inscription, altering stock report, letter to Garfield<)> double-facedness & treachery toward Grant, whose biography he wrote.)[16] Buy ground in N.Y., & erect it with great ceremony, getting enemies to subscribe. [#]

---

[15] President Garfield's nomination of Judge W. H. Robertson as collector of the port of New York City, opposed by Roscoe Conkling and supported by Reid and James G. Blaine, brought to a crisis the dispute between those Republicans who had bolted from Grant at the convention of 1880 (the "Half-Breeds") and the "Stalwart" faction of the party. The Senate confirmed Robertson's appointment on 18 May 1881. Reid's role in the protracted struggle gained him his reputation as a secret wire-puller, especially after the publication of a telegram he sent to John Hay urging the president to stand firm in Robertson's behalf (New York *Herald*, 6 January 1882). Garfield's assassin, of course, had proclaimed himself a Stalwart.

[16] Reid's biography of Grant has not been identified from among the numerous pamphlets supporting Grant's campaign. In *Ohio in the War: Her Statesmen, Her*

Tribune is indebted to House yet, for correspondence. Tribune was hard up at the time & H did not press the claim.[17]

W. R. receiver of stolen goods. Stole <Hayes's> Wash^{n} treaty (Alabama Claims) message?[18] Receiver worse than thief in this instance; for thief cannot *eat* message, & if there is no receiver there can be no message-thief.

locked up White & Ramsdell for [it]

Reid has The <proportions> aspect of a derrick without its dignity.

Tribune wanted Grant to have a Brutus & be assassinated.[19]

W. R. since marriage has arrived at dignity of pall-bearer at <rich> capitalists' funerals (Wagner's, Jan. 16/82)[20]

Take the malice out of you & your <altitude> <(bulk)> (stature) would be reduced <one-half> to three feet & one inch; then go on & <extract> (take) the vanity <from> (out of) you & you would disappear. [#]

Generals, and Soldiers, 2 vols. (New York: Moore, Wilstach & Baldwin, 1868), Reid's appraisal of Grant was ambivalent: he found Grant's manners "as unpretending as his person," yet "on political matters he is ignorant and careless" (1:414). Historians "will look in vain for such characteristics as should account for his being first in a Nation of soldiers; and will not fail to observe the comparative poverty of his intellect and his acquirements." But "such a career laughs at criticism, and defies depreciation. Success succeeds" (1:413).

[17] Edward H. House had resumed work for the *Tribune* after his return from Japan in 1880. He had worked for the *Tribune* during the 1860s.

[18] On 11 May 1871 the *Tribune* shocked members of the Senate by publishing a supposedly secret text of the "Alabama Claims" settlement with Great Britain. The Senate summoned and questioned two Washington correspondents for the newspaper, Zebulon L. White and H. J. Ramsdell; both were temporarily imprisoned when they refused to divulge the source for their copy of the treaty.

[19] During the 1870s the *Tribune* was one among several newspapers which accused Grant's supporters of "Caesarism" for their efforts to perpetuate his presidency.

[20] Within a year after Reid's marriage to Elisabeth Mills he attended the New York funeral services for Webster Wagner, sleeping car magnate and influential New York State Republican legislator, who had been killed in a train collision (New York *Tribune*, 17 January 1882).

Reid & Talmage equally judicious in selecting antagonists who can't hit back.—or who can but won't condescend.[21]

3—$450 each
Striped rug—$175. (bought)
Dining room $450.[22]

Funeral of Greeley—
<S. P.> Salmon P. Chase[23]
?

Wagner

Chas. Clark.	<drop one>
Twichell	
Parker	Friday 6 P.M.
Dunham.	
Robinson	

Hamersley.[24]

$200

Mrs. Morgan at Barth.[25] for 3 P.M. [#]

---

[21] Mark Twain resented the highly publicized diatribes against Robert Ingersoll's agnosticism which Thomas DeWitt Talmage delivered from his Brooklyn Tabernacle pulpit on 15 and 22 January 1882. He had chosen to single out Ingersoll in his sermons, Talmage declared, because Ingersoll is "the champion blasphemer of America" (New York *Times*, 16 January 1882). Contrary to Mark Twain's assumption, Ingersoll replied to his assailant with an often-delivered lecture titled "Talmagian Theology."

[22] As redecoration of the Hartford house neared completion, Clemens informed Howells on 28 January 1882: "All our rooms are finished & habitable, now—& there's rugs enough, you bet! for Mrs. Clemens has been to New York" (*MTHL*, p. 389).

[23] At Horace Greeley's funeral services in 1872 Reid had marched in a procession of *Tribune* employees, while Salmon Portland Chase, chief justice of the United States, had been one of the pallbearers (New York *Tribune*, 5 December 1872).

[24] Clemens' list of guests for a session of the Friday Evening Club on 3 February 1882 includes Charles Hopkins Clark, assistant editor of the Hartford *Courant*, Congregational minister Edwin Pond Parker, attorneys Samuel C. Dunham and Henry C. Robinson, and William Hamersley, state attorney for the Superior Court of Connecticut.

[25] Bartholomew & Company, Hartford brokers.

Fenn's[26]—cushions & soiled clothes hamper.

3 lb grapes & 12 bananas.

Shakspere Phrasebook—Little, Brown & Co[27]

Feb. 11/82, Twichell noticed his orderly's picture for first time after many years, & said "I wonder if he is alive yet."—Got a letter from him from Wisconsin next day.

Mr. <——>Keep[28] asked Mrs. —— "Do you remember a Va Senator in beginning of war who stoutly refused to side with secession? Yes. "I want his name." Can't remember it.—Few days after, (he had looked it out, meantime) he said to her "If I mention his initials can you fill out the name?" She said "I can without that—it was John Minor Botts."

Get Kellogg's Andersonville experiences through short-hand reporter.[29]

& write the "Hornet" wreck, putting in a sailor-man who gives birth to a child. <(Attribute>[30]

Dr. Frohlich in a red brick building opp the Seminary.[31]

Cases of pilots burning at the wheel. [#]

---

[26] The Linus T. Fenn furniture store in Hartford specialized in upholstery.

[27] John Bartlett's *The Shakespeare Phrase Book* had been published by Little, Brown & Company in 1881.

[28] Probably Charles D. or Howard H. Keep, both employed by the Phoenix Mutual Life Insurance Company in Hartford.

[29] From journals kept by Robert H. Kellogg a subscription publisher had edited *Life and Death in Rebel Prisons: Giving a Complete History of the Inhuman and Barbarous Treatment . . . at Andersonville, Ga., and Florence, S. C.* (Hartford, Conn.: L. Stebbins, 1865). *Geer's Hartford City Directory* for 1882 lists R. H. Kellogg as a general agent for the Connecticut Mutual Life Insurance Company.

[30] Mark Twain is considering embroidering his 1866 narrative about fifteen men who endured forty-three days in an open boat (see Notebook 5 in volume 1). He finally reworked the narrative for the November 1899 issue of the *Century* in "My Début as a Literary Person" with numerous notes and additions, but no childbirth.

[31] The home and office of Dr. Charles E. Froelich, physician, were at 49 Pratt Street, across from the Hartford Female Seminary.

Bixby running Island No. 10 during the war.[32]

House characterized 3 Cunard captains as rude & insolent toward passengers—gave personal instances & mentioned a newspaper anecdote where a lady asked one a question in navigation, who said, "I will call the cook—<he will give you such information as you may want."> "O I beg pardon, I thought you were that person."

But it *is*n't ship captains only—all ignorant persons, learned in one narrow specialty despise passengers—the rule applies to all *steam* boat officers, stage drivers, hotel clerks, &c—(give steamboating examples.)

Capt. Watson the silent, of the Parthia—& how I used to rage at him for "talking too much."

Tell about the sea-sick Scotch boy in the Parthia, & Westminster Abbey—& the solemn English clergyman who helped the boy explain to me that the Abbey was not a hotel.[33]

Monday.

House, Union Square Hotel till <day after to-morrow. (Wed.)> Thurs evening.[34] [#]

---

[32] The tenth island from the mouth of the Ohio River commanded a strategic channel on the Mississippi near the Kentucky-Tennessee state line. Confederate gun batteries successfully repelled all Union attempts to navigate the river beyond this point until 4 April 1862, when the gunboat U.S.S. *Carondelet*, lashing a cotton barge to her exposed side and taking advantage of a night storm, ran past the blockade and reached New Madrid. When the U.S.S. *Pittsburg* duplicated the feat on 7 April, Island No. 10 was surrendered. Bixby's service at the battle for Island No. 10 and his further war exploits are recounted in Notebook 21 (pp. 563–567).

[33] Clemens sailed on the Cunard line steamship *Parthia* from Liverpool to Boston in January 1874. The ridiculous conversation in which Clemens feigned ignorance of London's great tourist attraction is recounted in an undated, unpublished, seventeen-page manuscript entitled "Information About Westminster Abbey" in the Mark Twain Papers.

[34] House and his adopted Japanese daughter, Koto, began what was intended to be a brief visit to Hartford on 30 January 1882, but their stay as houseguests of the Clemenses was prolonged by illness. On 18 February House wrote from Hartford to John Russell Young: "I suppose you know I have had a fierce attack of gout—so fierce as to keep me in bed here for three weeks," he lamented. "I purpose

I am so indolent, & all forms of study are so hateful to me, that although I was several years living constantly on steamboats, I never learned all the parts of a steamboat. Names of parts were <d[u]> in my ear daily whose office & locality I was ignorant of, & I never inquired the meaning of those names. For instance, I think I never saw the day that I could describe the marks on a lead line. I never knew what <the> "in the run" meant—I couldn't find the run in a boat to-day, & be *sure* I was right.

After my first voyage at sea I never took any interest in knowing the parts of a ship. I cannot name ⅔ of the sails in a full rigged ship; I do not know the names or functions of ½ dozen ropes. The line "A wet sheet & a flowing sea" has always been meaningless to me. I do not know whether a *sail* is meant or the rope called a "sheet"—& I have never had energy enough to inquire.

Desperado when Piper's theatre was afire, who mounted a bench & said "I'll shoot the first — — — that stirs!—now, *you* go; now you, now *you*"—& sent them out in single file, saving every life, & nobody even scorched but himself—he went last.[35]

In Miss. book, put that game of billiards with redheaded X eyed left handed man, in Va.[36]

<Tiffany, about mantel.>[37] [#]

---

leaving here for N. York on Monday or Tuesday next. . . . I shall (in all probability) be at the Union Square Hotel on Tuesday or Wednesday" (Clifton Waller Barrett Library, University of Virginia, Charlottesville).

[35] In "The United States of Lyncherdom" (written in 1901), Mark Twain again would recall this incident which he purportedly witnessed at Piper's Opera House in Virginia City, Nevada: "I saw a noted desperado make two hundred men sit still, with the house burning under them, until he gave them permission to retire" (*Europe and Elsewhere* [New York: Harper & Brothers, 1923], p. 245).

[36] Mark Twain's anecdote about his defeat at billiards by a laconic stranger in Virginia City who offered to play left-handed, but who neglected to mention that he *was* left-handed, would not be incorporated into *Life on the Mississippi*. Later, however, it became a dependable gag for his public appearances; the 25 April 1906 issue of the New York *World*, for instance, repeated the joke as he had told it at a billiard tournament on the previous day. (See also *Mark Twain's Speeches*, ed. Albert Bigelow Paine [New York: Harper & Brothers, 1923], p. 302.)

[37] Louis C. Tiffany & Company notified Clemens on 14 February 1882 that "we have shipped today to your care, a case of glass which is to be used over the mantel."

<Thorp, $<5>4,500>[38]

<Charley, buy Kao remains.>

Criticise Thackeray.
Calling Tauchnitz a pirate.[39]

<Burglar alarm>

<Write Century artist>[40]

<Osgood, send me 100 criticisms>[41]

<Howells, your new book is fine.>[42]

My nightmares, to this day, take the form of running down into

---

[38] Clemens was dissatisfied with the results as well as the price of Alfred H. Thorp's architectural services during the 1881 expansion of the Hartford house, even though in making his drawings Thorp had collaborated with its original designer, Edward Tuckerman Potter. The $4,500 figure represented the total construction costs for the projects under Thorp's supervision, which included the kitchen, reception hall, and a verandah. Potter attempted to persuade Clemens that Thorp's rates were reasonable for a New York architect: on 24 March 1882 he sent Clemens a schedule of "the usual professional charges"; on 30 March he offered to relinquish his own fee to resolve the dispute; and on 14 June Potter again volunteered to yield the money owed him because "I would like to pay Thorp what he thinks is due him . . . ($300)." Soon thereafter Clemens settled with both men, but whether he accepted Potter's offer to forgo his fee is not clear.

[39] In anticipation of his own journey Clemens might have been reading "A Mississippi Bubble" in Thackeray's *Roundabout Papers,* which described a voyage from New Orleans to Saint Louis. But Thackeray, like Clemens, was on good terms with his Leipzig publisher, Christian Bernhard Tauchnitz, so the source for Clemens' charge is puzzling.

[40] W. Lewis Fraser, the *Century's* art editor, informed Mark Twain on 24 February 1882 that Abbott H. Thayer had been selected to draw his portrait for the September issue, which would contain an essay on Mark Twain by Howells.

[41] Evidently Mark Twain already had sent a similar request to the British publisher of *The Prince and the Pauper,* for on 3 March 1882 he would write to Andrew Chatto: "I am very much obliged to you, for sending me all those English notices of the book. They are surprisingly complimentary" (Yale).

[42] Serialization of *A Modern Instance* had begun in the December 1881 issue of the *Century.* Clemens' admiration for the novel increased: on 22 June he would call it "perfectly dazzling—it's masterly—incomparable"; on 24 July he would assure Howells that Bartley was enjoyable "to the utmost uttermost"; the final chapters he pronounced "prodigious" on 3 October (*MTHL,* pp. 407, 412, 417).

an overshadowing bluff, with a steamboat—showing that my earliest dread made the strongest impression on me (running steadily down into the deep shadows of Selma Bluffs & head of Hat Island.

Dr. Riggs, Dentist, Cheney Building, Wed. 10.

Chi[na] Boy $25 per an.[43]

Dean Sage.

Gen. Grant.

Am. Consul Abroad.[44] (Lee & Shepard)

Tiffany & Co.

Lan[n]igan's World Fables
Ahkoond of Swat.

Georgie on the Cars, Courant Mch 8.[45]
Teaching boy about Washn (Reader)[46]
Visits, Friday.

Gen. Grant, 2 Wall st. noon.[47]

---

[43] Perhaps one of the supporters of the Hartford Chinese Educational Mission, which had foundered the year before, now was soliciting contributions for a more modest scholarship program.

[44] Luigi Monti converted his experiences as United States consul at Palermo, Sicily, from 1861 to 1873, into a fictionalized account of the difficulties besetting such officeholders in *Adventures of a Consul Abroad* (Boston: Lee and Shepard, 1878), written under the pseudonym "Samuel Sampleton."

[45] The 8 March 1882 issue of the Hartford *Courant* contained a brief sketch with this title, reprinted from the Boston *Transcript*. Five-year-old Georgie embarrasses his mother by loudly repeating her comments about a red-nosed, bald-headed elderly man who is seated nearby. Clemens may have considered including the piece in *Mark Twain's Library of Humor*.

[46] A shortened version of "The Artless Prattle of Childhood" by Robert J. Burdette would be published in *Mark Twain's Library of Humor* as "The Simple Story of G. Washington." Burdette's sketch had appeared in *The Rise and Fall of the Mustache and Other "Hawk-Eyetems"* (Burlington, Iowa: Burlington Publishing Co., 1877).

[47] Clemens hoped to prevent President Arthur from replacing William Dean Howells' father as United States consul at Toronto. On Friday, 10 March, in New York, Clemens saw Grant, who a few days later assured Clemens that William Cooper Howells would be allowed to retain his post (see *MTHL*, pp. 393–394).

Maitland Armstrong, 10 A.M.[48]
Gilder (on the way), 9.30 A.M.[49]
Russell Sage & Dean, <3.30> 1 P.M.[50]

Telegraph Gen. Grant.
" Armstrong.
" Webster (Saturday.)[51]
" <Dean Sage?>

Telephone Bissell take $5000 Am Bk.[52]

Tinct. of Myrrh. ½ doz a day[53]

Stopping at H B[54] [#]

---

48 David Maitland Armstrong had a studio in New York City. He specialized in designing and constructing stained glass windows.

49 Richard Watson Gilder, editor-in-chief of the *Century*, had written to Clemens on 2 March 1882 reminding him that "you promised or half-promised Mr. Roswell Smith [president of the Century Company] you would help us in our Crusade for Copyright" and asking if Clemens would "reel something off—no matter how short—in time for the number we are now making up." Clemens did not comply with Gilder's request in 1882.

50 Multi-millionaire Wall Street speculator Russell Sage was distantly related to the much younger Dean Sage, an executive in a lumber manufacturing firm (H. W. Sage & Company) established by Dean's father. During 1882 Dean Sage operated as Clemens' broker in New York City. He had been trying to set a date for a dinner at which Clemens and Russell Sage could meet (Dean Sage to SLC, 2 March 1882); on 7 March he wrote Clemens that he had "just seen Mr Sage & fixed the date of the banquet for *Friday afternoon* the 10th at 3.15 at Room 4 Beaver St Delmonico's. . . . Now dont disappoint me as Russell is dying to meet you."

51 Clemens probably intended to notify Charles L. Webster that he would visit his house in New York City on 11 March. Jane Lampton Clemens and Pamela Moffett were staying with the Websters for a few days before proceeding on to Hartford for a visit.

52 On 3 March 1882 George P. Bissell & Company, bankers in Hartford, had sent Clemens an investment prospectus describing the American Bank Note Company of New York, "*a consolidation of all the leading Engraving Companies*" which "has virtually a monopoly of the business of engraving and printing" for banks, railroads, insurance companies, and world governments. "It prints all the stamps used by the United States," the brochure claimed.

53 Myrrh in solution was prescribed as an astringent for sore gums and as an expectorant for pulmonary congestion.

54 Clemens arrived in New York City on Thursday, March 9, and stayed at the Hotel Brunswick.

Forgot to buy accident ticket, but no matter now.

Golden Arm.
Incorporated Company of Mean Men.

Mark "top" of glass.—also "face toward hall."

Pasage Hotel, Havana.

Telegraph Hotel "

Dr. Burgess, No 2 Tacon.

Joshua Davidson[55]
Mrs. Lyn Linton

Kate Beaumont.[56]
A History of the Florentine Commonwealth—A. Trollope.[57]

The Ghost on the Aleck Scott[58] (it was a rat climbing the whistle rope.)

The ghosts that used to flock in the pilot house, nights, in their shrouds, from the old Caving-in Graveyard (in Kaskaskia Bend?) & chatter with their teeth about the wrong & insult being done them.

Fisher's old father, whom the wolves chased so swiftly that they *left no tracks!*
He brought home a cow's skull to sit on (called it buffalo) & said he had grown so used to it among the Indians that he couldn't sit comfortably anywhere else. Bully old liar. [#]

---

[55] Clemens purchased a copy of Mrs. Elizabeth Lynn Linton's *The True History of Joshua Davidson, Communist* (Philadelphia: J. B. Lippincott & Co., 1873) soon after he made this memorandum (A1911, item 290b).

[56] James R. Osgood and Company had published John William De Forest's novel about Reconstruction life and customs in South Carolina in 1872 after its serialization in the *Atlantic Monthly* the previous year.

[57] Thomas Adolphus Trollope, Anthony's older brother who settled in Florence in 1843, had written *A History of the Commonwealth of Florence, from the Earliest Independence of the Commune to the Fall of the Republic in 1531*, 4 vols. (London: Chapman and Hall, 1865).

[58] The *Aleck Scott* was built in Saint Louis in 1848 and still was on the river when Clemens became a pilot. Isaiah Sellers piloted this steamboat for many years.

A novel ought to be written wherein the hero, (a Mason,) is saved from perils by the usual signs, & saved from death by that sign which is made with the hands.[59]

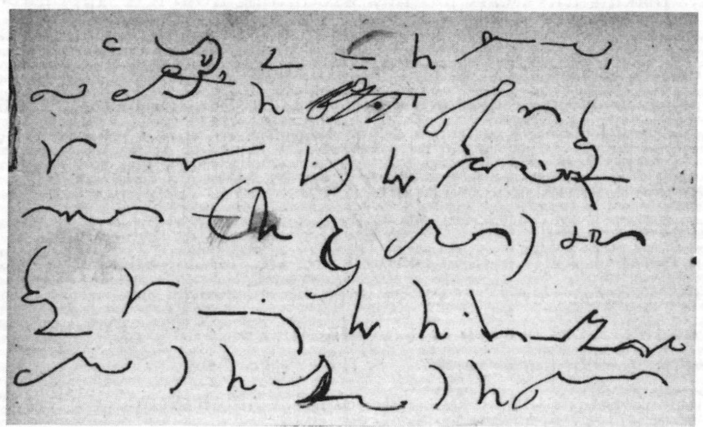

[*The shorthand reads:* A novel ought to be written in which the hero is saved from dire peril by masonic signs (the usual ones) & is saved from death by the cxtraordinary one of the lifting of the hands.]

Stranger instructed to wear white handkerchief on left arm—some other stranger, coming by the same train, had been instructed to display the same sign—they get *mixed*—& then comes the comedy of errors.

In the Brush. by Pierson[60]

That poor fellow at Tuttleville who entertained me on a long walk with enthusiastic talk about his wife, whom he was on his way to the

---

[59] Clemens' negotiations with Roswell Phelps in mid-March aroused his curiosity about stenography: he wrote out this entry in shorthand following the longhand version. Phelps himself may have instructed Clemens briefly when he visited his future employer on 15 March. Nine pages of additional shorthand practice from this period are in the Mark Twain Papers (DV 156).

[60] The Reverend Hamilton W. Pierson's memoirs might have seemed promising for descriptions of the backwoods, but there is no evidence that Clemens acquired a copy of *In the Brush; or, Old-Time Social, Political, and Religious Life in the Southwest* (New York: D. Appleton and Co., 1881).

next village to see, & who had been absent a week, that I had the strongest desire to look upon a woman who could inspire such worship. And to my deep pain & astonishment I found that he was *always* making this weary journey & returning from it disappointed & marveling. His wife had been dead <[1]>*23 years*. On her return from a week's absence, young & beautiful, the stage went over a precipice—& when he arrived, uninformed, expecting to take her in his arms, they <s> lifted a sheet & showed him her corpse.[61]

Tell, now, in full, the events preceding & following the Pennsylvania's explosion:[62] the fight with Brown; the boat steaming down Bend of 103[63] with nobody at the wheel—the white-aproned servants & passengers on deck applauding the fight—the prophetic talk on the levee between Henry & me that night in N.O. before Pa. sailed on her fatal voyage.[64]

McManus (Jimmy) robbed me of brass watch chain, & <robbed> $20—& robbed old Calhoun of underclothes.[65]

Leave out that wonderful dream.[66] [#]

---

[61] This story became the subject of "The Californian's Tale," finally written during January 1893 and published that year by the Authors Club of New York in *Liber Scriptorum*. In Notebook 4 (volume 1, p. 77) Clemens identified the deranged miner as "Boden."

[62] The phrasing of this entry suggests that in planning his "river book" Mark Twain initially contemplated extending the narrative of his piloting experiences in "Old Times on the Mississippi."

[63] Here Albert Bigelow Paine interjected a comment: "Bixby gives it as Eagle Bend, probably it was." In chapter 19 of *Life on the Mississippi* Mark Twain located his fight with the senior pilot of the *Pennsylvania* in Eagle Bend.

[64] The sidewheeler *Pennsylvania* exploded and burned at Ship Island, near Helena, Arkansas, on 13 June 1858. Twenty lives, including Henry Clemens', were lost. The pilot with whom Clemens had fought, William Brown of Saint Louis, was killed instantly by the explosion.

[65] Possibly Clemens was robbed of some money and valuables donated by fellow boatmen for relief of the *Pennsylvania* explosion victims. In "Villagers of 1840–3" (written in 1897), Clemens recalled that his friend Bart Bowen, a river pilot and captain, "Gave $20, time of Pennsylvania disaster. Young McManus got it" (*HH&T*, p. 32). "Old Calhoun" is not mentioned in that manuscript, however.

[66] Many years afterward—in an Autobiographical Dictation on 13 January 1906—Mark Twain recorded his dream of seeing Henry Clemens' corpse in a metal casket with a bouquet of white roses on his breast. The premonitory vision had to

The bear that Bill Hood[67] & I released from his chain "for fun" & he took possession of the boat.

Whenever want to lug in an incident, be *reminded* of it by passing Hat Island or some other locality.

Jim Kane the athlete who used to bring young jackasses aboard under his arms. He broke the jaw of a giant roustabout with his fist.

Kant's Critique of Pure Reason—Max Müller's translation. Macmillan, N.Y.[68]

Boston Sat. Morn. Club 5 Otis Place, 10 to 11 AM Apl. 15.[69]

Major Jones's Courtship.[70]

Cut the map of the Mississippi into 20 pieces (full page size) & interleave it along through the book, beginning at St Louis & going down section by section to N.O.[71] [#]

---

be omitted from *Life on the Mississippi* "because I never wanted my mother to know about that dream" (*MTA*, 1:307).

[67] In *Life on the Mississippi* Hood is identified as a cub pilot who served his apprenticeship under Ben Thornburgh, and with whom Clemens quarreled daily. "A heedless, reckless creature he was, and always in hot water, always in mischief" (chapter 49). While the two were pilots on the steamboat *Arago* J. W. Hood and Clemens jointly signed a burlesque "Pilot's Memoranda," which appeared in the Saint Louis *Missouri Republican* (see Allan Bates, "Sam Clemens, Pilot-Humorist of a Tramp Steamboat," *American Literature* 39 [March 1967]: 102–109).

[68] F. Max Müller's two-volume translation of *Critique of Pure Reason* was issued in 1881.

[69] Mark Twain was writing "a paper which I am to read before a club of young girls in Boston next Saturday, entitled 'Mental Telegraphy'" (SLC to Rutherford B. Hayes, 10 April 1882, Hayes Memorial Library, Fremont, Ohio). On 14 April he traveled to Boston to meet Howells, Osgood, and Aldrich, all of whom were to be guests at the April 15 meeting of the Saturday Morning Club of Boston.

[70] The author of these Georgian dialect sketches, William Tappan Thompson, died on 24 March 1882; perhaps his death notices reminded Mark Twain that *Major Jones's Courtship* (1844) might contain material suitable for *Mark Twain's Library of Humor*. One of Thompson's humorous letters—"Christmas in Pineville" —is in Mark Twain's collection.

[71] Clemens wrote to the office of the secretary of war on 6 April 1882, requesting a map of the Mississippi River. On 11 April the office of the chief of engineers of the United States Army replied, stating that "a copy of Map of the Alluvial

Going down, use the little packets all the way, & stop somewhere every day. At

Cape Girardeau & see Burroughs[72] under secresy.
(But run up to Hannibal, first, incog.)[73]
(See John Hamilton[74]—also, at Quincy, Wales Mc)[75]

Stop at Cairo.
Hickman or
Columbus.
New Madrid (1 hour). & ask about the old feuds.[76]
Memphis a day. Yellow fever.[77]

Basin of the Mississippi River, and 16 sheets of the new Map of the Mississippi River, have been sent to you by to-day's mail." Many years later Clemens referred to "the great War Department map of the Mississippi," which was "a yard wide and thirty-six feet long" (SLC to David R. Francis, 1903[?], newspaper clipping in MTP). *Life on the Mississippi* contains no such map, however.

[72] Jacob H. Burrough had lived with Clemens during one of the periods when Clemens worked in Saint Louis as a youth (see Notebook 1 in volume 1, note 45). In a letter to Burrough's son on 15 December 1900, Clemens affirmed that "he & I were comrades & close friends" (Kent Library, Southeast Missouri State College, Cape Girardeau). Later Burrough entered law practice and settled in Cape Girardeau where he was a probate judge until his death in 1883.

[73] Clemens did not visit Hannibal until after his voyage downstream to New Orleans. By that time he was no longer using the pseudonym "C. L. Samuels" which he had used during the first part of his journey.

[74] In 1855 Clemens jotted down an identical reminder about river pilot John Hamilton in his first notebook (in volume 1, p. 37).

[75] McCormick and Clemens had been fellow apprentices in the Hannibal *Courier* printshop. Clemens would later use him as the model for Doangivadam in "No. 44, The Mysterious Stranger," and would recall the joke they played on a minister in his notebooks, autobiography, and other reminiscences (see *HH&T*, pp. 33, 357). Clemens evidently did not meet with McCormick during this trip, but during his 1885 lecture tour with George Washington Cable he wrote to Livy that he had met this "giant printer-cub of 35 years ago" (23 January 1885, *LLMT*, p. 233).

[76] In chapter 26 of *Life on the Mississippi* Mark Twain placed the Darnell-Watson feuds on the Kentucky-Tennessee border across the river from New Madrid, Missouri. Walter Blair discusses Mark Twain's conception of Southern feuds in *Mark Twain & Huck Finn* (Berkeley and Los Angeles: University of California Press, 1960), pp. 225–227. Notebook 21 records Mark Twain's conversation with a pilot about the Darnell-Watson vendetta (pp. 567–569).

[77] Memphis suffered yellow fever epidemics in 1867, 1873, and, most severely, in 1878.

Compromise?[78]
Napoleon.[79]
Helena
Walnut Bend or some other wretched place.
<Compro>
Port Hudson
Lake Prov.
Natchez. (Duels) (Hanging the gamblers)
Baton Rouge
Donaldsonville
N.O.
Go up a bayou with Geo W Cable.

Bixby's boat is the Baton Rouge.

<Make pi>
At Memphis get facts about pilot who stood at wheel & was burned.[80]

Get notable steamer explosions.

Begin with a chapter of my experiences as a *pilot?*[81] [#]

---

[78] In chapter 26 of *Life on the Mississippi* Mark Twain states that the church attended by both the Darnells and Watsons was "at a landing called Compromise. Half the church and half the aisle was in Kentucky, the other half in Tennessee."

[79] Napoleon, Arkansas, was where Clemens first saw newspaper dispatches about the *Pennsylvania* disaster in 1858 (*Life on the Mississippi*, chapters 20, 32). In *Life on the Mississippi* the town provides the pretext for a story about fingerprints and a morgue (chapter 31), but in chapter 32 Mark Twain learns that "there *isn't* any Napoleon any more": the river has destroyed it. Walter Blair has noticed similarities between Napoleon and the fictional Bricksville locale in *Huckleberry Finn* (*Mark Twain & Huck Finn*, pp. 253, 305–306).

[80] It seems likely that Clemens is remembering William C. Youngblood, one of the pilots on the *John J. Roe*. In a 31 August 1906 Autobiographical Dictation Clemens called him "a good pilot" who "fully appreciated the responsibilities of that great position. Once when a passenger boat upon which he was standing a pilot's watch was burned on the Mississippi, he landed the boat and stood to his post at the wheel until everybody was ashore and the entire after part of the boat, including the after part of the pilot-house, was a mass of flame; then he climbed out over the breast-board and escaped with his life, though badly scorched and blistered by the fire."

[81] These musings about his piloting career brought a windfall to Clemens' sister,

Yarns about the great overflow of March '82.[82]

Let pilots tell me all sorts of lies & give me all sorts of taffy, thinking me to be green.

"Harris" is along, as usual.[83]

And I use false name because it is mysterious & stylish.[84]

Attend a colored religious meeting.

Locate Clara's[85] black swearing chambermaid (fat & black) in some Arkansas town & make her good-natured & perfectly overflowing with variegated profanity. Then "Did you think I said dat bad word? No, I said it's de con-demdest hotel, dat's all what I said—I ben converted las' week an' I <don'> doan use dem kine o' words no mo', now." Then let her heave in Scripture & piety <o>honestly, & occasionally forget & hurl in a sounding oath.

Find Ab Grimes.[86] [#]

Pamela Moffett, who was the Clemenses' houseguest from 13 March to 7 April 1882. She related her good fortune to her son on 31 May: "When I was in Hartford, Sam suddenly remembered that he stayed with me [in Saint Louis] all those years that he was learning to be a pilot, whenever he was in port; & that he had never paid any board. He insisted on giving me a thousand dollars. I told him I accepted it as a gift, but not in the way of board."

[82] Massive flooding occurred along the Mississippi River a month before Clemens toured the region.

[83] Harris was the narrator's companion in *A Tramp Abroad* (1880). Clemens finally settled on the names Rogers and Thompson to refer to James R. Osgood and Roswell H. Phelps, the men who accompanied him on his river journey.

[84] Mark Twain confided to Joel Chandler Harris on 2 April that "to escape the interviewers, I shall follow my usual course & use a fictitious name (*C. L. Samuel, of New York.*) I don't know what Osgood's name will be, but he can't use his own" (*Mark Twain to Uncle Remus*, p. 17). The travel address which Howells received on 16 April 1882 differed slightly: "Send a line, addressed to 'S. L. Samuel, Southern Hotel, St. Louis, Mo.' " (*MTHL*, p. 401). Olivia Clemens mailed a letter of 27 April to "Mr. C. L. Samuels/St. Charles Hotel/New Orleans." Mark Twain dropped this subterfuge after he reached New Orleans; on 5 May Livy used his correct name on a letter she sent to him at Saint Louis.

[85] Pamela Moffett, who was visiting the Clemens family in Hartford, reported to her son on 24 March 1882 that "Miss Clara Spaulding arrived yesterday from the south, where she has been travelling for some time."

[86] Absalom C. Grimes had been an Upper Mississippi pilot before the Civil

Mike Fink shooting tin cup off Carpenter's head.[87]

Murrell's Gang, Island 37.[88]

Our trip through Devil's Race Ground (Bill Hood & me.)

Kaolatype.[89]
Small hall chandelier.

Dean Sage
KAOLATYPE.

Gov. Fuller.[90] [#]

War; during 1883 he still was piloting steamboats regularly from Saint Louis. In his memoirs Grimes claims to have belonged to the same Confederate militia company that Clemens joined in 1861, but in "The Private History of a Campaign that Failed" (1885) Clemens assigns Grimes to another, similar group of local recruits. Grimes's autobiography was edited by M. M. Quaife and published as *Absalom Grimes: Confederate Mail Runner* (New Haven: Yale University Press, 1926).

[87] Fink missed the cup of whiskey atop his friend Carpenter's head and killed him instead; subsequently another keelboatman avenged Carpenter by murdering Fink. Thirteen versions of the fatal contest and Fink's death, selected from among the "more than a hundred accounts . . . which appeared in print between 1823 and 1955," are published in *Half Horse Half Alligator: The Growth of the Mike Fink Legend*, ed. Walter Blair and Franklin J. Meine (Chicago: University of Chicago Press, 1956), pp. 257–258, 260–277. A working note for *Huckleberry Finn* also recalls the shooting match (Bernard DeVoto, *Mark Twain at Work* [Cambridge: Harvard University Press, 1942], p. 65).

[88] The desperado John A. Murrell (1804?–1844) led a gang of river pirates and highway robbers in the Old Southwest. Murrell's outlaw band was the presumed source of the twelve-thousand-dollar treasure discovered by Injun Joe and his companion in the haunted house in chapter 26 of *Tom Sawyer*. Mark Twain chronicled a few of Murrell's cold-blooded operations in *Life on the Mississippi* (chapter 29).

[89] The following few entries are a list of reminders pertaining to Clemens' brief visit to New York on 17 April, the eve of his departure for Saint Louis. Clemens had planned to start from New York with Osgood early in the evening of 17 April (*MTLP*, p. 155), but an invitation from journalist William Mackay Laffan to attend a farewell dinner at the Union League Club on that date caused Clemens and Osgood to postpone the departure until the morning of 18 April (Laffan to SLC, 12 [April] 1882).

[90] Clemens' friendly business relationship with Frank Fuller had lapsed following the "steam-generator" venture of 1877 (see Notebook 13, p. 12) which had resulted in a loss to Clemens of five thousand dollars. On 23 March 1882 Fuller renewed the association, referring ruefully to the "harm so innocently wrought upon the

Abbott H. Thayer[91]

Gilder.

Telegraph Osgood.

Clara's darkey preacher who insisted & repeated that "Platto (Plato) was almost persuaded to be a Christian."

Academy Water Color Exhibition.[92]

Caroline Fox's Memories.[93]
The <Mendellson>Mendelsson Family[94]
Osgood get a Longfellow for Clara's birthday.[95]

<<Po>Terrapin soup>
1 doz raw
1 broiled spring chicken.
1 stuffed crab
<½ bot. Mu>

---

purse of a dear friend" and encouraging Clemens to buy shares in the Indiana, Bloomington & Western Railroad, "a stock not now generally believed in," but which Fuller had been assured "will take a considerable rise very soon." Clemens and Fuller corresponded in April about arrangements for overseeing Clemens' one hundred shares while he traveled.

91 Figure, landscape, and animal painter Abbott Henderson Thayer had been president of the Society of American Artists in New York since his return from Paris in 1879. Thayer had been selected by the *Century* to do a portrait of Mark Twain for the September issue (see note 40).

92 The American Water-Color Society held its fifteenth annual exhibition at the National Academy of Design in New York from 28 January until 25 February 1882. Clemens is not known to have been in New York while the exhibition was in progress.

93 The diaries and letters of Caroline Fox, recently published as *Memories of Old Friends . . . from 1835–1871*, ed. Horace N. Pym (Philadelphia: J. B. Lippincott & Co., 1882) contained her reminiscences about Carlyle, Mill, Coleridge, Wordsworth, and other prominent English authors.

94 Clemens' library included a copy of Sebastian Hensel's *The Mendelssohn Family (1729–1847) from Letters and Journals*, 2 vols. (New York: Harper & Brothers, 1882) (A1911, item 234).

95 Clara Clemens would be eight years old on June 8. Newspapers and magazines were eulogizing Longfellow, who had died on 24 March 1882. Boston publishers Houghton, Mifflin and Company published a one-volume edition of *The Poetical Works of Henry Wadsworth Longfellow* in 1882.

Potatoes hashed with cream
Sliced cucumbers, French dressing
½ bot. Mumm's extra dry.
1 bot. pale ale.
<H>[96]

Offer services to country editor in Arkansas—ask him $100 an hour—services declined.

Gillette ask Chas W Butler about Mrs. Bruner's play—"A Mad World."[97]

John's Restaurant Cor. Canal & [*blank*] board & lodge both.[98]

Man who ate a synapism.

Snobs (Routledges) waiting to glimpse the Prince of Wales. We said we wouldn't wait so long even to <Gen.> President Grant, after having seen him once. They said "Of corse not" (he being only a President) They had seen P. of W. 50 times. The world *is* full of snobs.

Flush Times on the Mississippi.[99] [#]

---

[96] The following shorthand notes in Clemens' hand have not been deciphered.

[97] Jane W. Bruner had known Clemens in California. On 29 March 1882 she wrote to ask him "to reach out a helping hand to an old friend struggling over the hard road a kind fate made easy for you" by attending the New Haven preview of her play *A Mad World* and to "use your gifted pen in saying a few kind things." Clemens wished to consult William Gillette because Jane Bruner's letter mentioned that Charles W. Butler, an actor currently appearing in Gillette's *The Professor*, had read her play with some interest. Although Clemens would meet briefly with Mrs. Bruner, he did not see *A Mad World*, pleading a bad cold. She then wrote him on 7 April, sending a copy of the play and soliciting his opinion: "Even if it is unfavorable—I want to know my fate, & get back to my children."

[98] Clemens stayed at the St. Charles Hotel in New Orleans, but he attended a dinner at John Strenna's popular restaurant.

[99] Mark Twain may have read Joseph G. Baldwin's volume of humorous sketches, *The Flush Times of Alabama and Mississippi* (1853), for either *Life on the Mississippi* or *Mark Twain's Library of Humor*.

War Diary of Gen. Geo. H. Gordon.[100]

Gen Dick Taylor's book.[101]

Autobiog of a Plumber

The bell rings in the Todt Gallerie & turns <to> the watchman's hair grey.[102]

He's an anteek, *ain't* he?

Put in Jehovah Gap.[103]

"Set down! I'll kill the first — — — that stirs!—Now—you go—now you—[104]

Millett's[105] fine story of the two men in the graveyard, searching, the one for the grave of his friend, the other for that of his enemy.

26th Apl 11 AM[106]

46⅝ + 7⅜ (large)

---

[100] Osgood probably told Clemens about General George Henry Gordon's *A War Diary of Events in the War of the Great Rebellion, 1863–1865* (Boston: James R. Osgood and Co., 1882).

[101] General Richard Taylor's *Destruction and Reconstruction: Personal Experiences of the Late War* (New York: D. Appleton and Co., 1879).

[102] The climax of "A Dying Man's Confession" in chapter 31 of *Life on the Mississippi* is the tale about the ringing of an alarm bell in a Bavarian morgue by a presumed corpse.

[103] See Notebook 19, note 75.

[104] This second reference (see p. 448) to an incident that occurred in Virginia City, Nevada, also resembles an allusion Clemens probably made during this same period: "When Aleck Scott blew up, mate stood with pistol, over life-boat" (*A1911*, item 427).

[105] Artist and journalist Frank D. Millet was living in New York City during most of 1881 and 1882. Clemens' entry on page 463 of this notebook indicates that he asked his friend's advice regarding some details of the redecoration of the Hartford house.

[106] Clemens was in Vicksburg, Mississippi, during the morning of 26 April 1882. Since this entry is in pencil, and all of those surrounding it are in ink, it seems to belong with notes which Clemens made while on the river. Perhaps he is noting the departure time for the *Charles Morgan*, which he boarded at Vicksburg for New Orleans.

This is *flush*—does not include beading, moulding or anything.

The two end spaces are 7⅜ square.

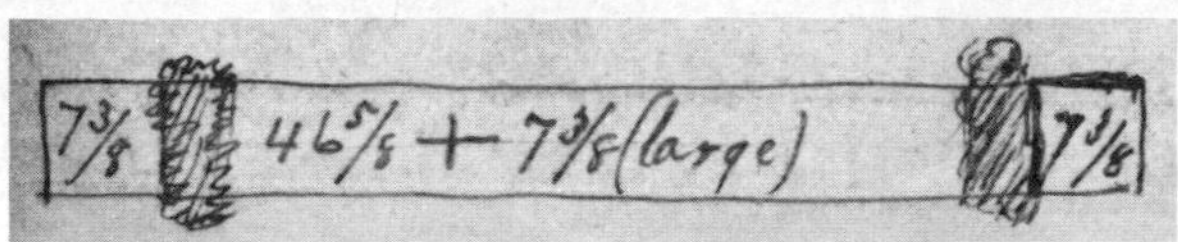

This is a long black walnut *frame*; & tiles can be inserted as in a picture—in fact can be framed & set *within* this frame.

Dark green (like seated musical Jap) for long space; & light olive green for the 2 squares. This is Millett's judgment.

John's, <cor>restaurant, cor Canal & Dryades sts.

Huxley's Hume[107]

"News from Taxidermist Johnson report &c." She thought it was the man's *name*—so she named her child Taxidermist Jones.

She said it was very teching.

Mistopher (Mr.)

Get $200 at hotel in N.Y.

Buy several flasks.

Ask W. why he is going to need money meantime.[108]

Bring raft of prepaid envelops[109] from the old store room.

Send Jno Russell Young a telegram Tuesday Apl 25.[110] [#]

---

[107] Thomas Henry Huxley's *Hume* (1878) was available in an edition published by Harper & Brothers in 1879.

[108] This question had been resolved by 17 April 1882, when Clemens wrote Webster: "I hope you wont run out of money while I am gone but if you should, apply to Mrs. Clemens and she will furnish it" (TS in MTP).

[109] Five of Clemens' eleven letters to Livy during his journey were mailed in prepaid envelopes with a printed Hartford return address.

[110] Young married Julia E. Coleman on April 25, 1882, in Hartford. Clemens wired from Arkansas City: "I send a thousand congratulations & add to them as many regrets that I can not be present."

<Take writing-pads
& env
& cards ditto.>

<Put away the Library of Humor books.>

Cigars & tobacco.

Lorne whisky.

from the *Liar*[111]

When clothes did not come from Bdgpt. ordered up my polyglot to do the swearing. He was hired for 5 years at high wages—his peculiar duty not named in the writing. At end of 2 yrs a minister converted him. I sued the minister for damages. Question of jurisdiction—local court, US Court, or Ecclesiastical—could take my choice. Said I would split the difference & have a military court. I should have won, of course. But then they forced me into a U.S. Court, without a jury. I would have been all right, but *judge* was converted, week before. He decided agst me *& raised the man's wages.*

They put in the "Sir"—Northerners don't.

Jessee James the Missourian[112]

JRO (hotel car)

Beck Jolly[113] [#]

---

[111] The entry was written in ink at the beginning of Clemens' journey; its heading ("from the *Liar*") was inserted later in pencil. *Life on the Mississippi* contains a number of yarn-spinning characters, but none of them introduces this scheme.

[112] James had been killed by a member of his own band at Saint Joseph, Missouri, on 3 April 1882.

[113] Sobieski ("Beck") Jolly piloted the *John J. Roe* when Clemens began his apprenticeship on the river. When Clemens visited the river in 1882 Jolly was living in Saint Louis and was captain of the Anchor Line steamer *William P. Halliday*. In a 30 July 1906 Autobiographical Dictation Mark Twain recalled that as a young man "Jolly was very handsome, very graceful, very intelligent, companionable —a fine character—and he had the manners of a duke."

Saml. Pepper—[114]
3016 Lucas ave
(Mrs. Essie Goodwin[115]

Tom Moore,
Poydras & Tchoupitoulas.[116]

Southern Hotel—Johnson drew bowl of water—then asked waiter to bring him some water to wash this water." (with).[117]

Phila man pronounced car *corr*; & carpet corpet. *stort* for start.

E[ss]ie Pepper[118] spotted me on train & asked if I knew her. I said sit down & let me look at you. I named her street correctly.

Lawrence Barrett[119] <knew us>stumbled on us. [#]

---

[114] Samuel Pepper was once a steamboat clerk, probably on the *John J. Roe,* whose captain, Mark Leavenworth, was his brother-in-law. Later Pepper changed his occupation: on 23 April 1867, shortly before the *Quaker City* sailed from New York City, Clemens advised Charles Warren Stoddard to address him "*care of Samuel Pepper of Gaylord & Leavenworth, Bankers, St. Louis, Mo.,*" because "I mean to have my letters forwarded to Europe" (TS in MTP).

[115] Presumably this is the former Essie Pepper—see note 118.

[116] John T. Moore, Jr. & Company, a wholesale grocery firm, was located at 37–39 Tchoupitoulas Street in New Orleans. On 4 May 1882 Clemens wrote to Livy: "I hunted up Tom Moore, who used to be mud clerk on the John J Roe when I was cub. He is short, & unwieldy with flesh, is a rich & respected burgher, & looks it. Good fellow is Tom; am going to his house to see his wife & six children, tomorrow."

[117] Mark Twain stayed at the Southern Hotel in Saint Louis. He is again experimenting with a fictitious name for one of his companions; in chapter 22 of *Life on the Mississippi,* where "Rogers" comments on the sediment in the city water supply, Mark Twain lists other fictional names he considered using.

[118] Clemens remembered Samuel Pepper's daughter from his years as a river pilot, when Pepper and his wife and Essie resided on Chestnut Street near the home of William Moffett's family, with whom Clemens stayed when he was in Saint Louis (Annie Moffett Webster, "Recollections of the Clemens Family in St. Louis When Sam Was a River Pilot," *The Twainian* 8 [March–April 1949]: 1).

[119] Lawrence Barrett was well known to both Clemens and Osgood. On 19 April 1882 he was performing at the Saint Louis Grand Opera House in a touring production of *Yorick's Love,* Howells' adaptation of *Un drama nuevo* by Manuel Tamayo y Baus. Barrett produced and starred in the play in 1878, revived it repeatedly, and included it in his troupe's repertoire for many years. James R. Osgood and Company had issued Barrett's biography of Edwin Forrest in 1881.

Clerk of hotel <as>answered question with—It's all right—I recognized you.[120]

The pretty southern accent.

Lo-oville (Louisville)

The r ignored, South. S. says b'fo' the waw. N.Y.$^{r.}$ says lawr for law.[121]

Southern Hotel,—plain & substantial—one may say *bald,* sterile in decoration—this is better than the tawdry shams the dreadful decorations of the Palmer House.[122]

St Louis death rate 15 & 16.19

Now & then, *look at* Scrapbook.

Map of a Reconnaissance of the Map of the Mis. River—from Cairo, Ill., to N.O. La.—To accompany the Report on that Portion of the 3^{d} Subdivision of the Missis— route to the seaboard made in accordance with act of Congress approved June 23^{d} 1874—by Chas R Suter, Corps of Engineers USA. Get this map.

From Chalk Pt below Columbus to Mo shore, said to be 6 m. None of the great bar showing, now—all water.

Send W. ashore & get preposterous accounts of Thebes, Grand Tower, Cairo, &c.

Sometimes he is drunk—sometimes they give him taffy—sometimes he gives *me* the article. [#]

---

[120] During his second stopover in Saint Louis, on his way up the river to Hannibal, Mark Twain would tell a newspaper reporter that in April he "passed twenty-four hours in the city without any one knowing it outside of one or two friends. Stopped a night here at the Southern, registering as C. L. Samuels, New York. The three of us were prowling under fictitious names, and we remained just as long as we dared. . . . We have been dodging people, making our way by stealth and keeping up a sort of swindle day by day" (Saint Louis *Globe-Democrat,* 13 May 1882).

[121] At the bottom of this entry Albert Bigelow Paine added in pencil: "(No Brooklynite)."

[122] The decorations of the Palmer House in Chicago "make one cry," Mark Twain declared in chapter 22 of *Life on the Mississippi.*

Visit Ste. Genevieve & old Kaskaskia[123] over in bend above Chester, where Miss has cut into Kaskia river & you can descend K river in <tug or> skiff to the old town.

Make my reception by <George> Ed. Gray in pilot house of Gold Dust very rough or sarcastic or something—afterward Len detects voice. Possibly G. recognizes me & "puts up" the rudeness on me. Use the most effective.[124]

The two little boys whom *Len* & I accused of being the late Jesse James & his brother Frank—this talk exposed my voice.

Farris' Landing <bel> below Wolf Island, where I went to sleep at wheel & came near getting a snag.

(Place above Walnut Bend where I nearly ran into a bluff sandbar —steering on a cloud—& Bob Kirkpatrick[125] saved us.)

Handsome, plump young mother with very sweet placid face suckling her baby in cabin.

The dredful music.

Get map of Missis from Jno B Lee & Co 106 Market st St Louis. [#]

---

123 The Kaskaskia River joins the Mississippi at Kaskaskia, Illinois, one of the earliest French settlements in the Mississippi Valley. Floodwaters gradually were destroying the old village site, which was across the river from Sainte Genevieve, Missouri.

124 In *Life on the Mississippi* (chapter 24) Mark Twain called the pilot who supposedly tricked him Rob Styles. This was necessary because the pilots whom Clemens met aboard the *Gold Dust,* Edmund and his brother, Lemuel S. Gray, were no longer suitable subjects for a humorous story. After his river tour Mark Twain had copies of his *Stolen White Elephant* sent to the men, but at the bottom of Edmund Gray's letter of thanks Mark Twain noted: "Just one month later (Aug. 23) <Len>Lem was buried. Died of wounds from explosion of the boilers." The explosion which demolished the *Gold Dust* occurred on 7 August 1882; Edmund Gray escaped serious harm, but his forty-year-old brother received fatal injuries. Chapter 37 of *Life on the Mississippi* gives an account of the disaster.

125 Robert Kirkpatrick piloted on the Lower Mississippi River. On 2 May 1882 the New Orleans *Daily Picayune* reported that this "old partner of Mark Twain, when the latter was a star gazer, arrived in the city yesterday on the Future City."

Mr. Guthrie[126] Monday evening, with Harris[127] &c

Tuesday Eve, dinner with Maj. Burke &c[128]

Wed morning, tug of Mr. Wood—down the river.[129]

Sunday 9.45 meet gentlemen of Art Union.

Sunday church with Cable.[130]

Winan's Chapel
corner First & Dryades[131]

Joel Chandler Harris, Upton<, (Prov>Station, (Province of) Quebec. Telegraph him upon arrival at Hartford. He returns 26th to 30th May.[132] [#]

---

[126] New Orleans attorney James B. Guthrie was the brother-in-law of David Gray, a Clemens family friend in Buffalo. Clemens paid a visit to Guthrie's home on the evening of 1 May, when he listened to "superb piano music by young ladies, & some excellent recitations by (myself) & others, & a song or two" (SLC to OLC, 2 May 1882, *LLMT*, p. 212).

[127] Joel Chandler Harris arrived from Atlanta on Sunday morning, 30 April; he registered at the St. Charles Hotel where Clemens was staying, and they then joined Cable in attending church services. This was Mark Twain's first meeting with the creator of Uncle Remus (New Orleans *Times-Democrat*, 1 May 1882).

[128] "We dine with the editors to-night," Clemens wrote to Livy on 2 May 1882 (*LLMT*, p. 212). Edward A. Burke, managing editor of the New Orleans *Times-Democrat*, hosted a dinner for Clemens and Osgood at John's Restaurant that evening. Several months after Clemens returned from his trip he received a letter from Page M. Baker, an editor of the *Times-Democrat*, which mentioned that "the evening we spent at John's—the good stories over the wine, the music, (in which Cables thin but melodious tenor mingled sweetly with [L. André] Burthe's magnificent barytone) & the flowers that graced the board—remains with me, & I trust with both yourself & Mr. Osgood, a delightful fragrant memory" (26 September 1882).

[129] Clemens changed his mind about this excursion. He wrote Livy on Tuesday, May 2, that on account of the strain of his social engagements, "we . . . pretend to go down to the mouth of the river tomorrow, but shall lie abed & sleep, instead" (*LLMT*, p. 212).

[130] At Prytania Street Presbyterian Church.

[131] Cable wrote this two-line address in ink at the top of a page. Winan's Chapel was an African Methodist Episcopal church in New Orleans (see Notebook 21, p. 552).

[132] Harris' father-in-law, Pierre LaRose, had a farm near Saint-Ephrem d'Upton in the province of Quebec.

Prevalence of poker in N.O. clubs.

It's as easy as killing your father whom you take for a burglar. It is as hard to hit as a burglar.—*Any*body can hit a relative, but a Gatling gun won't get a burglar.

And there is the Oldest Pilot,[133] full of strange lies & wordy brag, who is proud to remember how he started <as s> at the bottom round

N.O. is still in the dark ages of independent fire Co's. Nothing paid but a Babcock Co.[134] The town *belongs* politically to the independent organizations.

Used bar[135] & had no trouble with mosquitoes.

Warm, but not warm enough for my summer clothes.

Southerners ignore the r.

Where is it *at?*

What a splendid moon!
Laws bless you, honey you ought to seen dat moon befo' de waw.

People talk only about the war. Other subjects are *started,* but they soon pale & die & the war is taken up.

Bought a horse for $10,000 (Confed. money) & sold him for $800 (greenbacks) & made a heap of money.

$400 for pr boots, $250 for a drink.

Like the flag officer did.[136] [#]

---

[133] Clemens retained ambivalent feelings toward Isaiah Sellers, "the oldest steamboat pilot on the Mississippi River, and the most respected, esteemed and revered" (AD, 10 September 1906; *MTE*, p. 228).

[134] Clemens presumably is referring to a company which used a Babcock Fire Extinguisher. Upon his return to Hartford he requested information about a home model of the "Improved Babcock" (price $40) from the New York agent for the firm (S. F. Hayward to SLC, 9 October 1882).

[135] Mosquito netting.

[136] In chapter 44 of *Life on the Mississippi* Mark Twain cited this as an example of the "infelicities" of Southern grammar.

8 shirts
2 drawers
2 undershirts
2 w^{h} jackets
4 pr. socks.
4 hdkfs.

"I was a-asking the steward <was> where you was a-setting *at.*"

Where you been at?

Pilot house 14 ft square.

"Pretty *hord* to steer"

Lagniappe—any trifle over & above—the baker's dozen.

Make exhaustive picture of pilot Brown[137] & his snarling ways & meannesses.

Left N.O. $5.^{10}$, May 6, reached Natchez (300 m.) at <4.4> 3.40 May 7—$22.^{30.}$ First time I ever went to Natchez inside of 24 hours I believe.

Here they say "I *will*" do so & so, when they mean *shall.*

Negro passed the word Mark Twain—seemed odd he didn't say Mr as I was not acquainted with him.

Julio's picture[138]—Stonewall Jackson is saying Got a match about you

Jim Russell fell dead at the wheel above Memphis with heart disease. Capt on roof—saw boat breaking for shore—shouted & got no answer—ran up & found Jim dead on floor—1869.

In N.O. they always *interrupt*—conversation is impossible. One

---

137 William Brown died in the *Pennsylvania* disaster in 1858.

138 Clemens saw E. B. D. Fabrino Julio's equestrian oil painting, "The Last Meeting of Lee and Jackson," in the Washington Artillery armory building in New Orleans.

soon loses confidence & doesn't dare begin anything, knowing he will be interrupted with an irrelevancy. They like to hear themselves talk, but nobody else.

Big thunderstorm at Natchez, May 7

May 8—Got up at 4 A.M. in a roasting-room—some idiot had closed the transoms & I was over the boilers—& went on watch. Fog—Geo. Ritchie steered the watch out by compass, using his & Bixby's patented chart for the crossings & occasionally blowing the whistle. The chart is a great thing—many pilots use it, now.[139]

At 600 yards distance, the reflection of a tree in the smooth water of an overflowed bank was (or at least *seemed* to be) stronger & blacker than the ghostly tree itself. These faint spectral, shadowy trees, dimly glimpsed through the fog, were very pretty.

The Biblical absurdity of the Almighty's being only 6 days building the universe & then fooling away 25 years building a towhead in the Missississippi. (This one—6.[30] AM, May 8—is Diamond Island towhead—the island is grown up & only the

Towhead means *infant*—an infant island, a growing island—so it is said.

May 8—9. AM.
Vicksburg is now a country town. Instead of coming in *above* the town as we used to do, boats come through a cut-off now which is clear *below* the town. In low water boats can get up only to lower verge of town—there they land.

Delta, La., a few miles from Vicksburg, is left out in the country by this same cut-off. A vast willow bar has attached itself in front & in a few years what was river will be dense forest.

The cut-off turned 70 miles into 35, they say. [#]

---

139 George Ritchie was one of Horace Bixby's pilots on the Anchor Line *City of Baton Rouge* in 1882. He and Bixby had also invented a lamp to use in reading their chart.

Gen. Grant's cut-off didn't work. The other was the preferable place, but the enemy's guns wouldn't let working[140]

There is a cut-off at Eagle Bend (102), now, & boats of course don't run the bend any more.

Below Natchez now & then a reposeful alligator.

Get statistics of width, length & volume of Misspi out of Cyclopedia.

And something about La Salle's trip out of Parkman.[141]

Pilot said some French camped on the hills at Baton Rouge & were massacred by Indians, who stained a mast or stick with their blood & stuck up as a warning to other whites to keep away. Hence the name baton rouge.

Pilot house heated by steam—coil of pipes in middle.

Make an imaginary yarn <of> about a pilot struck dead at the wheel by lightning.

Pilot heroisms on burning steamers.

Let artist make picture of boat at country landing with electric light glaring on trees & white houses.[142]

It is said that pilots who suggested things to the M. River Commission were PAID OFF.

The R. C. have cut off the timber for 50 yards back, along long stretches of shore; & they propose<d> to slope that bank<s>

---

[140] During his siege of Vicksburg General Grant tried repeatedly to cut canals through the west bank of the Mississippi to create a new river channel. These efforts were futile. Then, in a crucial maneuver on 30 April 1863, Grant attempted to cross the river to the Vicksburg side at Grand Gulf, Mississippi, was repulsed by unrelenting enemy gunfire, but finally succeeded in landing unopposed further south at Bruinsburg.

[141] In chapter 2 of *Life on the Mississippi* Mark Twain acknowledges Francis Parkman's *La Salle and the Discovery of the Great West* (1879) as a source and quotes extensively from Parkman's "fascinating narrative."

[142] Such a drawing appears on page 260 of the first edition of *Life on the Mississippi*.

down to dead low water mark & put rocks & things on the slope to prevent washing. That looks kind of sensible.

Saw immense tree fall in, below Pilcher's Point—splashed yellow water up 40 ft & soon sank.

Big thunderstorm between Lake Providence & Pilcher's May 8.

The snag boats & beacons are a grand good thing—but *I* think (says pilot) the R. C. will fool away their money for nothing trying to tame & order this channel.[143]

Geo Ritchie was blown up on a boat above Memphis—blown into river from pilot wheel & disabled—clung to cotton bale in very cold water with his teeth <till> & floated till rescued nearly exhausted, by deck hands on piece of wreck who tore open the bale & put him in it & warmed the life back into him, & so got him to Memphis. He will never get entirely over the effects.

Bixby was blown up in Madrid bend & his partner lost.[144]

Dick Kennett blown up near Memphis & killed. <(Memphis battle?) No>

All the axidents, nearly, happen near Memphis & that generous town is heavily taxed.

The whistle-treadle is new, & the tube to hear the engine bells. [#]

[143] Mark Twain was essentially noncommittal in 1882 when newspaper reporters pressed him for his opinion about the recommendations of the Mississippi River Commission, but in an Autobiographical Dictation of 7 September 1907 he would castigate "the Mississippi Improvement conspirators, who for thirty years have been annually sucking the blood of the Treasury and spending it in fantastic attempts to ameliorate the condition of that useless river—apparently that, really to feed the Republican vote out there. These efforts have never improved the river, for the reason that no effort of man can do that" (*MTE*, p. 18).

[144] On its first voyage from New Orleans to Saint Louis on February 4, 1858, the steamer *Colonel Crossman*, with Bixby as one of its pilots, blew a boiler near New Madrid, Missouri. Bixby and the captain were saved, but the other pilot and thirteen officers and passengers died (New Orleans *Picayune*, 6 February 1858; Saint Louis *Republican*, 7 February 1858; William M. Lytle, *Merchant Steam Vessels of the United States 1807–1868* [Mystic, Conn.: Steamship Historical Society of America, 1952], p. 252). Clemens was not piloting with Bixby at this time.

A levee is 6 ft high & sometimes 18.

Pilot—Look at you little dam book.

These people have spent $11,000,000 since the war rebuilding & repairing the destroyed levees

Henry Eli—str. Sultan,[145] burned above Ste. Genevieve. He stuck to his post till he got her nose to the bank, then went overboard, the fire shutting him off, forward—got ashore frozen, & died after a few minutes.

Early In the war, when bullets flying, pilots used to hold up a spittoon or a cane-seat chair to protect their heads—& hide behind a bit of canvass or lie down on floor.

One in white linen held spittoon to his head, with the breaking glass rattling around him the contents spilt on his clothes & when he saw it he said "O God, I'm shot["] & fainted.

Dad Dunham[146] & the pet bear.

Consound him, he's got a memory like a memorandum book.

The histories of Will Bowen,[147] Sam,[148] & Capt. M^c^Cune[149] &

---

145 Twenty-three people were killed when the sidewheel steamer *Sultan* was destroyed by fire on 2 April 1858 at Sainte Genevieve, Missouri (Lytle, *Merchant Steam Vessels*, pp. 180, 247). Clemens was serving on the *Pennsylvania* at the time.

146 Second mate of the *Gold Dust*.

147 Will Bowen's wife died in 1873; he remarried in 1876 and about 1880 he moved to Texas to promote the insurance agency of Bowen & Andrews. He had been a childhood friend of Clemens, and the two men corresponded occasionally until Will's death in 1893 (see *HH&T*, p. 346).

148 Sam Bowen, Will's brother, was one of the youths whom Clemens joined in his brief soldiering expedition at the beginning of the Civil War. Sam Bowen had hastily married after discovering that his sweetheart's father had bequeathed a fortune to her as "Mrs. Sam Bowen." Her family successfully contested the will by proving that the marriage postdated the bequest. Clemens retells the story, with variations, in chapter 49 of *Life on the Mississippi* and in his Autobiographical Dictation of 9 March 1906 (*MTA*, 2:185–186; see also *HH&T*, pp. 32, 347). Bowen died of yellow fever in 1878 and was buried at the head of an island in the Mississippi.

149 During Clemens' tenure as a pilot on the river John S. McCune (1809–

Mrs. <B[a]>B.[150] make human life appear a grisly & hideous sarcasm.

Prodigious storm of rain, hail & wind opposite Buck Island in afternoon of May 9. It seemed the pilot house was bound to be blown away, so I went down in the hold to see what time it was. (Kept up till midnight).

Don't think our storms are quite so heavy

All through this overflow the beacons have been pretty faithfully kept alight—& many of the standards stood in water from 2 to 4 ft deep & in woods.

"See, right through there where it went *at*."

They say "evening," meaning afternoon.

At the Devil's Elbow, above Memphis, the river now runs several miles up stream where it used to run down. (This is at Fogleman's chute—which is ½ mile wide now, & is the channel, but in my time a fallen tree would almost bridge it.

Aged Lying Pilot—I've seen the river so low that it was so dusty you had to wear a veil at the wheel—dust flying from the sand-bars, you know."

The man who is mentioned in a book, or who is interviewed, always curses the man who did it—& the man who *isn't* mentioned does the same. Why is this thus?

The Apparitions & Miracles at Knock.[151] New Yk P. J. Kenedy &

1874) was president of the Saint Louis & Keokuk Packet Line, which he had founded in 1842. The unhappy portion of his history is not known.

150 Clemens could be referring to any one of five women named Bowen or Bixby. Will Bowen's first wife died in 1873; he married again in 1876. No further details are available about Sam Bowen's disinherited bride. Bixby married for the first time in 1860; after this wife died in 1867 he remarried the next year.

151 The book to which Clemens refers evidently was an American reprint of either John MacPhilpin's *The Apparitions and Miracles at Knock* (Dublin: Gill & Son, 1880) or *The Apparition at Knock . . . by Sister Mary Francis Clare* (London: Burns & Oates; Dublin: M. H. Gill & Son, 1880). The "apparition" was a vision

Co 5 Barclay st Compare one of these with a miracle from the Bible —& make a devout old Presbyterian fool contend that the ancient miracle proves the modern one

May 11

Beautiful precipitous & broken bluffs from Cape G up, richly clothed in lavish greenery.

Left Memphis 10 AM May 10. Arrived Cairo 7. AM May 11—the Cape at noon. Devil's Tea Table 2.$^{45.}$

Ring in Jehovah Gap.

Grand Tower & Devil's Bake-Oven at 3.$^{45.}$

At 5 PM got to where Hat Island *was*. It is now gone, every vestige of it.

Goose Island, at the Graveyard, below Commerce, is all gone but a piece about big enough for <a> dinner. (Lot of buzzards there on wreck of "Grand Tower" fishing for drowned men, etc.

Graveyard is all grown up.

Man living above Jessup timber <at> behind Hat Island says 29 steamboats have been lost in sight of his house.

Nicholson, opp. Laclede Hotel—6th bet. Ches^{t} & Market.[152]

---

of the Virgin Mary alleged to have been seen on 21 August 1879 in the parish chapel at Knock, a small village in County Mayo, Ireland. In 1880 two other visions—Saints Joseph and John—were reported at Knock; pilgrims began to visit the village, and several hundred miraculous cures were claimed within a year. Mary Francis Cusack, who adopted the name of her convent order (Clare) as a pseudonym, then published *Three Visits to Knock, with the Medical Certificates of Cures and Authentic Account of Different Apparitions* (London: R. Washbourne; Dublin: M. H. Gill & Son, 1882). Clemens' personal library would include his annotated copy of *Three Visits to Knock* (New York: P. J. Kenedy, 1898) which also reprinted, in the same volume, John MacPhilpin's *The Apparitions and Miracles at Knock* (Antenne-Dorrance Collection, Rice Lake, Wis.).

152 The Nicholson grocery in Saint Louis occupied five floors, employed fifty people, and specialized in imported goods (John Thomas Scharf, *History of Saint Louis City and County*, 2 vols. [Philadelphia: Louis H. Everts & Co., 1883], 2:1242).

Get 

Send photographs of the fambley to Bixby.[153]

Capt. Jim O'Neil.[154]
Supt. Anchor Line

May 13, left St Louis in the Gem City.[155] A sister of Writer Levering[156] on board with husband. She has grown sons (*one*, anyway.)

Mo river comes in <12> 14 m above St L. Was <18> 22 or 23 above when I first saw it. Will cut through & come in 2 miles lower within 5 yrs. [#]

---

[153] On 21 September 1882 Horace Bixby wrote to Clemens from the *City of Baton Rouge* at Saint Louis: "I am a thousand times obliged to you for your Elegant Photo and those of your Children which [I] suppose are good but never having seen them am not able to judge but will say *good looking Children* any way and if you can better them send me Photos when you establish the fact."

[154] The "River News" column in the Saint Louis *Post-Dispatch* reported on 12 May 1882: "Mark Twain visited 'Change today in company with his old friend Horace E. Bixby. The meeting between Mr. Clemens and Capt. James O'Neal was cordial in the extreme." Now superintendent of the Anchor Line, O'Neil was the "d–d Fenian" whom Clemens in 1866 had called "a bully boy, if ever there *was* one. . . . The whitest Captain I ever sailed with" (*Mark Twain's Letters to Will Bowen* [Austin: University of Texas, 1941], p. 14). The two men had become friends aboard the *Alonzo Child* in 1860, when Clemens piloted that boat.

[155] Clemens arrived in Saint Louis aboard the *City of Baton Rouge* on 12 May; he intended to depart the same day on the *Bald Eagle*, but the 13 May 1882 Saint Louis *Post-Dispatch* explained that "the Bald Eagle failed to get out for Keokuk last night, and Mark Twain remained in the city and goes North on the Gem City this afternoon."

[156] Evidently this is another name for Clint Levering, the ten-year-old boy who drowned in the Mississippi River on 13 August 1847, according to Mark Twain's "Villagers of 1840–3" (*HH&T*, pp. 36, 357; see also Dixon Wecter's *Sam Clemens of Hannibal* [Boston: Houghton Mifflin Co., 1952], pp. 169–170). In chapter 54 of *Life on the Mississippi* the boy is called Lem Hackett.

Many of the people I once knew in Hannibal are now in heaven. Some, I trust, are in the other place.

Phelps fell backward down pilot house stairs—long & steep.

I couldn't sleep in 46—hog chain making intermittent thumping noise. Moved to 58 but no use. Got up at 2.30 & went on watch below draw of Louisiana bridge[157]

New Orleans College of Languages.[158]

Garth's coachman[159] called for me at 10 instead of 7.30—excused himself by saying "De time is mos' an hour & a half slower in de country en what it is in de town—you'll be in plenty time, boss—sometimes we shoves out early for church, Sunday mornins, & fetches up dah right plum in de middle er de sermon—diffunce in de time—a body can't make no calculations 'bout it."

As to the river: Eccl. VII, 13: "Consider the work of God: for who can make that straight which he hath made crooked?"

Stavely's Landing.[160] [#]

---

157 Louisiana, Missouri, is about twenty-five miles below Hannibal.

158 There is no record of a school with this name. Far up the river from New Orleans, Mark Twain may be reflecting on the cultural intermixture which distinguished that city. In a passage deleted from *Life on the Mississippi* he reproduced four random pages from *Soard's New Orleans Directory for 1882* in order to illustrate the population's "variegated nationalities."

159 The Hannibal *Daily Courier* for 15 May 1882 reported that Clemens registered at the Park Hotel upon his arrival in town on Sunday morning. On Monday, 15 May, he "was driven over the city and viewed the different points of interest" as a guest of John Garth, with whom he dined that day. Clemens wrote to Livy on 17 May: "I spent my nights with John and Helen Garth, three miles from town, in their spacious and beautiful house" (*MTL*, p. 419).

160 John Stavely was a Hannibal saddler who greeted every steamboat despite the fact that his business with each packet was purely imaginary. This conspicuous and pathetic figure appears in chapter 55 of *Life on the Mississippi*. When writing "Villagers of 1840–3" in 1897, however, Mark Twain attributed this behavior to another harness-maker and saddler, James Pitts (*HH&T*, pp. 37, 362). Yet his 1882 recollections actually were correct, for a Hannibal historian, C. P. Greene, mentions that Hannibal gained notoriety among rival river towns as "Stavely's Landing" owing to "John W. Stavely, who came here in 1842" (*A Mirror of Hannibal* [Hannibal: C. P. Greene, 1905], p. 71). The 26 October 1854 issue of

The water above Dubuque is olive green—rich & beautiful & semi-transparent with the sun on it.

Upper Miss the home of superb sunsets.

Railway along river bank pretty much all the way from St Louis from St Paul.

The bluffs all along up above St Paul are exquisitely beautiful. <Some> Where the rough broken, turreted rocks stand up against the sky above the steep verdant slopes, they are inexpressibly rich & beautiful/mellow in color—soft dark browns mingled with dull greens—the very tints to make an artist worship. Remind one of the old houses in Spanish New Orleans.

Let a Rock I man tell what a dead town Davenport is—but with handsome residences.

Get photos of R I bridge & Government works.

Let a man give me some agricultural information about sugar & cotton in the style of How I Edited an Agricultural Paper[161]

Alas! everything was changed in Hannibal—but when I reached third or fourth sts the tears burst forth, for I <sa> recognized the mud. *It*, at least, was the same—the same old mud—the mud that Annie McDonnold got stuck in.

Met G. & McD [102] & many other boyhood friends of ninety yrs

---

the Hannibal *Missouri Courier* refers to wags who were calling the city port Stavely's Landing.

161 This sketch appeared in the July 1870 *Galaxy* and after several reprintings it was collected in *Mark Twain's Sketches, New and Old* (1875). Since the temporary agricultural editor in that piece assumed that turnips grow on trees and pumpkins are berries, the advice about sugar and cotton from this new expert is easily imaginable.

162 Presumably Clemens means John Garth and Jimmie McDaniel, his former Hannibal schoolmates. McDaniel had been a fellow member of the Cadets of Temperance in 1850 (Wecter, *Sam Clemens of Hannibal*, pp. 152–153). Clemens recalled in his 16 March 1906 Autobiographical Dictation that "he was the first human being to whom I ever told a humorous story"—the tale about Jim Wolf and the cats (*MTA*, 2:213).

ago—they told me of this that & the other comrade who passed away during <Washingtons administration> the war with England &c.

The atrocious grammar of Hannibal & the West.

8 yrs ago boats like the Minneapolis[163] used to go into St Paul with 150 people. Man used to say "Got 28 cars of wheat, Captain." "I'll take 2 of 'em."

Now the *Captain* inquires "What you got for us?" "Nuth'n."

The RR has done it.

Used to carry loads of harvesters—now they've invented a self-binder & don't *have* harvesters any more.

May 21 Sunday 7 AM—Arrived per Minneapolis at St Paul & put up at the Metropolitan. Cold as the very devil. Gold-band hat would give us ticket for a carriage & fetch it in 30 minutes if we paid *in advance*—no other way to get a carriage in St. P. Walked to hotel.

Wretched poor family on boat going to the frontier—man on deck with wagon; woman & several little children allowed in cabin for charity's sake. They slept on sofas & floor in glare of lamps & without covering. Must have frozen last night.[164]

Walked all over town—infernally cold.

May 22—Snowed a few flakes. We left at 1.45 east.

Tell some big yarns about blizzards.

On the Northwestern they always run 2 miles beyond each station, then back down 2 miles behind it—thus you pay for <800> 400 miles & they give you 800.

Tell how I once saw a planter gamble a negro away.—Make it

---

[163] Clemens left Hannibal on 17 May aboard the *Minneapolis*, "desperately homesick" and dreading "this hideous trip to St. Paul," as he wrote to Livy later that day from Quincy (*MTL*, p. 419).

[164] In a letter to his wife Clemens told how he and Osgood befriended this pitiable family and succeeded in obtaining meals and blankets for them (20 May 1882, *LLMT*, p. 214).

realistic.—The negro appeals dumbly to the passengers. Or put this tale in another man's mouth.[165]

The Duke of Manchester[166] & party were at St Paul.

This day, *May 23*, three inches of snow fell in Iowa.

Entering Philada, May 24, cut an Italian laborer's foot off. The train stopped, & <hundreds> crowds gathered to gaze. Our tracks ought to be fenced—on the principle that the majority of human beings being fools, the laws ought to be made in the interest of the majority.

Describe a profane & irritable man in a hurry, writing a letter with a stylographic pen that won't go.

Cypress-root razor-strop—weightless.

Sugar is <[r]>made & plowed & planted in this way: (Go on with a confused & absurd statement, & wind up with wishing I had taken notes. Editing Agricultural paper style.)

How I edited a religious <newspaper>Newspaper. (Same style.)

Down south the trees cut down for food for the poor starved cattle & mules—a pathetic spectacle, the stripped bark.

Put in the *sick* comrade, who whines over imaginary ailments,

---

165 Sometime during the 1890s Mark Twain carried through this intention: in "Randall's Jew Story" a young Negro maid, realizing that a slave-trader has just won ownership of her in a poker game, "was crying and sobbing; and she looked timidly from face to face, as if hoping she might in her extremity find a friend and savior there. It was a pitiful thing to see" (*Mark Twain's Fables of Man*, ed. John S. Tuckey [Berkeley, Los Angeles, London: University of California Press, 1972], p. 287). Mark Twain described the same situation in "Newhouse's Jew Story," written in the late 1890s (*Fables of Man*, pp. 279–282).

166 William Drogo Montagu, the seventh duke of Manchester, arrived in Saint Paul on 20 May on his way to Manitoba to purchase large tracts of wilderness from the Canadian Pacific Railroad for a land company of which he was president. He was accompanied by six business associates and his son, Viscount Mandeville. Clemens and the duke both registered at the Metropolitan Hotel, but there is no indication that they met.

forecasts disaster, never enjoys the present, &c. "You wait till you *get* the malaria—that'll be time enough to get in a sweat about it."

Pitch into the idiot who invented the present musical notes <inste>instead of "shape" notes.

Punch's Advice to Persons about to Marry—Don't—was 1000 yrs old when Punch was born.

$10 in Jeff Davis' pocket if he never born.

Burned up the tramp in Hannibal.[167]

See Dickens for a note on Cairo[168]

Throw in incidents from many lands—Cal., the black negro we saw entering Jerusalem, &c

Get La Salle's discovery of Mississippi

Well dressed wenches in Helena. Where got they such clothes in so desolate a place?

No *gentleman* ever swears—<Da> this obscure pup who shouts this from his pulpit or his goody-goody paper sees no immodesty in setting himself above Wellington, Washington &c
Cheap obscure maxim-mongers are loathsome people.

Give the Malley boys a shot, & a good strong one<.>—for they are guilty, no matter what the evidence may fail to prove. They

---

167 The tramp's death in jail and the youth's consequent sense of guilt for having given matches to a drunken man are described in chapter 56 of *Life on the Mississippi*.

168 In chapter 12 of his *American Notes for General Circulation* (1842) Charles Dickens called Cairo, Illinois, "a hotbed of disease, an ugly sepulchre, a grave uncheered by any gleam of promise: a place without one single quality, in earth or air or water, to commend it." Dickens also made use of his unpleasant memories of Cairo in depicting "Eden" in *Martin Chuzzlewit* (1844). Mark Twain comments in chapter 25 of *Life on the Mississippi* that "Cairo is a brisk town now; and is substantially built, and has a city look about it which is in noticeable contrast to its former estate, as per Mr. Dickens's portrait of it."

ought to be taken from Court & lynched—if I were kin to the girl I would kill them on the threshold of the court.[169]

A State that permits a lottery is pretty far behind the age. (La).

The Mascot pow-wow in N.O.[170] The Mayor ordered the paper to be suppressed! And another big man resented its attacks & jumped its sale up to 15,000 & made it a good property when it would have died if left alone. Its proprietors are fighters. [#]

---

[169] The death of twenty-year-old Jennie Cramer resulted in one of the most notorious trials in Connecticut history. The girl's body was found on the New Haven shore in August 1881; an autopsy disclosed the presence of arsenic in the corpse and witnesses testified that shortly before her disappearance Miss Cramer was in the company of two cousins of a well-to-do family, Walter E. Malley and James Malley, Jr., and Blanche Douglass. In a trial which was beginning in New Haven when Clemens left Hartford for New Orleans and which was still in progress when he returned, the prosecution alleged that Jennie Cramer had been seduced by James Malley, Jr., who refused to marry her and, fearing publicity, enlisted his cousin and Blanche Douglass in a murder plot. Since the evidence was largely circumstantial, the Malley family hired a battery of detectives and defense attorneys to discredit the victim and the presumed motives. After deliberating less than an hour on 30 June 1882 the jury acquitted the three defendants.

[170] The weekly New Orleans *Mascot* published a cartoon and article in its April 22 issue accusing Watson Van Benthuysen of bribing members of the city council to procure an extension of the Carrollton Railroad franchise. On the day of publication Van Benthuysen and his son entered the *Mascot* office with revolvers and a walking stick; after a tumultuous confrontation one of the newspaper editors filed charges of assault with dangerous weapons against the Van Benthuysens. At this point New Orleans Mayor Joseph A. Shakspeare ordered the chief of police to suppress publication of the *Mascot*, but on 27 April the publishers obtained an injunction against the mayor's action. At the same time Van Benthuysen was granted an injunction which restrained the *Mascot* from publishing defamatory caricatures of him. On 29 April the *Mascot* nevertheless resumed its campaign against Van Benthuysen, and consequently its three owners, editors, and publishers —Joseph Liversey, George Osmond, and J. S. Bossier—were summoned for a court hearing. Despite their appeal to press freedoms, the judge found the men guilty of contempt of court and sentenced them to ten days in jail (New Orleans *Times-Democrat*, 5 May 1882). Less than a week later the State Supreme Court reversed this verdict and ordered the release of the three prisoners (New Orleans *Times-Democrat*, 11 May 1882). Clemens arrived in the city prior to the second *Mascot* attack on Van Benthuysen; he left New Orleans before the higher court reached its decision.

Talks, there, with Weightman[171] & others about dueling.

That killing case <whi> (Devereux)[172]

<J M White>[173]

Baton Rouge cost $125000—sound boats cost toward a million.—one is sham & the other real.

Not even electrical bells. Everything cheap & primitive & paltry.

Bugbee & Soule—300 Celebrated Cases. Just published.[174]

Life of Jon. Edwards about 1820 Northampton Mass.[175]

Maj. E A Burke of Times-Dem duel with C H Parker, of the

---

[171] Richard W. Weightman of the New Orleans *Times-Democrat* served on the reception committee at the Southern Art Union benefit mule race which Mark Twain attended on 29 April (New Orleans *Daily Picayune,* 23 April 1882). Weightman also attended the dinner hosted by Edward A. Burke at John's Restaurant on 2 May (New Orleans *Times-Democrat,* 7 May 1882).

[172] Thomas Devereaux was killed and Michael Hennessey was wounded when a fusillade of gunfire on 13 October 1881 climaxed a feud between three New Orleans police detectives. Michael and David Hennessey were charged with the murder of Chief of Aids Devereaux, and were dismissed from the police force. On 27 April 1882, the day before Clemens' arrival in New Orleans, a jury in the Criminal District Court found the two former detectives not guilty.

[173] Mark Twain mentioned this famous steamboat, which in 1844 set a record on a trip from New Orleans to Cairo by averaging fourteen miles an hour, in "Old Times on the Mississippi" (*Atlantic Monthly,* August 1875, p. 192).

[174] Soule & Bugbee was a Boston firm which published books concerning the legal profession. In the 10 June 1882 issue of *Publishers' Weekly* they announced publication of Horace W. Fuller's *Noted French Trials: Impostors and Adventurers,* a copy of which Clemens acquired and signed "S. L. Clemens/Hartford, June 1882" (University of Illinois at Urbana-Champaign). Walter Blair believes that Fuller's first chapter, "The False Martin Guerre," was germinal to the Wilks episode in *Huckleberry Finn,* and that Mark Twain's depiction of the King may have been influenced by Fuller's lengthy account of "The False Dauphins" who claimed to be Louis XVII (*Mark Twain & Huck Finn,* pp. 327–328).

[175] Clemens acquired a copy of Samuel Hopkins' *The Life and Character of . . . Jonathan Edwards* (Northampton, Mass.: Andrew Wright, 1804), which contained eighteen of Edwards' sermons, several miscellaneous writings, and extracts from his diary. The volume is now in the Mark Twain Papers.

Picayune—at the Slaughter House June 7—at 5th shot Burke shot through both thighs.[176]

Young negro in Grand Pacific Chicago who never forgot a hat.

I think I could wipe out a dishonor by crippling the other man, but I don't see how I could do it by letting him cripple *me*.
(Insert my duel with Laird).[177]

In the south is little or no architecture, but New England is full of it. The town hall in Belmont[178] is finer & more beautiful & more pure & elegant art than anything in South, perhaps.

Boston's about the prettiest city in the world; & the new part has the prettiest & elegantest architecture

Write Chatto send me Hood's Annual for 73, 74, 75.[179]

Say I remember Rev. <P>Dr Palmer's eloquence & was sorry not to hear him again.[180] [#]

---

176 Edward A. Burke was state treasurer of Louisiana and managing editor of the New Orleans *Times-Democrat*; C. Harrison Parker was editor-in-chief of the New Orleans *Picayune*. Their duel took place after a *Picayune* editorial charged Burke with dishonesty in manipulating state bonds.

177 James L. Laird, a proprietor of the Virginia City *Daily Union* in 1864, was offended by Clemens' editorial remarks in the *Territorial Enterprise* about the United States Sanitary Fund. Despite a heated exchange of insults, the anticipated duel never took place (*Mark Twain of the "Enterprise,"* ed. Henry Nash Smith [Berkeley and Los Angeles: University of California Press, 1957], pp. 24–29). Albert Bigelow Paine wrote "Speaking of duels" at the top of the notebook page.

178 Howells lived in this Boston suburb.

179 Mark Twain's "How I Escaped Being Killed in a Duel" had appeared in the London periodical *Tom Hood's Comic Annual, for* 1873. The 1874 issue contained a version of "Jim Wolf and the Cats." Clemens sent his request to Chatto & Windus on 10 June 1882.

180 The Reverend Benjamin Morgan Palmer, pastor of the First Presbyterian Church, had been a clergyman in New Orleans since 1856. Upon arriving in the city Clemens told a newspaper reporter that he intended "to hear Dr. Palmer as I used to do in the old days" (New Orleans *Times-Democrat*, 29 April 1882). But since he spent only one Sunday in New Orleans, Clemens deferred to Cable's custom and attended services at the Prytania Street Presbyterian Church with him (New Orleans *Times-Democrat*, 1 May 1882).

Mention the fine music at Guthrie's[181]

Emerson died while we were in N.O. So glad I visited him 2 or 3 weeks before.[182]

Say a word about that visit—but mainly about our going in the evening to reverently look at his *house*. At first he did not remember me, but the voyage with his sun recalled me.[183]

Mention went from Hannibal [to] join Confederate army with Sam Bowen & Ed. Stevens.[184]

By the Times-Democrat I see that murderers are promptly found guilty & hanged in the South.

Mention meeting Darwin at Grasmere, by the landlord's introduction Both of us embarrassed, as in Gen. Grant's case. Tell how Norton said Darwin always read himself to sleep with my books—& then (Norton) blushed & apologized. I am glad to have seen that mighty man.[185]

<<Wer>Where <were the> she got the dance cards & where engraved? pencils. (Barrows)>[186]

---

[181] See note 126.

[182] Emerson died on 27 April, the day before Clemens' steamboat reached New Orleans.

[183] Clemens and Emerson's son, Edward Waldo, had been fellow passengers aboard the *Batavia* sailing from Liverpool to New York in November 1872.

[184] Five years had passed since Mark Twain made a humorous speech before a joint convention of Hartford and Boston artillery companies about his impulsive enlistment in a secessionist militia group in 1861 (New York *Times*, 7 October 1877). He did not include this episode in *Life on the Mississippi*; "The Private History of a Campaign that Failed" (1885) is his fullest account of it.

[185] Darwin's death on 19 April 1882 elicited Clemens' recollection of their meeting in the English Lake District three years earlier. Evidently Clemens' encounter with Darwin was as awkward as his first meeting with Grant in 1868. Then, finding himself at a loss for words, Clemens had remarked: "Mr. President, I am embarrassed. Are you?" (*MTA*, 1:13–15; *Following the Equator*, chapter 2). Charles Eliot Norton and his family became well acquainted with the Darwins during a visit to England in 1868.

[186] Samuel W. Barrows & Company was a Hartford book, news, and stationery firm. This and the next three entries note preparations for a party attended by

<Get dances from Alice Day[187] & order the cards & pencils—60.>

<Ask Miss Dunham to give us 2 names about that age from each of the Knight & Frank Cheney families.>[188]

<Ask her <about> if Dr. Parker has any little people.>[189]

Ask about the Webb & Parsons[190] ch^{n}, sex, No. & age.

<Telegraph Fairchild we can't come.[191] *& Orion*>[192]

Box of fancy paper.

Holland fountain pen [#]

---

sixty-seven children to mark Clara's eighth birthday on June 8. At the party "Jean picked up scarlet fever & was a prisoner some weeks. It delayed our journey to Elmira by six weeks, & delayed 'Life on the Mississippi more than twice as long," Clemens noted in "A Record of the Small Foolishnesses of Susie & 'Bay' Clemens (Infants)" (Clifton Waller Barrett Library, University of Virginia, Charlottesville).

187 Alice Hooker Day was a friend of Livy, and her daughters Katharine and Alice were playmates of the Clemens girls.

188 Miss Mary Dunham of Hartford had visited the Clemenses while they were staying in Paris in 1879. Frank W. and Knight Cheney operated large silk mills in nearby South Manchester, Connecticut.

189 Mark Twain undoubtedly knew that the Reverend Edwin Pond Parker was the father of both boys and girls, but he may have been uncertain about their ages.

190 James S. Parsons was president of the Continental Life Insurance Company in Hartford. Webb's identity is not known.

191 Boston broker Charles W. Fairchild, Howells' friend and neighbor in Belmont, had invited the Clemenses to a dinner on 22 June for James R. Osgood, who was leaving for Europe. Clemens decided not to attend because the banquet was scheduled for the day on which he planned to take his family to Elmira. On 16 June 1882, a week or so after he wired Fairchild, Clemens asked Howells to assure Fairchild that "if we *could* have got to Boston for his dinner, it would most surely have been done. We both wanted to go, badly enough" (*MTHL*, p. 405).

192 Jane Lampton Clemens was seriously ill at Charles L. Webster's house in Fredonia. Orion Clemens notified his brother on 7 June 1882 that he and Mollie and Pamela "have had a terrible fright about Ma, this morning"; Orion reported that she was suffering "cerebro-spinal" spasms, and that "the doctors have the gravest doubts." On 9 June he wrote: "When your dispatch came this afternoon, I told Ma I had received a dispatch from you, in which you sent the love of all that family, and wished to be kept informed. She was much affected." Jane Clemens recovered enough to be able to travel to Keokuk in August.

<Phenix printg office Pearl st.[193]

Another just this side of Park church (high up)>

1. It is *real* terra cotta.
2. It is very fine, yes—I have a house built of it.

Maj. Burke was shot in the backside! Not really hurt, but can't sit down.

Let us have a law that *all* duels shall aim at that part—then it shall not be crime. Would soon kill the custom. Possibly this one case has already killed it, & Burke is a martyr in a good cause.

Story that Bob Tombs challenged an old deacon who resigned from his church, made a will, then went to practising with a rifle —whereupon Tombs backed out & was forever ruined in the eyes of the South.[194]

Man down south from New England said "if I had heaven or home placed before me, wouldn't know which to choose"—reflected & added, "would take home—can go to heaven *any* time"

Champagne—"Why papa, it's snowing *up!*"

A Rapture in Pine & Hemlock. [#]

---

[193] There was a printing and bookbinding establishment at 141 Pearl Street in 1882, the Case, Lockwood & Brainard Company. The president of this firm, Newton Case, also served on the board of directors for the Phoenix Mutual Life Insurance Company (*Geer's Hartford City Directory*, 1882, p. 243).

[194] Robert A. Toombs resigned as United States senator for Georgia in 1861, served briefly as Confederate secretary of state, and entered law practice after the war. In 1872 Toombs challenged the former governor of Georgia, Joseph E. Brown. According to the Atlanta *Constitution* (29 August 1880), Brown "made his will, put his estate in order, withdrew from the church, and clipped all the trees in his orchard practicing with the pistol. Had the duel come off . . . Governor Brown would have . . . sent his bullet within the eighth of an inch of the place he had selected" (quoted in William Y. Thompson, *Robert Toombs of Georgia* [Baton Rouge: Louisiana State University Press, 1966], p. 233). Thompson confirms that Toombs's reluctance to follow through with his published challenge diminished his political reputation for a time.

Solomon has said According <to a mans> to a man's character, even so also is his fence likewise. Sol was always throwing/flashing/flirting off some neat little thing like that, when the women were quiet.

A Threnody in iron.
A Saturnalia in [*blank*]
A Symphony in [*blank*]

Work in <*lanniappe*> lagniappe

Muscatine—Bill Israeel, who drew a butcher knife gaumed with red ink on me once in a lonely place & made me apologize for some imaginary affront.[195] (A stranger

Saw them in the South toting bricks & mortar up a ladder in the old fashioned way.

It was odd to hear person speak of a "blue" bucket, in the way I hadn't heard for many years.

"So sorry you warn't here at the Mardi-Gras" (silly, but they admire mystery, romance &c. For instance, nobody knows who is Rex. Remus & Cable.

Make no end of Chas. Lamb, & people who have been educated to think him readable, & really *do* think him so. The same prejudice of education in favor of some other passè authors.

The romance of boating is gone, now. In Hannibal the steamboatman is no longer a god. The youth don't talk river slang any more. Their pride is apparently railways—which they take a peculiar vanity in reducing to initials ("C B & Q")[196]—an affectation

---

[195] The menacing lunatic appears in chapter 57 of *Life on the Mississippi,* where he demands to be acknowledged as "the sole and only son of the Devil."

[196] Six railroad lines operated through Hannibal in 1882, but the Chicago, Burlington, & Quincy was becoming the major railway system in the area.

which prevails all over the west. They roll these initials as a sweet morsel under the tongue.

South still in the sophomoric (gush) period. All speech there is flowery & gushy—pulpit, law, literature, it is all so.

<Barber scissors.>
Engineering Co[197] X
<Telegraph Holden[198] & Ch. Webster.>
Cut coupons & put in 2 bonds.
<Telegraph Gov. Fuller.>[199]
Call at Perkins's[200] X
List & number those securities.[201]

See Bunce[202] X

Pack hat trunk. [#]

---

[197] With his 145 shares Clemens was the second largest stockholder in the Hartford Engineering Company. Its president, Drayton Hillyer, reminded him from Hartford on 17 July 1882 that "the note . . . endorsed by you falls due to day." He enclosed "a new note" for Clemens to sign and requested its "return by earliest mail" from Elmira. Whether the Xs here and below were added to emphasize that these tasks remained undone or to indicate that they were completed is not apparent.

[198] E. R. Holden was a New York official of the Delaware, Lackawanna & Western Railroad Company. Clemens had intended to leave Hartford for Elmira on 22 June but was compelled to cancel arrangements for a special railroad car because of his children's illnesses. On 26 June Holden assured him by letter that "your message countermanding order for car was in time so that no expense was incurred." Finally on 13 July the Clemenses made the trip to New York and departed the next day for Elmira. After the journey Clemens thanked Holden for "a new sleeping car which was the perfection of comfort & cleanliness" (16 July 1882, Henry E. Huntington Library, San Marino, Calif.).

[199] See note 90.

[200] Charles E. Perkins was Clemens' Hartford attorney. Some of his tasks were trivial: he was responsible for sending Orion a monthly allowance from his brother (generally seventy-five dollars), but he also served as secretary for the Kaolatype Engraving Company.

[201] Clemens had rented a safety deposit box in Hartford for the storage of his stocks and securities. Presumably the list of investments that follows represents its contents.

[202] Cashier of the Phoenix National Bank, Edward M. Bunce belonged to Clemens' Friday Evening Club. Clemens probably deposited his stock certificates in Bunce's Hartford bank.

Go Hubbard first, & get N.Y. Cent <certif>Certif.[203]

O, see her bow! (Have a foreigner write me & ask me in bad English to explain this exasperating sentence.

<4 pr *closed* drawers #24
1 " " " 22>

Co-Op. Dress Ass^{n} Certif of stk #No. 2. (ticket No. 2002 . . $	25
Am. Bk. Note Co. certif #1701 20 shs ($1000)	1,000
Ditto #1740—(80 shs)	4,000
N.Y. Central & Hud River 50 shs (A31929)	5,000
Adams Express #9261 (50 shs)	5,000
Norfolk & Western Bonds, Nos. 325, 326, 327, 1618, 1619 . .	5,000
Little Rock M. R. & T. Bonds, 883, 884, 881, 880, 879, . .	5,000
Little Rock, M. R. & T. Bonds, 1531, 1530, 1532, 1533, 1534	5,000
Independent Watch Co. <(50 shs)>	5,000
N.Y. Vaporizing Co.	5,000
Hartford Engineering Co. 145 shs (No. 26)	14,500
Am. Exchange in Europe 500 shs (<— — — —>24001 to 24500	5,000
Conn. Fire Ins. 12 shs (No. 1515	1200
Jewell Pin Co 15 shs No. 19	1500
Farnham Type-Setter Mf Co, 200 shs (No 229	5000
Kaolatype Eng Co, 120 shs (No. 6)	3,000
Crown Pt. Iron Co. (No 339) 100 shares	10,000
Hartford Sanitary Plumbing Co. 40 shs	1,000
Watch Co (Howard Bros) Note in J L & Co's hands due Sept. 1883	3,600
St Paul Roller Mill stk.	5,000
New stk of Am Ex in Europe	5,000
Metford, 100 shs	3,125.
Burr Index Co	2,500

[#]

203 Hubbard & Farmer was a Hartford brokerage firm from which Clemens received monthly statements of his stock purchases and profits during 1882. The list following shows that Clemens owned fifty shares of New York Central & Hudson River stock.

Dunham.[204]

Get up a rambling yarn about a fellow who went into battle with a Testament in front & 6 decks of cards behind. The man & the Testament uninjured but all the cards ruined.

The frightfullest time I ever saw? It was the time I was up in my balloon & seemed to have got into that (fabled) stratum where, once in, you remain—going neither up nor down for years—forever—& I came across first one balloon & afterwards another & we three lay (apparently) motionless beside each other, the green, mummified (frozen) corpses of Prof. Wise, Donaldson & the journalist <lookin> <gazing> gloating mournfully from the tattered baskets.[205]

No domestic architecture 20 years ago—now it booms in the very

---

[204] Eventually Mark Twain decided against modeling a central character after "Dad" Dunham of the *Gold Dust* for *Life on the Mississippi*, but several entries like this one preceded his decision to assign these tales to other narrators. Dunham is introduced in chapter 25 as "Uncle" Mumford, a profane "mate of the blessed old-time kind"; in chapter 28 he testifies about the uselessness of attempting to control the waters of the Mississippi.

[205] During the 1870s two balloonists, John Wise and Washington H. Donaldson, vanished mysteriously in separate voyages over Lake Michigan. Donaldson and a journalist, Newton S. Grimwood of the Chicago *Evening Journal*, disappeared in 1875 when a storm broke after their ascent from Chicago. Although Grimwood's body was found a month later, no traces of Donaldson or his balloon ever were located. In 1879 the seventy-one-year-old Wise came out of retirement to make a balloon ascension at Saint Louis. He agreed to drop advertising circulars from the car over a local region; winds carried the balloon so far northward, however, that his trail of jettisoned leaflets led to the brink of Lake Michigan. The body of Wise's companion, a young Saint Louis bank teller, washed up on the Indiana shore; Wise never was seen again. The manuscript of *Life on the Mississippi* reveals that Mark Twain expanded these notes into a passage which was deleted before publication of the book. The invented narrator was a *Gold Dust* passenger, Mr. Harvey, who commences a ghoulish tale of entrapment in the "stratum of dead air" where the grinning corpses of previous balloonists hover eternally. Interrupted by a business interview, Harvey fails to complete the story and leaves his listeners, like his hapless balloonist, hopelessly suspended. Mark Twain would revive the idea of trapped vessels in a brief manuscript of 1896, "The Enchanted Sea-Wilderness" (*Mark Twain's Which Was the Dream? and Other Symbolic Writings of the Later Years*, ed. John S. Tuckey [Berkeley and Los Angeles: University of California Press, 1966], pp. 7–8, 74–86).

villages—& improves all the time. The Stewart Mausoleum[206] (to be given N.Y. for a picture gallery when he died!—like old Whatshisname's Park[207] at Elmira!) would not be built now.

Mixed-up Scripture yarn like Man went down from Jericho to Jeru & fell among thieves.

Couldn't sleep & overheard negroes between decks, on freight piles: "Wanted to send message to <his>His Chillen, & didn't know no way but to sen' it in read'n & writ'n, w'en he know'd pow'ful well dey warn't no niggers could read it—& wouldn't be *'lowed* to learn, by de Christian law of de <Sof> Souf—& more'n half <o'> er de white <w>folks! Ki-yi-yi-yi! (derisive laughter)—if 'twas a man dat got up <su>sich a po' notion, a body'd <se>say he sick er he <don't know noth'n> can't invent worth shucks; but bein' its *Him*, you got to keep yo' mouf shet."

"Well, how He gwine to let um know de message ef he don't sen' it in a book?—you tell me dat."

"Shucks, plenty ways, *plenty* ways! Wanted de whole worl' to breave, didn't He?—white folks 'n' niggers 'n' all. *Well* den!—he sent de *ar* to *all* <on> un um!—sent it to *all* um <mind>min' you,—dem dat kin read & dem dat can't—dey ain't no dam unsuttainty 'bout de *ar*, is dey? Suppose he got any *yuther* message

---

[206] Alexander T. Stewart, the New York merchant who made a fortune in dry goods, built a two-million-dollar Italian Renaissance mansion on Fifth Avenue at Thirty-fourth Street. During its construction in 1867 Mark Twain ridiculed Stewart's taste in his May 28 letter to the *Alta California*: "Verily it is one thing to have cash and another to know how to spend it," he declared. Marble is "cold, ghostly, unfeeling stuff. . . . Stewart's house looks like a stately tomb" (*Mark Twain's Travels with Mr. Brown*, ed. Franklin Walker and G. Ezra Dane [New York: Alfred A. Knopf, 1940], p. 246). After Stewart died in 1876 there were persistent rumors that Mrs. Stewart intended to leave the monumental structure to the city as a public art gallery (New York *Times*, 26 October 1886), but upon her death in 1886 it would be learned that her will contained no such bequest.

[207] Clemens probably was thinking of Eldridge Park, given to the city of Elmira by Dr. Edwin Eldridge three years before his death in 1876. This amusement park was decorated with huge cast-iron statues; its grounds were dominated by a four-story wooden casino with an observation platform and restaurant. Inside the casino a lever was rigged to raise or submerge a mermaid statue in the nearby lake.

to sen', you reckin he don' know enough to rig up some way to make it go to de whole blame worl' if he want to?"

Further along:

<"*Why* ain't He 'sponsible? Didn't he make de men so dey'd sin? Coase he did: den He sponsible f'r dem sins his own seff.

"O de hell you say!"

"Yes, de hell I say.—> Do a dove ever want to hurt anybody?

"Coase not."

"Do a rabbit?"

"No."

"Do a fishin'-worm?"

"Ke-he!—no."

"Do a cat fish ever want to soak whisky en git drunk?"

"No—coase he don't."

"<N>Do a butterfly ever <w>cuss & swäah?"

"O hell no, coase he don't<?>."

"Do de bull-frog tell lies en steal?"

"No."

"*Well,* den! <Hit sho> He don't make *no* dove dat's bloody-minded; He <don>doan make *no* catfish dat loves whisky; He doan make *no* butterfly dat cusses & swäahs; He doan make *no* bull-frog dat lies & steals! What do all dat show? It show dat He kin make a cretur any way He *want* him—*dat* what it show. He could a made de <mu>mankind so *dey* wouldn't ever want to rip & cuss & kill folks, & git drunk & so on, 'f he'd a wanted to. But he didn't *want* to. Dat's de pint!—he didn't *want* to. He *made* <no> most all of 'em so dey'd be a set of ornery blame' <rascals> scoun'ls,—& now you reckon he gwine to roas' 'em to all everlast'n for what He done his own <sel>seff? No, *sir*—He's 'sponsible—shore's you's bawn he is; & dey jist ain't no way for Him to git <around>aroun' it."

Further along:

"When a fox take a goose & a wolf take a sheep, it's embellishment,* ain't it? He's done a mighty wicked act, ain't he?"

---

*Embezzlement. [*Clemens' footnote*]

"No, he ain't—it's his natur."

"Well, when a rattlesnake bite you & kill you, hit's murder, ain't it?"

"Coase it ain't. Dat's <he>de way de rattlesnake's made—its his natur.

"Den dey ain't no man dat's gwyne <to> ter accuse a rattlesnake of murder & a fox of embellishment?"

"Why what a fool you is! Coase dey ain't."

"*Well*, den! What do dat show? It show dat a man is a pow'ful sight mo' juster en what de Lawd is! Kase de Lawd take en buil' up a man so he <jes>jis *boun'* to kill people, en lie en steal en embellish, en den he take en jam him into de <everlastin>everlast'n fire en brimstone for it! Doan talk no sich blame foolishness to *me!* De Lawd ain't no sich po' trash. *I'll* resk it, dat <de> any book dat's got any sich stuff as dat in it warn't ever writ by de Lawd—en you kin pen' 'pon it de Lawd warn't even roun' in de neighborhood when she *wuz* writ, nuther."

(What did Moses say to Goliah?—dats it.)

(Referring to a clergyman) *Who?* Dat old stallion?—Mf!—*he* doan know nuffin!

<Osgood said he would divide the $2500 loss by <de[v]>defaulting general agent with me.>[208]

There was no default on Tramp Abroad.

Like my late publishers, who declared no div. in 7 years, on several shiploads of books; then as soon as business left them declared 3 in 18 months. [#]

---

[208] Osgood had relied on the subscription canvassing apparatus of the American Publishing Company for marketing *The Prince and the Pauper*, but both he and Clemens felt that this arrangement was unsatisfactory. In several letters to Osgood in January and February 1882 Clemens had condemned the "unfaithful genl agents," vowing that "we'll have a very different genl agent system, hereafter, and not any Bliss's in it" (*MTLP*, pp. 150–152).

Expert may find they have sold 50,000 Sketches—which brings them in for $2000 rebate.[209]

Moral abscess like Congressman Hubbell[210]—a hypocritical virtue-mouthing sham, the loathsome representative of the loathsomest of systems, the present civil service—a robber who waylays poor clerks & department women & demands "voluntary contributions" to election funds. *Seven*, more & more sharp, were sent to one man by the *N. Y. State* repub. committee. The later ones, while asking "voluntary" cont., used manifestly threatening language. [#]

---

[209] Clemens had become convinced that the American Publishing Company had cheated him out of thousands, and he had directed Charles L. Webster to obtain proof of the Blisses' malfeasance. On 28 June 1882 Webster reported jubilantly that Frank Bliss had consented to allow an auditor to examine company records. Clemens most likely made these notebook entries around 8 July 1882, when he complained in a letter to Webster that since he had sold his shares of American Publishing Company stock in 1881 the firm had declared three dividends, whereas "in over *nine years* they paid no dividend" while they sold 300,000 copies of his books. Clemens admonished Webster to instruct the auditor to "do his level best to find out exactly how many of each of my books have been sold, if possible. And especially how many *Sketches*—for when they have sold 50,000 Sketches they will owe me a rebate of 2½ per cent on each copy of the whole 50,000" (*MTBus*, p. 190). Although Webster would concur on 12 July that "it certainly looks as if some one had stolen a good deal of money those years that no dividend's were declared," he also pointed out, "in regard to the 'Sketches' . . . I have been watching that, but at present they have sold but about 38000." By 8 August Clemens' desire to prosecute Frank Bliss was cooling. "Look here," he remarked to Webster, "have the Am. Pub. Co. swindled me out of only $2,000? I thought it was *five*. It can't be worth while to sue for $2,000, can it?" (*MTBus*, p. 192). Although Webster continued his investigation through the summer he uncovered no actionable evidence of financial misdoings by the Blisses.

[210] Jay A. Hubbell of Michigan was chairman of the Republican Congressional Campaign Committee which requested "voluntary contributions" from government employees for the 1882 elections. Attorney General Benjamin Harris Brewster declared Hubbell exempt from the law of 1876 that prohibited Federal officers from soliciting civil servants for campaign funds, since congressmen technically are not "officers" of the United States. "Though gifts in name, the vigorous mode of solicitation made the returns in fact, assessments," George Frederick Howe would remark in *Chester A. Arthur: A Quarter-Century of Machine Politics* (New York: Dodd, Mead & Co., 1934), p. 197.

McWilliams & Hubbell—Mc resigns office.

McW & Scarlet fever—for Miss. book.[211]

Write Sue a letter for mother.[212]
<Get <shoes> blocks for Jean.>
< " picture books.>
Transfer closet stock & take it to safe Deposit.

<Return <to> jug to Rathbun[213] & fill it with sulphuric acid.>

<Brush & comb for Chn.>

<Barber come this afternoon.>

Get compartment & 4 seats *sure.*
Powder for Jean.

<1000 pencils.>
June 21—Crane We should be delighted to see any one of you here, but as the children have been exposed we don't dare move them.
SLC

<<Co>Closet stock
Telegraph Office
Twine
Rubber bands.
Railway Compartment.
1000 pencils.>

Ring into the book the pathetic tale of the Obituaryist.—&

Is anybody brave when he has no *audience?* [#]

---

211 In June and July of 1882 Jean Clemens was seriously ill with scarlet fever. Mark Twain never implemented this idea for a domestic sketch resembling "Experience of the McWilliamses with the Membranous Croup" (1875), "Mrs. McWilliams and the Lightning" (1880), and "The McWilliamses and the Burglar Alarm" (1882).

212 Olivia Clemens undoubtedly was afraid that news of Jean's grave illness contained in letters to Susan Crane would alarm their seventy-one-year-old mother, Olivia Lewis Langdon.

213 Julius G. Rathbun was a Hartford druggist.

Is *any*body or any *action* ever unselfish? (Good theme for Club Essay)[214]

Charles Snowden 10th Baron Fairfax, died in Baltimore in '69. He spared Ferguson's life, after taking Deringer from, saying he spared him on account of his wife & children. Mention him. Meet somebody who knew this American baron, whose family still figures in Burke's peerage.[215] <[--]>

Write Courant & Times-Democrat change to Elmira[216]

Met a passenger who spoke good English, & who, after hearing a good deal of brag about great men, said his country was very small & remote but had produced 2 or 3 pretty big men; named a couple

---

214 On 19 February 1883 Clemens delivered a paper titled "What Is Happiness?" to the Monday Evening Club of Hartford; subsequently he developed this examination of human motives into the dialogue published as *What Is Man?* (1906).

215 Mistaken in certain details, Clemens' information about Charles Snowden Fairfax nevertheless is correct in its general outline. The deaths of all lineal heirs in 1846 qualified Fairfax to become the tenth baron of Fairfax, but the Virginia-born American citizen refused to travel to England to establish his claim to the peerage and, like his father, never assumed the title. Fairfax moved to California in 1851; the town which developed where he settled in Marin County was named after him. He was elected clerk of the State Supreme Court in 1854. Versions of the affray to which Clemens refers differ somewhat, but most agree that it occurred in Sacramento in 1858, and that Fairfax's opponent was a reporter of the court, Harvey Lee. A vivid account of the incident is contained in autobiographical recollections dictated in 1877 by Stephen J. Field: after Fairfax and Lee quarreled, Lee drew the sword from his sword-cane and thrust it into Fairfax's chest. "By this time Fairfax had drawn his pistol. . . . But [he] did not shoot. . . . While the blood was trickling from his own person, he said, 'You are an assassin! you have murdered me! I have you in my power! your life is in my hands!' And gazing on him, he added, 'But for the sake of your poor sick wife and children I will spare you.' He thereupon uncocked his pistol and handed it to his friend, into whose arms he fell fainting" (*Personal Reminiscences of Early Days in California with Other Sketches* [privately printed, copyright 1880], pp. 110–111). Fairfax died of consumption on 4 April 1869 in Baltimore at the age of forty. Mark Twain would refer to the American Fairfax heirs in the first chapter of *The American Claimant* (1892). When he recounted Fairfax's magnanimous act in an undated Autobiographical Dictation, Mark Twain added, "I knew him, but not intimately" (*MTA*, 1:81).

216 Clemens had subscribed to the New Orleans *Times-Democrat* in addition to the Hartford *Courant*.

nobody ever heard of—then offered to bet the third had been heard of—named Jesus Christ! He was born close to the grotto & was familiar with it! It seemed like meeting a person who had known him.

<Want a couple more quarts to-day.>
In N.O. Have you got any rotten strawberries?
Rotten ones?—*no.*"
"What, you ain't out a'ready?
Out—we hain't never been *in.*"
"Sho, <how you talk> look at your daybook—<you sent me> 2 quarts <of 'm yesterday,> there 't I got yesterday, I reckon.

How early can Rosa get her break?[217]

2 Big slices of bread soaked in beef juice—beef just warmed & squeezed—at <$7.^{30.}$>$7.^{30.}$

Call us at <7.> $6.^{30}$

A pint bottle<.>, *tonight*

Small pitcher <at>of *morning's milk* at $6.^{30}$.

Euchre cards[218]

Breakfast[219]

1 broiled chicken.
Potatoes hashed with cream
Coffee
bread & butter.

Luncheon

2 broiled chickens.
Soft shell crabs for 1

---

[217] Rosina Hay, nursemaid to the Clemens children since 1874, was caring for Jean.

[218] Euchre became a family pastime for the Clemenses during 1882; on 27 April eleven-year-old Susy had written to her father that "we are lerning to play Eucher now, and we like it very much, today played with mamma, Rosa, Katie, Clara and Jaurge" (*LLMT*, p. 209).

[219] Olivia Clemens entered these menus in black ink.

Loads of bread & butter.

Some plain bread without butter.

1 bottle claret.

<dispatch to Katy.[220]

We are [*blank*] this morning. Have Dr. Hooker[221] comes to see about fumigating have him look at *chairs* in Susys room.>

The pleasant old maid (passenger) whose false teeth would fall out while she was talking interestedly, & she would catch them in her hands & go right along. slap them in with a dull snap.

<<Man (Dad Dunn,)>[222] Our liar, who had a fight, all alone, at midnight, on the forecastle, at Arkansas City, with a mosquito,—bricks & capstan bars used. Had a bill like a swordfish.>

On this trip 4 great men died—Emerson, & Longfellow here, & Darwin & Dr John Brown[223] abroad. Had some personal acquaintance with all of them<.>—with Brown intimate.

The physician's is the highest & the worthiest of all occupations—or would be, if human nature did not make superstitions & priests necessary.

Board of Foreign Missions—I have saved a Turk's soul.

---

[220] The following message to be telegraphed to Katy Leary was written in Livy's hand after the family left for Elmira on 13 July 1882. It was customary for Katy to remain in Hartford when the Clemenses went to Quarry Farm.

[221] Edward Beecher Hooker, son of John and Isabella Beecher Hooker, had begun his Hartford medical practice four years earlier.

[222] Mark Twain was sketching another tall tale for attribution to "Dad" Dunham, second mate on the steamboat *Gold Dust*. By the time he made this entry, he may have learned that Dunham suffered a shoulder injury and minor wounds when the *Gold Dust* exploded on 7 August. Dunham soon was back on the Saint Louis levee, "jovial as ever," assuring his friends that he "*made a pretty hard landing and broke a fender or two*. That's all" (J. W. Bryan to SLC, 12 August 1882).

[223] On 1 June 1882, soon after he returned to Hartford from the Mississippi River, Clemens addressed a letter of condolence to Dr. Brown's son which began: "I was three thousand miles from home, at breakfast in New Orleans, when the damp morning paper revealed the sorrowful news among the cable dispatches" (*MTL*, p. 420). Actually Brown died on 11 May as Clemens was approaching Saint Louis on board the *City of Baton Rouge*.

What did it cost?
$2,000,000.[224]
Is it worth that?

U.S. Govt.—I have killed <a whole> 200 Indians.
What did it cost?
$2,000,000.
You could have given them a college education for that.

The Foreign M Board is <largely> mainly supported by legacies now. This represents people of a past generation. <A>This generation contributes little & will leave few legacies.—Next one may possibly do nothing.

<Coals>
"Give us but 8 men!" appeals the board pathetically—"4 for China, 2 for Japan & 2 for Africa, & we will hold our peace for the present." So there is *one* trade which is not overdone.

Title, <"Abroad on the Great River."> <"Abroad on the Father of Waters."> "Abroad on the Missisippi"[225]

Was told that South they don't keep negro mistresses as much as befo' the waw.

Bummer & Lazarus.[226] [#]

---

224 The American Board of Foreign Missions held its annual meeting in Portland, Maine, between 3 and 6 October 1882. At the 4 October session Dr. L. T. Chamberlain reported that an intensive effort to extend knowledge of the Christian gospel to five hundred thousand additional heathen souls would require an expenditure of two million dollars (New York *Tribune*, 5 October 1882).

225 Mark Twain's indecision about a title for his new subscription volume caused his publisher some uneasiness. James R. Osgood finally would write on 22 September 1882: "We particularly need the title at once, that we may have the cover-stamp prepared" (*MTLP*, p. 158, n. 3).

226 Clemens had written about these two dogs, the famous Bummer and his "obsequious vassal" Lazarus, when he was a reporter covering local affairs in San Francisco (see *Clemens of the "Call": Mark Twain in San Francisco*, ed. Edgar M. Branch [Berkeley and Los Angeles: University of California Press, 1969], pp. 49–50). The pair were associated with Emperor Norton, an eccentric who believed himself to be ruler of California and Mexico.

Emperor Norton.

Bought 8 tickets for <[Staines]>[227] & return—ticket taker said return the <5>4 & get money back—which I did. They were special—for that day & date only.

Funerals in our stupid & expensive way—cremation <prevalen>preferrable. Poor Moore had to pay $26 for *cheapest* coffin.[228] You can cremate a body for one. Plague has been produced by bodies 200 years buried.

Parallel Fijian slavery with political assessment slavery.

Mrs.	C.	Mrs	C[229]
2	5	2	0
4	3	1	0
4	4	4	2
6	4	0	5
2	6	2	4
1	3	3	3
1	2	2	5
4	2	1	2
1	5	4	6
0	5	5	3
1	6	0	2
1	2	1	4
0	5	3	2
1	3	3	4
4	4		

"To remember one worthy thing, how many thousand unworthy things must a man be able to forget!" [#]

[227] Although it seems unlikely, Clemens may have been thinking of Staines, England, a town on the Thames River west of London which he visited briefly in 1873 on his way to Windsor. The entry remains cryptic.

[228] In *Life on the Mississippi* (chapter 42) Mark Twain cites the case of an impoverished Negro laborer who was required to pay this exorbitant sum in order to bury his small child.

[229] Presumably these are card game scores.

French language—"Very lean & shallow, if very clear & convenient."

Fred the Great was a bad speller—& Carlyle can't account for it![230]

Take a lot of <des> romantic rescues from fire, shipwreck, &c, & marry them. Then give the sequel, with fights & divorce—the parties being miserably mismated.

Superior independence of the present day. <Couple of grave> old New Englander & thoughtful young one. "If the Prodig'l Son belonged *here* & was to come back busted, he wouldn't go a-beggin' around his old father." "Wal, no, With his reputation, he wouldn't need to<;>—<he could go into the lecture field;> becuz he could lecter."

Human nature cannot be studied in cities except at a disadvantage —a village is the place. There you can know your man inside & out— in a city you but know his crust; & his crust is usually a lie. Dr. Purdy[231] & the clergyman's wife who dislocated her wrist rescuing a child from a pit. P & the family were on cold terms—he would not relieve her. It was night & she had to walk to Up de Graff's[232]—could get no car. Nearly fainting, then. Pain & so swollen had to have chloroform. Should be sued.

Blaine[233] the Nickel-Plated Statesman. Brass, *covered.*

Nothing left of you but this sad faculty of sowing chaff in the fashionable manner! F. II v. iv 252[234] [#]

---

230 Clemens was reading Thomas Carlyle's *History of Friedrich II of Prussia, Called Frederick the Great* (1865).

231 Henry H. Purdy had been an Elmira physician for more than twenty years.

232 Thaddeus S. Up de Graff was a well known eye, ear, and throat specialist in Elmira. It is probable that Clemens heard this story from Dr. Up de Graff when the physician made a house call to Quarry Farm on 21 July 1882.

233 Clemens' anti-Blaine feelings would lead him to join the mugwumps in 1884.

234 Clemens is quoting Thomas Carlyle's assessment of the career of the duc de Belle-Isle, whose achievements in the court of Louis XV soon fell into oblivion. Clemens owned a thirty-volume set of Thomas Carlyle's collected works. His citation is to the ten-volume *History of Friedrich II of Prussia, Called Frederick the Great* included in the collection (London: Chapman and Hall, 1871), 4:252 (A1911, item 65).

Old friends. But sentiment aside, I know very well what became of them. Some of them were hanged, the rest escaped.

Orpheus C. Kerr.[235]

<So much noise> Such a big lie entered my ear that it swelled & spread till I could not see out around it. It has always remained so, to this day; & strangers often come miles to see me <[-]>fan myself with it.

Write a good story, but cov[e]rtly introduce winter into summer, sugar <c>fields into the North, &c., & now & then kill off a character, & some time introduce him again with no other than a calm cold footnote explanation that he was necessary to the story. Or, a lunatic might tell it & have all alive at end; the audience complain. Draws knife & says "No dead? we will remedy that."

Write a novel with a *real* M.C or two in it—not the customary wretched exaggeration. Draw Sunset Cox, Proctor Knott, Jay Hubbell, Bulkley, <& to>&c to the life. Conkling, Ben Butler.[236] Let them invent back-pension<s> bill of $100,000,000 a year in order that two or three people may make a thousand dollars in the lobby.

RR man in Canan[a] [237] scared off a thief & wheeled the barrow ½ mile up hill in 6 inch of snow, put it in his woodhouse expecting detect thief by marks on barrow in the morning. Thief removed the barrow <in the> before morning!

Mamma, I've got a dog <[--]> & he's a half-shepherd—only ½ shepherd, Mamma, but <[he's]> a whole dog! [#]

---

[235] Orpheus C. Kerr was the pseudonym of Robert Henry Newell. One of his doggerel poems, "The Great Fit," was included in *Mark Twain's Library of Humor*.

[236] Mark Twain refers to Samuel Sullivan Cox of Ohio, James Proctor Knott of Kentucky, Jay A. Hubbell of Michigan, Roscoe Conkling of New York, and Benjamin F. Butler of Massachusetts. No one by the name of Bulkley had served as a member of Congress by 1882.

[237] Clemens' superscript *a* renders any reading problematical, but he may mean a town called Canaan or Canandaigua.

Mental Teleg. The things which <I>pass through my mind when I lie awake in the morning are pretty sure to be the topics introduced by the others at breakfast or dinner that day or the next.

Sept. 20/82. Livy says "I have *no* memory." My own thought (but about<)>myself) last night.

Southern speech. "It is curiously soft & gentle; & expressive<;>, when the speaker will, of a caressing deference."

You could excite her interest as you can a poor relation's.

<As>He was as dirty as Adam.[238]

Difference between an 8-months child & an 8-months-old child. The latter is 8 months older than the former.

Write a tale, pretty & sweet girl &c married to natty, sappy young chap. First baby. II. Their silver weddin.[239] III Their golden ditto.

Speech on Arctic searches for Arctic explorers for the N.E. dinner, Dec. 22.[240]

House with all the modern inconveniences. [#]

---

[238] In his manuscript for chapter 38 of *Life on the Mississippi* Mark Twain declared that the dirt on the *Charles Morgan* "would have attracted the attention of Adam himself, while his own dirt was still damp"; the passage is not in the book. Mark Twain had taken this steamboat from Vicksburg to New Orleans.

[239] William Dean Howells followed a similar plan in *Their Wedding Journey* (1872) and its sequel, *Their Silver Wedding Journey* (1899).

[240] Upon his return from the Mississippi River, Mark Twain consented to be one of the guest speakers to respond to toasts following the Forefathers' Day Dinner to be held by the New England Society of New York City. Arctic exploration was not the topic he eventually used; Mark Twain would propose that the assemblage drink to "Woman—God Bless Her!" He explained, "I threw aside all my other subjects—they were too solemn" (SLC to Horace Russell, 12 December 1882, Clifton Waller Barrett Library, University of Virginia, Charlottesville). Joining General U. S. Grant, Joseph H. Choate, Chauncey M. Depew, and other dignitaries in raising toasts during the banquet at Delmonico's, Mark Twain delivered "an address which kept the tables in a roar for a quarter of an hour. The speaker brought his words out in an indescribable drawl, and puffed a cloud of smoke from his cigar between every two sentences" (New York *Times*, 23 December 1882).

See St Gaudens, ask about rent, restaurant, lessons & models.[241]
Have Brunswick man come to <Y>Hoboken.[242]
Write Charley we shan't stop—get the address[243]

The ignorant are afraid to betray surprise or admiration—sometimes they think it ill manners

N.O. stands on made ground, but not now known who made it.

Finish Agricul speech for <New Eng dinner.> Ashfield.[244] [#]

---

241 Clemens is presuming that the sculptor Augustus Saint-Gaudens would be familiar with European rates because of his extended residence in Paris and Rome during the preceding decades. Karl Gerhardt's sculpture lessons were proving more costly than his patron had intended, and on 30 September 1882 Clemens wrote a lengthy and disjointed admonition to Karl and Hattie Gerhardt to signal his growing uneasiness about the young couple's expenditures.

242 The Clemenses returned to Hartford from Elmira by way of New York City during the last week in September. The Delaware, Lackawanna & Western Railroad depot was located in Hoboken; passengers were ferried from the New Jersey side of the Hudson River to the city, and Clemens wished to have a Hotel Brunswick porter present to attend to their baggage. The 29 September 1882 New York *Times* noted that Clemens had registered at the Hotel Brunswick on the previous day.

243 By now Clemens had realized that his business affairs must wait "until I get my book finished. The weather turned cold, and we had to rush home [from Elmira], while I still lacked thirty thousand words" (SLC to Howells, 3 October 1882, Henry W. and Albert A. Berg Collection, New York Public Library). Charles L. Webster meanwhile was preparing to become the New York general agent for Osgood's subscription organization. On 27 September Webster conveyed Osgood's opinion "that I would have to get a better office near the book business in the neighborhood of Bond St. near Broadway," and reported to Clemens that he already had found a suitable room in that locality. Within a few months Webster's stationery bore a new letterhead: "Office of Charles L. Webster/General Agent for Mark Twain's Books./658 Broadway/Corner Bond St."

244 Clemens had been asked to speak at the mid-summer Ashfield Academy Dinner, a benefit sponsored annually by Charles Eliot Norton in Ashfield, Massachusetts. For the second time in two years Clemens belatedly withdrew from the event, pleading his daughters' illnesses and his difficulties in writing the river book. Norton assured Clemens on 18 July that he understood the circumstances which caused his cancellation, although "the good farmers of Ashfield and their wives and children will be greatly disappointed that they are not to greet you at our Annual Festival." Its topic suggests that the undelivered lecture would have been modeled on the July 1870 *Galaxy* sketch, "How I Edited an Agricultural Paper Once." Possibly Clemens was thinking that if he completed the speech now in

Annoyed by <s>tight man commenting appreciatively on the sermon. "To be good is to be great, to be pure is to be godly." "999 out of a possible thousand!" comments this fellow in reverent scarce-audible voice. And so on, all through sermon. Suggested by the NO Talmage,[245] but happened further up the river.

Ingersoll "<Egod>Egad he didn't get left,"[246] put it in book, describing the guests.

Lubbock[247] shows that ants are warriors, statesmen, &c. which led me to think they might have religion. Read Col. x. 14—3 ants signified approval, the rest went away.[248] Various verses showed some were Baptists, Pres &c. [#]

September he would have a humorous talk ready in case he accepted another speaking engagement.

[245] The pulpit style affected by the Reverend J. H. Nall of the Prytania Street Presbyterian Church in New Orleans evidently resembled that of the Reverend Thomas DeWitt Talmage of Brooklyn, Clemens' old adversary whom he reproached earlier in this notebook (see p. 445). On 30 April Clemens and Cable heard Nall preach a sermon from John 14:2, "In My Father's House Are Many Mansions" (New Orleans *Times-Democrat,* 30 April 1882). Five years later Clemens would entertain guests at Frederick E. Church's "Olana" with a rendition of this religious service. Among the group assembled on Church's piazza overlooking the Hudson River on 9 June 1887 was Grace King, who wrote the next day: "In the evening Mark Twain just let himself out. . . . One of his funniest hits was an imitation of the sermon Cable took him to hear in the little Prytania St Church when he was in N O" (Grace King to Nina Ansley King, quoted by Robert Bush in "Grace King and Mark Twain," *American Literature* 44 [March 1972]: 35). The incident of the whispering worshiper may have "happened further up the river" in Hannibal on 14 May or in Saint Paul on 21 May; during his Mississippi River journey Clemens spent the other Sundays on steamboats.

[246] The details of this anecdote emerged in an 1885 Autobiographical Dictation: at the Chicago Palmer House banquet given to U. S. Grant by the Army of the Tennessee on 13 November 1879, Clemens talked with a young Union soldier who admired Ingersoll's ideas but feared his oratorical reputation would suffer by comparison with the other illustrious public speakers at the event. Much to the private's relief, however, Ingersoll delivered a spellbinding speech that evoked a massive ovation. Obviously gratified, the young man turned to Clemens and declared, "Egod! He *didn't* get left!" (*MTA,* 1:18).

[247] Sir John Lubbock's *Ants, Bees, and Wasps* was published in 1882.

[248] Whatever Mark Twain intended by this parody, he was not referring to the Book of Colossians: Paul's epistle contains only four chapters.

Shove in episode of Jennie Bruner & Miss Campbell, recalled by Jennie's coming with a play 18 yr after—(& a book?)[249]

The divice in colored glass on the Hotel Brunswick dining-room is a tape-worm! (apparently.)[250]

McWilliamses & false case of Scarlet Fever—ruined all metal work in the house with sulphuric acid[251]—nothing but a rash.

Write short article about Dr. Brown<,>.

Sky get feet wet (Jean)
Aldrich wittiest man in 7 centuries.
Joe's account of that London tramp.[252]
That convict's wonderful letter.[253]
Joe's Fiji cannibal defender.

---

[249] Clemens is confusing the name of Jane W. Bruner, who approached him in March 1882 for assistance in promoting her play, *A Mad World,* with that of her daughter, Jennie. The episode involving Miss Campbell must have taken place long before in California. Jane W. Bruner had written a melodramatic novel about love and marriage in the Sierra Nevada foothills, *Free Prisoners: A Story of California Life* (Philadelphia: Claxton, Remsen, & Haffelfinger, 1877). This may be the "book" to which Clemens refers, since he had purchased a copy of *Free Prisoners* through James R. Osgood & Company on 19 July 1877 (Scrapbook #10, p. 69, MTP).

[250] H. Edwards Ficken designed the new addition to the Hotel Brunswick restaurant which the New York *Tribune* praised as a "gratifying contrast to the gilded mirror steamboat saloon style of decoration" (26 February 1882). Clemens' "tapeworm" could be any of the motifs which Ficken used on the walls, tiles, and stained glass windows of the restaurant.

[251] When John Howells was ill with scarlet fever in 1884, Clemens advised his father: "*Please do remember this*: Mrs. George Warner grasped some door-knobs while her hands were greasy with Vasiline. When she came to fumigate, after scarlet fever, all other metals were destroyed, but those knobs were not affected. This knowledge could have saved us three or four hundred dollars if we had had it when we fumigated" (*MTHL*, p. 464).

[252] Twichell returned to Hartford early in September 1882 after three months in Europe. His stories about London and a "Fiji cannibal defender" are unknown.

[253] Chapter 52 of *Life on the Mississippi* describes a clever literary hoax perpetrated upon Twichell and other unsuspecting pastors and their congregations in 1873 by a "gifted rascal, Williams—burglar, Harvard graduate, son of a clergyman," who was scheming to procure his release from state prison.

Make portrait of old Davis the mate.[254]
Barnum's prize baby[255]
Harte's story of the man in restaurant—about man's life saved &c.[256]

Sketch old Mrs. Mooney for Century—simple & straightford, no effort at effect.

<Ablithnit>Ablishnist's-a-comin! Patter-rollers.[257] [#]

---

254 In an Autobiographical Dictation of 31 August 1906 Mark Twain described "old Davis," chief mate of the *John J. Roe,* who interspersed his "regular orthodox profanity" with terms borrowed from a geology book. Mark Twain seems to be considering Davis as a name for the character in *Life on the Mississippi* modeled after "Dad" Dunham. On 22 July Edmund Gray of the *Gold Dust* wrote to ask, "Did you receive the Photo of 'Dad,' our Second Mate." Mark Twain replied from Elmira on July 31: "Hang it, *no*! I haven't received Dad's photograph. Maybe it was sent to Osgood, Boston, instead of to me, at Hartford. Was it?" (Southeast Missouri State College, Cape Girardeau). John H. Carter of Saint Louis sent Dunham's picture on 23 August 1882. The pen and ink drawing of "Uncle" Mumford on page 305 of the first edition may safely be presumed to be a likeness of Dunham.

255 Early in his career P. T. Barnum began to stage "baby shows" with cash awards and prize medals for winning babies and their mothers. Barnum recounted the success of these publicity stunts in *Struggles and Triumphs,* an autobiography that was among Clemens' favorite books. Barnum's show received widespread attention when one of its elephants gave birth to "Bridgeport," the second elephant ever born in captivity, on 2 February 1882. And Barnum's celebrated British acquisition, "Jumbo" the elephant, arrived from London on 9 April 1882. Clemens may be intentionally conflating one of these "prize babies" with Barnum's previous "baby shows."

256 Clemens is recalling an anecdote he heard Bret Harte relate. An Autobiographical Dictation of 20 December 1906 published in the *North American Review* (186 [September 1907]: 17–21) provides the full version: Harte told of being present in a San Francisco restaurant when a penniless tramp introduced himself to a sea captain and claimed to be Burton Sanders, the sailor who had saved him from drowning at sea a dozen years earlier. Gratified at meeting the man for whom he had long searched, the captain rewarded Sanders with $200 and a free dinner. Harte learned afterwards that the tramp merely impersonated Burton Sanders after overhearing the captain's description of his narrow escape from death. Clemens would make a similarly cryptic entry about the story in Notebook 23.

257 Joel Chandler Harris explained this Negro idiom in a footnote to "Mr. Fox Is Again Victimized" (collected in *Uncle Remus: His Songs and His Sayings* [New York: D. Appleton and Co., 1880], p. 41). The term referred to the various town-

Emerson & Artemus Ward—[258]

Conversations heard in the elevator (hotel).

A dozen young people privately agree that during a whole evening they will deceive one of their number by pretending they see & hear nothing which he sees & hears—& they will glance wonderingly at each other & seem to make furtive comments. An hour after he goes to bed they (the males) slip up & peep into his room & find him avoiding imaginary creature—a staring-eyed maniac.[259]

Some rhymes about the little child whose mother boxed its ears for inattention & presently when it did not notice the heavy slamming of a door, perceived that it was deaf.[260] [#]

---

ship and county patrols which enforced curfew laws and other rules regulating slave activities in the pre-war South. Harris noted that the "patter-roller" figured in a song once current among Southern slaves. Clemens read Harris' stories in 1882 and selected this piece to appear in *Mark Twain's Library of Humor*, where it was published as an extension of "Mr. Rabbit Grossly Deceives Mr. Fox." Marion County, Missouri, had patrollers to thwart Illinois abolitionists, as Mark Twain would recall in Notebook 22 (1884) and in "Tom Sawyer's Conspiracy" (see *HH&T*, pp. 12, 152, 172).

[258] Not until late in his life did Clemens explain this incongruous pairing, which he repeated in Notebook 43 (1900). The details finally emerged in Notebook 48: the incoherency of a lecture by Emerson ("losing his scraps & his place") allegedly caused his uninformed audience to mistake him for the literary comedian Artemus Ward. One confused listener remarked, "He's tolerable funny, but my, he ain't up to his reputation." Since Clemens credited this story to Edward Waldo Emerson, it is possible that he heard the anecdote while visiting Concord with Howells in April 1882.

[259] The theme of practical jokes with tragic consequences intrigued Mark Twain. For *A Tramp Abroad* he invented "The Legend of Dilsberg Castle," relating a prank which left a youthful knight permanently deluded by the conviction he was fifty years older than his actual age (chapter 19). Several times thereafter Mark Twain wrote about pranksters who frightened their victims into insanity simply by donning false-faces: see chapter 53 of *Life on the Mississippi* and "Doughface" (*HH&T*, pp. 143–144).

[260] Mark Twain's notes for *Huckleberry Finn* refer to this situation, specifying that the child's deafness resulted from scarlet fever (DeVoto, *Mark Twain at Work*, p. 67). In chapter 23 of the novel Jim remorsefully blames himself for punishing his daughter Elizabeth for inattention, when in fact scarlet fever had rendered her "plumb deef en dumb."

Put a grave kind character in a play who always tells people the thing that will give them present relief or comfort or pleasure—these lies of course make no end of confusion & complications.

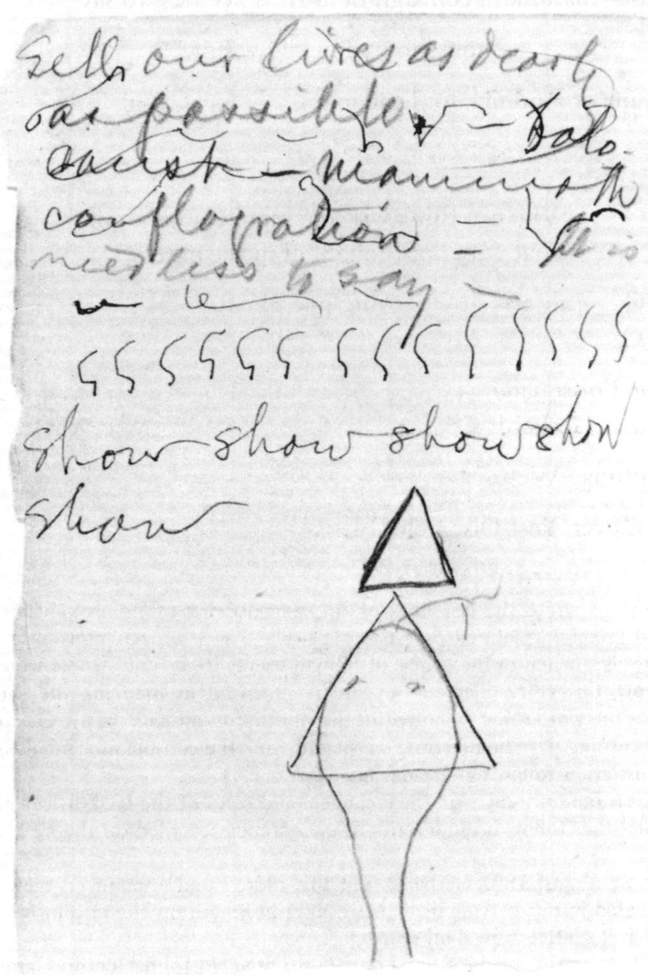

devouring element

"Rejoiced in the euphonious cognomen" &c beggars description—accomplished his hellish purpose—watery grave—I regret to say—

a wellspring of joy—afforded a spectacle more easily imagined than described—It is needless to add.—in durance vile—Giving ourselves up for lost—sickening [*page torn*] Sell our lives as dearly as possible.—holocaust—mammoth conflagration—It is needless to say—[261]

show show show show show[262]

Guavana or Paulinia, for headaches.

Who can think wise or stupid things at all
That were not thought of in the past?[263]

Mrs. C. July 30— || Aug. 1— ///|
C " " ///| " " |||

11 rue Boissonade
Atelier Gerhardt's[264]

Schnutlinge We[in]

J. H. Carter, Post-Dispatch St L[265]

---

261 Clemens wrote the last lines of this penciled list of literary clichés over a shorthand exercise (pictured on page 511) which was written previously in blue ink and reads: "when in the course of human events it becomes [*three words*]."

262 Above this entry Clemens repeatedly practiced in blue ink the shorthand symbol for the word *show* (pictured in the illustration on page 511). On the verso of the succeeding page he practiced in the same ink the consonant symbols pictured in the illustration following "headaches." (p. 512.6).

263 This is the only entry on the cream-colored recto of the back flyleaf; the card game scores that follow begin a series of memoranda recorded on the blue verso of the flyleaf.

264 On 13 August 1882 Gerhardt sent this address and announced that "we are nicely situated in our cosy atelier." An Elmira postmark on the envelope indicates that Gerhardt's letter arrived on 28 August.

265 As river editor for the Saint Louis *Post-Dispatch*, John Henton Carter made frequent announcements in the "River News" column about Clemens' progress during his Mississippi tour, based in part on information which Clemens supplied personally. Carter published humorous annual almanacs under the pseudonym "Commodore Rollingpin"; in 1881 he had written for permission to use one of Mark Twain's sketches in the next edition, and on 24 March 1882 he sent a note of

Mrs. Jno. Ford,[266] Campbelltown, N.Y.
Gen. Lucius Fairchild,[267] Madison, Wis.
Geo. MacDonald, c/o A P. Watt.[268] 34 Paternoster Row.
Jno. Garth[269]
Mrs. Cox,[270] Care G. W. Cable
Dean Sage[271] [#]

---

thanks for Mark Twain's cooperation, along with a proposal to include a passage from "Old Times on the Mississippi" in a future almanac. Walter Blair has noted that *Rollingpin's Humorous Illustrated Almanac* (New York, 1883) contains the report of an interview with Clemens in Saint Louis (*Mark Twain & Huck Finn*, pp. 286–287). On 19 July 1882 Clemens wrote Osgood: "Won't you please send to Commodore Rollingpin and get a photograph of Capt. Isaiah Sellers' Monument in Bellefontaine Cemetery" (*MTLP*, pp. 156–157).

266 Mrs. John K. Ford, Livy's cousin by marriage, lived near Elmira in Campbell, New York. Like most of the people whose names Clemens listed on the back flyleaf, she was probably to receive a complimentary copy of either *The Stolen White Elephant* or *Life on the Mississippi*.

267 Lucius Fairchild, former governor of Wisconsin, had been consul general in Paris during Clemens' 1879 stay there. Fairchild had resigned from his post as United States minister to Spain and returned to Wisconsin earlier in the year. He visited Clemens in Hartford on 7 April 1882.

268 A. P. Watt was the literary agent for George MacDonald, the Scottish minister, novelist, and poet whom Mark Twain met in 1873. MacDonald provided this address in a letter of 26 August 1882 which recommended Watt's services to Mark Twain. Clemens replied to MacDonald on 12 September 1882 informing him that he was not in need of a literary agent and promising to send him a copy of *Life on the Mississippi* when it issued (Greville MacDonald, *George MacDonald and His Wife* [London: George Allen & Unwin, 1924], p. 458).

269 John H. Garth was president of the Farmers & Merchants Bank in Hannibal. Several miles outside of town he maintained a country estate named "Woodside" where Clemens stayed during his visit to Hannibal. On 7 July 1883 Garth wrote to Clemens after receiving a copy of *Life on the Mississippi*: "Thanks for the book. Each and every one at Woodside has enjoyed it greatly."

270 The widowed Mrs. Frances Antoinette Cox and her three children lived across the street from her brother, George Washington Cable, in New Orleans. Clemens sent copies of *The Stolen White Elephant* to Mrs. Cox and her daughter Helen ("Nellie") Morton Cox. Helen Cox thanked him in a letter of 3 July 1882: "I was greatly pleased to receive the book that you sent me especially as it was written by yourself, I have read several of the stories, and I like them very much because they are different from others that I have read, and now since I know you it seems like I could hear you talking."

271 Dean Sage acknowledged enigmatically on 29 July 1882: "I received this morning from an unknown source a copy of a literary production of yours which I

Joe Goodman[272]
Susie Crane <3>5
Gerhardt
<Capt. Edmund Gray.>[273]

The Chas A. Vogeler Co. Balto.[274]

Stedman
Parkman[275]
O W Holmes.
Lowell, Whittier.

Den wie vielten Januar

18 rue de l'Abbè de l'Epeé (Gerhardt)[276]
Father said, "Take care of yourself, & then attach just as many people as you can drag." [#]

---

shall consign to my box in safe deposit co in N Y next time I go there. I am much obliged to you for it." The "literary production" was Mark Twain's *1601*, recently printed in a fifty-copy edition by Lieutenant C. E. S. Wood at the United States Military Academy, West Point.

272 Mark Twain understandably wished to send copies of *The Stolen White Elephant* and *Life on the Mississippi* to his old friend from the *Territorial Enterprise*. After reading *The Prince and the Pauper* Goodman had written from his California ranch on 29 January 1882 to complain that the novel "is the first of your works in which I have ever been disappointed. . . . You went entirely out of your sphere." Goodman's advice was explicit: "Your forte is existing people and things. No one but a mere romancer should travel out of his age."

273 Gray, a pilot for the *Gold Dust*, wrote to Clemens on 22 July 1882 from Memphis: "Capt. J. T. McCord, Lem S Gray and my self each received a White Elephant, Etc. without the aid of detectives, and this acknowledgement though slow in coming, is accounted for, by saying that we have perused the books with a great deal of pleasure."

274 A wholesale drug firm located at 184 West Lombard Street in Baltimore.

275 Mark Twain quoted from Francis Parkman's description of the La Salle expedition in chapter 2 of *Life on the Mississippi* and undoubtedly wanted to send him a copy of the book. The names of Stedman, Parkman, Holmes, Lowell, and Whittier were the last addition to this list, written in blue ink rather than pencil.

276 With the foregoing German sentence fragment Clemens continued his memoranda onto the blue endpaper of his notebook. Hattie Gerhardt informed the Clemens family on 26 December 1882 of her move from Karl Gerhardt's workshop to "a little chamber" on the rue de l'Abbé de l'Epée because of the impending birth of their child. Her note arrived in Hartford on 13 January 1883.

Want a carved board 3 ft long & 7¼ wide The full width is 8¼ inches.[277]

Roswell Smith[278]— Picture
Proposal
2 songs

3125—
100 sh
Me[-----] Co[279]

---

277 On 25 January 1883 Charles L. Webster wrote from New York City: "I called at Tiffanys yesterday & saw Mr De Forest. He promised to send one of the carved boards right away, the price is $20⁰⁰. They are very beautiful indeed." Clemens replied two days later, "I think that the carved board is going to be just the thing" (*MTBus*, p. 209). The moulding was to be an ornament for one of the fireplaces in the Hartford house.

278 Clemens noted the name of the president of the Century Company in ink; the items following his name were listed in pencil.

279 This entry repeats the information (100 shares of Metford stock worth $3,125) noted by Clemens in a list of his investments on page 491 of this notebook.

XXI

"Setting Down Volumes of Literary Stuff"

(April–May 1882)

NOTEBOOK 21 is a travel journal kept by a secretary during Clemens' return to the Mississippi River in April and May 1882. Although not written in Clemens' hand, the entries in this document record with apparent fidelity his impressions of the people and scenes he encountered on a voyage down and then up the river. In order to free himself for sightseeing and conversation, Clemens was attempting again to employ a stenographer-companion, as he had in his 1873 experiment in England with a theological student, S. C. Thompson. Since the earlier attempt had failed not only because Thompson lacked qualifications, but also from personal incompatibility, Clemens used great care in selecting a secretary to accompany him. He began to look for candidates during the Christmas holidays in 1881, well in advance of his departure. He wrote to James R. Osgood on 28 December, giving specifications: "Osgood, remind me to speak of a short-hand reporter to travel with us in the spring. I want a bright, companionable *gentleman*" (*MTLP*, p. 147). At that point Clemens received a recommendation from Livy's relatives in Elmira, and he hastily notified Osgood on 31 December, "Never mind. Crane says the coal-firm's young phonographer will suit me, and the firm would like him to have the trip and the holiday as a testimony of their satisfaction with him. He will not be expensive" (*MTLP*, p. 148). However, this arrangement did not work out, and although Osgood then tried to procure the services of a New York legal stenographer, the "companionable *gentleman*" who finally accompanied Clemens on the trip was Roswell H. Phelps, a stenographer for the Continental Life Insurance Company of Hartford. Phelps was a thirty-seven-year-old bachelor who boarded at the City Hotel; he had taught school in Connecticut, Delaware, and California before beginning a career as a shorthand secretary and newspaper reporter.

The letters written by Phelps to Clemens which establish their arrangements for the excursion survive, although Clemens' replies are not available—if they still exist. On 14 March 1882 Phelps wrote to say that he "should like to go, and *think* I could," but that before he formally consented they ought "to come to a mutual understanding as to terms, etc." and he then must "immediately explain the matter to the Secretary & Pres[t]. of the Co." Among other things, he wished to know "if *typewriting* is a disideratum," for in that case he "must proceed at once to acquire that occult science." He suggested a meeting the next day with Clemens. On 16 March 1882 he outlined acceptable conditions for his employment in a letter to Clemens, explaining that "this would be *much* below my income if I remained here,—but the various advantages of the trip may compensate." Phelps's terms were agreeable to Clemens, for on 20 March 1882 he wrote to Charles Webster, requesting him to "thank Mr. Whitford for his efforts to get me a stenographer, but I had already secured one, just before your letter came" (TS in MTP).

The arrangements were concluded on 12 April, when Phelps mailed Clemens a contract stipulating the terms of his employment for a "trip to the Southwest" to begin on 17 April 1882 and to last "at least four weeks." The contract, Phelps explained, was "merely out of desire to prevent possibility of misconception." As Clemens' "stenographic secretary" Phelps was to receive $100 a month and all traveling and living expenses; for transcribing his stenographic notes (to be completed by 1 June) he was to earn in addition one dollar per thousand words. A copy of the agreement, with Clemens' signature, is in the Mark Twain Papers.

On 17 April Clemens and Phelps left Hartford for New York City, where they were joined by Osgood for their overland trip by rail to Saint Louis. Aboard the *Gold Dust* bound for New Orleans, Clemens expressed exuberant delight with the tour: "We are having a powerful good time & picking up & setting down volumes of literary stuff," he wrote Livy on 22 April (*LLMT*, p. 208). Phelps's notebook was the major repository for Clemens' observations and revived memories, and he found the task of dictating to be pleasant. "Having a most serene & enjoyable time," he assured Livy; "Osgood says he never enjoyed any trip more" (25 April, *LLMT*, p. 210). An itinerary of the river voyage appears at the end of the headnote to Notebook 20.

Traveling in the wake of such celebrities as Mark Twain and his prominent publisher, Phelps naturally was overlooked by interviewing reporters in the cities along the river. Some newspapers observed that Osgood and Clemens were accompanied by a stenographer, but very few mentioned Phelps by name. Clemens himself was strangely silent about the personality of his employee; virtually his only reference to the man occurs in Notebook 20, where he noted on 13 May after leaving Saint Louis for Hannibal that "Phelps fell backward down pilot house stairs—long & steep." This incident may explain Phelps's disappearance from view on the tour after 15 May. On that date the Hannibal *Daily Courier* alluded to Phelps in reporting Clemens' arrival, although the final dictation in Notebook 21 was made on 10 May before the men reached Saint Louis on their way north. If Phelps boarded a train in Hannibal to return East, this may have been because of an injury from his fall. Or, since his contract simply specified that he was to accompany Clemens "to the Southwest," possibly he never was expected to go any further north than Hannibal. Whichever the case, there is no evidence that Phelps completed the journey to Saint Paul.

If Phelps failed to impress his employer sufficiently to be mentioned in Clemens' private notebooks or his later Autobiographical Dictations, at least he also escaped his wrath. Upon returning to Hartford Phelps resumed his position with the Continental Life Insurance Company and continued to work for that firm during much of the remainder of his life. In 1887 he moved to the town of his birth, East Granby, a community north of Hartford. There in 1896 and again in 1898 he was elected probate judge for the district. Phelps died in 1907.

Although Roswell Phelps's secretarial notebook has sometimes been referred to as a shorthand notebook, his original shorthand notes are not known to have survived. In his letter of 16 March proposing terms to

Clemens, Phelps indicated his intention to transcribe his notes day by day during the trip. The existing manuscript is the longhand transcription the stenographer had contracted to produce. It is all in pencil and all in Phelps's legible handwriting except for a single entry interpolated in ink by Clemens reminding himself to criticize the "filthy-clothed waiters" aboard the *Charles Morgan* (p. 548.13) and a calculation (at p. 571.9–11) possibly by Phelps or Clemens, but equally possibly by someone else. The notebook contains only five use marks (at pp. 532.14–533.17 and p. 544.21–29), all probably by Clemens. The marked passages were used with few changes in *Life on the Mississippi,* but other passages also used in the book were not struck through in the notebook.

It is reasonable to assume that the notebook represents substantially what Clemens and his companions said, but the limited evidence available suggests that the specific language of the transcription does not exactly reproduce the original dictation and may at times depart markedly from it. Phelps's task of transforming casual speech into reasonably correct, if colloquial, prose must have required him to supply some details of the text himself. Clemens can hardly have interrupted the narratives of his companions or his own informal dictation to specify for the stenographer details of spelling, capitalization, hyphenation, punctuation, or paragraphing. Hence these parts of the text—its "accidentals"—must have been provided by Phelps. The number and variety of Phelps's revisions of accidentals show how freely he exercised independent judgment in these matters.

Analysis of the manuscript revisions offers clues to the kinds of contributions Phelps may have made to the language of the notebook. For example in the phrases "<th> Capt. Ed. Montgomery's coat" (p. 536.9) and "<f>the first time" (p. 542.21–22), the first revision appears to delete an article, partially written, where none was needed, and the second adds an article where it had been omitted. From these and similar revisions it appears likely that Phelps followed the practice of omitting at least some articles from his original notes and inserting them during transcription of the final draft on the basis of his sense of context.

Doubtless some of Phelps's revisions are corrections of simple transcription errors, but the significance of a change may be quite ambiguous. It is probable that Phelps was merely correcting an eye-skip in the phrase "this <stage> excellent stage of the water" (p. 525.11), although it is not impossible that he inserted the word "excellent" on his own initiative, perhaps to clarify the meaning. On the other hand, in the sentence "I have <only> seen the lead hove only once" (p. 525.21), in which the second "only" was part of the initial inscription, not interlined later, the revision does not look like a corrected eye-skip. It seems improbable that Phelps could have written "only" so far out of place the first time simply by accident. He might, however, have written "I have only seen the lead hove once" in his shorthand notes and then have moved "only" while transcribing the statement in order to improve the diction.

Even when the reason for a revision seems apparent, there may remain a question whether Phelps made the change on his own or at Clemens' direction. Such a problem occurs in the sentence "After that <he> <Watson> Darnell got into trouble with a man who run the ferry & <some of the family> killed the ferryman" (p. 568.7–8). Presumably it was Phelps who decided to replace "he" by "Watson" and then realized his mistake and changed the name to "Darnell." Like other revisions apparently made by Phelps, this change clarifies the sentence without altering the meaning. However, the cancellation of "some of the family" changes the meaning radically. Clemens may have struck out the phrase himself, or he may have directed the stenographer to do so, perhaps when Phelps read the day's dictation back to him. In any case, it seems improbable that Phelps decided on his own to cancel it. A similar problem occurs where Phelps interlined "rigid ferocity" above "ferocious smile" (p. 522.6–7) without canceling either one. Clemens sometimes left such unresolved alternative readings in his own manuscript, and it seems more probable that he told Phelps to add the second version than that Phelps experimented independently with the language of the notebook.

The one revision in the notebook most probably initiated by Clemens is the change from "shoot" to the author's preferred spelling "chute." Phelps wrote "shoot" consistently until the point at which he changed the spelling to "chute" twice in two lines (p. 540.1–2), after which he always wrote "chute." Since "shoot" was accepted as an alternative spelling of "chute" by the 1884 edition of Webster's *American Dictionary of the English Language* (Springfield: G. & C. Merriam & Co.), Clemens' preference seems much the most likely reason for Phelps to have changed his own practice.

To present the complete record of the manuscript, the editorial procedures followed for this notebook are the same as those followed for the notebooks in Clemens' hand even though the errors and idiosyncracies preserved are Phelps's. The recorded details cannot be taken as evidence of Clemens' literary practices, of course, but some of them provide the best clues available about the confidence with which a passage may be accepted as what Clemens said.

Following the entries written by Phelps, sixteen pages of the notebook are occupied by shorthand texts of eleven letters Clemens dictated after his return to Hartford from Elmira in the fall. Although the letters are not dated in the notebook, October dates can be supplied for four of them from the typed transcriptions Clemens sent. Clemens dictated these letters to an unidentified secretary-typist whom he employed in Hartford. No sample of shorthand written by Phelps is available for comparison, but proper names in the notebook texts of the letters are written out in a longhand unlike Phelps's. Since the letters have no connection with the journal contents of Notebook 21 they are not included here.

Notebook 21 is a stenographic notepad, hinged at the top, rather than at the side. It now contains 132 ruled pages, 4 of them blank. At least four leaves have been torn out and are missing. The pages measure 9 by 4⅜ inches (22.9 by 11.2 centimeters) and are ruled with twenty light red lines. The stiff cardboard covers are hinged with black leather and are covered with paper marbled in red, gray, and yellow. The endpapers and the three flyleaves (two in the front) are white. The covers, the gatherings, and many single leaves are loose.

[*two short canceled unrecovered lines*]
<April 18th 1882>

New York to St. Louis
Apl. 18, 1882

The grace and picturesqueness of female dress seem to disappear as one travels west away from N. York.

Orthodoxy <(in re Ingersol)> <for> trembles not so much <at> because Ingersol's arguments are old (stale) as because they are <true.> good.[1] [#]

---

1 On the evening before Clemens arrived in New York City Robert G. Ingersoll

Scene near Greenville, O.

Tendency to the esthetic:—A rather plain, white-painted wooden house<;>, facing the R.R. In the yard two composition Dogs guarding the walk; both with glass eyes—one with a fire-red head & ears; nearer the door two <lions>Lions couchant, regarding <pas> our train and other passing events with a ferocious smile/rigid ferocity; aspect of the dogs more benignant;—half a dozen <[a]> urns and vases;—near the center a cast-iron swan, not dying but evidently pretty sick. All these and other adornments in a door yard barely 50 feet square!

April 19th—This morning struck into the region of full "goatees" —sometimes in company with moustaches, but usually not.

All the R.R. station loafers west of Pittsburgh carry *both* hands in their pockets. Further east one hand is sometimes out of doors. Here never. This is an important fact in Geography.

Mem.:—Monument to Adam[2]

Apl. 20th. A.M.—Went aboard the "Fannie Tatum" purposing to take passage to St. Genevieve. She was just in with a big trip of all sorts of odds-and-ends; and would probably miss going anyway.[3]

---

delivered the first of two lectures assailing the theology of Thomas DeWitt Talmage. The 17 April 1882 New York *Times* reported "some sample Ingersollisms" from his Sunday speech to a large audience in the Academy of Music: Ingersoll belittled the orthodox belief in damnation, miracles, the biblical account of creation, and the divine "calling" of ministers; throughout his address he defended his own character and credibility against Talmage's recent disparagements.

[2] Clemens still toyed with his campaign for erecting Adam's memorial in Elmira, a scheme he had promoted to near success in 1880. Twenty-five years later he incorporated the project into "The Refuge of the Derelicts" (*Mark Twain's Fables of Man*, ed. John S. Tuckey [Berkeley, Los Angeles, London: University of California Press, 1972], pp. 158–202 *passim*, 449–452) and explained its origins in "A Monument to Adam" (*Harper's Weekly*, 15 July 1905).

[3] The *Fannie Tatum* arrived in Saint Louis on April 19 and was scheduled to leave at 5 P.M. the next day for Cape Girardeau, Cairo, and points on the Ohio River. While being loaded at the Saint Louis wharf, however, the boat sprang a leak and her captain, J. B. Conway, was obliged to move the freight and bring in a pump. After repairs the *Fannie Tatum* left on 21 April (Saint Louis *Globe-Democrat*, 18–22 April 1882).

Wanted to make some inquiries of the solitary sentry at the saloon door (a colored boy). He was n't authorized. Could nt make the inquiries of the head steward in the purser's office because the 13 bbls. flour he had brought up from somewhere overslaughed him with business. *He* hadn't the time to talk.

The companionway was less than 2 inches deep in dirt, showing that she had n't been washed down for perhaps a couple of days. The saloon round about the stove was guttered up and splintered, showing that she had n't been repaired as to floors since I was in St. Louis last.

Four iron spittoons around the stove—not particularly clean, but clean enough to show that there hadn't been any passengers aboard this year. Green, wooden chairs, cane seated, all more or less venerable; a venerable colored chambermaid;—everything venerable. No decoration except a painted, pale-green diamond over the state room doors. This boat built by Fulton; has not been repaired since.

Mem:—Comparative scarcity of steam boats now. In old days the boats lay simply with their *noses* against the wharf, wedged in, stern out in the river<.>, side by side like sardines in a box. Now the boats lie end to end.—The "Anchor Line"[4] appears to <line> monopolise

Boarded the "Gold Dust" 5 p.m. Apl. 20th.

Encountered on the deck before starting a vender of books and papers. His name is Sullivan—of pure Irish extraction. He says he came into the world on the 23^{d} Sept 1800. Has lived here 34 years and never crossed the Miss. Says if you meet an Irishman *prove* he is an Irishmn. Not an Irishmn because he is born in Ireland no more than a man is a horse because he's born in a stable. Thousands born in Ireland who are not Irishmen. His ancestors came to Ireland 300 years after the flood and he gave their names. Referring to his business

---

4 Easily visible "anchor" insignia identified steamboats of the company which now dominated passenger service on the river. The Anchor Line owned the *Gold Dust*, on which Clemens went to Vicksburg, and Captain Horace Bixby's *City of Baton Rouge*.

of vending literature, he says:—"I read quite a little in my youthful days. Some say a person has no right to read fiction but I tell ye that all the great men of the day read fiction. I niver met a great man who didnt rade fiction. When you rade the Greek and Latin languages you're rading fiction. Go to-night and rade the firmament; the stars, <are> ivery <o> wan of 'em tells of fiction. Indade, its nicessary for a man to rade fiction to be a scholar."

(By Johnson)[5] "Do they have Scotch whiskey in Ireland?"

"They have *Irish* whiskey sir. They have the best kind.<"> But I don't use much mesilf. I am not a hard drinker, sir. Give an Irishman lager beer for one month and he's a dead man. An Irishman is lined inside with copper and the lager beer corrodes it."

(By Sampson) I suppose the whiskey, on the other hand, tends to polish off the copper."

"Bedad that's the truth of it, sir."

<Said>Says he has a watch for which 20 years ago he was offered $250. He now watches and waits for any offer.

Evening of 20th—10 p.m.

Four hours have elapsed and we have gone a mile, i.e., across the river to E. St. Louis.

April 21—

Landed at 6 o'clock this morning at a God forsaken rocky point where there was an old stone warehouse, gradually crumbling to ruin; two or three decayed dwelling houses, and nothing else suggestive of human life visible. X Nobody put in an appearance except a tallow-faced <man o[f]> beardless man of about 30 carrying one cubic foot of baggage tied up in a red handkchf. As he came aboard his eye caught our Mr. Johnson seated on the forward deck. Something in the stern aspect of Johnson convinced this passenger that he was actually gazing upon the Captain of the Boat. <and a>A self-deprecatory look immediately overspread his features and he quickly crept in out of range of Johnson's eagle glances. X

We put ashore a gentleman and a lady, well-dressed<,> with

---

[5] Mark Twain was trying out fictional names for his traveling companions.

good Russia leather bags; also two very nicely dressed lady like young girls. There was no carriage awaiting and they marched off down the road to go God knows where. It seemed a strange place for civilized folks to land. But the mystery was explained when we got under way again for these people were evidently bound for a large town which lay in behind a tow-head two miles below the landing. I couldn't remember that town; couldn't place it; couldnt call its name; couldn't remember ever to have seen it before; couldn't imagine what the damned place might be. I guessed that it might be St. Genevieve—and that proved to be correct. The town is completely fenced in. Even at this <stage> excellent stage of the water a boat can't land within two miles of it. It is one of the oldest towns in Mo. Built on high ground, handsomely situated; once had good river privileges, but <is>it is no longer a river town. It is town out in the country.

I noticed a beacon at the foot of the crossing—the first one I have seen.

Met the steamer "Centennial"[6] in that crossing.

Can't really tell anything about the stage of the river except I know by the signs that it is falling, and I judge it must be at half-bank stage, at least, because I have <only> seen the lead hove only once. It was below that St. Genevieve crossing where they had quarter less 3 coming into shore and quarter twain after straightening down.

Went up to the pilothouse when we were approaching Chester (where the big Illinois penitentiary is located). Found everything familiar in the pilothouse except that they blow the whistle with a foot-treadle and have a bell-pull that I wasn't acquainted with to call for the electric light, and a big speaking tube under the breast board, whose use I don't know.

Something which suggests short packet lines and quick trips is the absence of spars.

Another brand new thing is the suspending of the "stages" from

---

[6] The *Centennial* was headed for Saint Paul. She was attracting much attention on her way up the Mississippi, for the *Centennial*, 325 feet in length, was reputed to be the largest steamboat ever to undertake a voyage on the upper river.

derricks, letting them swing in the air projecting forward. Admirable contrivance both for quickness and convenience in handling. There is no nighthawk on the jack staff. There is an electric light where it used to be, and that is used in place of the ancient torchbasket. There is an electric head-light over the companionway which can be turned in any direction by the Capt. from his position on deck—so that the landing of a steamboat at night is as easy work as in the day time. They couldnt use the nighthawk lamp to land by because it would blind the pilot.

The officers of this line will go into uniform on the 1st of May. They are quiet and dignified according to the ancient custom. Also the mates; whereas it used to be required of the mate to rip and curse by way of emphasizing orders. One of the 3 mates on this boat is of the ancient tribe.[7] He is one of the old-fashioned, God-damn-your-soul kind. Very affable and sociable. Pointed out a country residence saying, "There, thats a God damned fine place. That place was built out of the profits of the flesh brokerage business in St. Louis. The old bitch that owns that place has the biggest <[h]> whore house in St. Louis. She don't know how much she's worth. Brings the girls down here into the country to freshen them up for work. A man told me he had seen 47 "shimmies" hanging on one line there. She's got a husband and if he don't go straight she licks him. She makes him do as she God damn pleases.

This other place down here is owned by old what's-his-name He's got an income of $100,000. a month. *He* don't give a God-damn. He Don't know how much he's worth."

(This man talks like the machine Barnum had around with his circus for a while. Has that same guttural indistinct, jumbling, rasping way of talking. But this mate can out-swear the machine.)

Our passenger from Nebraska thinks the dinner on the boat was the best he ever "sot" down to. Soup & fish & two kinds of meat and several kinds of *Pie!*

He said to Phelps to-day, "Say, that friend of yours is up in the pilot house. I jest heard him talking & he's an old pilot himself.

---

[7] "Dad" Dunham, second mate of the *Gold Dust*.

Now, he's been giving me taffy, representing that he didnt know much about this river. Judging by his conversation I think he knows *all* about it."

Friday Eve'g Apl 21st.

Visited the pilot house this morning to get warm, and was betrayed by one of the boys—the pilot on watch. He said, "I have seen somebody sometime or other who resembled you very strongly and a great many years ago I heard a man use your voice. He is sometimes called Mark Twain—or Sam Clemens."

I said, "Then don't give me away" and made no further effort to keep up the shallow swindle. The pilot said he recognized me partly by my voice and face and this was confirmed by my habit of running my hands up thro my hair.

Had a great deal of talk about the river and the steam boat men, most of whom are dead now. He located a dozen for me who were still alive. One Sam Bowen died of yellow fever in 1878. Buried at Jackson's point near the head of "<68>65." Another one Bill Krebben[8] died at the same time—or, at least on same trip. He was Bowen's fellow-pilot on the boat. Died of yellow fever, and was buried at Island 68. Will Bowen[9] is an insurance agt. in St. Louis.

Ben Thorndyke[10] is dead. His cub is also dead.

Billy Molloy[11] was pilot of a rebel boat during the war She was

---

[8] William S. Kribben began piloting between Saint Louis and New Orleans in the mid-1850s. At the end of the Civil War he became secretary of the Pilots' Association. In "Villagers of 1840–3" (*HH&T*, p. 32) Clemens identifies Kribben as "the defaulting secretary" whose theft helped wreck the association.

[9] Bowen retired from piloting in 1868; in 1870 or 1871 he moved to Saint Louis, where he formed the Bowen & Andrews insurance firm. Because his agency had increasing business in Austin, Texas, Bowen moved his family there in 1881 (*Mark Twain's Letters to Will Bowen* [Austin: University of Texas, 1941], p. 7), although he probably made frequent trips to Saint Louis.

[10] In the manuscript of *Life on the Mississippi* he is identified as Ben Thornburgh, which was the name used in the first edition. *The St. Louis Directory, for the Years 1854–5* lists "B. T. Thornburgh" as a licensed Mississippi River pilot. Thornburgh's cub pilot was J. W. ("Bill") Hood, whom Clemens recalled in Notebook 20, p. 455.

[11] Clemens no doubt had known William Molloy when they both piloted on

about to fall into the hands of the federals so they blew her up as a matter of precaution, and blew Billy up with her.

Ed. Montgomery[12] who was commodore of the rebel fleet in the battle of Memphis has lost his eyesight in a large measure.—

Horace <Bigsby>Bixsby[13] is capt. of the "Baton Rouge."

An old partner of mine is capt. of another boat.[14]

Mike Gavin[15] is dead.

Strother Wiley[16] is alive. All the Cables[17] are dead.

There is a new Association two or three years old, numbering over 80 members. 30 are employed by the "Anchor" line; about 20 are employed by towing, freight lines; the other 30 subsist upon odd jobs. The Association is not as strong as the old one was.

I found that the river was as brand new to me as if it had been built yesterday and built while I was absent. I recognized no single feature of it until I got to Grand Tower. Then I recognized the reach to the right of the Island because I had snagged a boat there once. I recognized the bend around the Island before we got to the foot of it because I tried to snag another boat there once.

---

the Lower Mississippi River. Molloy is listed in *Kennedy's Saint Louis City Directory for 1857* and the *St. Louis Directory 1859.*

[12] Evidently James E. Montgomery, a former steamboat captain for whom Clemens piloted. See note 27 and p. 536.

[13] Mark Twain soon saw Bixby again. The New Orleans *Times-Democrat* (4 May 1882) reported that the two men "met and embraced" in New Orleans on 3 May.

[14] Sobieski ("Beck") Jolly, formerly a pilot on the *John J. Roe,* was captain of the Anchor Line steamboat *William P. Halliday* in 1882.

[15] His name was spelled "Michael Gaven" in the list of "Licensed Pilots" for the Lower Mississippi published in *Kennedy's Saint Louis City Directory for 1857.*

[16] Calling him Stephen W., Mark Twain wrote about pilot Strother Wiley's "delicious impertinences to steamboat captains" in the sixth and seventh installments of "Old Times on the Mississippi."

[17] Between 1854 and 1859 the Saint Louis city directories contain listings for Chauncy Cable, steamboat captain; Isaac C. Cable, steamboat captain and pilot; and George W. Cable, steamboat captain. Arlin Turner has documented the fact that various distant relatives of the writer George Washington Cable were engaged in steamboat trade on the river (*George W. Cable: A Biography* [Durham, N.C.: Duke University Press, 1956], p. 8).

I didn't find Hat Island and upon inquiry learned that it has utterly disappeared.

I "run" the crossing above Cape Girardeau and did it right. Found an old friend at the cape whom I had n't seen for 21 years.[18] I run the bend below Cape Girardeau—which is the first bend I ever did run. It is about the only one that a cub was permitted to run in low water in the old times. <I>

I was able to recognize Grand Chain, but the rocks are all under water.

Recognized Commerce, but didn't remember Cat Island at all—if that is the name of it. Didn't seem to me that any island belonged there. Found Beaver Dam Rock after it was pointed out to me; but it was in the middle of the river and we went down to the left of it—whereas there wasn't room to the left of it in my day.

The place where we grounded the A. B. Chambers[19] has long ago ceased to be anything but sand with a little water on top of it. Nothing left of Goose Island but a patch the size of a steamboat; and the grave yard where we used to hug the Ill. shore is a deserted grave-yard now. Boats go down the right of Goose Island. Dog Tooth bend has ceased to be the channel—one goes down the middle of the river now. The Missouri Sister is gone entirely. The Ill. Sister has moved over to the Missouri side. The shoot is closed up and the Sister is joined to the Mo. land with hardly a low place between and with a mile of river in front of it. It is thoroughly joined to the Mo. shore. But the people on it pay taxes in Illinois and work on Ill. roads.

At Cairo the Illinois Bend is made away down. The Big Rock which used to be in the middle of the crossing moved away up the

---

18 Before leaving Hartford Clemens had resolved to look up his one-time Saint Louis roommate, Jacob H. Burrough, now a fifty-seven-year-old attorney in Cape Girardeau, Missouri (see Notebook 20, p. 456).

19 The *A. B. Chambers*, a side-wheel steamboat built in 1855, was not seriously damaged in this mishap. The boat eventually snagged and sank near Saint Louis on 24 September 1860; on that date Clemens was piloting the *Alonzo Child* toward New Orleans (SLC to Orion Clemens, 28 September 1860, *MTL*, p. 48; William M. Lytle, *Merchant Steam Vessels of the United States 1807–1868* [Mystic, Conn.: Steamship Historical Society of America, 1952], p. 248).

river and then exposed itself and was blown up by the government.

The moving down of the point has moved Cairo away up the river far above where it ought to be.

Saw the boat landed at Cairo where my partner Joe Bryan[20] sunk a coal boat once, and where I next trip ran into a stern-wheeler by order of the Capt.[21] He said there wasn't any steamboat there and I tried to prove it to him and succeeded by mashing that stern-wheeler all to pieces. He tried to get me to go into court and swear that I didn't see any stern-wheel boat there, but I said "No, I did see a stern wheeler there" and promised to drive it out into the state of Ill. if he gave the order and he did; I did the best I could. It cost him $900.

The river is so thoroughly changed that I can't bring it back to mind even when the changes have been pointed out to me. It is like a man pointing out to me a place in the sky where a cloud has been. I can't reproduce the cloud. Yet as unfamiliar as all the aspects have been to-day I have felt as much at home and as much in my proper place in the pilot house as if I had never been out of the pilot house. I have felt as if I might be informed any moment it was my watch to take a trick at the wheel.[22]

To-night when some idiot approaching Cairo didn't answer our

---

[20] Joseph W. Bryan was listed in *Lloyd's Steamboat Directory* (1856) as a Mississippi River pilot based at Saint Louis. He wrote to Clemens on 12 August 1882, recalling their last meeting at the outset of the Civil War when "you gave me your picture which I have at home yet." In 1882 Bryan was an officer on the Anchor Line steamboat *City of Greenville*.

[21] Clemens recalled this incident again in a 1906 notebook entry: "Drove Alonzo C into sternwheler." The *Alonzo Child*, a side-wheel steamboat, was built in 1857; Clemens served aboard her during the last segment of his piloting career—from September 1860 until April 1861.

[22] According to his later recollections, Clemens soon was granted the privilege for which he yearned: "When we got down below Cairo, and there was a big, full river—for it was high-water season and there was no danger of the boat hitting anything so long as she kept in the river—I had her most of the time on his [Lem Gray's] watch. He would lie down and sleep, and leave me there to dream that the years had not slipped away; that there had been no war, no mining days, no literary adventures; that I was still a pilot, happy and care-free as I had been twenty years before" (*MTB*, p. 738).

whistle but rounded to across our bows and came near getting himself split in two I felt an old-time hunger to be at the wheel and cut him in two,—knowing I had fulfilled the law and it would be his fault. By shipping up and backing we saved him, to my considerable regret—for it would have made good practical literature if we had got him.

Found Cairo looking very natural by the light of the gas and our own electric light from the pilot house, and concluded to wait till morning and go ashore and examine it.

Found government lights everywhere all down the river. This is too much. It takes away <all the> a great deal of the agony of piloting and must make it even more enjoyable than it used to be,—and it was always enjoyable enough.

Hove the lead three times. Had Quarter Three at the foot of Jacket Pattern; Quarter Twain at another place, and Deep Four at another. But this information will not be valuable because I don't know where those places are. Didn't know at the time; don't know yet.

Birds Point looked as it always looked, except that the river has moved Mr. Bird's house ¾ mile nearer to the front than it used to be.

Mem:

The only thing that remains to me now of the technical education which I got on the river is the faculty of remembering numbers, streets and addresses,—which I trace to the automatic remembering of the depths of water by the lead.

THE HANDCAR EPISODE.

The second mate "Dad" Dunham said he went out on the Iron Mountain R.R. with Elevator Dodge and Joe Smith to look at some property they wanted to buy. They were rich men, and on coming back he said:

"We took one of these God-damned hand cars propelled by a couple of damned niggers. Presently we came to a down grade and along there was a lot of shanties occupied by a lot of damned niggers. Just as we passed by one of these shanties, going like Hell out came an old sow. She jumped right ahead of the hand car across the track.

But she got left. So did we. The hand car chopped the sow into two pieces. I went down the bank about 60 feet amongst the rocks and things. Elevator Dodge he come down, too, and then he sung out 'Are you hurt?' and I says 'By God, give me a chance to examine.' The other fellow went to Hell on the other side. We scrambled up, examined ourselves and found there wasn't a Goddamned bruise on any of us. Wasn't nobody hurt but that hog, and by God they taxed us $16. for that hog. If it was to do over again I would come on those niggers for damages to myself.

Mem: Piano playing and singing aboard the "Gold Dust."

Song "When I am far away, Oh then you'll love me still." Deep pathos.

Mem: Regarding a pilot who disappeared three or four years ago.[23]

Capt. McCord[24] (In re Beulah Lake, Isl. 74) When the state of Arkansas was chartered she controlled to the center of the river. Since then a cut off has been made. Some years after a cut off was made throwing part of Arkansas over onto the Miss. side. After that the state made a new charter and adopted the same language—that the boundary line should be to the channel of the river. That leaves this island on the other side <as>and Missippi has no control, Arkansas has no control, and the owner is monarch of all he surveys. Has about 4000 acres. [#]

---

[23] Phelps repeated this same entry in the "Memoranda" section of his notepad (p. 569). The description fits William C. Youngblood, a pilot on the *John J. Roe* whom Mark Twain discussed in an Autobiographical Dictation on 31 August 1906. Then he spoke of him as a "fine" man who "had a young wife and two small children —a most happy and contented family." Youngblood risked his life to save the passengers on a burning steamboat he was piloting (see Notebook 20, p. 457); but "a year or two later, in New Orleans, he went out one night to do an errand for the family and was never heard of again. It was supposed that he was murdered, and that was doubtless the case, but the matter remains a mystery yet."

[24] John T. McCord was captain of the *Gold Dust*. Mark Twain drew a vertical slash mark in blue ink across this entire entry, which would appear as part of chapter 33 in *Life on the Mississippi*. He similarly marked the entries "Avoiding the liquor law" (used in chapter 33), "Change of river course" (discussed in chapter 29), and "Island No. 10" (included in chapter 26).

Avoiding the liquor law.

The State of Miss. allowed no liquor to be sold. A fellow got possession of Isl. 92 which belonged to Ark. but is really joined to the Miss. shore. He established a whiskey shop there & so got Miss. patronage under protection of Ark. where there were no restrictions.

Change of river course.

Channel used to cut thro' above Isl. 37 by Brandywine bar and went down towards Isl. 39. Afterwards changed its course & went from Brandywine down to Fogleman's shoot in the Devil's Elbow, & passed thro that shoot to Isl. 39—part of this course reversing the old order, the river running *up* 4 or 5 miles instead of down and so cutting off throughout say 15 miles of distance.

This in 1876. All that region now called Centennial Island.

ISLAND NO. 10.

<[-]> The river passes from Ky. into Tenn., back into Mo. then back into Ky. and thence into Tenn.

That is, a mile or two of Mo. sticks over into Tenn.

A *model contract.*

The pilot's brother rented his farm. Contract with his tenant that he (owner) should get every *third* load of corn. When harvest time came didnt get any corn. Asked tenant why & his reply was "I didn't have but 2 loads." That threw out the proprietor altogether.

Island No. 8.

War times. Bombarded for 2 weeks. Jeff Thompson[25] took command & slipped out through the swamp. Federals evacuated same night and got 20 miles off before they heard <we> rebels had gone.

Feds then came back & took possession.

Opposite Isl. No. 8 is Jim Bayou where they kill a white man for

---

25 Lieutenant Colonel M. Jeff Thompson, a former mayor of Saint Joseph, Missouri, organized troops who became known as "Thompson's Swamp Rats." In 1861 he staged a series of raids around Cape Girardeau and New Madrid. His operations along the Mississippi did not end until his surrender in 1865.

$10. and a nigger for $5. A nigger had rather go overboard than be landed at Jim Bayou.

This region remains the same everlasting stretches of unbroken forests

In Grand Tower there were two hotels and a hall as I could see by the signs. There were 2 hotels in New Madrid as I could see by the same sign. Old frame shanties, shabby affairs. Both of these places and the average village on the banks of the river were mere collections of tumble-down frame houses unpainted, looking dilapidated and miserable.

We landed <at> a drunken man at Point Pleasant who failed to get ashore at New Madrid.

The village of Point Pleasant consisted, as usual, of perhaps a dozen frame shanties of an <und><and> uncared for sort. The only life visible at Point Pleasant was a brisk man in his shirt sleeves, a nigger on a mule and an unoccupied hog. More life at Point Pleasnt than we saw in any other village of its size.

The scenery all day has been just what it always was in my time—everlasting stretches of almost unbroken forests on both sides of the river amid soundless solitude. Here and there a miserable cabin or two standing in small opening on the gray and grassless banks of the river,—cabins that had formerly stood a quarter or half mile further in and gradually pulled back & further back as the banks of the river caved in.[26]

The verdure is in its fresh spring green, and so is in pleasant contrast to the leafless New England region. There is nothing clean except nature.

We are glad we struck the "Gold Dust." She is clean <and> comfortable and well-ordered. All she needs is to sand-paper the table bill of fare, which is the same old bill of fare they had last year.

Hickman looks about as it always did; and so does Columbus

---

[26] Mark Twain enclosed this paragraph within diagonal lines in black ink. He employed these two sentences near the beginning of chapter 33 in *Life on the Mississippi.*

where the battle of Belmont was fought. Hickman is said to be decaying. They raised a good deal of money there to get a railway built to some place or other. As soon as the <r>R.R. was finished it walked off with all their trade, carried it eastward<.>, whereas in former times Hickman had a prodigious tobacco trade—a prosperous place.

The river goes down the right hand shore at No. 21. The tow head has closed down under the head of 21.

Reached Plum point after nightfall. Saw government fleet there with its colored lights. Had three or four lights in the Bend below Plum Point. The old avenue was still there. Bulletin tow head still there. Just missed a big snag at the head of the tow-head. So many government lights that piloting is a very easy matter. There was a light on Craig Heads point. At the foot of Plum Point bend <and that> was where the federal fleet was stationed and where the rebel fleet came up from Fort Pillow which was in sight on the Tenn. shore and fought a battle on the 10th May 1863. Capt. Ike Fulkerson had command of the rebel fleet. His tiller rope was cut by a shot. He had to draw out of the fight and the rest of his fleet followed and, (the pilots say) gave up the fight when they had really whipped the federals and didn't know it.[27]

Big cut-off at Commerce below Memphis has left Walnut Bend out in the cold.

<Mem:—Irregularity of the street walks (board walks) in Memphis. Habit of rising up at one end [& striking] a fellow's eye.>

Mem: Irregularity of the street pavements in Memphis. Roses in full bloom there climbing up the trellises and posts. [#]

---

27 Clemens' account is mistaken in several particulars: the engagement actually took place on 10 May 1862 with Commodore James E. Montgomery in command of the Confederate fleet; Isaac D. Fulkerson was captain of the *General Earl Van Dorn*; the accident to the tiller rope occurred aboard the *General Bragg*. It was Montgomery who ordered the retreat when he realized that the Union forces were regrouping in water too shallow for his fleet (U.S., Naval War Records Office, *Official Records of the Union and Confederate Navies in the War of the Rebellion*, series 1, 27 vols. [Washington, D.C.: Government Printing Office, 1894–1917], 23:55–57).

Ship Island is grown up. The tow-head has closed down on it & shut it off. The Pennsylvania was sunk just above this place.[28]

The St. Nicholas <blue>blew up near Ship Island and the mate stood at the stern with a pistol and kept the rush of passengers back until the women and children could be got into the boats.[29]

<The>Between Cairo and St. Louis there is <one> a wreck to every mile on average. Distance 200 miles.

Boats used to burn wood; now burn coal.

One time I mistook <th> Capt. Ed. Montgomery's[30] coat hanging on the big bell for the Capt. himself and waiting for him to tell me to back I ran into a steamboat at New Orleans

Landed at Memphis, morning Apl. 23, and took an hour's drive. Was recognized by a lawyer (Brown) at the hotel. He said he noticed the name W. Clemens on register.

All around Memphis and up & down this section there is a monotonous sound of profanity. It begins to sound almost wicked.

Reached Helena Ark. about 5:30. P.M. Went out for a stroll about <to>the town. All been under water. (Vide Photographs.) The plank walks loosened and irregular. Had to <be> step careful or a

---

[28] With Henry Clemens aboard, in 1858.

[29] The *Saint Nicholas* (built in 1853) exploded near Helena, Arkansas, on 24 April 1859 with a loss of sixty lives. Clemens had alluded to the *Saint Nicholas* calamity in "A Curious Experience," published in the November 1881 issue of the *Century*. This third reference in Notebooks 20 and 21 to a level-headed figure of authority echoes Clemens' comment on Harriet Martineau's story of some gamblers who seized a lifeboat and refused to take aboard other survivors from their sinking river vessel. "Not like mate of St Nicholas & man in Va City theatre," Clemens noted in his copy of *Retrospect of Western Travel*, 2 vols. (London: Saunders and Otley, 1838), 2:12 (in MTP) which he received and inscribed in December 1877.

[30] James E. Montgomery was captain of the *City of Memphis* when Clemens piloted that boat in 1860. In 1874 Clemens informed a correspondent: "Edward Montgomery is worthy to be an admiral of the blue. I ran the *City of Memphis* into a steamboat at New Orleans one night under his orders and he never went back on me—shouldered the responsibility like a man" (Saint Louis *Times*, 2 May 1874).

loose board would fly up and hit Johnson on the nose. Rude boats, box shape, improvised for the sudden flood lying around in the streets and vacant lots by the dozen.

Saw a garden which a man had planted with oyster cans. Couldn't raise anything else, so tried to raise oysters.

Johnson noticed a young lady in a door yard—a stylish pretty lady—quite a relief to the dismal monotony of the town.

Battle of Belmont.[31]
Pilot's[32] story.

It was the 7th November. The fight began at 7 in the morning. I was on the R. H. W. Hill.[33] Took over a load of troops from Columbus. Came back and took over a battery of Artillery. My partner said he was going to see the fight. Wanted me to go along. I said no, I wasn't anxious I would look at it from the pilot house. He said I was a coward, and left.

That fight was an awful sight. Gen. Cheatem[34] made his men strip their coats off and throw them in a pile and said "Now follow me to Hell or victory!" I heard him say that from the pilot house; and then he galloped in at the head of his troops. Old Gen. Pillow[35] with his white hair mounted on a white horse sailed in, too, leading his troops mighty lively. By & by the federals chased the rebels back, and here they came down under the bank where they took shelter. All at once

---

[31] The Battle of Belmont, Missouri, was a one-day engagement in 1861 which cost each side more than six hundred men. Grant attacked the fortified Confederate camp of Belmont with over three thousand troops, using gunboats to protect his men from enemy artillery. Grant occupied the camp and burned it, but was nearly cut off from his river transports by rebel reinforcements brought to the scene in steamboats from downstream. Grant's supporting gunboats managed to open an exit for his forces, and they withdrew with captured guns, horses, and a few prisoners.

[32] Lemuel Gray and his brother Edmund divided the pilot watches on the *Gold Dust*, so this narrative is attributable to one of them. Mark Twain repeats the story in chapter 26 of *Life on the Mississippi*.

[33] The *H. R. W. Hill* was among four transport ships which ferried Confederate troops across the river during the battle.

[34] Brigadier General Benjamin Franklin Cheatham led a flanking attack by Confederate forces after he arrived from Columbus, Kentucky.

[35] Brigadier General Gideon Johnson Pillow.

I noticed a whizzing sound passing my ear. Judged that was a bullet. I didn't stop to think about anything. Sit with my leg hanging out of the pilot house window. I just tilted over backward and landed on the floor and stayed there. The shots came booming around. Three cannon balls went thro the chimney; one ball took off the corner of the pilot house; shells were bursting around. Mighty warm times—wished I hadn't come. I lay there on the pilot house floor while the shots came faster and faster. I crept in behind a big stove in the middle of the pilot house. Presently a minnie ball came thro the stove and just shaved my <hat> head & cut my hat. I thought it was time to get away from there. The Capt. was on the roof with a red-headed major—a fine looking man—from Memphis. I heard him say he wanted to leave here but "that pilot is killed." I crept over to the starboard side to pull the bell to set her back. Raised up and took a look and I saw about 15 shot holes thro the window panes came so lively I had n't noticed them. I glanced out on the water and the spattering shot were like a hail storm. I thought best to get out of that place. I went down the pilot house guy <hed>head first. Before I <reached> struck the deck the Capt. said I must <get> leave there. So I climbed up that guy and got on the floor again. About that time they collared my partner & were bringing him up to the pilot house between two men. Somebody had said I was killed. He poked his head in and saw me on the floor reaching for the backing bells. He said "Oh, Hell, he aint shot," and jerked away from the men who had him by the collar and ran below. We were there until 3 o'clock in the afternoon and then got away all right.

The next time I saw my partner I said "Now, come out, be honest and tell me the truth. Where did you go when you went to see that battle?" He says, "I went down in the hold."

All thro that fight I was scared nearly to death. I hardly knew anything I was so frightened, but you see nobody knew that but me. Next day Gen. Polk[36] sent for me and praised me for my bravery and

[36] General Leonidas Polk commanded the Confederate force which compelled Grant to give up the captured Belmont camp. In a report to his headquarters after the battle Polk complimented the pilots and officers of the transport steamers that

gallant conduct. I never said anything; I let it go at that. I knew it wasn't so but it wasn't for me to contradict an able general. Pretty soon after that I was sick and used up and had to go off to the Hot Springs. When there I got as many as 25 letters from commanders of fleets saying they wanted me to come back. I declined because I wasn't well enough or strong enough. But I kept still and kept <my> the reputation I had made.

Napoleon, Ark. Apl. 24.

The town (2000 inhab.) used to be where the river now is. Washed entirely away by a cut-off and not a vestige of it remains—except one little house and the chimney of another which were out in the suburbs once.

THE CAPTAIN'S[37] STORY.

Senator Bogy of Mo.[38] had a son a pompous sort of a fellow. His name was Joe. Joe was fond of being known as the son of Senator Bogy, and liked to be introduced at parties and gatherings as "Mr. Bogy son of Senator Bogy."

He got to be quite well known in this respect. A man once got off this parable:—

"I had a very singular dream last night. I dreamed I was dead & in next world. The Lord was up there sitting on his throne with the angels around him. Directly who should walk in but Joe. His name was announced "Joe Bogy son of Senator Bogy." The Lord at once spoke and said:—<">'Christ, my son, get up and give a seat to the son of Senator Bogy of Missouri.

Island No. 63.—A story connected therewith:—Capt. Jesse Jimerson of the "Skylark" had <an> a friend an old, old pilot—superannuated old fellow. The Capt. left him at the wheel for a little while.

---

had ferried troops and ammunition. Under "heavy fire," he wrote, they "stood firmly at their posts, and exhibited a fearlessness and energy deserving of the highest praise" (Polk to Colonel W. W. Mackall, 10 November 1861, *Official Records of the Union and Confederate Navies,* 22:409).

37 John T. McCord entertained Clemens with the three anecdotes which follow.

38 Lewis Vital Bogy, a Saint Louis attorney and businessman, had served as United States senator from 1872 until his death in 1877.

That ancient mariner went up thro the <shoot> chute down the river up thro the <shoot> chute and down again all thro' his watch. Supposed was going down the river all the time. A darkey saw the boat passing so often and said, 'Clar to gracious! I reckon dar must be a whole line o' dem ar Skylarks.

The "Eclipse" was <th> noted as being the fastest boat.[39] She had just passed an old darkey on shore who happened not to recognize her name. Presently some one asked him, "Any boat gone up?" "Yes sah." "Was she going fast?" Oh, so-so, loafing along." "Now, do you know what boat that was?"

"No, sah."

"Well, that was the Eclipse."

"Oh, well, she just went by here a sparkling!"

The pilot thinking I was a greenhorn put up a good deal of remarkable river information on me.

The Capt. said that if this boat were to sink right here (Ark. section) in less than one hour there would be a hundred pirates out here in skiffs after plunder.

Down here we are in the region of boots again. They don't wear shoes.

Fence-rail quarrel.

During the high water one man's fence rails washed down on another mans ground and the latter's rails around on to former's ground. Kind of exchange of rails. In the eddy they got mixed somehow. One said to the other "<let>Let it remain so; I will use your rails & you mine." But the other wouldn't have it so. One day the first man came down on the other's place to get his rails. The other said "I'll kill you, you son of a bitch, and went for him with a revolver. The other said "I'm not armed" and the assailant threw

[39] In 1852 and 1853 the *Eclipse* made record runs from New Orleans to Natchez, Cairo, and other upstream ports. Mark Twain described her exploits in "Old Times on the Mississippi" (*Atlantic Monthly*, August 1875) in a section published as chapter 16 of *Life on the Mississippi*.

down his revolver and came at him with a knife, cut his throat all around but not severing the jugular vein or arteries. Struggling around the man whose throat was cut got hold of the other's revolver on the ground and shot him dead<.>, but survived his own injuries.

Another.

Two shop-keepers in adjoining stores had a quarrel. One of them put his hand back in his hip pocket to get some documents. The other thought he was going for a weapon, drew his pistol and began firing. The first called out "Im not armed; don't kill an unarmed man." But the other kept on firing and killed him. Was acquitted by the jury.

When the niggers move from one plantation to another by these boats they carefully get all their dogs aboard—mangy, yellow dogs—and are so interested in the dogs that they sometimes forget their children. In one instance they brought aboard six miserable dogs and left a child on the landing. The people had to take care of that child.

Neither this country nor any other can ever prosper until the votes of the two parties are nearly equal

Stopped at Arkansas City April 24. This is a Hell of a place. One or two streets full of mud; 19 different stenches at the same time. A thriving place nevertheless. A R.R. here—the Little Rock, Miss. river & Texas R.R.[40]

April 25.

Landing at head of what was Kentucky <bend>Bend. Up at 4 o'clock in the morning.

The filling up of this Bend was the result of that Shirt Tail Bend cut-off, which was made in my time.

Birds singing here at sunrise; foliage green in the distances very effective. The strong green of solid walls of forest near at hand paling gradually with the distance and vanishing. Shadows thrown by projecting trees produced fine effect. The first blush of the rising sun

---

[40] Clemens owned stock in this railroad: see his list of holdings in Notebook 20 (p. 491).

out on the over-flow, was pink, then purple; and the reflections in the still water beautiful.[41]

UNPROFITABLE BUSINESS.
(Pilot)

A fellow was persuaded by his friends to start a hotel at a sort of R.R. junction thinking he would pick up a good business. He fitted up his place all nice—ice coolers, water-closets &c. But his expectations not realized. People didn't patronize him much except to drink his ice water & urinate there.

One of his friends asked him how was business. He replied, "Well, I can't say exactly yet. Haven't struck a balance."

"What do you mean? Can't you judge whether you are making anything?"

Well, it stands like this:—They come here and exchange their piss for my ice water and I have n't sold the piss yet."

Used to be a great many snags below foot of Kentucky Bend. Hard wind blowing and boat ran over snags & began to sink. Old Capt. Poe's wife was in her state-room. Door locked. The Capt. broke in door with a heavy axe but in so doing cut open his wife's head.

Apl. 25 p.m.

Off Hilliard's took soundings and found *mark twain* for <f>the first time.

15 feet of water on some portions of the overflowed country.

Capt. McCord says there is not an old planter who does not favor abolishing the levees altogether. [#]

---

[41] On this same day (25 April 1882) Clemens mailed a letter to his wife which expanded upon the language of this passage:

> It was fascinating to see the day steal gradually upon this vast silent world; & when the edge of the shorn sun pushed itself above the line of forest, the marvels of shifting light & shade & color & dappled reflections, that followed, were bewitching to see. And the luxurious green walls of forest! & the jutting leafy capes! & the paling green of the far stretches! & the remote, shadowy, vanishing distances, away down the glistening highway under the horizon! *and* the riot of the singing birds!—it was all worth getting up for, I tell you. (*LLMT*, p. 210)

Pilcher's Point, La.

The river here has cut off 300 yards from the bank by this flood. The steamboat now sails over the spot where was a garden last season.

(Col. York[42] lands here.)

River now 44 ft. above low water. Has fallen 8 ft.

(When this river gets a mortgage on a man's farm it is bound to foreclose.)

Here is where "Old Dad" (2^{d} mate) said to the roustabouts—"Come, come God damn you, circulate around. Do ye think you're pall bearers!"

Land Co.

Col. Calhoun,[43] (gr.son of J. C. Calhoun) went to Boston and formed a syndicate which purchased an immense tract of land on this river in Chico Count, Ark.,—some 10,000 acres,—for cotton growing. Banker Corbin in Boston[44] at head of syndicate. They purpose to work on a cash basis, buy at first hands and handle their own product<.>; to supply their negro <b>laborers with provisions & necessaries at a small profit, say 8 or 10%.; to furnish them comfortable quarters &c., and encourage them to save money and remain on the place.

If this proves a financial success (as it seems certain) they propose to establish a banking house in Greeneville & loan money at reasonable interest—say 6%.

The trouble heretofore has been that the planters altho owning the land, were without cash capital. Had to hypothecate their land

---

42 General Zebulon York had directed relief operations in this region during the March floods. Mark Twain included in Appendix A of *Life on the Mississippi* an article from the New Orleans *Times-Democrat* which praised York's efforts to rescue farm families and their livestock and distribute rations in the northern Louisiana parishes.

43 For more than a decade John Caldwell Calhoun (1843–1918) had been colonizing his Arkansas plantation with Negro freedmen from throughout the South; in 1884 he would sell his land holdings and move to New York City, where he gained control of numerous railroads and mines.

44 Probably Austin Corbin, president of the Corbin Banking Company; his offices were in New York City.

and crop to carry on the business. Consequently, the commission dealer who furnishes the money takes some risk and demands big interest—usually 10% and 2½ per ct. for negotiating the loan. <Had to buy all th> Planter has also to buy all his supplies thro same dealer paying commis. & profits Then when he ships his cotton the dealer adds his commissions insurance &c making altogether about 25% which he (dealer) gets out of the crop. So the eastern capitalist thinks 20 or 25% profit a good venture. (Syndicate's capital about one million.) One man and mule will raise 10 acres cotton—giving

10 bales cotton worth say	500.
Cost of producing	350.
net profit	150.

Or $15. per acre

There is also now a profit from the cotton *seed* which used to be deemed worthless.

In 1600 lbs crude cotton there is 400 lbs. lint @ say 10c

There is 1200 lbs. seed which is worth $12. or 13. per ton.

The oil made from cotton seed is colorless tasteless and odorless.

They used to ship so much of it to Italy that it interfered with their Olive vineyards & the gov^t put duty on it.

The inhabitants along here in Miss. & La. will send up the river to buy vegetables rather than raise them & they will come aboard the steamer at landings & buy fruits of the bar keeper. They don't know anything but "cotton." The bar keeper says he believes they don't know how to raise vegetables & fruit.

He says a nigger will go to Hell for a watermelon. Bar keeper buys watermelons for 5c up the river, brings them down & sells them for 50c. A bar used to make $2000. a trip in old times. A father who left his son a steamboat bar left him a fortune.[45]

Vicksburg Nat. Cemetery. See reverse portion of this book.[46] [#]

---

[45] A single vertical pencil mark was drawn through this entry. Mark Twain used its material in chapter 33 of *Life on the Mississippi*.

[46] Phelps placed Clemens' observations about this landmark in the "Memoranda" section at the back of the notebook (p. 572).

On board "Chas. Morgan" Apl 26 p.m.[47]

At Rodney's Reach the plantations all gone. (Petit Gulf.)

Pilot of the "Morgan" says river is not as easy to navigate as it used to be. The bars are sharper and harder to get over.

In 1873–4 water only 7 feet deep in channel below Vicksburg. Pilot thinks levee system wrong.

Passed Bruin's Burk 50 miles below Vicksburg where Gen Grant crossed the river.[48]

It used to be 60 miles from Vicksb. to Grand Gulf. <only>Only 35 now. No gain <fur>for the boats as the shortening has increased the current.

Pilot says "The crookeder the river the better navigation."

Very few, if any, boats now run up the White, Red & Ark. rivers. The railroads have taken the traffic. Only two or three boats go up the Mo. river. Pilot says that river is difficult to navigate. Once he sailed up 1000 miles, by using great care, & then run into a snag & sunk. Worked 6 weeks trying to raise the boat but failed. Used to be 8 or 10 boats from St. Louis up in to the mountain country<.>; now none.

The sugar plantations begin near the mouth of the Red River and continue towards New Orleans. (The Cotton raising territory begins a little below Cairo.)

Below Bayou Sara the plantation buildings & most of the cabins are whitewashed. Occasionally painted brick color. These buildings are over behind the levee and lower than our boat. [#]

---

[47] Since the *Gold Dust* ran only between Saint Louis and Vicksburg, Clemens and his companions boarded the *Charles Morgan,* whose captain was Albert Stein, for the final stretch of their voyage to New Orleans (New Orleans *Daily Picayune,* 29 April 1882).

[48] In the spring of 1863 Grant had resumed in earnest his campaign against Vicksburg. He intended to cross the river from the west to the Vicksburg side at Grand Gulf, Mississippi, but his gunboats were unable to subdue the Confederate batteries there so he made an unopposed landing downstream at Bruinsburg, Mississippi, on 30 April 1863.

Many northern men just after the war bought plantations at low price. One man bot. plant. of 1200 acres with nice buildings, sugar house &c. for $20,000.

Apl. 27. Landed for half an hour at Baton Rouge. In the Capitol (now being repaired.)[49] Much damaged during the war. Magnolia trees past bloom. Quite warm here. Trees in full foliage.

Found the river about as it always was below Baton Rouge; so I went to bed at <Placquem> Plaquemine. Lay in berth all the afternoon listening to the big colored laundress on guard gossiping with a subordinate. Among other things she said:

"You jest go and look at that curi's shirt. Did you ever see anything like that? It belongs to that Mark Twain."

"Who is Mark Twain," the other said.

"I dun'no. But you look at that long shirt—that gown."

"What does he do with it?"

"I dunno. They say he sleeps in it. I never see anything like that befo'. What you reckin it is?"

"Why that; that's a shimmy of course."

"No, 'taint no shimmy—too long."

"Well, its a kind of a shimmy anyhow."

She went on with her work diligently. The other laundress stood back to back with her, and they discussed all sorts of things. They talked of religion; they black-guarded the colored barber; they discussed distances from Donaldsonville & other points to N. Orleans; they talked about <the> colored people who lived in Cincinnati only two or three miles from their mothers & never went to see them. They discussed the ways of rich men—how they come to get their shirts & say they haven't got the change but will bring it presently. Never see them again. They told how this entire steamboat is in debt

---

[49] At the Louisiana State Convention of 1879 this ante-bellum capital had been redesignated as the seat of state government. Baton Rouge citizens then assisted the legislature in raising funds to rebuild the State House, which was burned in the war. The shift of the capital from New Orleans to Baton Rouge had officially taken place on 1 March 1882, shortly before Clemens' visit.

to them—some of the officers for this trip, some for last trip, some for both trips,—others for a longer term.

At one place one of them said: "That's a mighty beautiful plantation."

The other replied, "Lordy, Lordy, many a poor nigger has been killed there, jest for nuffin, & flung into that river thar' & thats the last of-em."

After a pause the <o>first said, "If we could only have the old times back again, just for a minute, just to see how it would seem."

"Oh, Lordy *I* dont want 'em back again for a minute. It was mighty rough times on the niggers."

"Thats so. I come mighty near being sold down here once; & if I had been I wouldnt been here now; been the last of me."

The other said, "I was sold once down as far as Miss. I was afraid I'd go furder down. If I had I'd never been here."

Occasionally the big laundress would drop into song & sang all sorts of strange plantation melodies which nobody but one of her race would ever be able to learn.

She expressed her opinion about one of the colored waiters who had got himself burnt in a low down house in Cincin. She could hardly pity him, altho' sometimes he was really in no condition to wait on table because he was in such pain & suffering. She said, "I jest tell you this: Some women takes up with everybody and anybody that comes along. But I jest tell you if I was a girl I wouldn't sleep with no stranger, don't care what he'd pay."

She chaffed a young colored chap who went off saying, "I was pretty close to it." She said, "Could n't get much closer." After he had gone she said, "That's just as close as I allows one of them young fellows to go. I don't want anything to do with *boys*. If I want anybody I want a *man*."

On the boat at breakfast table this morning a man got to discussing oleomargerine <with> and butter with another idiot who sat opposite. He was contending that oleomargerine could be made, and was made, so that you couldn't tell it from good butter; and that there were plenty of other things done in same way.

The opposite man said, "Yes, plenty of other things same way. For instance, they make olive oil out of cotton seed oil so that you can't tell them apart."

"That's so," said the other. "They send it to France & then bring it back labeled French olive oil."

"Ha!," exclaimed the first, "we know a trick worth six of that. We simply take the regular foreign oil *label* and put it on our bottles of cotton seed oil which we make in our factory in N. Orleans, and send that around this country, all over the U.S., as French Olive Oil. All but the label is made in our factory in New Orleans."

He seemed to think the funniest part of that was the ingenuity & dishonesty of it.

Give this gilt-&-filth sty *rats*. Filthy-clothed waiters.[50]

Wary Stratagem of a *Fellow-passenger*.

I was pacing the cabin when a man came along and said "Are you Mr. Mark Twain?" I said "Yes," and he walked along with me saying "I heard you were aboard. I am an old scenic artist of St. Louis, and my wife is aboard here with me and also another lady. This other lady belongs up the Yazoo & she's very rich—owns plantations there. They'd like to see you. It would be a great treat to them to see you. They're sitting back there in that place. Would you mind just walking by where they are?"

I said "Are they going to be aboard to-morrow, too?"

He replied, "Yes."

"Very well," said I, "suppose I call on them in the morning."

Oh," said he, "you needn't mind *calling* on them. Just walk by."

"Well, of course I should want to be introduced" I said. "It would embarrass me to go by on exhibition.<"> <Th> <He said> It

---

[50] Written in blue ink at the bottom of a page, this is the only entry made by Mark Twain in this notebook. In the manuscript of *Life on the Mississippi* Mark Twain adhered to his intention: he denounced the steward of the *Charles Morgan* as one who "must have learned his trade in a sewer." He did not specifically name the *Charles Morgan* in the published book, but in chapter 38 he complained that the boat he boarded at Vicksburg for New Orleans was caked with "ancient and obdurate dirt" and was "ably officered in all departments except the steward's."

looks simple but I don't think I could get through that alive. Let me speak to them; introduce me." But he seemed to have some objection to that. Presently it occurred to me that those women were not in his secret and so I need not be embarrassed. I said "Do they know of this little game you are getting up? Have you said anything to them about it?"

He said, "Oh not at all. They dont know."

"Well," said I, "I dont mind walking by in that case."

So we started back there. As we approached the two ladies he said (as if continuing an important conversation,)

"As I was saying, the more I think of it, sir, the more I am convinced that the opinion you have expressed is the correct one."

About that time we got to the ladies. I was going to pass by <a>when he said

"Mrs. Johnson, this is Mr. (aside, to me "What name shall I call you?")

I said "<any>Any name."

"This is Mr. Williamson, Mrs. Johnson."

I said, "It's a pleasant even'g." We sat down and I tried to talk with the one who was his wife, but I couldn't get a word out of her nor a sign of life. Meantime he was conversing with them. One of them said "Yes the clerk told me on the wharf-boat that Mark Twain was coming on this boat, and he said he was on the boat now." The man said, "Well, I hear that he is a very long, lank creature with long hair down his back—a kind of a youngish-oldish person—a man that anybody would think at once is a kind of remarkable person."

She said, "Yes, I suppose anybody would know him from anybody else. The clerk told me he was aboard, but I guess he changed his mind, perhaps went to New Orleans by rail."

This fellow then said to her "You've read his books, I suppose?"

"Oh, yes."

"Well, what do you think of them?"

She replied "Oh, they're well enough but—"

"But what?"

"Well, they are very funny in places but they——"

I arose and said, "I guess I'll move along. It's getting warm here, and the ladies want to talk. I will see you again, Mr. Smith" and I bade them goodnight.

Apl. 28

Landed at New Orleans this a.m. about 8. Took a carriage after breakfast<,> and drove about the old French part of the city. Visited the old "St. Louis Hotel."[51] Reminds one of a vast privy. Place where the legislature has met. Hasn't been swept for 40 years. Saw old ornamental iron railings on balconies & before windows; much of it quite pretty and unique. Great deal of this iron work.

Old cemetery surrounded by high wall just over the top of which could see the roofs of the quadrangular tombs

One old pirate[52] buried here. Was a fine pirate, an ornament to his profession. But he fell by mixing in ward politics & finally sunk so far from his former estate as to be elected alderman. But his grave is remembered to this day—more because of his early record.

Evening 28th Drove to the "West End". Cable with us. All around N. Orleans there seems to be a line of forest but one never reaches it. Cemetery on the way. Monument to Stonewall Jackson.

Sat. Apl. 29th

Mule race with Burke<,> & Houston.[53] Latter mentioned the

---

[51] For almost a decade the forty-year-old St. Louis Hotel had served as the state capitol. After refurbishing it would reopen as the Hotel Royal.

[52] Dominique You, one of Jean Laffite's lieutenants, preyed principally upon Spanish vessels. He joined Laffite in protecting New Orleans against the British, for which he was praised by Andrew Jackson in 1815 and pardoned for his previous crimes by President Madison. You settled permanently in New Orleans, where he became a Jacksonian ward politician, but died in poverty. George Washington Cable would publish an essay in the April 1883 issue of *Century Magazine*, "Plotters and Pirates of Louisiana," that discusses "Captain Dominique's" varied career and mentions his immense funeral procession, which even included the city militia. Dominique You was buried in Saint Louis Cemetery Number Two with an epitaph declaring him "*sans reproche et sans peur*"; his tomb is mentioned in chapter 44 of *Life on the Mississippi*.

[53] Edward A. Burke was managing editor of the New Orleans *Times-Democrat* as well as state treasurer. On 2 May James D. Houston was present at Burke's dinner for Mark Twain at John's Restaurant (New Orleans *Times-Democrat*, 7 May 1882). Houston was a tax collector in New Orleans.

<Boudou>Boudoo superstitions. Among old creoles if one meets a funeral he removes his hat & walks back with procession one block.

At the mule race managers wore rosettes large as sunflowers. Riders dressed in silk and velveteen costumes of the gayest colors. All leaders of fashionable society here.[54]

One of the mules got unmanageable & took a heat by himself before the regular start. Nigger braced up against another mule to hold him in. 13 mules in first heat. Best time 2:22 (1 mile) but 8 of them were distanced. Much merriment. Last mule got around just in time for 2ᵈ heat.

Police regulations require the doors & shutters in French part of town to be closed. A hole for observation is left by the inmates.

Cockfight Sunday, Apl. 30.[55]

Circular, amphitheater arrangement <fille> partially filled (200 or so) with an audience of <c> whites, negroes, creoles, Mexicans, Spanish &c.

Honor of an introduction to the proprietor—a Frenchman.

Fighting pit about 30 feet diameter. The birds first weighed; must be same weight. Negro called the "pitter" encouraged his cock in Spanish language. Didn't seem to understand that tongue for he was getting worsted.

At end of each round the pitters would blow water on their heads & legs, & lick off the blood. After 3 rounds one chicken had both eyes gouged out; the other had one eye left but couldnt see out of it first rate on account of blood. He crowed however. [#]

---

[54] The race was staged to benefit the Southern Art Union, a newly formed organization for promoting exhibitions of New Orleans artists.

[55] Joel Chandler Harris recalled leaving the cockpit in mid-fight. Although "wonderfully lively," the "affair was disgusting in the extreme, as Mr. Clemens's party discovered as soon as they reached the cool, refreshing serenity of the quiet streets." Harris was especially appalled at the juxtaposition of this Sunday entertainment with earlier church services where they had "heard a sermon which can only be described as bold, logical and powerful, and the contrast between the two events (or episodes) was simply shocking" (Atlanta *Constitution*, 20 January 1884). Interestingly, Mark Twain changed the day of the week in *Life on the Mississippi*: "We went to a cockpit in New Orleans on a Saturday afternoon," he reported in chapter 45 of his book.

Colored church Sunday eve'g.[56]

Opened with singing of a choir. 12th Chap. Daniel read by black clergyman, during which an aged deacon back by the door chided some young dusky damsels saying "Takes yo' long time get seated. Settle yo' d'rectly ef yo do' get seated."

Clergyman then lined a hymn. Offered prayer very well,—better than some white ministers because it was short. The whole thing was a failure because too good for literature.

White woman preached.

Tues. May 1.

Tug Boat "W. M. Wood".[57] Sailed up & down river front for 10 miles. Saw Chalmette Cemetery 5 miles below N. Orleans. 12,600 soldiers of last war buried here. <[b]>Saw battle ground of 1815 near here.

Note the absence of "R" from the southern dialect. They also eliminate the final "g" in -ing

A boy six years old and a <boy> girl four played the balcony scene in Romeo & Juliet in a private house.[58] [#]

---

[56] On 30 April Clemens visited Winan's Chapel, also known as the First Street Methodist Episcopal Church; George Washington Cable had supplied its address in Notebook 20. The Reverend Stephen Priestly was the pastor.

[57] According to the "River News" column in the Wednesday 3 May 1882 issue of the New Orleans *Times-Democrat*, "Capt. Mumf. Wood had Mark Twain on the Wm. Wood yesterday, giving him a sight of our harbor, and at the same time a pleasant ride on one of the finest tugs afloat." Clemens wrote enthusiastically of the tour in a letter to Livy on 2 May: "A big, fast steam-tug was offered us, & this morning we steamed up & down the river a couple of hours at a tremendous rate. I did the steering myself. There was a fine breeze blowing, the sun was bright, & orange groves & other trees about the plantation dwellings in full & sumptuous leaf. Splendid trip" (*LLMT*, p. 212).

[58] New Orleans attorney James B. Guthrie and his wife entertained Clemens and Osgood on Monday evening, 1 May. Guthrie gave a recitation from Shakespeare and then presented Birney and Laura Guthrie (New Orleans *Times-Democrat*, 7 May 1882). The children performed "in the quaintest most captivating way, with good emphasis, elocution, earnestness, & perfect simplicity & unconsciousness. I never have seen anything that moved me more. They required prompting only once. There was an audience of twenty-five ladies & gentlemen" (SLC to OLC, 2 May, *LLMT*, p. 212).

The better class of dwelling houses here in New Orleans are white, framed, with ample porches & surrounded by orange and other trees. Are very homelike and attractive. But there is little other architecture worthy of the name. Commercial buildings are excessively plain and ugly & old-fashioned. The New Orleans of to-day in all respects is the N.O. of 40 or 50 years ago. They use the electric lights here pretty lavishly. Canal st. has more lights of the kind than I ever saw before; and several adjoining streets are so lighted. There are 4 miles of electric lights on the river front.

The only sewerage seems to be in open gutters that pretend to carry water both ways but it seems to be generally taking a rest and stinking. Some of the commercial parts of the town never seem to be cleaned at all. I suppose they are but don't look like it. The smells are the liveliest things in N. Orleans and the most variegated.

Are building a fine Cotton Exchange[59] of stone, carved and ornamental; very massive, stately & handsome, a credit to any city. Will have a good effect because it will start a new departure in that direction.

The Custom House is a fine building but that is national not domestic architecture. N. Orleans has nothing to do with that.

It is still in the romantic dark ages here. They fight duels for the merest trifles, but the French fashion of small swords probably prevails; also the French immunity from danger. The newspapers do not generally consider such duels worth making a local item about.

They have started an Art Union which is a couple of years old & promises to prosper.

They have not got rid of flowery and fulsome speech in the newspapers and are consequently high-colored in expression high-wrought rhetoric & eloquence. Too much puffery & mention of personal names.

While here on the ground one does not see the bloody shirt waved

---

59 The directors of the Cotton Exchange were preparing a show place in anticipation of the World's Industrial and Cotton Centennial Exposition which would be held in New Orleans in 1884/1885. Edward A. Burke was director-general for the exposition.

nor hear of outrages of a political nature. Everybody seems so humane and decent and orderly that one is not conscious of being out of his own country or in anything of a strange land. The fire-eater may exist, but one does not run across him.

Here are the large shrimp and very delicious crawfish about as big as a man's thumb. The boss fish is the Pompano; soft-shelled crabs the best of their kind; sheepshead, red snapper & Spanish mackerel. A very choice market for fish.

Strawberries have gone out at the end of April, and the roses are gone from the rose trees in the gardens & over the houses. Magnolia dropping its blossoms; but many of the magnolia trees are still a fine spectacle with their shining green leaves luxurious foliage and snowy blossoms.

The pomegranate & oleander are in blossom.

Noticeable paucity of steamboats as at St. Louis. One tug now brings down barges[60] containing 6000 tons of grain—stuff which in my time would have come down in 4 or 5 steamboats. Big stern wheel boats are used as tugs for this commerce because they handle better than side-wheelers & there is a better application of power. One stern wheeler will bring down from Pittsburg 30 flat boats (in one tow) filled with coal—22000 tons, or about 6 acres of coal afloat. Distance 2250 miles. This is done in high water during Spring & Fall freshets. (This statement made by Col. B. D. Wood,[61] a large coal dealer here.)

It is said that cotton crops raised on the sediment of an overflow are almost sure to be chawed up right away by a worm bred by the overflow. So the annual overflow is not as useful as it would be on the Nile. [#]

---

[60] Towboats and barges were beginning to recapture some of the river trade lost to railroads: in 1875 only four tugboats and thirty barges were in service between Saint Louis and New Orleans; by 1887 sixteen tugboats would be towing one hundred and twenty barges (Harold Sinclair, *The Port of New Orleans* [Garden City, N.Y.: Doubleday, Doran & Co., 1942], pp. 265–266).

[61] The B. D. Wood & Brothers coal firm owned several tugboats for towing barges of coal down the river from Pittsburgh to New Orleans. Burris D. Wood made one of these boats available to Clemens for scenic tours of the delta vicinity.

The great Isaiah Sellers died in Memphis about 1863. Buried in Bellefontaine Cemetery St. Louis. There is a monument over him which he had constructed during life. It <prese> represents him standing at the pilot wheel. He was detested by all the other pilots because he could antedate them so far in river reminiscences.[62]

Had my row with Brown the pilot[63] in Eagle Bend.

The big bar of the St. Charles Hotel with its sawdusted floor and groups of mint-julep suckers is as it was 25 years ago, and they seem to be the same juleps and the same suckers; no change noticeable.

The cool porch overlooking the street just the same, with its big columns.

The people in this section are active talkers but poor listeners. They like to hear themselves talk. This is noticeable from St. Louis clear down.

Thurs. May 4.

On tug "W. M. Wood"[64] to plantation of ex-Gov. Warmouth[65] 47 miles below N. Orleans. Party numbered 15—7 ladies. Parrot on

---

62 Isaiah Sellers (ca. 1802–1864) piloted between Saint Louis and New Orleans for nearly forty years. He was supposed never to have sunk a boat of which he was pilot and it is claimed that the phrase "Sellers is at the wheel" was "the expression used to quiet the nerves of timid travelers" (Walter B. Stevens, *St. Louis, The Fourth City, 1764–1911*, 2 vols. [Saint Louis: S. J. Clarke Publishing Co., 1911], 1:271). The monument is a bas relief sculpture of Sellers at the wheel with a map of the Mississippi at his feet. Mark Twain would write to Osgood on 19 July 1882 to request that his publisher obtain a photograph of the monument. "I stole my nom de plume from him," Mark Twain explained, "and shall have considerable to say about him, for out there he was 'illustrious' " (*MTLP*, p. 157). A sketch of the sculpture appeared in chapter 50 of the first edition of *Life on the Mississippi.*

63 William Brown, the pilot who died in the *Pennsylvania* steamboat explosion and fire in 1858. Clemens' graphic account of his fight with Brown and of the steamboat disaster is in chapters 19 and 20 of *Life on the Mississippi.*

64 "Mark Twain, Mr. Osgood, Capt. and Mrs. H. E. Bixby and Capt. Burr Wood and his wife took a trip to the lower coast yesterday as far down as the Magnolia Plantation, on the W. M. Wood" (New Orleans *Times-Democrat,* 5 May 1882).

65 Henry Clay Warmoth had been the Republican governor of Louisiana from 1868 until 1872.

board keeping up constant stream of remarks, some irrelevant, some not. Parrot's swearing *very* inappropriate. (Elaborate this: Parrot makes extremely naughty remarks and the ladies gradually withdraw.) Passed a cotton factory on way down. Three in city but this one closed up because every stock holder wanted to be an officer & get a fat salary.

Warmouth met tug in river opposite his plantation. Tall, witty, self-possessed man of 40. Took us in <plant> carriages over his place. Contains 2600 acres—650 to cane which will produce <$>1,500,000. lbs. Has 4700 orange trees 150 Fig trees.

<600) 1,500,000 (2500
<1½ to 2 tons sugar, cane.> 1 200
3000
3000>

Will make from one & one-half to 2 tons sugar per acre. Juice before evap. is passed thro' filters of bone black. 12 of these filters. In sugar house had seven clarifying tanks from which juice is drawn into two (open) evaporating pans; thence to vacuum pan where condensed to granulating point. Then drawn off into centrifugals—(6 of them) The molasses thrown out by centrifugals is put thro former process (clarifying, open pan, vacuum pan & centrif.)

French Market, N. Orleans.

Consists of 3 buildings—meat market, Bazaar (dry & fancy goods) & vegetable & fruit market. But occasional meat stall in midst of dry goods. Nothing covered from flies. Saw tripe covered with flies; tripe invisible except at edges. One woman trying to brush flies from legs of mutton. Mutton covered with mashed flies; must be very nutritious mutton. The brush she used had been used for number of years; blacker and dirtier than the dirtiest fly. Cobwebs hung in graceful festoons from market ceiling.

Saw dirty old barrel half full of sour kraut; board across top of barrell with 2 plates of the sour kraut as samples,—look^{d} as if it had the jaundice.

2 policemen (lazy) for the whole market. Market Ordinances

containing 35 sections. Only one section is obeyed viz. that no OYSTERS should be sold. Policeman nor anyone knew why oysters should not be sold there.

Market stalls rent for 50 to 75c per day.

One <we> little weazened faced old French woman had a curbstone space (rent 15c per day) Had little conical piles of potatoes as large as marbles—could cover with tea cup; little piles string beans built like log cabins—could <[p]> carry on a table spoon; small messes of onions & cauliflower. Her whole stock would inventory as much as 50c.

The sights here are bad, but the smells heart-rending. Stick to a fellow's clothes all day.

The beeves <slaugh> before they are slaughtered for this market are so poor and discouraged that <they> a man holds them up on their legs while the butcher goes thro' the form of knocking them down with his axe.

The meat is lean & shriveled, so they blow it up with air giving it a fat, plump appearance. Same performance with fowls.

May <5>6.—Visited Armory of the "Washington Artillery". Hanging there is an equestrian portrait of "Stonewall" Jackson & Lee (by Julio.)[66] Also an original portrait—full length—of Andrew Jackson.

Flag of the Wash. Artillery with names 60 noted engagements embroidered thereon. Also flag of the Cross and Stars—the first one made after adoption of change from <B>Stars & Bars.

In another room were portraits of Gen. Beauregard[67] & Gen Owens[68]—our chaperone.

---

[66] The painting was E. B. D. Fabrino Julio's "The Last Meeting of Lee and Jackson," to which Clemens gave the burlesque caption "Got a match about you?" in Notebook 20, p. 470.

[67] Pierre G. T. Beauregard commanded the attack on Fort Sumter and directed troops at Bull Run.

[68] William Miller Owen had been commandant of the Washington Artillery from 1876 until 1880. He served as adjutant of the military company in the Civil War, and in 1882 was appointed inspector-general of the Louisiana State National Guard on the governor's staff, which gave him the rank of brigadier general. In

In the hall above witnessed drill of the "Sweet Sweepers"—a company of 24 young ladies armed with brooms. The manual exercise was pretty well done, but the marching partook a little of a slight bouncing movement. They had the waltz in their minds. Also an occasional halting to arrange skirts especially after a right about face. <F> Drill in fancy movements was the best. To storm *breast works* defended by such sweet troopers would be very difficult.

The Spanish Moss growing in profusion on trees here is gathered, cleansed and used in upholstering. Is becoming a staple article of trade.

The Jetties.

The jetties at the S. E. Pass into the Gulf are 2 parallel walls confining the current. Built 1000 feet apart. Capt. Eads[69] found this too wide and he built wings on the inside 125 from each wall—thus confining current to 750 feet. The current then had a narrower space and dug it out "scoured" it out to an average depth of 27 or 28 feet where before it had been only 8 or 10 feet in places. The jetties are 1½ miles in length. Each wall consists of 2 rows of piling between which they sunk mattresses made of willow &c. & then piled stone upon them; then another mattress & then stone and bags of sand. When they had got built well out to sea they put on a sea wall by making board boxes 8 feet high filled with brick, stone & sand & poured into it liquid Portland cement. Then took away the boards leaving a solid wall.

The sea is undermining it some & they have to make repairs occasionally.

Ships now pass thro'.

(The above by Mr. <Pe>P. B. Sexton,[70] substantially.) [#]

1885 Owen would publish *In Camp and Battle with the Washington Artillery of New Orleans.*

[69] James B. Eads designed his system of jetties to maintain a navigable channel at the mouth of the Mississippi; he successfully completed construction in 1879, and the feat earned him a national reputation as a hydraulic engineer.

[70] Peter B. Sexton was listed as an engineer in the New Orleans city directories.

He says that at Plum Point on the river they are going to start a cut-off & work down the stream. Preparing to put in mattresses & save the bank. Big undertaking. May be able to do something in the heaviest bends. If they can make gradual bends, keeping about the same distance so as to have no more current thinks the river can be kept in. Long job. They are going to throw the water against Plum Point. Capt. Quinn U.S. Eng. Corps is there in charge. The River Commission[71] consists of 3 belonging to the army & 2 civilians—prominent engineers. No pilot in the commission.

Alex Scott Jack-o-lantern Chute Paupau Isl. above Vicksburg.—Build wing dams opposite Paupau Isl. throw the water over and cut off the foot of Paupau Island; go into the bend of the *old* river and make what was formerly an upstream bend, a down stream bend and follow it into the shore above Vicksburg.

<Made landing at Greenville, Miss. at 8 p.m. Monday May 8th.>[72]

The high willow bar above Lake Providence. River Commission have driven piles from one end to the other up into the willows and clear out to both ends of the bar—a bar that is out of water 40 feet in dead low water. What on earth their idea of it is nobody can guess.

Took Steamboat *Baton Rouge*
Up the River
May 6th 5 p.m.

This boat is 300 feet long. 49 feet wide 9½ feet depth of hold. All *bed*-rooms aft the middle gangway, each with 2 beds. Six bridal chambers.

Dimensions of pilot house: 14 feet square 8½ high. 4 window sashes on each of 3 sides. Double-circle wheel. Nickel plated bell-pull:

---

[71] The recent floods had focused national attention upon the projects proposed by the Mississippi River Commission. On 18 April 1882 President Arthur requested that Congress pass the recommendations of the commission and provide appropriations to realize its proposals for controlling floodwaters and improving navigation channels.

[72] Phelps copied this entry out of chronological sequence. He recorded the memorandum again on the next page of the notepad in its logical context.

Electric lights worked from the bell pull. Compass & chartbox. Tubes to hear the engine bells through. Steam radiator to heat pilot house, instead of stove.

Tonnage of Baton Rouge 2300 tons. By hoisting arrangements can unload a full cargo in 10 hours. Besides the Boat Engines she <s>has 4 smaller steam engines: 1 for capstan 2 for the stages 1 for hoisting, & 1 for electric light.

Reached Baton Rouge at 4:10 a.m May 7th—Bayou Sara at 7:30 a.m. Morgan's Bend 9. Gen. Whitman sunk there.[73]

Made Natchez, Miss., at 4:15 p.m. May 7th
Vicksburg 8 a.m May 8th

Greenville, Miss 8 p.m. Mond. May 8th

An experience of Ritchie the pilot[74] in the war:—We were at Columbus.[75] All the boats stopped there for fear of the Confederates. Laid there all one day. Captain taken sick there with sick-headache. Had somebody bathing his head in <room>rum. A boy came up from below & Capt. asked if everything was all right. The boy said yes all right, and the Capt. said "Ring the bell & go on down the river." He had n't heard of any change of signals. We went down to the island & landed. Well, they *had* changed the signals, but Capt. didn't know it. We got ready to put out the lights & got in sight of Isl. No. 10 & there was a signal gun fired.

Presently the Confederates opened out six or eight guns. At the 3^{d} gun the Capt. rushed up <cr> shouting away "O my God, what shall I do! O my God what shall I do!" dancing around the <f> room. His headache was completely cured. I was at the wheel steering & every time I saw a flash of a gun I'd dodge. They would

---

[73] The *General Quitman*, built in 1859, sank at Angola, Louisiana, above Morgan's Bend and Bayou Sara in 1868. Mark Twain mentioned the *General Quitman* in "A Curious Experience" (*Century Magazine*, November 1881, p. 36) as one of the "old familiar steamboats" associated with New Orleans.

[74] George Ritchie, on Bixby's *City of Baton Rouge*.

[75] Southern troops effectually blockaded the Mississippi near Columbus, Kentucky (at Island No. 10) until April 1862.

call up to me from below "Run by the battery, pilot!" and I was standing here shaking and dodging. Finally I happened to hit on a signal and I made down to the Island and found everything all right.

There was an old nigger barber at Natches when the gunboat Essex[76] was coming down. The barber said, "God-damn <tha> dat Yankee gunboat; Dey wont dare fire; an de white folks got an old cannon down to de wharf thinking they would jest take dat gunboat. Fire at her two free times and den go out and take her. Well, de old black thing come floatin down de river lookin like an old turtle. Den de white folks fire at her supposin she give up right away. But all a sudden "bang, bang bang," de gun boat said—all de white folks took up de hill. Didnt stop to fire dat gun on de wharf any more. I had a man in my chair half his face shaved de udder half lathered. Didn't hab time to finish. I run up de hill too but de soldiers run by me. Overtook a woman with a baby & she asked me to carry de baby. So I grab de child skersely knowin what I did. I got out in de fields & got up on a fence. A shell tore dat fence all down. I fell flat wid de child in my arms & says I I aint got time to carry dat child any furder. De woman offered to pay me for what I <c>had carried de child but I sez "I aint got time to take pay. Goda'mighty <pa> will pay me for dat," and I <f> left de place right-away.

Symbols in Pilothouse.

Little anchors are fixed in between the strands of rope on bell pulls; anchors are indicated in various ways signifying "Anchor Line."

There is a stick (natural crook) <s>painted red & suspended from ceiling of pilot house, signifying *Baton Rouge.*

Sam Bowen buried at Parker's Bend at head of "65." The river has cut away the banks & Bowen is washed into the river.[77]

---

[76] On 3 September 1862 the "U.S.S. *Essex,* Commodore W. D. Porter, in pursuit of C.S.S. *Webb,* had a landing party fired on at Natchez, Mississippi, from which Union forces had withdrawn on 25 July. *Essex* bombarded the town for an hour, after which the mayor 'unconditionally surrendered' the city to Porter" (U.S., Naval History Division, *Civil War Naval Chronology 1861–1865,* 6 vols. in 2 [Washington, D.C.: Government Printing Office, 1961–1966], 2:95).

[77] Bowen and William Kribben both died of yellow fever while piloting in 1878;

(Bill Krebbin is buried at the head of 68 in Arkansas)

Minstrels.

Evening on Baton Rouge. Two colored <[h]> cabin hands; one *more* colored than other. One played banjo & both sang. Concert opened with "Golden Slippers" in Negro dialect, followed by "Old Black Joe" "Empty is the cradle" &c.[78] Following are the words to

Mary's Gone Wid de Coon.[79]

1. Oh, <there's> dar's heaps of trouble on the old man's mind,
Come darkies weep wid me;
My Mary Ann's gone away wid de Coon.
He's black as black as he can be,
But I would n't care if he was only yaller,
But he's black all o'er, he's a porter in a sto'
No matter what he owe
That de chil' I bore should think of me no mo'
Dan to run away wid a black coon.

Chorus.

Mary's gone-a-wid-a coon
Mary's gone wid-a-coon
Dar's heaps o' trouble on de old man's mind
Since Mary's gone away wid de Coon.

2. I <never>nebber would a' thought when I raised dat chil'
She'd-a-be dat trouble to me;
She had ebber-y <[d]>thing dat her heart could wish,
She was raised in de lap o' lux*urie.*

Absalom Grimes reported that Clemens made arrangements at his own expense to have Bowen's coffin reinterred because floodwaters had exposed the gravesite (Absalom Grimes, *Confederate Mail Runner*, ed. M. M. Quaife [New Haven: Yale University Press, 1926], pp. 18–19).

[78] The words and music for the spiritual "Oh! Dem Golden Slippers" were copyrighted by James A. Bland in 1879. Stephen Foster's "Old Black Joe" was published in 1860. "Empty is the cradle, baby's gone" is the last line of a song copyrighted by Harry Kennedy in 1880, "Cradle's Empty, Baby's Gone."

[79] Neither the origin nor any other transcriptions of this folk song have been discovered.

But I nebber once for a moment suspected
But that she would 'a' reflected—
So highly connected,
A man mo' respected
Dan to run away wid a black coon.
(Chorus)

3. Now all yo' people who hab chil'n to raise,
Take warnin' at my fate;
Watch ober dem carefully or else you find
Like-a-me you'll be too late.
For girls are wild when in dar teens
<T> Dey're allus after beaus,
A-wearin' good clothes,
A-goin to shows
And nobody knows
What de trouble & woes
From a parent heart flows,
Since-a Mary ran away wid de Coon.
(Chorus.)

May 9th 30 miles below Memphis tied up to the bank while they washed out the boilers and let a hurricane, thunder & hail storm pass over. The wind snapped off several forest trees near by making <a> sounds like reports of a rifle. At Memphis (where we arrived in early morning May 10) several sheds were blown down & the hail stones were nearly 3 inches in circumf.
Unusual for this latitude.

A War Pilot.

Capt. Bixby gave a little experience as follows:
I was a pilot on a Miss. river gun boat fleet for 10 months. Our first engagement with the enemy was at No. 10. Went into the service with Commodore Foote. It was by a scratch that I got into that service. I happened to be on the train from Buffalo to St. Louis and Commodore Foote was also on the train.[80] He seemed to take a fancy

[80] Historical documents generally corroborate these reminiscences by Horace

to me, learned I was a Miss. river pilot, Pres. of the Asso., a Union man &c. Every little while when he spoke with me on the train he would say something about making me confidential pilot. He wanted some one in that capacity. So I consented. He had received an injury on the gun boat Essex at Fort Henry[81] and was relieved from charge of our gun boat flotilla at Plum Point & Com. Davis[82] took his place. We lay around <their>there 6 weeks. One morning the rebel fleet came up and attacked our picket boat—a mile below. We got under way, went down & repulsed them<.>, but they sunk 2 of our iron-clads. We saved them as they were on a bank.

From Fort Pillow we dropped down to Memphis & on our way captured the rebel transport Sovereign<.> with a little tug.[83] This was at foot of Isl. 35. I had told the flag officer<s> if he would give me the tug, a few marines & Lieut. Bishop to command that I would catch that boat. He said All right<.>, and we started after her gaining pretty fast.

The Lieut. ordered me to turn back. I asked him what for & he said he thought we would suddenly find a masked battery. But I had started to catch that boat & was going to do it. He ordered me the second time to go back & by that time we had gained upon her &

Bixby. His chance encounter with Andrew H. Foote must have occurred during the first week of September in 1861. Foote was detached from the New York Navy Yard and given command of the Western waters on 30 August 1861; he notified the secretary of the navy on 5 September that he had arrived in Saint Louis and had reported for duty (*Official Records of the Union and Confederate Navies*, 22:307, 313).

[81] Foote actually received his wound aboard the gunboat *St. Louis* during an attack on Fort Donelson on the Cumberland River on 14 February 1862. Fort Henry on the Tennessee River had been captured by Foote's naval forces a week earlier (*Civil War Naval Chronology*, 2:17, 22). Foote's injury did not heal and he remained on crutches. On 9 May 1862 he reluctantly gave up his command of Federal naval forces on the Mississippi. He would never recover from the wound which caused his death a year later.

[82] Captain Charles H. Davis assumed temporary command of the Western Flotilla on 9 May 1862 until his permanent appointment was confirmed on 17 June.

[83] The Confederate transport ship *Sovereign* was captured on 5 June 1862 by the *Spitfire*, a tugboat assigned to the U.S.S. *Benton*. Commodore Davis described the steamer as "a valuable prize" (*Official Records of the Union and Confederate Navies*, 23:671, 119).

fired a shot which exploded right over her. She run up a flag of truce & we came alongside and took possession<.>, towing her out in the stream ready for our flotilla when they came along. The Lieut. in his report said he did not deserve any credit; that he had ordered me back twice & if I had obeyed we wouldn't have got that boat.[84]

Next morning at day-light the drum beat to quarters & signal was made to move up the river. I suggested we drop *down* the river & bring the rebel gun boat flotilla in full view for I was confident they were down there. So we dropped down & the whole fleet came into view. They steamed up and came for us, firing. Com. Elliott/Ellet[85] of our ram fleet cut loose with his rams on the opposite side of the river & went down among the rebel gunboats. Com. Davis said "Where is that d—d fool going?" I said, "He's going down to get gobbled up<.">, unless we help him."

He signalled the balance of the fleet to follow. We headed down the stream, and were just 40 minutes in using up that whole fleet—except one boat which run away.[86]

Then we dropped down to Vicksburg, and were there when the rebel ram "Arkansas<.>" came out of the Yazoo and ran thro' our fleet to get by. Two deserters had come aboard our vessel & reported that the ram would come out on that Sunday morning but we paid no attention to it.

Com. Farragut was there and they were sent aboard his vessel, he being the senior officer. He sent up 2 boats early that morning to reconnoitre. About daylight in the morning the officer of the deck reported to the fleet captain heavy firing in the direction of the Yazoo river. About 15 minutes later same report—apparently growing closer.

---

84 Nevertheless, shortly after this triumph Lieutenant Joshua Bishop was named to take command of the captured Confederate steamer *General Bragg* (*Official Records of the Union and Confederate Navies*, 23:141).

85 Colonel Charles Ellet, Jr., had converted a number of river steamers into a Union ram fleet in the spring of 1862. Ellet was fatally wounded in this encounter on June 6, known as the Battle of Memphis. Most of the Confederate River Defense Fleet was demolished, and Memphis surrendered to Captain Davis.

86 Only the *General Earl Van Dorn*, because of her superior speed, was able to escape from the engagement; the other Confederate ships were either captured or destroyed.

The next thing was drum-beat-to-quarters. The reconnoitring gun boat A. O. Tyler was coming in the lead and the Ram 300 or 400 yards behind shooting at her, the Tyler shooting back. The Tyler & the Carondelet had met the ram up in the Yazoo. She carried away the tiller rope of the Carondelet which caused her to run on a bank & get left for the time.

As soon as the Ram came in sight Farraguts fleet, consisting of the Richmond, the Hartford & 10 other lesser vessels & all our iron-clads began shooting at her. But we being so high & she so low we overshot her. The gunboat Essex (Commander Porter)[87] was lying there without steam up. She had a 10-inch Dahlgren pivot gun on her stern. She hit the ram with a shell which exploded inside<r> her. <pilothouse.> I know the pilot was killed by that shot.

We followed her down among the batteries with the Benton, and as soon as the batteries opened fire on us we rounded to and got out of the way as fast as we could, (which was very slow, indeed, with the Benton.) After we had gotten her out of range & out of sight we came to anchor. Com. Farragut and three or four of his old sea-captains held a council of war and determined to exterminate that ram Arkansaw before dark that night. Accordingly we dropped down and brought the rebel upper batteries into view for his gratification. Then he issued an order for the flotilla to be ready to sail at 4:30—three of our gun boats to drop down and draw the fire and the flotilla to sail around & broadside the town, especially the Arkansas which would be laying at Vicksburg. The gun boat "Sumpter" (which we captured at Memphis)[88] was to bring up the rear and go in "head on" & sink them. There was something the matter with her pumps and 'twas late when the flotilla got started,—<so late> pitch dark[89]—and she never did find the Arkansas. But

[87] Commodore William David Porter.

[88] The *General Sumter* was captured in the Battle of Memphis on 6 June 1862. She was damaged by cannon shot in this attempt to locate and destroy the Confederate ironclad *Arkansas*.

[89] Commodore David G. Farragut reported later that "it was so dark by the time we reached the town that nothing could be seen except the flashes of the guns" (*Civil War Naval Chronology*, 2:81).

we went head on into the wharf boat & sunk *it* & then went on down the river with balance of Farraguts flotilla.

Shortly after that the troops were withdrawn from opposite Vicksburg Farragut dropped down the river & we went back up to Helena.

Cairo being the naval headquarters Com. Davis went to Cairo.

I lay around three or four weeks & finally took the chills & fever. When the Benton started for Milligan's bend to capture the "Fairplay"[90] I got permission from the fleet captain to go aboard the hospital boat Red Rover—not as an invalid but for recreation. The Red Rover went to Memphis. While there the John H. Dickey despatch boat from below came up on her way to St. Louis The Captain, an old acquaintance of mine was walking on deck & recognized me. He called out "What are you doing there?" I said "<I a>I'm sick & I want to go to Cairo.<"> Can I go with you?" He said I could & I got aboard.

I called on the flag officer at Cairo[91] who <s[-]> said he was surprised to see me there. I told him I was a little surprised myself<.>; but that I was unfit for service. I applied to the fleet captain for sick leave & he wouldn't grant it at first. Finally granted leave of absence "until<—> fit for service."

I afterwards wrote him from St. Louis that my continued ill health & my duty to self & family compelle[d] me to resign my position. He answered my letter accepting with regret my resignation;—and that's all I know about gun-boating.

Family Feuds.

Darnell & Watson[92] were the names of two <f> men whose

---

[90] The Confederate steamer *Fairplay* was captured while transporting arms and munitions on 16 August 1862 by a naval force which included the *Benton* (*Civil War Naval Chronology*, 2:91).

[91] Commodore Charles H. Davis had left the flagship *Benton* and returned to naval headquarters in Cairo on 3 August 1862 (*Official Records of the Union and Confederate Navies*, 23:281).

[92] Before his trip Clemens made a notation in Notebook 20 reminding himself to stop in New Madrid "& ask about the old feuds" (p. 456). The Darnell-Watson

families had kept up a long quarrel. The old man Darnell & his 2 sons came to the conclusion to leave that part of the country. They started to take steamboat just above "No. 10". The Watsons got wind of it and as the young Darnells were walking up the companion way stairs <they> with their wives on their arms they shot them in <their>the back.

After that <he> <Watson> Darnell got into trouble with a man who run the ferry & <some of the family> killed the ferryman. But the ferryman's friends shot old Darnell through & through—filled him plumb full of bullets. <That was>

One time a man & his wife were working for Darnell.<—[-]> Old Darnell tried to get advantage of his hired man's wife & she told her husband. He sent for Darnell to come over & settle up wages. Just as he got near the cabin he shot him with a gun. Then Darnell's friends killed the hired man.

(By Mr. Clemens:)[93]

One of these families lived on the Kentucky side the other on Missouri side near New Madrid. Once a boy 12 years old connected with the Kentucky family was riding thro the woods on the Mo. side. He was overtaken by a full grown man and he shot that boy dead.

I was on a Memphis packet & at a landing we made on the Kentucky side there was a row. Don't remember <wh> as there was anybody hurt then; but shortly afterwards there was another row at that place and a youth of 19 belonging to the Mo. tribe had wandered over there. Half a dozen of that Ky. tribe got after him. He dodged among the wood piles & answered their shots. Presently he jumped into the river & they followed on after & peppered him & he had to make for the shore. By that time he was about dead—did shortly die.[94]

---

vendetta is described in chapter 26 of *Life on the Mississippi* and was a source for the Grangerford-Shepherdson feud in *Huckleberry Finn.*

[93] This comment by Phelps was inserted to identify the following remarks as products of Clemens' own experience.

[94] On 28 March 1885, replying to Reginald Cholmondeley's inquiry of 12 March about whether "blood-feuds really existed in Arkansas within 50 years" as portrayed in *Huckleberry Finn,* Clemens affirmed the account from personal experience: "I

Pilot: Well, nearly all of those old parties were killed off.

They used to attend church on the line (part of church in Tenn. part in Ky.) Both Darnell & Watson went to that church armed with shot guns, & neither party would allow the other to cross the line in that church.

This old Dan Watson couldnt write, but he kept his books by pictures or hieroglyphics. One day a wood chopper came around to settle his a/c. Watson had him charged with a *cheese*. The fellow said he had never bought any cheese. Well, they had a fight & the wood chopper got the best of old Dan. Finally old Dan happened to remember that he had made a mistake. <Sai> He had forgotten in making his symbol for <a chees> the entry to make a hole in it. It was a grindstone which the woodchopper had bought.

A *gentle hint*.

One day Old Dan had company for dinner. There was a red-headed fellow who used to like his daughter but old Dan did n't like him. The red headed fellow sat down to dinner, however. They had chicken-pie. Old Dan helped everybody & himself quite liberally & by that time the chicken pie was all gone. Then he said to the fellow, "May be *you*'ll have some chicken pie, you old red-headed devil."

MEMORANDA.[95]

Mem: Regardg a pilot who disappeared three or four years ago.

Grave of Col. Sellers at St. Louis.

During the War Isl. No. 10 bombarded from Donaldson's Point for 13 days, and all the damage done was to break the leg of a yellow dog. Near head of the big timber It was a rebel dog. claim for pension in Congress. [#]

---

came very near being an eye-witness of the general engagement detailed in the book. The details are historical and correct."

95 Phelps recorded this final group of dictated entries in a section he set aside for chance remarks which occurred to Clemens in the course of the journey. These brief observations and reminders, written with the notepad inverted, begin on the second leaf from the back and run toward the front. The intervening pages between Clemens' day-by-day dictations and these random memoranda were later filled in with shorthand transcriptions of letters.

Murrell's gang Isl. 37

The gambler who used to bet niggers is gone. Used to be called the "nigger better."[96]

What used to be big corn-fields when I was pilot is now the channel of the river.

The whole Miss. river is on the Ky. side of Isl. No. 10. Used to be a narrow place.

Length of the Island reduced to half-a-mile.

New Madrid<;>, Mo., is still here but gradually receding.

Mem: Everybody likes to see his name in print but he covers up his vanity by abusing the man that put it there. The records of the so-called society papers prove this by original doc^{s}.

Apl. 23.

Passed the wreck of the "Golden City" below Memphis. Caught fire early in the morning Mch. 30/82. The negro crew jumped ashore and deserted her. They ran her into shore but she got out of line. Great many lives lost—people asleep. She drifted down inside of President Island and sunk[97] [#]

---

[96] The poker-playing slave trader in "Randall's Jew Story" (written in the 1890s) resembles this recalled figure (*Mark Twain's Fables of Man*, ed. John S. Tuckey [Berkeley, Los Angeles, London: University of California Press, 1972], p. 285).

[97] The Cincinnati and New Orleans packet *Golden City* had caught fire as she approached Memphis on 30 March 1882. Although the pilot managed to dock at the city wharf, flames spread so rapidly in the cargo of jute, oakum, creosote, and cottonseed oil that the lines could not be properly secured and the burning steamboat drifted downstream until it sank. Following an investigation, charges of murder through negligence were brought against the watchman who had dropped his ignited lamp upon jute stored in a deck room. A coroner's jury also blamed the crew members for failing to cover the cargo properly. Hero of the disaster was young Robert Kelly, second engineer, who died at his post after giving the alarm. But only Kelly and three other Southern Transportation Company employees perished, whereas the reported passenger casualties—mostly women and children—numbered approximately forty (New Orleans *Daily Picayune*, 30–31 March, 4 April 1882).

<L>Mem:—Look up the Fort Pillow massacre.[98] Also the great naval battle at Memphis.

<Mem: Regarding a pilot who [disappeared] some three or four years ago.>

Jeff Thompson's war chief.

The Linsey Woolsey Beauty of Walnut Bend. The Bend being shut off could only see the possible place in the distance. But the boats do not go nearer now.

Will Bowen—measles 1844.—I got them.[99]

$$\begin{array}{r} 1844 \\ 1835 \\ \hline 9 \end{array}$$

Landing at mouth of Arkansas river—Alexander, Postmaster.

Down here on the boat college-bred men use the most atrocious grammar—doubling up their negatives &c.

Our Lord & Saviour Jesus Christ the forgotten Son of God

Like captain, like crew. Steamboat men of a feather flock together

(*Je ne comprend pas*
Johnny Comprong.) [#]

---

[98] Fort Pillow, Tennessee, was seized by Confederate forces commanded by General Nathan Forrest on 12 April 1864. The events which followed the attack kindled a bitter controversy. A congressional board of inquiry concluded that the Confederate soldiers murdered most of the garrison after it surrendered, that atrocities were committed upon the Negro troops who had helped defend the fort, and that tents which contained Federal wounded were wantonly set afire. Southern spokesmen dismissed these claims as mere war propaganda, and blamed the large Federal losses—231 killed, 100 seriously wounded—on a refusal to surrender in the face of overwhelming odds (Mark M. Boatner, *The Civil War Dictionary* [New York: David McKay Co., 1959], pp. 295–296).

[99] In at least two other instances Clemens recalled deliberately exposing himself to measles as a child, once in his autobiography (*MTA*, 2:219) and again in "The Turning Point of My Life" (1910). In the first version he would set his age at the time as ten; in the second he would give it as twelve and a half. Dixon Wecter has confirmed that the Hannibal measles epidemic occurred in 1844 (*Sam Clemens of Hannibal* [Boston: Houghton Mifflin Co., 1952], pp. 140, 297).

The Jews who have <floc> come in great numbers to this valley have at many points on the river rather got the ascendency. In some cases they were made distributing agents for the rations sent by the gov't. One of them with a zeal for <the> economical management of government affairs held forth as follows:—

To a darkey applying for rations: "Vat is your name?"

"Ginger Jones, Sah."

"How many beeples you got in your familee?"

"Me and 7 children, sah."

"Vell, here ees 10 lbs. meal and 3 rips (lbs.) bacon. Now don't pee extravagant. Don't you come back for a veek!<"> Who's next von?"

2nd Mate "Dad."

"I was brot. up before a negro commissioner once in New Orleans, charged with striking another nigger with a *left*handed axe handle. Now, who in Hell ever heard of a lefthanded axe handle?

Apl. 25.

Alsatia crevasse at Melbourne.[100] First point where we saw the country overflooded.

Vicksburg Apl. 26.

Rode to National Cemetery. <16,600> Motto over gateway: "Here rest in peace 16,600 who died for their country in the years 1861 to 1865."

(Motto at Arlington, Va.—

"On fame's eternal camping ground
Their silent tents are spread,
And glory guards with solemn round
The bivouac of the dead.")[101] [#]

---

[100] The citizens of New Orleans had become gravely alarmed about the flood stage of the river when in northern Louisiana an extensive crevasse opened in the Alsatia Levee, which had broken previously in 1874 (New Orleans *Daily Picayune,* 22 March 1882). This huge breach was still causing the inundation of a region below Lake Providence when Clemens passed by on the *Gold Dust* on his way to Vicksburg and New Orleans more than a month later.

[101] These lines from Theodore O'Hara's "The Bivouac of the Dead" adorn

On our ride saw nigger & a pair mules drawing ¼ cord wood 5 miles. Sells it for 50c.

Large cannon are planted for monuments. Perhaps watching over their own dead.

Scene of surrender Gen Pemberton to Gen Grant. (See sketch.)[102]

Jews.

Mr. Campbell thinks that the fact of the Jews buying property and settling in this cotton district is a good augury, as they are a shrewd people.

A *Gourd Float.*

<Just> In the overflow a negro's cabin surrounded by water 2 feet deep. Woman & 2 children on roof. Man wading around by the door fixing a <s>platform. One of the little niggers fell off the roof into the water. The old man called out "Look-a-dar! Look-a-dar Millie fell overboard.

The woman replied "Nebber mind, nebber mind. She's got a <gour> gou'd on."

Ques. Can they really dam the Mississippi?

Ans. The river *has* been damned a good many times by pilots on dark nights.

Conundrum.

Ques. Why don't they build mills on the banks of this river?

Ans. Dam it, how can they?

2nd Mate "Dad" Dunham says he was mate on the Fannie

---

numerous military monuments and burial grounds, including the Arlington National Cemetery.

[102] After withstanding a lengthy siege, Vicksburg was surrendered to Grant by General John Clifford Pemberton on 4 July 1863. Pemberton's capitulation was particularly humiliating because it took place on a patriotic holiday. Without identifying its author, Mark Twain would quote from "a Vicksburg letter of the time" to describe the surrender ceremony in a chapter of *Life on the Mississippi* which was discarded from the final version. This unidentified letter evidently was the "sketch" referred to here.

Tatum[103] Trip up Missouri river 3300 miles made fastest time on record viz. 3 days 9 hours and 4 months. (Capt. Ed Gray misconceived the spirit of this joke & said: "You mean 4 months 3 days and 9 hours.)

Old Uncle Ben raised game chickens. One day he caught a bald eagle and took him to a match. The other man Frenchman let out his boss game chicken & Uncle Ben put out his bald eagle. The eagle just reached for the game chicken & in two strokes tore him to pieces. The Frenchman cried out "Oh save de gaffs! Save de gaffs!"

They do not <*sing* at> call in the *singing* tone at the heaving of the lead as they used to, nor do they sing when leaving port

Fly Trap.

Up the Red River the alligators lie on the bar in the sun, mouth open, with upper jaw stretched wide back. The poor flies are beguiled in and after they have covered all the tongue & inside of the mouth then the alligator flops that upper jaw down and chaws. The chief engineer of Baton Rouge says that is taking a very mean advantage of the flies.

---

[103] Clemens may have told Dunham that he nearly took passage at Saint Louis on the *Fannie Tatum* instead of the *Gold Dust*.

TEXTUAL APPARATUS

Textual Introduction

THE MANUSCRIPTS of the nine notebooks in this volume, the only authoritative versions known to exist, are copy-text for this edition. Eight of the notebooks are in Clemens' hand; Notebook 21 is an amanuensis notebook in longhand, consisting of remarks Clemens and his acquaintances dictated to the secretary Clemens had hired to accompany him down the Mississippi River in 1882.

As far as possible, the entries in these notebooks appear in their original, often unfinished, form with Clemens' irregularities, inconsistencies, errors, and cancellations unemended. The same treatment has been accorded the secretarial notebook. The details of inscription in that notebook are reported for the sake of the clues they provide about the nature of Clemens' original dictation and the modifications the secretary may have made when transcribing it.

The headnote to each notebook includes a physical description of the manuscript and a discussion of textual characteristics or problems peculiar to that notebook. Although the footnotes do not often contain textual information, they do discuss textual matters that significantly affect the meaning of the text. All textual details brought to the reader's attention in footnotes are repeated in the fuller listings in the Textual Apparatus.

The Textual Apparatus contains two lists for each notebook: Emendations and Doubtful Readings, and Details of Inscription. These lists report all recoverable significant facts about the manuscript not fully represented in the text itself and enable the reader to trace the course of a notebook's composition. Emendations and Doubtful Readings reports all departures from the language of the manuscript, except for the points of holographic or typographic style described below, and records editorial conjectures about ambiguous and unrecovered passages. Details of Inscription records such readings as interlineations that apparently were added by Clemens after the initial drafting of a passage, describes complex revisions, and reports other aspects of the manuscript that may bear on the evolution of the text.

The list of emendations includes editorial corrections of obvious author's errors in the few cases when there is no doubt about the intended reading, when the error is excessively distracting, and when the emendation makes no appreciable change in the meaning of the text. In Notebook 19, for example, "hoes" has been emended to "does" at p. 412.19.

Sometimes letters are missing because Clemens inadvertently wrote off the edge of a page or because part of a page has been torn away. When such a gap is very short and there can be little doubt what letters are missing, the probable reading is supplied in the text in square brackets and is reported as an emendation, as in the word "Fin[ally]" at p. 120.8.

A few emendations report the substitution of words for ditto marks. The printed text follows Clemens' use of ditto marks, *ditto*, and *do* except when the vertical alignment of words is not naturally the same in print as in the manuscript notebooks. In such cases, to avoid awkward spacing of words or lines, the appropriate word is supplied in place of the abbreviation and the substitution is reported as an emendation.

The doubtful readings reported in the list include possible alternative versions of words which are partly or completely illegible in the manuscript or whose form is unclear. For example, Clemens' habit of running words together when writing hastily and his inconsistent use of hyphens in compound words (usually *to-day* and *good-bye*, but occasionally *today* and *good bye*) sometimes make it difficult to say whether the author intended to write two separate words, a hyphenated compound, or one solid word. Similarly, possible compounds hyphenated at the ends of lines in the manuscript could be transcribed either as hyphenated words or as solid words. Whenever the intended form of a compound word is in doubt, the form Clemens used most frequently at the time is printed in the text. If no authorial preference can be established, the conventional form according to dictionaries of the period appears in the text. In either case, the editorial decision is reported in Emendations and Doubtful Readings.

Clemens' grasp of the use of accents in foreign languages, especially French, was never firm: he omitted them, placed them over the wrong letter, used the wrong accent mark, and occasionally resorted to the schoolboy trick of using a flat mark that can be read as either an acute or a grave accent. All Clemens' accent marks are retained in the text, whether they are right or wrong. His ambiguous mark is rendered in the text as the accent it most resembles, and the alternative possibilities are noted in Emendations and Doubtful Readings.

When Clemens changed writing materials the fact is reported in Details of Inscription as evidence of a possible lapse in time between entries, but minor peculiarities of ink and paper, vagaries of handwriting, and the points in the text where manuscript pages begin and end are mentioned only when they cast light on the meaning of an entry or the sequence of composition. The lengths of lines and the position of words or lines on the manuscript page are not reproduced in the texts, except for headings, verse, addresses, tables, lists, and similar formal elements. Clemens' regular division of the text into entries has been followed, but no attempt has been made to reproduce the inconsistent means by which he separated entries. In particular, the horizontal lines or flourishes following many but not all entries have been omitted; the separation of entries is indicated here by extra space between lines or, when the end of a manuscript entry coincides with the end of a page of the printed text, by the symbol [#].

Uniform paragraph indentation has been imposed on the first lines of all entries except those that require special alignment, such as the formal elements mentioned above. Clemens indented most entries, but neither this fact nor his occasional failure to indent affects the meaning of the text. Moreover, the depth of indentation (which has been standardized in this text) varies so widely throughout the notebooks that in places it is difficult to tell which lines are indented and which are not. Indeed, occasionally when Clemens neglected to indent the first line he indicated paragraphs by indenting the second and succeeding lines instead. Since in such cases the author's intention to form paragraphs is clear, these are also presented in the conventional manner. When the separation of entries is in doubt or an ambiguity in paragraphing affects the meaning of the text, the problem is reported in the apparatus and if it is crucial is discussed in a footnote.

The occasional dots and lines under superscript letters, which Clemens tended to write indistinctly when he used them at all, have been silently omitted. Thus words which might at different times be interpreted as $M^{\underset{.}{r}}$, $M^{\underset{..}{r}}$, $M^{\underline{r}}$, or $M^{\underline{\underline{r}}}$ are all rendered as M^{r}. However, a period following a superscript appears on or above the line as Clemens wrote it, thus: $M^{r}.$ or $M^{r\cdot}$.

Although Clemens' cancellations are generally retained, cancellations to repair such purely mechanical problems as misspellings and miswritten words or letters are omitted. However, every authorial change which might possibly provide a clue to anything more significant than a moment's inadvertence is included in the text. Thus, words originally written clearly and spelled correctly which nevertheless were canceled and then rewritten are retained in the text as evidence of possible authorial indecision. While most spelling errors corrected by Clemens are omitted, when he misspelled and then corrected a proper name, both the error and the correction are included in the text as evidence that Clemens may have been unfamiliar with the subject.

Drawings related to the text or having some other intrinsic significance are reproduced in positions which reflect as clearly as possible their relationship to the text. Scrawls and random marks are reproduced or described only if they may bear on the meaning of the text. When Clemens, and later Paine, copied or adapted a passage for use in a work intended for publication, they frequently indicated the fact by marking the section with a simple stroke or two of pencil or pen. Most such "use marks" reveal nothing about the meaning of a passage or the use made of it, if any, and are omitted. Occasionally when revising a passage Clemens used proofreader's marks such as *stet* and ¶, or he indicated the placement of passages with lines, arrows, or written instructions. His intention is followed in each case, and the mechanism is described in Details of Inscription.

Clemens underlined words in the notebooks so unsystematically that it is often impossible to say whether he intended to convey different degrees of emphasis by single, double, and triple underlining. While no attempt has been made to impose a system where Clemens apparently intended none, differences in the manuscript are reported by means of the normal typographic conventions: letters underlined once have been set in italic type, letters underlined twice in small capitals, and letters underlined three times in full capitals. Triple underlining is recorded in Details of

Inscription, to preserve the distinction between words underlined and words actually written in capital letters.

Most entries are presented in the physical order they follow in the manuscript notebooks, although that order is not necessarily the order in which they were written. Endpapers and flyleaves, in particular, usually contain notes jotted at various times during a notebook's use. Since such short notes cannot usually be precisely dated and since their aggregation at either end of a notebook is typical of Clemens' practice, these groups of entries have been presented intact. Elsewhere in the notebooks, however, occasional entries or blocks of entries have been moved into chronological order when a reconstruction of the order of their inscription can be defended and the rearrangement does not separate passages deliberately juxtaposed by the author. Entries are moved most often when Clemens turned a notebook and began writing from the opposite end. When the order of entries has been changed, Details of Inscription describes the original manuscript sequence and any textual peculiarities bearing on the rearrangement. When the order of entries has been left unchanged because the chronology of their inscription cannot be firmly established, the list nevertheless reports aspects of the manuscript that suggest a chronological sequence different from the physical sequence, such as the fact that an entry was written with the notebook inverted. Footnotes explain the external evidence for moving or dating a passage.

Passages whose intended position Clemens did not clearly indicate and pages which have come loose from the notebooks are placed in the text where the available evidence suggests they belong. Words written at an angle across other entries or in the margin are usually placed following the entry with which they are associated. A special problem arises in parts of some notebooks where Clemens used only the right-hand pages for the main sequence of his remarks but wrote a few scattered entries on the otherwise blank left-hand pages. In such cases the context sometimes suggests that Clemens deliberately placed the isolated entry opposite a particular passage on the facing manuscript page, while at other times it seems more probable that he simply picked a convenient blank space to write in. In the present text an isolated entry of this kind normally is placed in a position which reflects as nearly as possible its manuscript location and its logical relationship to other entries, but it may be moved, to avoid interrupting a continuing sequence of entries. Problems of the appropriate sequence or placement of entries vary so widely from case to case that no general statement of editorial principles can cover them all. In each instance the situation in the manuscript is described in Details of Inscription and is discussed if necessary in a footnote. Clippings and notes not in Clemens' hand which are interleaved in the notebooks or attached to them are described or printed in full, according to their importance and length, in the footnotes.

Clemens occasionally wrote in his notebooks while on horseback or aboard ship, in a carriage or a crowd, or in very bad light. Such passages may be chaotic scrawls. Even in passages written under more favorable conditions, minor lapses and inaccuracies sometimes produce puzzling ambiguities. These characteristics cannot be rendered in type, and some of them defy verbal description. But, except under unusual circumstances, Clemens' handwriting is clear, and a description of the occasional problems makes it appear more challenging than it is in fact. The sometimes confusing resemblance of *a* and *o*, *n* and *u*, and *w* and *m*, and Clemens' occasional crossing of an *l* mistaken for a *t* or dotting of part of an *n* or *u*, misread as an *i*, are characteristic of hasty and informal notes. Finally, a terminal *s* may be no more than a hook on the penultimate letter. Context easily resolves most of these problems. When a word is so badly written that it is impossible to tell whether it is spelled correctly or incorrectly but there is no question what word was intended, it is assumed that Clemens spelled the word correctly. When an obscurity cannot be resolved, the alternatives are registered in Emendations and Doubtful Readings and, if crucial to the understanding of an entry, are discussed in a footnote as well.

Clemens used both the exclamation point and the question mark as internal punctuation, and he frequently followed a terminal period with a dash. He also sometimes used a terminal dash in place of a period or extended a period so that it looks like a dash or a comma. Colons, semicolons, and commas sometimes resemble each other. These difficulties are often compounded by the similarity between the capital and lower-case forms of some of Clemens' letters such as *t*, *s*, *c*, and *m*. Problems caused by these characteristics of the author's handwriting and punctuation are resolved silently here on the basis of familiarity with Clemens' hand and practice and of any other information available. Ambiguities are reported in Emendations and Doubtful Readings when doubt persists.

To keep the text as uncluttered as the demands of completeness and clarity will allow, the number of special symbols used has been held to a minimum. Readings canceled by Clemens have been enclosed in angle brackets, and the spacing following the closing angle bracket indicates how a cancellation was made. When Clemens canceled a word or word-ending simply by striking it out, a normal space follows the closing angle bracket, thus: "<American> passengers" and "bell<s> rang." When he canceled a word or word fragment by writing something else over it, the original reading is enclosed in angle brackets and the new reading follows the closing angle bracket without the customary intervening space. Thus, when Clemens wrote "organ" over "part" the text reads "<part>organ," and when he wrote "take" to cover and cancel the false start "s" the text reads "<s>take."

On the rare occasions when Clemens revised a word by writing over a part of it or by striking out one or more letters within it (other than the terminal letters), the entire original reading is given within angle brackets, the entire revised reading follows the closing angle bracket without an intervening space, and an entry in Details of Inscription explains exactly how the change was made. Thus, when Clemens wrote "sen" (possibly intending originally to write "sent") and then changed it to "stayed" by writing "tayed" over "en," the text reads "<sen>stayed" and the revision is explained in Details of Inscription. Similarly, if he had written "t" over the "s" of "sake" the text would read "<sake>take," and if he had simply canceled the "t" of "stake" the text would read "<stake>sake." The process of revision in such cases is described in Details of Inscription. The same procedure applies to revised numerals: when the text reads "<10>30-ton rocks" Details of Inscription records that "3" was written over "1" (that is, "30" was not written over "10"). For ease of reading, punctuation marks have been spaced normally even when they fall within or immediately follow a cancellation. Therefore, the lack of an extra space after the closing angle bracket in readings like "<">How" and "I will <not>!" does not necessarily mean that the canceled material was overwritten by what follows it. When a mark of punctuation is written over a word or letter, or when something is written over a mark of punctuation, Clemens' revision is explained in Details of Inscription.

Interlineations and other readings apparently added by Clemens after completion of the initial inscription appear in the text unaccompanied by special symbols except for one limited category. When Clemens interlined a word or phrase as an alternative to a previously inscribed reading but canceled neither version, both readings are printed in the text, separated by a slash mark and with the earlier reading first, thus: "Turn/Flee."

All Clemens' identifiable additions are recorded in Details of Inscription, where they are enclosed within vertical arrows, thus: "↑innocently↓." To help the reader find the additions in the text, a word or two of context may be included in an entry in Details of Inscription, thus: "↑the↓ noted occasions." Similarly, for the reader's convenience, extra words, often including cancellations associated with additions, may be presented in an entry if doing so provides enough context to clarify the revision, thus: "<mighty> ↑very↓" or "Hotel↑s↓ gouge<s>." (All cancellations, whether or not they are repeated in Details of Inscription, are enclosed in angle brackets in the text.)

Conjectural reconstructions of illegible readings and of letters where the manuscript is torn or words are written off the edge of the page are enclosed in square brackets in the text. Hyphens within square brackets stand for unreadable letters. Editorial explanations are in italics and within square brackets. Thus "[------]" stands for an illegible word of about six letters and "[*three words*]" stands for three unrecovered words. (To preserve square brackets for editorial insertions, Clemens' square brackets, which he used interchangeably with parentheses, are rendered as parentheses.) In the apparatus a vertical rule has been used when necessary to indicate a line-ending, thus: "to-|day." An asterisk in Emendations and Doubtful Readings refers the reader to the corresponding entry in Details of Inscription.

In descriptions of Clemens' revisions, words identified as written "above" other words are interlined, while words written "over" other words are written in the same space, covering the reading they supplant. The word *follow* indicates a spatial but not necessarily a temporal relation. The word *endpaper* designates the pasted-down page inside either cover of a notebook and the word *flyleaf* refers to the leaf next to an endpaper.

Line numbers in tables and citations refer to Clemens' text only and do not count editorial language on the same page.

Key to Symbols

<word>	Clemens' cancellation
↑word↓	written later than the surrounding passage

[word]	doubtful reading, marginally legible
w[- -]d	illegible letters
[*page torn*]	editorial remarks
word/word	alternative readings proposed but never resolved by Clemens
word|word	end of a line
[#]	last line of text on the printed page is the end of an entry in the manuscript
*	cross-reference in Emendations and Doubtful Readings to Details of Inscription

Notebook 13

Emendations and Doubtful Readings

	MTP Reading	MS Reading
13.6	midnight	mid-|night
18.14	to-day	to-|day
20.11	snow-white	[*possibly* 'snow white']
22.8	light colored	[*possibly* 'light-colored']
24.13	nearly	[*possibly* 'nearby']
31.20	moonlight	moon-|light
32.16	sea-sick	sea-|sick
36.1	sweetheart	sweet-|heart

Details of Inscription

11.1–37.1 J. R. Locke . . . laughter. [*written from the back of the notebook toward the front with the notebook inverted*]

11.1–12.3 J. R. Locke . . . Fuller [*written on the back endpaper pocket flap. The remainder of the endpaper is blank except for Paine's note* 'Idle Excursion' *which is not included in the present text. The adjoining ruled leaf is blank except for the inscription at 12.4*]

12.4 First . . . May. [*written immediately above the hinge of the page facing the entries beginning* 'Bar-keep' *(12.5) and possibly added after those entries were begun. This is the only inscription on the notebook's last ruled leaf*]

13.5 ↑Slow railroad↓ [*squeezed into the top margin of the page above* 'Two elderly men' *(13.3) and boxed*]

13.14–15 ↑(suspicious . . . . manners↓

13.26 <[o]the>the other [*the first letter of what appears to be* 'othe' *canceled, producing* 'the']

14.2 there<–>↑.↓ <we>We [*originally one sentence; the dash canceled, the period added, and* 'W' *written over* 'w' *to create two sentences*]

15.23 ↑Then . . . clerical.↓

15.24 <wa>when ['h' *written over* 'a']

18.1 ↑Sunday.↓

18.6 ↑Governor Gardiner↓ [*interlined below* 'Boston student's' *and above* 'fine clothes']

18.12 <[¶]S> ['S' *indented to begin a new paragraph, then canceled, and the preceding paragraph continued*]

18.19 ↑Sea-sick resurrection.↓ [*squeezed into the space between the surrounding entries; written in purple ink*]

19.1 ↑Fine . . . carriage.↓ [*written lengthwise on the page across portions of the preceding entries,* 'Narrow channel . . . dandy canes.' *(18.18–27)*]

19.8 <↑done↓ in co>

19.13–14 <& it h>with ['w' *written over* 'h']

20.1 Eternity." [*a flourish originally ending the entry here was overwritten and the entry was continued*]

20.13–14 road↑.↓ <so> This

20.16–17 <bow> ↑military salute↓

21.3 dresses [*follows a caret; there is no interlineation*]

21.5 ↑Fool↓ [*written in purple ink*]

21.13 ↑Monday↓ [*written diagonally on the page across the following entry*]

21.14 6 AM ↑Monday↓

22.1 pipe-clay. [*a flourish originally ending the entry here was overwritten and the entry was continued*]

23.11 base like ↑a↓ pillar

24.3 ↑undefinable↓

24.14 <↑to 15,000↓> ↑to 15,000↓

25.7 ↑dogs↓

27.1 ↑Tuesday↓ [*written diagonally on the page across the two following entries*]

27.17 ↑or purple↓

27.20 ↑Morning . . . day.↓ [*written lengthwise on the page across the preceding entry*]

27.24 ↑wholly↓

27.25 <↑shap↓>

28.25 <fees> ↑fine↓

29.9–10 ↑Iron clad chicken.↓

31.12 ↑Simple Negro–↓

31.17 ↑Locate it in St. George's.↓ [*written lengthwise on the page across the two preceding entries*]

31.19 day–|–came

32.1 ↑Dogs . . . nights.↓ [*written lengthwise on the page across the preceding entry*]

33.2 ↑high &↓

33.11 ↑Fool . . . passengers.↓ [*written lengthwise on the page across the preceding entry from* 'aboard' *to* 'presently.' (33.6–10)]

35.5 ↑country↓

35.9 <Hartford.> [*a flourish originally ending the entry here was overwritten and the entry was continued*]

36.21	↑Close↓ [*written in black ink above the following entry*]
37.1	laughter. [*followed by 19 blank pages, the one-page drawing of a gate, another blank page, and the end of the sequence of entries at 37.2–40.11*]
37.2–40.11	Pen-knife . . . signs [*written from the front of the notebook toward the back*]
37.2–39.3	Pen-knife . . . Broadway. [*written on the front endpaper*]
37.2	2–Toys. [*boxed on three sides*]
39.1–3	Capt . . . Broadway. [*written with the notebook inverted*]
39.4–40.3	Write . . . Leather head [*written on both sides of the front flyleaf; an additional flyleaf and one ruled leaf have been torn out following these entries*]
39.10	Butter-tongue/↑mouth↓
40.7	car. [*followed by one blank page; then one ruled leaf has been torn out*]

Notebook 14

Emendations and Doubtful Readings

	MTP Reading	MS Reading
50.6	mad-house	mad-|house
50.9	gamekeeper	game-|keeper
51.4	bell	[*possibly* 'hell']
52.6	Roehn	[*possibly* 'Rochu' *or* 'Rocher']
54.20	to-morrow	[*possibly* 'tomorrow']
56.3	dry-goods	dry-|goods
59.12	<di Le>	[*possibly* '<<d'>de Leu>']
61.13	overhead	over-|head
62.9	*every*body	*every*-|body
62.12	graveyard	grave-|yard
62.13	Chuckleheaded	Chuckle-|headed
*63.30	[G]rumbler	[*page torn*]
65.2	undertaker	under-|taker
65.8	sea-sickness	sea-|sickness
*65.15	<jay-birds>	<jay-|birds>
68.23	bull's-eye	bull's-|eye
70.21	Degetan	[*possibly* 'Degetau']
71.5	open-work	open-|work
71.22	shove	[*possibly* 'show']
72.16	to-day	to-|day

76.18	drawing-room	drawing-|room
77.6–7	is not natural	is not | not natural
77.19	schoolboys	school-|boys
77.21	sunshine	sun-|shine
81.10	to-day	[*possibly* 'today']
81.14	middle-aged	middle-|aged
84.6	sunset	sun-|set
85.13	Degetan	[*possibly* 'Degetau']
85.19	thunder	[*possibly* 'thunder,']
86.4	1½ to 3 minutes	[*possibly* '½ to 3 minutes']
86.7	<twi>	[*possibly* '<noi>']
88.7	to-night	[*possibly* 'tonight']
88.24	bedchamber	[*possibly* 'bed-chamber' *or* 'bed chamber']
89.20	good-bye	good-|bye
89.26	moss covered	[*possibly* 'moss-covered']
90.1	Woman	[*possibly* 'Women']
90.20	<the curling s>	[*possibly* '<the curlings>']
91.2	Seubert	[*possibly* 'Scubert']
93.22	hand organ	[*possibly* 'hand-organ']
93.26	heart-breaking	heart-|breaking
94.20	landlord	land-|lord
96.7	to-day	[*possibly* 'today']
97.9	to-morrow	[*possibly* 'tomorrow']
98.5	to-day	to-|day
101.18	generat	[*possibly* 'general']

102.2	Stole	[*possibly* 'State']
102.17	near-sighted	near-|sighted
103.13	cars	[*possibly* 'car']
106.6	F. Humelsheim	[*possibly* 'F. Hundsheim']
107.3	named . . . spring	[*possibly* 'named, . . . sprung']
*109.7	*gas.* in hotel.	[*possibly* '*gas,* in hotel.']
*109.12	<*herr*[rs]>	[*possibly* '<herr[rs]>']
109.23	Unabhängigkeitserklärunge[n]	[*written off the edge of the page*]
*110.8	Marie Rieu	[*possibly* 'Marie Rien' *or* 'Marie Bien']

Details of Inscription

49.1–51.9	Nov. 23 . . . Dromios. [*written from the front of the notebook toward the back on 3⅓ right-hand pages*]
49.1–51.3	Nov. 23 . . . Durham [*written in purple ink except for the word* 'Written' (49.6)]
49.6	↑Written↓ [*penciled diagonally across the preceding entry*]
51.9	Dromios. [*followed on the manuscript page by the entries at 108.18–109.2, which were written with the notebook inverted*]
51.10–109.19	Tie up . . . coffee pot. [*written from the back of the notebook toward the front, with the notebook inverted*]
51.10–52.5	Tie up . . . village [*written on the back endpaper*]
52.6–53.1	Frau Emma . . . himself. [*written on the recto of the back flyleaf*]
52.8	↑1st & 2^{d} story,↓

53.2–53.9 From Zurich . . . Venice. [*written on the verso of the back flyleaf*]

53.2–3 ↑(Hotel . . . best.)↓

53.10–65.6 Mch 15/78 . . . wife wh made [*29 leaves are inscribed on right-hand pages only, except for entries at 54.5, 54.23–24, 57.13–15, and 63.1–5 written on left-hand pages*]

53.15–18 ↑*Mem* . . . world.↓ [*written in blue ink lengthwise on the page across the preceding paragraph and the two following entries*]

54.5 ↑Write . . . form.↓ [*written at the top of a left-hand page opposite* 'The First . . . Harper' *(54.6–8) on the facing right-hand page; the left-hand page is otherwise blank except for* 'Mch. 13 . . . promises.' *(54.23–24) written at the bottom; since the 29 leaves beginning at 53.10 are inscribed almost entirely on right-hand pages only, it is likely that these entries were written later*]

54.23–24 ↑Mch. 13 . . . promises.↓ [*written at the bottom of a left-hand page opposite* 'Mch. 19—Susie's . . . Lester was to have' *(54.15–16) on the facing right-hand page; the left-hand page is otherwise blank except for* 'Write . . . form.' *(54.5) written at the top; it is likely that Clemens added this entry at some time after he completed the entry at 54.16–22,* ' " " Lester . . . appointment.)']

55.17 obscurity<,>. <& thinks this> [*the period written over the comma*]

56.2 W. is years [*the top quarter of the leaf has been torn out above this entry, leaving the flourish that probably followed a preceding entry*]

56.17 ↑& fittest↓

57.13–15 ↑1¼ . . . 2¾↓ [*written on an otherwise blank left-hand page opposite* 'No such . . . Scribner.' *(57.16) on the facing page; since surrounding leaves (beginning at 53.10) are inscribed almost entirely on right-hand pages only, it is likely that Clemens added this entry later than at least some of the entries that follow* 'No such . . . Scribner.']

57.16 No such pictures [*the top quarter of the leaf has been torn out above this entry, leaving the flourish that probably followed a preceding entry*]

58.12 <Buried> ↑Coffined↓

58.14 <visitor's>visitors [*the apostrophe canceled*]

59.9 <suf>supplicating ['p' *written over* 'f']

59.16 ↑Dine . . . Pavilion↓

59.18 ↑Write Robt. Watt.↓ ↑2 Nordgate↓

60.12 <Frederichs-Thal>Frederichshal [*originally* 'Frederichs-|Thal'; *the* 'T' *canceled*]

60.19 ↑Prettiest . . . world.↓ [*written lengthwise in the left margin of the page beside the preceding paragraph*]

61.1 ↑Switzerland,↓

61.7 <Mayence> ↑Mainz (fresh)↓

61.8–9 ↑& Heidelberg. . . . trip.↓

61.12 <Königsberg> ↑Rheinstein↓

61.16 ↑& occupation.↓

61.20 <dong[- -]>donkey ['key' *written over* 'g[- -]']

61.23 ↑Grumbler.↓ [*written lengthwise in the left margin of the page beside the preceding and following entries*]

63.1–5 ↑1.75 . . . 262.50↓ [*written on an otherwise blank left-hand page opposite* 'the nation . . . don't have' (62.22–23) *on the facing page; since surrounding leaves are inscribed almost entirely on right-hand pages only, it is likely that Clemens added this entry at some time after he completed the entry at* 62.19–26 ('Going abroad . . . domestic.')]

63.23 ↑male & female↓

63.30 ↑[G]rumbler.↓ [*written lengthwise in the left margin of the page beside the preceding entry; the bottom half of the leaf has been torn off, leaving the flourish below the preceding entry and removing the* 'G' *of* 'Grumbler' *and perhaps additional entries below the flourish*]

64.1–22 Write . . . bell [*written on three leaves which have lost their conjugate halves and have been placed here because they appear to have been inscribed at the same time as the surrounding pages. The first two leaves, which are loose, clearly belong together because the sentence beginning* 'I' *at the bottom of the first continues with* 'know you will refrain' *(64.4–5) at the top of the second. The third leaf, beginning* 'Transfer' *(64.17), has been glued along its inner edge to the following leaf. Although its contents do not indicate whether it originally preceded or followed the two loose leaves, it is placed after them here because of the possibility that it was tipped in by someone who did know the correct order of the pages—perhaps by Mark Twain himself. The top half of the first loose leaf has been torn off. It appears probable from the torn edges of the two loose leaves that their missing conjugate halves originally preceded them. Moreover, if this gathering was originally a full one of 12 leaves, then two more leaves, forming another conjugate pair, are also missing here.*]

64.13 ↑Peruvian dollars↓ [*interlined at an angle above* 'Gillette, Roe, Beach.' *(64.14)*]

65.15 <jay-birds>↑blue↓ jay↑s↓ [*originally* 'jay-|birds'; 'birds' *canceled,* 's' *written over the hyphen, and* 'blue' *interlined*]

66.11 <Sonnenschien>Sonnenschein ['ei' *written over* 'ie']

66.15 Grumbler. [*written lengthwise in the left margin of the page beside* 'hohe . . . Folgung.' (66.11–14)]

66.17 <dieses>dieser ['r' *written over* 's']

66.18 <sie>seiner ['ei' *written over* 'ie']

67.3 <ze>zwei<n> ['w' *written over* 'e']

68.9 ↑large↓

68.17 ↑inviting↓ [*written in black ink diagonally across the preceding paragraph*]

70.12 ↑Hamburg-↓Americanische ↑Packet*fahrt*↓

70.29 <my heart!"> ↑me here!" putting . . . heart.↓

71.12 Grumbler [*written lengthwise in the left margin of the page beside the preceding entry*]

72.6–7 ↑Gr:=↓ ↑The Kronprinz . . . anyway.↓

72.21 ↑Bergedorf to.↓

73.1 Hotel . . . Cassel [*originally* 'Hotel ---- Cassel'; 'du Nord' *written over the hyphens*]

73.22 <there>they ['y' *written over* 're']

74.4 <su>stubborn ['t' *written over* 'u']

74.19 year. [*a flourish originally ending the entry here was overwritten and the entry was continued*]

74.28 <pro-> [*canceled at the end of a manuscript line*]

75.1 Even ↑in↓

75.6 the<y> ↑courier↓

75.13 <Geutenburg>Geutenberg ['e' *written over* 'u']

75.18 ↑Carl↓

76.3 <Gutenburg>Gutenberg ['e' *written over* 'u']

76.7 ↑The Trinity.↓ [*written in purple ink*]

76.10 In . . . us, [*two-thirds of the page is blank below this entry*]

76.18–19 Fresco . . . balloon. [*the illustration that follows is drawn over this entry*]

78.13 6 ↑to 9↓ hours

78.18 <This>The ['s' *canceled; the same character used for* 'i' *and* 'e']

79.10 <father-> ↑mother-↓dog . . . <mother-> ↑father-↓dog's

79.20 <10>12 ['2' *written over* '0']

79.21 ↑Cheap . . . days.↓

79.23 <40>20 ['2' *written over* '4']

80.21 -----/↑verb?↓

80.22 drink. [*a flourish originally ending the entry here was overwritten and the entry was continued*]

80.24 study<,>! [*the exclamation point written over the comma*]

80.25–26 ↑& spreading↓

81.6 *pr*<*o.*> ↑if an o comes after it.↓

82.16 Student↑s at↓ tables

82.21 ↑Alway . . . within (—).↓

83.1–2 ↑(the hyphens are mine):↓

83.3–5 der in- . . . begegnet [*small crosses in purple ink appear above* 'der' *and below* 'begegnet']

83.9 <— —>↑godam godam↓ [*the words interlined above the two dashes, one word above the other, apparently to replace the dashes*]

83.9 THE's ['the' *underlined three times*]

83.10 ↑young lady↓ [*interlined above* 'turnip' *with a line to indicate placement*]

83.14–17 Where . . . church. [*what may be an arrow, perhaps pointing to the entry at 83.10–11, appears beside this entry*]

84.18 Werden to it<.>, [*a flourish originally ended the entry after* 'it.'; *the period was mended to a comma, the flourish overwritten, and the entry continued*]

84.20 ↑(May 22)↓

87.6 <J[-]>Jim ['i' *written over an unrecovered letter*]

87.10 ↑By far↓

87.15 <"Er ist in ihr aftern."> [*canceled in purple ink*]

87.23 <& *then*> [*a line below* 'th' *may represent an abandoned intention to italicize* 'then']

88.8 <zahlreis>zahlreich ['c' *written over* 's']

88.12 wind [*a flourish originally ending the entry here was overwritten and the entry was continued*]

88.20 <bahnhoof>bahnhoff ['f' *written over* 'o']

88.23 ↑May 26↓

88.25 ↑Will hide . . . & *stay* hid.↓

88.27 <missing> ↑steering safe among↓

89.5 *der* <h>Hund ↑*the* dog;↓;

89.6 ↑<a>the wom[an]↓ [*written off the edge of the page*]

89.10 Hund↑e↓↑n↓(?)

89.17 ↑singular↓

90.6 <996>896 ['8' *written over* '9']

91.3 LOHENGRIN . . . ALBERT NIEMANN ['Lohengrin' *and* 'Albert Niemann' *written with initial capitals; then underlined three times*]

91.11 <aufge>aufheben [*originally* 'auf-|ge'; 'ge' *canceled and* 'heben' *added*]

91.18 sub- [*end-of-line hyphen; word not finished*]

92.16 ↑V.N.↓

92.20 ↑(this is John)↓

92.23–24 ↑tremulous↓ voice <tremulous with tears>

93.10–12 ↑the tenor &↓ the soprano . . . alternately hold<s> out <her>their arms toward <the tenor> ↑each other↓ ['her' *expanded to* 'their']

93.16 <fellow> ↑rioter↓

93.25 ↑long, arid↓

93.26 ↑between-times↓ <expanses>expanses ['expanses' *canceled, then restored by stet marks*]

93.28 <who>which <↑always↓> ['ich' *written over* 'o']

93.34 <what>who ['o' *written over* 'a'; 't' *canceled*]

94.13 <A week> ↑10 days↓

94.15 Du↑t↓chess

95.3 <miene>meine ['ei' *written over* 'ie']

95.3 ↑haben ge↓lacht

95.5 *<ungefëhr>ungefähr* ['*ä*' *written over* '*ë*']

95.8 ↑a something which we have lost↓ [*interlined without a caret above* 'had this beautiful Castle']

95.10–11 ↑(A natural thought)↓

95.21–22 <die des> meine Schwester↑s↓

96.12 Wirt↑h↓schaft

96.20 fish wife [*followed by a caret; there is no interlineation*]

98.1 ↑Unintelligibility↓ [*written lengthwise in the left margin of the page beside the preceding entry and underscored by a row of dots*]

98.2 Stadtverord↑n↓etenversammlung.—↑27↓ ↑tapeworm↓ ['tape-worm' *interlined without a caret above* 'Stadtverordnetenversammlung']

98.9 ↑(movement↓

98.11 ↑(quiet)↓

98.17 <married,> ↑painted,↓

98.21 <emp> ↑President↓

99.9 <sind> ↑waren↓ heute <↑hier↓> viele

99.10 <heir>hier ['ie' *written over* 'ei']

99.11 <Win>Wunderschön ['un' *written over* 'in']

100.13 ↑Ponderous . . . jaws.↓ [*written in purple ink lengthwise across the preceding paragraph*]

100.14–24 noble . . . bark. [*the exact order of inscription is unclear*]

100.14 ↑noble *un* sound↓ ['noble' *possibly added later*]

100.15 ↑Great ↑big↓ *guns*<!>.↓ [*the exclamation point mended to a period*]

100.15 ↑Grosse Gewehre↓

100.16 ↑London↓

100.16 Schlacht [*possibly added later*]

100.17 ↑Thunder↓ ↑Donner↓

100.17–23 Boom . . . Bellow ['Boom', 'Burst', 'Crash', *and* 'Bellow' *struck through in purple ink, probably to indicate use rather than cancellation*]

100.19 ↑Blitz is good as Lightning.↓

100.20–21 ↑The spitting of the lightning–Blitz.↓

100.20 –Hölle [*possibly added later*]

100.21–23 Cannon | Artillery | Bellow [*possibly added later*]

100.23–24 ↑–<bark–bellt:>↓ ↑bellt is . . . bark.↓ ['bellt is . . . bark.' *written lengthwise in the right margin of the page*]

100.25 The roar . . . crash! [*about three ruled lines have been torn from the leaf above these words on the recto and above* '(Per literature)' *(101.16) on the verso, apparently before these entries were written*]

100.25–28 The roar . . . roar. ['The roar . . . yell.' *and* 'The howl . . . roar.' *struck through in purple ink, probably to indicate use rather than cancellation*]

100.25 booming [*follows a caret; there is no interlineation*]

100.26 ↑long↓

100.28 ruhig ↑peacefully↓ ['peacefully' *interlined without a caret below* 'ruhig']

101.4 <Hieligen>Heiligen ['ei' *written over* 'ie']

101.5 ↑wind↓

101.6 stürm↑ish↓ <(sh)> (weak) ['weak)' *written over* 'sh)']

101.12–15 Heilig . . . ruhig [*listed in purple ink on the right side of the page beside* 'wind Blows . . . Explosion–' *(101.5–8)*]

102.3 bird-shot. [*a flourish originally ending the entry here was overwritten and the entry was continued*]

102.7 ↑jetzt↓

102.7 ↑(spread.)↓ ↑out.↓

103.7 ↑official↓

103.12–13 Walldürn . . . Seckach [*not in Clemens' hand*]

103.16 ↑oak↓

103.18 <Ro>Rubbed ['u' *written over* 'o']

104.1 ↑found out the mystery.↓

104.11–12 Breakfasted . . . combed. [*boxed*]

104.21–23 Who has . . . has it. [*boxed*]

104.29–105.3 Das . . . 30 Juni [*boxed*]

104.29–105.2 *hielt* <↑pre-↓> ↑with-↓/↑de-↓ . . . *ab.* ↑(vented).↓/↑held↓/↑layed↓ ['<pre->' *interlined above 'hielt',* 'with-' *below 'hielt', and* 'de-' *below* 'with-'; '(vented).' *squeezed in at the end of the line beside 'ab.',* 'held' *squeezed in beside* '(vented).', *and* 'layed' *squeezed in below* 'held'; *all without carets*]

105.4 I will take my um . . . . brella. [*written lengthwise in the left margin of the page and linked to the preceding paragraph by a short connecting line*]

105.10 ↑July 2↓

105.11–12 ↑July <3>7 . . 5 PM↓ [*squeezed in between the preceding and following entries*]

105.15 German hotels . . . are dark. [*written in black ink*]

106.10 ↑K. Gallo.↓

107.1 *Rache!* (What for?) [*struck through in purple ink, probably to indicate use rather than cancellation*]

107.2 <of [-]>from ['f' *written over an unrecovered letter*]

107.25 ↑II Tage↓

107.26 Dieser . . . Tage. [*an arrow in the left margin beside this sentence points to* 'K. Müller' (107.25)]

108.2 ↑with ribbon↓

109.1 <21>22 ['2' *written over* '1']

109.2 township map. [*followed on the manuscript page by*

the end of the sequence of entries at 49.1–51.9, which were written with the notebook held right side up before it was inverted]

109.3–4 <same . . . a mark a> ↑½ mark a↓ minute

109.7 *gas.* in hotel. ['in hotel.' *possibly added later; see Doubtful Readings*]

109.11 <*ëchzen*>*ächzen* [*'ä' written over 'ë'*]

109.12 <*herr*[rs]>*herr*↑.↓ [*originally apparently 'herrrs'; the end of the word was canceled and the period added; the italics may have been added when the inscription was revised*]

109.15 Ceremonies. [*followed by the page of inscription in purple ink at 50.7–51.3, which was written with the notebook held right side up before the notebook was inverted*]

109.19 coffee pot. [*the bottom half of the page is blank below this entry; followed by the page of inscription in purple ink at 49.10–50.7, a blank page, and the page of inscription in purple ink at 49.1–10; the inscriptions in purple ink written from the front of the notebook toward the back before the notebook was inverted*]

109.20–110.5 ↑Tabaksuntersuchung.↓ . . . Grocer. [*written on the verso of the front flyleaf*]

109.20–110.2 ↑Tabaksuntersuchung.↓ . . . Lebensversicherungsgesellschaft [*written with the notebook inverted*]

110.6–111.2 Hotel . . . Hoboken. [*written on the recto of the front flyleaf*]

110.6–18 Hotel . . . Stadtverordnetenversammlungen [*written with the notebook inverted*]

110.8–10 Madame . . . Lausanne. [*not in Clemens' hand*]

110.11 Miss . . . address [*written by Olivia Clemens*]

110.12–14 8 . . . 32[-] [*the following four lines written over this entry*]

111.3–112.2 Marine . . . Platz. [*written on the front endpaper*]

111.3–111.11 Marine . . . Heidelberg. [*written with the notebook inverted*]

Notebook 15

Emendations and Doubtful Readings

	MTP Reading	MS Reading
*119.18	Em[press.]	[*page torn*]
*119.18	O[ur]	[*page torn*]
*119.18	wa[s]	[*page torn*]
*120.4	[B]aden	[*page torn*]
*120.4	[ta]ble	[*page torn*]
*120.5	[(S]unday)	[*page torn*]
*120.5	Amer[i]cans	Amer-|[i]cans [*page torn*]
*120.5	[o]ld	[*page torn*]
*120.6	[b]eyond	[*page torn*]
*120.8	Fin[ally]	[*page torn*]
120.16	*good*-bye	*good*-|bye
121.13	daylight	day-|light
122.7	to-night	to-|night
123.12	monopolies[–]	[*page torn*]
124.6	on	[*possibly* 'ou']
126.6	make-shift	make-|shift
133.17	twilight	twi-|light
136.12	He	[*possibly* 'We']
138.24	to-night	to-|night
138.27	uplifted	up-|lifted

139.6	cap-stone	cap-|stone
139.11	[it]	[*page torn*]
143.4	clothes-line	clothes-|line
144.10	to-night	[*possibly* 'tonight']
145.27	stage-coach	stage-|coach
148.4	keepsake	keep-|sake
148.12	to-morrow	[*possibly* 'tomorrow']

Details of Inscription

115.1–116.1	Miss Elizabeth . . . Roosevelt. [*written on the front endpaper with the notebook inverted*]
116.2–3	Heiliger . . . <n>Nacht! [*written on the front flyleaf*]
116.15	Openau . . . Ofenberg & change. [*boxed*]
117.1	↑25th↓
117.6	↑Pretty girl here.↓
117.7	↑Offenbosen↓
117.14	<Luisa R>Luisaruhe [*originally* 'Luisa | R'; 'R' *canceled and* '-|ruhe' *added*]
118.11	prince. [*a line across the page originally ending the entry here was overwritten and the entry was continued*]
118.23	<↑For 6 marks↓> [*interlined in heavy pencil*]
119.17–18	↑for an Em[press.]↓
119.18–120.8	Em[press.] . . . Fin[ally] [*the outside and bottom edges of the leaf are torn; emended*]
120.2	<move>make ['k' *written over* 'v'; *the same character used for* 'o' *and* 'a']
121.14	↑& get-up↓

121.15 suffers. [*a flourish originally ending the entry here was overwritten and the entry was continued*]

123.8 endurable. [*a flourish originally ending the entry here was overwritten and the entry was continued*]

123.12–13 ↑Would . . . here.↓

123.14 <can> <↑could↓> ↑might possibly↓

124.22 <some> ↑many↓

130.4 ↑Aug 8↓

130.16 <Alfa>Alva ['v' *written over* 'f']

131.25–26 ↑is a . . . building–↓

132.7 ↑Stopped for beer at↓ [*interlined above* ' "Machen . . . board." ' *(132.6); a line drawn to* '<Neckar>' *indicates placement*]

133.11 ↑No Name.↓

133.14 ↑Name it.↓

133.17 ↑(heads against sky)↓

134.13 ↑Baden↓

134.20 ↑on stret↓

135.2 ↑made by <St> Stüber.↓

136.3 ↑Always↓

136.5 ↑walking↓

136.6 <25> ↑15↓

137.12 ↑he was↓

137.16–17 <fetched down> ↑touched↓

137.23–24 <idle> ↑foolish↓

137.29 ↑Man's . . . agent.↓ [*written lengthwise on the page across the preceding entry*]

138.4 left <side> ↑half↓

138.24 Sunday Night ['Music' *is written above this entry, probably by Paine*]

139.24 <a rap> an ecstasy ['rap' *canceled and* 'n' *added to* 'a']

140.6 ↑because of the crowd↓

142.25 <Removed> ↑Collected↓

146.5 <Visp> ↑Locchi-Suste↓

148.3 ↑Crazy wooden↓

148.3 <a> ↑the↓

151.2 ↑for the poor↓

152.3 The Rhone [*follows a blank page*]

Notebook 16

Emendations and Doubtful Readings

	MTP Reading	MS Reading
158.2	Glossary	[*possibly* 'dctionary']
160.3	fr[om]	[*page torn*]
160.8	overhung	over-|hung
161.5	anywhere	any-|where
161.19	to-night	[*possibly* 'tonight']
162.5	crossbones	cross-|bones
164.17	up	[*possibly* 'UP']
168.9	to-day	to-|day
168.10	to-day	[*possibly* 'today']
171.5	over-confident	over-|confident
171.6	cornstalk	corn-|stalk
171.26	soap-bubble	soap-|bubble
172.8	sugar-loaf	sugar-|loaf
172.12	Chamounix	[*possibly* 'Chamonnix']
172.15	good-natured	[*possibly* 'good natured']
172.17	Chamounix	[*possibly* 'Chamonnix']
172.20	post office	[*possibly* 'post-office']
180.5	mountains	[*possibly* 'mountain']
182.16	wood saw	[*possibly* 'wood-saw']
182.20	up stream	[*possibly* 'up-stream' *or* 'upstream']

183.19	ill-fitting	ill-|fitting
185.24	overtook	over-|took
188.22	pew-rent	[*possibly* 'pew rent']
189.7	door-frame	door-|frame
190.8	to-day	to-|day
191.3	bowman	[*possibly* 'bow-man']
193.8	forehead	fore-|head
201.2	to-morrow	[*possibly* 'tomorrow']
204.27	whitewash	white-|wash
205.9	pour-boir	pour-|boir
206.26	powwow	[*possibly* 'pow-wow']
207.6	red hot	[*possibly* 'red-hot']
*207.22	High lights	[*placement uncertain*]
207.27	baggagemaster	[*possibly* 'baggage-master']
209.11	starboard	star-|board
210.18	steamboat	steam-|boat
212.5	Miserére	[*possibly* 'Miserēre' *or* 'Miserère']
213.17	Watchmakers	[*possibly* 'Watch makers']

Details of Inscription

158.1–159.7	Fred'k . . . Verona. [*written on the front endpaper*]
159.5–7	↑Sticks . . . Verona.↓ [*written lengthwise in the left margin of the front endpaper*]
159.8–21	Geo. . . . Vienna [*written on the recto of the front fly-leaf*]

160.1–2 Marks . . . Venice. [*written on the verso of the front flyleaf*]

160.2 Venice. [*two leaves have been torn out following this entry*]

160.3 <Beyond> ↑At↓

161.7–9 The poet . . hat. [*Clemens drew a wavy vertical line through this entry and wrote the instruction* 'STET' *diagonally across the entry; see note* 8]

162.5 <scull>skull ['k' *written over* 'c']

162.20 ↑poor↓

163.11 <he.>him ['i' *written over* 'e.']

163.23 <ten> <ten> 10 ['ten' *miswritten twice*]

164.8 ↑Aug. 28↓ [*circled*]

165.12 <the> ↑his↓

165.13 <roc>rolling ['l' *written over* 'c']

165.20 on his summit [*a flourish originally ending the entry here was overwritten and the entry was continued*]

166.3 ↑the base of↓

167.12–13 ↑Houses . . . Interlaken↓

169.16 ↑DRUNK↓

170.10 Mary <McDowling>M^{c}↑Dillon↓ ['Dillon' *interlined above canceled* 'Dowling']

171.4 <steep> ↑perpendicular↓

172.25 <other> ↑back↓

173.1–2 ↑vast . . . shadows.↓ [*interlined in brown ink above and below the illustration*]

173.6 ↑6,500 ab Cham↓ [*written in brown ink*]

174.2 <[co]>took [‘to’ *written over what appears to be* ‘co’]

174.17 <a[m]>as [‘s’ *written over what appears to be* ‘m’]

175.4 <[¶]Later when> [‘Later when’ *indented to begin a new paragraph, then canceled, and the preceding paragraph continued*]

175.6 ↑idyllic odic↓ [*written in brown ink,* ‘idyllic’ *above* ‘ray’ (175.2) *and* ‘odic’ *following* ‘affords.’ (175.4)]

175.12 <d’>de [*originally* ‘d’ ’; *the apostrophe canceled and* ‘e’ *added*]

176.1–5 Grateful . . . bills. [*written in brown ink*]

176.12–14 ↑(Samuel . . . Geneva.↓

179.11 ↑*climb*↓

179.13 72 yrs old. [*a flourish originally ending the entry here was overwritten and the entry was continued*]

179.15 ↑waved hdkf↓

179.18 <defects> <↑wh↓> ↑great qualities↓

181.15 <Dreadfully dangerous> ↑But . . . dangerous↓ [*altered in brown ink*]

182.17 ↑Jacks . . . 8.↓

185.15 100 m. [*a flourish originally ending the entry here was overwritten and the entry was continued*]

186.26–27 ↑shops . . . sides↓ [*interlined without a caret above* ‘on great piers’]

187.9 Hamburg. [*a flourish originally ending the entry here was canceled and the entry was continued*]

189.1 <up> ↑back↓

189.5 ↑almost↓

189.9 fruits &c. [*a flourish originally ending the entry here was overwritten and the entry was continued*]

190.17–18 ↑Bran . . . wine.↓

190.24 "VIETATA L'AFFISSIONE" [*written with initial capitals* 'V', 'L', *and* 'A'; *then underlined three times*]

191.5 or ↑else↓ look

191.10 <One or two>Two or three ['Two' *written over* 'One'; 'three' *written over* 'two']

192.8 <Reubens'>Rubens' ['u' *written over* 'eu']

192.16 <f>at ['a' *written over* 'f']

192.18 ↑Sept. 21.↓

193.5–6 <Twenty> ↑15↓

194.14 Valpolicella wine. [*a line below* 'Valpolicella' *may originally have been a flourish ending the entry before* 'wine.' *was written*]

195.4 ↑with yellow of egg.↓

195.6 troppo caro [*not in Clemens' hand*]

195.14 week. [*the bottom third of the leaf has been torn out following this word on the recto and* 'sailing' (195.18) *on the verso*]

196.11 ↑for the pope–↓

196.16 ↑Not so . . . hour.↓

197.5 <Riley> ↑Myer↓

197.6–7 ↑At . . . in 67.↓

197.14 <Conyellyana>Conyellyano [*the final* 'o' *written over the final* 'a']

197.14 ↑WINE↓

198.14 describe [*boxed*]

199.19 <60.> ↑asked . . . 60.↓

199.26 <is a> ↑in the↓

200.13–14 ↑–a most . . . activity.↓

200.17 <Gover>Gov't [' 't' *written over* 'er']

200.20 ↑Agent's report:↓ [*interlined without a caret above* 'The 15 or 20']

202.13 ↑(left-legged man↓

202.17 <Raphael's> ↑Titian's↓

203.13 <S><Church> ↑Scuolo↓

207.6 <–>which ['w' *written over the dash*]

207.20 heat/↑fervency↓ ['fervency' *written in brown ink*]

207.22 The handle/↑High lights↓ on the end ['High lights' *written in the top margin of the page above* 'handle on the end', *apparently as an alternative reading to* 'The handle' *but possibly as a separate note*]

207.32 <his left> ↑one↓ hand

208.16 <worst>worse ['e' *written over* 't']

208.20 position. [*a flourish originally ending the entry here was canceled and the entry was continued*]

208.20 have come. [*the top half of the following leaf has been torn out; the recto of the torn leaf is blank;* 'Hotel . . . Spania' (*209.1–2*) *is on the verso*]

209.4 Union.– [*a flourish originally ending the entry here was canceled and the entry was continued*]

209.6 ↑No.↓

209.9 ↑(Fusina)↓ [*interlined without a caret above* 'point']

209.12 ↑½↓

209.19–20 ↑<Arr.> . . . 10.45↓

210.9 pour-boire. [*a quarter of the page is blank below this entry; the bottom half of the leaf has been torn out;* '1.50' (*210.10*) *is on the otherwise blank verso*]

210.11–12 Pension . . . apiece [*written at the top of an otherwise blank page*]

210.21–211.4 was 10 min . . . I got no premium . . . inquire. [*three-quarters of the leaf below* 'I got' *has been torn out, as has the entire following leaf; the passage was written across the torn edge onto the next remaining leaf so that* 'was 10 min . . . I got' *appears on the top remnant of a right-hand page and* 'no premium . . . inquire.' *appears on the bottom three-quarters of the next surviving right-hand page*]

210.22 ↑(*they . . . cab*)↓

211.3 ↑(last . . . train)↓

211.5–12 At Bellagio . . . agreed. [*written on the recto of the back flyleaf, the first available space following the list of tunes for the music box and G. K. Mayer's address* (211.20–212.20)]

211.13–18 Hotel . . . 493 [*written on the verso of the quarter leaf noted at* 210.21–211.4]

211.15–18 ↑83 . . . 493↓ [*written lengthwise in the top margin of the page above* 'Hotel Grand']

211.19–*illustration* ↑San Stefano . . . [*illustration*]↓ [*inscribed on the top quarter of the page above* 'no premium' (210.24); *see* 210.21–211.4]

211.20–212.18 <Father . . . Hymn. [*written, with the exception of the words noted at* 212.1, *on the last ruled page of the notebook*]

212.1 ↑where . . . regions.↓ [*beginning on the last left-hand page of the notebook and continuing across the gutter on the recto of the back flyleaf*]

212.18 ↑<Mendellson's>Mendelsson's Hymn.↓ [*written lengthwise in the left margin of the page beside the preceding titles; the first* 's' *written over the second* 'l']

212.19–20 G. K. Mayer. | Vienna [*written, below the words noted at 212.1 and above the concluding three paragraphs of the complaint (211.5–12), on the recto of the back flyleaf; not in Clemens' hand*]

212.21–213.12 1. America. . . . 705 [*written on the verso of the back flyleaf;* '1. America. . . . Waltz.' *written lengthwise on the page; not in Clemens' hand*]

213.13–22 From . . . Verona. [*written on the back endpaper*]

213.13 <to> ↑arrives at↓ Bouveret

213.22 <Golden> . . . Verona. [*written lengthwise in the right margin of the back endpaper*]

Notebook 17

Emendations and Doubtful Readings

	MTP READING	MS READING
219.1	Go to	[*ditto marks below preceding* 'Go' *and* 'to']
219.6	best	[*possibly* 'last']
*222.19	shape & size of	shape of & size
223.8	to-night	to-|night
223.8	news-man	news-|man
224.9	table cloths	[*possibly* 'tablecloths' *or* 'table-cloths']
229.6	right-handed	right-|handed
229.10	to-day	[*possibly* 'today']
229.22	hat box	[*possibly* 'hatbox' *or* 'hat-box']
230.1	re slate	re-|slate
230.20	cross-ways	cross-|ways
230.20	sunrise	sun-|rise
231.19	chuckleheaded	chuckle-|headed
233.20	left-handed	[*possibly* 'left handed' *or* 'lefthanded']
237.16	to-day	[*possibly* 'today']
237.17	custom house	[*possibly* 'custom-house' *or* 'customhouse']
238.8	doorway	door-|way

238.14 to-day — to-|day

238.17 To-morrow — [*possibly* 'Tomorrow']

238.20 noticed — notied

239.1 Wood fire — [*possibly* 'Wood-fire']

239.25 *raised work* — [*possibly* '*raised* work']

241.14 knee-joints — knee-|joints

241.19 umbrella stand — 'umbrella | stand' [*possibly* 'umbrella-|stand']

242.4 overcome — over-|come

242.24–25 sugar plums — [*possibly* 'sugar-plums' *or* 'sugarplums']

242.25 Godspeed — [*possibly* 'God-speed' *or* 'God speed']

245.16 <Le>Lv. Salzburg — ['Salzburg' *replaces ditto marks below preceding* 'Salzburg']

246.10 slop-shop — slop-|shop

247.12 fir[e] — [*page torn*]

250.18 blow-out — [*possibly* 'blowout']

252.5 Dec. 18 — [*possibly* 'Dec. 78']

254.13 To-day — [*possibly* 'Today']

255.20 folk lore — [*possibly* 'folklore']

256.10–11 earthen ware — [*possibly* 'earthenware']

257.7 Boot blacking — 'Boot | blacking' [*possibly* 'Boot-|blacking']

257.8 whitewashing — [*possibly* 'white washing']

257.8 water color — [*possibly* 'water-color' *or* 'watercolor']

260.18	what 's	what | 's
261.7	wood-splitters	wood-|splitters
263.16	bedroom	[*possibly* 'bed room']
267.4	a picture	[*possibly* 'e picture']
267.10	chambermaids	chamber-|maids
270.26	copyright in books	copy-|right in books
272.11	whitebait	[*possibly* 'white bait']
272.12	Catfish	Cat-|fish
272.21	belly aches	[*possibly* 'bellyaches']
272.24	Butter milk	[*possibly* 'Buttermilk']
272.25	buckwheat	buck-|wheat
273.4	Canvas back	[*possibly* 'Canvasback']
273.17	Pine nuts	[*possibly* 'Pinenuts']
273.20	god-dam	god-|dam
276.6	<(10 Aug>	[*possibly* '<(18 Aug>']
277.13	does	[*possibly* 'day']
283.25	f20.40^{c}	[*possibly* '£20.40^{s}']

Details of Inscription

218.1–219.6	Telegraph . . . court. [*written on the front endpaper*]
219.7–220.1	Douvernak . . . ink. [*written on the recto of the front flyleaf*]
220.2–5	Oct 14/78. . . . perceptible. [*written on the verso of the front flyleaf*]
220.3–5	Ich . . . perceptible. [*written lengthwise on the verso of the front flyleaf*]
220.11	↑only↓

221.2 ↑Shipped from Rietti's.↓ [*written lengthwise in the left margin of the page beside* 'Articles . . . $66' (*221.3–11*) *and bracketed with these entries*]

221.8 <Conve>Concave ['ca' *written over* 've']

221.12 ↑Shipped from Besarel's.↓ [*written lengthwise in the left margin of the page beside* 'Jardiniere . . . $<85>89' (*221.13–21*) *and bracketed with these entries*]

221.21 $<85>89 ['9' *written over* '5']

222.2 frame<.>, [*the period mended to a comma*]

222.5 $400<.>, [*the period mended to a comma*]

222.11 ↑(finger to temple.)↓

222.19 shape ↑& size↓ of ['& size' *interlined with a caret inadvertently placed after* 'of'; *emended*]

222.23 <one> ↑an antique↓

223.3–4 good for <me> ↑you↓

226.25 ↑Make a Legend?↓

227.5 <Piete>Pieti ['i' *written over* 'e']

228.12 <give> ↑transfer to↓

229.3 Benvenuto's. [*a flourish originally ending the entry here was overwritten and the entry was continued*]

230.8 <all>always ['w' *written over* 'l']

230.13 <cowdung>dung ['cow' *canceled*]

230.17–18 much ↑as↓ an

231.13–14 ↑thin↓ <unpretentious m> hair

231.14–15 ↑& along his jaw—↓

231.15–16 noble dignity. ↑—chain large links, falling on breast—↓ [*the intended position of* '—chain . . . breast—' *is uncertain; it is squeezed in following* 'noble' *at the bottom of a page*]

232.4 blanket <↑shirt↓>. ['shirt' *interlined above* 'blanket' *and canceled*]

232.12 ↑Comes . . . retouching↓ [*written diagonally across the preceding paragraph*]

232.22 ↑fearful perspective,↓ [*interlined without a caret above* 'imagination, or absence']

232.24 <Belli>Belle ['e' *written over* 'i']

233.4–5 <they ought to> ↑one would . . . them to↓

234.12 <vou>voo <francay>fransay ['o' *written over* 'u' *and* 's' *written over* 'c']

234.16 ↑Oct 27↓ ↑Uffizzi . . . day,)↓

234.21 free again<,>. [*the comma mended to a period*]

235.1 by | ↑by↓

235.9–10 <scrawny sick> ↑unchildlike↓

235.10 <holy>Holy ['H' *written over* 'h']

235.21 <knotte>knotty ['y' *written over* 'e']

235.24–25 ↑upon the following questions–↓

236.4–5 2.50 f. ↑(50 cents)↓

238.9 Peter is. [*a flourish originally ending the entry here was overwritten and the entry was continued*]

238.14–15 ↑showed . . . engrave.↓ [*the intended position of this passage is uncertain; interlined without a caret above* 'allowed . . . asked']

239.7 ↑black↓ negro

239.18 toss/↑pitch↓

239.25 ↑<or>–it was *raised work.*↓ [*the dash written over* 'or']

240.1 ↑Nov. 3↓

240.5 <tired>tiresomeness ['s' *written over* 'd']

240.12 Picture/↑Vision↓

241.7–8 <on ear>in heaven ['i' *written over* 'o'; 'hea' *written over* 'ear']

242.11 from ↑2↓ to ten feet

242.27 <cards>yarns ['y' *written over* 'c'; 'ns' *written over* 'ds']

242.31 ↑(3^{d} floor):↓ Prices<:> <↑pr day↓> ↑per day:↓

242.32 ↑fr.↓ 45

243.5 ↑Both . . . Spagna.↓

243.13 <hotel>Hotel ['H' *written over* 'h']

244.10 <history>History ['H' *written over* 'h']

244.15 <To>Turganieff's ['u' *written over* 'o']

245.12 Get ↑to↓ Venice

245.16 <Le>Lv. ['v' *written over* 'e']

247.11 shapeless. [*the bottom third of the page is blank below this entry*]

248.3–4 start ↑or arrive↓

248.10–11 <same> ↑former↓

248.11 <our> ↑European↓

248.13 cream. [*a flourish originally ending the entry here was overwritten and the entry was continued*]

249.21–22 ↑on 14th↓

250.12 ↑Call them "Works."↓

250.14 <hereafter,> ↑hereafter,↓

250.22–23 <verse> ↑stanza↓

251.5 intion [*a line-ending* ('in-|tion') *probably accounts for the missing syllable* 'ten']

252.5 ↑Dec. 18.↓

252.14 <reisee>reiste ['t' *written over* 'e']

253.2 <without this>with ['out' *and* 'this' *canceled*]

253.15 <in>on ['o' *written over* 'i']

254.4 museum. [*a flourish originally ending the entry here was overwritten and the entry was continued*]

255.14 <Last> ↑2↓ line

255.25 aloud. [*a flourish originally ending the entry here was overwritten and the entry was continued*]

256.20 <Too pompous> ↑Too . . . occasion↓

256.21 <killing> ↑hunting↓

256.21 harpoon. [*a flourish originally ending the entry here was overwritten and the entry was continued*]

257.10–11 ↑Said . . . Art.↓ [*written lengthwise on the page across the two preceding entries*]

258.4 ↑Miss Benfey said:↓

258.5–6 ↑(Trouble . . . here↓ [*added at the end of the paragraph with an arrow indicating placement*]

259.17 <stocking> ↑ancle↓

260.1 ↑Jan. 13–79–Munich↓

260.7 victimized [*a flourish originally ending the entry here was overwritten and the entry was continued*]

261.5 <youn>youth ['th' *written over* 'n']

261.7 <slice> ↑chop↓

262.14 <15> ↑14⅔↓

262.14 <16>15 ['5' *written over* '6']

262.15 <2½>2↑⅝↓ ['½' *of* '2½' *canceled*]

263.2 <⅓>⅕ ['5' *written over* '3']

263.13 ↑The noises at Heilbronn.↓

263.14 <up> ↑around↓

263.21 <all>always ['w' *written over* 'l']

264.4 dim ↑white↓

264.19 <3> ↑3↓

265.7 want↑ed↓

265.14 Cold–|–the thermometer

266.16 carefully/↑strictly↓

267.19 institution. [*a flourish originally ending the entry here was overwritten and the entry was continued*]

267.22 "Funny"–↑Beastly↓

267.23 ↑Damp fog (d–d fog)↓ [*squeezed in below* '–Beastly']

267.24 ↑We . . . nasty.↓ [*squeezed in below* '"Funny"' *and to the left of* 'Damp . . . fog)']

268.11 <it>is ['s' *written over* 't']

268.22–23 <Tay in>Taylor ['lor' *written over* 'in']

268.23 7. [*someone, possibly Paine, taking the* '7' *for a* 'T', *has added* 'aylor' *to it*]

269.9–11 ↑At that . . . interrupt.↓ [*written lengthwise on the page across the preceding entry from* 'chap' *to* 'Providences?' *(269.2–8)*]

270.1 ↑particularly & progressively↓

270.3–4 he <↑at last↓> becomes<.>, <↑at↓> ↑at last,↓ [*the period mended to a comma*]

270.25 ↑Little . . . raw↓

271.17	↑*real*↓
272.3	English toast! ↑Execrable↓
272.4	Muffins. ↑good, but indigestible↓
272.6–7	↑OYSTERS.↓ ↑*Blue points*↓ ['OYSTERS.' *written in the top margin of the page above* 'variety (at' (*272.1*); '*Blue points*' *written in the middle of the preceding passage, below the ditto marks* (*272.4*) *and above* 'In Europe' (*272.4*)]
272.11	↑whitebait↓ sole
272.22–29	Biscuits . . . table d'hote. ['Biscuits . . . greens–', 'breakfast bacon,', 'succotash', 'cabbage . . . pork', 'buckwheat . . . cream–', *and* 'roast . . . table d'hote.' *struck through, probably to indicate use rather than cancellation*]
272.23	chitlings ↑hot eggs, bread.↓–
272.23–24	↑corn-cake,↓ . . . ↑Butter milk.↓ . . . ↑Iced milk↓ . . . ↑Ice water.↓ [*interlined without carets:* 'corn-cake,' *above* 'bacon,–boiled'; 'Butter milk.' *above* 'corn–'; 'Iced milk' *above* 'succotash'; *and* 'Ice water.' *above* '–cabbage']
272.26–27	potatoes–↑*mussels* in S.F.↓ baked ['*mussels* in S.F.' *interlined without a caret above* 'potatoes–baked']
272.27	baked apples ↑with cream↓–
272.28	↑& *steamed* in Wash^{n}↓ [*interlined without a caret below* '(Describe)']
273.11	↑baked & boiled↓ beans
273.19–21	Baroness . . . word. [*heavily bracketed in the margin*]
273.20–21	↑(Baron . . . word.↓
273.22	swearin [*written off the edge of the page*]
273.27	↑Had . . . June.↓

275.15	<He>His ['i' *written over* 'e']
276.5	<2^{d} of> ↑10th↓
276.5–6	<& 5th (or 10th?)> ↑2^{d}↓ Sept.
276.6	↑(9th Thermidor) <(10 Aug>↓ [*squeezed in at the bottom of the page below* 'to such an extent' (276.8)]
276.10	subsided. [*a flourish originally ending the entry here was overwritten and the entry was continued*]
276.12–15	16th May" &c. ↑(Orator . . . benefactor.↓ [*a flourish originally ending the entry after* '&c.' *was overwritten when* '(Orator . . . benefactor.' *was squeezed in at the bottom of the page*]
276.17–18	<hup!!>hupp! 10,11, <hup!!>hupp! <hup!!>hupp! ['p' *written over the exclamation point three times*]
276.21	↑mis-↓correcting
277.8–278.2	30th Jan, . . . Convention [*Clemens wrote the instruction* 'See 2 pages further on' *lengthwise across the first page of this entry; see* 278.3–19]
277.9–10	↑Louis Philippe's Govt↓
278.3–19	There was . . . Ham [*written on an otherwise blank left-hand page, apparently chosen at random, sometime before the entry at* 277.8–278.2 ('30th Jan, . . . Convention') *was written on the two surrounding right-hand pages*]
278.10	<ha[te]d> ↑<[- -]>never↓
278.15	<a> ↑it↓
278.22	↑Swearing.↓ [*written in the upper left corner of the page and boxed*]
279.2	*Ibid* [*the bottom half of the page is blank below this entry*]
279.11	↑O, I *am* . . . *was* so dry!↓

279.12 <Small chapter> [*the bottom third of the page is blank below this entry*]

279.21–22 ↑I like my whisky . . . pie↓ [*written lengthwise on the page across the preceding entries from* 'Strifenhofer' (279.13) *to* 'married!' (279.20). *This entry and the entry at* 280.8–9 *are on facing pages and were written with the notebook held in the same position*]

280.8–9 ↑JOHN . . . SHINE↓ [*written lengthwise on the page in large uneven letters across the preceding entries from* 'I copper that.' (279.26) *to* 'aftern." ' (280.7). *See* 279.21–22]

281.2 Geneva. [*two leaves have been torn out following this entry; there are fragments of inscription on the remaining page stubs*]

281.3 180 [*the bottom half of the leaf has been torn out following this number on the otherwise blank recto and* '48.25' (281.11) *on the verso. The following leaf has been torn out*]

281.12 ↑Little Pedlington↓ . . . Frau Kratz [*written on the recto of the back flyleaf*]

282.2–283.6 Quanto . . . Piano [*written on the verso of the back flyleaf*]

282.4–8 180 . . . 1448 [*written in the left margin of the page beside Clemens' drawing of the mirror*]

283.4–6 Vincenzo . . . Piano [*not in Clemens' hand*]

283.7–284.6 Continental . . . Artists [*written on the back endpaper*]

283.10 (small [*the inscription is so light as to be almost illegible and is partly overwritten by the following line*]

283.12–14 <Hanfstaegel . . . Munich.> [*not in Clemens' hand*]

283.19–23 ↑John . . . Judy.↓ [*written across the fold between the flyleaf and the endpaper; boxed*]

284.1 ↑musical↓

Notebook 18

Emendations and Doubtful Readings

	MTP Reading	MS Reading
291.13	handcuffed	hand-|cuffed
294.9	pic—poor	pic— | poor [*possibly* 'pic-| poor']
294.26	humbugs	hum-|bugs
297.2	lash	[*possibly* 'rash']
298.10	masterpiece	master-|piece
299.21	midnight	mid-|night
302.8	hod-carriers	[*possibly* 'hod carriers']
303.12	cup-bearer	cup-|bearer
303.24	thot that	[*possibly* 'that that']
306.2	Post office	[*possibly* 'Post-office' *or* 'Postoffice']
309.1	Tourgènieff	[*possibly* 'Tourgénieff']
*309.14	Good-<night>nice	[*possibly* 'Good-<nice>night']
310.4	fiancée	[*possibly* 'fiancèe']
310.7	Horror:	[*possibly* 'Horror!']
310.11	peop[le]	[*page torn*]
312.22	to-night	[*possibly* 'tonight']
313.2	Rosière	[*possibly* 'Rosiére']
313.3	Rosière	[*possibly* 'Rosiére']

313.5	Rosières	[*possibly* 'Rosiéres']
313.7	Rosière	[*possibly* 'Rosiére']
314.14	morrocco covered	[*possibly* 'morrocco-covered']
314.19	it.["]	[*page torn*]
318.3	wood-pile	[*possibly* 'wood pile' *or* 'woodpile']
318.3	show-case	show-|case
318.4	woodyards	wood-|yards
326.7	drawback	draw-|back
327.16	Carrall's	[*possibly* 'Carroll's']
327.17	note-book	note-|book
329.1	masterpiece	master-|piece
329.10	miracle-working	miracle-|working
329.18	hard-working	[*possibly* 'hard working' *or* 'hardworking']
329.28	middle-class	middle-|class
330.12	Gaye's	[*possibly* 'Gaze's']
331.7	homelike	home-|like
332.9	after-dinner	after-|dinner
333.13	re-division	re-|division
333.25	copyright	copy-|right
340.11	*statero*[*om*]	[*page torn*]
340.29	daylight	day-|light
341.3	life-boat	life-|boat
342.16	Second-hand	[*possibly* 'Second hand' *or* 'Secondhand']

342.20	self-sacrificing	self-|sacrificing
343.14	sap	[*possibly* 'sop']
344.2	["]Mighty	[*page torn*]
344.8	[lied]	[*possibly* 'hid', 'bid', *or* 'died']
344.23	[i]n	[*page torn*]
348.1	André	[*possibly* 'Andrè']
349.23	Gaye	[*possibly* 'Gaze']

Details of Inscription

290.1–2	100,000 . . . Times. [*written on the front endpaper*]
290.3–9	<19 Boulevard . . . st. W. [*written on the recto of the front flyleaf*]
291.1–11	<REMEMBER . . . crockery. [*written on the verso of the front flyleaf*]
292.6	↑Feb. 27, at Strasburg.↓
292.11–13	Madame . . . Chaillot [*written by Olivia Clemens*]
292.15	place . . . français [*written by Olivia Clemens*]
292.18–293.3	Hotel de Fleurus . . . also [*written by Olivia Clemens*]
293.11	<Huntingdon>Huntington ['t' *written over* 'd']
293.14	↑& size↓
293.16	the↑y↓
293.22	↑& coarsest↓
293.24	<4> ↑5↓
294.6	<28>26 ['6' *written over* '8']
294.16	↑& sunk↓
294.30	<yearn f>hunger ['h' *written over* 'f']

295.2 <is>it ['t' *written over* 's']

295.15 glahs/↑gloss↓

295.16 bahsket/↑bosket↓

295.20 <american>American ['A' *written over* 'a']

295.26 ↑because not good American,↓ [*interlined without a caret above* 'an American, & we' (295.26)]

296.6 ↑See 3 leaves ahead.↓ [*written diagonally in the left margin of the page beside* 'Eng . . . bloody.' (296.3–5); *refers to the boxed entry* 'Funny . . . xtrordnry.' (298.17–18)]

296.11 ↑four . . . &c↓ [*written in black ink at the top of the page above* 'Shoshones . . . country people' (295.7–14)]

296.12–14 ↑Directly . . . humble↓ [*written lengthwise on the page across* 'for <is>it . . . Shoshone Indians' (295.2–6). *These lines and those at 296.15–22 are on facing pages and were written with the notebook held in the same position*]

296.15–22 ↑From a . . . the H.↓ [*written lengthwise on the page across* 'Shoshones . . . country people' (295.7–14); *see 296.12–14*]

296.23–297.1 ↑o is pron. . . . three.↓ [*written lengthwise on the page across* 'In words . . . either.' (295.32–296.10)]

297.2 ↑lash . . . Hog.↓ [*written lengthwise in the left margin of the page beside* 'Cabman . . . adultery.' (297.7–12)]

297.3 <lan>literature ['it' *written over* 'an']

297.3–4 branches/↑divisions↓/↑specialties↓

297.5 <wea[thes]>wears ['rs' *written over what appears to be* 'thes']

297.20 <$7>$17,500 ['1' *written over* '7']

298.14 ↑(Harris trans)↓

298.16	<that>than ['n' *written over* 't']
298.17–18	Funny . . . xtrordnry. [*boxed*]
298.19	↑Can't speak—lowspirited.↓
298.23	invited? [*followed by a caret; there is no interlineation*]
298.24	salary [*followed by a caret; there is no interlineation*]
299.1	↑as a RR ticket↓
299.3–4	↑in order . . . mystery,↓
299.8	<but> ↑&↓
299.15–16	allowed↑."↓ <to sleep>
299.17	↑Doug. Straight↓ [*written in the top margin of the page above* 'each of her parks' *(299.14) and boxed*]
300.9	<8> ↑52↓
301.3	<& murder> ↑burn & butcher↓
302.1	<old>Old ['O' *written over* 'o']
302.15	↑far severrer↓
302.15	<oppo>oppressions ['r' *written over* 'o']
302.16	↑& persecutions than↓
302.17	Irish↑;↓
302.17	<The Jews>They ['Jews' *canceled and* 'y' *added to* 'The']
302.19	<They>There ['re' *written over* 'y']
303.4	↑witless, poverty↓ [*interlined without a caret above* '(beastly) & dispraise']
303.10	↑Lord Bacon↓ [*interlined without a caret above* '<4 maids of honor,>']
303.18	furnish him one. [*a flourish originally ending the entry here was overwritten and the entry was continued*]

305.10 ↑somewhere↓

308.1 hair↑s↓

309.11 <where>what ['at' *written over* 'ere']

309.14 <night>nice ['ce' *written over* 'ght'; *see Doubtful Readings*]

309.15 Coward. [*a flourish originally ending the entry here was overwritten and the entry was continued*]

309.20 <received>receives ['s' *written over* 'd']

310.10 ↑2↓

310.13 ↑A↓ ↑Talk with the departed.↓

310.14–15 <move to> ↑try the↓ | the

311.7 <the[-]>that ['at' *written over* 'e' *and another letter*]

312.7 <are> ↑are↓

312.7–8 ↑in the upper classes↓

312.11 battle-picccs<—>↑.↓ <because>Because [*originally one sentence; the period added, the dash canceled, and* 'b' *of* 'because' *underlined three times to create two sentences*]

313.9 <suppote>supports ['s' *written over* 'e', *and* 'r' *added*]

313.10 ↑&↓ 200

313.18 ↑by calling him the↓ the

314.9 ↑June 1.↓

314.13 <take> ↑study↓

315.1 <St>San ['a' *written over* 't']

316.7 <oc>causes/↑makes↓

316.8 <but which> ↑and↓

316.10 ↑"Church of the↓ . . . Lesson.↑"↓

316.13 <&cc>&c &c ['&' *written over the second* 'c']

317.2 ↑A French marriage & funeral.↓

317.10 ↑Put this with D'Aiguillon↓ [*written diagonally across the preceding paragraph*]

317.15 processed. [*a flourish originally ending the entry here was overwritten and the entry was continued*]

317.19 <he>his ['i' *written over* 'e']

319.13 <n[--]>no ['o' *written over two unrecovered letters*]

319.14 <nude> ↑naked↓

319.22 ↑to↓ say

319.24 <The glory of>*Glory* ['The' *and* 'of' *canceled;* 'G' *written over* 'g' *of* 'glory'; 'Glory' *heavily underlined*]

320.1 <glories>glory ['y' *written over* 'ies']

320.5 <A><Disciples> ['D' *written over* 'A']

320.7 <↑Prove↓>

320.22 ↑bright↓

320.23 conveying↑,↓ <of>

321.1 <<victories>victorious time> ['ous' *written over* 'es'; *the entire cancellation follows a caret; there is no interlineation*]

321.7 <is> ↑was↓

321.12 <maintain>tain ['main-' *canceled at the end of a line;* 'tain' *left standing at the beginning of the next line*]

321.22 ↑Bastile↓ [*written at the top of the page above* 'I mean in Xdom–' (*321.18–19*)]

322.2 <both> ↑they↓

322.11–14 Chastity . . . plainly [*apparently the list* 'Chastity', 'Lying', 'Honor' *was written first; then* 'Honor' *was canceled, '–constant* in books' *was added after* 'Lying', *filling out the line, and the discussion was continued with* '–plainly' *on the line below* '<Honor>']

322.21 <kings> ↑bachelors & its husbands↓

323.4 <country> ↑nation↓

323.17–18 <He put . . . & then> [*written and heavily canceled at the top of the page above* 'things is not perceptible' *(323.22), apparently sometime before the paragraph* 'All . . . erroneous.)' *(323.19–23) was written around it*]

323.21 ↑protection would be wise↓

324.28 ↑body's↓

324.30 <unchastity>chastity ['un' *canceled*]

324.33–34 <His> ↑A F.'s↓ home is where another <woman's> ↑man's wife is.↓

325.2 Liberte . . . Fraternité [*circled*]

325.4 <great>Great ['g' *underlined three times*]

325.5–6 They . . . is. [*circled*]

325.7 <Untran>Unrepeatable ['repea' *written over* 'tran']

325.8 time. [*followed by* 'X' *written three times and circled*]

325.17 <11>12 ['2' *written over* '1']

325.21 <<chi>darling> ['dar' *written over* 'chi']

326.7 <the [r]a>them ['m' *added to* 'the' *and* '[r]a' *canceled*]

326.8 <civilizati>civilized ['ed' *written over* 'ati']

326.16 L'Assomoir<.>illustrated ['il' *written over the period*]

326.18 <& he is no>in dread ['in dread' *written over* '& he is no']

327.7–8 Paris . . . news. [*circled*]

327.7 ↑small & dirty↓ [*interlined without a caret above* 'papers are']

329.1–2 ↑Rubens . . . acrobat.↓ [*written diagonally across the preceding paragraph*]

330.11 ↑or burglars, have forgotten which.↓

330.20 ↑smelt like↓

332.18 ↑But I wander from my subject.↓ [*written lengthwise on the page across the preceding paragraph*]

332.24 <Moral> ↑Esthetic↓

333.15 <all>always ['w' *written over* 'l']

337.2 <Saturday> ↑Sunday↓

337.2–3 <Saturday> . . . Wyndham. [*seven-eighths of the page is blank below this entry*]

337.4 ↑Room↓

337.15 <10th> ↑1st↓

338.10 ——↑(capital)↓ ['(capital)' *interlined above the dash with a caret*]

338.11–15 Saturday . . 20– [*apparently not intending to compile a list, Clemens originally wrote* 'Saturday Aug 16.| Gave Joseph–£5.' *and then wrote the August 17 entry that begins at 338.16. He subsequently interlined* 'Monday . . . 10' *below* 'Gave . . . £5.', 'Windermere . . . £10.–' *below* '——(capital) £5.4.4.' (338.10), 'Grasmere . . . 5.–' *below* 'Windermere . . . £10–', *and* 'Coniston . . . 20–' *below* 'Saturday Aug 16.'. 'Windermere . . . £10.–' *is written above a flourish that originally ended the entry with* '£5.4.4.' (338.10)]

339.9 <keeper> ↑theatre↓

339.12 <">a ['a' *written over quotation marks*]

339.14 ↑Talked with the great Darwin.↓

339.19–340.23 1 box . . . ship trunk. [*written on two facing pages apparently chosen at random sometime before the paragraph beginning at 340.24 was written on the surrounding pages; see 340.25*]

339.19–340.7 1 box . . . Besarel– [*written by Olivia Clemens*]

340.8 *12 Trunks.* [*circled*]

340.25 about 9 PM [*at the bottom of the page below these words Clemens wrote* '(run 2 pages)', *indicating that the paragraph continued following the list that appears at 339.19–340.23 of the present text*]

340.30 <12>↑15↓

340.30–31 complete arch) in [*two leaves have been torn out following these words, apparently before this entry was written*]

340.32 <colorado>Colorado ['C' *written over* 'c']

341.6 them<,>. [*the period written over the comma*]

342.13 <pc>pkg ['kg' *written over* 'c'; *one leaf has been torn out following this entry*]

344.4 <paw>prawfut ['ra' *written over* 'aw']

344.13 <———>Go-to-h– ['Go-to-h–' *written over the dashes*]

345.2 <–>& ['&' *written over the dash*]

345.20 ↑entirely↓

346.7 ↑(Traverse.)↓

346.11 ↑sterom'↓

346.11 <knecht>necht ['k' *of* 'knecht' *canceled*]

346.16 <Tho>Townsend ['ow' *written over* 'ho']

347.31 same time. [*followed by one and one-half blank pages; then two leaves have been torn out*]

348.1 Monuments . . . Arnold– [*written at the top of an otherwise blank page*]

348.12–21 cease. . . . Holmes. [*written on both sides of the bottom half of the leaf; the top half was apparently torn out before this entry was written*]

348.22–349.22 An heroic . . . *don't-you.* [*written on the recto of the back flyleaf*]

348.22–349.7 An heroic . . . say. [*struck through in brown ink*]

349.5–7 This . . . say. [*written on the right side of the page beside* 'An heroic . . . definitions.' *(348.22–349.13)*]

349.11 –↑(↓strong.↑)↓ [*the first added parenthesis may have been meant to cancel the dash*]

349.14–18 Nasty . . . N. h'*yaah* [*the exact order of inscription is unclear;* 'female (woman)' *appears between* 'h'yaah! (negro. & Eng.' *and* '& *hee*-er & N. h'*yaah*']

349.17 ↑(negro. & Eng.↓

349.18 ↑(Amer . . . h'*yaah*↓

349.20 <En>in ['i' *written over* 'E']

349.23–350.3 Joseph N. Very . . . 29 Pall Mall [*written on the verso of the back flyleaf*]

349.27 <1.10>1.20 ['2' *written over* '1']

350.4–10 Bible . . . Jacob [*written on the back endpaper*]

350.5 ↑St Gaudens↓

350.6 ↑49↓

350.7 ↑Mr. Dubois.↓

Notebook 19

Emendations and Doubtful Readings

	MTP Reading	MS Reading
358.2	Corn[wall.]	[*possibly* 'Cornhill.']
359.11	Supernaturals	Super-|naturals
368.2	deep[ly]	[*page torn*]
369.1	orang-outang	orang-|outang
369.25	cloth-worker	cloth-|worker
373.9	First floor.	[*ditto marks below preceding* 'First' *and* 'floor.']
373.15	<ᶜ/ct[-]s>	[*possibly* '<ct[-]s> ↑¢↓']
*375.15	existence.	existence. | 80
*376.4	speculative	speculative 100
*376.10	–a battle	145 | –a battle
*376.18	degrading	degrading 200
*376.26	citizen!	citizen! | 275.
*376.27	By this	2 | By this
377.9	to-day	[*possibly* 'today']
380.7	Yrugy	[*possibly* 'Yrngy']
381.9	mouthpece	mouth-|pece
381.13	[M]ind	[*page torn*]
392.5	stock	[*possibly* 'stack']
400.12	Sitz	[*possibly* 'Sitg']
406.10	charmé	[*possibly* 'charmè']

406.11	refusé	[*possibly* 'refusè']
406.11	après	[*possibly* 'aprés']
407.5	snowstorm	[*possibly* 'snow-storm' *or* 'snow storm']
410.2	housemaid	house-|maid
411.7	Brébeuf's	[*possibly* 'Brèbeuf's']
412.14	block	[*possibly* 'black']
412.19	does	hoes
*412.23	trio<;>:	[*possibly* 'trio<,>:']
412.25	block	[*possibly* 'black']
417.9	132[2]	[*page torn*]
424.6	on whisky	['whisky' *replaces ditto marks below preceding* 'whisky']
*425.4	GENERAL	1 | GENERAL
*425.12	& as the	2 | & as the
*425.21	civilization	3 | civilization

Details of Inscription

357.1–359.9	W[--]dens . . . station [*written on the front endpaper; the front flyleaf and the first ruled leaf have been torn out; blot marks on the endpaper suggest that the flyleaf was inscribed in ink*]
357.1–358.2	W[--]dens . . . Corn[wall.] [*written in pencil and covered by the succeeding entries,* 'A. St. Gaudens . . . New York.' *(358.3–359.6), written in ink*]
358.10–14	Conway . . . London [*written in black ink*]
358.15–17	↑care Prof . . . Pa.↓ [*written lengthwise in the right margin of the page beside* 'Conway . . . London' (358.10–14)]

359.7–9 ↑Chas. Sneider . . . station↓ [*written lengthwise in the left margin of the page beside the preceding three entries,* 'Conway . . . New York.' (358.10–359.6)]

359.10–360.3 Running . . . Smith [*written on both sides of the first surviving ruled leaf; the bottom half of the page is blank below* 'Smith'; *the following leaf has been torn out*]

359.10–18 Running . . . truth. [*written in pencil*]

359.19–20 ↑Miss . . . 1 PM↓ [*written lengthwise on the page across the preceding entries,* 'Running . . . successfully.' (359.10–12)]

360.1–2 ↑Charley . . . 57th st.↓ [*written lengthwise on the page across the preceding entries,* 'The principle . . . *habitual* (I' (359.13–16)]

360.4–14 Mrs Colt . . . high. ['Mrs Colt . . . drops.' *written in pencil; the bottom quarter of the leaf has been torn out following* 'drops.' *on the recto;* '8000 . . . high.' *is written at the top of the otherwise blank verso. The top half of the following leaf has been torn out and the remaining half is blank; the two following leaves have been torn out*]

360.15–17 Beefsteak . . . 2 [*written in pencil at the top of an otherwise blank page*]

361.7 ↑Burton's . . . 1858.↓ [*crowded in beside* 'Bill Arp' (361.8)]

362.1 ↑Talmage's Sermons.↓ [*written lengthwise in the right margin of the page beside* 'Brownell . . . Adler' (361.9–15)]

362.2 ↑–Dick & Fitzgerald.↓

362.3 <Old Si> (?) ↑Uncle Remus↓ ['Uncle Remus' *interlined without a caret*]

363.11 ↑Lowell↓

363.16 ↑Arthur . . . (rot)↓ [*written in the right margin of the page beside* 'Doesticks | John Phoenix' (363.6–7)]

363.17–18 ↑Cousin . . . Bedott.↓ [*written in the right margin of the page beside* 'Harte . . . Holmes' (363.12–14)]

363.19 ↑Neal, Charcoal sketches.↓ [*written lengthwise in the left margin of the page beside* 'Danbury . . . Downing.' (362.6–363.5)]

363.20 ↑The South . . . poets &c.↓ [*written lengthwise in the right margin of the page beside* '3 Gnaw . . . Slick' (362.4–363.1)]

363.21 ↑Look . . . Pirates.↓

364.3 ↑Widow Bedott.↓

364.10 ↑—Josh Billings↓

364.11 ↑Josiah Allen's Wife.↓

364.12 <Dictionary>Dictionaries ['ies' *written over* 'y']

364.16 ↑page↓

365.3 Don't . . . mama? [*written in pencil*]

365.6–7 ↑Livy . . . truth↓ [*written lengthwise along the left margin of the page across the preceding two entries*]

365.13–16 "Numbered by days." ↑"this afternoon . . . mind us.↓ [' "Numbered by days." ' *is written at the top of a left-hand page, followed by* 'If . . . Crusoe.' (366.1–12); ' "this afternoon . . . mind us.' *is written on the facing right-hand page and marked to follow* 'days." ']

365.13 ↑(July 26)↓

365.14 ↑in 2 yrs↓

366.3 ↑D$^{r.}$↓

366.11 ↑funy↓

366.11 <gur>got ['ot' *written over* 'ur']

368.12 ↑Tight↓

368.14 <Who><↑Well,↓ who>Who [*originally* 'Who';

'Well,' *added and* 'Who' *mended to* 'who'; *then* 'Well,' *canceled and the* 'W' *of* 'Who' *restored*]

368.18 <not a single> ↑hardly a↓/↑not a single↓

368.19 ↑of the↓department↑s↓

368.20 <assassination, lynching,> ↑murder,↓

368.24 <Chinaman,> ↑Digger,↓

368.24–25 <nasty Frenchman> ↑Fejeean↓

369.18 <teetotalers,> ↑Turks,↓

370.4 <15>10 ['0' *written over* '5']

370.7 X10U8 [*circled*]

371.3 book. [*the bottom half of the page is blank below this entry*]

371.14 <Su>Mrs. ['M' *written over* 'Su']

372.1 ↑Send Music box man.↓

372.4 Holmes . . . N.Y. [*circled*]

372.5 ↑in . . . afraid?↓

372.6 decrease/↑surcease↓

372.15 <love> ↑serve↓

372.16 <lord>Lord ['L' *written over* 'l']

372.20 <that loves> <↑'t adores↓> ↑serves↓

373.2 dear/↑firm↓/↑high↓

373.3 love/↑trust↓

373.4–6 And . . . intirely.–/↑had "got left."↓/↑it was . . . left."↓

373.14 *elsewhere.* [*most of the leaf following the page that ends here has been torn out; the remnant is blank*]

373.16 Sept. 28/80. [*the bottom half of the leaf has been torn out following this date on the recto and* 'misplaced–of de' *(374.2) on the verso]*

374.1–2 <–& I>My fel . . . of de [*written on a left-hand page opposite both* '<You . . . speeches.>' *(373.19–20) and* 'I am . . . built.' *(374.3–6) on the facing right-hand page;* 'My' *written over* '–&'; 'fe' *written over* 'I'; *see note 57*]

374.3–6 ↑I am . . . built.↓ [*may originally have ended with* 'Hartford' *or* 'Oak'; 'I am . . . Hartford' *crowded into the top margin of the page above* '<You . . . speeches.>' *(373.19–20);* '–the city . . . built.' *written between the lines of* '<You . . . speeches.>', *either when* 'I am . . . Hartford' *was written or later*]

374.5 <↑historic↓>

374.8 immortal/↑imperishable↓

374.9 <Let us> ↑We shall best↓

374.10 <P>As ['As' *written over wiped-out* 'P' *which may have been indented to begin a new paragraph*]

374.13–14 ↑as↓ the pioneer

374.15–16 <the> <rude><savage> [*the order in which these words were canceled and whether they were canceled at different times or at the same time cannot be determined*]

374.19 ↑has sunk . . . patriot,↓

374.25 <–>1880 ['18' *written over the dash*]

375.5–377.2 <After> . . . disaster. [*written on right-hand pages only, except for later additions at 375.16–23, 376.5–6, and 376.10–13 written on left-hand pages*]

375.5 <After> ↑Through↓/↑By↓

375.10 ↑loyally↓

375.11 ↑permanently↓

375.12–15 generalship↑.↓ <which . . . possible> <–you . . . for> ↑& resigned . . . existence.↓ ['<which . . . possible>' *canceled at the bottom of a right-hand page and* '<–you . . . for>' *canceled at the top of the following right-hand page; then* '& resigned . . . existence.' *crowded into the bottom and left margins of the first page below and beside* '<which . . . possible>']

375.14 approaching age/↑accumulating years↓

375.15 existence. [*the number* '80', *Clemens' word count of the speech through* 'existence.', *is written at the top of the otherwise blank facing left-hand page; emended*]

375.16–23 <↑By this . . . way.↓> [*written and canceled on the left-hand page preceding* 'You . . . that.' (376.1–4)]

375.16 ↑present tedious & exhausting↓

375.17 ↑<&> by↓

375.17 ↑by↓ the wisdom

375.18 ↑by↓ the magic

375.20–21 ↑dishonor &↓

376.2 <against> <↑upon↓> against ['against' *restored by stet marks*]

376.3 <but>because ['ec' *written over* 'ut']

376.4 speculative [*followed by Clemens' word count number* '100'; *emended*]

376.5–6 ↑You are doing . . . them.↓ [*written lengthwise in the right margin of the left-hand page inscribed* '<By this . . . way.>' (375.16–23) *and in the adjoining left margin of the facing right-hand page; its intended position on the right-hand page indicated by a caret*]

376.8 ↑loaded him . . . dignities,↓

376.10 $5,000,000<,>. <besides> <& also a long list of> [*the period written over the comma*]

376.10–13 ↑–a battle . . . $4000 000↓ [*written on the left-hand page facing the preceding cancellation at 376.7–10; the number* '145', *Clemens' word count of the speech through* '$4000 000', *is written at the top of the page; emended*]

376.18 ↑so↓ degrading [*followed by Clemens' word count number* '200'; *emended*]

376.21–22 wave↑.↓ <& this . . . exist.>

376.23–24 ↑measureless↓ love, <her> ↑&↓

376.25 Hartford<!>, [*the top stroke of the exclamation point canceled and the period mended to a comma*]

376.26 <↑patient,↓>

376.26 citizen! [*followed by Clemens' word count number* '275.'; *emended*]

376.27–377.2 By this . . . disaster. [*the number* '2' *written above this paragraph indicates that it was added to replace canceled* 'By . . . *disaster.*' (375.16–21), *which is on the second page of the draft speech; emended*]

377.8 <republican>↑Conn.↓

377.12 Food. [*five leaves have been torn out following this entry*]

378.1 ↑–Mr. Carter↓

378.2 ↑Anne Trumbull↓

378.3 ↑Miss Wheeler↓

378.4 ↑Prof. Holbrook.↓

378.5 ↑–Berguin↓

378.7 ↑Mr. . . . Trobridge↓

378.8 ↑–Miss Barnard↓

378.9 ↑–Mr. Carpenter↓

378.10 <Peter Piper> [*the bottom quarter of the page below these words was originally left blank; probably* 'Peter Piper' *was canceled when* 'Valet . . . Utterback.' *(381.1–2) was written in the blank space*]

378.11–379.8 Emily . . . Islander [*the leaf bearing these entries was torn out, removed from the notebook, and later restored to its original position; it was in the notebook when* 'surprising people with it' *(379.6) was written on its verso (ink blots on the following page match that inscription), but it was missing from the notebook when* 'Valet . . . Utterback.' *(381.1–2) was written on the preceding page and when* 'hebenly sho' ' *(381.25) was written four leaves later (see Details of Inscription entry at 381.1–2); two pin holes in the leaf indicate that it was at some time attached to another document*]

378 *illustration* ↑Precinct↓ [*written in pencil*]

380.3 Gillette<.>— [*the dash written over the period; a flourish originally ending the entry with the period was overwritten and the entry was continued*]

380.4 Man . . . failure [*the bottom third of the leaf, bearing these words on the recto and* 'Susan Sarepta . . . Loammi' *(381.3–8) on the verso, was torn out and removed from the notebook; it was found in an assortment of miscellaneous manuscript fragments in the Mark Twain Papers; the fragment was missing from the notebook when* 'Valet . . . Utterback.' *(381.1–2) was written two leaves earlier and when* 'hebenly sho' ' *(381.25) was written three leaves later (see Details of Inscription entry at 381.1–2); two pin holes in the fragment do not match those reported above at 378.11–379.8*]

380.7 Cas↑e↓y

381.1–2 ↑Valet . . . Utterback.↓ [*written in the space originally left blank below* '<Peter Piper>' *(378.10). Originally* 'Susan Sarepta' *(381.3) followed* 'Earl Douglas'

(380.12) on a left-hand page; then the bottom third of that leaf was torn out (see entry above at 380.4), leaving ‘Earl Douglas’ *the last line on the surviving portion; and the preceding leaf was also torn out (see entry above at 378.11–379.8); thus with the notebook opened to the page now ending at* ‘Earl Douglas’, *the bottom third of the left-hand page that had preceded the torn-out leaf appeared immediately below the torn edge, revealing the line* ‘<Peter Piper>’ *followed by blank space (see entry above at 378.10); when* ‘Valet . . . Utterback.’ *was written in that blank space, a line was drawn across the torn edge from* ‘Douglas’ *to* ‘Valet’ *to indicate the intended relationship. The inscription of* ‘Valet . . . Utterback.’ *produced matching ink blots on the page bearing* ‘hebenly sho’ ’ *(381.25), and the inscription of* ‘hebenly sho’ ’ *produced matching blots on the page bearing* ‘Valet . . . Utterback.’; *so all or part of each of the four intervening leaves was missing from the notebook when these inscriptions were made (the missing leaves and portions of leaves are reported in entries at 378.11–379.8, 380.4, 381.8, and 381.12)*]

381.2 Valett <de>D. Utterback [‘D.’ *written over* ‘de’]

381.8 Loammi [*one leaf has been torn out following this entry; it was removed from the notebook before* ‘Valet . . . Utterback.’ *(381.1–2) was written three leaves earlier and before* ‘hebenly sho’ ’ *(381.25) was written two leaves later (see Details of Inscription entry at 381.1–2)*]

381.12 Chicago. [*the bottom half of the leaf has been torn out following this word on the recto and* ‘afternoon’ *(381.14) on the verso; the fragment was removed from the notebook before* ‘Valet . . . Utterback.’ *(381.1–2) was written four leaves earlier and before* ‘hebenly sho’ ’ *(381.25) was written on the following page (see Details of Inscription entry at 381.1–2)*]

381.16 <boost> <↑shove↓> <↑highst↓> ↑yank↓

381.19 <pull him out> <↑drag↓/↑snake↓> ↑yank him home↓

381.20 <de>dat ['a' *written over* 'e']

382.3 Gap. [*the bottom half of the page is blank below this entry*]

382.4–6 House . . . result. [*the top half of the leaf has been torn out above this entry on the recto; the verso is blank*]

382.7 ↑Ned Bunce↓

383.7 <↑Charley Stoddard, Honolulu.↓>

383.10 <Charley,> ↑Julia↓

384.5 ↑Dr. Burton.↓ [*written in the right margin of the page beside* '<Mrs. Whitmore.>' (383.2)]

384.6 ↑Dr. John Brown.↓ [*written in the right margin of the page beside* 'David . . . Hay' (383.4–5)]

384.7 <↑"Hawkeye" R. J. Burdette.↓> [*written in the right margin of the page beside* 'H. H. . . . Howells.' (383.6–8); *boxed*]

384.8 <↑Wattie Bowser.↓> [*written in the right margin of the page beside* '<Ma,> . . . Holmes.' (383.11–12)]

384.9 ↑T. W. . . . Chas.↓

384.11 ↑G. W. Curtis.↓

385.1 ↑Lt. . . . West Point.↓

386.3 ↑Seaver.↓ [*written in the right margin of the page beside* 'Elihu Vedder.' (384.13)]

386.4–5 ↑W. P. Hanscom . . . Chicago.↓ [*written lengthwise in the left margin of the page beside* 'J. R. Lowell. . . . Will Bunce.' (384.12–386.1)]

386.6–8 <↑Wattie . . . Lemon.↓> [*written lengthwise in the right margin of the page beside* 'Rose Terry . . . Club.' (384.15–385.7)]

386.17 <D[i]> Liver poem [*heavily circled by a looping line*]

387.4–5 <'F . . . myself,> ↑'Rah . . . 'rah!↓

387.8 <gathered all> <↑came↓> ↑swarmed↓ the ↑joyful↓ ['swarmed' *written over* 'came']

387.11 ↑without going,↓

387.11 WITH [*underlined three times*]

387.20 <verse>*ver*-her [*originally* 'verse'; *then* 'ver' *underlined and* 'he' *written over* 'se']

387.20 ↑for↓

387.22 Write Mrs. Swisshelm [*a third of the page is blank below this entry*]

387.23–24 *–*ture* . . . <which> [*footnote written at the bottom of the page below* 'Rep.' (387.12)]

387.24 rhyme<,>. <which> [*the period written over the comma*]

389.2–16 P. . . . unframed. ['Jno Stokes . . . unframed.' *written beside* 'P. . . . 562' *which is written along the left margin of the page*]

388.21 <66,000,000>65,000,000 ['5' *written over* '6']

388.25 1,040,000 00↑0↓ [*the final* 'o' *added in pencil*]

388.26 2,080,000 00↑0↓ [*the final* 'o' *added in pencil*]

389.2 <50>40 ['4' *written over* '5']

390.13 friend. [*the bottom half of the page is blank below this entry*]

390.14–393.16 They were . . . yard.) [*written on right-hand pages only, except for later additions at* 391.13–392.4 *and* 393.6 *written on left-hand pages*]

391.13–392.4 ↑Pay . . . Ask him.↓ [*written on the top half of an otherwise blank left-hand page*]

393.6 ↑Bring . . . <[--- --]>↓ [*written at the bottom of an otherwise blank left-hand page beside* 'Must . . . too?' (*393.4–5*) *on the facing page*]

393.9–10 color↑.↓ <& confining & any color>

395.1 Tear-drop<s> [*the top third of the leaf has been torn out above this word on the recto and* 'Dunnigan' (*395.10*) *on the verso*]

395.1–2 <3,000> <↑2 to 2500↓> ↑1,500↓ barrels.↑–⅛ . . . diam.↓

396.4–6 ↑Webster . . . Providence↓ [*written lengthwise on the page in pencil; one leaf has been torn out following this entry*]

397.10–14 Mrs Warner . . . Paris [*written in pencil on the top half of an otherwise blank left-hand page; the following leaf has been torn out*]

397.15–17 1–10 | 2 17 | 3 20 [*boxed*]

399.5 ↑Col. Valentine↓

399.5 Club. [*the bottom quarter of the page is blank below this entry and the following leaf has been torn out*]

399.7 kings! [*a flourish originally ending the entry here was overwritten and the entry was continued*]

399.9–400.4 Get rooms . . . somebody. [*written in pencil*]

400.7–16 Nursery . . . leaks. [*written in pencil*]

400.7 <|||> ↑3↓ [*Clemens counted three with three strokes, canceled them, and interlined* '3']

401.5–9 Chatto's . . . 374.16.9. [*written in black ink except for* 'Depos. . . . '81.' (*401.6*) *added later in blue ink*]

402.13 <Louise Messina> ↑her.↓

404.5 ↑Boot black . . . cold.↓

404.16 <">Ticket ["T" *written over the quotation marks*]

405.15 <I think>Think ['I' *canceled and* 't' *underlined three times*]

406.13 ↑Before reaching Essex,↓

406.16 <25>20 ['o' *written over* '5']

407.11 ↑Monday↓

407.11 ↑sifted↓ snow<ed>

407.16 ↑generally↓

407.20 ↑Abrahams, Fortescue, Dalhousie↓

407.23 W/↑Windsor↓ Hotel

408.5 <*it*> ↑*me*↓

408.21 ↑The children . . . the↓

408.23 <Mince—> ↑Irish stew—↓

409.2 <'em>'m [*originally* ''em'; *the* 'e' *canceled*]

409.4 with<'em>'m [*originally* ''em'; *the* 'e' *canceled*]

409.9 <tha>there ['e' *written over* 'a']

409.10 <po>pile ['i' *written over* 'o']

409.23 tin ship<?>hanging ['h' *written over the question mark*]

409.26 color<.>— [*the dash written over the period*]

410.4 ↑Je↓

410.5 ↑yet↓

410.10 excited<,>. <Pauline.> [*the period written over the comma*]

410.12 <rip> ↑blast↓

410.13 <discharged> ↑delivered↓

410.17 sœur [*ligature indicated by a line above* 'oe']

410.18 <meet> ↑revoir↓

410.27 ↑an average of↓

411.6 <Breboeuf>Brebeuf ['o' *canceled*]

411.14 ↑with . . . heart↓

411.15 <[hun]>I will ['I w' *written over what appears to be* 'hun']

411.16 ↑him↓

412.1 ↑City of Burglars.↓

412.23 trio<;>: [*the colon written over a partially canceled semicolon; see Doubtful Readings*]

413.4 ↑Dec. 3.↓

413.8 <Doncona>Don↑na↓cona [*originally* 'Don-|cona'; 'n' *written over the hyphen, and* 'a' *and a second hyphen added to create* 'Donna-|cona']

413.14 ↑meaning, I suppose,↓

414.4 short. [*a flourish originally ending the entry here was overwritten and the entry was continued*]

414.13 ↑, probably old.↓

416.5 <conscious>conscientiously ['ent' *written over* 'ous']

416.8 ↑78 ½↓

416.8 ↑101.↓ [*a flourish originally ending the entry here was overwritten and the entry was continued*]

416.10 compassionate/↑(nobler)↓/↑magnanimous↓/↑generous↓

416.18 Anæsthetics [*ligature indicated by a line above* 'ae']

416.21–25 ↑Sewing machine . . . Chromos.↓ [*written in the right margin of the page beside* 'Railway– . . . Anæsthetics' *(416.14–18)*]

417.3 & applies ['&' *underlined twice*]

417.8 <Logariths>Logarithms ['m' *written over* 's']

417.9 <wor>earth ['ea' *written over* 'wo']

417.13 "Apologia . . . Newman [*not in Clemens' hand*]

418.9 ↑ask Grant.↓

421.4 ↑First Smith↓

421.8 ↑Attacked↓

421.8 ↑on . . . 73.↓

422.3 <McCo>McCullough ['u' *written over* 'o']

422.7 ↑Madcap Violet. £200↓ [*crowded into the top margin of the page above* 'Reform Club' (*422.5–6*)]

424.9 Reid. [*three-quarters of the page is blank below this entry*]

424.12 Whitlow [*what may be an* 'e' *is scrawled above the final* 'w']

425.1 pall-bearer. [*the bottom half of the page below this entry and the following leaf are blank; three leaves have been torn out following the blank leaf*]

425.2–3 Geo. . . . Clemens [*three-quarters of the leaf has been torn out following these entries on the verso; the recto is blank*]

425.2 Geo. E Blackham [*not in Clemens' hand*]

425.4–22 General . . . Republic! [*written on right-hand pages only; page numbers* '1', '2', *and* '3' *have been deleted by emendation; followed by six blank pages*]

426.8 <190>170 ['7' *written over* '9']

426.18 (our) [*one leaf has been torn out following this entry; the following page is blank*]

427 *illustration* [*followed by one blank page*]

427.16 ↑Mr . . . pts.↓

427.24 <200>300 ['3' *written over* '2']

427.25 <400>600 ['6' *written over* '4']

428.11 47,563. [*the bottom half of the page is blank below this entry*]

428.12–13 <Alabama> ↑California↓

428.18 Habberton. [*one leaf has been torn out following this entry*]

429.4 <fan>fables ['bl' *written over* 'n']

429.11–13 Phenix's . . . tickets [*written in pencil*]

430.1–4 ↑These . . . S.L.C.↓ [*written lengthwise along the right margin beside and partially across* 'Phenix's . . . Aldrich' (*429.11–28*) *on the final ruled page of the notebook, which faces* 'He lost 3 . . . won—even' (*430.5–27*) *on the back endpaper; the back flyleaf was apparently torn out before* 'These . . . S.L.C.' *was written*]

430.1 ↑of cigars↓

430.3 <cigs>cigars ['a' *written over* 's']

430.5–27 He lost 3 . . . won—even [*written on the back endpaper*]

Notebook 20

Emendations and Doubtful Readings

	MTP Reading	MS Reading
*443.20	<on>in	[*possibly* 'on' *written over* 'i']
*444.7	[it]	[*page torn*]
446.3	Phrasebook	Phrase-|book
446.13	short-hand	[*possibly* 'shorthand']
447.17	to-morrow	[*possibly* 'tomorrow']
448.8	to-day	[*possibly* 'today']
450.1	steamboat	steam-|boat
452.15	Graveyard	Grave-|yard
454.16	underclothes	under-|clothes
458.7	chambermaid	chamber-|maid
458.8	good-natured	[*possibly* 'good natured']
467.10	<bel>	[*possibly* '<bet>']
474.14	shot["]	[*page torn*]
*475.1	<B[a]>B.	[*possibly* '<B[o]>B.']
479.7	<Some>	<Some-|>
480.6	Captain."	[*possibly* 'Captain'!']
481.12	razor-strop	razor-|strop
483.5	suppressed!	[*possibly* 'suppressed?']
484.8	1820	[*possibly* '1870']
494.22	bull-frog	bull-|frog

495.22	agent	[*possibly* 'agents']
499.15	*tonight*	[*possibly 'to-night'*]
504.8	cov[e]rtly	[*page torn*]
508.4	tape-worm	tape-|worm
509.7	Patter-rollers	Patter-|rollers
512.6	Guavana	[*possibly* 'Guarana']
512.13	Schnutlinge	[*possibly* 'Schmitlinge']

Details of Inscription

437.1–468.7	Charley's . . . Dryades [*written in blue ink except for entries in pencil at 438.3, 439.1–5, 462.12, 464.7, and 466.11 and the cancellation in pencil at 438.1*]
437.1–438.3	Charley's . . . Box. [*written on the front endpaper*]
438.1	<Gerhardt . . . Michel.> [*canceled in pencil*]
438.3	603 . . . Box. [*written in pencil*]
438.4–5	Dam-*na*-tion . . . unsung! [*written on the recto of the front flyleaf*]
439.1–5	May . . 1681.50 [*written in pencil on the verso of the front flyleaf*]
439.13	<heroes>hero↑'↓s [*the second 'e' canceled and the apostrophe added*]
439.15	decent. [*the bottom half of the page is blank below this entry*]
440.2–3	↑H. L. Stewart.↓
440.13	<a> ↑the future↓
441.2	↑<Alas,> I have no nuts!↓
441.4	↑upon him↓

441.6 ↑temptation↓ [*written in the top margin of the page above* 'his motto, through life–' (*440.17*)]

441.12 meaning. [*followed by about two lines of blank space*]

441.17 ↑Individuality↓

441.19 ↑Constructiveness (lying & slander).↓

442.5 <give> ↑put↓

442.7 children<.>↑;↓ [*the period canceled and the semicolon added*]

442.8 <there>this ['i' *written over the first* 'e'; *the second* 'e' *canceled; the same character used for* 'r' *and* 's']

442.10 <friends> ↑himself↓

442.11 ↑a defect in↓

442.13 west. [*a quarter of the page is blank below this entry*]

443.4 <never> ↑only↓

443.16 ↑Sign . . . them.↓ [*written lengthwise in the left margin beside* 'Write . . . sillily.' (*443.13–18*)]

443.20 <on>in [*either* 'i' *written over* 'o' *of* 'on' *or* 'on' *written over* 'i'; *see Doubtful Readings*]

444.3–4 <Hayes's> ↑Wash^n treaty↓ ↑(Alabama Claims)↓

444.7 ↑locked up . . for [it]↓ [*written in the top margin of the page above* 'W. R. . . . stolen' (*444.3*); *the page torn following* 'for']

444.8 ↑Reid has↓ The <proportions> ↑aspect↓

444.13–14 <altitude> <↑(bulk)↓> (stature)

444.14 <↑one-half↓>

444.15 ↑go on &↓ <extract>

445.2 ↑–or . . . condescend.↓ [*written lengthwise in the right margin of the page*]

445.8 Wagner [*the bottom half of the leaf has been torn out following this word on the recto and* 'Hamersley.' *(445.14) on the verso*]

446.2 bananas. [*the bottom two-thirds of the leaf has been torn out following this word on the recto; the verso is blank*]

446.3 Shakspere [*the top quarter of the leaf has been torn out above this entry on the recto and* 'Yes.' *(446.9) on the verso*]

446.7 Mr. <——>Keep asked Mrs. —— ['Keep' *written over a line indicating a blank to be filled*]

446.15–448.20 putting . . . in Va. [*written on right-hand pages only except for the entries at 448.21–449.8*]

446.16 <↑(Attribute↓>

448.21–449.8 <↑Tiffany . . . is fine.↓> [*written on the left-hand page opposite* 'has always . . . in Va.' *(448.12–20) on the facing right-hand page*]

449.1 $<5>4,500 ['4' *written over* '5']

450.13 (Reader) [*the bottom half of the page is blank below this word*]

451.3 <3.30> ↑1↓ P.M. [*Clemens left blank lines following this entry and following* '<Dean Sage?>' *(451.7) and* 'Am Bk.' *(451.8), probably to permit the addition of new items*]

452.4 hall." [*a quarter of the page is blank below this entry*]

452.11 Trollope. [*a quarter of the page is blank below this entry*]

453.8 ↑by↓ Pierson

454.5 <[1]>23 ['2' *written over what appears to be* '1']

456.9 ↑& ask . . . feuds.↓

456.10 ↑Yellow fever.↓

457.1 ↑Compromise?↓

457.12 Geo ↑W↓ Cable

459.4 ↑Kaolatype.↓

459.7 ↑KAOLATYPE.↓

460.8 <Mendellson>Mendelsson ['s' *written over* 'l']

462.4 <to>the ['h' *written over* 'o']

462.6–7 He's . . . Gap. [*the top half of the leaf has been torn out above* 'He's' *and the bottom quarter of the same leaf torn out following* 'Gap.' *on the recto;* ' "Set down . . . you–' (*462.8–9*) *is written on the verso of the remaining quarter*]

462.11 enemy. [*three-quarters of the page is blank below this entry*]

462.12 26th . . . AM [*written in pencil*]

464.7 ↑from the *Liar*↓ [*written in pencil*]

465.1 ↑Saml. Pepper–↓

465.2 ave [*a flourish originally ending the entry here was overwritten and the entry was continued*]

465.8 ↑*stort* for start.↓ [*the bottom half of the page is blank below this entry*]

465.11 <knew us>stumbled ['st' *written over* 'us']

466.1 <as>answered ['ns' *written over* 's']

466.11 Now . . . Scrapbook. [*written in pencil; a quarter of the page is blank below this entry*]

467.4 <George> ↑Ed.↓

467.8 ↑little↓

467.17 S↑^{t}↓ Louis

468.6–7 Winan's . . . Dryades [*written by* G. W. Cable]

468.8–491.5 Joel Chandler Harris . . . 22> [*written in pencil except for the interlineation in blue ink at* 479.9]

468.8 Upton<, (Prov>Station ['Stati' *written over* '(Prov']

470.7 <was> ↑where↓

470.20 ↑Julio's picture↓

471.4 ↑Big . . . May 7↓

471.10 ↑smooth↓

474.4 levees [*followed by about two lines of blank space*]

474.9 ↑Early↓ In

475.1 <B[a]>B↑.↓ [*what appears to be* 'a' *canceled, and the period added; see Doubtful Readings*]

475.5 ↑in the hold↓

475.7 ↑Don't . . . heavy↓ [*written lengthwise on the page across the preceding paragraph*]

475.15 ↑½ mile↓ wide now, & ↑is↓

477.8 <12> ↑14↓

477.8 <18> ↑22 or 23↓

478.7 ↑New Orleans College of Languages.↓ [*written in large script lengthwise on two facing pages across the five preceding entries* (477.5–478.6)]

479.7 ↑rough↓

479.9 beautiful/↑mellow↓ ['mellow' *interlined in blue ink*]

480.12 ↑Sunday 7 AM↓

480.24–25 <800> ↑400↓

481.16 <newspaper>Newspaper ['N' *written over* 'n']

482.4 <inste>instead ['inste' *canceled, then* 'ad' *added, reinstating the original reading*]

482.19 one<.>– [*a flourish originally ending the entry at*

'one.' *was overwritten and the entry was continued; the dash written over the period*]

484.7 ↑Just published.↓

484.9 ↑E A↓ . . . ↑C H↓

486.14 apologized. [*a flourish originally ending the entry here was overwritten and the entry was continued*]

486.16 <Wer>Where ['h' *written over* 'er']

486.17 ↑pencils.↓ ↑(Barrows)↓ ['pencils.' *interlined above* 'dance cards' *(486.16), and* '(Barrows)' *interlined above* '<were the>' *(486.16), both without carets*]

487.6 ↑*& Orion*↓

488.1 ↑Pearl st.↓

488.2 (high up) [*one leaf has been torn out following this entry*]

488.3 ↑1.↓ It is

489.2–3 throwing/↑flashing↓/↑flirting↓

489.8 <*lanniappe*> ↑lagniappe↓

489.16–17 ↑(silly . . . &c.↓ ↑For instance . . . Rex.↓ ['For . . . Rex.' *written lengthwise along the left margin of the page across portions of the preceding entries,* 'up a ladder . . . to think him' *(489.12–20)*]

490.3 ↑(gush)↓ [*interlined without a caret above* 'sophomoric']

490.5 <↑Barber scissors.↓>

490.6 ↑X↓ [*here and at 490.10 and 490.12*]

490.12 ↑*See Bunce*↓

491.1 <certif>Certif. ['C' *written over* 'c']

491.2 ↑& ask me↓

491.6–497.21 Co-Op. Dress . . . 1000 pencils. ['Co-Op. Dress . . .

10,000' *(491.6–23) written in black ink;* 'Hartford . . . 1,000' *(491.24) written in blue ink;* 'Watch . . . 3,125.' *(491.25–29) written in pencil;* 'Burr Index . . . 1000 pencils.' *(491.30–497.21) written in blue ink, except for revisions and additions in pencil as noted*]

491.17–18 <— — — —>24001 to 24500 ['24001 to 24500' *written above the dashes indicating a blank to be filled*]

491.27 s↑t↓k.

492.1 ↑Dunham.↓ [*written in pencil*]

493.4–5 ↑Mixed-up . . . thieves.↓ [*written in pencil*]

493.7 <his>His ['H' *written over* 'h']

493.8 ↑well↓ [*written in pencil*]

493.10 <o'> ↑er↓

493.12 <su>sich ['u' *mended to* 'i']

493.12 <se>say ['a' *written over* 'e']

493.19 sent it ↑to↓

493.19 <mind>min↑'↓ ['d' *canceled and the apostrophe added*]

494.13 ↑cat↓ fish

494.16 don't<?>." [*the question mark mended to a period*]

494.20 <don>doan ['a' *written over* 'n']

494.24 <mu>mankind ['a' *written over* 'u']

494.27 <rascals> ↑scoun'ls,↓ [*altered in pencil*]

494.29 <sel>seff ['f' *written over* 'l']

494.30 ↑ain't↓

494.30 <around>aroun↑'↓ ['d' *canceled and the apostrophe added*]

495.4 <he>de ['d' *written over* 'h']

495.11 <jes>jis ['i' *written over* 'e']

495.12 <everlastin>everlast↑'↓n ['i' *canceled and the apostrophe added*]

495.14 <de> ↑any↓

495.18 ↑(What . . . it.)↓ [*written in pencil in the top margin of the page above* 'dat a man is a' (495.9)]

495.19–20 ↑(Referring . . . nuffin!↓ [*written in pencil*]

495.21–22 <Osgood . . . me.> [*canceled in pencil*]

495.22 <de[v]>defaulting ['f' *written over what appears to be a* 'v']

497.2 ↑for Miss. book.↓

497.4 <Get <shoes> ↑blocks↓ for Jean.>

497.7 Rathbun [*a flourish originally ending the entry here was overwritten and the entry was continued*]

497.9 <Barber . . . afternoon.> [*canceled in pencil*]

497.12 <1000 pencils.> [*canceled in pencil*]

497.16–21 <<Co>Closet . . . pencils.> [*canceled in pencil*]

497.16 <Co>Closet ['l' *written over* 'o']

497.22–512.8 Ring . . . the past? [*written in pencil except for entries in blue ink at 499.18–500.6 and 510.2*]

499.3 with it! [*a flourish originally ending the entry here was overwritten and the entry was continued*]

499.4 <↑Want . . . to-day.↓>

499.9–10 <how you talk> ↑look at your daybook↓—<you sent me> 2 quarts <of 'm yesterday,> ↑there . . . yesterday,↓ I reckon.

499.12 ↑2↓ Big slice↑s↓

499.13 <7.$^{30.}$>7.↑$^{30.}$↓ [*superscript* '30.' *canceled, then rewritten*]

499.15 bottle<.>, [*the comma written over the period*]

499.18–500.6 Breakfast . . . Susys room.> [*written by Olivia Clemens in blue ink; two leaves have been torn out following this entry*]

500.9 ↑slap . . . snap.↓ [*interlined without a caret above* 'right along.']

500.10 <Man (Dad Dunn,)> ↑Our liar,↓

500.15 them<.>↑—with Brown intimate.↓ [*the dash written over the period*]

502.3 did. [*a flourish originally ending the entry here was overwritten and the entry was continued*]

502.5–25 cremation . . . 4 ['crema-' *is at the bottom of a left-hand page; the top quarter of the facing right-hand page was apparently torn out before this entry was written, as the entry continues with* 'tion' *just below the torn edge;* 'tion . . . slavery.' *(502.5–9) is written on the recto and the card scores at 502.10–25 on the verso of the torn leaf; the bottom half of the surviving portion of the recto is blank below* 'slavery.']

502.6 <prevalen>preferrable ['ferra' *written over* 'valen']

503.10 ↑around↓

503.10 ↑Wal, no,↓ With ['Wal, no,' *interlined without a caret*]

503.11 need to<;>— [*the dash written over the semicolon*]

504.4 <So much noise> ↑Such a big lie↓

504.16 <& to>&c ['&' *written over* '&'; 'c' *written over* 'to']

505.5 about<)>myself) ['m' *written over closing parenthesis*]

505.6 gentle↑;↓ & expressive<;>, [*the comma written over the semicolon*]

505.13 ↑First baby.↓

506.7 <New Eng dinner.> ↑Ashfield.↓

507.6 <Egod>Egad ['a' *written over* 'o']

508.7 Brown<,>. [*the period written over the comma*]

509.7 <Ablithnit>Ablishnist's ['sh' *written over* 'th'; 's' *written over* 't']

510.2 Conversations . . . (hotel). [*written in blue ink*]

511.4 ↑devouring element↓ [*written above* ' "Rejoiced . . . euphonious' (511.5)]

512.3 sickening [*the bottom fifth of the leaf has been torn out following this word on the recto and the drawing of a snake's head (illustration on page 511) on the verso*]

512.3–5 Sell . . . show ['Sell . . . say—' *written in pencil over the shorthand transliterated in note 261 and followed by a line in which Clemens repeated the shorthand symbol for the word* show; *the shorthand and the words* 'show . . . show' *written in blue ink (illustration on page 511)*]

512.6 Guavana . . . headaches. [*written at the top of an otherwise blank page; followed by one line of shorthand symbols for consonants written in blue ink (illustration on page 512) at the top of the next page, which is also otherwise blank*]

512.7–8 Who . . . past? [*written on the recto of the back flyleaf; the bottom three-quarters of the page is blank*]

512.9–514.9 Mrs. C. . . . Whittier. [*written on the verso of the back flyleaf in pencil except where blue ink is noted*]

512.13 Schnutlinge We[in] [*written in blue ink*]

513.3 ↑A P. Watt . . . Row.↓

513.5 ↑Mrs. Cox, Care G. W. Cable↓ [*written in blue ink on the right side of the page beside* 'Jno. Garth' (513.4)]

514.6–9	Stedman . . . Whittier. [*written in blue ink*]
514.10–515.8	Den . . . Co [*written on the back endpaper in pencil except where blue ink is noted*]
514.12–515.3	Father said . . . Roswell Smith [*written in blue ink*]
515.3–5	↑–Picture . . . songs↓
515.6–8	3125– . . . Co [*written in blue ink*]

Notebook 21

Emendations and Doubtful Readings

	MTP Reading	MS Reading
523.4	overslaughed	over-|slaughed
529.19	grave-yard	grave-|yard
530.5	stern-wheeler	stern-|wheeler
531.31	God-damned	God-|damned
535.3	was finished	was was finished
535.4	walked off	walked of
538.12	red-headed	red-|headed
542.18	state-room	state-|room
545.24	whitewashed	white-|washed
546.29	They	The
551.23	lick off	lick of
555.7	sawdusted	saw-|dusted
556.20	put	put put
556.34	2 policemen	2 policeman
556.34	whole market	whole markets
558.25	have to make	have to made
560.1	chartbox	[*possibly* 'chart-box']
560.4	arrangements	arranegments
561.5	God-damn	God-|damn
564.10	iron-clads	iron-|clads

566.13	<pilothouse.>	<pilot-|house.>
566.28	and	at
567.23	compelle[d]	[*written off the edge of the page*]
570.4	corn-fields	corn-|fields
571.1	the Fort	the the Fort
572.19	overflooded	over-|flooded

Details of Inscription

521.1 [*two short canceled unrecovered lines*] [*erased; follows two blank flyleaves*]

521.2 <April 18th 1882> [*written diagonally in the upper right corner of the page, then erased*]

521.3–4 New York . . . 1882 [*written across the erased lines at 521.1*]

521.5 ↑female↓

521.6 ↑west↓

522.3 house<;>, [*the semicolon mended to a comma*]

522.5 <lions>Lions ['L' *written over* 'l']

522.6–7 ferocious smile/↑rigid ferocity↓

523.19 river<.>, [*the comma written over the period*]

524.7 ↑to↓ be

524.16 <Said>Says ['ys' *written over* 'id']

524.16 ↑for↓ which

524.25–32 ↑X↓Nobody . . . glances.X [*the cross marks possibly written by Clemens; the second as well as the first may have been interlined*]

524.30–31 Boat↑.↓ <and a>A [*originally one sentence; the period added,* 'and' *canceled, and* 'A' *written over* 'a' *to create two sentences*]

524.33 well-dressed<,> ↑with↓

525.9 damn↑ed↓

525.14 <is>it ['t' *written over* 's']

526.26 ↑He↓ Don't

527.17 <68>65 ['5' *written over* '8']

528.5 <Bigsby>Bixsby ['x' *written over* 'g']

531.10 Found government [*marked to begin a paragraph with a paragraph sign*]

532.20 <as>and ['nd' *written over* 's']

534.14 an <und><and> uncared ['u' *of* 'und' *mended to* 'a', *then* 'and' *canceled*]

535.4 eastward<.>, [*the comma written over the period*]

536.3 <blue>blew up ['ew' *written over* 'ue']

536.6 <The>Between ['B' *written over* 'Th']

536.17 Helena ↑Ark.↓ about 5:30. ↑P.M.↓

536.18 <to>the ['h' *written over* 'o']

536.19 to <be> ↑step↓ careful [*possibly revised by Clemens*]

538.18 <hed>head ['a' *written over* 'd']

538.19 <reached> ↑struck↓

539.24 <">↑'↓Christ

540.1–2 <shoot> ↑chute↓ . . . <shoot> ↑chute↓

540.25 "<let>Let ['L' *written over* 'l'; *the quotation marks possibly added*]

541.4 dead<.>, [*the comma written over the period*]

541.24 <bend>Bend ['B' *written over* 'b']

541.26 Shirt Tail ↑Bend↓

542.4 ↑(Pilot)↓

543.17 product<.>; [*the semicolon written over the period*]

545.9 Gulf. <only>Only ['O' *written over* 'o'; *the period possibly added*]

545.10 <fur>for ['o' *written over* 'u']

545.18 country<.>; [*the semicolon written over the period*]

548.13 Give . . . waiters. [*written in blue ink by Clemens*]

549.17 "<any>Any ['A' *written over* 'a'; *the quotation marks possibly added*]

551.1 <Boudou>Boudoo ['oo' *written over* 'ou']

552.15–16 ↑They . . . in -ing↓

552.17 <boy> ↑girl↓

556.10 <$>1,500,000. lbs. [*the dollar sign crossed out*]

556.12 ↑to 2↓

556.12 tons sugar, cane [*written in shorthand*]

556.15–16 ↑Juice . . . filters.↓ [*written following* 'centrif.)' (556.21); *a circled* 'A' *preceding* 'Juice' *corresponds to a circled* 'A' *interlined following* 'acre.' (556.15), *indicating the intended position of the passage*]

557.23 ↑names↓

558.19 ↑&↓

558.28 <Pe>P. [*the period written over* 'e']

559.25 chambers. [*followed by one blank line, probably to allow the description to be extended*]

560.16 <room>rum ['u' *written over* 'oo']

562.8 ↑1.↓

562.22 <never>neb↑b↓er ['b' *written over* 'v'; *the second* 'b' *added*]

564.7 <their>there ['re' *written over* 'ir']

564.9 them<.>, [*the comma written over the period*]

564.15 right<.>, [*the comma written over the period*]

565.2 possession<.>, [*the comma written over the period*]

565.10 Elliott/↑Ellet↓ ['Ellet' *interlined below* 'Elliott']

565.14 up<.">, unless [*the comma written over the period*]

566.1 ↑reconnoitring↓

566.12–13 inside<r> her↑.↓ <pilothouse.>

566.25 which ↑would↓ be

567.15 <I a>I↑'↓m ['m' *written over* 'a'; *the apostrophe added*]

567.19 myself<.>; [*the semicolon written over the period*]

568.6 <their>the ['e' *written over* 'ei'; 'r' *canceled*]

568.7 <he> <↑Watson↓> ↑Darnell↓

568.17–21 One . . . landing [*a line drawn in the margin beside this passage*]

569.21–574.18 Memoranda . . . flies. [*written from the back of the notebook toward the front, with the notebook inverted; follows the blank back flyleaf, the stubs of three leaves which have been torn out, and one blank ruled leaf*]

569.26 ↑Near . . . timber↓

570.9 New Madrid<;>, [*the semicolon mended to a comma*]

570.10–12 Mem: . . . doc^{s}. [*boxed*]

571.3–4 <Mem: . . . ago.> [*crossed out, then all but* 'Mem: Regarding' *erased*]

571.9–11 1844. | 1835 | 9 ['1844.' *is in Phelps's hand;* '1835', *the subtraction bar, and* '9' *may have been added by Clemens*]

573.1 ↑&↓ a pair

574.6 man ↑Frenchman↓

Index

Webster's Biographical Dictionary is normally the authority for accepted forms and spellings of names of people of public record. People of little historical note or those whose identification is uncertain or incomplete have been included selectively. Newspapers, periodicals, and scholarly publications which appear merely as citations are not listed. Mark Twain's writings are indexed by title.

The text of this book is set in Electra, a type face designed by W. A. Dwiggins (1880–1956) for the Mergenthaler Linotype Company and first made available in 1935. Electra avoids the extreme contrast between "thick" and "thin" elements that marks most modern faces, and is without eccentricities which catch the eye and interfere with reading. It is a simple, readable type face which immediately conveys a feeling of ease, vigor, and speed, characteristics that were much prized by Dwiggins. Headings are set in Michelangelo and Palatino, two display faces designed by Hermann Zapf for Stempel Type Founders in 1950. These graceful types blend admirably with the text face.

The book was composed by Heritage Printers, Inc., Charlotte, North Carolina, printed by Publisher's Press, Salt Lake City, Utah, and bound by Mountain States Bindery, Salt Lake City, Utah. Paper was manufactured by P. H. Glatfelter Company, Spring Grove, Pennsylvania.